SOMETIMES YOU HAVE NO OTHER CHOICE BUT TO WATCH SOMETHING GRUESOME OCCUR. YOU DON'T HAVE THE OPTION OF CLOSING YOUR EYES BECAUSE IT HAPPENS FAST AND ENTERS YOUR MEMORY.

HAVING TWO OR THREE PEOPLE IN LOVE WITH YOU IS LIKE MONEY IN THE BANK. THE SMALLEST THING CAN MAKE SOMEBODY SEXUALLY UNAPPEALING. A MISPLACED MOLE OR A PARTICULAR HAIR PATTERN CAN DO IT. THERE'S NO REASON FOR THIS BUT IT'S JUST AS WELL.

YOU CAN WATCH PEOPLE ALIGN THEMSELVES WHEN TROUBLE IS IN THE AIR. SOME PREFER TO BE CLOSE TO THOSE AT THE TOP AND OTHERS WANT TO BE NEAR THOSE AT THE BOTTOM. IT'S A QUESTION OF WHO FRIGHTENS THEM MORE AND WHOM THEY WANT TO BE LIKE.

IT'S NO FUN WATCHING PEOPLE WOUND THEMSELVES SO THAT THEY CAN HOLE UP, NURSE THEMSELVES BACK TO HEALTH AND REPEAT THE CYCLE. THEY DON'T KNOW WHAT ELSE TO DO.

OBVIOUSLY YOU STRIKE OUT AGAINST PEOPLE WITHIN RANGE. IT'S CATHARTIC TO AFFECT SOMEONE WHEN YOU'RE ANGRY. ALTERNATIVELY, CHOOSE ENEMIES IMPOSSIBLY FAR AWAY SO YOU NEVER HAVE TO FIGHT.

HANDS-ON SOCIALIZATION PROMOTES HAPPY INTERPERSONAL RELATIONS. THE DESIRE FOR AND THE DEPENDENCE UPON FONDLING ENSURE REPEATED ATTEMPTS TO OBTAIN CARESSES AND THE WILLINGNESS TO RECIPROCATE.

THE MOUTH IS INTERESTING BECAUSE IT'S ONE OF THOSE PLACES WHERE THE DRY OUTSIDE MOVES TOWARD THE SLIPPERY INSIDE.

THE RICH KNIFING VICTIM CAN FLIP AND FEEL LIKE THE AGGRESSOR IF HE THINKS ABOUT PRIVILEGE. HE ALSO CAN FIND THE CUT SYMBOLIC OR PROPHETIC.

HOW DO YOU RESIGN YOURSELF TO SOMETHING THAT WILL NEVER BE? YOU STOP WANTING THAT THING, YOU GO NUMB OR YOU KILL THE AGENT OF DESIRE.

I SAW THEM STRIP A MAN SO THAT IN A MATTER OF SECONDS HE LAY CURLED AND NAKED ON THE SIDEWALK.

IF YOUR CLOTHES CATCH ON FIRE, DROP DOWN IMMEDIATELY, ROLL UP IN A BLANKET, COAT OR RUG TO SMOTHER THE FLAMES, REMOVE ALL SMOLDERING CLOTHING AND CALL A DOCTOR OR AMBULANCE.

YOU HAVE TO MAKE THOUSANDS OF PRECISE AND RAPID MOVEMENTS TO PREPARE A MEAL. CHOPPING, STIRRING AND TURNING PREDOMINATE. AFTERWARDS, YOU STACK AND MAKE CIRCULAR CLEANING AND RINSING MOTIONS. SOME PEOPLE NEVER COOK BECAUSE THEY DON'T LIKE IT, SOME NEVER COOK BECAUSE THEY HAVE NOTHING TO EAT. FOR SOME, COOKING IS A ROUTINE, FOR OTHERS, AN ART.

IF YOU'RE SMART, YOU WATCH FOR CHANGES IN COLOR. THIS CAN APPLY TO SEEING THAT FRUIT IS RIPE OR NOTICING THE FLUSH THAT GOES WITH FEVER, DRUNKENNESS OR FURY.

WHEN YOU'RE ON THE VERGE OF DETERMINING THAT YOU DON'T LIKE SOMEONE, IT'S AWFUL WHEN HE SMILES AND HIS TEETH LOOK ABSOLUTELY EVEN AND FALSE.

IT CAN BE STARTLING TO SEE SOMEONE'S BREATH, LET ALONE THE BREATHING OF A CROWD. YOU DON'T BELIEVE THAT PEOPLE EXTEND THAT FAR.

IT IS HARD TO KNOW WHAT SOMEONE WANTS BECAUSE YOU CAN'T ACTUALLY FEEL HIS NEEDS. YOU DEVELOP WAYS TO READ OR ANTICIPATE DEMANDS, OR YOU WAIT UNTIL YOU'RE ASSAULTED AND THEN HIS REQUIREMENTS BECOME TANGIBLE.

**5000 Artists
Return to
Artists Space:
25 Years**

5000 Artists Return to Artists Space: 25 Years

Claudia Gould & Valerie Smith, editors

Artists Space | New York

PUBLICATION TEAM

5000 ARTISTS RETURN
TO ARTISTS SPACE: 25 YEARS

EDITORS
Claudia Gould
Valerie Smith

DESIGN/PRODUCTION
Design/Writing/Research:
J. Abbott Miller
Paul Carlos
Scott Devendorf
John Corrigan
Jane Rosch
Paul Makovsky

RESEARCHER/EDITORIAL ASSISTANT
Mariani Lefas-Tetenes

COPY EDITOR
Cathy Peck

INDEXER
Meryl Schneider

RESEARCHER
Debra Singer

EDITORIAL COORDINATOR
Debi Sonzogni

SPECIAL THANKS TO
Liz Dalton, David Joiner, and Sarada Rauch

Library of Congress Catalogue Card Number
98-073099

ISBN 0-9663626-0-8

PUBLISHED BY   Artists Space
                38 Greene Street
                New York NY 10013
                (212) 226-3970
                fax:(212) 966-1434
                artspace@artistsspace.org

DISTRIBUTED BY Distributed Art Publishers (DAP)
                155 Sixth Avenue
                New York, NY 10013
                800 338-2665

CONTENTS

6
SPONSOR'S STATEMENT
BY Stephanie French

7
BOOK FUNDING

8
CURRENT FUNDERS

9
BOARD OF DIRECTORS
1998–1999

10
INTRODUCTION AND
ACKNOWLEDGMENTS
BY Claudia Gould

13
EDITOR'S NOTE
BY Valerie Smith

15
DESIGNER'S NOTE
BY J. Abbott Miller

16
INTERVIEWS INDEX

DIRECTOR INTERVIEWS

20
Trudie Grace AND Irving Sandler
INTERVIEWED BY Joan Rosenbaum

52
Helene Winer
INTERVIEWED BY Matt Mullican,
Cindy Sherman, AND Valerie Smith

114
Linda Shearer
INTERVIEWED BY Valerie Smith

194
Susan Wyatt
INTERVIEWED BY Evelyn B. Leong

226
Carlos Gutierrez-Solana
INTERVIEWED BY Amy Wanggaard

264
Claudia Gould
INTERVIEWED BY Denise Fasanello
AND Ronald Jones

CHRONOLOGY OF ACTIVITIES AT
ARTISTS SPACE AND INTERVIEWS

17
1970s

112
1980s

224
1990s

320
KEY TO CHRONOLOGY

ARTISTS SPACE SERVICES

321
HISTORY OF THE IRVING SANDLER
ARTISTS FILE

322
HISTORY OF THE EMERGENCY
MATERIALS FUND, INDEPENDENT
EXHIBITIONS PROGRAM, AND THE
INDEPENDENT PROJECT GRANTS

324
BOARD HISTORY

326
STAFF HISTORY

328
PUBLICATIONS HISTORY

335
HISTORY OF BENEFIT
ARTISTS' MULTIPLES

FUNDERS HISTORY

338
DOMESTIC AND INTERNATIONAL
GOVERNMENT SUPPORT

339
FOUNDATIONS

340
CORPORATIONS AND GALLERIES

341
BENEFIT CONTRIBUTORS

342
INDEX

ENDNOTE BY Jenny Holzer
LIVING | 1980–82

Artist-centric may be the most succinct way to describe the mission of Artists Space, an institution dedicated to the work of emerging artists for more than 25 years. When it began in the early 1970s, few opportunities existed for nonestablished artists to show work, and virtually none where artists selected and curated exhibitions. By offering gallery space and resources to the growing artistic community of Lower Manhattan, Artists Space had a hand in creating the most vibrant artist's community in the world.

Over the years, Artists Space has consistently mounted exhibitions that challenge perceptions of contemporary art, as well as discovering and promoting new trends and styles of work as it emerged fresh from artists' studios. Its philosophy—to serve only unaffiliated emerging and under-recognized artists—renders Artists Space a unique environment in the multifaceted world of art.

For its immense contribution to contemporary art and artists, Philip Morris is proud to support Artists Space's 25th-anniversary publication. Our association began in 1981 and has been sustained through a mutual commitment to innovation, creativity, and support for contemporary artists whose work delves into the far reaches of experimentation.

Stephanie French
Vice President, Corporate Contributions and Cultural Programs
PHILIP MORRIS COMPANIES INC.

5000 Artists Return to Artists Space: 25 Years
is sponsored by Philip Morris Companies Inc.

Major support for the design and production of *5000 Artists Return to Artists Space: 25 Years* has been provided by the National Endowment for the Arts, the Mark Rothko Foundation, and Sotheby's. Earlier contributions toward research and development were provided by the Cowles Charitable Trust, the Bohen Foundation, General Atlantic Corporation, the National Endowment for the Arts, and the New York State Council on the Arts, a state agency.

This season of Artists Space is made possible,
in part, by the support of the following foundations, corporations,
and government agencies:

CORPORATIONS AND FOUNDATIONS
Harriett Ames Charitable Trust
J.M.R. Barker Foundation
Bohen Foundation
Chase Manhattan Bank N.A.
Robert Sterling Clark Foundation, Inc.
Cowles Charitable Trust
Daimler-Benz of North America
Dynamic Systems, Inc.
I. J. Feldman Foundation
Foundation for Contemporary Performance Arts
Stephen A. and Diana L. Goldberg Foundation, Inc.
Herman Goldman Foundation
The Horace W. Goldsmith Foundation
J. P. Morgan
Jerome Foundation
The Netherland—America Foundation
Betty Parsons Foundation
Philip Morris Companies Inc.
Larry Rivers Foundation
Saul Rosen Foundation
Mark Rothko Foundation
Sotheby's

PUBLIC
National Endowment for the Arts
New York State Council on the Arts
City of New York Department of Cultural Affairs
City of New York Department of Cultural Affairs Cultural Challenge Program

*To those individuals and businesses who have provided financial support and
donated products or services, we are extremely grateful.*

List in formation as of October 19, 1998.

This book tells many stories about Artists Space. Our triumphs and failures, hopes and misgivings, recoveries and discoveries are all presented here, narrated by the artists, curators, staff, and critics who have helped to build our organization. By providing a comprehensive chronicle of the development of Artists Space, this book also recounts the history of the alternative exhibition space movement in the United States, a phenomenon for which we served as both catalyst and model. It also stands as a record of the New York art world during the years leading up to a new century.

Most importantly, this volume represents the spirit of more than 5,000 artists who have shared in the life of Artists Space. It is only with the perspective which time brings that one is able to recognize and articulate the accumulative contribution our constituency has made to history. Our future will be informed by all these individuals, as well as those yet encountered. This book has allowed us at Artists Space to reflect upon our past activities and to evaluate our position within the art community. Artists Space will continue to be an organization dedicated to artists and their work, devoted to programs and events in the spirit of our mission.

This project began 10 years ago with Susan Wyatt, then the Executive Director, who worked on a publication commemorating 18 years of Artists Space. Susan's work, and the work of her editor, Nancy Princenthal, became the basis for our book, *5000 Artists Return to Artists Space: 25 Years*. In 1996, the Board of Directors and I committed ourselves to completing the book project in celebration of Artists Space's 25th anniversary. We brought up to date the exhibition chronology begun by Susan and added more current interviews to some which had already been done. I contacted Valerie Smith, Curator at Artists Space from 1981 to 1989, and asked her to write a history of the organization. While thinking about the book, Valerie felt a more dynamic approach should be taken in order to capture the innovation and excitement, the successes as well as the failures, of the past 25 years. The controversies, anecdotes, and everyday aspects of Artists Space were as important to our history as were the accomplishments. She suggested we include as many interviews of artists, writers, curators, staff, and Board members as possible, and have the past Directors' interviews, as well as my own, be conducted by people who worked with them. In this way the book became a publication about the individuals and by the individuals who made up this complex organization. In the course of the interviewing process it was apparent that people were not just telling stories about Artists Space, but giving a history of the contemporary New York art world of the past 25 years, which all of us have helped shape. We felt very strongly that a history is built upon many different opinions, and so we included artists and people whose views we knew might not necessarily be complimentary toward Artists Space. This is the open approach we felt was necessary in order to truly represent the organization that has been such an important part of our lives.

I am indebted to Valerie Smith, for whom this book was a daunting but thoroughly absorbing task. Her spirited determination and enthusiasm for this project were an inspiration to all who worked with her. She felt strongly that we must examine the legacy of Artists Space not only from the perspective of those who functioned within its framework, but also from the perspective of those outside that structure who participated in and were affected by our choices and ideology. If Valerie had not insisted on this, and that we *are* our history, I am certain this book would not be the document it is today. For this my Board and I are grateful.

This book is the sum of many parts, and I would like to begin by thanking Susan Wyatt, who began this process. Her template served as an important point of departure. She has also been invaluable in guiding Valerie and me through some of the more controversial points of our history. Susan worked closely with Nancy Princenthal from 1989 to 1992. I would like to thank Nancy for keeping us on track and always remaining calm. Jack Bankowsky also deserves my thanks for his initial work on this book. Along with Nancy, Jack conducted some of the early interviews from which Valerie and I took our cue. Susan worked with a number of individuals researching and proofing the chronology, archiving the photo collection, and coordinating the book project. Thanks to Barbara Hertel, Stacey Jamar, Vincent Katz, Cathy Peck, Emily Russell, and Sarah Wagner for the many hours spent on these details.

Valerie and I thank all who shared with us their thoughts, contained in over 200 interviews within these pages, as well as all those whose views for various technical and editorial reasons are not here. While the majority of the interviews were conducted by Valerie and myself, we did have assistance. When circumstances deemed it fitting, we made a more personal pairing between interviewer and interviewee in order to maintain the feeling of a private dialogue we felt so important to the project. Thanks to Connie Butler, Pip Day, Denise Fasanello, Ronald Jones, Matt Mullican, Joan Rosenbaum, Cindy Sherman, and Amy Wanggaard for their generous contribution of time. Their relationship to the individuals interviewed ensured an honest recounting of Artists Space's history.

Because of her history with Artists Space and because her work is text based, Jenny Holzer was a natural choice for our endnote. We invited her to provide a piece that would commemorate both her own work and the publication. Her original text, *Eating Friends,* was exhibited as a collaborative work with Peter Nadin at Artists Space, January 9 to February 13, 1982. She later reworked this piece, and it appears here in its revised form. It is a wonderful tribute to the organization, and we thank Jenny for the opportunity to publish this most apropos selection.

There are numerous individuals who have been hired specifically to work on this book. For the 1996–97 season, Debra Singer began compiling and fact-checking an early version of the chronology, and Debi Sonzogni started coordinating the different aspects of the publication. In the 1997–98 season, Debi had the laborious task of transcribing the interviews and conducting general troubleshooting on the editorial side. Debi is someone who has been close enough to Artists Space to recognize essential places, names, and information. I would like to thank them both for their hard work in these areas of research and coordination.

Also in this past season, Valerie and I have had the good fortune to have Mariani Lefas-Tetenes join us as general editorial assistant and researcher. Although asked to wear many hats, Mariani never lost her good-natured enthusiasm for the project and remained unfazed by the enormous pressure of deadlines, technological pitfalls, and potential disasters. We cannot be grateful enough to Mariani for all she has done. As we neared the eleventh hour, she was assisted by David Joiner and Sarada Rauch; thanks to both of them.

Valerie and I are very pleased to have Cathy Peck as copy editor for this book. Since she worked with Susan Wyatt during its early stages, her closeness to the material was very important to us in its final stage. Finally, thank you to Liz Dalton who, with a fresh eye, gave this book a final read and to Meryl Schneider our diligent indexer.

We are also fortunate to have worked with Abbott Miller of Design/Writing/Research (DWR). I have known Abbott since before his exhibition at Artists Space (January 20 to March 16, 1996) and I knew from the start that I wanted him and his team to design this book. Besides their award-winning design work, they are able to deal with vast and varying amounts of information with ease. At DWR we worked with Paul Carlos, John Corrigan, Scott Devendorf, Tracy Hummer, Paul Makovsky, and Jane Rosch who whipped this book into shape.

My staff, most notably Assistant Director Elizabeth Metcalf and former Curator Pip Day, have played key roles in this publication. Lisa was responsible for the fundraising of this project. Without her convincing proposals, this book would not have been as ambitious as it is. Valerie and I relied on Pip to interview artists who had more recently exhibited at Artists Space and to help fill in the gaps in the recent years of the chronology. I also want to thank my former Assistant Sara Reisman and Artists File Coordinator/Development Associate Elizabeth Hires for helping with further details, such as lists of limited editions produced by Artists Space, a comprehensive list of funders, and a complete index of all the artists in our chronology. I would also like to acknowledge two new staff members, curator Jenelle Porter and my assistant Tara McDowell who have helped me pull together different aspects of this book at very short notice.

Our auditors, Lutz and Carr, under the supervision of Karen Kowgios, CPA, have done a great job of making a graph illustrating government support of Artists Space for the past 25 years. This has taken a bit of research on their part, and I thank Karen for agreeing to do this for us.

We are fortunate to be working with Distributed Art Publishers for distribution of this book. DAP has been an ideal match for us, and I would like to thank Avery Lozada and Sharon Gallagher for their interest in our project. We are also working with Bill Bartman of Art Resources Transfer to donate books to public libraries in underserved communities nationwide.

On behalf of the Board of Directors, I would like to thank the following foundations, corporations, and government agencies for their generous financial support of this project. During Susan Wyatt's tenure, initial funding was provided by the National Endowment for the Arts and the New York State Council on the Arts. Significant support from the Cowles Charitable Trust, the Bohen Foundation, and General Atlantic Corporation moved the project forward. Recent support has been provided by the lead sponsor of both the book and our 25th-anniversary season, Philip Morris Companies Inc. Additional major support has been provided by the National Endowment for the Arts, the Mark Rothko Foundation, and Sotheby's.

It is a pleasure to thank my Board of Directors, under the direction of President Virginia Cowles, who have been supportive and excited about this undertaking. I turned to a few Board members in particular for guidance, encouragement, and their expertise during the course of this project. I would like to thank Carolyn Alexander, Ann Gibson, Ronald Jones, Irving Sandler, Allan Schwartzman, and Beverly Wolff for their help with everything from the initial conceptualization to fundraising to reading the book in draft form. Andrea Schwan, our publicity magician, has performed miracles for our 25th-anniversary season, and we are eternally grateful.

Finally, I would like to especially thank Elizabeth and Anthony Enders, A.G. Rosen, and Tom Slaughter, all of whom have significantly contributed to Artists Space during my tenure as Director.

While every precaution has been taken to ensure accuracy in this record of 25 years, we may have made errors. We apologize if our fact-checking has not been completely accurate. I hope the reader and anyone directly affected will understand.

Ultimately, this book has been the concerted effort of everyone involved in Artists Space, from the 1973 inaugural season to the present. We are a very close team, that's how we work. All that has transpired in these 25 years has touched us. I thank everyone for helping to create this history and for making it so spirited and memorable.

Claudia Gould
EXECUTIVE DIRECTOR

As an undergraduate I did a little interview with Laurie Anderson. It was my first. I asked her what her favorite books were. She told me *The Dancing Wu-Li Masters: An Overview of the New Physics* by Gary Zukav and *Working* by Studs Terkel (the latter may have been a subtle suggestion that I had some homework to do in the area of interviews). In any case, ever since then, *Working* has been a model and inspiration and definitely in the back of my mind when I thought of the concept for *5000 Artists Return to Artists Space: 25 Years*. This is not to say that there is any real resemblance between *Working* and this book, only that I wanted to include within these pages as many varying opinions from as many people with different cultural and professional art backgrounds as time and space allowed.

An early version, Artists Space's 18th-anniversary catalogue, contained some interviews. However, the questions were specifically about Artists Space, and the interviewees few and select. For the 25th-anniversary book I wanted to broaden this process by interviewing a large number of people: artists who come from diverse cultural backgrounds, angry artists, excited artists, critical artists, grateful artists, artists for whom the process is everything, and artists for whom success is the product of commercial recognition. Everyone had a legitimate story to tell. In addition to artists, I felt it was important to hear what Artists Space's Board and staff members, writers, architects, and curators had to say. The perspective of those individuals who navigated and witnessed Artists Space through its significant maelstroms is invaluable in the reconstruction of its history. It is also interesting to read the variations in the different accounts, not only because they flesh out the story, but in order to understand the significance these tumultuous events had and still have on those who effected and observed them and the enormous repercussions for those who didn't.

Unlike *Working*, this book is not a record of the here and now, but a multivoiced history of an art institution. The majority of interviews are full of reflections and anecdotes on experiences from people who were at Artists Space in the 70s and 80s. But the tone changes in the interviews with artists who showed their work in the mid- to late 90s. Their memory is still fresh and full of promise for the present, and there is an invincible optimism in their descriptions of what they are doing.

For the most part I kept the interview questions very open to allow for the maximum of random souvenirs, including those tangential to a direct Artists Space exhibition experience. What came out of these conversations were candid statements about the pioneering hardships of the 70s, the financial and cultural complexity of the 80s, and the retrospective position of the 90s. The direction these accounts took was left entirely up to the interviewee. My only intervention was to preface the interviews by saying our approach to the book attempted to be democratic, so we were inviting critical as well as happy memories to be voiced. The reasons for this should be clear. Too often retrospective catalogues are embarrassingly laudatory or weepy recollections of the good old days. To be honest, there is some of that in here; however, for the most part we have been able to preserve the purity of the open interview approach, where the emphasis is not on the pat on the back, but on a sharp examination of the past 25 years.

This critical take on Artists Space's history does not come out of the blue. It is inherent in the very best work shown at Artists Space and endemic of the continuous self-reflective mode of the institution. Born out of the necessity to critique the imbalances of the New York art system, over the years Artists Space, like other alternative institutions, has had to ride the socioeconomic wave and suicidally doubt and reevaluate its mission, ironically, in order to remain in existence.

In this book a conscious effort has been made to construct a balance between concrete and colloquial information and how one supersedes the other in a succession of words, numbers, and images. But it was important to us that the artist get the last word. Therefore, it was fitting that Jenny Holzer write the endnote, and appropriate that she present a revised edition of a work she had originally shown at Artists Space in 1982. Jenny's atomic sentences tightly contain all the critical spots of her generation. They crunch into a microcosm a spectrum ranging from worldly to gut-felt issues in which the mundane concerns of Artists Space and artists are subsumed. It was important to us that readers go out with a kick, propelling them to the understanding that the concerns within the book are just a frame for the larger issues without.

In compiling the photographs and documents for this book we came across the problem of how to represent the artwork. This is an issue which is never successfully resolved unless the book is a monograph. The true essence of any artwork, from the most ephemeral to the most concrete, is largely lost to the reader in a book like this. So we opted to select mainly anecdotal and familial material (there is nothing so curiously narcissistic as seeing yourself way back when), in the hope that the distinct atmosphere of each decade, administration, exhibition, or event will infuse these pages with the spirit of the place.

In the chronology there was an initial attempt toward consistency that hung a false homogeneity over the material. For the 25th-anniversary book we have gone back to the original announcement cards, posters, and general printed matter to use the language of the times to identify and describe artwork. For instance, the reader may come across "visible and invisible structures" instead of sculpture, or "tape works" instead of audio, and "situations" versus film and performance. We have decided to keep these complex and colorful designations linked with the 70s in order to give the reader a flavor for the language of the time and to respect the certain mystery they give to the artwork. We felt the labels were intentional, not arbitrary, part of the work and not separate from it, so we have retained them in homage to these ephemeral projects. It is interesting to note a lot of new media made its first appearance in the early and mid-70s. What we take for granted as an installation or a performance today was then just beginning to be articulated. These ambiguous names reveal a playful search for meaning and individuality as well as an attempt to carve out a new genre or expand on an old one.

In so many retrospective studies the financial history is strangely absent. We felt it would be a radical step to acknowledge both the ups and downs of support Artists Space has experienced over the years. Given that Artists Space was initially solely funded by NYSCA (New York State Council on the Arts), we thought it would be valuable to present a graph of government support, from 1973 to the present. In addition, we have provided readers with the names of government, foundation, and corporate funders as well as benefit contributors over the years. It is a preliminary account of Artists Space's complex fiscal history, and like any compilation, it invites further research.

As we were interviewing artists for the book, a surprising number of sharp leitmotifs occurred in the accounts, and we have decided to use them as sight lines that intersect specific events at Artists Space. In this way we have been able to develop a chain of radically different generational positions in our oral history on such topics as multiculturalism, censorship, and government funding. It is interesting to keep in mind what is important to one generation has a different meaning for the second and a completely new one for the third. Thus one can trace the transformation in the significance of certain political, social, and aesthetic issues through the succession of nearly three decades as represented here.

The editing process is not a cold and bloodless activity inflicted on the unknowing and vulnerable voice. Oddly enough, it's like curating an exhibition at Artists Space. There is all this raw primary material of seemingly conflicting points of view, tentative statements as well as passionate opinions, and what holds it together is the latitudinal line of the chronology and the longitudinal critical points that periodically drop down into each decade. Without this grid there would be nothing to grab on to but a collection of disconnected speculations. What we have suggested in *5000 Artists Return to Artists Space: 25 Years* is that there is something more here for the reader who is up to the challenge.

Valerie Smith
EDITOR

Artists Space has pushed the boundaries of artistic practice and the institutional framework in which artists present their work. Under the directorship of Claudia Gould, the number of exhibitions presenting designers and architects has increased. In architecture and design, the scope of a project is often defined by a conceptual or programmatic brief that responds to the needs of a specific commission. Artists Space has provided a different context, one in which the fertile exchanges between design, art, fashion, and architecture can be explored.

For my studio, the invitation to show at Artists Space provided a far more open-ended framework in which to think about design. It allowed us to present a more speculative vein of research and experimentation, work that did not have an immediate practical application. The open forum of Artists Space encouraged us to think about the status of words and letters in electronic media, leading to an exhibition, and, later, a book called *Dimensional Typography*. Our project for Artists Space explored the concept of letters in three dimensions, bridging the formal and spatial concerns of sculpture with the technological and editorial issues confronted in design.

Artists Space has now invited us to collaborate on this publication documenting their 25th anniversary. While our exhibition at Artists Space provided an exhilarating lack of constraints, the commission to design this book was daunting for several reasons. As an institutional history there is a temptation to simply open the archive and let the material speak for itself. But in the case of Artists Space, and the very anti-institutional terrain it pioneered, there is not a definitive list of greatest hits and brightest moments. Rather, the significance resides in a sustained determination to show the work of many artists, especially those who might not otherwise be seen. So quantity (5,000 artists) and duration (25 years) became significant reference points in the design.

As a documentary history, we were also intent to show Artists Space as a *place* (actually several places throughout its various changes of address). Wherever possible, we show the work as it was displayed in the gallery, rather than presenting isolated reproductions of individual works. This desire to communicate the often modest and makeshift character of the organization was the overriding criteria for editing the thousands of available images.

As an oral history, we wanted to convey the idea of a polyphony of voices—many contradictory—that comprise that very communal phenomenon sometimes called "institutional memory." Within the interviews we typographically signal the conversational character of the tape-recorded sessions. From an editorial standpoint we also felt it was important to convey the sense of six different episodes in the 25 years of Artists Space, reflecting the distinct tenures of its past six directors. In preserving the multiple, overlapping, and sometimes conflicting accounts of specific events we acknowledge the problems inherent in oral history. As a result of this insistence on multiple vantage points, the index to the book becomes a critical tool for navigating and comparing these various accounts.

Perhaps the most challenging aspect of the book was how to convey its chronological structure without succumbing to the formality or tedium of a timeline. It would overstate the clarity and coherence of Artists Space to represent its first 25 years as an orderly progression. Instead, we have tried to represent it as an organic, discontinuous phenomenon, laced with conversations and controversies. The book adopts a calendrical format, based on a 25-square grid, presenting the exhibition history against an armature that refers to two of the institution's greatest claims: it was among the first of its kind, and it has survived for 25 years.

Publishing a 25-year history is an essentially conservative undertaking, particularly for an experimental institution. Books, as repositories and containers of records and histories, are a literally conservative medium. Our intention with the design of this project was to bring these texts and images together in a way which acknowledges Artists Space's pioneering history while also representing it in the present as an established cultural institution. In other words, to reconcile the chaotic and organic aspects of an evolving phenomenon with the clarity and structure of creating an historical record.

J. Abbott Miller

Design/Writing/Research, *Letter J & F*, design.
Project: Exhibit A: Design/Writing/Research, Jan. 20–Mar. 16, 1996.

DIRECTOR INTERVIEWS

Trudie Grace and Irving Sandler interviewed by Joan Rosenbaum, 2/25/97 — — — — — — — — — page 20

Helene Winer interviewed by Cindy Sherman, Valerie Smith, and Matt Mullican, 1/6/98 — — — — — — — — — — — 52

Linda Shearer interviewed by Valerie Smith, 5/10/97 — — — — 114

Susan Wyatt interviewed by Evelyn B. Leong, 12/93 — — — — 194

Carlos Solana-Gutierrez interviewed by Amy Wanggaard, 4/3/97 — — 226

Claudia Gould interviewed by Ronald Jones and Denise Fasanello, 4/5/97 — — — — — — — — — 264

Valerie Smith Interviews

Stan Allen, 4/21/97 — — — — — 192
Anastasia Aukeman, 10/27/97 — 292
Mowry Baden, 3/10/97— — — — 155
Mirosław Bałka, 1/10/98 — — — 221
Judith Barry, 2/25/97 — — — — 167
Gretchen Bender, 12/10/97 — — 139
Ashley Bickerton, 2/9/98 — — — 158
Dara Birnbaum, 3/10/97 — — — — 87
Marc Blane, 2/4/97 — — — — — 68
Douglas Blau, 2/4/97 — — — — — 182
Barbara Bloom, 2/9/98 — — — — 74
Jennifer Bolande, 4/22/97 — — — 146
Gregg Bordowitz, 2/11/98 — — — 215
Troy Brauntuch, 5/1/97 — — — — 92
Tim Burns, 5/12/97— — — — — — 134
Connie Butler, 5/13/97 — — — — 245
David Cabrera, 12/2/97 — — — — 152
Cynthia Carlson, 2/4/97 — — — — 34
Linda Cathcart, 5/12/97 — — — — 147
Charlie Clough, 2/3/97 — — — — 82
Edit deAk and
 Walter Robinson, 11/5/97 — — 37
Jane Dickson, 4/24/97 — — — — 136
Mark Dion, 11/25/97 — — — — — 176
Nancy Dwyer, 2/11/98 — — — — 80
Jean Fisher, 3/18/97 — — — — — 189
Andrea Fraser, 3/27/97— — — — 178
Ellen Gallagher, 5/17/98 — — — 256
Leslie Gill, 4/21/97— — — — — — 193
Gilles Jean Giuntini, 2/13/97 — 140
RoseLee Goldberg, 4/15/97 — — 111
Guillermo Gomez-Peña, 5/18/98 216
Sharon Greytak, 3/10/97 — — — 141
Peter Halley, 2/18/97 — — — — 159
Ann Hamilton, 12/15/97 — — — 191
Biff Henrich, 3/26/97 — — — — 149
Julia Heyward, 2/9/98 — — — — — 91
Chris Hill, 5/8/97— — — — — — — 188
Jenny Holzer, 5/15/97 — — — — 137
Pamela Jenrette, 2/4/97 — — — — 69
Kellie Jones, 4/28/97 — — — — — 185
Ronald Jones, 4/25/97 — — — — 138

Mike Kelley, 3/10/97— — — — — 180
Rick Klauber, 2/13/97 — — — — 70
Silvia Kolbowski, 12/1/97 — — 123
Jeff Koons, 2/11/98 — — — — — 139
Justen Ladda, 2/24/97 — — — — 159
Ernest Larsen, 4/16/97 — — — — 237
Louise Lawler, 2/21/97 — — — — 100
William Leavitt, 3/21/98 — — — 107
Zoe Leonard, 4/11/97 — — — — 214
Lucy Lippard, 4/28/97 — — — — 106
Robert Longo, 4/16/97 — — — — 81
Ken Lum, 3/5/97 — — — — — — 145
Joseph Marioni, 2/13/97— — — — 35
Tim Maul, 4/23/97 — — — — — — 152
Allan McCollum, 2/25/97 — — — 127
Micki McGee, 4/12/97 — — — — 248
Annette Messager, 5/1/97 — — — 136
Alan Michelson, 3/26/97 — — — 189
John Miller, 3/6/97— — — — — — 169
Gerry Morehead, 3/11/97 — — — 73
Robert Morgan, 2/18/97— — — — 72
Lee Mullican, 3/19/97 — — — — 175
Tony Oursler, 5/7/97 — — — — — 308
Michael Paha, 4/14/97 — — — — 174
Judy Pfaff, 3/4/97 — — — — — — 126
Patricia C. Phillips, 5/14/97 — — 184
Adrian Piper, 5/7/97— — — — — 31
Lari Pittman, 3/11/97 — — — — 154
Tim Rollins, 5/12/98 — — — — — 141
David Salle, 5/1/97 — — — — — — 90
Keith Sanborn, 3/7/97 — — — — 181
Robert Sanchez, 4/21/97 — — — 217
Carolee Schneemann, 3/25/97 — — 29
Cindy Sherman, 4/22/97 — — — 241
Cindy Sherman, 3/18/98 — — — — 84
Kiki Smith, 3/26/97 — — — — — 219
Dan Walworth, 3/14/97 — — — — 187
Megan Williams, 2/26/97 — — — 154
Fred Wilson, 5/9/97 — — — — — 186
Martha Wilson, 2/10/98 — — — — 76
Mel Ziegler, 5/15/97 — — — — — 162
Michael Zwack, 2/26/97 — — — — 82

Claudia Gould Interviews

Philip Aarons, 11/97 — — — — — 218
Vito Acconci, 5/97— — — — — — 35
Dennis Adams, 2/97 — — — — — 108
Charlie Ahearn, 11/97 — — — — 49
Carolyn Alexander, 11/97 — — — 312
Laurie Anderson, 1/98— — — — — 33
Janine Antoni, 1/98 — — — — — 244
Richard Armstrong, 11/97 — — — 173
Beth B, 11/97 — — — — — — — — 92
Jonathan Borofsky, 2/97— — — — 28
Eva Buchmuller, 5/97 — — — — 288
Chuck Close, 5/97 — — — — — — 31
Binda Colebrook, 5/97 — — — — 277
Diego Cortez, 3/97 — — — — — — 47

Virginia Cowles, 6/97 — — — — 315
Douglas Crimp, 2/97— — — — — 89
Bryan Crockett, 4/97 — — — — 284
Constance De Jong, 4/97 — — — 153
Carroll Dunham, 5/97 — — — — 130
Elizabeth Diller, 2/97— — — — — 182
Elizabeth Enders, 11/97 — — — 247
Denise Fasenello, 6/97 — — — — 286
Hermine Ford, 2/97 — — — — — 170
Steven Frailey, 11/97 — — — — 148
Andrew Ginzel, 11/97 — — — — 46
Neil Goldberg, 4/98 — — — — — 290
Kathryn High, 5/97— — — — — — 170
Perry Hoberman, 1/98 — — — — 148
Barry Holden, 6/97 — — — — — 70
Alfredo Jaar, 3/97 — — — — — — 162
Joan Jonas, 1/98— — — — — — — 96
Mel Kendrick, 3/97 — — — — — 28
Jon Kessler, 2/97 — — — — — — 152
Carole Ann Klonarides, 2/97 — — 171
Tom Lawson, 3/97 — — — — — — 296
Annette Lemieux, 4/97 — — — — 156
Kristin Lucas, 4/97 — — — — — 291
Greg Lynn, 5/97 — — — — — — 285
Anthony McCall, 3/97 — — — — 29
Paul McMahon, 4/97 — — — — — 85
J. Abbott Miller, 11/97 — — — — 287
Mary Miss, 11/97 — — — — — — 168
Frank Moore, 11/97 — — — — — 298
Matt Mullican, 5/8/97 — — — — 71
Elizabeth Murray, 4/97 — — — — 220
Shirin Neshat, 6/97 — — — — — 280
Donald Newman, 2/97 — — — — 109
Patrick O'Connell, 4/97 — — — — 94
Tom Otterness, 1/98 — — — — — 96
Ellen Phelan, 5/97 — — — — — — 72
Howardena Pindell, 4/13/98 — — 110
Richard Prince, 4/97 — — — — 124
Hani Rashid, 2/97 — — — — — — 183
Janelle Reiring, 11/97 — — — — — 98
Peter Schjeldahl, 1/98 — — — — — 68
Richard Shebairo, 11/97 — — — — 280
Laurie Simmons, 2/97 — — — — 101
Mike Smith, 4/97 — — — — — — 78
Valerie Smith, 5/8/97 — — — — 222
Nancy Spero, 5/97 — — — — — 105
Haim Steinbach, 2/97 — — — — 111
Donald Sultan, 2/97 — — — — — 105
Lynne Tillman, 3/97 — — — — — 153
John Torreano, 3/97 — — — — — 30
Bernard Tschumi, 5/97— — — — 95
Ben van Berkel, 6/97 — — — — — 300
Julie Wachtel, 1/98— — — — — — 131
Robin Winters, 1/98— — — — — — 75
Beverly Wolff, 11/97 — — — — 234
Michael Zahn, 4/97 — — — — — 292

Claudia Gould and Valerie Smith Interviews

Nan Goldin, 5/97— — — — — — — 172
Ragland Watkins, 3/97 — — — — 135

Connie Butler Interviews

Mike Ballou, 9/97 — — — — — — 250
Willie Cole, 6/97 — — — — — — 287
Renée Green, 6/97 — — — — — — 239
Rita McBride, 9/97 — — — — — — 242
Beverly Semmes, 5/98 — — — — 236
Chrysanne Stathacos, 6/97 — — — 242

Denise Fasanello Interviews

Alejandro Berlin, 11/97— — — — 288
Ken Buhler, 11/97 — — — — — — 251
Victor Wong, 5/97 — — — — — — 278

Pip Day Interviews

Adam Ames, 1/9/98 — — — — — 289
David Arnold, 1/9/98— — — — — 301
Andrew Bordwin, 1/30/98 — — — 309
Anne Gardiner, 2/4/98 — — — — 310
Karen Kimmel, 1/9/98 — — — — 301

Nancy Princenthal Interviews

Félix González-Torres, 1991 — — 186
Barbara Kruger, 1991 — — — — — 28

Jack Bankowsky Interviews

Scott Burton, 1989 — — — — — — 70
Roberta Smith, 1989 — — — — — 222

Statements

Eric Bogosian, 5/9/97 — — — — 101
Michael Byron 4/98 — — — — — 143
Christopher D'Arcangelo, 1977— — 97
Pip Day, 6/97 — — — — — — — — 310
Hudson, 2/16/97 — — — — — — 138
Ladd Kessler, 5/13/97 — — — — 131

155 Wooster Street, Summer 1973.

Mel Kendrick, *Dinnever Hill*, 1974, installation view.

October **1973** to October **1975**

Trudie Grace and Irving Sandler interviewed by Joan Rosenbaum

In 1972 the Committee for the Visual Arts was incorporated as a service and arts organization. Its gallery, Artists Space, opened its first season in October 1973 at 155 Wooster Street. Trudie Grace became the first Executive Director of Artists Space and remained so until October 1975. Irving Sandler served as first Board President, until 1980. He remained a Board member until 1995, when he became an honorary Board member. Joan Rosenbaum was an Artists Space Board member from 1980 to 1992. This interview took place on February 25, 1997.

JOAN ROSENBAUM: We're going to be talking about Artists Space in the early years, 1972 through 1975. I remember when you, Trudie, were Director of the Visual Arts Projects Program of the New York State Council on the Arts (NYSCA). You, Irving, and the Visual Arts Projects panel were thinking of ways that NYSCA's funds might best benefit artists.

TRUDIE GRACE: At NYSCA, the Museum Aid Program had a budget of millions, while the Visual Arts Projects Program had a budget of about one million dollars. We were receiving requests from visual arts organizations all over the state, including many art centers serving upstate towns as well as New York City groups offering children's workshops in poor neighborhoods. Our mandate did not allow us to fund cooperative galleries. Nor were we able to fund already existing alternative galleries, unless they were serving a large constituency and conducting programs that could be considered a "public service."

So, at a time when the gallery scene was tightly closed, we did not have a way to serve a huge body of artists. We began to hear some grumbling about it, particularly from the cooperative galleries.

IRVING SANDLER: There was another consideration. The state legislation mandated that only not-for-profit organizations could get funds. Just about everybody in the arts—dancers, actors, video people—formed a not-for-profit group, except artists, who were still like old-fashioned entrepreneurs. They couldn't get funding.

Around 1971, I was asked to be a consultant to the Visual Arts Projects Program to organize an artists lecture project to serve nonprofit organizations in New York State. A small educational organization became the conduit for the monies. I ran the lecture program out of Trudie's office at NYSCA.

TG: In the spring of 1972, in response to an obvious need, Irving and some of us at the Council began to mull over ways to fund more programs of direct benefit to visual artists. Lucy Kostelanetz, Director of NYSCA's Visual Arts Program, which incorporated both Visual Arts Projects and the Museum Aid Program, strongly encouraged Irving and me to develop some plans. That's when we started to have meetings with artists working in different disciplines to get their opinions on the subject. This whole effort had the strong backing of the Visual Arts Projects funding panel. It was composed of prominent people in the visual arts in New York State—administrators, critics, and artists. Irving had served on the panel for several years and was an eloquent spokesman for artists.

JR: I remember the artists' meetings after-hours in the office.

TG: Yes, Richard Nonas, Jene Highstein, and Kes Zapkus were there.

IS: I think Jeff Way and George Segal were also among those who attended. There were maybe three or four meetings during which we simply asked the direct question, "What is it that the art world needs at this moment, aside from grants to individual artists?" (This was being done by other organizations funded by NYSCA.) The purpose was to identify the needs of artists and suggest what might be done to meet them.

TG: **It was Richard Nonas who talked about funding a presentation of shows in artists' studios.**

IS: We shot that down because we felt people wouldn't come. Too many lofts were not easily accessible. We needed something really more established, something to induce people to come see the work of totally unrecognized, unaffiliated artists.

TG: **The idea of establishing a gallery space where artists would select artists emerged from these meetings. Those of us involved were naturally delighted and, to tell you the truth, surprised that the plan met with such unqualified support from Lucy Kostelanetz and the Visual Arts Projects panel. We saw the idea as an almost impossible ideal. Lucy, though, went on quickly to obtain approval from Eric Larrabee, who was Director of NYSCA, and from the members of NYSCA's governing council. The first budget was $100,000—all of it directly from the Council. I've always thought that Irving's stature within the art community and his reputation for knowing many artists greatly contributed to the swift acceptance of the idea of Artists Space.**

JR: Initially, it was remarkable to have all Council money.

TG: **However, Lucy Kostelanetz, without being adamant, did encourage fund-raising and warned us that the organization would not always have the Council's support. But we knew that our association with the Council, and Irving's good contacts at the National Endowment for the Arts, would help us raise other funds. Ultimately, it took three years for Artists Space to no longer be viewed as an arm of the Council.**

IS: I knew the imaginativeness of the artists we brought together would produce a good idea, but I was worried that the Council might balk at giving artists so much decision-making power and the high visibility that Artists Space would project because of this.

What if it turned out to be scandalous, as it did, every now and then, later? The Council would have been on the spot. But it went along with the establishment of Artists Space.

TG: **One reason was that Artists Space was to have several service programs for artists that would also benefit nonprofit organizations involved with artists on short- or long-term projects. The Artists Lecture Program was going to continue, and the Emergency Materials Fund was going to be initiated. The idea for the latter emerged during the discussions with artists prior to the establishment of Artists Space.**

JR: Right, that was one of the founding programs, just like the Unaffiliated Artists File was one of the founding programs.

TG: **We wanted to make the organization as open and clean as possible because there was such an acute sense of the gallery system being locked up and controlled by critics, curators, and dealers.**

JR: I remember that.

IS: We meant for artists to have major decision-making power right from the start. We decided that half our Board would be artists. We believed that this would make us different from the typical arts organizations, which are controlled by nonartist administrators and trustees. And artists would choose who was to show.

JR: You decided it would work, because artists' choices were the heart and soul of it. The next level is how you actually established Artists Space.

IS: First, we had to incorporate. Jerome Hausman, David Ecker, and myself formed the Committee for the Visual Arts, Inc. Once this was done, Trudie left the Council early in the summer of 1973, just three months after all the discussions with artists had begun, to become Director of the Committee, which administered Artists Space and its programs. Then we got the third-floor space above the Paula Cooper Gallery—full of floor-to-ceiling junk.

TG: **Irving found the space, at the corner of Wooster and Houston Streets. It was a choice spot.**

IS: Then, I left for the summer, and you cleaned it out and created one of the handsomest galleries in New York. It was spacious, well-lit—a wonderful spot.

TG: **I hired various artists to help. Phil Glass even came in to see whether he wanted to take on the plumbing job.**

IS: Before leaving for the summer, I had drawn up a list of 21 well-known artists, to cover nine months of one-person shows. They represented a fairly broad spectrum. Then we asked each of them to choose one

unaffiliated artist. An artist could choose or be chosen only once.
That way, no person or group could dominate the gallery and what we
exhibited would always be surprising. The gallery would assume all costs.
If works were sold, all the money would go to the artist.

TG: He especially considered artists who were in contact with a lot of unaffiliated artists.

IS: Yes, people who knew artists and who wouldn't be self-serving. What
a list it was: I remember Chuck Close, Donald Judd, Romare Bearden, Vito
Acconci, Philip Pearlstein, Sol LeWitt, Dorothea Rockburne, Richard Serra,
Jackie Winsor, and Nancy Graves.

JR: So it was in the first year that you started this system of choosing three artists to select
three artists.

IS: Yes. Each artist had a one-person exhibition, with three people able to
show simultaneously because of the size of the space.

**TG: The selectors responded quickly. Some of them visited artists' studios, which is just what we had
hoped would happen. A few selected their assistants, and that was also fine. We were simply interested
in unaffiliated artists whose work was thought worthy of exposure by exhibiting artists. As we
predicted, curiosity about whom this or that artist had selected contributed to getting people to come
to the gallery. We were sometimes asked who had selected the selectors, and Irving's solid reputation
helped when we had to substantiate that question.**

IS: Of course, there were so many artists around who really needed
shows. But I asked, "Why should I choose the selectors? Why not turn that
over to artists?" So we drew up a list of about 660 artists. We sent this list
to each of the artists on it and asked each of them to choose 10 to be
selectors. We were astonished at the return—420 of these came back. We
hadn't even provided return envelopes.

TG: The response told us we had a good deal of support.

↑ *Cobb, Edelheit and Morton*
exhibition opening, Oct. 6, 1973.
Photo: Henry Edelheit

22

IS: We collated the returned lists and came up with the selectors for the second and third seasons. It was a great group. I recall Louise Bourgeois, Christo, Red Grooms, Al Held, Lynda Benglis, Mel Bochner, Robert Ryman, Mel Edwards, Brice Marden, Mary Frank, and Rafael Ferrer. The selection process was now even more the artists' choice. And by then, we had set up the Unaffiliated Artists File.

TG: **We started the File when we first opened and it grew fast. So, before the artists selected for the second and third seasons, we suggested that they consider not only artists they already knew, but also artists in our File.**

IS: Yes, we wanted to include artists who were completely unknown. Then we began to use the File innovatively. At the end of the first season, when the File contained about 400 artists, we invited all artists with material in it to come to Artists Space, view slides from the File, and vote for 12 to be in a group show. The idea was that artists, who often felt victimized by juries, now would become the jury-of-the-whole. They would choose. We also asked groups of artists to select shows from the File.

JR: The records of Artists Space indicate that a jury of all 130 artists of the Unaffiliated Artists File actually participated in this process. What also interests me is that you started in October, and by February you presented an *Artists As Filmmakers* series. This shows that you weren't just dealing with painting, sculpture, printmaking, and the like. There was a lot of boundary-crossing.

IS: Yes, there were poets and multimedia artists scheduled for two or three evenings a week. Also, there were panels that first year. I remember a panel of critics who wrote for *Artforum*.

JR: Yes. You did do panels.

TG: **For the most part, many of these evenings were not generated in-house. The artist community knew we were approachable and reviewing proposals. Also, since we were supported by the Council, it was almost expected that we would be responsive to outside ideas. Alida Walsh came to us with her proposal for the *Artists As Filmmakers* program.**

Due to our substantial support from the Council, we actually felt obliged to keep the place going night and day, if there was demand. We weren't open to just any group; but, if it seemed as though we were dealing with responsible people, we made Artists Space available. We only made restrictions if there was going to be some danger to the art on exhibition. Most often additional programming was done between shows.

JR: You had dancers in March of that year. Suzy Harris organized *The Natural History of the American Dancer*. And you had some plays by Bruce Serlen and Gregory Lehane. Then Edit deAk, who began to work for you part-time, organized *PersonA*, a series of video and performance evenings focusing on autobiography.

Then you did this big group show from the Unaffiliated Artists File. And Irving moderated a panel, on *What Are the Issues in Art Today?* with Chuck Close, Barbara Rose, John Coplans, Lucas Samaras, and Nancy Graves. A week later, there was *Pop Art*, a panel discussion with Rudolf Baranik as moderator and the panelists Lawrence Alloway, Robert Indiana, Robert Rosenblum, and George Segal. Then four films by and about Charles Simonds, and two by Rudy Burckhardt. So it was an incredibly impressive first season.

IS: Again, that was in part because of our openness. We would just let things happen.

TG: **Sometimes we weren't even present at the evening event, if we felt that we could trust the person organizing the program. One night, for instance, John Cage and a large diverse group read from Gertrude Stein's writings through the night. I came back the next morning, and to my surprise some of the readers were still in the gallery, sitting on mattresses scattered all over the gallery floor.**

JR: Do you have a memory of how you were different, say, from Art and Urban Resources?

TG: **Yes, absolutely. Alanna Heiss had control over everything that happened with that organization, or so it seemed.**

JR: That's true. Because she was the Director and the Curator. Her organization *was* different. I think it's important to emphasize that.

TG: **We admired her work, though, and we were encouraged by her ability to survive in the nonprofit world.**

JR: Artists Space, however, was an amazingly democratic process that sprang from the artists.

TG: **And we showed the work of a whole range of people, including older artists. Sidney Geist, for one, had a show at Artists Space.**

JR: That's an important policy, to program artists in their mid-careers, or older artists who haven't been recognized. They were always a part of the mix. I can remember, from the earliest discussions, that it wasn't just going to be the young or the most avant-garde who were going to show at Artists Space.

IS: Yes, that's right.

TG: **Also, we wanted to give exposure to as many unaffiliated artists as possible whether they were showing at Artists Space or not. That's why, during the second season, we held two slide shows to which we invited dealers, critics, and curators.**

We were stunned at the number of people who attended. We showed slides from the Unaffiliated Artists File at a time, you have to remember, when most dealers wouldn't look at slides at their galleries.

IS: We really did do things right. That first evening, for instance, everyone was given a list of the artists, about 400 in all, whose slides were going to be shown. If there was anything that they liked, they made a note and ticked it off. The phone numbers were there for them to follow up later.

In the back of our minds, we could see that there were two contradictory things going on. First, we were going to try to get these artists accepted in the art world. And second, there might be the possibility of creating an alternative art world, which, of course, we never succeeded in doing. This is because collectors, the people who put bread into artists' mouths, won't buy in an alternative space. They must have a dealer stand behind the work he or she chooses.

JR: But did you really make an effort to sell?

TG: **Only if someone walked in and showed an interest. We would certainly talk to them and pass on the artist's telephone number.**

IS: One of our policies was not to show an artist more than once. So, in that case, we couldn't have represented anyone in any significant way.

JR: That's true.

IS: Also, there would have been too many to promote. We were completely democratic, as democratic as we could be.

TG: **We didn't even make the decisions as to what work artists showed. In most cases, they had the good sense not to overhang. We stepped in when it looked like that was going to happen. These were serious artists, though, and most knew how to present their work well. The shows looked good.**

IS: And the gallery itself always looked beautiful.

JR: Who was on the staff?

TG: **I was there all the time. Irving, who was President of the Board, came into the gallery several times a week and, overall, gave the organization a great deal of his time.**

JR: Trudie, did you have an assistant? Or did you use interns?

TG: **I believe Edit deAk was there on a part-time basis toward the end of the first season. I also had interns, one of whom was Susan Wyatt. She later worked as Assistant Director with Helene Winer and then Linda Shearer before becoming Director of Artists Space. Susan and her friend Abby Turner were students at Sarah Lawrence College, where Irving taught briefly. For a time, they helped us about once a week. I was very tight with money and didn't want to spend it on staff. We didn't know what unforeseen expenses we might have with this new organization, and we were very sensitive to the fact that we were using the taxpayers' money.**

JR: What about the Board? What's your memory of it all? It was half artists. Is that correct?

IS: I know George Segal, Chuck Close, and Lucy Lippard were there the first year.

JR: I just wondered if you had any memories about how the Board functioned.

TG: **They were very supportive of the organization's mission; however, there were not many decisions to be made at first, because we had received Council money for such specific programming. Our system was set for the first couple of years, and it was going well.**

JR: It sort of hit the ground running in a way. It worked instantly, didn't it?

IS: It did, right from the start. We didn't need much outside advice.

JR: Now, what about the Emergency Materials Fund? That was a program from the very beginning, right?

TG: **The idea for it came from artists who attended those early meetings at the Council. It so happened that two of them, Richard Nonas and Jene Highstein, kept running into the same sort of problem. They'd be invited by a nonprofit organization to do a sculpture, but not necessarily as the result of a paid commission. Then they wouldn't have the money to buy all the materials they needed or to transport them to the site. They thought a program that helped artists with various costs would go toward ensuring the completion of works. This would be particularly welcome in the final phases of a project resulting from the collaboration between an artist and a nonprofit. Even a few hundred dollars, they noted, would make a difference with a sculpture project or with the transportation of works of art for a show. Indeed, we ended up by giving a lot of grants, with three hundred dollars as the maximum.**

IS: It was done on a first-come, first-served basis. All we needed was a letter from the sponsoring organization to show that the request was legitimate.

TG: **And each artist gave us a specific budget for the project.**

JR: And the staff just handled it.

TG: **Yes. The budget for the program was only somewhere between three and five thousand dollars, but it funded many projects.**

IS: One program that I was particularly fond of involved putting artists in residence in towns and small cities where they could use the local resources. It was such a wonderful idea. The project that worked most successfully, I think, was the one involving Richard Friedberg.

JR: What was that?

IS: He went to Clinton, New York, where an old steam engine and boiler factory was made available to him. The Kirkland Art Center was his host. We provided a stipend. He left a work of his there. The program was so promising that the Council said, "It's too big for you. We want it." And I said to the Council, "If you take it, you'll kill it. It's our inspiration, our energy. You won't do it right." And of course they took it, and it died.

JR: Tell me about some of the memorable shows.

TG: **Well, a memorable incident actually occurred at Jonathan Borofsky's show. He had placed, near the gallery door, a three-foot-high stack of graph paper filled with consecutive numbers. One day, a woman, who seemed a little strange, studied this piece rather intently. Then she suddenly reached down and took some of the sheets from the top of the stack, and walked out the door. We ran after her down the stairs and informed her she was taking away part of an artwork. She thought she had picked up publicity material. The sheets were returned, and after the show Borofsky presumably continued his numbering of this work in progress.**

IS: Laurie Anderson did a stunning show. It was mostly conceptual art, but she also did a performance, then or shortly afterwards. She was selected by Vito Acconci.

JR: What was the piece? Do you remember?

IS: Well, it was a multi-unit conceptual piece, which was a rumination on the Mercator globe, on an orange and a breast. I also remember the Mel Kendrick show, with the pieces along the floor. The Sidney Geist show was very important, in part because, as we said before, he was an older artist.

JR: I remember that show myself.

IS: It was a beautiful show.

TG: **There were a number of pedestal pieces, and many of Geist's longtime art world friends came to the show.**

IS: Marvin Torffield did a huge sculpture using sound, and Judy Pfaff's show was sensational.

TG: **We also showed works by a group of graffiti artists, whom many people thought were very good.**

JR: I remember you had that important graffiti show.

IS: A little before its time. Peter Schjeldahl wrote the introduction. There was a time when somebody had forgotten the key to Artists Space. A bunch of these kids were outside, and one said, "Oh, don't think about it. I'll just break and enter." That was funny.

JR: Let's talk about Artists Space in relation to other alternative spaces that were emerging at the time.

IS: Many of them were modeled on us. We would have visitors coming in from out of town, looking us over, asking questions, figuring out our funding. The one space with which I was most personally involved was the Sculpture Center in Utica. We were an inspiration to I don't know how many of the 300 artists' spaces, because we were the first. That was really important. Also, when you begin to look back, not only on the artists of our time, but the artists that Helene Winer showed…it is astonishing, the number of artists who had their first one-person show at Artists Space and who later went on to become leading artists of their generations.

The organization was really serving a need. The gallery system wouldn't or couldn't accommodate the many artists who deserved shows. Also there were artists working in ways that didn't lend themselves to commercial representation.

TG: We got very little criticism. I only recall that some cooperative gallery members, who would have liked Council funding for their organizations, felt a bit disgruntled by the size of the support from the Council.

JR: Right. Exactly.

IS: Later, in 1983, the Mark Rothko Foundation gave us a grant to do a series of one-person shows of work by more mature artists. Immediately, we were faced with the problem of how to help older unaffiliated artists, and it did present a problem. It sounds like a great idea, but how do you avoid the loser image? We got around that by showing the older artists with the young ones, and giving them special treatment, like handsome catalogues. It really worked.

JR: Artists Space always had that struggle between being a small organization that had invented itself and continued to have the flexibility to reinvent itself, and becoming institutionalized. This happens once you get recognized, begin to raise grant money, and have benefits. There was always that tension.

IS: But it did reinvent itself several times.

JR: Nevertheless, you had to have a Board that was giving money or raising money.

IS: With this development, we ran into a very big problem. In order to raise money, et cetera, you need high visibility. But in order to show unaffiliated artists, you're not going to get high visibility. It remains a problem.

JR: What would you say about Artists Space today? Is there a major shift in policy? Is the art world different?

IS: No, I think Artists Space is still trying to do its thing. The wonderful aspect about it is that each director was more or less able to do what he or she wanted to do, as long as it seemed reasonable and he or she could justify it to the Board. That worked most of the time.

On the one hand, a major reason for the success of Artists Space was our openness to the imagination, the enthusiasm, and the energies of artists. That may have been somewhat my role. And we ran a tight administrative ship, which was Trudie's role. We had a solid organization that was fiscally and administratively responsible. The mix just worked.

1972–1999

Chronology of Activities at Artists Space and Interviews

Originally incorporated in 1972 as the Committee for the Visual Arts, Inc., Artists Space begins as a pilot project of the New York State Council on the Arts (NYSCA), dedicated to assisting young, emerging artists. Trudie Grace, at that time Director of the Visual Arts Project Program at NYSCA, becomes Artists Space's first Executive Director, Irving Sandler, a consultant at NYSCA, becomes the first Board President, and Edit deAk eventually becomes Assistant Director. Located at 155 Wooster Street, Artists Space follows a general trend toward the alternative art space beginning with such organizations as 112 Workshop (later named White Columns), located at 112 Greene Street and founded in 1970 by Gordon Matta-Clark and Jeffrey Lew, and the Institute for Art and Urban Resources (later named P.S. 1 Contemporary Art Center), founded in 1971 by Alanna Heiss.

During its first year, Artists Space's exhibitions are organized by three artists, each selecting another artist to show. In these early years, Artists Space also opens its doors to a variety of events, performances, and cultural meetings, organized both in-house and out. In addition, it establishes several artist services, including the Visiting Artists Lecture Series, the Emergency Materials Fund, and the Independent Exhibitions Program (see page 322), designed to provide financial assistance to artists as well as opportunities to exhibit outside of Artists Space.

Ree Morton, *Souvenir Piece*, 1973, installation view.

Names in parentheses are the selectors or organizers of the exhibitions
Blue boxes refer to related exhibition photographs and illustrations

1973

Oct. 6–27: J.B. Cobb, sculpture with video (Richard Nonas); Martha Edelheit, painting (Lucas Samaras); Ree Morton, sculpture installation (Nancy Graves).

← J.B. Cobb, *Ocular Optical*, video installation, 1973.

Nov. 3–24: McArthur Binion, painting (Ronald Bladen); Jonathan Borofsky, sculpture (Sol LeWitt); Mary Obering, painting (Carl Andre).

→ Jonathan Borofsky, *Counting from 1 to 2,048,775*, Jan. 1, 1974.

Dec. 1–29: Ben Berns, sculpture (Peter Agostini); Paul Colin, painting (Edwin Ruda); David Crum, painting (Michael Heizer).

1974

Jan. 5–26: Laurie Anderson, *Systems*, objects and photo-text pieces (Vito Acconci); Don Gummer, sculpture (Richard Serra); Barbara Kruger, painting (Jane Kaufman).

↙ Barbara Kruger, painting, 1973.

Feb. 2–23: Mel Kendrick, sculpture (Dorothea Rockburne); Lois Lane, painting (Jackie Winsor); Christopher Shelton, sculpture (Romare Bearden).

ARTIST **Jonathan Borofsky** It could have been Sol LeWitt who knew my work, because we were both teaching at the School of Visual Arts and I might have shown him a book of my counting. I recall I had brought it in because it was my first year teaching there. I'd seen Sol's work in the minimal art show at the Jewish Museum in the 60s. So I made some connection there in my head. At a later time, he came to my apartment and the two of us sat in chairs staring at this column, a stack of paper in the bedroom. There was this large studio and there was this stack of paper I had been counting for several years. It went into the show, just that stack of paper.

The idea of Artists Space to have artists select artists seemed novel. It had a unique placement. Artists Space, at that time, was above Paula Cooper's gallery. I wasn't showing with Paula, but I was in a group show, *No. 7* (May 18–June 17, 1969), which Lucy Lippard organized at the gallery. I felt at home above Paula's place. Maybe I looked forward to Paula seeing my piece at Artists Space because she was downstairs. I remember my stack of paper sitting in the middle of the room and thinking that it was pretty hot, pretty exciting as a presentation. To celebrate that moment, I bought something at one of the stores to put around my neck. It was a Persian object and I still wear it today. It looks a little like a figure eight, but it isn't. It's a circle pulled in at the center. When I bought it, they said it was 2,000 years old. At the moment, at that time, a power object appealed to me. Just like the counting did.

ARTIST / WRITER **Barbara Kruger** Artists Space, along with Franklin Furnace (two so-called alternative spaces, though I don't use that term), were places where I first started reading my writing. I had also shown paintings at Artists Space, but the painting came to a screeching halt when I started reading the poetry and prose I was writing at the time. My very first reading was at Artists Space and it really put the brakes on that other work.

I don't know what an alternative space is and I don't know what a noncommercial space is. I never knew anyone, my colleagues or myself, who ever resisted commerce. In '74, when I showed at Artists Space, there simply were fewer galleries. The schools were vomiting out 20 million artists every semester, so most people couldn't possibly find a place for themselves. Artists Space accommodated a few of those people. Of course, you still had to go there and show your slides and someone had to choose you, it wasn't an entirely open process. But it was a very important space, because it did allow people to show their work. I always appreciated their support and I continue to support them. I don't know an artist who doesn't want his or her work to be seen.

ARTIST **Mel Kendrick** I spent a year working for Dorothea Rockburne, installing her shows around Europe. I had not shown my work to many people at that point, but she knew my work quite well. You basically knew who was doing what. The art world was a closed system in the 70s. It was much more emphatic, far less pluralistic. There didn't seem to be much interest in supporting or looking at what younger artists were doing. Nobody was thinking or writing about art. There was nothing, no emphasis on younger artists, and no such thing as a young gallery. Paula Cooper was a young gallery, but it was still all a generation older than me.

I knew I wanted to go to New York and make art, but the best I could hope for was a teaching job or to work for an artist. Artists Space put me into the grid in some way, although I was not thrilled about the sponsorship of established artists selecting unestablished artists. Artists selecting artists seemed derivative. But I realized, as a form of public relations, it was extremely important in order to get attention for the shows. I think the fact that Irving Sandler and Trudie Grace organized it meant their system was genuine in intention. It was good and there were interesting choices all over the place. Artists Space introduced me to Scott Burton's work. I also saw the work of Laurie Anderson and Judy Pfaff for the first time. The gallery space was unequivocally great. It was as good a space CONTINUED

Feb. 8–16: **Artists As Filmmakers** series (Alida Walsh)

Feb. 8: Doris Chase, *Squares*, *Moon Gates*; Eunice Goldin, *Blue Bananas* and *Other Meats*; Walter Gutman, *The Grape Dealer's Daughter*.
Feb. 9: Bob Cowan, *This Space in the Shaking of the Light;* Jane Dobson, *Shadow-graph* and *Water Forms*; Martha Edelheit, *The Albino Queen and Snow White in Triplicate*; Silvianna Goldsmith,*Orpheus Underground*; Storm de Hirsch, *An Experiment in Meditation*, *Shaman*;

Leonard Horowitz, *Loft Life and Sufi Dance*; Nancy Kendall, *Sound Movie*; Maria Lassnig, *Chairs*.
Feb. 15: Anthony McCall, *Line Describing a Cone*; Mark Rappaport, *Casual Relations*; Olga Spiegel, *Alchemy Blues*.
Feb. 16: Susan Brockman, *Depot*; Irving Kriesberg, *Out of Into*, Mike Lovell, *Birds of Paradise*; Frank Mouris, *Frank Film*; Carolee Schneemann, *Plum Line*; Rosalind Schneider, *Dream Study, Tulips*; Patricia Sloane, *A Knee Ad*; Alida Walsh, *The Martyrdom of Marilyn Monroe*.

1974 FEBRUARY

as there was in Manhattan to show at that time. This lent credence to the whole thing. The next year we were invited to be on selection committees and to get involved in the process.

I showed some very quiet panels that leaned low against the bottom of the wall. Working in this very shallow area of white, I painted the wall onto the floor to effect the perception of where the floor ended and the wall began. The effect was an empty room where some people felt the work hadn't even been hung yet. It related to Mel Bochner, Richard Tuttle, and, of course, Dorothea. My show was reviewed in *Artforum* by Angela Westwater.

At Artists Space, there was no talk of sales, no one ever expected it. New York was in the middle of a fiscal dilemma and everybody thought it was going down the tubes. There was no money going into art, except to the established artists. Money and art did not cross or coexist. Art was a philosophy. It is totally different now. The art world is viable and making art seems to be a viable occupation. When I first came to New York, it felt like the edge of the earth. Between 1974 and 1984, the art world changed dramatically. As things come around, the work I did in '74 fits in better in '97 than it did in '81, because '81 was the beginning of "new image" and "bad" painting, which was a whole other thing.

The idea of Artists Space to have artists select artists seemed novel. It had a unique placement.

FILMMAKER

Anthony McCall *Line Describing a Cone* explored the sculptural dimension of film as a medium. It existed between the screen and the lens of the projector, and people walked around it. The film was a three-dimensional narrative experience.

Unlike the Collective for Living Cinema or the Millennium, which were only for film, Artists Space was unique for independent filmmakers, because it showed work of many colors and different media. It was very open and, for this reason, much more catholic. Nevertheless, there was always a frame of reference, but it wasn't judgmental. People went, showed their stuff, and then there was a lot of discussion about it. One also has to remember, SoHo was a deserted community, very quiet. The only way you knew you were in the right place was to see someone you may have seen before in the same stairwell. So Artists Space also fulfilled a social function. You went there knowing you'd see interesting work and to reinforce acquaintances because you'd keep meeting the same people there.

ARTIST

Carolee Schneemann Artists Space provided a situation where one could experiment, try things, take risks, and these risks were unprecedented. The atmosphere was raw. There was something exciting and communal in terms of a shared imaginative position, a desired imagination. In those days, long ago, the considerations were not about media, financial gain, making a product, pursuing a self-reflective narrative, getting on TV, or flying to Hollywood. It was a deep mind coupled with new material.

I don't like to do performances in New York anymore. It's very expensive and it's calibrated to a standard based on the history that was, to some extent, created by my own work. In many ways, I can't feel as if I'm really naked and working in a new territory. It feels occupied. Sometimes I'll perform unexpectedly in very odd places. Somewhere in Canada, or in Italy, where the cultural expectations haven't already established themselves with predictability. When you're working in a raw blind form you need a context that hasn't much conviction, and in it you can trace a double position. That's what Artists Space represented and made possible for its artists.

I hold the reactionary politicians who dismantled the NEA responsible for the demise of the creative community, the very active imagination, and the purposefulness of bringing important exhibitions into a community — a purposefulness that was so hard-won. We had a moment when work could flourish and organizations were selfless and dedicated to what art could be. But it's not just that they're dismantled, it's the denigration and misinterpretation that has warped the cultural understanding of what art does, what art means. Now we have to go to Europe not to feel like a terrorist fool who should go out and get a real job. Basically, I'm talking about the popular feeling in the United States and what it means to have to be predictable and predetermined, predigested. It's precensoring, too. The organization and the artist, the printers and publishers, everyone precensors themselves. We censor ourselves over issues that are already moving around in the popular culture, that are on television and in movies. We have to think about that. Creativity has never been a very strong value here, and that's why it's important to look to Europe, even to places as paternalistic as Austria or Germany. They have the historic conviction that art is their future and their history, that it is their deepest value. When their boards and politicians have disappeared there will still be the cultural artifacts that distinguish them. That's so deep in the cultural consciousness of Europe. They're willing and able to engage with difficult, challenging, unpleasant, contemporary artists because they have that larger perceptual pattern. We're so Puritan, we're so Lutheran. I grew up in a town where I was asked, "Why do you have to make art? Isn't life good enough for you just the way it is? And besides, you're wasting you're time, you could be typing or raising children or having a normal life."

Feb. 23: Chris Jones, *Basic Elements*, performance; Fred Krughoff, *St. Louis Hand Saw*, performance.	Mar. 2–30: Sidney Geist, sculpture (Philip Pearlstein); Marvin Torffield, installation with sound (Don Judd); John Torreano, painting (Chuck Close).	Mar. 2: Bob Harding, *Diagonal*, videowork.
Mar. 30–31: Carmen Beuchat, Suzy Harris, Cynthia Hedstrom, Rachel Lew, and Mary Overlie, *The Natural History of the American Dancer* and *Line Drawings*, dance performance.	Apr. 5–6: *Doomed Love, Grocery,* and *Two Love Figures,* plays by Bruce Serlen, author, and Gregory Lehane, director; *The Comeback*, play by Jack Gilhooley, author, and Jack Marks, director.	

↑ John Torreano, painting, Judy Pfaff, sculpture
35 Artists Return to Artists Space: A Benefit Exhibition,
Dec. 4-24, 1981.

← John Torreano

ARTIST / BOARD

John Torreano At Artists Space, I showed some paintings about outer space. They had four large quarter-round frames which made them bulge out toward the viewer. The frames and the paintings were painted the same; some of them had jewels and dots like stars. Judy Pfaff and Marvin Torffield were other artists showing that same year. It was high energy. After Artists Space, I did a group show at Paula Cooper (1974) with Elizabeth Murray and Marilyn Lenkowsky. It was the first important show for all of us.

I met Chuck and Leslie Close when I first moved to New York in '68. They lived right behind me. I remember seeing his first big photo image paintings and even a big nude. A year later, Jennifer Bartlett moved in across the street. I also met Bob Israel, a good friend of Joe Zucker's. Joe and Chuck were friends. Later, they went in on a building together where the restaurant Jerry's is now. I met Joel Shapiro around then and, later, Paula Cooper. I got to know people very quickly. We were all from the same generation. The art community was pretty small in 1974, relative to what it is now.

Chuck was the first one to try and legalize artists living in commercial buildings. I didn't like the concept of a SoHo Artists Association. I knew legalization would solve a problem, but would bring a lot of problems, too. Of course, you can't stop progress. This was before it was even called SoHo. At 4:00 p.m., when business closed down, you could park your car on the street. Anybody out on the street after 4:00 was probably an artist. It was that empty. There were only a couple of places you could go for food—places like Fanelli's didn't stay open late. The Broome Street Bar was the first bar open to the art community. But, the first real artist's bar was Spring Street Bar, on the corner of Spring and West Broadway. It was *the* SoHo bar and restaurant.

Around 1975 or later, I started doing stand-up comedy using material about SoHo. I said, "SoHo is the only place I know of in the world where it's illegal to live if you're *not* an artist. Most places in the world want to get rid of the artists. Here, if you're not an artist, it's illegal. Now, that doesn't mean that you can't have a hobby." Then I'd talk about an artist who does brain surgery on the weekends, I role-reversed the situation. "At a party, a guy asked if I was a sculptor, and before long he's showing me castings of somebody's teeth." A dentist who had to pretend he was a sculptor. It was funny then, it's not so funny now.

In the 80s, I was on the Board with Elizabeth Murray, Richard Armstrong, Greg Amenoff, Mary Miss, and Cindy Sherman. That was very good, because I realized just how vulnerable a living organism an institution like Artists Space is and how difficult it is to keep it going. Although it wasn't as difficult then as it is now—there was a lot more support during the 80s. For a number of reasons, Artists Space's dependency on grants during the 80s required there be a lot of shows that served ideas focused specifically for the grant. There was even one for people over 50 years old. Because we got money from different countries, we did a Spanish show and a Korean show, etc. So it seemed that unless the exhibition was part of some larger socioeconomic image, it wouldn't have as much of

Artists Space — that name is what it should always be about: artists.

a chance to get funding. Yes, there were individual shows for artists, but curatorially, it wasn't the main thrust. There was always another social or political agenda.

Artists Space—that name is what it should always be about: artists. It was a good idea to have artists on the Board and it's still a good idea to have artists choosing artists. Artists Space was great when it first started with this concept. It had clarity. Now there are so many places competing for the same attention. It's a general problem in our culture. I call it the tyranny of choice. We're consumed. If you try to pick a shampoo for your hair, you're traumatized by the number of potential choices. Then add to it a cacophony of other choices. That's how our culture controls and manipulates. It's the opposite end of fascism. Freedom is lost by the tyranny of too much choice. That's the dilemma.

30

Adrian Piper The series of six photographs of me at the typewriter refer to the text, *Talking to Myself, the Ongoing Autobiography of an Art Object.*

It is about the *Catalysis* series of street performances I did between 1970 and 1972. If the *PersonA* series at Artists Space was 1974, I would probably have done a street performance of the *Missing Being*. The texts would have referred to the work I was doing at that time, as a continuation of *Talking to Myself, the Ongoing Autobiography of an Art Object*, which stemmed from the *Catalysis* series, but with certain specific alterations. The *Catalysis* series was a series of untitled and, I thought at the time, undocumented street performances in which I altered my physical presentation in very odd ways that would have been unproblematic if I had been a three-dimensional sculpture. But, being a person, they looked weird, and they reinforced my sense of alienation from everyone around me. The one described the most was the one in which I soaked my clothes in a mixture of cod liver oil, eggs, vinegar, and all sorts of awful stuff for about a week. Then I wore them on the subway. For another performance, I wore very, very baggy polyester clothes stuffed with Mickey Mouse balloons. You had the three heads, the three bulging shapes coming out all over me, and I rode the subway during rush hour. Of course, the balloons started to break.

The performances were done independently. I started them in April 1970. The first one I did was in connection with an event of performance works organized by John Perreault on the street in front of Max's Kansas City. After that I did a number of others and they continued up to about 1972. Then around 1972 or 1973, I started working more intensively on the *Missing Being* series, in which I dressed in drag as a young black male. I wore an Afro, shades, a mustache, I had a cigar, and all that.

I wasn't living in New York during *The Nigger Drawings* show. I learned about it from Howardena Pindell. I felt very, very conflicted about joining the protest, because Helene Winer had really been very good to me. After *Aspects of the Liberal Dilemma* installation, she told me about the new NEA grant for artists and strongly encouraged me to apply for one, which I did, and I got it. That was my first NEA grant. I felt very indebted to her, and I think a lot of her. I felt very bad about having to be in a position of chastising Helene about this. I wrote in my *Selected Writings* volume that *The Nigger Drawings* incident was not a matter of anyone's bad intentions, but of people simply not thinking through the implications of what they were doing. We were all relatively naive in those days. Americans share a history of naiveté and they are known all over the world for it. Part of the problem was American society, certainly by no means just Artists Space. It's this continuing tendency to want to pass, begin afresh, and do it better. This way of manifesting one's good intentions has the unfortunate consequence that people can't learn from their mistakes.

Chuck Close I was a founding Board member of Artists Space. Nobody really knew how to do it. It was on-the-job training, and my participation wasn't a lot.

Initially, we came up with the idea of artists choosing artists, because we didn't know what it should be. We were worried about a committee decision. When you're trying to find consensus, often nobody gets the person they really want and there's a compromise. The whole idea of an alternative space was somewhere between a commercial gallery and a museum. I suppose the model was more museum than gallery. Nobody ever expected to sell anything, and nothing ever sold. We would ask, "Is this the way it ought to be? Is this different enough from a gallery? What needs does it serve? How do you identify the needs of artists?" We didn't want to duplicate what the gallery system was doing. There were cooperative galleries like Razor Gallery and 55 Mercer Street, but they were a little embarrassing. For the most part, we were just trying to figure out what would work and what it might look like.

There was a lot of nepotism in the early selections. Something about this system makes it a bit like being on a jury. You try to transcend your prejudices and be better than you are. Of course, there are pressures. Some people have never forgiven me for not picking them. In fact, one friend brings it up all the time. I didn't get the person I originally selected. Joe Zucker declined because he was very close to getting Klaus Kertess to make a decision to show him at Bykert Gallery. Klaus was very slow to commit and Joe thought if he shot the work at Artists Space he wouldn't have anything to show at Bykert. He had a wonderful piece I wanted him to show, but he didn't get a chance to show it for many, many years and it really would have made a difference. He had a 100-foot or 100-meter-long painting of all these panels. In the old Artists Space, it could have wrapped around three walls and would have been really interesting. I also wanted to show Judy Pfaff and then somebody else showed her. So I selected John Torreano, who worked for Richard Artschwager. I knew him because we hung out together.

SoHo barely existed when I moved there in '67. There were maybe 10 people living between Canal and Houston Streets. There was the bodega where the jewelry store is now on the northwest corner of Prince and West Broadway. There were two bars, Fanelli's and another Italian bar where Ken and John's Broome Street Bar is today, but they got rubbed out by the Mafia. I first lived down on Greene between Canal and Grand. Then, around '69, I moved to a building where the restaurant Jerry's is now. A bunch of artists lived there, some had been there for a long time. Actually, Paula Cooper opened right across the street. Artists Space was above her second gallery when she was on Wooster Street, but her first gallery was on Prince Street right across from where the catalogue clothing store currently exists. Everyone thinks she was the first gallery in SoHo, but the first was actually Richard Feigen's. His space was where Aesthetic Realism is today. During the week there were trucks, rats, and rags. Garbage trucks, because it was part of the carting area, so rats were just running everywhere. And the streets were filled with bales of rags and stuff like that. All the light manufacturing and sweat shops had pretty much left. CONTINUED

There wasn't the sense that great careers were to be had. You seemed to have your whole life to figure out who you were and what you wanted to do.

There are some funny stories about that. When Al Held was a kid, his father owned one of those little sidewalk stands where Kenny Scharf is now. He delivered donuts and coffee to the sweat shops. One of the shops he used to deliver to is the loft Al now lives in on West Broadway and Prince. It was one of the earliest ones to convert. On Saturday or Sunday you could have laid down all day in the middle of Greene Street and not a single car would have driven around you. It was that empty. I was surprised SoHo remained an art community and worked as long as it did. It was a time in which the art world was very inclusive, where musicians and composers like Philip Glass and Steve Reich got their first support in the visual art world, not the music world. All of the first support for visual and performing arts was in the galleries and alternative spaces. Paula Cooper owned all the foam rubber pads, which people borrowed for every event. It was a community, a grassroots support system. There wasn't the sense that great careers were to be had. You seemed to have your whole life to figure out who you were and what you wanted to do. It wasn't until the 80s that rampant careerism raised expectations for a major rewarding career early in one's life. In those days, people really helped each other a lot more. I think they're helping each other again.

There were certain things that worked well at Artists Space and certain things that didn't. For instance, the Slide File never really made much sense. Did anybody ever get anything out of it? Initially, it wasn't being used. We used to have those open slide viewings. The first time we did the Slide File screening, major critics and other people showed up. About halfway through there was a lot of groaning and people got up and left. Democracy and art are weird together. It is finally a rather elitist activity, I'm afraid. I'd love to see it open up—every effort should be made to make it inclusive. It's interesting how the art world has,

without quotas and without an effort, readdressed wrongs, specifically in an Affirmative Action way. The women's movement hit downtown like a ton of bricks at approximately the same time Artists Space opened up. I would bet there were probably more women showing at Artists Space in the early to mid-70s than any other period. Although it may be true today as well. It was out of a general awareness that things had been really wrong and it was naturally corrected. For instance, half the people graduating from art schools were women and why weren't they in the galleries? For me, it was a time of incredible social change and ferment. Nineteen sixty-eight was a watershed year in this country, especially in lower Manhattan and what's now SoHo—everything changed. It was a year in which many of us became visible. I first showed my work in '68. It was a time when you didn't believe in anything. It was an interesting time to try to form an organization.

I came to New York with no job, having given up a teaching position in Massachusetts to move here. At that time in New York, you could still get a teaching job and I was able to pick some up right away. A lot of people slammed up sheet rock. Phil Glass was doing plumbing and driving cabs. A 2500-square-foot loft cost between $50 and $100 a month, that's all. I made less than $4000 a year and lived on it, although it wasn't from my painting. My first painting, one of the early black and white portraits, sold for $1300. Of course, the gallery took its cut. The sale augmented my teaching salary. In '73 I was just beginning to show regularly and live off my work, so I hadn't been around that long. But, we all helped each other, that's what you did. I helped Richard Serra build all his early lead prop pieces and Nancy Graves' camels. We used to carry them up and down her goddamn stairs. But it's not so different now. I've been trying to convince one of my assistants he ought to be in Brooklyn. If I were a young artist today, I would want to be in Brooklyn where everybody else is. You need to be where other people in your position are so you can help each other. SoHo is now what the Village was and what 10th Street was when I moved to the City. That's where all the established artists lived. We were early pioneers in SoHo, then later in TriBeCa, Long Island City, or wherever. You need to be where people share concerns and can help each other. It's great. I'm not necessarily saying that Artists Space ought to follow the artists, although that's not such a bad idea. It might be okay to move it to Brooklyn.

Apr. 6–27: Liz Phillips, sound structure (Peter Campus); Marlene Scott V., tape (Dan Flavin); Jim Tribe, painting (Jack Youngerman).

Apr. 22: Barbara Kruger, reading. Juan Hamill, reading.

Apr. 23–26: **PersonA**, video and performance series focusing on autobiography (Edit deAk, editor of *Art-Rite*).

Apr. 23: Jennifer Bartlett, reading; Eleanor Antin, *Caught In the Act: January 20, 1649*, video.

Apr. 24: Nancy Kitchell, *Visiting Hours*, audio; Peter Hutchinson, *Foraging*, film; Alan Sondheim and *Black Tarantula*, Kathy Acker, video.

Apr. 25: Laurie Anderson, *As:If*, performance; Scott Burton, *Performance Portrait of the Artist with Cothurni and Ithyphallus*, 1973, performance; Roger Welch, *Welch*, 1972, film.

Apr. 26: Adrian Piper, *Talking to Myself, the Ongoing Autobiography of an Art Object*, performance/photo-texts; Dennis Oppenheim, selections from films, 1970–73; Jack Smith, *Life with Mekas*, performance.

← Roger Welch, Apr.25, 1974, film. *PersonA* series. Photo: Yuri

Apr. 27: John Fischer with the Composer's Collective, *Participation Cantata…*, a musical evening for audience and instrumentalist(s).

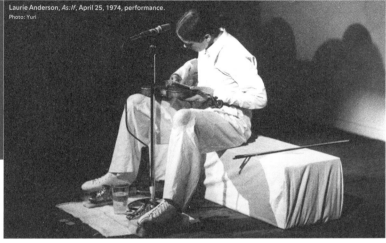

Laurie Anderson, *As:If*, April 25, 1974, performance. Photo: Yuri

Laurie Anderson

ARTIST

I probably met Vito Acconci in 1973 through Dan Graham and Dan through Richard Nonas. I was in a couple of different groups then. One was a group with Gordon Matta-Clark, Richard Serra, Philip Glass, Dickie Landry, Tina Girouard, Suzy Harris, and Jene Highstein. It was the party group. We had a lot of fun and worked on each other's projects. The other group was more serious, or just different. They overlapped a bit. It was made up of Dan, Sol LeWitt, and Vito. Vito got plunked in there because he was starting to do things in galleries, even though they were poetry readings turned into installations. That group was wild. It was so much fun.

During the Artists Space show, I was always running over to Richard's because he had a lot of stuff there and I would say, "I need to get this and that." And he'd say, "Jene will help you." It was really this very loose way of helping each other. That was the most fun I ever had as an artist. We just had a wonderful time together.

Everybody left at a certain point. They all started to tour or whatever our versions of touring were—go over and do an installation in Stockholm or a show here or there. We just couldn't keep up that daily contact. Places like Artists Space are for young artists starting out, clumping together, and doing stuff together. Most young artists are dependent on banding together. The physical base for us then was right around Food restaurant, the Kitchen, Artists Space, and the Paula Cooper Gallery.

I wore a white dress that went to the floor for my performance at Artists Space, *As:If*.

The projections were meant to be a film screen. Every performance I have ever done has had some basic shape. In *As:If* it was an arc. Many of these images come from where I live. Outside my window is this huge bridge that spans Canal Street. Every single thing I did often described a 180-degree arc: fans, windshield wipers, hand gestures, rocking chairs. Often, that's enough to hold something together visually for me. I was very interested in comparisons, so the grammatical structure was the colon in between *As:If*. A lot of the language stuff in my work was a play on words; they were reason rhymes. There was one piece in which all the words had to do with words and things relating to water.

The evening I performed *As:If*, I was very nervous about whether a microphone I had strapped around my right underarm with an improvised mike clip would fall out. It really looked ridiculous, but I gave it a try. I wanted to have my hands free to do other things. This was before reliable remote wireless microphones. At that time, I did a multimedia show, which meant slide projectors, Super 8 film, big cables, and microphones strapped with a belt to my chest. I wasn't that nervous at Artists Space, probably because I had done so much public stuff early on. I felt more vulnerable than nervous. Like, "Why am I saying these things about my own life and my grandmother?" It was a very unusual thing to do then. There was no such thing as autobiographical art, which is what it was called a few years later.

As a kid I was very used to getting up in front of people, having been in the Talented Teens U.S.A. I was a dorky American teenager from Illinois. We did shows for people like the mayor of Brighton, England, or U.S. sailors on a ship in Nice, France. I would give these things called "chalk talks," which meant I'd draw really fast on huge pieces of paper on a topic, say, American life. Because I was really fast at cartoons, I would ask someone from the audience to come up and I would do caricatures of them while we talked. That was the entertainment, and it was really fun.

May 4–25: Group exhibition (149 artists respond to a call for slides, 130 of them attend a viewing of their own work and vote to select 12 to participate in the exhibition). Paula Barr, Cynthia Carlson, Byoung Min, Annette Oko, painting; Arthur Gibbons, Ken Hubbell, Marsha Liberty, Joe Neill, Barbarie Rothstein, Marsha Vander Heyden, sculpture; Joan Lee Goldberg, books; Mimi Smith, drawing.

→ Installation view, group exhibition.

May 4: Jeriann Hilderley, music and poetry.

May 10: **Panel discussion:** *What Are the Issues in Art Today?* (Irving Sandler). Chuck Close, John Coplans, Nancy Graves, Barbara Rose, Lucas Samaras. Irving Sandler, moderator.

May 17: **Panel discussion:** *Pop Art* (Rudolf Baranik). Lawrence Alloway, Robert Indiana, Robert Rosenblum, George Segal.

May 23: Charles Simonds, *Birth, Landscape-Body-Dwelling, Dwellings, Dwellings Winter,* 1974, films; Rudy Burckhardt, *Slipperella, Doldrums,* film.

ARTIST

Cynthia Carlson It was my first exhibition, and also the first for my dear friend Ree Morton, so it was a big coming-out for her, too. It's sort of a cliché, but we were young and ideas were free, just flying around, it wasn't territorial. You could do anything, we all felt our muscles.

We also attended a lot of pretty bad events in those days, when you look back on some of those stupid performances, where we all sat so seriously like life and death. A lot of the work was like that, too. One of the artists in the show with me at Artists Space was Barbara Kruger, who was doing these big organic things with sexual parts. They weren't overtly sexual, but they were dime-store material, they were horrible! I'm sure she wants nothing to do with them today, given her more severe political bent, but they were part of that period in time.

1974–75

The three one-person shows per month continue, but a new process of identifying selectors is developed. A list is circulated of 657 artists, most represented by galleries in New York State, who are asked to vote among themselves. 420 artists respond to the ballot, and the results are used to determine the selectors for the 1974–75 and 1975–76 seasons. The Unaffiliated Artists File is established as a new resource for exhibitions. Slides submitted for the May 1974 group show serve as its foundation.

Sept. 3–18: **Eight Upstate**. Faculty exhibition in cooperation with the Art Department, SUNY Potsdam. Charlene and George D. Green, painting; Joe Hildreth, prints and drawings; Stephan Sumner, photographs; William T. Gambling, James S. Sutter, Charles Swanson, sculpture; Arthur Sennett, clay works. Charlene and George D. Green, artists in residence at Artists Space, July–August 1974.

Oct. 5–26: Gwynn Murrill, sculpture (Lynda Benglis). Judy Pfaff, painting installation (Al Held); Don Wynn, painting (Jack Beal).

↙ Judy Pfaff, *J.A.S.O.N.,* Sept. 1974, installation.

Oct. 8: First slide screening of work by the 220 New York State artists in the Unaffiliated Artists File. Screening is part of a series that aims to be a service to art dealers, curators, and critics.

Oct. 15: **Panel discussion:** *A Forum on Artforum* with the editors of *Artforum.* Lawrence Alloway, John Coplans, Max Kozloff, Rosalind Krauss, Joseph Masheck, Annette Michelson, Robert Pincus-Witten, Angela Westwater. Diane Kelder, moderator.

Joseph Marioni I moved to New York in late 1972, worked as a carpenter and an artist and was just beginning the process of going out into the art world to see who's who and how it worked. My main reason for moving to New York was because Bob Ryman and Brice Marden lived there. I am a painter, always have been a painter, and New York was where painting was going on. Shortly after my arrival, I was told this was the end of an era, not the beginning. So things have changed considerably in the art world. It has made a complete turn around in the past twenty years.

I was in a couple of group shows. The first was a new talent show with Ivan Karp in 1973. But in March 1975 Brice was asked to pick someone for a show at Artists Space. I had just met him a few months earlier. I was introduced to Brice by Klaus Kertess who told him to see my stuff. After about twenty minutes in the studio he told me he had been asked by Artists Space to choose an artist and would I participate in a show. So two years after my arrival in New York I had my first one man exhibition. The combination of just having arrived and Brice seeing my work was very significant for me. Then, for him to offer me this exposure, this public exhibition was even more of a validation. My show was up the same time as his show at the Guggenheim. It was the kind of exposure to the art world you just don't get walking in cold and knocking on doors. Brice Marden is a hero figure in the art world. So, this was not only a validation, it was a turning point in my life which had to do with self esteem, personal recognition, and a sense that I had found my milieu in the art world. I had arrived in the place I belonged. It wasn't the great coming out or the great public event in art world terms. It was more about a personal satisfaction and recognition from an artist I looked up to. And, it was an acknowledgment that I, too, was a player. It was one of the great highlights of my career and life as an artist. It's where I consider my public career begins. This was Day One.

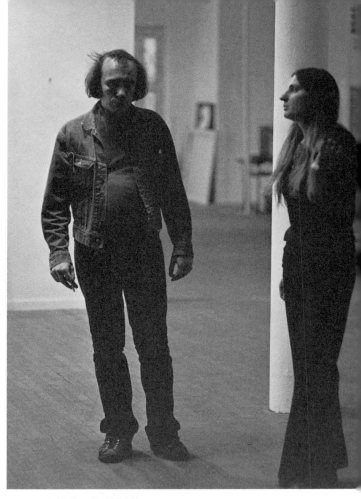

↑ Vito Acconci and Edit deAk,
during *PersonA* series, Apr.23-26, 1974.
Photo: Yuri

Vito Acconci When I was asked to choose an artist to show at Artists Space, I didn't know Laurie Anderson. The person who suggested her to me was Dan Graham. Was I tremendously interested when I went to see her stuff? I'm not exactly sure. But I was interested enough to think I would like to select her. She had photos with little texts, little narratives, little beginnings of stories, certainly the start of stuff she was going to do very soon. I liked her show. It was funny, though, because at the same time Richard Serra had picked Don Gummer and Barbara Kruger was also showing. And, everybody kept asking how I could have picked Laurie when Don was hot or seemed to be or was going to be. Laurie's stuff was more casual looking, much more off the cuff, almost intermittent. Laurie was cute. When I chose her, I hadn't seen her performances, I didn't even know about them. I'm not sure she'd done any before.

It's funny to think of my connection to Artists Space and the fact that I chose Laurie. What the early Artists Space meant to me was exactly what its title stated: a space determined by artists. Artists would choose other artists, younger, newer artists. The other things I did at Artists Space I didn't think of as specific to Artists Space's mission. They were showing a film, my conversation with Lawrence Alloway as part of the *Art-Rite* interviews, which I remember really, really vaguely, and the series of audio works. I don't remember them, probably, because that's not what Artists Space meant to me. It wasn't a part of me. By that time I was quasi-established and it seemed like Artists Space wasn't a space for established people. The work I showed there was stuff peripheral to what I showed in commercial galleries.

I don't remember who brought me on the Board, but I was an inactive member. I never knew what I was doing there. The objections that came up and the reason Artists Space started to change a little was the suspicion that established artists were choosing their assistants or people they were going out with. Maybe that was true. I tried to take it seriously and find out about people I didn't know. Which is why I asked around and came upon Laurie. However, it could happen that you go out with someone because you like their work, too. It would be ridiculous to eliminate that possibility. Unfortunately, that situation does get tricky, even if you have valid reasons to choose that person. On the outside, it appears very different, which is too bad.

I showed at 112 Workshop on Greene Street, in the *Avalanche* offices, and in all those places back in the days when an alternative space was what it said it was going to be. It wasn't like a baseball minor league for commercial galleries. Now, alternative spaces are like tryouts for the big time—places to be seen so a commercial gallery can take you on. It's not an alternative system. I have to admit, when it was artists choosing artists, the notion of Artists Space interested me more. Then again, I was more interested in the notion of art and being an artist and doing art. Now, I'm not.

Scott Burton, *Portrait of the Artist with Cothurni and Ithyphallus*, Apr. 25, 1974, performance. **PersonA** series.
Photo: Yuri

↑ Walter Robinson and Edit deAk.

I would kid the artists who walked in.
I told them we had so many rules, forget it.
Nothing you want to do applies.

CURATOR **Edit deAk** Artists Space was not like *Art-Rite* (published 1972–79, editors Walter Robinson and Edit deAk), which came from the people, establishing our own voice, our own style and category. Artists Space was something grown-ups and institutions like NYSCA dreamed up. I was a *schulkie* for two dollars an hour. I lived next door and they thought that was great because I could come over any time, day or night. I was a golden find because I was the real kid giving the sauce, the juice of the real art mode of the time, to an institution that was organized from above. I did everything from being the cleaning lady to making it possible for artists to breathe the air there because they had so many rules and regulations. I would kid the artists who walked in. I told them we had so many rules, forget it. Nothing you want to do applies. Then I would teach them how to rephrase it according to our codes between the door and the supposed desk.

Artists came in to find out what we were about, to try and do something. Sometimes a person like Demi would show up who was a real idiosyncratic strange young man. He would have rolls of tissue paper and drawings chewed around the edges under his arm. Automatically he'd be told, "You can't do anything here, we have rules and regulations, artists have to choose you and you don't qualify for that," etc. Trudie Grace wouldn't even talk to them. At least I sat down and looked at their work. I knew exactly who was working where in the art galleries and the alternative system. I would teach them how to show their work, how to leave slides, "don't go to the main guy, go directly to the assistant, that will flatter." I would describe the profile of the galleries and which ones they should try. It was extraordinarily useful information, a magical little service that Artists Space had. Sometimes, I would ask artists to leave their drawings overnight. Then I'd take them to Mike (Walter Robinson) and see what he thought. We'd show it to some of our art friends. Maybe nothing could happen for that artist at Artists Space, but we would do something in *Art-Rite* for them. INTERVIEW CONTINUED

Irving Sandler was the Chairman of the Board and Trudie Grace was the Director. I don't know who she really was, but she was definitely having a frustrating time in her life. She had a pretty plush job, even though it was very important to look almost dilapidated so it wouldn't seem as if money was spent with any kind of style. She sat there taking up almost the entire surface of her desk with these giant oversize pads of accounting sheets, constantly entering expenditures into these categories with a sharp pencil. This was pre-computer. But there was no desk, just a table, so she couldn't really hide, her legs would show. For that she got a tremendous salary, considering. You don't need to be the director to do accounting, you hire an accountant to come in once a month. She was just a frustrated person doing her Ph.D. She came in, sat there eight hours a day and worked hard. Two years later the directorship was up for grabs, so what to do with me? Let me be the Director? Everybody thought I was the Director anyway, which was a problem. I was always very humble, I never wanted it to look like I was the Director, but unofficially I had the Artists Space job. They asked me to interview which was ridiculous. I worked there, interview me about what? Irving said I was so wonderful, valuable, priceless, and unique. I had the real spirit and *Art-Rite* was the real thing, not like Artists Space, and I shouldn't be wasting it on Artists Space. I think he meant it. *Art-Rite*, which existed from about '72 to '79, had a connection to Artists Space because of our generation and because I had a job there. I thought Susan Wyatt, who started to work at Artists Space at the end of my stay, should be the Director. She was very loyal. She was a very quiet girl from a fancy girls' college. At lunchtime, she'd always be reading *The New Yorker* on a little bench. I thought reading *The New Yorker* was so old fashioned or grown up. I always liked her. I left Artists Space after the whole director issue came up.

CURATOR *Walter Robinson* **Edit had good ideas for shows.**

ED: *Art-Rite* opened up the space for performances in the evening. That was tremendous because we could show a lot more artists. At 6:00 p.m. I would close up, take the paintings down, and by 8:00 the whole place was transformed into a nightclub. Everyone loved it! This was the real thing. The shows were about how an institution is afraid to show what they like because it's public money. They can't show their taste, because who are *they* to show it. So, there's this elaborate mechanism set up to choose people to show and it was gearshifts away from a directness: artists who never showed before were chosen by other artists, so that none of the staff, nobody could say we chose an artist, they didn't have the nerve. Then there was the question of who chooses the artists who choose the artists.

In those days we didn't have a name for performance art. I designed the invitation. The title was not "Persona," it was graphically expressed "person" and then a rubber stamp for the "A," "*PersonA*." In *Art-Rite* we still didn't publish the term performance. Although Laurie Anderson and others were doing it. We called it *Pieces on Pieces*, like various pieces in a magazine. We experimented with how to present performance, by description, by photo essay, by critical review, by publishing a script. For Robin Winters's performance we published a list of props.

So, our generation of artists, during the unofficial hours, would take over the gallery and perform at night. It was almost like a guerrilla activity of getting into the gallery system with a different medium.

ED AND WR: Vito (Acconci) chose Laurie Anderson. She exhibited like a regular artist, on the wall, and she did a performance in *PersonA*. It was fantastic, just breathtaking. It was an elongated metaphor of water. She came out with ice skates in blocks of ice. She was like an angel in a long white tunic, playing the violin excellently. She had projected words behind her, much like what came later. She had the bravura coordination of a filmmaker with still images in the back while she was in front talking in unison with what was behind her, which she couldn't see.

WR: She projected this incredible charm and warmth and narrative interest in distinct contrast to the minimalism that came before. This was actually a performance that was interesting and amusing to watch as opposed to minimalist performances that were boring and trials to watch.

← Adrian Piper, *A109 #1–6*, September 1975
(refers to: …*Ongoing Autobiography*…,
Apr. 26, 1974, performance. **PersonA** series.)

ED: Dennis Oppenheim and Vito and the previous generation who did live conceptual work were in the audience. They were more in the Richard Foreman vein, not about pleasing the public. But Laurie was. If you watched the faces in the audience, you could see they were being charmed by the minute, which was an extremely risqué, rough, and new thing to do.

WR: It was the first return of narrative after minimalism. Bill Wegman started doing the same thing with those early videotapes, making tapes that were funny. People would stand around and laugh. That, of course, was unheard of. Videotapes were long and tedious and demonstrated some analytical proposition.

ED: Do you remember Kathy Acker's videotape with this collaboration about a famous book, *Lovejoy*?

WR: It was *Love's Body* by Norman O. Brown and the other artist was Alan Sondheim. He's still around. They had sex while having an intellectual discussion.

ED: It was a videotape we showed at Artists Space. How long can they go on? An orgasm is coming, but they have to keep on trying to have this discussion, which one of them gives up first and just goes with the orgasm.

WR: It was ridiculous. Do you think it was radical? Kathy Acker had a certain connection to Artists Space, wouldn't you say? Didn't she do some of her earlier readings there?

ED: Again, through us a lot of these people searched for their medium. At that time, there weren't myriads of open venues for young people. So, our generation of artists, during the unofficial hours, would take over the gallery and perform at night. It was almost like a guerrilla activity of getting into the gallery system with a different medium. There were lots of performances and Artists Space was good about offering its space for that. The Kitchen came later and it was definitely for media, à la Canada. Each night there were more and more people and the little gray flat foam pillows that Artists Space had for years were thrown out on the floor for people to sit on. They looked like a Carl Andre in chaos.

Scott Burton's performance *Cothurni and Ithyphallus* was like a living sculpture, before Gilbert and George. *Cothurni* is a platform used in the Greek amphitheaters to elevate the actors and *Ithyphallus* is a dildo. Scott was standing there for a certain amount of time dressed in this super wacko 70s outfit. That was his performance.

WR: This was before he was making furniture. He was doing performance tableaux. I would run a tape and he'd have the lights turned on only for one minute and then go out. I remember because I couldn't make the tape recorder work and there was no sound and I was mortified. So it was a brief performance. There was also some document or relic, a work on paper or photo or something.

ED: Scott also did a regular show at Artists Space, which was a bronze chair downstairs. It was one of these chairs like the kind you find discarded on the street.

WR: We had an article on him in *Art-Rite*. He did pictures of furniture out in the woods. We liked those. He'd set up an old living room suite in the bushes and take some snapshots. That was funny.

> **ED:** I had a real William Morris chair with leather pillows, which was limping a little bit, but in pretty good condition. I gave it to Scott with what seemed like a million-dollar job. He put a lot of money in professionals, really fixing it. The furniture was very important in terms of the tableaux.

WR: In Jack Smith's performance, *Life with Mekas,* he just got up there and gave a rambling, difficult-to-follow monologue about Jonas Mekas.

> **ED:** And he was selling pieces of bread for a dollar. It was about this Marxist idea of unalienated art.

WR: All he wanted to do was show his films, and Mekas wanted to control everything. I don't really know about Mekas. He probably wanted to represent Jack and his work as well as possible. So there was a joke about selling art and getting money. It was fairly incoherent and very loose.

> **ED:** Like the artist and his daily bread. He was also sprayed with green dollar signs. It was interesting because of his timing. At that point, there was no sense of time in his life. The previous period was over, his Broome Street loft where he had the theater, was over in real life, in real time. He was in between, not many people knew who he was. Later on he was performing more and more here and there.

Artists Space was the focus of one of the great battles of the culture war.

WR: That's the way we felt anyway. He was totally obscure even though he was famous for his films and theater. This must have been the beginning of his downslide. He showed again at Artists Space. My friend Willy Lenski was chosen to operate the slide projector. Although he was just a drunken kid, a bohemian, he gave the impression of being competent. So Jack explained to him in great detail how he wanted to show each slide for 10 seconds and Willy said, "Gee, I don't have a watch." Jack said, "Just count." So he counted to 10 after the first slide and changed to the next and Jack blew his top because Willy was trying to control Jack's show, he ruined it, he hadn't done it right. But Jack was drunk. That was in '77 when Artists Space was downtown in the Fine Arts Building.

> **ED:** I remember thinking then it was strange that Artists Space was showing Jack, because Artists Space didn't have that kind of funk. It was too straight for Jack.

WR: I remember Jennifer Bartlett reading from her autobiography. And Adrian Piper must have read from her autobiography, too. But the *Forum on Artforum* was the panel of the season (October 15, 1974). That was the most interesting evening of all. The editors sat at a big table in the front and complained about their power. I specifically remember Carter Ratcliff rising from the audience to protest *Artforum's* exclusionary cliquishness. On the level I was operating, *Artforum* was a clique of all the coolest kids in town. It was interesting to see Carter, who was active and accomplished, protesting this in public.

Carlo McCormick called one of CoLab's (Collaborative Projects) first group shows *The New Capital*. You have a group of associates, your artist friends, who you think are good, and they're your capital, so to speak. So, I curated a show of my friends from CoLab. You know how it is. Even though I was never a curator I put them in this show at Artists Space. I couldn't come up with a title or an essay. That was before I learned how to talk. I couldn't think of anything to say.

> **ED:** In addition to *PersonA*, there was also a performance of John Torreano as a comedian. And I did panels and *Artists as Filmmakers* series. Later the *United Graffiti Artists* show was dumped on my lap. It was the opening show in September 1975, with 15 young kids from the subway, and Trudie and the staff disappeared for the summer. They were scared shitless. The people who owned the building were trembling in fear that the hallway would be hit with graffiti. But, these kids were totally on the opposite wavelength. They were going to paint the hallway clean and put carpet down. The kids were living in my house and I acted like a mother or sister. I'd make phone calls to their weird shit jobs and say, "Coco can't come in today, he has a cold or the flu." They wanted a catalogue, which my cousin in New Jersey printed in color for them. I was left there alone with no budget, I even had to borrow money to buy stamps.

WR: Peter Schjeldahl wrote an essay for the catalogue. He had written something earlier about graffiti.

> **ED:** The United Graffiti Writers had had a show the year before. But 1975 wasn't yet the moment for graffiti. It was too early and not the scene. It came in later through the music and clubs. The art around that time was lyrical and abstract. Maybe they saw graffiti in terms of these nice vaporized hues of pinks and blues.

I was thinking about Artists Space's upcoming "silver jubilee," and that it takes 25 years for the polyurethane to wear off, because everything was newly polyurethaned in the SoHo of the 70s. SoHo was just shining with polyurethane. But Artists Space didn't have that. We had raw gray floors because it was supposed to be rough. When we had the *Graffiti* show, the graffiti kids wanted to put down carpet at their own expense. They wanted to show off the fact they were exhibiting at Artists Space, a real gallery. How could they do that with all these barren walls and wood floors? They didn't understand.

Artists Space had been stinking of democracy. It was stuff like who should choose the artists who choose the artists. Was it going to be the artist who was chosen before who chooses the artists who can choose the others? It was endless, I used to make jokes about it. Then there was the Committee for the Visual Arts Slide Registry, which was a way to deal with artists we couldn't show. This is what Artists Space should have really been about. Helene organized this big jury of the Slide Registry. It was narrowed down to a certain number of people who would visit artists in order to choose who was going to show. On Sundays, a dozen of us, critics, artists, dealers, high pressure people, were organized together in a little bus and would go and visit 20 artists' studios. I'll never forget all of us piling into a studio and having half an hour to look. I thought of these poor artists. It's so difficult to show people your work in your studio. It takes skill. But how overbearing to have a dozen people show up! I called painting "fast art" for a while after that because, with painters, we could go in and out before these poor artists could even wake up to the fact that there had been a regiment of people through their studio. But video, we'd be staring at it for 40 minutes, so I thought that was unfair.

WR: Artists Space was the focus of one of the great battles of the culture war. *The Nigger Drawings* was the first incredible display of cynicism by the art world progressives. To come down on Artists Space for daring to allow the title *The Nigger Drawings* was ridiculous. It was fueled by liberals like Lucy Lippard.

ED: You ask me about black protesters? What black protesters? There were no black people in the art world.

WR: Lucy Lippard and assorted other art world liberals, like Richard Goldstein at the *Village Voice*, called up black people and said, "There's this white gallery down in TriBeCa that has this show *The Nigger Drawings,* what do you think of that?" And they all thought it stunk. It was a cynical exploitation of something harmless for political purposes. Poor Helene! They battered her left and right. The problem was, as Edit said, the art world was, if not racist, certainly a white bastion. Only today is there any substantial change. I certainly felt guilty about the whole thing. You feel a certain amount of shame for not having a better integrated art world. But, on an individual level, there was some difficulty in knowing what to do about it. Try to hook up with your colleagues in the uptown scene. You can only do so much.

↑   Don Gummer, sculpture installation, 1974.

Oct. 26: Minoru Yoshida, an ionospheric piece with aerial performance and electronic sound.

Nov. 2–23: Albert M. Fine, drawing and text (works from the collection of Richard Tuttle); Martica Miguens, painting (Robert Ryman); Billy Omabegho, sculpture (Mel Edwards).

→ Albert M. Fine, post card sent to Artists Space.

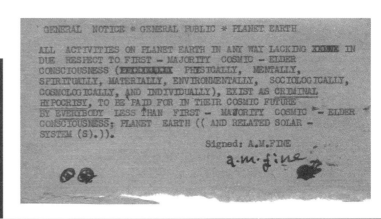

Nov. 28–Dec. 3: **Artists As Filmmakers** series (Alida Walsh).

Nov. 28: Jack Smith, *Thanksgiving Slide Show of Lucky Consumer Paradise*, performance.

Nov. 29: Walter Gutman, *Benedict Arnold*, film; Maria Lassnig, *Shapes*, film.

Nov. 30: Madeleine Ge Kiere, *Ratatouille* and *Horizontal Transfer*, film; Richard Milner, *Tree in Nine Parts*, film and film installation; Marian Oken, *Myself, Camera,* and *Lake*, film; Virginia Piersol, *Film for Step Motion II, Clock Tower, Tower, Chair, Chair*, film; Richard Protovin, *Ungah Ungah,* and *Eternal Duck*, film; Robert Wolff, *Erotic Self Portrait*, film.

Dec. 1: Carolee Schneemann, *Up To And Including Her Limits*, performance with video, film, and drawing.

Dec. 2: Anthony McCall, *Partial Cone, Cone of Variable Volume, Partial Cone, Conical Solid*, 1974, film; Sakai, *Interbound* and *Exposure*, film; Sylvia Whitman, *Red Cone*, dance/film performance.

Dec. 3: Juan Downey, *Representation*, performance with dancers (Carmen Beuchat, Suzy Harris), film and painted environment.

Dec. 4: Juan Downey, *Representation*, installation.

Dec. 7–28: Thomas Lanigan-Schmidt, religious and secular art installation (Christo); James Biederman, sculpture; Charles Simonds, *Mythologies,* film (chosen from the Unaffiliated Artists File by artists who showed at Artists Space during the previous season).

Dec. 31–Jan. 1: Marathon reading of Gertrude Stein's *The Making of Americans.* Readings from 12 noon Dec. 31, continuously through Jan. 1, late afternoon, in celebration of the New Year and Gertrude Stein's birthday (Alison Knowles, Anna Lockwood, and Jean Rigg, with **Participation Projects Foundation).** Readers: Ruth Anderson, Jackie Apple, David Behrman, Jim Burton, John Cage, Ruth Coran, Phil Corner, Sari Dienes, Sari Fine, Fontana, Elaine Hartnett, Geoff Hendricks, Dick Higgins, Nelson Howe, Tom Johnson, Jill Johnston, Franz Kamin, Alison Knowles, Anna Lockwood, Mary Lucier, Linda Lutes, Jackson MacLow, Charlie Morrow, George and Susan Quasha, Jean Rigg, Armand Schwerner, Charles Stein, Diane Stevenson, Julie Winter.

Jan. 4–25: Louisa Chase, floor pieces (Joan Snyder); Ted Stamm, painting (Julius Tobias); Meryl Vladimer, sculpture (Louise Bourgeois).

Jan. 7: Ralston Farina, *Time Art*, performance.

↑ Committee for the Visual Arts, Inc. logo.

Jan. 25: Francesc Torres, *Almost Like Sleeping*, performance with film, slides, and sound.

Jan. 26: Benefit for *Letters*, reading/performance.

Jan. 27–28: Jim Barden, continuous performance and installation.

Jan. 29: Carl Andre, *False Creek*, reading.

Feb. 1–22: Deborah S. Freedman, painting (Audrey Flack); Judy Rifka, painting (Mel Bochner); Ernest Silva, sculpture (Rafael Ferrer).

Feb. 6: Bruce McClelland, George Quasha, Susan Sherman, poetry reading.

Feb. 7–8: Maurice Amar, *A Visit with Philip Pearlstein*, *A Visit with Sue Fuller*, and *A Visit with Ron Kleeman*, film.

Feb. 14: Lil Picard with Charles Schwartz, *Heart on for Valentine's Day*, video and performance.

Feb. 18: **Panel discussion:** *Perimeters of Protest* (Rudolf Baranik). Carl Andre, Rudolf Baranik, Mel Edwards, Hans Haacke, Linda Nochlin, Nancy Spero, May Stevens. Carl Baldwin, moderator.

Feb. 19: Jean Dupuy and Olga Kluver, slide and film performance.

Feb. 23: Harvey Bialy, Theodore Enslin, Ken Irby, Nathaniel Tarn, poetry reading to benefit His Holiness The Gyalwa Karmapa, Kagyu Order of Tibetan Buddhism.

Mar. 1–22: Andrew Ginzel, sculpture (Red Grooms); Joseph Marioni, painting (Brice Marden); Barbara Schwartz, painting (Nancy Grossman).

Mar. 6: Meeting of American section of International Association of Art Critics.

ARTIST

Andrew Ginzel I was in high school in Chicago when I met Red Grooms, then I went on to Bennington College for two years. I was 21 when I first showed at Artists Space. Edit deAk was there then. I remember her distinctly making a comment about my age and being pleasantly surprised. It was definitely before the time when 21 was a respectable age to be having a show, but before the era when it was assumed you should. I knew where I wanted to be. I lived on Crosby and later on Prince Street next to the post office. The neighborhood seemed intimate. There was a sense of a better community and of adventure for everybody.

For my show at Artists Space I created a work with a narrative structure. There were collages mounted perpendicular to the wall so you could proceed down the line, encountering them front and back, like a book, but brought out of that bound context. There were also a couple of freestanding pieces, less narrative in the strict pagelike structure, but more so in general composition.

The idea of artists choosing artists to show created a real sense of nurturing. It would normally happen except most artists don't necessarily have opportunities to give their acquaintances or people they know a show. There's no mechanism for it, even though it's probably one of the most valuable ways of seeding the future. Artists Space was a catalyst for that procedure. So the people who are involved in Artists Space have a different perspective because of their time there. In a way, it's a never-ending epic.

Mar. 14: **Panel discussion:** *Is There a Renaissance Woman?* (Ruth Vodicka). In cooperation with the *International Women's Arts Festival*: Martha Edelheit, Shirley Fuerst, Juliette Gordon, Donna Marxer, Nadine Valenti, Alida Walsh. Ruth Vodicka, moderator.

Mar. 22–30: **Artists As Filmmakers** series (Alida Walsh).

Mar. 22: Nancy Graves, *Izy Boukir*, 1970, *Aves: Magnificent Bird, Great Flamingo*, 1973, and *Reflections on the Moon*, 1974, film.

Mar. 23: Dianne Arndt, *Man Walking in Light and Audio Space*, film; Timothy Binkley, *Portrait of Sean*, film; Louva Irvine, *Elegy for My Sister*, 1972, *Waterdance*, 1973–74, *Blue Moment*, 1974, *Rain*, 1972, film; Vicki Peterson, *Variations to Sea*, film; Michael Siporin, *Openings*, film.

Mar. 27: Diego Cortez, *Palming: A Means of Relieving Strain*, slide performance; Bob Harding, *Walking Past*, video performance; Kristina Nordstrom, *Broadway Crazy Quilt*, film; D. Samatowicz, *Actuate, Actuate II, Actuate III*, film.

Mar. 28: Douglas Turnbaugh, film with photography, sculpture, dance, and poetry.

Mar. 29: Laurie Anderson, *For Instants* and *Songs and Stories for the Insomniac*, performance with slides, song, and film; Donn Aron, *Exchange*, performance with film; Steven Lowe, *Freddie Film for Dziga Vertov*, film; Mary Miss, *Cut-Off*, film.

Mar. 30: Al Hansen, *The Hamlet of Gertrude Stein*, performance.

Mar. 26: **Interview:** Vito Acconci (Irving Sandler). Led by Lawrence Alloway and the editors of *Art-Rite*, Edit deAk and Walter Robinson.

ARTIST

Diego Cortez

I moved to New York from Chicago in 1973. I was interested in performance, video, and film. The places I gravitated to for my work were Artists Space, the first place where I performed, the Kitchen, and Anthology Film Archives. They were the main alternative spaces that gave artists a chance. Almost every artist in the 70s from my generation who developed a professional career in the art world came through Artists Space. It definitely created a whole generation. Artists Space is where I met Laurie Anderson, my best friend then and still a very good one, and Julia Heyward, my girlfriend for a long time. Artists Space is where I met most of my initial friends—Robin Winters, Michael McClard, and Liza Bear, who later found CoLab (Collaborative Projects).

I performed for only two or three years, and the performances were always about medical metaphors. I worked nights at a medical center gathering videotapes of brain surgeries, which I then edited for the interns. I filmed cataract operations, various types of surgical procedures, and medical problems, which I then cut into my narrative performances in video, slide, or film visuals. I did pieces on skin diseases, cataracts, brain surgery, etc. I did many film performances using a single frame or freeze frame, called an analytical projector, which was 16-millimeter. Doctors use them to analyze images using stop frame or for slow motion. Conceptually, I was interested in an extension of body art. I worked as a studio assistant for Vito Acconci. I was also very interested in Joseph Beuys and the connection between the artist and the doctor or shaman. I wanted to reunite the two functions of artist and doctor as it was in earlier civilizations. In the end, I decided it would be better if I helped promote art as opposed to making it. I felt there was more of a need for that then, so I organized shows, made books, and worked in the music scene.

You have to give credit to artists from the late 60s who brought about that creative atmosphere and developed SoHo as a neighborhood. Although Paula Cooper and Leo Castelli were pioneers, the generation of Keith Sonnier, Tina Girouard, Suzy Harris, and Philip Glass had more to do with the development of SoHo as an artist's neighborhood and the global art capital for international artists. Gordon Matta-Clark, Dickie Landry, and Tina Girouard started the first restaurant, Food. I wish there was a book documenting the step-by-step development of the neighborhood and an account of what these artists did. SoHo has come full circle and has become a completed project.

> **Almost every artist in the 70s from my generation who developed a professional career in the art world came through Artists Space. It definitely created a whole generation.**

Apr. 1: **Interview:** Leon Golub (Irving Sandler). Led by Carol Duncan and Carter Ratcliff.

Apr. 5–26: Henrietta Bagley, drawing, objects (Mary Frank); Susan Heinemann, sculpture (selected from the Unaffiliated Artists File by artists who showed at Artists Space in 1974–75); Albert Terris, sculpture (Darby Bannard).

Apr. 8: Second slide screening of work by the 360 New York State artists in the Unaffiliated Artists File. Screening is part of a series that aims to be a service to art dealers, curators, and critics.

Apr. 14: **Interview:** *Strategies of Art Criticism* (Irving Sandler). Interview with Phoebe Helman, Budd Hopkins, and May Stevens. Led by Carter Ratcliff.

Apr. 15: Jeff Way, *Catlin with Chief with Cherries*, slide lecture.

Apr. 18: Ernie Gazella, video performance.

Apr. 22: Janet Hamill and Barbara Kruger, reading.

Apr. 24: Franz Kamin and John Beaulieu of Hydragyral Elevator presents an evening of music, dance, and reading.

Apr. 25: Paul Tschinkel, video performance.

Apr. 30: Brendan Stecchini and Thom Thompson, *Collaborations, Art and Film*, performance; Cherly Katz, multimedia performance.

May 3–24: Group exhibition (selected by volunteer jury of 285 artists in the Unaffiliated Artists File). Charles Ahearn, Margia Kramer, Eliot Lable, painting; Kathleen Ferguson, Pamela Hawkins, Diane Kaiser, Joyce Robins, Sue Sayre, F.O. Smith, Chris Zeller, sculpture; Robert Kerns, tapeworks; Ann Marie Rousseau, drawing.

May 8: **Performance:** The Voice Group. Fred Farrell, Carol Flamm, Ed Hasselbrink, Joan LaBarbara, Jeanne Lee, Genie Sherman, Alexandra Stavrou. Jay Clayton, director.

May 10: Bob Harding, video performance.

May 10–11: Eve Packer, presentation of one-act plays.

May 15: Henry Geldzahler, *SoHo: Past and Future*, benefit lecture for Artists Space.

May 22: Peter Gordon, music and multimedia performance.

May 27: **Panel discussion**: *Feminism and the Art of the Seventies* (Cindy Nemser and Irving Sandler). Douglas Davis, Audrey Flack, Dorothy Gillespie, Barbara Haskell, Lila Katzen, Gloria Orenstein. Cindy Nemser, moderator.

May 28: Antonio Muntadas, multimedia performance.
May 29: Gary Brown, multimedia performance.

FILMMAKER

Charlie Ahearn The work selected from the Artists File caught me in an in-between stage. During this period, I submitted slides of paintings I eventually showed at Artists Space. It was great to have them there. And from that time on, I continually returned to Artists Space to show new developments in my work.

In 1976, I went to Arizona with two brand-new friends, Scott B and Beth B. We lived there for a month and made films. I made these poetry landscape movies about going down into the coal mines. The result was a film called *Mass Guide*, a 16–millimeter with sound that was not synchronous. It certainly wasn't narrative filmmaking. It was more poetic, independent filmmaking. And Beth and Scott each in turn created sound visual pieces using slides, video, and music. Together the three of us made an exhibition of it at Artists Space.

A big part of my feature film *Wild Style* was going out, taking photographs, recording music, and just documenting as much as possible, to work into a foundation for the film. Every weekend I went to rap clubs and gave slide shows. The slide shows were projected onto sheets that hung behind the rappers. At some point, I decided to bring that slide show down to Artists Space. I brought together Nan Goldin, Jack Smith, Peter Grass, Christof Kolhofer, Robert Smith Cooney, and Fred (Fab 5 Freddy) Brathwaite; we all created slide works for a weekend at Artists Space in 1981.

As a young artist, I felt Artists Space was a workshop where you could go and exhibit stuff that was in progress. It was a place I certainly went to a lot and where I collaborated with other artists. As I look back on it, I can see how close together all those dates are. Whereas at the time, they seemed to stretch on forever. The *No Wave Music Shows* were memorable. That changed a lot of things right there. Artists Space became really hot when they moved to 105 Hudson Street. It was a great time because the art world was going in lots of directions.

October **1975** to January **1980**

Helene Winer interviewed by Matt Mullican, Cindy Sherman, and Valerie Smith

Helene Winer was Director of Artists Space from the fall of 1975 to the winter of 1980. She hired Cindy Sherman as Program Assistant in the fall of 1977 and Sherman worked there until 1981. Sherman first showed her work at Artists Space in November 1976 and subsequently in September 1978. Valerie Smith was hired as Curator by Linda Shearer, Director of Artists Space from 1980 to 1985, in the fall of 1981 and stayed until the spring of 1989. Matt Mullican first showed his work at Artists Space in March 1976. Winer began her tenure in Artists Space's first location at 155 Wooster Street. In January 1977, she moved the organization to 105 Hudson Street. This interview took place on January 6, 1998.

VALERIE SMITH: When you were hired did the Board give you carte blanche?

HELENE WINER: No. Artists Space was founded with a particular premise of showing art that didn't have other outlets by using a method of selection that didn't represent one person's taste. So the Board assumed I would continue those methods that were in place. I was never explicitly informed about that expectation. I wouldn't have taken the job if there was no possibility for innovation or change. I just went ahead and did what I thought was necessary to have an effective program for exhibiting interesting new art.

CINDY SHERMAN: Had you known Irving Sandler or Trudie Grace previously?

HW: I believe I knew them slightly — and a few of the Board members, like Lucy Lippard and Kynaston McShine. I had been in New York for a year doing freelance projects for the NEA (National Endowment for the Arts) and NYSCA (New York State Council on the Arts) and organizing some exhibitions.

VS: No one was watching your back and shaking their finger?

HW: No. Prior to moving to New York, I was the gallery director of Montgomery Art Center at Pomona College outside of Los Angeles and was expected to organize the exhibition program without oversight. So, that's what I thought I was hired to do at Artists Space, or at least what I thought I should do.

VS: How did you turn the place around?

HW: It didn't require turning around. I didn't think it had an identity, at that point it was a neutral space. I just saw it as a good opportunity to do something with the art that was emerging at that time.

CS: Were there shows already programmed when you started?

HW: There were a few. But, I thought what was going on wasn't very successful and that there were problems with the exhibition process of showing unknown artists selected by well-known artists. The intention was good, but the result was inconsistent and suffered from a lack of continuity. The result was still that only a limited number of artists had exhibitions, and then only those with a connection to an established artist who might choose them. The nepotistic aspect of some of the shows didn't mean the artists didn't deserve the exhibition, just that there was no connection between the three artists who exhibited together each month and an audience.

VS: There was this funny moment that took place when you came in and Trudie went out. Pamela Jenrette, a formalist, assistant to Larry Poons and friend of Clement Greenberg, showed at Artists Space simultaneously with the cool conceptual gay guy, Scott Burton. Pamela arrives in the gallery ready to hang her paintings and she sees an old beat-up chair, which she drags over to her work (it is very heavy). She steps up on it to hammer a nail into the wall, when all of a sudden, dashing out of the office comes an Artists Space staff person ranting, "You can't do this! This is a $30,000 chair. Get off it!" Shortly after Scott comes running out and…

HW: He could be pretty emotional.

vs: No, no. On the contrary. He liked it and said it was exactly what he wanted to have happen. Then, Pamela goes on to describe the opening where her crowd and his crowd were so far apart theoretically they moved around like ghosts in the same gallery. It sounded like a good analogy of Trudie's administration versus yours.

HW: Probably, as things developed.

vs: On the other hand there was the Vito Acconci and Laurie Anderson combination.

HW: A lot of interesting artists showed there during the first couple of years. As much as artists might resent the inherent exclusivity of curatorial behavior, it isn't the idea of a selection that artists really object to, it's the pain of not being selected. Art is ultimately an individual act that requires positive response and special support to succeed. Artists *do* want to hear that someone in a position to offer support is especially interested in their work and they all want to be associated with other artists and the work with which they feel a relationship. It's part of the process. Like the situation you, Cindy, with others set up at Hallwalls in Buffalo, so you could get closer to finding out what the art world was about. You were all involved in this special arrangement, but not because you had intentions of being just one in a large mass that occasionally had a show somewhere.

cs: No, no. It was mostly Robert's (Longo) and Charlie's (Clough) thirst for what was going on. The college and the museum weren't all that interesting. There were other places like media studies at the university which tried to pick up some action, but they didn't target the right people.

HW: Banding together, or gravitating to like-minded artists to create your own platform, is the most useful way to go after your interests.

vs: This is very much what I saw happening in London three or four years ago, young artist-initiated exhibitions and wandering groups that collectivized and then expired.

HW: All the best new work seems to come out of that type of situation.

cs: When we came to New York there was a Cal Arts (California Institute of the Arts) faction and then a Buffalo faction with whomever was already in New York.

vs: Toward the end of your time at Artists Space there was a filtering-out process. There must have been some competition then, when groups drifted apart as they were vying for positions. Was there any tension between those two factions?

cs: There was no tension. We automatically got together, especially in the early days before careers started and people began getting competitive. If anything Artists Space was the defining place for those two factions. It was just a question of politics for a lot of other artists who didn't get attention or exposure from Artists Space.

HW: There were individual competitive feelings, especially when attention from the outside began to develop. But no one got very much attention. The system's response to young artists was very limited at that point.

vs: When the Board discovered what you were up to did you have a showdown?

HW: I'm not sure what you mean. While there was a group of artists I felt personally involved with, there were many other artists who had exhibitions and did projects of all sorts. We initially had Board meetings at Irving Sandler's house. They may not have liked the change of direction, but it never became an issue.

cs: When did they start asking questions?

HW: Right away. There was always some concern on the part of the Board. Basically, I was just too single-minded to deal with it. Then after a few meetings I began to feel that the Board, as it was constituted, was not very effective. It was a Board that, at that time, didn't raise money or, with the exception of Irving, play an active role. Ultimately, there were very few Board meetings.

vs: They phased out completely?

HW: Not completely, but almost.

cs: I like that. That's great. What did the Board say?

↑ Stefan Eins, Diego Cortez and Seth Tillett

HW: I don't believe that they were very concerned. They were people in the art world who were involved with forming the organization around certain egalitarian principles, but for the most part they didn't have an ongoing interest. I do remember that some Board members were available to talk about problems or ideas that came up. Irving was of course very committed. Kynaston McShine was also very helpful and supportive. A very broad range of exhibitions and events occurred during that time. I didn't organize the shows directly, I found people who were actively involved with artists and new work to organize the exhibitions or the staff together would come up with ideas. That's when I met Cindy, Robert, and Charlie. They (Robert and Charlie) just came in and more or less said, "Well, we're really great young artists from Buffalo and we want to invite some artists up and we want to have a show at Artists Space." They came to New York often and got to know Paul McMahon, the Assistant Director, and met Matt (Mullican), David (Salle), Jack (Goldstein), and others in New York. They invited them to Hallwalls to do an exhibition and give talks. They were really energetic and enthusiastic and knew everything that was going on.

CS: During the installation of the Hallwalls exchange show, I remember we cooked at Artists Space on Wooster Street and slept in one of the back rooms. One morning, we woke up to a group Irving brought in who just stepped over our sleeping bags!

HW: There were political meetings at night. I'm afraid I wasn't very sympathetic to this other world of activity that wasn't associated with the rest of the programs scheduled by us.

VS: Was this the Artists Meeting for Cultural Change, which would meet at Artists Space on Sundays?

HW: I think so. The space was available for use for various activities from the time it was formed by NYSCA.

CS: And then, they seemed to stop, just phased out.

VS: Cindy, did you get the job at Artists Space right after the exchange show?

CS: The show was a year or so before we moved to New York. We moved here in the summer of '77 and that fall I started at Artists Space.

HW: I had almost hired someone else and Robert told me that Cindy got a job at Macy's in the cosmetics department and was very unhappy.

CS: No, it wasn't even that, it was in the robe department. It was so horrible, I only went for one day.

HW: It was just right for what we wanted to have happen at Artists Space because Cindy had a very easy relationship with the artists who came in and would sit at the front desk and chat.

VS: It must have been intimidating for some artists coming to Artists Space for the first time not knowing the ropes.

HW: No, I don't think so. It wasn't an institution. It was pretty low key, not a daily scene of any sort. All the young artists were intimidated by the commercial galleries because there weren't any small galleries at that time. The only places to go were 112 Workshop—which later became White Columns, Artists Space, P.S.1, or Franklin Furnace, and places like that.

VS: Were you competitive with or did you talk shop with other places like 112 Workshop and Franklin Furnace?

HW: It wasn't competitive at all. There were no formal discussions or organized meetings, but we all knew each other well and went to each other's events. We were all quite distinct.

CS: In those days, the only way to get funding was to prove the differences between the spaces. This is why there wasn't direct competition.

HW: There was a little resentment of Artists Space because it was founded and initially funded by NYSCA; and we performed other functions, we held meetings and provided small grants to artists based on immediate needs for their art. The budget was very small and the whole thing wasn't very professional, much less institutional.

VS: I am curious about how the jury you organized to go on group studio visits functioned.

HW: I invited artists who I thought would be in touch with what was going on to a few versions of the selection committee. There were only four or five people and they changed. One group lasted maybe a couple of rounds of shows. We pursued artists who had been recommended from inside and outside the group. If anybody felt very strongly about an artist and no one strongly objected then they had a show. I felt this method would elicit good information to follow up on and somewhat continue the spirit of the old process. Actually Matt, you were one of the first artists to show your work in this way. If I recall,

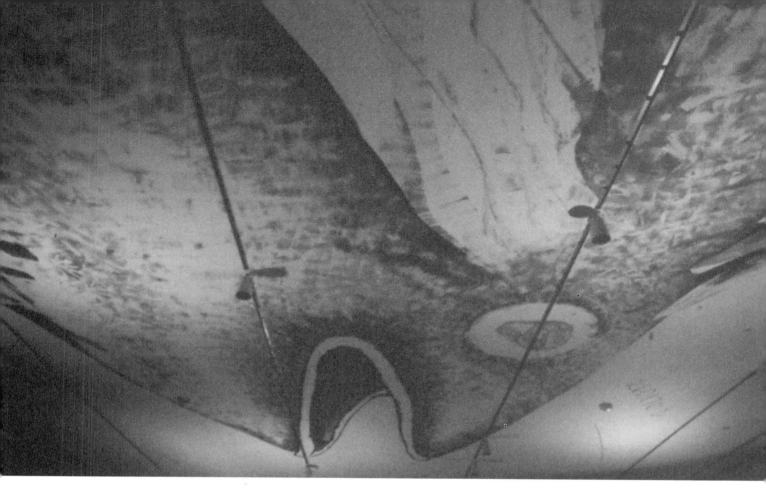

Bill Wegman was one of the artists on the committee who chose you, which makes sense. The committee looked at slides and visited studios. In one instance we invited David Salle to show his work and to invite someone he would like to show with. He picked Barbara Bloom who was living in Holland at the time. We rarely organized exhibitions in a formal way.

> VS: There were curators involved such as Linda Shearer, but there were also artists in that group such as Bill (Wegman) and Jennifer Bartlett.

HW: It was a segue to an entirely unstructured program.

> CS: How often would you get together?

HW: Fairly often at first. It was hard to get everybody to come in once a week, probably we did it once a month. After that point, it became a casual process of selection, where the staff discussed artists or curators who might do something exciting.

> VS: Cindy, do you remember hanging out in Helene's office?

> CS: I remember hanging out more in the central area with whomever was around, which was really Susan's office. I don't remember the meetings.

HW: In the afternoons when everyone finished doing what they were doing I remember sitting around that long green couch and talking. For instance, we would try to figure who was in touch with something about Super 8 movies or performance and then get them to organize a program.

> VS: Cindy, when you worked at Artists Space, some of the events and exhibitions you saw must have impressed you. Or was it more like the artists were all your friends and it was just a job for a period of time?

> CS: Yes, it was just a job.

HW: But you kept the job well beyond the point you had to financially, didn't you?

↑ Jonathan Borofsky, installation on the ceiling. *Sixth Anniversary Exhibition,* Neuberger Museum, Purchase, NY, Sept. 9–Oct. 15, 1979.

cs: No, I stopped exactly when I should have stopped. By the last year or so I was only working two or three days a week anyway. It was just the perfect balance. I wasn't making that much more outside of it, but it was giving me just a little bit so I could do both.

I didn't start working until one o'clock in the afternoon. I was part-time. Even though in the beginning it was maybe five days a week, it was only from one to six o'clock. In those days I was staying out, going to the Mudd Club until two or three. So I was probably rehashing the night's events. We all were.

MATT MULLICAN: That *was* the scene. The music scene was very important, because we spent all our time in clubs. Remember the evenings of bands? The Contortions jumped into the audience and there was a huge fight, but the only guy who kept on going was the drummer. It was fantastic.

HW: The bands were great and I remember the poster being so perfect with the band's incredible names in huge bold yellow letters on black paper. It was timely.

cs: In a way, it was the right moment to have Mike Zwack organize it, because so many artists were also in bands at that point like Robert (Longo), Richard (Prince), and Kim (Gordon).

HW: The connection made sense, but it really wasn't that appropriate to have that music at Artists Space, it just seemed like the right thing to do. A lot of people came who wouldn't have ordinarily, even though it wasn't like a club — I remember Brian Eno being there.

cs: It seemed like a nice thing, but it was competing with the Kitchen, which did things like that then.

HW: I think they programmed much more avant-garde music, performance, theater, and video/film events. I don't remember the Kitchen with that kind of punk music.

MM: I remember Robin Winters's performance at Artists Space and how he kept everybody out. He had us out on Wooster Street, because that was part of the way he wanted to treat it... it was a David Bowie thing. He showed a Mercedes crash test and he submerged his entire body into that tank of cold water. We were really involved, but no one was allowed to...

CS: Go inside to watch the performance?

MM: We had to wait until he was ready for us. He wanted a line outside, because culturally a line represented importance. Later, when we did the *Memory Jam* performance at Artists Space, we shared the same night and he told me, "Let's keep them out. Let's get some tension going." So he was like quoting a rock star.

HW: I don't remember it as a staged part of the performance. I didn't feel entirely responsible for everything that occurred. Artists Space had the luxury of programming a lot of exhibitions and events without worrying about the long-term commitment that a commercial gallery has.

vs: That's the beauty of Artists Space.

HW: Yes, I even miss it now. I would like to have the freedom that was there, to show whatever appears of interest and not worry so much about how successful or resolved the work is at any given point.

vs: So, why not go ahead?

HW: I would certainly show anyone whose work I liked now, but there was a different level of expectation and a different audience in the mid-70s. Artists Space was fun in that way. Nobody was necessarily expected to do a great show, just an interesting one.

MM: When you took over, Artists Space changed radically — I was there before, when all the shows were chosen by other artists. It was a joke. You could tell this artist looked like him or her and therefore that must be the artist's assistant, because the work looked identical. Of course, there were exceptions like Ree Morton, who was chosen by Nancy Graves, or Jonathan Borofsky, who was chosen by Sol LeWitt. That was an excellent show. Great things happened. Scott Burton... But it became much tighter when you were involved, much stronger. It gained architecture and meant something. It had a lot to do with you.

cs: You were open to other things.

HW: Well, I just wanted to set up a situation that would introduce a lot of challenging work. Artists Space took on an identity that a lot of artists wanted to be associated with. Also it was a different time in the art world. It was the beginning of this notion that art could be both visually seductive and conceptually serious. There was a very clear division between the different types of art being done. I had no confusion about what needed to be shown or what didn't require an alternative outlet.

© Cindy Sherman

art talks

So, if someone was doing a certain type of painting at that time there were galleries available to them. But if an artist was doing work like you two (Matt and Cindy), which was very new, then there were few opportunities. There were no galleries that exhibited young artists' work, and with the exception of fantasizing that Leo Castelli or Ileana Sonnabend would discover them, these artists didn't really have galleries appropriate for their work.

MM: And I really didn't expect it to happen, because there was no gallery around I wanted to be a part of. Artists Space was the scene I was into and Cal Arts was like that as well. When we all came to New York, we were smart enough to realize we had to create our own situation.

VS: Cindy, how did your dressing up and impersonations come about?

CS: Originally, I did it in Buffalo only a couple of times. And also in New York just a couple of times, too. It would be a spontaneous thing. Maybe I was playing in my studio and there would be an opening in a couple of hours and I would just stay in character. Or there were times when I turned into a character and went out and watched TV with whomever else was hanging out at Hallwalls. But in New York, in the morning, I would be futzing around with some character in my studio and I might decide to go to work that day as this secretary. For the show Janelle (Reiring) organized, part of the idea was that I would occasionally come to work dressed up.

HW: As a secretary or nurse or something. But I thought you had refused to do that.

CS: Well, no. It happened maybe four times, and then I just couldn't do it anymore.

VS: And Helene, you were charmed.

HW: I was more than charmed. I thought it was great of Cindy to do it in such a normal way that blurred the lines between her art and her job. It wasn't quite a performance. However, one time, I was being interviewed for a museum job, which took place at Artists Space, and Cindy showed up in the now-famous secretary suit. It made it difficult to be serious—I didn't even try to explain our odd receptionist.

VS: So you thoroughly embarrassed your boss?

HW: I wasn't Cindy's boss exactly.

CS: You weren't like a boss. I didn't even know what a boss was. It was probably the only real job I had.

MM: There was always that edge. You were rigorous. Of course, you hung out and there was wine and the Mudd Club later at night, but there was a rigor. When you talked there was no bullshit. Nobody could get away with anything, because you wouldn't let them. If someone made a statement about anything, it was clear they had to be conscious. That was a time when we were tough on ourselves and tough on each other.

HW: I must have lightened up since then. But you were all incredibly serious. You seemed to think you had to make a huge break from the kind of conceptual art that was so restrictive and at the same time avoid a lot of art none of you wanted to be associated with. That early conceptual art was not something to continue in its pure form, even though it was the primary influence. You had to invent a completely new way to do it. I was very involved in that idea, I felt excited about it.

MM: You were *completely* involved in it. And you were a tremendous sounding board. You really reflected all of our ideas and constantly challenged us. But that kind of criticality was everywhere.

VS: Where did you have these discussions?

CS: At openings or...

HW: Openings only had about 25 people in the beginning or we were just around hanging out at some bar or at a party.

MM: It was social. We hung out together at bars, on the street...

CS: Or just at the gallery. Because of all the grant applications Artists Space did every year, there was always a main group of people who would come back to the gallery; not just to see the shows, but to reapply to the Independent Exhibitions Program and the Emergency Materials Fund. Or people would come in to update their slides. Artists hung out at Artists Space during those times.

HW: It's hard to imagine, now, how inhospitable the art world was to young artists then. There were no young dealers with comfortable unintimidating galleries, like the ones artists started in the East Village and others which exist today. So if you didn't have a place like Artists Space to go to, you couldn't really go anywhere.

MM: We'd go to the openings, but we were invisible. It was fine.

HW: Sure, it was exciting, but hanging around an opening at a place where you were welcomed was what developed. Now, it's a much less exclusive situation with so many galleries and openings they are public social events rather than a private gathering of insiders.

VS: Tell me about *Pictures*. Ronald Jones said he thought your tenure at Artists Space was marked by the construction of *Pictures*.

HW: Well, that's probably not so far off. Many other things happened, of course. I do regret that neither Matt, Cindy, nor David Salle specifically were in that show. That was because they had already had one-person shows at Artists Space, and we had this one-time rule that now seems silly. Of course, we had no idea the show would be a sort of marker. I really thought there was a particular type of art being formulated and I wanted to have a serious look at it. I raised some money to do a catalogue and travel the show and invited Douglas Crimp to be the curator. That's when we went to Buffalo and looked at everybody's art. I knew at the time it was a mistake that the other artists were not included.

You both did very resolved work very early. Cindy, when you brought in the first film stills everyone just went crazy. The same with Matt's stick figure drawings. Actually seeing your drawings is one of my clearest memories of being turned on about new work. It was incredible work for artists who were just 22 years old.

CS: Maybe it seemed that way because it was a transitional time in the late 70s. Even though the *Pictures* show had been up, it hadn't really caught on. It was still a minor phenomenon that didn't affect the rest of the art world. It was a slow time.

MM: I remember seeing the photographs Cindy took at Alice's (Phillips) house on her trip to L.A. with Nancy (Dwyer). Alice is a childhood friend of mine. The context around that time was very familial. It was the right illustration of our time and its fascination with celebrity.

HW: Obviously that work struck a chord.

VS: David is critical of *Pictures*. Still to this day!

CS: Really? Oh, that's interesting.

MM: Of course. He was upset about not being involved.

↑ Thomas Lanigan-Schmidt, installation. *Sixth Anniversary Exhibition*, Neuberger Museum, Purchase, NY, Sept.9–Oct.15, 1979.

HW: I didn't know that. When Douglas first started working on the show, we talked about the ideas and the artists. It got fairly serious in relation to postmodernist concepts he was involved with critically. *Pictures* didn't really attract a lot of attention at the time, but it is remembered as an important show.

VS: How did you know Douglas?

CS: Was he already writing for *October*?

HW: I met him when I first arrived in New York, and we became good friends. He was writing criticism and had returned to graduate school to study with Rosalind Krauss. He had worked at the Guggenheim for a time before I knew him. This was the first appearance of postmodernism and he became quite interested in the art you were making. He wrote an important text for the catalogue that introduced many of the issues and language which became associated with a certain type of art. When he rewrote it for *October* he included additional artists, realizing he hadn't quite covered the territory. I'm sure it sounds very basic, especially if you consider how outdated an idea such as appropriation seems now.

VS: That was a hot word back then. I remember bantering it around in bars with Tom Lawson and Jeff Koons. It was on everybody's lips.

HW: Oh, yes, it was a big thing. I first heard it from Sherrie Levine.

MM: *Pictures* really affected me more socially than anything else. Especially in the way I related to the guys who were in it and how I felt they related to me. At that point, Robert, Troy (Brauntuch), and Jack became this trio. But I was very close to Jack before and remained close to Jack after, as well as Troy. It was a social thing. Robert changed more than anybody.

CS: It's weird the way *Pictures* changed some people in it. I hadn't realized it was the show that did that.

HW: Robert was the one who got a lot of response from that show, which wasn't expected by the other artists.

MM: At the opening he changed. His demeanor towards me changed. I challenged him on this point, because I was hurt. I thought we were becoming friends and then this wall came down. Very cool. And this is just because I wasn't in the show; I figured, well, I already had a show, and so forth.

HW: Oh, I'm surprised to hear that. I don't know how aware I was of those feelings around the show, though I remember how sensitive you were in general during that period.

MM: That's a minor point. The show did do that. It was a powerful show and it did create an "in" and an "out." It did have this quality about it. In the long term, it doesn't mean or change anything. But the show itself became a marker.

HW: It's funny that you remember those things so well. I guess we all have our significant memories.

MM: But we all knew it was important. Not the show itself, but the moment the show represented, which we *were* a part of.

CS: Many people assume I was in the show, but I always have to correct them. I get the impression people just assumed the idea of the show included a wide group of artists. I never got the sense it was so accurately remembered. Maybe because I am in a different position now, people are more generous with their memory of me.

HW: Matt's talking about the people right around him at the time.

MM: Yes. It was about personal relationships.

CS: Being a woman artist, *Pictures* wasn't a thing for me. It was mostly a guy thing.

MM: Yes, the guy thing with those long dark coats. They would never come in, and would never take off their coats, and would stand by the door...

CS: Oh God, that's right! I totally forgot about that. It's so funny about the coats. I used to tease Robert all the time about that. It's true, whenever we would go to parties, the three of them — Troy and Jack as well — would stand around with their fucking coats on and probably their sunglasses too, ready to leave at a moment's notice.

HW: Well, they were competing with each other.

MM: They never took off their coats because they would never commit to a space they were entering.

HW: It was before people were concerned about social behavior.

MM: Getting back to *Pictures* being a marker, it's ironic how, in history, Cindy, you are the star of that exhibition. According to the public, not only were you in it, but you were the most important artist in it!

↑ William Leavitt, tableau and drawings.
Exhibition: May 5 – June 9, 1979.

HW: Although a German curator recently asked me if I had an extra copy of the catalogue, because he's organizing a show that relates to that period, frankly, I don't think many people remember the show itself.

cs: I don't either. People just blur all of us together into this group of *Pictures* people.

HW: I've read the term "pictures generation" used as a catchall.

cs: Then again, just a year ago, I had an assistant who didn't even know what appropriation was! He was talking about rephotographing some found imagery and asked if this had been done before.

MM: The art world has changed so dramatically. Its amazing what 20 years does.

HW: Well, you had to dope something out for yourselves that now has a literature behind it that young artists have essentially been raised on.

vs: The same year there was the *New Image Painting* exhibition at the Whitney.

HW: There was some concern about that show, because of the possible confusion about the work all of you were doing and new image painting. The work had little in common with yours except the use of images.

vs: And two years later *The Nigger Drawings* episode occurred.

HW: That was a marker for the end of that era, for me at least.

vs: So what did you do? You had to confront all those protesters, what was it like?

HW: It was terrible personally, like being under siege.

cs: How did it all start? How did we find out about it?

HW: We didn't find out directly, which was why I was furious that people, whom I knew perfectly well, didn't call me to say that there was a real problem with the title. I knew Howardena Pindell and Lucy Lippard, who were active in the protest. They organized a letter-writing campaign to the NEA and NYSCA, which we knew nothing at all about. I didn't know until I was at an unrelated meeting and Kitty Carlisle Hart said, "Oh, I understand you're having some problem over your current exhibition." I just said, "No. Not that I know of." I honestly didn't know. I then called up some friends at NYSCA and asked

what was going on. I was angry because those who were objecting really didn't want to talk to us about the problem and how to address it. They just used it as an opportunity to protest against Artists Space. At that point I hadn't realized that the protest was about a larger problem concerning racism in the art world.

CS: It was like the birth of "PC."

HW: The title Donald Newman gave his show of drawings was on his invitation. It was a word that was used, I thought, comfortably enough given the art context. It was stupid, insensitive, ignorant, and uninformed not to realize that the source, both Artists Space and Donald, might make the use of that title a problem.

VS: Since it was sent out to the entire mailing list, Cindy, you must have been barraged by people calling Artists Space?

CS: Frankly, I remember making a lot of jokes about the whole situation. To us it was such a bizarre thing, because it…

HW: It seemed misplaced. We were also critical of the title. Prior to learning of the protest we had received only one phone call about the title and that was only to ask why the title was being used.

CS: Yes. None of us stood up for the title, but, at least, for the freedom to title it whatever Donald wanted. That's why we didn't question it. Also, we thought the whole thing was so stupid, because the work had nothing to do with the title. I thought, "Why are people making it an issue?" It didn't seem worthy. Right away, it was just sensationalistic on Donald's part.

HW: It took us awhile to figure that out. It had to do with our lack of comprehension and sensitivity to the circumstances of African American artists at that time. And it was also about that community's discomfort with places such as Artists Space and our lack of awareness or effort to correct what was obviously a problem with access and communication.

VS: How did you know Howardena?

HW: We had been friends since the early 70s when I was working at Whitechapel Gallery in London and she was traveling for MOMA. When I moved to New York from Los Angeles in 1973, I took over her apartment when she moved to a loft, and then when I moved, Matt lived there for awhile.

VS: Adrian Piper had a philosophical take on the situation. She didn't point the finger at you per se, but at American society and our unwillingness to learn from history.

HW: That's generous of her actually, because she had every reason to believe we should have been more aware and concerned, even though many of the relatively hidden issues of racism were not as well understood as they are now.

VS: But the flip side is, you're left with a censorship issue. Are you going to censor this guy or are you just going to say, "This is a problem, but I can't censor you, so just be aware that this is a problem."

HW: I wouldn't have censored him, but had I really been aware of what was at play, I probably would have told him that I just didn't believe he required that title for the drawings he was showing. It's not as if I went to him and said, "I know this is a deeply felt language necessity of yours so I won't censor it." Had it been discussed or had I been alert enough and tuned into his intention and the possible reaction, I would have just told him to fuck off. It wasn't ultimately a matter of censorship, as the title was totally extraneous to the work, which didn't contain any related visual or language reference.

CS: You could have intimidated him. "You don't get a show mother fucker!"

HW: I wouldn't have quite said that, rather that it just made no sense and had nothing to do with the show and I didn't want him to use it. He apparently just wanted to attract some attention, which frankly didn't occur to me or, at least, I wasn't troubled by it.

VS: What a bizarre way to attract attention. What was his motivation?

HW: Later, I remember Paul McMahon telling me it was just a punk thing. That's in fact how it was viewed in general, as some punky thing.

MM: It was a punky thing. That's what I saw it as, because Patti Smith, less than four months earlier in a club uptown, had these buttons painted "Rock 'n Roll Nigger" that everyone was wearing.

HW: Donald's explanation was that, like Patti Smith, he was comparing an "artist" to a "nigger," because it was about devalued labor in society without compensation or respect or regard.

> **MM:** He did a show with Mary Boone because of all the press. That's why he's "Mr. Hot" in his head.

HW: Why did he leave the art world and become a computer salesman? Does he still consider himself an artist?

> **CS:** Oh no. It totally sounded crazy. Claudia Gould told me he said it was better to go underground and work with computers, because he was too big for the art world. He had some ridiculous rationalization.

HW: During the ordeal, I asked him to please not make statements to the press and that I would appreciate his not getting involved in escalating the situation, because we were in enough difficulty. In his favor, he didn't. And he could have exploited it and become a bad-boy celebrity of some sort.

> **VS:** He probably didn't calculate the public's response and must have been stunned by the fact his title had such an incredible effect.

HW: And that I was furious at him, which really meant I was angry at myself for not anticipating a problem and at least questioning what he was doing, and being prepared.

> **MM:** If the show hadn't had that word attached to it, it would have come and gone.

> **VS:** But you had these people booing Artists Space outside.

> **CS:** It was kind of exciting, actually.

HW: I thought it was a nightmare. I really was upset by it, because I couldn't believe the protesters wouldn't talk to us and didn't want to correct this particular episode directly. It was being used to make a larger point, and I wasn't very happy to be the villain. And I doubt my undeveloped statements to the press helped.

> **CS:** There was some big meeting at Artists Space where we allowed them to come in at a certain time, on Saturday, to have an open forum.

HW: Yes, somebody, possibly Irving, arranged a meeting. But only after the ad hoc group had scheduled their own meeting at Artists Space without informing us — I guess it was to be a sit-in or something. I knew in advance only because I got a call from someone at the NEA, who had been invited for this big meeting and told me he would be there. Since no one told us about it and I had no idea what was planned, I closed the gallery that day, partly because I was angry, but also because the building was a co-op and already they didn't like all the traffic in and out of their building. Since I didn't consult the Board, I believe they were quite upset about that.

↑ Dara Birnbaum, *Lesson Plans (To Keep the Revolution Alive); May Day(s) 77*: installation with film and video, May 7–14, 1977.

* The Hatch-Billops Collection, Inc., archives of Black American cultural history in New York City, is directed and maintained by James Hatch and Camille Billops.

vs: Didn't you have lots of meetings about this? At the Hatch-Billops Collection* I found photographs that show several meetings in different locations. I saw Irving, Rudolf Baranik, Martha Wilson as well as other familiar faces in these photographs.

cs: If there were meetings they didn't involve us. There was just one meeting that I know of, unless it was on the street. Maybe in front of the building.

HW: I was on a panel at the NEA while all of this was going on and so was Benny Andrews, who is a very nice guy and who was one of the more active protesters. He suggested we fly back to New York together. I said I was surprised he wanted to fly back with me since we were in the midst of this big conflict, in which I was the enemy. I remember that he said, "Oh, you're all right. You just left the door open a little bit. And you don't seem to understand something about this. We had to do what we had to do." It was an opportunity to make an important point on the part of African Americans. This was my first clear sense that the protest wasn't about me or Artists Space in particular. And it did end up initiating some change. It made people aware of the serious inequities and lack of comfortable access. Whereas we hadn't previously thought there was any problem at all and that we were open to anyone who wanted to approach us about a show. We were naive. To not understand that now would be incredibly hostile, out of touch, and ignorant.

vs: Recently, Kellie Jones was talking to me about Kara Walker, an artist who showed large silhouetted images at the last Whitney Biennial. Essentially, she is exploring the derogatory image of African Americans in a very direct way. As an African American she can do this. But as a white person you can't.

HW: That's what we didn't understand. You could not consider yourself one with black artists. I considered myself one with other art people, intellectuals, and liberals, and that we were all together in this. As if we were all so special. I thought the problem people were elsewhere—that people having problems and people causing problems with issues like racism were in another world entirely. I hadn't realized that a part of the group was really alienated and uncomfortable and not invited to the dance. I simply didn't know that then. It's unimaginable from this vantage point not to realize the many levels of discrimination that existed.

vs: It came up again in the 80s. NYSCA started asking for quotas, not specifically, but something to the effect that we had better cover our bases in terms of gender and color.

HW: Gender was always covered.

vs: Perhaps not exactly 50/50.

HW: It was 50/50 when I was there. I didn't plan it to be, but it *was* amazingly so.

vs: We did an in-house account in the mid-80s and it was pretty good.

HW: It was certainly the best of any place. There were a lot of serious young women artists working then. I think it marked a real generational change.

cs: So in order to get grants Artists Space had to prove they were giving equal opportunities?

vs: Sure. One day, Susan Wyatt came up to me and said there was grumbling going on at NYSCA. We realized we had been pretty white across the board and so I felt I had to go out there and do some corrective work.

HW: It was smart of you to realize it required some immediate action. So even then it still hadn't been addressed?

vs: No, it hadn't consistently been addressed, because there we were—Susan, myself, and Linda Schearer—for better or for worse, all white girls.

HW: Daughters of the American Revolution.

vs: The program had definitely become unacceptable. When the responsibility became real, I didn't feel badly, I just felt ignorant about it and thought, "I had better get my act together and do something." I talked to Fred Wilson, who was then working at Longwood Gallery, and asked him what was happening, met some people, and then it started rolling naturally.

HW: I eventually decided — this is now, at Metro Pictures — it wouldn't roll naturally. I wouldn't run into the black artists I wanted to show in my normal course of interaction — finding out by word of mouth, or through people I relied on telling me about new artists to consider. Since this wasn't going to happen and being receptive just wasn't good enough, we had to make a specific effort.

VS: You do. In the 70s and then again in the 80s and again now in the 90s. It's always a corrective step you have to make.

CS: Hopefully it will eventually equalize.

VS: Oh it's a hell of a lot of better.

HW: I am sure it is better. First of all, this generation of artists is much more confident about what they are after and how to pursue it. They're not as alienated and not as uncomfortable in their ability to deal with the system. The artists I know are different, not as angry in the same way as the artists who were around in the 60s. Of course, they may be angry and have every right to be, especially over the residual difficulties still in place. But the artists I know are not as overwhelmed by the problems that exist. *The Nigger Drawings* was a miserable episode in my life. I was labeled a racist, which is about the worst thing imaginable. Though it was a significant event in my career, I thought it was a long forgotten incident for others. Then I had a meeting with David Hammons, whose work I like very much and would have liked to show at Metro Pictures, and his response to me made it clear that the incident was anything but forgotten, at least by him. That realization did cause me to rethink the episode. I am careful to bring up this event when planning something with artists who are black, in case they have a strong feeling about it or reservations, so they aren't blindsided by it later.

VS: In her interview, Linda (Shearer) makes a parallel between *The Nigger Drawings* incident and her dilemma regarding censorship and a performance by Eric Bogosian when he flashed images from Amnesty International — some of the most gruesome images of tortured people. When she heard about it she had to figure out how to deal with it. So she discussed it with a Board member and told Eric about her concerns, but finally she couldn't censor it.

↑ Barbara Bloom, participatory installation. Exhibition Sept. 18 – Oct. 9, 1976.

HW: No, you really cannot.

VS: You could say, "If you show these images we could lose some funding and I just want to lay it out on the table."

CS: To leave it in his hands? If he wants to self-censor? But I can't believe you could lose funding for something like that.

MM: Would you have done it that way: let Eric know that if he does this, Artists Space could lose its funding, but he can do it if he wants to?

HW: No. That is censorship. I don't think artists should be held responsible for the response of government funding requirements, which would imply that everything exhibited has to have a PG rating. By putting the responsibility of the space on the artist it fundamentally alters the intentions of the work. It puts artists in a position in which their work becomes an aggressive act against the organization.

MM: You would have let him do it without saying anything?

HW: Yes, I think it would be a given, because he was already invited to show his work, and his diatribes always have difficult content. There's no reason that it can't be discussed, but I think there is a limit to how much influence ought to be put to bear. Although I don't really know the specifics of what Linda was referring to, I'm sure there are some circumstances in which certain events or exhibitions would be totally unacceptable or literally dangerous.

Apropos, I remember when Tom Otterness did a film of a dog being shot. I couldn't watch because it was so troubling, but I didn't really question the validity of his intentions.

CS: Oh gosh, that was another big incident. Not as big as the others but… When I first heard all about it, it really disturbed me, then I watched it. Apparently the dog was set to be exterminated that day anyway. It was going to be put to sleep.

HW: We showed the film at Artists Space in a Super 8 film show and there were no repercussions. Later, it was shown at the Kitchen where it drew the attention of the press and became an issue regarding the abuse of public funds. We were interviewed about it and there was never any question about defending the artist's right to free speech.

VS: At that point did you feel you had to move cautiously, because NYSCA and the NEA were your only funders?

HW: I didn't. I did try to raise additional funds from corporations and individuals, but very half-heartedly. The Board at that time did not contribute financially or raise funds — it was made up entirely of art professionals. We had a couple of lame benefits at the Mudd Club.

CS: Those benefits were great.

VS: I noticed one benefit gave 100 percent of the proceeds to the artists. I thought that was great!

HW: It was a benefit auction for artists that was essentially an exhibition.

VS: Why did you move Artists Space?

HW: We lost our lease on Wooster Street. It was a co-op on the second floor, above the Paula Cooper Gallery, and they objected to the public coming in and out of the building.

VS: Artists Space then moved to a great space.

HW: The TriBeCa space was beautiful. It felt so perfect for the situation. It was the entire second floor and had a variety of rooms so we didn't do any redesigning or construction, just painted it white and it worked.

↑ Invitation card for Sixth Anniversary Benefit, Oct. 25, 1979.

1975–76

Trudie Grace leaves and in October 1975 Helene Winer is hired as Executive Director. Winer hires Paul McMahon as Assistant Director, and unless otherwise noted, they work collaboratively to select programming for Artists Space during this season. A committee of artists and art professionals is organized by Helene Winer to view slides, conduct studio visits, discuss artists' work, and organize exhibitions. Beginning in 1976, Artists Space holds regular weekly screenings of films by artists, the **Artists Film** series.

Sept. 9–27: **United Graffiti Artists**. Group show of painting on canvas (Edit deAk). Richard Admiral (AMRL or BAMA), Darius Dent (T-REX 131), Gary Fritz (WG), Roberto Gualtieri (COCO 144), Anatasio Kesoglides (SJK 171), Thomas Lee (LEE 163), Lonnie Marrow (PHASE 2), Rodolfo Martinez (STITCH I), Jaime Ramirez (MICO), Eduardo Rodriguez (SNAKE I), Eduardo Salgado (FLINT 707), Juan Tapia (CAT 87). Catalogue published by United Graffiti Artists, with essays by Hugo Martinez and Peter Schjeldahl.

Oct. 4–25: Marc Blane, sculpture (Hans Haacke); Ken Hubbell, sculpture (selected from the Unaffiliated Artists File by artists who showed at Artists Space during the previous season); Carole Stein, wall installation (Joyce Kozloff).

Nov. 5: **Panel discussion:** *Critics' Responsibility to the Artist.* Bruce Boice, David Bourdon, Douglas Crimp, Rosalind Krauss, Marcia Tucker. Irving Sandler, moderator.

Nov. 8–29: Ruth Hardinger, piece in three parts (Robert Morris); Richard Klauber, painting (Robert Motherwell).

Nov. 14–15: Simone Forti/Peter van Riper, two performances.

CURATOR / WRITER

Peter Schjeldahl I had been an art critic for the *New York Times* for some years at that point, although I was working freelance. I got a call from a man named Hugo Martinez, who was working with young Puerto Rican graffiti artists, and he wanted me to organize a show of their work. I got to Artists Space probably through Irving Sandler. I remember Trudie Grace not being terribly pleased with the idea of the graffiti show. I felt as if I was energetically used by Hugo Martinez to inject this work into the art world and I was happy to do it, although it ended up being exhausting. Hugo really kept the artists away from the next group of graffiti artists, who were from the Lower East Side. As a result, they had no prospect to make it over into the art world. A couple of them certainly could have.

The works were all paintings on canvas, including one that was the size of a subway car—it was gigantic. The show, which was spectacular, got reviewed a lot. Everybody panned it. It was most likely one of the first graffiti shows around. I've never curated anything since then. The experience has given me a lifelong respect for mediocre curators.

ARTIST

Marc Blane The people who worked at Artists Space believed in what they were doing. They weren't jaded. But the art world wasn't as large as it is today. It was a very intimate art experience. There was no business attached to it. It was the business of thought and there really was no money to be made anywhere. Artists Space was usually the first show in SoHo for almost all the artists who showed there. It was also part of a happening thing, the right kids were noticed, and a new generation had a place where they could actually dialogue. It was much looser than it is now. It was much easier to get around and negotiate relationships with people. There weren't as many barriers.

I remember art spaces being informal, low budget, everybody worked. Sue Wyatt, who was a student intern, stuffed my envelopes and helped me with all kinds of stuff. She was very gracious. Helene Winer, who was the Director, was very involved in helping out and being an intellectual. It was exciting working with her, she was bright and aggressive. She turned Artists Space into an organized machine and really made it fly. Formerly it had been more funky. Artists Space helped me an extraordinary amount. It was crucial, it gave you your chops.

The fact that Hans Haacke chose my work for Artists Space was not rooted in a bond between us. He was my advisor in sculpture for maybe a year and a half at Cooper Union. I was very influenced by his thought, although my show didn't reflect it. I have absolutely no clue as to his reasons for picking me. They definitely weren't personal. And my work was way out of line with what was being done at the time. It wasn't minimal or conceptual. I really don't know what it was.

I did a performance at Artists Space. I proclaimed myself "Art Champ of the World" and made a lot of enemies. I displayed posters on the street of famous artworks by Pop and minimal artists—anybody more successful than myself or whose work I envied or thought was great. I dipped my glove in a bucket of paint and punched a poster. Then I autographed it and gave it to anyone. That was a work by "the Champ." I wore a pair of boxer shorts that had things written on them like "Big Leo da Vinci," "Mike Angelo"—just turning the classical thoughts into a bit of a comedy routine. I also showed sculpture that I actually made up in the gallery.

68

Dec. 6–27: Scott Burton, two chair pieces (Claes Oldenburg); Pamela Jenrette, abstract painting (Larry Poons).

← Scott Burton, *Bronze chair (Street Furniture)*, 1974-75

Dec. 12: Connie Beckley, *Performance in Sound No. 2: Song Contained, Question of Perception, Spiral, Sound Split*, and *Conversion, Feat,* art performance and music.

ARTIST

Pamela Jenrette An exhibition was canceled at Artists Space and they needed a replacement show to go up in two weeks' time. I had been Larry Poons's studio assistant for a year or two and he trusted me totally. I had just been canceled from Documenta in Germany, so I had a whole show framed and sitting right inside my front door when this instant show came up at Artists Space. But Larry was just getting close with his girlfriend, now his wife, so he was tortured because, of course, this was his chance to do something for her. So, I'm thinking, "Oh boy, there goes me, I'll never get it now because he'll be on the spot and she'll be mad." But I didn't let it go that easily and I said, "Well, Larry, just do the right thing" or something loaded like that. So he thought about it and then he said, "Okay, it's only fair, it's only right, you're ready to go and she's not and this is for now." That's how I got it, by being ready to go at that moment.

I had my show with Scott Burton. I didn't know that much about him. He was in a gay world and his work was conceptual and environmental. It wasn't really my brand of art. My world was the formalists' world. In addition to Larry, I had also assisted Jules Olitski and hung out with the formalist branch of the art scene. I went to their openings and museums with them and I was a friend of Clem Greenberg and that whole crowd. So, if you can imagine this hysterical opening, it was like ghosts gliding in and out of each other. His people acted as if they didn't even see my people and my people acted as if they didn't even see his people. Artists Space liked him, but they weren't so keen on me because I was an abstractionist, a color field painter. He was hot, more hot, more cutting edge, and getting more articles written about him. I'm more mainstream. So, on the day of the opening, I am there trying to hang my show and I see some awful Bowery-bum-like chair of garbage and I thought, "Oh, what is that doing in here? How hideous! How gross!" Galleries are not even supposed to have furniture! You're supposed to stand around with your plastic glass of bad wine and that's it. But I shoved it over to the wall and I stood on it in order to get my paintings up. It weighed a lot more than I thought it would, the thing was really hard to move, but I shoved it around some more, wherever I needed it. Then a gallery woman starts screaming at me, "How dare you? That's a $40,000 Scott Burton bronze sculpture of a Bowery bum chair!" Scott was there and he said, "Let me introduce myself, I'm Scott Burton. I just loved what you did, that's why I do this." That was his whole thing, setting up situations and observing what furniture makes people do socially. He said, "That was so wonderful. You just took 20,000 pounds of chair and shoved it wherever you needed to bang in the nail." He loved it and that is how I found out what a with-it guy he was.

Dec. 18: Cynthia Carlson, *Grassroots Art in America*, slide lecture.

Jan. 2–3: **Artists Film** series. Dan Graham, *Sunrise to Sunset*, 1969; *Two Correlated Rotations*, 1969; *Binocular Zoom*, 1969-70; *Roll*, 1970; *Body Press*, 1970-72; *Helix/Spiral*, 1973, film.

January 2: *Performer/Audience Sequence*, performance.

January 3: videotape of performance.

↓ Announcement card for Dan Graham film screening; **Artists Film** series, 1975.

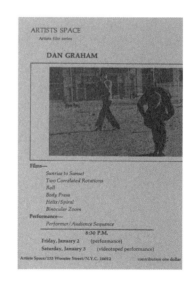

ARTIST **Rick Klauber** In 1975 I had just finished a body of work I started in '73-'74. I hadn't worked for Robert Motherwell since '71 and he hadn't seen these paintings, although he had been very supportive of my work earlier and was a guru in the true sense of the word for me. I lived with him three days a week while I was in college. We traveled through Europe together with his daughter and my girlfriend. He kept saying, "This is more than a graduate education." I still think about him, not only for the very powerful personal relationship we had, but the fact that he was the most eloquent person I've ever heard talk about abstract painting. He was extraordinary in that way.

I remember distinctly finishing a bowl of cereal and getting a phone call from someone who said Robert Motherwell had suggested me for a show at Artists Space. I was delighted and immediately went over and met Helene Winer and looked at the space. It was a miracle, because the space went hand in glove with my work. The size of the walls and the size of the paintings, which were quite large, were going to be a perfect match; this included room for a couple of drawings, too. So, there was really no anxiety. There was no preparation, nothing had to be done. When I made the paintings, I had no idea they would ever be shown. The very moment I put my brush down I was called and given a place. I thought my art career was going to be a breeze after that. I brought the paintings over to Artists Space and hung them up with Paul McMahon, who later became known as "the Rock and Roll psychiatrist." Murray Reich, a former teacher of mine at Bard, happened to be there and had a good eye for placement. So it seemed to be a seamless experience for me. The show just melded into the openness of that space, which had the flavor of typical SoHo spaces of the time, where work changed because of the loft architecture.

ARTIST **Scott Burton** The first Artists Space on Wooster Street was a product of the 1950s and 60s: the 50s because of its pre-Castelli, pre-commercial roots in abstract expressionism and the 60s because of the whole idea of alternative culture. It wasn't as if young artists would automatically get shown at Janis or Emmerich in the early 70s, thus the "do-it-yourself" idea. Artists Space in its early years had a fantastic record. It was the best thing going. They were very responsive to feminist politics when it was first hitting the art world and were very fortunate to get Helene Winer as Director. She was plugged in to new styles of art. Before that, Edit deAk was the living link to the artist community. I can't overstate her importance.

I had a one-person in '75, though it seems like a hundred years ago. That was back when artists still recommended artists. It was absolutely the best thing in the world for me. The Clocktower was the only other place that seemed like it might show my work then and they didn't offer me anything. Although I didn't show mature work, my Artists Space show was a turning point, the foundation of my later career. It was just as essential to many other artists—just look at the roster of names in the 10th-anniversary exhibition, *A Decade of New Art.*

Scott Burton, *Pastoral Chair Tableau,*
1971-74. Exh. Dec. 6-27, 1975.

ARTIST **Barry Holden** I started N.A.M.E. Gallery in Chicago in 1973. Artists Space and P.S. 1 started around the same time. There were four or five other places and they all happened independently which was quite amazing. Like the others, N.A.M.E. started out of necessity. There was a vacuum for innovative art, installation art, and, believe it or not, abstract painting and sculpture other than figurative. At that time, I was a graduate student at the Art Institute of Chicago and five or six of us got together and, in a nutshell, started a nonprofit gallery. We decided to just do it, although we didn't really know what we were doing. If we couldn't show in other places, we would show in our own place. We immediately applied to the NEA, but they were not funding spaces then. They tried very hard to give us a grant, which they finally ended up doing, but only after opening up a new category, Special Projects, for artist-run spaces. N.A.M.E. Gallery members paid dues, but only until there was funding. We each paid $25 a month at the most. Basically, we were participating in the space and supporting it. All members were also on the Board, and amazingly enough in the first year all the decisions were unanimous. After that year, it changed a little. If work sold through the gallery, we didn't take a commission. If people wanted to make a donation from sales to the gallery, that was great.

The founding members of N.A.M.E. knew of Artists Space, because we were both at conferences together in Washington, D.C. One day in 1976, I made a motion at a gallery meeting to close N.A.M.E. We were at the peak of our popularity. N.A.M.E. had achieved all of the goals it had set out at the beginning. I thought, "What a great time to go and avoid becoming an institution." I didn't want it to become an organization so full of bureaucracy that the spontaneity had left. I really felt strongly about this. Needless to say, I was outvoted ten to one. Everybody thought I was insane. To this day, I believe I was right. At any rate, it continued. But, if it had closed, it would have made its mark in a different way. I left along with many of the original members. It has changed hands many times in the last 24 years. I don't know exactly why it finally closed.

70

Matt Mullican, *Explaining the Exhibition to the Audience*, Mar. 26, 1976, performance.

When Helene took over Artists Space, it marked a shift, because she was acutely aware of history and politics.

Matt Mullican I had seen almost all the Artists Space shows prior to mine. There weren't so many places to go. You had the alternative spaces plus the galleries. I would start uptown and work my way downtown. When friends came over, we hit every gallery in one day. I remember seeing Scott Burton's chair on the street chained to a pipe and hearing the stories about it. It was a Queen Anne– style chair made in bronze. Of course, the show was wonderful and it stood out. Jonathan Borofsky was also an exception. But, by and large, I didn't find many of the exhibitions all that interesting. Often, I saw similarities between the artist selectors and the artists they chose. It was almost as if they were clones. Even as a student it was very obvious. It was always funny.

When I first arrived in New York in '73, I hung out with Jack Goldstein and Helene Winer. When Helene took over Artists Space, it marked a shift, because she was acutely aware of history and politics. Much more so than before she came to New York. She was very conscious of showing the best artists she could. Helene was tough and she ran that space in a very tough way. She was wonderful, very articulate, very ambitious, and we'd have great debates about the art situation and what was important. It was a good time.

I was Helene's first show in 1976. She didn't choose me per se, but I was the first show she was really involved with. I was staying in the tiny basement at the house of James Agee's widow, Mia Agee. A selection committee stuffed themselves in there while I showed them my work. Edit deAk arrived late and stayed late, too. When they chose me I was very happy. It was a major event in my life. I turned the space into a large chart and I put everything in a certain order, so all the work in the show interrelated. I had photographs, big drawings, signs and symbols broken down, and signs and symbols broken up. I had a head and body and color swatches, and then the chart describing the whole thing. I also did some performances, which I had done three years earlier at Project, Inc., Paul McMahon's space up in Boston. I went into a picture, I read a woman's life story from birth to death, and I acted out bits of the cosmology. There was pressure, because I knew what Artists Space meant. Everyone hopes their first show is important. I count '76 as the beginning of my professional career. It was a creative period, but emotionally it was really tough.

I remember Robert Longo's performance. He was a central figure, just in the way he commanded a lot of space; people were almost satellites around him. Cindy (Sherman) was the opposite. You never even noticed her, except for her really cool haircut. And Robin Winters really understood the audience. During his first performance at Artists Space, he submerged himself in a tank of water. We all sat out in the front waiting, it was like a big star fuck to get into this event. Michael McClard did a performance with these big bleachers inside the space. Then there was Jack Goldstein's performance and films. He placed a hired contortionist under a green light, just to do that. It was a beautiful piece. It was the vocabulary of what was going on at the time.

One of my favorite events, because it was so surreal, was Jack Smith's performance. It was supposed to start at 7:00 or 8:00. There was a marine in the back howling, he had really short hair and wore a beige outfit. My memory tells me it was a marine, but he might have just been dressed like one. Maybe he even was a real marine. In any case, we sat there waiting and waiting. There was also a big table on which some people were cutting up slide sheets to put in slide frames. By now, it was 8:30, 9:00, and Jack hadn't even seen the slides yet. Someone came out to say "Okay, this is obviously not going to be happening right away, why don't you come back at 11:00." So, we all went out and it started to snow: just wonderful little flakes of snow. When we came back around 11:00 not much had happened, it still looked about the same. Jack was still working on his performance. Finally, around 1:00 a.m., it got going. It was a beautiful performance involving these stuffed animals and a bizarre story. Now Jack, who was in the third row, had been drinking wine, when suddenly he looked up at the screen, and at one point he bent over and vomited; and as he was vomiting he coughed "fffocuuus, fffocuuus!" Susan Wyatt and Paul carried him out, and that was the end of Jack Smith. Meanwhile, there was this weird entourage of personalities including this guy howling like a dog, which wasn't part of the performance. It lasted until 2:30, 3:00. He was just incredible.

The concert series, *Bands*, was something else, too. When James Chance and the Blacks or James White and the Blacks broke into a fist fight. Michael Zwack organized all the *No New York* guys to come and play. *No New York* was the album that came out of those evenings. The Contortions were playing and in the middle of it there was a fist fight. James Chance had somehow insulted this guy's girlfriend and they started swinging and blood started to spurt up. Everyone put their instruments on the ground and joined in the brawl, except for the drummer who kept on drumming. Slowly it ran its course, they were pulled apart, and the guys eventually got back on stage to finish the song.

Jan. 7: **Artists Film** series. Jack Goldstein, *Metro-Goldwyn-Mayer*, 1975; *Knife*, 1975; *Chair*, 1975; *Butterflies*, 1975; *Shane*, 1975; *White Dove*, 1975; *Ballet Slipper*, 1975, film and performance with contortionist.

Jan. 10–31: Sigrid Burton, painting (Helen Frankenthaler); Bruce Colvin, visible and invisible structures (Mary Miss); Ellen Phelan, fans (Joel Shapiro).

Jan. 16: **Artists Film** series. Vito Acconci, *My Word*, 1974, film.

Feb. 7–28: Susan Leites, painting (Alex Katz); Lauren Ewing, video; Inverna Lockpez, wall pieces (both selected from the Unaffiliated Artists File by artists who showed at Artists Space during the previous season).

Feb. 22: Theodora Skipitares, *Mask Works*, two performances.

ARTIST

Ellen Phelan The real reason I left Detroit was because there were other women like me in New York. It was because of my friendships with Jackie Winsor, Jennifer Bartlett, Elizabeth Murray, Jackie Ferrara, Lynda Benglis, Brenda Miller, Mary Heilmann, Joan Jonas, Susan Rothenberg, and Nancy Burson, and the fact that they were women who were also very serious about making art. It wasn't about feminist art. It was about being out there and participating in a dialogue with the art world. That was the high of it. So, I was connected with a whole scene before I actually moved to New York. I met Joel Shapiro a month after I got here. Jennifer introduced us and the rest is history. I was embarrassed about being Joel's girlfriend and that he picked me for the show at Artists Space. But, when you look back at the artists who pick other artists, they were all good.

Being a young artist, I was totally oblivious as to what it meant to have a one-person show at Artists Space. I was making big, 6-foot-tall, freestanding fan pieces. I showed four of them. Some artists felt showing at Artists Space would prevent something else from happening or would put them in a lesser category. I actually think that was accurate. At that time, there was this very active downtown scene. Everybody knew everybody and those people were pretty serious. We were all born during the Second World War and went around in the small circle of the art world. There were passionate arguments about art, which took place on the streets at 5:00 or at Fanelli's or the Spring Street Bar or else up at Max's Kansas City. That's what I miss in the art world. Nobody talks about art now. They only talk about real estate or money. Maybe the younger artists have a real scene.

Feb. 27: **Artists Film** series. Lawrence Weiner, *A Proposition + Some Questions As To Moved Pictures*: *Done to*, 1974; *Green As Well As Blue As Well As Red*, 1976, film.

Mar. 6–27: Susan Eder, photo pieces; Matt Mullican, installation (both selected by Jennifer Bartlett, Edit deAk, Paul McMahon, Linda Shearer, William Wegman, and Helene Winer).

Mar. 12: **Artists Film** series. David Lamelas, *Time As Activity*, 1968; *Study of Relationship Between Inner and Outer Space*, 1969; *Interview with Marguerite Duras*, 1970; *Cumulative Script*, 1971; *Pour Milk Into A Glass*, 1972; and *The Desert People*, 1974, films.

Mar. 13: Valery Taylor, *Map Reading*, performance.

ARTIST

Robert Morgan I remember a talk at Artists Space, *Art and Class*, organized by Leon Golub, Carl Andre, May Stevens, and Rudolf Baranik. I was a young graduate student at that time and I went to this forum at Artists Space that was an incredibly exciting event. I remember the dialogue between Golub and Andre. That's when I really understood Andre's concept of the anti-monument in relationship to his work. This talk was tremendously helpful to me. The heated argumentation that took place was terrific, people really took positions and talked with conviction. It assumed a certain hegemony or a certain relationship to the power structure. That was a great aspect of Artists Space. I think all the shows had a certain radical edge. Helene (Winer) also had a knack for that and it would provoke a tremendous amount of interest and discussion. Nothing was settled, nothing was assumed. There wasn't all this fashion world complicity that has become endemic to the art world today. It was much more about art and really trying to understand art. Curiously enough, there wasn't so much talk about economics or politics in the art world sense. There was a lot of talk about politics in the real world sense. It was an exciting time in those early days and Artists Space was a major forum for opening up a lot of serious art that developed in the late 70s and early 80s.

Paul McMahon really needs to be given credit in those early years of Artists Space for being a dynamic force in bringing artists together. Paul had a tremendous sensitivity, maybe too much sensitivity. He had this ability to empathize with artists and I know he was responsible for a lot of the energy there.

← Robert Morgan, *Turkish Bathers*, 1977, photo assemblage. Exh. Mar. 5-26, 1977

Mar. 19: **Artists Film** series. Robert Morgan, *Locations*, recording with diagrams; *Turkish Bathing*, film event.

Mar. 26: Matt Mullican, performance pieces.

Mar. 27: **Artists Film** series. Chris Langdon, *Venus Ville*, 1972; *Picasso*, 1973; *Last Interview with P. Pasolini*, 1975; *Bondage Boy*, 1973; *Bondage Girl*, 1974; *999 Boy*, 1973; *Now You Can Do Anything*, 1972, film.

Apr. 2: **Artists Film** series. Diego Cortez, *Hospital Colors*, 1975; *Like a Job*, 1974; *Vienna*, 1976; *City of Song*, 1976, film.

Apr. 3–24: Gerry Morehead, painting and drawing; Jim Pavlicovic, installation (both selected by Jennifer Bartlett, Edit deAk, Paul McMahon, Linda Shearer, William Wegman, and Helene Winer).

Apr. 9: **Panel discussion:** *Art and Class: A Forum (Some Marxist Viewpoints)*. Amiri Baraka, Carl Andre, Lee Baxandall, Kay Brown, Leon Golub, Lucy Lippard, May Stevens, Alan Wallach, Kevin Whitfield. Patricia Hills, moderator.

→

Apr. 17: Gerry Morehead, *Barrington*, *I Think*, 1973; *Black Sambo*, 1974; *Mulatto*, 1975; *Old Trick All Ready*, 1975; *Counter Place Weight Series*, 1973–74; *The Last Line*, 1975, film and video.

Helene Winer and Gerry Morehead

Apr. 23: Martha Wilson, *Rose*, performance.

↑

ARTIST

Gerry Morehead When I went to Artists Space to look around and see the space I was going to show in, Scott Burton had an exhibition in the back room. It was his early furniture tableaux that had a flimsy velvet rope in front of it. A friend and I easily violated the velvet rope and sat down to have a little breakfast on the vinyl chairs and tables, much to Helene's dismay and to the chagrin of Scott. Helene thought it was inappropriate. I would venture to say that Scott thought it was interesting. Subsequently, his work became more private than public and at the same time his work was catapulted, because he had cast-bronze chairs, like the kind you find in Little Italy, which Italo Scanga was guarding downstairs outside on Wooster Street.

The first show I had at Artists Space of painted records was also the first sale I made. During one of those community meetings, which happened while my show was up in April, I remember Paul McMahon had an interesting argument with Leroy Jones on the relative importance of German contemporary art over Andy Warhol. This was well before it was a standard art world party line that Paul was articulating.

Within two years, from '75 to '77, Artists Space changed drastically. They moved to Hudson Street and, along with 112 Workshop, consolidated an aesthetic line carried over to Metro Pictures by way of Sherrie Levine and Jack Goldstein. But there was a severe critical cut-off point and the forum closed. I still bear the wounds from that Douglas Crimp show. I remember the comment, "Well, Gerry's more interested in magic and shamanism and not so much in pictures." But this is not my fondest nor my most objective memory of Artists Space. It was a tremendously important place to become acquainted with ideas other than one's own and to broaden one's perspective of a potential peer group. The months around the time I had my exhibition were very fertile. Every other night there was something going on at Artists Space.

A friend and I easily violated the velvet rope and sat down to have a little breakfast on the vinyl chairs and tables, much to Helene's dismay and to the chagrin of Scott.

Apr. 24: Marcel Just, *Showing the Outline*, performance.	Apr. 27–28: **Artists Film** series. David Shulman, *Untitled*, 1976; *(A Premonitory...)*, 1974; *(...On a Continuous...)*, 1970; *Specious Present*, 1975; *(A Current...)*, 1973; *(A....B)*, 1976; *Untitled*, 1976, film. *No Recourse*, sculpture.	May 1–22: Gary Bower, Fontaine Dunn, Hermine Ford, painting (all chosen by Jennifer Bartlett, Edit deAk, Paul McMahon, Linda Shearer, William Wegman, and Helene Winer).	May 9: *Gradual Progress*, a collaboration: Maureen Connors, shadow drawings; Wendy Greenberg and Elaine Hartnett, movement studies.	May 12: Meeting of artists in the UAF to discuss programs, grants, exhibitions, and other issues of interest to independent artists.
May 14: Alan Sondheim, *Failure, Ideology, and the World Order*, lecture.	May 28: **Artists Film** series. Robert Attanasio, *FILM-OM (#2)*, 1975; *Sound Film*, 1976; *Sea Composition*, 1973; *Echoes*, 1974; *Indecent Exposure*, 1973; *Window Light*, 1973-76; *Explorations*, 1973-76; *STR(L)IFE*, 1975; *Seeing is Bereaving*, 1973; *Sound/Camera Rotation: On Location*, 1976; *Running Time*, 1976; *The Split Screen Reconsidered*, film and performance.		June 5–26: Eleanor Magid, drawing and prints; Tony Vevers, painting (William White); William White, sculpture (William King).	
June 9: Meeting of artists in the UAF to discuss the possibility of forming an association to consider the common interests of its members.	June 11: Scott Billingsley, *Trespass*, situations.	**1976–77** Programming in 1976–77 continues to be determined by Winer and McMahon, with assistance from Susan Wyatt, Program Administrator. In January 1977, Artists Space moves to 105 Hudson Street. At its new location, a separate gallery, **Room 207**, is made available to artists who submit proposals for individual installations and projects, and is programmed in this way through the 1977–78 season.		Sept. 18–Oct. 9: Barbara Bloom, participatory installation (David Salle); David Salle, constructions and works on paper (Helene Winer).

↑ (L) Barbara Bloom and,
(R) David Salle, installation view.
© D. James Dee

Barbara Bloom David Salle was going to do a show and he wanted to do it with someone else, so he asked me. I think his idea was that I would come up with something that was between language and image, something that was similar to what he was doing. But, it was the first time I thought about the possibility of doing a work which was a cross between an exhibition, a set for a performance, and a game room that ultimately became an installation.

In the piece there was a boardroom, a photograph of three girls, and a game that you played, a literary and logical game with cards, which maybe interrelated with the photograph and maybe didn't. Each person got an envelope. It was a detective game, not Clue, but like it. Although it was quite vague, there was a logic problem that could be solved. In a way, it was strangely prescriptive and participatory, much more so than anything I would do now. It was the first time I ever did a work which was not about the objects, but the relationships between the objects and how you think about them in the space. It was also about bringing people together—you couldn't play the game with fewer than two or three players. I liked the idea of a group of people trying to figure out what the fuck was going on and other people watching them do that.

It was about a collective trying to figure something out, and in so doing they get a picture of someplace. It was really nice. I was quite happy with it. I have no idea if anyone else understood what was going on. It was very literary and very philosophical, as though I didn't want to make any more of the picture than what the public could make of it. The photograph of the three girls was a suggestion and a red herring. I wanted the piece to be between performance-fluxus-installation. It was some weird hybrid of that time. I shipped the piece to Artists Space, because I was living in Holland. I don't think I even saw the show.

The Green Lounge was a performance. There was me and the audience and we hung out in this lounge or waiting room area we'd set up. I just sat, listened to the radio, and changed the station from time to time. But I had little transmitters that would transmit on certain bands of the radio and I transmitted prerecorded programs, songs, interviews, a variety of things, on these bands. Some of it was regular radio and some was the prerecorded stuff. I may have exhibited something on the wall. Also people in the room were supposed to talk about certain things that would coincide with what was on the radio. But my idea was, if you were listening to the radio and hanging out, you would feel this weird coincidence between what was happening in real life and what was happening in the media, i.e., on the radio. It would seem as though nothing was going on at all but, in fact, there *was* something going on. It was a paranoiac's field day.

ARTIST

74

The question is, how do you coalesce and get monies funneling directly to artists?

Robin Winters I locked the doors to Artists Space and everybody waited in the hallway. I constantly had people go out to explain that they really did have to wait and not to leave because it wasn't just about waiting. I made a plywood oversized box of water with fiberglass on the inside, which filled up with water while the performance was supposed to start. Finally, it was filled, and I let people in. I wore a pinstripe suit and lay down asleep on this table in a room where the lights were dim and James Brown was singing "The Money Song." It went "It's money, money, money. Money can't change you." In the background was the sound of the ocean with a narrator giving relaxation lessons, very New Age before its time. There was a sign on the wall that said "RELAX" in big letters and "GO ANYWHERE YOU WANT, BUT GO." In the corner of the room was an umbrella with lights underneath it spinning around. It was motorized and looked like a flying saucer. The doorway had two film projections on it: a spinning door with screens on both sides, which was motorized. The projected images were cars spinning around and around in a circle with a talking parrot in the middle. The cars and the parrot made a figure eight with each other when the door spun. Suddenly, a light came on. I got up, walked over to the tank of water, and put on a snorkel and mask. I climbed up the ladder and got into the water, which was ice-cold. Once underwater, I gave a talk about relaxing. My teeth were chattering, I was freezing, and absolutely *not* relaxed. I was in the water for about 20 minutes. Then I got up and took a bow. This was a kind of immersion therapy, along with relaxing and going anywhere you want to go.

CoLab (Collaborative Projects) started in reaction to or in relation to P.S. 1, Creative Time, the Kitchen, and Artists Space. I had a meeting with the heads of each of these organizations as a representative of CoLab. My basic thrust and opinion, which I still believe, is that real estate and administration take too much money away from artists. CoLab, as a group of 50 indigent maverick artists, supplied more money and more direct show space to more artists, with less funding, no real estate, and no administrative costs. This has been my political argument for years. I'm not against any of the spaces that are functioning and actually servicing artists. The question is, how do you coalesce and get monies funneling directly to artists? CoLab started with these issues and was formed in order to try to get a piece of the pie. Ultimately, all of us were cooks, stirring the soup, and writing grants. But most of the time the girls did more of the work and the boys got more art credit. It was interesting, as a group we were very mixed, male to female, pretty equal. In fact, today, if you look at it economically, the girls have made more money than the boys.

I was happy when Helene Winer opened Metro Pictures. I was not really happy when she directed Artists Space. I thought it became a very elitist, exclusive place supporting only a few artists and promoting their careers. It was a misuse of government funds. If you're going to run a private gallery in a public space, don't call it Artists Space, open a private gallery. And she did. I'm rather Machiavellian. I even sympathized with her because, for my taste, I wouldn't want to deal with a whole lot of people, either. It's a really tough job. I think Artists Space is more interesting now, more grassroots, the angles are different.

75

Martha Wilson Franklin Furnace was made possible by Helene Winer, Director of Artists Space, and Paul McMahon, her Program Director. They allowed me to use their nonprofit Committee for the Visual Arts, Inc., indicia on a mailer which was sent to people in the art world. The mailer said, essentially, "I know you're a painter or a sculptor but I bet you have these little artist's books tucked away in the basement somewhere and you're not quite sure what to do with all of them."

The learning curve was fairly steep at the very beginning. I sent out a letter in two different-sized envelopes. When I got to the post office they refused all my mail. So I came back and Helene Winer patiently explained to me that the mail can only be sent in like-sized batches. I had to reshuffle all the zip codes and make sure all the same-sized envelopes were together. As a young arts administrator, I was very grateful to the older institutions and their pioneering nonprofit status.

When Artists Space was at 155 Wooster, I was there with Lauren Ewing looking at an exhibition of black sculpture on which letters were stenciled. It made a big impression on me because I marveled at the way artists were smashing together words and images. Up to that point, I hadn't seen sculpture with words on it. Although I thought it wasn't very successful, the effort was very interesting. Artists Space was at the vanguard for work I hadn't seen anywhere else.

Then there was that moment on Hudson Street in 1979, when Donald Newman titled his charcoal drawings *The Nigger Drawings*. A section of the art community erupted in moral outrage. Lucy Lippard and Howardena Pindell were at the head of the morally outraged pack against Helene Winer, who defended the artist's right to say whatever he wanted to say. This stood out as the first time in the art world when racism was confronted in a direct way. It had been lurking around for some time. It may have been a not-so-pleasant first for Helene Winer, but it was a very important first for the art world.

I did a performance, *Mudpie*, at the 155 Wooster Street space, but I didn't want to be visible in it because it required a naked lady. So I hired a woman I met in California to be the naked lady. The piece involved sweeping flour off the floor and making some kind of loaf, while an audio piece based on Alice in Wonderland was being bellowed in the next room. The audience watched the naked lady sweeping and listened to me bellowing, fully clothed.

Martha Wilson, *Mudpie*, Oct. 29, 1976.
Performance Series.
© Babette Mangolte

Oct. 15–30: **Performance series**:
Oct. 15: Poppy Johnson, *Writing* (*about this art is this art*), a continuous performance.
Oct. 16: Donn Aron, *A Strategy for Two Players*.
Oct. 17: Robert Longo, *"THINGS I will regret "/" TEMPTATION to exit" art in heaven (for Richard Stance)*.
Oct. 20: Michael Smith, *Busman's Holiday Retreat Revue*.

Oct. 22: Robin Winters, *Wait*.
Oct. 23: Amy Taubin, *Superimpositions*, never to be shot footage.
Oct. 24: Susan Russell, *Magnolia*.
Oct. 27: Michael McClard, *Clamor Clobber Comb*.
Oct. 29: Martha Wilson, *Mudpie*, accompanied by the artist's book, *The Annotated Alice*, chapter five, *Mudpie*.
Oct. 30: Marcel Just, *Gimme a Break*.

Nov. 3: **Evening event**.
Anthony McCall, *Line Describing a Cone*, 1973; *Conical Solid*, 1974; *Cone of Variable Volume*, 1974; *Partial Cone*, 1974, film.

Poppy Johnson

ARTIST

Michael Smith
I first performed at Artists Space in 1975 in a private performance for a select group. I was living in Chicago at the time. I was able to rent Artists Space through Martha Wilson or Jacki Apple. Helene was very open about it and let me have the space for a nominal amount. Because of that evening, I was included in a performance series at the Whitney Museum, which was great.

I was already included in a performance series Helene had put together when I moved to New York in the summer of '76. I did *Busman's Holiday Revue*, *Minimal Message Movement,* and *Baby IKKI*. *Busman's Holiday* was a song and dance routine with a really loose narrative. It was more abstract than *Go for It Mike*, but sillier, with more art world references. *Go for It Mike* had real world references and a narrative with a lot of notations and ideas. It was this pastiche of found music and type. This cowboy had a toaster for a sidekick on which he rode around, treating the audience like sightseers. I conducted a tour through a landscape of kitschy artifacts. There was some adventure, I rescued a set of neckties, a crib, and a buckle boot out of some kitty litter.

The *Minimal Message Movement* was a satire of minimal dance. I got the idea after seeing a piece of Trisha Brown's in a magazine for rooftops of New York. I wore the outfit of minimal dancers, white pants, white top, and had a couch made of plinths and some cushions. I also had a chair. I came out and I started the piece by saying, "The name of this piece is *Minimal Message Movement*. I originally thought of this piece with two other people, but I couldn't find two other people with legs as short as mine. So I want you to imagine two other people doing exactly what I'm doing, starting now." Then I did a series of very pedestrian movements around the space. I played with the couch. I told jokes structured according to the golden rule of comedy

with threes. I did a lot of punning and double entendres off the idea of the theatricality of minimalism and this pedestrian quality of minimal dance.

Then there was the *Baby*, which came out of an idea about neutrality. But it was actually a crowd pleaser, so I did the *Baby* at the end. The finale was arty songs. One looked good on paper: "White, white, white, white." I came out of a doorway with a roller handle for painting with white paper towels. I went right into another song, "Take a hammer and notebook wherever you go, put it down real fast, a hammer and notebook wherever you go."

Down in the Rec Room was very important for me. It was the first time Mike came out as a full-fledged character/persona. I'd been performing about three years and had a sense of staging, a sense of what made a show. I created this rinky-dink theatrical theatrics, where I could perform within the space. I worked in that back room on Hudson Street and used the windows. I put a door on the frame and made it into the side of a house. The rec room is also an Americana idea. *Down in the Rec Room* was a retreat for Mike, a place where he could be alone. I was out of the loop. But for him it was real solitude, real loneliness. It had a ring to it. The energy was great.

Artists Space was an incredible hub of activity. I met a lot of people there and hooked up with artists who responded to my work. I don't know if I knew exactly what they were doing, but we became friends and it created a community. I met artists who performed: Robert Longo, Cindy Sherman, Paul McMahon, and through Paul, I met Matt Mullican. I was also friendly with David Salle at that time. Matt and David were part of a whole group of former Cal Arts students associated with Artists Space. Paul had these events called "party bands" and "party clubs," where I met Tom Lawson, Troy Brauntuch, and Barbara Kruger. Some of these people later became an extended family to me.

Susan Russell

Michael Smith, *Busman's Holiday Retreat Revue*,
Oct. 20, 1976. **Performance** Series.
© Babette Mangolte

Robin Winters, *Wait*, Oct.22, 1976.
Performance Series.
© Babette Mangolte

1976 NOVEMBER

Nov. 6–27: **Hallwalls,** an exchange exhibition. Artists associated with Hallwalls, Buffalo, N.Y., show at Artists Space. Diane Bertolo, painting; Charles Clough, installation; Nancy Dwyer, painting; Robert Longo, performance documentation; Cindy Sherman, photo installation; Michael Zwack, sculpture. **Resemblance,** the other half of the exchange, takes place at Hallwalls, Buffalo, N.Y., March 11–31, 1977.

ARTIST / BOARD

Nancy Dwyer It was the Hallwalls couples show. Robert (Longo) and Cindy (Sherman) were together, Charlie (Clough) had a girlfriend, Diane Bertolo, who was also in the show, and then there was me and (Michael) Zwack. We were the six people in that show. Cindy and I had just graduated from college. Zwack and I took the opportunity of the show to move to New York. We may even have driven to the city with all our artwork, kind of like the Beverly Hillbillies. That was the level of sophistication: "Let's all pile in the car and get on down there sometime."

Robert and Charlie had somehow convinced Helene Winer to do an exchange show, "Artists Space at Hallwalls**."** Hallwalls was very much fashioned after Artists Space. We used it as a role model to organize shows and get funding for Hallwalls. Somehow I got included in that exchange show. I felt very lucky for that because I didn't think Helene liked my work. But it was about friends of friends. At the time, I did this goopy amorphous sculptural painting. But they did have words in them. They were like writing-painting, a stream of consciousness. They were oddly shaped and they had a lot of roplex and feathers. My work and use of language have always been personal and never formally referred to art.

I was really young, I had just turned 21 and was completely naive. It was a positive experience in the sense of, "Gee, this is my artwork in SoHo." That's why having a show was a wonderful way for an artist to move to New York. You hit the ground running. Going to openings was something to do. We'd drink as much of the free white wine as we could get our mitts on and if they had food, we'd try to fill up on it. We were really struggling and extremely poor.

The key person to introduce me to people in New York was Linda Cathcart, then Curator at the Albright-Knox Museum in Buffalo. She was friends with everybody and completely open to all. She was great. She wasn't like a regular museum person. She introduced me to Marcia Tucker. Marcia was so generous, she invited us to everything. I met Eric Bogosian at one of her events. Michael and Eric became really close friends.

Nov. 10: **Artists Film** series. Michael Harvey, *Sub Rosa, Emit 'T' Time, Bonaparte (A tragicomedy for 2 TV's),* and *Igor Orig,* film and video.

↑ Robert Longo, "*THINGS I will regret"/"TEMPTATION to exit,"* art in heaven (for Richard Stance), Oct. 17, 1976. **Performance** Series.

→ Robert Longo, *The American Soldier,* 1977. **Pictures,** exhibition Sept.24-Oct.29, 1977.

← Cindy Sherman, cutout detail from a photographic installation. **Hallwalls,** exchange exhibition Nov. 6–27, 1976

"Gee, this is my artwork in SoHo." That's why having a show was a wonderful way for an artist to move to New York. You hit the ground running.

A year later, when Robert moved to town, a lot more happened because he was so aggressive. It was depressing before Robert moved to New York, so I have to give him a lot of credit. He was great about meeting people and getting them involved in making a community. I always liked meeting people, but didn't know how to get things going.

In those days, Jack Goldstein was our biggest hero. I thought Jack was the star of the whole bunch, because of his talent. We really revered his artwork and short films, especially *The Diver* and *MGM*. Those were seminal works for a whole bunch of people. He was one of the first who showed me that Pop art wasn't all done, that it was just scratching the surface of something. He said, "You can take a little piece of that and just meditate on it as an image." I could go into it and find a means of expression that meant something to me. And that's something to do as an artist. It was very important.

Linda Shearer asked me to be on the Board. It was always 50 percent artists, so I wasn't shocked to be asked. But it was a completely new experience. I wasn't sure what to do. Little by little, though, I did my duty in one way or another with a benefit and an edition. I thought of it as community service. Whether or not Artists Space was actually providing a service to the community was the big question the entire time I was there. It was right after the East Village explosion, when very small, very modest spaces were proliferating commercially, which sent the nonprofit spaces into an identity crisis. They didn't know whether they were still viable as showcases for under-represented artwork. The East Village was providing a venue for those artists and feeding them directly into the commercial machine. The noncommercial spaces were trying to figure out what their role was, who they were.

Nov 13: **Evening event**.
Kevin Boyle, *Trace*,
performance.

Nov. 19: **Evening event**.
Vincent Trasov (a.k.a. Mr.
Peanut) and John Mitchell,
*The Rise and Fall of the
Peanut Party Journal:
Twenty Days in November*.
Book-signing party, slide
reading, off the air
coverage of the Peanut
Campaign.

← Vincent Trasov

1976 NOVEMBER

ARTIST

Robert Longo

Artists Space was definitely the center of the art world for us and the best arena in which to be seen. It was a place where my generation seemed to be and where we just had a really good time. It was also the gallery everybody tried to emulate, because it was a place where artists who didn't have a gallery or money could find a beginning. Artists Space had the Emergency Materials Fund, which Charlie Clough and I used, and it was great. But the criteria and quality of the work shown were heads above everything because the work was being chosen by artists. I remember seeing a great Scott Burton show there. I also remember seeing the work of Matt Mullican, Jack Goldstein, David Salle, and Troy Brauntuch. I felt some affinity for that work and it probably helped me make the decision to move to New York. In particular, Helene Winer was incredibly helpful in steering me to artists she found exciting. People like Troy were on the top of the list. He was going to be the next Jasper Johns, and Matt was going to be the next Joseph Beuys. I remember Matt's show and I was even there for a night of hypnotism, which was great. Helene introduced me to all these people, who subsequently have become important artists in my life. I also became involved in what they were doing as artists and this encouraged me to move to New York and insinuate myself into their group as a friend. Then I curated an exhibition with those artists, which was the last I curated for Hallwalls before I left for New York. And that's how the group of Buffalo artists I was associated with merged with artists from Cal Arts. These friendships still exist. We were really eager to learn and Helene was eager to provide information and help us. There was a lot of generosity at that point. Although I haven't had time to deal with it lately, that generosity hangs out in you as an artist to the point where you want to continue it.

Franklin Furnace somehow plugged into this new scene too. After Artists Space moved over to Hudson Street, the Kitchen, Franklin Furnace, and Artists Space became the triangle of activity. In the beginning, Helene didn't come up to Buffalo, we went down to New York and bugged the shit out of her. Charlie and I would always come down to look at the slides and see the shows. Artists Space was the place to be, for sure. Helene was doing a performance series, so I made a pitch to her. I did my performance and then I did the Hallwalls exchange show. During that show I slept on the gallery floor with five other people from Buffalo and we woke up to hear Irving Sandler giving a lecture. Howard Cosell was there. It was the weirdest experience. But the work I had in that group show was lame compared to Charlie's. The best work he'd ever done was in that show. I also remember bringing down Cindy's (Sherman) book about the rent collection courtyard in China. It's a narrative of figures cut out in an interesting way.

Cindy had just received an NEA grant and I got this gig with the *Pictures* show, so we finally had a reason to leave Buffalo, which we did in the beginning of the summer. Cindy had wanted to move to New York for a long time. When we finally moved, we sublet Troy's loft on Fulton Street, which didn't have a phone, and she was having a hard time going out of the house. I stumbled into this job at the Kitchen, but she was going to get this job working for this big fat German woman who was a lingerie buyer. I remember calling up Helene from a phone booth and saying, "You've got to help me, Cindy's flipping out. She can't go work there, what can she do?" She said, "Ask her to come in the next day." That's when she became the person at the desk, getting dressed up every day, which was always pretty funny when she went to work. But Artists Space was never a place to hang out. I guess there was a little bit of hanging out when Cindy worked there, but not a lot of people, always just one or two. Yeah, hanging out in Helene's office was like hanging out with the school principal. We'd go there and you'd see shit and you'd want to go home and work. That's the best thing you could say about it.

Prior to *Pictures*, I was working on a piece called *Missouri Breaks* which was being cast in a foundry in Buffalo, and I was teetering between different versions of how to finish it. David Salle, who was in Buffalo for the show I curated, had one idea; Troy and Jack were also very verbal and helpful, it was interesting to talk to them about it. Then I showed the piece in a Western New York exhibition in which Cindy was also included. It is usually a competition but that one year Linda Cathcart curated it. Linda had come to the Albright-Knox Art Gallery in Buffalo at the time when Charlie and I were just starting Hallwalls. She was like a breath of fresh air. She became our co-conspirator, only she was located in a high art institution. Helene and Doug Crimp came up to see the show, which was when I first met him. He saw the piece, *Missouri Breaks,* and next thing I knew I was in the *Pictures* show. When I got to New York I wanted to make new work for the show. I saw the CONTINUED

Nov. 20: **Evening event.** Beth Anderson with Paul Cotton, performance.

Nov. 30: **Evening event.** Cid Collins, *AMASS (Grace Jag Stacks Grace)*, performance.

← The *Communists*, May 2, 1978, **Bands** series of "New Wave" musical groups.
Photo: Glenda Hydler

Dec. 17: **Artists Film** series. Charlie Ahearn, *Dolphins Amazing People, Chalk Octagon, Stairway, Five Days and Nights,* film; Jill Ciment, *Chinatown, Food, and Wallet,* film.

Dec. 18: **Evening event.** Tannis Hugill, *Dialogues with a Single Performer,* performance.

ROBERT LONGO / CONTINUED

Fassbinder retrospective and then I made that piece, a small relief for *Pictures,* which started my career.

There was such a healthy camaraderie surrounding the *Pictures* show. We all thought we would get a lot of attention after the exhibition, but no, because the Whitney opened with the exhibition *New Image Painting* (December 5, 1978 – January 28, 1979) at the same time. In addition, there was that confusing shit that happens between generations, like the way it is with painting now; it's the same thing. The other day, Gary Simmons was complaining about how nobody in his generation has done anything like the writing that accompanied our generation; and the *Pictures* essay was one of the examples he pointed out. But, critically, aesthetically, and in the sense of colleagues, we were definitely noticed in *Pictures,* because someone had helped identify what we were doing as artists. I remember reading Doug's essay a bunch of times and wanting to understand it. It was a really interesting experience and incredibly helpful to have that kind of clarity at an early stage in one's career. *October* started up shortly after *Pictures,* and Doug's essay reappeared. My work was on one page and you'd turn to see Cindy's on another, as well as Troy's. But all the theoretical stuff that came out of the late 70s and early 80s didn't really have an effect on me. It probably had more of an effect on Charlie. Charlie, as far as I can see, is probably one of the best-read, most knowledgeable guys on art that I know.

It's embarrassing to talk about this early time at Artists Space and to start to read how important and pivotal it was for my development. It's almost too much. But if I hadn't met those artists and Helene, I probably wouldn't have a career. I think being an artist is not so much about making art, but also about finding the medium in which you want to function and who your soulmates are and their relationship to how you're thinking. Those bonds are so critical, especially when you're younger.

ARTIST

Michael Zwack Brian Eno came every night to hear the bands play, which ultimately resulted in the making of that album, *No New York*. It was an album of the current music in New York, which was basically the punk scene that was going on then. Many of the people in those bands went on to do other things. Arto Lindsay had a band called The Ambitious Lovers. Of course, Lydia Lunch, she's a favorite and famous poet. But none of the bands exist anymore. The evenings were well attended and it was an important event for that moment. It was Helene Winer's and Rags Watkins's idea. Helene wanted to do something like this and I knew Rhys Chatham, who was the Music Director at the Kitchen. I was working at Artists Space under the CETA (Comprehension Employment Training Act) artists program and Helene said, "Why don't you do this?" So I talked to Rhys and called up all these bands and got them to do it. There wasn't a lot of money around or huge tours planned for these people, so they were enthusiastic, and all the bands knew each other and wanted to participate.

There was one strange moment. James Chance had a very confrontational way with the Contortions and a confrontational way of singing. Lots of times he got into fisticuffs with people from the audience. At the Artists Space gig I had to get in between him and Robert Christgau because he was pouring beer on Christgau's head while they were playing. So I separated them, but it was more show than real, it was just part of the act. It was a really fun thing for me to do and it brought a lot of people there to Artists Space.

ARTIST

Charlie Clough Between the quantity of art students in the late 60s and early 70s, and the fact that the government was willing to give money to artists and art programs, it seemed like a biological inevitability that Artists Space and places like the Clocktower and 112 Workshop on Greene Street, later called White Columns, would sprout like mushrooms after the rain and become part of the system. Artists Space served me and my friends really well. I was looking for free money and chances to show. There was a program at Artists Space where $250 was available for exhibitions, and I got in on that as soon as I could. At that point $250 made a big difference. I remember getting a handwritten letter from Trudie Grace — she said their typewriter had broken down, but here was the check and good luck.

105 Hudson Street, January 1977.

Jan. 7–22: **New Art Auction and Exhibition**. An exhibition and auction of small works where the total proceeds of sales go to the artists (chosen from the Unaffiliated Artists File): John Ahearn, Ida Horowitz Applebroog, Alice Aycock, Diane Bertolo, Martha Hall Boyden, Troy Brauntuch, Charles Clough, Paul Colin, Diego Cortez, John Cross, John Cates Curtis, Scott Davis, Louie R. DeWitt, Fontaine Dunn, Nancy Dwyer, Susan Eder, Peter Grass, Colin Greenly, Julia Heyward, Marcel Just, Margia Kramer, Suzanne Kuffler, Eliot Lable, Susan Leites, Marilyn Lenkowsky, Sherrie Levine, Susan Lewis, Paula Longendyke, Robert Longo, Michael McClard, John Mendelsohn, Richard Milner, Antonio Miralda, Gerry Morehead, Robert Morgan, Matt Mullican, Gail Nathan, Howard Nathenson, Donald Newman, Lil Picard, Judy Rifka, Thor Rinden, Faith Ringgold, Walter Robinson, Christy Rupp, Aldona Sabalis, David Salle, Cindy Sherman, Jenny Snider, Alan Sondheim, Donald Sultan, Dianne Talan, Susanna Tanger, Peter Tkacheff, Peter Van Riper, Gail Von Der Lippe, Kevin Walz, Jeff Way, Robin Winters. Catalogue with reproductions of works shown. Live auction Jan. 22.

↙ Installation view.

Feb. 2–26: John Mendelsohn, painting; Donald Sultan, painting.

Feb. 4: **Room 207**. Jack Smith, slide show.

Feb. 23: **Evening event**. Peter Grass, projections and film.

ARTIST / BOARD

Cindy Sherman

I took a required film course in college and produced an animated film with cutouts of myself that came to life. I shot pictures of myself, cut them out, and then made an animated film using those photos. I didn't go anywhere with the film, but I liked doing these jittery paper dolls. I would take just one roll of film to have 36 pictures and spread them out like a deck of cards. They looked so neat with one arm sticking up here or there. Each was a separate cutout, but they progressed from standing still into a narrative. In the film, the doll picked up a piece of its little cutout clothes, tried it on, looked in a mirror, and then took it off. Each doll showed a different part of that movement. After doing the film, I started to shoot rolls of regular still film the same way. I would do 36 shots of some dumb little movement. It was always me in costume. I'd print them up and cut them out. The characters weren't very dynamic except for two, the Giant and the Fairy. The Giant was large and looked like a lumberjack—I was thinking of Paul Bunyan. For the other, I dressed in a little fairy costume and printed it up 32 x 3 inches. Then I started to write out these storyboards, which were more narrative and developed a plot from scene to scene, with different characters in each scene. It was a mini movie, hung up on the wall. If I wanted a man and woman embracing, I would shoot myself as both characters, then cut out the dolls so that one arm went behind the other doll. I made women smaller than men and children even smaller.

In late '77, shortly after I moved to New York, I started work for a group show at Hallwalls. I decided to do a series using one roll of film shots that looked like they were different pictures from one actress's life. I was also using more filmic concepts, zooming in and out. Characters would get smaller as they disappeared into the distance or larger if they were close up. I purposefully developed the film in chemicals that were slightly too hot, which caused reticulation, cracks in a pattern. I wanted it to be extra grainy. For that show I titled my piece *Murder Mystery*, because it was a story that starts and ends the same way. In the beginning everybody's at a funeral, and then it flashes back. It's just some really corny narrative about some 1930s actress who falls in love with the director. She was a has-been, an actress trying to make a comeback. She was a little matronly, trying to play younger parts. The press takes pictures of her and later she's poisoned by somebody, maybe the director's wife. She dies and the detectives have to figure out what happened—I forget how it all ends up. I figured out each scene in terms of the characters and how big they would be. If one character was walking away, I'd have a notation for the scale. Then I would figure out the scenes each character was in. On a simplistic level, it was what you would do if you were making a real movie. I figured out the actress's scenes, shot all of them, then referred to a sheet, which would tell me that this is the scene where she's doing this, take the picture. That would be on the roll of film, and I would print it up according to the same notation. So, in scene 11A she has to be this size, following my storyboard and putting it all together.

The first paper dolls were fanned out like a deck of cards and looked more decorative. I could see half of their bodies blending in and making a pattern. Then I actually put the different figures together. The final piece was the dolls tacked on the wall with tape. For the show, you'd walk in the door and immediately start to read the story as if it were a comic book or a Spanish or Italian photo novella. The scenes progressed around one room without words.

I worked for Paul Sharits. All those film people would hang out at Hallwalls. Tony Conrad hung out around there, too. Paul did these films with color flickers and I helped make these drawings with colored markers that would dictate the frames of the film. Then I shot the film in color so each frame was a different solid color and a constant flickering of color. Paul showed the strips of film as well as the drawings. The actual films became more like objects. I wasn't influenced by Paul, because I didn't do experimental work. My work was closer to Hollywood, and actually, European film was more of an inspiration, like Godard or Antonioni. It wasn't so much about seeing a lot of films as having a lot of books. I must have seen some films in Buffalo at the University, but more when I got to

CONTINUED

New York. I definitely wasn't doing the cutouts anymore when I moved to New York, but I didn't know what I wanted to do at that point.

Robert (Longo) and I were visiting David Salle's studio. Really, Robert was visiting the studio, I was just hanging out, snooping around to see what was on the coffee table, while they were talking art stuff. I think David worked for some magazine, because he had all these photos lying around. They must have sparked an idea, because this series had something to do with those photos. And I think he was using some of them in his paintings, too, at that time. That's when I got the idea that I could take these photos, because I was tired of cutting out. It was so labor intensive and the idea of paper dolls seemed trite and very girlish. I liked the idea that I could still have a narrative and some tension within the frame of the photograph if it was implied that someone was outside the photograph. That's when I did this one roll of film for that show at Hallwalls. At that point, I thought, "Well, that's it." Later, I decided I wanted to try different wigs, different characters, and it gradually progressed.

Whenever I had to go visit my parents in Arizona (actually, it was just one trip to Arizona and a trip to L.A. in 1977–78), I would bring my camera and tripod and maybe some lights. In those days I was just using clip-on lights. I would go to thrift stores, buy an empty suitcase, fill it up with Salvation Army clothes, and we would drive around Arizona. We'd stop and I'd set up the camera and get changed in the back of the station wagon. When I visited Nancy (Dwyer) in L.A., I did the same thing. She was house-sitting this really beautiful house, owned by Gifford and Ann Phillips. That's where some of the shots with African sculpture come from. The project suddenly had a different life. This character was no longer the has-been actress. Actually, the first roll of film with the has-been actress became the first six pieces of that series. I had this body of work and I wanted to show it. I didn't do it specifically for Janelle's (Reiring) show. But she had seen that work or she knew of it through Helene (Winer). I had four or six 30 x 40 prints blown up and hanging in the reception room where I sat. The rest, whatever number I was up to at that point, were in a flip book on the desk in glassine pages. I wanted them to be like posters and 8 x 10 glossies. I sat at the desk with the flip book—I don't even remember people going through it. Part of the idea was to occasionally dress up in costume and come to work as the character.

Adrian Piper was really a big influence on me when I was in Buffalo. I read about her work in *Avalanche* magazine. I'd never seen any of the performances except for a couple of documentation photos of what she would do on the bus. I loved that work and the ideas behind what she was doing. It didn't inspire me to go out and get dressed up, because our work was coming from different points of view. But the idea of revulsion definitely made an impression on me that came out more in my later work.

I would go out from the studio dressed up more often in Buffalo than I did in New York. I didn't realize until Janelle's show that I didn't want to do it anymore. It was a lot harder to lose your identity in New York than it was in Buffalo. Buffalo didn't seem as threatening for someone temporarily assuming some other weird personality. In New York, I felt like just another weirdo, no big deal. But I was pretty vulnerable at that point, being so young and new to the city. For some reason, I remember men on the street being a lot more disgusting to women. But then, I was coming from Buffalo, and maybe I still wasn't wearing a bra. I immediately started wearing bras. I really changed my identity to be more butch, almost military. I wore an army coat to be more neutral on the streets. Maybe, because I am older, people don't say those kinds of things to me anymore. And hopefully men have changed since then.

Paul McMahon Helene Winer was a friend and the gallery director at Pomona College, where I went to school. After college, I moved back to Boston and started a proto-alternative space, Project Incorporated. The space had finger painting and photography, after-school stuff for kids, and the occasional lecture. In 1972, they began to use the space to show conceptual performance art. I did about 31 night shows of Sol LeWitt, Lawrence Weiner, Douglas Huebler, Laurie Anderson, Matt Mullican, David Salle, and Jim Welling. I was connected to Cal Arts students, Dan Graham, and the conceptual art world. Then the phone rang. It was Helene, who had been asked to be the Director of Artists Space. She knew about the shows I had been doing and asked me to be her Assistant Director.

I'll tell you the real story. It wasn't always a political thing. My impression is that Helene was asked by NYSCA to take over Artists Space from Trudie Grace, because there was a sense of stagnation.

It was a difficult political end run that had to be accomplished, because the artists-choose-artists modus operandi was never going to open up into an interesting situation. I just had a funny flash come to mind. It was like Marxists choose Marxists. I was thinking of doing a show called *Former Lovers, Relatives, and People I Owe Money To*. Most of the people shown were either lovers of the artists, studio assistants, or slavish imitators. You'd have a group of artists together, choosing three other artists together, whose work didn't particularly have much to do with each other. It was messed up. The question was, how do we create this fig-leaf way of showing work we want to show? It did happen and it worked.

One of the best and most enjoyable aspects about working at Artists Space in the early days was reading Edit deAk's correspondence. It was out there. People wrote letters to Artists Space and Edit wrote back some of the funniest things in the world. A woman art student from the Midwest wrote to say she was broken-hearted because she wanted to be an artist and move to New York, but she heard that in the art world the only way you get ahead is by whom you blow. She was just crushed by the whole concept and didn't know what to do. Edit wrote back, and the first line was, "It is indeed an ill wind that blows no one good."

I came into the position Edit had occupied. Susan Wyatt was the constant thread. She was very much devoted and oriented toward a service organization. The three of us, Helene, Susan, and I, talked all the time. We had to devise various Machiavellian strategies to do shows that we found interesting, which we thought other people would also find interesting and which looked interesting. But we couldn't get arrested.

CONTINUED

One of the best and most enjoyable aspects about working at Artists Space in the early days was reading Edit deAk's correspondence. It was out there. People wrote letters to Artists Space and Edit wrote back some of the funniest things in the world.

Mar. 5: **Room 207**. Contextual evening from the Center for Experimental Art and Communication, Toronto, directed by Amerigo Marras. P. Dudar, *Crash Points*, film; Lily Eng, *Wall to Floor*, performance; Brian Kipping, *11 Minutes*, film.

Mar. 5–26: Robert Morgan, photo assemblage, film, slides, and books.

Mar. 11–31: **Resemblance**. (Helene Winer) Exchange exhibition of artists associated with Artists Space show at Hallwalls, Buffalo, N.Y. Troy Brauntuch, drawing; Paul McMahon, painting; Matt Mullican, installation; David Salle, painting.

Mar. 27: **Evening event**. Robin Lee Crutchfield, *Nursing Is an Art*, performance.

Mar. 29–Apr. 2: **Room 207**. Taka Iimura, *1 Sec and □*, film installation; *Time Pieces*, text.

Apr. 2–23: Michael Brewster, *An Acoustic Sculpture* and *A Clicker Drawing*, six concealed clickers sounding at three-second intervals. An exchange exhibition with the Los Angeles Institute of Contemporary Art.

Apr. 16–17: **Evening event**. Charlemagne Palestine, *Battling the Invisible*, performance of body works from 1972 to 1977.

Apr. 5–9: **Room 207**. Gary Schneider, *TOWARDS ANDROGEN, A Mating*, installation of performance photographs.

Apr. 11: Performance with slide projections.

←

PAUL MCMAHON / CONTINUED

People came up to me on the street to tell me they liked such and such show or artist and I'd think, "My God! I didn't think there was anybody there!" I believe that if anybody even has a thought, then somehow, everybody in the world knows what it is. So, when stuff gets shown it has an effect almost at the molecular level. But from the inside looking out, we definitely felt ignored. The only attention we got from the press, when we finally got attention, was in the form of an attack by Lucy Lippard on Donald Newman.

We formed the Unaffliated Artists Slide File by soliciting slides from everybody we wanted to show. Actually, everybody period, because we were curious to see the work. We got a group of people together to look at them and found that we tended to like more the people we wanted to show anyway. There were several people nobody had ever heard of whom we hunted down to look at their work, and it turned out to be interesting or not.

Jack Smith was the greatest. He was like a Cecil B. De Mille without money. Once, Andy Warhol said that he started making movies because he wanted to make a movie of Jack Smith making a movie. Jack Smith's movies are incredible. He only made two and then he ran out of money. He was quite frightening and eccentric and had a habit of showing up two to four hours late for his performances. He was about two hours late the night he did a slide show at Artists Space. He brought a couple of gallons of home wine with him and was pretty far gone. For a performance he had at Edit's (deAk) and Peter Grass's loft, he sat at the table ironing the film into the slide holders for the first two hours. Then he held the slides up to the light, agonizing five minutes over each to determine which end was up, and all the while music was playing.

At Artists Space, the carousels were already loaded, but loaded wrong. Upside down and/or backwards and/or on their side. And the audience was peppered with wild characters. One guy was prancing around in a little cowboy outfit. There was definitely a gay element in the performance, pre-AIDS. Jack was acting out and amazingly intoxicated. At one point he was up front giving a little explanation of the slides. A slide would come on, he looked at it for a long time, and then he would turn around and say something like, "The horses." He had the most incredible voice, it was the way he naturally talked. Now, the thing about his slide shows, which is a little hard to imagine if you haven't seen one, was that he took pictures of normal things. But something about the way he took them made you see something else in them. For instance, a picture of a cloud looked like an elephant, so when you saw it you saw the elephant, not the cloud. That's the way his slides were, visually extremely disorienting; you're seeing something that isn't there and the more you try to see, the less you see, because it goes away and you start to see what's really there. The person projecting the slides had a tantrum and quit. The performance was two hours late, Jack was in a completely fearful state of

CONTINUED

intoxication, and everybody else was also getting drunk. It was the worst wine in the world, giving you a hangover even before you got drunk. Then Jack started throwing up and two guys dragged him into the bathroom. He finished up his business in the bathroom, we cleaned up the puke, and the show went on. And it was fantastic. If I had to pick the best thing that ever happened at Artists Space, that would be at the top of half a dozen.

The performance series we did at Wooster Street was really powerful: Diego Cortez, Michael McClard, Robin Winters. Matt Mullican's performance was great and Paul Cotton's performance was way up there, just mind-blowing. It was a religious experience. Robin and Michael were both very exciting to work with because their demands were to the limits of possibility. Robin came in the day before and built a 6 x 6 foot cube in plywood screwed together and covered with a layer of fiberglass, which dried in the gallery. He proposed to fill it the next day with water. On the surface, it might not sound like such a big problem, until you start thinking about the weight of 6 cubic feet of water. After we calculated that the floor could take the load, we just went with it. But we still weren't sure if the box would hold together under the tremendous pressure. Charlemagne Palestine was also very interesting. His performance was at Hudson Street. It was subtle, a lot about the energy of his will, forcing and controlling the space in an interesting way.

When we moved to Hudson Street, we set aside one room for me to use as a studio. I made a lot of chaos in there, it got a little out of hand. In retrospect, if I were to put myself in Helene's position, having to deal with my studio, it would bother me. And it did bother her. That's part of the reason why she thought it was time for me to be an artist and stop being an administrator. Helene's aesthetic is quite well defined. I always find the work at Metro Pictures has a neatness about it. She doesn't like sloppy, drippy, eruptive, or dusty things. You'll find very challenging and provocative work, but it wouldn't be messy or expressionistic.

Artists Space was necessary, it was good. It was a wedge whereby our team forced a chink in their team's armor and then our team took over. By that time, I wasn't on it anymore. I don't have any second thoughts about supporting the work I did. Anything that has to do with art and artists is completely bound by the laws of paradox and contradiction. Jasper Johns said, "The artist is the highest rank of the servant class." That's why it is very paradoxical that artists with very high ethical and social motives, like those of the conceptualists and minimalists, were every bit as exclusionary and elitist as any other group. It was a very interesting moment in the late 70s. The reason so many artists played in rock bands was because it was the nature of their soul to want a lot of attention. Donald Newman is a perfect example, and also James Nares, who was in the Contortions. There were a bunch who then went back into the galleries when they were able to show their work, and if they couldn't, they were in the clubs. There was something squarish about it.

ARTIST

Dara Birnbaum I had been in Florence, Italy, and while I was there I met Vito Acconci, Dan Graham, Dennis Oppenheim, and Richard Landry. They were visiting artists, just passing through, and they told me to go back to New York. I was very naive, very young in every sense of the word. I was only starting to break out of architecture which I had been practicing for two years and I began to develop work with a video camera that someone had lent me. In those days, I was part of a peer group that included Robin Winters, Julia Heyward, Willoughby Sharp, and Scott Billingsley. Dan Graham would come on occasion. He was our elder wiser statesman. But, because I basically joined into that group, when it met the idea became about finding _their_ idea, so that wasn't going to work. One day an artist recommended me to Paul McMahon, so he came to see my new video work, but he didn't understand it. Paul thought something had happened to me and that I was trying to reveal this in my work. Later I heard a rumor that the work had been discussed and I had been turned down. The only way I got in was because Helene Winer wanted to show Suzanne Kuffler very badly. Helene had a fondness for people from Cal Arts. Then Suzanne came to me and said, "I'm supposed to do this show, but I don't want to do it without showing with another person." She didn't believe in the idea of individual shows. I told her I had been turned down from Artists Space. But she made a stipulation that I had to show with her. So they had to take me. CONTINUED

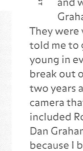

↑ Announcement card for Room 207.

ROOM 207
Artists Space

Room 207 is now available, upon application, for artists' film and video works, performances, installations and other short term projects.

Apr. 27–30: **Room 207**. Mitch Corber, _Apt. to Share, Rent free: Exchg.lt.hskpg_, continuous interviews and selected other works.

Apr. 29–30: David Hykes with the Harmonics Choir, _Hearing Solar Winds: Solo Singing, Choir Singing_, and selected other works, musical performance.

May 3: **Room 207**. Willy Lenski, _Shots from my old place on Duane St._ and _Non-elaborated Melodrama_, film.

May 5: Ted Titolo, _Whose is whose, is whosewhose?_ and _The partial return of the abducted_, two slide presentations with sound.

May 7–14: **Room 207**. Dara Birnbaum, _Lesson Plans (To Keep the Revolution Alive). May Day(s) 77, 15 shots at it_, installation with film and video; Suzanne Kuffler, _Talk/Personal Tenderness_, video installation.

1977 APR–MAY

↑ View into the entrance gallery, 155 Hudson St.

May 11–June 4:
Super 8 film exposition.

May 11–18: Laurie Anderson, *At the Shrink's*, continuous loop film installation; Marcia Hafif, *Notes on Bob and Nancy*; Charles Clough, *Drawing and Paint Boy*; Tim Burns, *Why Cars?*; Willy Lenski, *Forest Film/Pan Red Velvet*; Mitch Corber, *Rigoletto, Don Giovanni,* and *La Boheme*; James Collins, *Watching Sheilah* and *Imagining Sheilah;* Paula Longendyke, *Antarctica* and *Domino Theory;* Paul McMahon, *Table on Cape Cod* and *Film of TV;* Alan Saret, *Hole-in-the-Wall;* Charlie Ahearn, *Sinatra;* James Nares, *Pendulum Study;* Katy Martin,

A Family Passion Passing.

May 18–21: Colleen Fitzgibbon, *Real Estate;* Scott B, *Hold Up*; Judy Rifka, *Moving;* Bill Brand, untitled; Ann Flash DeLeon, *In Crastinum Defferre;* Susan Russell, *Seduction;* Dennis Oppenheim, *Aspen Projects I and II;* Donn Aron, *Three Commercials;* Andrea Callard, *Standard Adult Wheelchair* and *Temporary Participation for an Analogous Situation;* Robert Morgan, *Release Rescue (Dual Version);* Carolee Schneemann, *Kitch's Last Meal*.

May 25–28: Peter Grass, *Man and Moon* and *Savages of Asterisk;*

Jean Dupuy, *Central Park* and *Skin;* Peter van Riper, *Holographic Rainbow Window* and *Fluxus Tour (Soho Curb Sites);* Michael Harvey, *Dissolve, Cut, Emit T Time,* and *Photo Black and White;* Roger Cutforth, *Valerie and the Sea, In a Dark Wood, Lynnie by a Stream, Pat and the Lake, Dawn and Dusk,* and *Laura and the Sea;* Cathy Billian, *Long Shadows;* Michael Oblowitz, *Theatre of Long Words* and *Ontological Surgery;* Anthony McCall, *Demonstration at the Opening of the Rockefeller Show at the Whitney, September 15, 1976;* Betsy Sussler, *Sedition ;*

Marcia Resnick and Don Rodan, *How to Mount an Exhibition (Artful Bangers);* William Wegman, *Bubble Gum;* Christa Maiwald, *Ending*.

May 29–June 4: Vito Acconci, *Angeleno, Vamoose!,* 1977; Jared Bark, excerpts from *Krishna Concrete,* 1977; Ericka Beckman, *Pointing To,White Man Has Clean Hands,* 1977; Beth B, *Impress,* 1976; Leandro Katz, *Twelve Moons,* 1975; Jacki Ochs, *Trap;* Lan Payne, *Westchester Thumbs,* 1977; Virginia Piersol, *Film for Step Motion* and *Blowpipe,* 1973; Gregg Powell, *Skyline,* 1973;

Walter Robinson, *Untitled (Four Parts),* 1977; Seth Tillett, *The Role of Practice in the Objective Process of the Universe/The Unity of Knowing and Doing,* 1970; Roger Welch, *Burial, Flagpole (Star Spangled Banner),* 1970.

→ Charlie Ahearn

↓ Carolee Schneeman

May 22: **Evening event**. Ralston Farina, *Fun with Time Time*, performance.

May 24–28: **Room 207**. Tom Lawson, *In Camera*, four boxes and a wall drawing.

May 31–June 4: **Room 207**. George Griffin, *Step Print*, color film cycle.

DARA BIRNBAUM / CONTINUED

We were given Room 207, it was the first time that space was used for exhibition. It was a room dedicated to even more experimental work. The idea was that we would both develop work, not collaborate on it, but cooperate on how we displayed it. We met a lot to give each other the full extent of our individuality in the work. It broke down very easily. In fact, our work ended up being side by side.

Although Artists Space was an alternative space, it was more established and more in the public eye than the alternative spaces where I had been showing. So, confronted with this show, I had to think very carefully and in a different way about what I really wanted to say. I had been looking at the language of film a lot. But I didn't understand why no one was writing, for example, in *Screen*, on the language of television. So, I started looking at television. At that time, I had no equipment. I would just shoot straight off a TV set and try to catch these images.

It was during Watergate and the time of the David Frost/Richard Nixon interviews. People were coming back to me from one week to the next saying, "I just saw these interviews on TV." It was incredible! I really started to notice when they were cutting away who was speaking. Everyone said to me that my pictures were about cutaways and reverse angle shots and what's really being said in the statement, both pictorially and in the text. Sometimes the words go by so quickly. But when they're printed out and you see the exact moment being shown, it's rather astonishing; a lot of the hidden

agendas start to open up. Certain images can be carefully controlled, and cutaways are not necessary. But when you freeze it all, the truth becomes outstanding. *Lesson Plans* was the first work I did and it was for Artists Space, and while it has often gone in different directions, it has carried me through until now.

I had one little thing go wrong. By accident, I took someone's cassette, which had been left out on the floor, to test the video and make sure it was working. It should have been put back on a shelf. I got in a lot of trouble. I just didn't realize what it was. But to be honest, even bad memories are inside of a great memory of exhibiting. I had a lot of lesson plans from Artists Space, everything from feeling a little like someone rejected but allowed in and on my best behavior to feeling exhilarated because of a wonderful opening and show and a great dialogue that happened afterward.

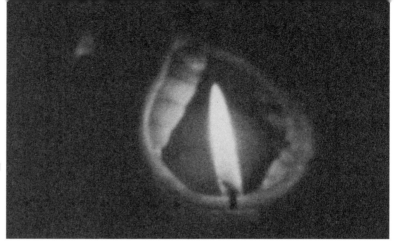

Douglas Crimp I had just started
graduate school when Helene Winer invited
me to curate *Pictures*. Previously, I had
curated a show of paintings by Agnes Martin
for the School of Visual Arts gallery; this was
at a time when Agnes had dropped out of sight and
people didn't know who she was. I had also been
writing criticism for six or seven years, so I had a
fairly strong knowledge of the art of that period in
New York. But I wasn't someone who went around
making studio visits. So, I took my lead from
Helene, who gave me a list of artists she thought
were interesting to visit.

That period marked the beginning of an
attitude about contemporary art, which was later
called pluralism. However, it was an uninteresting
notion of pluralism. An "anything goes" notion,
with a sense that all these different things were
happening and it was just fine, there was no reason
to make any distinctions, art no longer had any
particular direction or movement. But I was
committed to the idea that the critical purpose of
critical thinking about contemporary art was to be
able to discern direction, to see a coherent
development in an historical sense. I was still
committed to some notion of avant-gardism. I was
interested in an historically grounded newness
that offered a new paradigm for art-making,
taking art in a radically new direction. I went to the
studios without any preconceived ideas except
that one. I didn't have my finger on the pulse
because I hadn't seen enough art by younger
people. The studio visits made a big difference.
I had done it once when I worked at the
Guggenheim in the late 60s. It was actually part of
my job to make studio visits. And, of course, I had
artist friends and visited their studios. But the art
I saw at the time was emerging into the public
sphere, that is, in gallery exhibitions or in places
like Artists Space.

In the mid- to late 70s, Artists Space had a very
major constituency. It was relatively unique as a
place to see emerging art. There were people who
regularly visited Artists Space who were very
attuned to the art shown there. Consequently, a
lot of people came to the *Pictures* opening and the
show did have some immediate repercussions.
People found it interesting. Perhaps they also
found my writing about it persuasive. There were
certainly a number of artists whose work I
overlooked who might have been more interesting
in context. Cindy Sherman, for example, was doing
these narrative pieces. Right after that she began
her film stills. But the work I saw, when I put the
show together, was photographic cutouts. I saw
Robert Longo and Cindy Sherman in an exhibition
that Linda Cathcart curated in Buffalo at the
Albright-Knox Art Gallery. Robert had one piece
that really impressed me. I found Cindy's work
really interesting, but it didn't seem to work as

well with what I was doing, although I was wrong. I recognized this later when
I rewrote the *Pictures* catalogue essay and published it in the eighth issue of
October in the spring of 1979. It is probably the more famous of the two
Pictures essays. I refer to the show in the text, although I revised it almost
completely from the catalogue, but kept the title. I did it partially because
there was enough buzz around the show that Rosalind Krauss, my co-editor at
October, asked me to republish it. At the very least she wanted me to write
about those artists. At that point, I decided to write about Cindy Sherman,
for example, but not Philip Smith.

There is a retrospective interest in the *Pictures* show because a number of
the artists connected with it became very well known. So, the idea that
Douglas Crimp did an exhibition in 1977 and, thereby, made the careers of a
bunch of artists, is completely and historically wrong. There are so many
other factors that play into it. For example, a few years after *Pictures*, Helene
and Janelle Reiring started Metro Pictures and showed some of the artists
who were in *Pictures* as well as others with similar tendencies. They built a
public for a certain kind of art, as did other dealers and other critics. It just
happens that the exhibition, the catalogue essay, and the later *October* essay
struck a chord with some people, which resonated with what happened later.
But after all, it was only one tendency of the 80s and not necessarily the most
central one. There were others, unrelated to what I was talking about—for
instance, in the work of Louise Lawler, which Janelle included in the show she
organized for Artists Space after *Pictures*. And some of the artists in *Pictures*
are, at this point, not as important as they once appeared to be. At the same
time, feminist issues were incredibly central to what was going on and I
didn't recognize that aspect. I can't say *Pictures* was necessarily a founding
moment. Neither can I say it wasn't important or that I didn't do a good job.
But retrospectively, it has assumed an overblown importance.

Now I'm at a very different place in relation to contemporary art. It would
be very difficult for me to do something like that again because I've had a
very detached relationship to the art world for the last five or six years. I was
propelled into doing AIDS work, and in 1987 I did the AIDS issue of *October*.
Then I started work on gay sexuality and cultural studies. So contemporary
art has not been at the center of my own critical practice. I still try to keep up,
but it's such a different world. There's so much going on and other people
know it much better than I do. If I were asked to do an exhibition, it would be
thematic and on a subject which interests me now. I wouldn't try to identify
some new tendency in art. It doesn't have the same meaning as it did in 1976.
However, in '76 I didn't think I was discovering a new tendency in art, either.
It's easier to say that in retrospect. No, I was looking for something like
coherence. It was partly against a background of not accepting this weak
notion of pluralism.

Historically, it's a very, very different moment right now. That was
already discernible in the *Pictures* generation or what became known
as the postmodern generation of artists. The notion of specifically relevant
historical movements following one another is no longer the way art
functions. If you put the art world in a somewhat larger perspective, from
the time I entered it in the late 60s up to now, then you will find historical
necessity is perhaps no longer pertinent to the historical moment we live in.

CONTINUED

1977-78

From 1977 to 1980, programming of individual and group exhibitions is determined primarily by Helene Winer, Director, Ragland Watkins, Associate Director for Exhibitions, Susan Wyatt, Associate Director of Artists Services, and Cindy Sherman, Program Coordinator. During this time, a number of resources are used to identify artists, including the Unaffiliated Artists File and artists' proposals as well as informal suggestions from artists, art critics, and curators.

↑ Jack Goldstein, film still from *Shane*, **Pictures**, exh. Sept.24-Oct.29, 1977.

↑ Installation view, **Pictures**, exh. Sept.24-Oct.29, 1977.
© D. James Dee

↑ Souvenier

DOUGLAS CRIMP / CONTINUED

I remember when the art world was a tiny place. You knew almost everyone you ran into on a Saturday of gallery hopping. The New York art community would include the most interesting work in dance, music, and sculpture. It was a completely interconnected scene that you could be part of. One night you could see Yvonne Rainer perform, the next hear Philip Glass's *Music in Ten Parts,* and then see a Richard Serra exhibition. That was the world as I experienced it. The art world is *completely* unlike that today, partly because of the difference in the market. There was a relatively small market for art as late as the late 60s. Now art is many, many different things to many, many different constituencies and individuals. For example, I am interested in the development of "queer art." Some of it will be in a Whitney Biennial and some will be in a marginal scene, which only a certain constituency would really find important and interesting. In other words, there is a certain fragmentation of the art world, not strictly determined by the market, that I actually find valid, quite interesting, and useful now. The need for a single avant-garde, a single coherent movement, which I felt when I did the *Pictures* show, we now see as a fiction. It is not the way art works anymore.

ARTIST

David Salle I met Helene Winer quite early in California when she was working at Pomona College. I met her because Jack Goldstein was at Cal Arts. Then everybody moved to New York more or less around the same time and there was a little social club that grew up around Helene and Jack. When Helene became Director of Artists Space, the first thing she did was form a selection committee that went around visiting artists' studios to choose who would be invited to make an exhibition. The committee consisted of Helene, Linda Cathcart, Bill Wegman, and some others. After due process of sifting through this or that, I was invited to make an exhibition. At that time, in that big space, they made two exhibitions at once. I remember my work taking up a lot of space. What I also remember, and I could be remembering it incorrectly, was that after this brief, modest quasi-public exposure, after this moment of not quite total obscurity, I slipped back into total obscurity.

The people I had gone to school with who moved to New York all lived within a 10 block radius of each other, so I basically hung out with them. Whether we constituted an aesthetic alliance, I'm not really sure. But the galvanizing member of this unusual club was someone who hadn't gone to Cal Arts, but whom we all knew at Cal Arts, and that was Paul McMahon. Paul became Helene's Associate Director. Paul was the one with the day job. I don't know if he made anything happen. And I don't mean any of this in terms of the worldly sense—it was all very private. But he did make people realize they had some kind of collective identity. It was not a big deal and it didn't manage itself in any particular way.

I wasn't in the *Pictures* exhibition, that was much later and seemed like another era. The whole thing was straining to make a conflict. Again, Paul was the central person in this. It wasn't a club, it wasn't a school, it wasn't anything really, just a bunch of friends. Paul wasn't in the show either. Maybe he'd already been fired from Artists Space at that point. But Doug Crimp, in his very doctrinaire and minimally aesthetic training, tried to accommodate the next generation. That's all it was, nothing more nor less. When I think back on it, the whole thing was incredibly dry and thin. Often, in very first efforts, the real central component is humor, because humor is a measure of an expression of alienation. CONTINUED

And you could not find anyone less well equipped to make a show that accommodated or in any way expressed humor than Douglas Crimp. I haven't seen Doug Crimp in 15 years. I think the whole thing was essentially misguided. Because of that, I keep coming back to the same point: *Pictures* was all really ephemeral, it was never meant to last and didn't last, not really. The key intelligence here was always Paul McMahon, and the keynote of Paul McMahon, as an art critic, was humor. He was essentially a postmodern comedian. Artists Space presented that kind of humorous sensibility in other ways, with Eric Bogosian and others. What was really interesting about that moment, if anything, was something so ephemeral it could hardly be presented in any form. It was best presented at a party in the form of jokes, which is not really Artists Space's mission. You had to have been there. But it's something I recognize essentially in very new, very young art. It's something that happens with people with a certain sensibility, who come to art at a certain age or are impacted by the world in some way. It is not something that anybody invents.

Sept. 24–Oct. 29: **Pictures** (Douglas Crimp). Troy Brauntuch, prints and photography; Jack Goldstein, records, film, photography; Sherrie Levine, drawing; Robert Longo, sculpture; Philip Smith, drawing. The exhibition travels to the Allen Memorial Art Museum, Oberlin, Ohio, February 28–March 25, 1978; Los Angeles Institute of Contemporary Art, April 15–May 15; University of Colorado Art Gallery, Boulder, September 8–October 6. Catalogue with essay by Douglas Crimp.

1977 SEP–OCT

↑ Julia Heyward, *This is My Blue Period*, Nov. 26-27, 1977. **Performance** series.

ARTIST

Julia Heyward *This Is My Blue Period* was my first monologue. It was fairly unusual for a piece to turn around a text, and that's what people responded to. I remember Eric Bogosian saying something to me about how it hit him. It was connected to a persona in a psycho-emotional way, more centered around the artist as the persona as opposed to vice versa. It seemed so revelatory at the time. It was a very important piece for me—I don't do that many. In the last two decades I've mainly worked on larger pieces, so this was my first and last monologue.

The difference between my work and the generation that came before me was they had this detachment from their bodies. There was this hangover of conceptualism and minimalism and it bled, consciously or unconsciously, into performance work. It seems to start with Dada and certainly surrealism when narrative, which actually had a linear progression and a connection to the actors, was thrown out. Our generation brought back content and narrative.

In Yvonne Rainer's films and Joan Jonas's work there was a lot of "He said," "She said." I remember that was in almost everyone's work. But, who's "he" and who's "she"? What did they say? But they would never give you any of that. They would just use this stilted speech and it said, "I want to speak, but I don't have anything to say." Somehow conceptual art and minimalism washed out a lot of the adjectives, color, persona, the gradations of emotion. Because you can be angry. You can be violent. You can be irritable. You can be extreme. The generation before us was, across the board, deadpan. I wondered why people responded to it, because it really did get a great response.

I didn't think about my place in the context of my generation or another generation. We just did what we did. I was called an autobiographical artist, which I thought was a misnomer. I hated it. It was a small picture frame and I was dealing with larger, more abstract issues. I didn't say I was born here and my father was this, etc. I thought I was working with the way we think. Still there was a persona; I looked and acted a certain way. It was the beginning of developing myself as a medium for various extraneous topics. But somehow I held it all together. If you took Laurie Anderson out of her performances there would be a bunch of her smart bits and pieces, but she's what focuses it. *This Is My Blue Period* also represented a solid step in that direction.

In the performance I wore a sweatshirt, which went to a hooded point. I would pull that hood over my head and behind my ears so they stuck out and I would pull my skirt between my legs. I looked really ugly. That would be the goal. When I pulled the hood over we were in Jerusalem. The Virgin Mary. If you didn't know, we just time-traveled. Simple props. The skirt was one of those polyester dancer skirts. It would fall so I could hold my hands underneath the skirt to make it look like I was holding a tray table or a podium. Quite often, I went between feminine and various kinds of political dogmas. If you look at *Saturday Night Live* in '77 everybody wore bell bottoms. There was a lot of the same rhetoric around, so I was making fun of these things. I could go from the podium to blue collar in the same gesture. With the waitress tray I could go from a servant to an intellectual.

Nov. 5–Dec. 3: **Performance series**: 10 performances.
  Nov. 5: Madeleine Burnside, *Glyphs*; Andrew Kelly, *H.2., Tongue of Tongues*.
  Nov. 11: Ann Wooster, *Meditations on the Alphabet*.
  Nov. 12: Jill Kroesen, *Previews of Lou and Walter*.
  Nov. 18: Virginia Piersol, Brian Piersol, *Border Relations*.
  Nov. 19: Eric Mitchell, *Mass Homocide*; Susan Ensley, *No Conscience*.
  Nov. 25: Barbara Bloom, *The Green Lounge*.
  Nov. 26-27: Julia Heyward, *This Is My Blue Period*.
  Nov. 8–Dec. 3: Video and photo documentation of performance events.

Dec. 10–Jan. 7: **Group exhibition and silent auction** (selected by Artists Space staff from the Unaffiliated Artists File). An exhibition and auction of small works where the total proceeds of sales go to the artists. Kathleen Agnoli, Dike Blair, Farrell Brickhouse, Vincent Ciniglio, R.M. Fischer, Fred Gutzeit, Michael Harvey, Diane Jacobs, Tom Lawson, Michael Malloy, Allan McCollum, Paul McMahon, Judy Pfaff, Earl Ripling, Livio Saganic, Mira Schor, Joanne Seltzer, Terise Slotkin, Michael Zwack. Catalogue with reproductions of works.

↓ Eric Mitchell

Jan. 8: Norma Jean DeAk, *Travel Log*, performance.

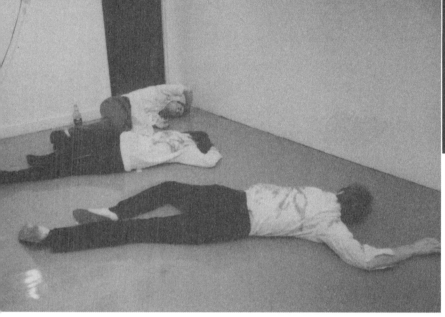

ARTIST **Troy Brauntuch** Alternative spaces were great in the mid- to late 70s. When I went to Artists Space, I felt very comfortable going in and taking a chair. But in terms of somewhere to go and hang, no. For that, there was Magoo's.

I met Helene Winer through Jack Goldstein not long after I came to New York, which was about 1975. Doug Crimp was putting this show together so he came to my studio. It happened fairly quickly. *Pictures* was great, a lot of fun, and very exciting for me as a young artist. Did it change the way I think? No. Did it change the way other people think? I think so. Some of the theory attached to it was accurate, and some of it not so accurate. Some of it was eventually abused and some remained true to its original concept. But I never looked at the work in the show in theoretical terms. In retrospect, I was just doing my work. One nice thing about *Pictures*, which Artists Space did for other shows, was the catalogue, which I still have. There's this object. Theoretically, it certainly still stands as an interesting piece of writing for its time. It was very professional and it was the first time I was around that kind of professionalism. It was helpful because it got people very interested in what was being done. And it generated a lot of energy for those artists both in and out of the exhibition. We were all making a certain kind of work that was new. The fact the show was taken seriously and the work seriously written about was certainly a wonderful step. It was part of an evolution of events. However, the last thing my generation really thought about was the idea of any kind of major representation by a gallery. But my show at the Kitchen and my first gallery, Metro Pictures, was pretty much a direct result of doing the *Pictures* group show. Metro Pictures was founded on the relationships that date from that period.

ARTIST **Beth B** In 1977, I was doing sculpture, stencils on the street, and photography. I had just started to do Super 8 film and video. It was a time when a lot of people questioned the whole gallery structure and alternative spaces— everything. In those days we were a little less precious about showing in other venues. That's when shows in rock clubs started. I was working with musicians and people who crossed boundaries between different mediums. CoLab eventually came out of that group with musicians, writers, artists, filmmakers, and photographers.

The audio piece I played at Artists Space came out of my experiences working as a phone girl at a whorehouse. While I was there, I recorded my phone conversations with the men who called. I eventually got arrested. It was not a happy affair. It was in a house where I was a madam and I would introduce the men to the girls. I was 19 or 20 at the time. From that experience I created this piece where people walked into this curtained-off room in which there was a blow-up doll on a bed and an audio playing the telephone conversations between myself and the men asking for various things they wanted to have done to them. It was a very valuable piece of research and information, especially at my age. It opened up a lot of issues I still deal with in my work. For instance, the dilemma of dominance and submission, the way power is used in our culture, both privately and publicly, and the denial of people's actual realities.

Jan. 21–Mar. 4: **Audio Works**. Sound pieces by 80 artists on records, cassettes, reels, installations, and performances : Vito Acconci, *Ten Packed Minutes* and *Gangster Sister from Chicago Visits New York;* Laurie Anderson, *Two Songs for Tape Bow Violin: Ethics is the Esthetics of the Few-Ture (Lenin), Song for Juanita, Is Anybody Home, It's not the Bullet that Kills You—It's the Hole, Break It,* and *From Photos and Other Good Designs;* Carl Andre, poem from a text describing a *Raid on Harpers' Ferry;* Ant Farm, *Car-Men;* Jacki Apple, *Black apples/blue sky dreams;* Art & Language, *Corrected Slogans;* Beth B, *House* (installation); John Baldessari, *Dorit Crypis attempts insults in the second language trying for the worst;* Robert Barry, *Variations (No.2);* Liza Bear, *Hartford, Hartford, Gloria/Breaux-bridge,* and *Subtropical;* Connie Beckley, *Triad Triangle;* Laurel Beckman, three

works; Ronald Benom, *Room, #1;* Nancy Blanchard, *Language Problems, Encounters with Michael Caine,* and *Memoirs;* Christian Boltanski, *Fais dodo Colas mon petit frère, Il était un petit navire,* and *Sainte-Elisabeth Works;* Nancy Buchanon, *C. S. Opera;* Chris Burden, *Wiretap;* Donald Burgy, excerpts from the notebook: *Things to do in the future;* Jim Burton, *High Country Helium;* Rhys Chatham, *Ear Ringing* (installation); Mitch Corber, *My Ideal Videotape;* Diego Cortez, *Arbiter, You Pay,* and *Cataract Monologue;* Guy de Cointet, *TSNX C 24V47ME;* Norma Jean DeAk, *Having a Wonderful Time;* Constance De Jong, *Modern Love;* Demi, *Ocher Moon;* Dr. Earl, untitled; Peter Downsborough, *A Place to be Brought Back To;* John Duncan, *No;* Bruce Fier, *The Sound Frame;* Terry Fox, *Lunar Rambles* and *The Labyrinth Scored for the Purrs of 11 Different Cats;* Fern Friedman,

Circumstantial Release; Cheri Gaulke, *The Red Shoes;* Jack Goldstein, *The Unknown Dimension* and *Three Felled Trees;* Ilona Gramet, *The Tables are Turning 'All Come to Order';* Jana Haimsohn, *Hav'a Lava Flow;* Terry Hanlon, *Circumstantial Release;* Newton and Helen Harrison, untitled; Michael Harvey, *Wind, Storm* and *Rain;* Julia Heyward, *Mongolian Face Slap, Big Coup (part one), Nose Flute,* and *Big Coup (part two);* Douglas Huebler, *Sound Drawings;* David Hykes and the Harmonics Choir, *Hearing Solar Winds;* Tom Jenkins, untitled; Poppy Johnson, untitled; Scott Johnson, *What Happened* (installation) and *Involuntary Songs Loops 2 & 3;* Allan Kaprow, *Courtesy;* Leandro Katz, *Animal Hours;* Laurel Klick, *Secrets for the Public, Part 2;* Christopher Knowles, *Who's the King of the Castle and Who's the Dirty Rascal?;* Jill Kroesen, *Hall Song;* Barbara Kruger, *Crosstalk on Language;* Suzanne Lacy,

3 Weeks in May; Les Levine, *What Can the Feds;* Paul McCarthy, *Paid Strangers;* Paul McMahon, *Maybe You Didn't Notice, Are You Fearless?,* and *Let the Moment Be the Moment;* George Miller, *Story of Uncle Curt;* Larry Miller, *Talk About It* and *Ho-Day;* Susan Mogol, *A. M. Mogul in the P. M. On FM;* Meredith Monk, *Rally* and *Procession;* Linda Montano, *When You Hear This;* Ian Murray, *Keeping on Top at the Top Song;* Richard Nonas, *What do you know?;* Dennis Oppenheim, *Broken Record Blues;* Charlemagne Palestine, *2 fifths (a minor third apart), Strumming Music;* Carlos Pazos, *Canta;* Tom Radloff, untitled; Tom Recchion, *14'7";* Stuart Sherman, *Sounds from Spectacles;* Alexis Smith, untitled and *Sensitivity;* Barbara Smith, *Vaya con Dios;* Michael Smith, *Traffic…short bits;* Keith Sonnier, *Air to Air;* Bart Thrall, *2 Stories;* James Umland, *10 to 10 - 5 to 5 - 10 blue 10 - 10 red 10;* Bernar Venet, *The Infrared*

Polarization of the Infrared Star in Cygnus; William Wegman, *Hartford, Hartford;* Lawrence Weiner, *Niets Aan Verloren* and *Having Been Done At/Having Been Done To-Essendo Stato Fatto A;* Bob Whilhite, *Buckaroo, Marriage Announcements & Portraits;* John Zorn, *Easy Beat.* For a related description of the exhiibition refer to: *Sound Selection: Audio Works by Artists,* catalogue, Jan. 1980.

Performances.
Feb. 11:
John Zorn, *The Creation Story* and *San Francisco.*

Feb. 17–18: Scott Johnson, *What Happened.*

Feb. 22–23: Rhys Chatham.

↓   Rhys Chatham

↑ **Audio Works**, installation view.

Patrick O'Connell I started as a volunteer out of the Mayor's Volunteers File. I had just come down from graduate school and I needed a job. I was a classics person, but art history is what I wanted to do, although I didn't have the time or the money to go back and get another degree. I also wanted to work with living and breathing artists who were my contemporaries. I was 21-years-old, and I didn't know what I was getting myself into. It was more about the fact I didn't want to take the bus uptown to the Metropolitan Museum of Art.

I was duded up in a nice Italian suit when I had an interview with Susan Wyatt. I'm sure they thought they were getting one thing. The next time I showed up, I was in your standard downtown T-shirt, and I never changed out of that. At first my position was part-time. I assisted Susan in program administration. She was working heavily with the Unaffiliated Artists File, the Visiting Artist Program, and the Artists in Residence Program. The programs were supported through NYSCA, who gave us funds to invite artists from around the state to do residencies or short gigs at Artists Space. This is how we ended up meeting all the people at Hallwalls. My job was supposed to be one or two days a week, but I started coming in every day and just never left. Essentially, I was the front desk, gallery, and telephone boy. And then there was always gallery prep; I'll never pick up another paint brush in my entire life! Remember, it was 1976, artists were doing installations with oil stick directly on the wall!

Being at Artists Space was very special for me. I was a typical, naive 21-year-old. Maybe more so than others because I'd been in school doing all that nonsense for years. Helene (Winer), Paul (McMahon), and everyone there gave me permission to look at art and showed me how. They were incredibly helpful. Helene took her job very seriously, and one of those responsibilities was to get the best out of her staff, volunteer or paid. Helene has a very definite eye. Probably through her, I look at art in the same way, too. That was the period before there was money in the contemporary nonprofit art world. Yet we did a lot of things and just kept doing them. New exhibitions and installations went up every month. There were evening programs as well, so we were constantly busy. Helene kept it together, we all rowed in the same boat. It was a lot of fun. There was always something going on at Artists Space, a new problem to solve, finding a way to get an artist's work into the gallery, and how to support that artist while you're doing it. At that time, SoHo was terribly amusing, but also very innocent and fresh. Then in late 1976, Helene announced it was

getting too crowded. That's when you'd meet maybe three people on a Saturday. So, we picked up and headed down to TriBeCa. We were the first tenants in the Fine Arts Building. The community was very small, but constantly expanding and exciting.

The politics of Artists Space and artists' organizations appealed to me. It's more geared toward empowering the artist, not just paternalistically protecting them. There is more of an equal partnership than you would have in museums or commercial galleries. I really admire Susan Wyatt and Helene. I'll always be eternally grateful for the 16 months I spent there. They provided the opportunity for me to meet, work and become friends with artists like Matt Mullican, Jack Goldstein, and the whole Hallwalls crew: Robert Longo, Cindy Sherman, Charlie Clough, Nancy Dwyer, Michael Zwack, and others.

One of the real high points, and absolutely the craziest night of my life, was working with Jack Smith. They were vomiting down the hallways and I had to clean it up. Paul was absolutely useless. It was hilarious, it was great. Helene wasn't on the premises, she was out on a speaking gig, and Paul was running the show. It was hours late. But the moment Jack started, it was worth everything. This is what art is about and what Artists Space is about, having a physical space and a mental space that allows things to happen. Artists Space worked for me, not because everything is going to be great or end up in a history book, but it's as close as you can get to the pulse of the moment. Go through the hit parade: the fact that Artists Space gave David Salle his first New York show and probably his first show out of school. Artists Space got Matt, Jack, Cindy, Robert, Donald Sultan, a slew of people, who became the name brands of the late 70s and 80s. It's terribly exciting to have been there to help facilitate those careers and consummate those friendships. Helene and Susan were very specific about networking, so we weren't just an isolated outpost. Helene thought it was a fabulous idea that I go up to Buffalo to Hallwalls because then we could start joint programming. There was a commitment to art as an instrument of change and a commitment to a vision with as broad a discourse as possible.

It's very easy to focus on our hits, but there are many other artists who made very interesting work, and Artists Space was the catalyst for that. But when we made mistakes, they were *big,* very *big.* They were not really mistakes, but good accidents. I was the first person Donald Newman spoke to in New York. He came directly from Penn Station to the desk at Artists Space and said, "Do you have any place for me?" and I said, "Excuse me?" He said, "Oh, John Baldessari sent me here and said you'd take care of me." I just leaned back and called, "Helene, I think we're into rentals now, what does this mean?" Donald was a fabulous artist. I don't think the controversy surrounding that exhibition did him particularly any good, although it has informed a lot of our behavior since then. The front-page problem helped temper our spirits but invigorated our commitment to what we were doing. The organization and the individuals in it strongly and adamantly supported the work. It's not pleasant having people say very mean things about you. It's not good for an artist or an organization. But the commitment remained true, and for that I'm proud. I'm also proud of the support we were able to give to artists like Tom Otterness. I'm proud of the support that was provided for David Wojnarowicz and Nan Goldin. Artists Space can be proud of the way their staff has behaved over the years. I'm thrilled to have been the person lucky enough to have walked up those stairs that afternoon to be interviewed by Susan.

I've worked in other places and built other organizations and Visual Aids is my last offspring, so to speak. But I think about the 16 months I was at Artists Space daily, and the commitment to the organization over the years is what created me.

Feb. 28–Mar. 11: **Room 207** (Jimmy de Sana, Colleen Fitzgibbon, Lindzee Smith, Betsy Sussler). *X Motion Picture Magazine*, installation of visual material used in the publication of the first three issues: Kathy Acker, Charlie Ahearn, Beth B, Scott B, Tim Burns, Robert Cooney, Mitch Corber, Diego Cortez, Philippe de Montaut, Jimmy de Sana, Stefan Eins, Colleen Fitzgibbon, Philip Fraser, Craig Gholson, Jeff Goldberg, Duncan Hannah, Scott Johnson, Leandro Katz, Tina Lhotsky, Jeremy Lipp, Chrisopher Makos, Katy Martin, Aline Mayer, Michael McClard, Sonia Miranda, Eric Mitchell, Alan Moore, James Nares, Michael Oblowitz, Jacki Ochs, Amos Poe, Marcia Resnick, Judy Rifka, Terence C. Sellers, Terence Severine, Duncan Smith, Lindzee Smith, Susan Springfield, Leisa Stroud, Betsy Sussler, Robin Winters.

Mar. 17–Apr. 1: **Artists Films** (Regina Cornwell).
Mar. 17–18: Tim Burns, *Why Cars?-CARnage!*, 1978, film and performance.
Mar. 22–23: John Baldessari, *Title*, 1971, *Script*, 1974.
Mar. 24–25: Manuel De Landa, *Itch, Scratch, Itch Cycle,* 1978; Ken Feingold, *Hysteria*, 1978; Martha Haslanger, *Frames and Cages and Speeches*, 1976, *Syntax*, 1974.
Mar. 29–30: Ericka Beckman, *Hit and Run*, 1977; David Haxton, *Cube and Room Drawings*, 1976-77, *Pyramid Drawings*, 1976–77, *Cubes*, 1977; Henry Jones, *New Glasses*, 1976, *Palm Tree*s, 1976, *Walking Man*, 1977.
Mar. 31–Apr. 1: Tom DeBiaso, *Polaroid*, 1976; Morgan Fisher, *Documentary Footage*, 1968; Joan Jonas, *Three Tales: Pt. 1 Cape North, Pt. 2 The Frog Prince*; *Pt. 3 Joshua Tree,* 1976–77.

Mar. 18–Apr. 1: **Room 207**. *ArtpArkArt III*, photo-documentation of Artpark's summer 1977 artists' projects. Organized in conjunction with Hallwalls, Buffalo, N.Y.

Apr. 8–29: Bernard Tschumi, **Architectural Manifestoes.** Manifesto 1, *Fireworks*, 1974; Manifesto 2, *Question of Space, or The Box*, 1975; Manifesto 3, *Advertisements for Architecture, 1976*; Manifesto 4, *Joyce's Garden*, 1977; Manifesto 5, *Birth of an Angel,* 1977; Manifesto 6, *The Park*, 1977; Manifesto 7, *Border Crossing*, 1978; Manifesto 8, *The Room*, 1978. Catalogue preface by Helene Winer with statements by Bernard Tschumi.

→ Bernard Tschumi lecturing on his work.

Bernard Tschumi Between '76 and '78 a number of people arrived in New York. My work was theoretical then. There was not a building to be built, it was more an investigation. Helene Winer had seen my large pieces on the floor and one day, almost out of the blue, she asked me to have a show. It was unbelievably important for me because some of the work had to be focused toward a major exhibition. I believe that *Architectural Manifestoes* at Artists Space was the first show of architectural drawings in a gallery or a public space.

I was interested then in something I still find essential today: questioning the idea of what happens in a space. And I was more interested in something like, he meets her, she kills him, she walks away, playing out the actions of characters, their movement in space, and the space itself. There were direct connections with the performance art of the time and an interest, which many of us had, in black and white B movies of the 40s and 50s.

Five years later I organized a show, *Architecture: Sequences,* and continued this interest with film and with the idea of spatial sequences. I looked for people who dealt with these ideas, either in terms of the process in which they produced their work or the movement of bodies in space.

In reality, there haven't been many places to show young architects' work. Places like Artists Space or Storefront for Art and Architecture have done a remarkable job, considering it's an acrobatic act. They've continued to sustain it for so many years and with a high level of quality. There's always a strange twist to their program and also an occasional surprise or something you don't expect at all. Artists Space never falls into the pattern of an establishment institution. Quite often during the late 70s to the early 80s institutions were more interested in conventional architectural drawings, such as what Michael Graves produces, work that does look like architecture. That always disturbed me, because I felt in many ways the art context was an incredible one in which to push the boundaries and limits of architecture and to explore areas you cannot in the context of normal architectural practice. That's why it's great that Artists Space did exhibitions with Greg Lynn and Ben van Berkel, where they clearly attempt to push the capability of what architecture can do as far as they can.

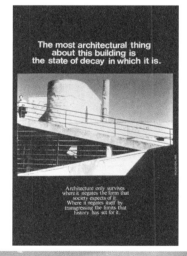

The most architectural thing about this building is the state of decay in which it is.

Architecture only survives where it negates the form that society expects of it. Where it negates itself by transgressing the limits that history has set for it.

→ Bernard Tschumi, Advertisements for Architecture, 1976.

Apr. 8–22: **Room 207**. Christy Rupp, *Goose Encounters*, installation with film by Charlie Ahearn.

Apr. 8: Christy Rupp, performance.

Apr. 29–May 13: **Room 207**. Krzysztof Wodiczko, *Guidelines*, a viewer-operated installation.

May 2–6: **Bands**. Series of "New Wave" musical groups with artist members (Michael Zwack).

May 2: *Communists*: Iosta Black, Gerry Hovagimian, Bob Mason; *Terminal*: Johnnie Dynel, Ann Flash (Ann Flash DeLeon), Charlie Nash.

May 3: *Gynecologists*: Robert Appleton, Nina Canal, Jim Sclavonas; *Theoretical Girls*: Glenn Branca, Margaret Dewys, Jeffrey Lohn, Wharton Tiers.

May 4: *Daily Life*: Glenn Branca, Barbara Ess, Christine Hahn, Paul McMahon; *Tone Death*: Robert Appleton, Nina Canal, Rhys Chatham, Peter Gordon.

May 5: *Contortions*: Adele Bertei, James Chance (James White), Don Christenson, Jody Harris, Pat Place, George Scott III; *DNA*: Robin [Lee] Crutchfield, Ikue Ile, Arto Lindsay.

May 6: *MARS*: Nancy Arlen, China Burg, Sumner Crane, Mark Cunningham; *Teenage Jesus and the Jerks*: Bradley Field, Lydia Lunch, Gordon Stevenson.

May 13–June 10: **Traditions/Five Painters** (Linda L. Cathcart). Charles S. Clough, William Fares, Sidney Leon Goldberg II, John Lees, Ann Thornycroft. Catalogue with essay by Linda L. Cathcart.

May 20–June 3: **Room 207**. Bart Robbett, *The Queen's Rules Suspended* and *Brachiating*, two installations.

June 10–24: **Room 207**. Alain Middleton, wall pieces.

June 10: Alain Middleton, concert, sound and instrument pieces.

ARTIST

Joan Jonas I showed *Three Tales* in Documenta, but the only time I actually ever showed it as film was at Artists Space. It was a Super 8 shot in the early 70s at three different locations: Joshua Tree, Nova Scotia, and San Francisco. I consider them related to each other. *Three Tales* is unique in my work. It was three little poetic narratives, each maybe 10 minutes long. They were pieces I made more or less spontaneously by taking a day of shooting in each location. I worked with a group of people in San Francisco. We went to different locations like the botanical gardens and the beach with some costumes and props, and improvised. I did a lot of editing in the camera, plus slow-motion effects. In Los Angeles, I went out to the desert with one performer and Joyce Nereaux, who ran the video section at Leo Castelli's. I made up a little narrative about a mystery and shot it on the spot. In Canada, it was the same situation.

The screening didn't have a big audience, but it was a very nice intimate situation, everybody knew each other. We all went to each other's performances and shows and concerts. There was a very close dialogue between artists. It's changed radically since then, of course. It was an audience that moved from place to place. I was part of a group of composers, sculptors, painters, and performers. For instance, Gordon Matta-Clark, Caroline Goodden, Pat Steir, Susan Rothenberg, Richard Serra, Jene Highstein, Philip Glass, Dickie Landry, and, just at the end of that time, Kiki Smith.

ARTIST

Tom Otterness It was like a Christmas sale. I sold my sculptures for $4.99 and made four or five hundred bucks. I averaged my time and figured I was making as much as I earned hanging sheetrock. It was my first success and the first sculptures I had made since I was a teenager. It was the most commercial venture I had done. Before, I'd done two-dimensional sign stuff using international sign figures; so, I just popped them into 3-D. There was a sitting guy, a pair of boxers, a couple fucking, and another pair, a death figure with wings, mating with another figure. One went up for auction at $1,500. I thought that was a good turnaround from $4.99. I think of it like selling stock options. They were unlimited editions, or you might say self-limiting in that I sold as many as I wanted. Because of breakage and everything else, only a few have survived over the years. So they're actually pretty scarce.

Artists Space is a great place. We used to go there to get money for projects. All you needed was a little idea and you got $250 bucks. That is really important for a young artist.

I showed the dog film at Artists Space. But I can't talk about it.

Christopher D'Arcangelo

Four Texts, for *Artists Space*

1. *Artists Space: Where are you and What's in a name?*

Space is a common commodity. In our current social context space is divided by design and name to fill a specific function, for example, street, house, store, bank, museum. Once these divisions are made, it is often difficult to ascertain their meaning.

At this time you are in a divided space, *Artists Space*. Your reason for being here can be one of many, but your being here subjects you to the limitations imposed by design and based on the function of this space. How can you see its function? How can you know its limitations?

As stated before, design and name make this division. First look at the design. The rooms you have passed through are architecturally complex—there are many doors, windows, walls, and corners. But the overall space is austere. The walls are painted white and there is no furniture except the desk in the reception room.

One could say that the austere design of this place helps to obscure its function. At this point one must be careful, for all this austerity can show the function of the space when it is connected with the idea that an object alone is more visible than an object in a group.[1] Thus the design of *Artists Space* shows one aspect of its function: to help us see (better) the objects placed in the space.

Now look at the name *Artists Space*. It is important to note that most names do not include the word *space*, yet space is what is being classified by those names. For example, *Citibank* does not call itself *Citibank Space*, but in fact the location of *Citibank* is a space whose function is that of a bank. In the case of the name *Artists Space*, the tricky problem of an obscure function, or space for the sake of space, returns. The use of the word *space* in the name conveys the idea that the space is unqualified. (This has been shown not to be true for design as well, as name gives function to and helps qualify space.)

Carrying the *Citibank* analogy one step further, it is a bank owned by Citi Corporation, the people who have invested in *Citibank*. Just as *bank* is qualified by *Citi*, *Space* is qualified by *Artists*. But *Artists Space* is not directly owned by artists. It is supported by federal and state tax dollars and some private money. It is not controlled by artists, though artists do have some input into what happens at *Artists Space*. What does seem to be the case is that *Artists Space* is for artists, a space for artists to make visible their objects/works of art to themselves and each other.

So, where are you? You are in a space that is designed to make any object in the space more visible.

So, what's in a name? In this case the name *Artists Space* is literal. It is a space for artists.

At this moment you are a viewer. You may also be an artist, but if you are not an artist beware, for by design and name this space is for artists.

It has been said that a lawyer who defends himself has a fool for a client.

[1] This is a common idea in the exhibition of 20th-century art. Go and look at the design of most galleries and modern museums. You will find this to be true with few exceptions, especially in galleries where it is economically important that the merchandise is highly visible

2. *Design, Name, Propaganda*

Design and name can show the function of space, but propaganda does so in an even broader sense.

"Propaganda is a method for the spread of certain ideas, doctrines, etc., or the ideas, doctrines, so spread."

It is more difficult to follow the connection between propaganda and function because propaganda may 1) be produced by someone without direct interests in the limitations of the space, i.e., any artist who exhibits at *Artists Space*, and 2) be seen by viewers at a time when they have no direct contact with the space.

There are many pieces of propaganda for *Artists Space*, but this text will only concern itself with one: *Artists Space, Committee for the Visual Arts, Inc.*, brochure for 1978–1979.

There are two points in the brochure that are important in terms of ideology. One is the credibility of *Artists Space*; the other is the relationship of *Artists Space* to the existing system, i.e., galleries and museums.

Credibility must be verified by the viewer. Credibility, in the form of propaganda, i.e., such phrases as "serious new art," can help to mislead you. Works of art shown at *Artists Space*, of art in general, need not be seen as serious or new or even art.

To the point of the relationship of *Artists Space* to the existing system. It is implied in the brochure that *Artists Space* shows work that is not shown in galleries and museums. Perhaps this is so. But the support for *Artists Space* is, in an indirect way, the same as support for galleries and museums. *Artists Space* receives its main support from tax dollars; galleries and museums from private money. The government invests our money to maintain itself and, at the same time, to maintain the full social, cultural, and economic system (capitalism). This is the very system that *Artists Space* implies does not support the art and artists it shows. Once it is understood that the support of *Artists Space* and the support of galleries and museums are one and the same, that the systems are one system, a discourse for change may be opened that will lead to tangible results, i.e., unqualified space and/or revolution.

When *Artists Space*, through its propaganda, leads you the viewer to believe that what is shown in *Artists Space* is not supported ("adequately exposed") by galleries and museums, it gives you the viewer a false perspective, a false view of the system, and thereby fulfills one of its functions in the system. In art and in all aspects of our lives, it is the false views, the false divisions that help to kill all discourse for change.

Although false discourse may bring results, the results are illusions.

Does propaganda support illusion?

Read the brochure, look around.

3. *Propaganda/Context*

Context/Propaganda: About this work.

This work may or may not be a work of art.
This work is the removal of propaganda about this work.
This work is propaganda, i.e., the frame of this work is the frame of the propaganda about this work.
This work is propaganda in its context, *Artists Space*.

The process used to install this work on the wall was the same process as that used to make the printing plate for the announcement and catalogue for this exhibition. The negative that would have been used to make the printing plate was, in this case, used to print this work on the wall.

Three copies of this work were made. The typeset and the negative were destroyed at the time the work was exposed.

Note: My name appears in the *Gallery Guide* because of my tardiness in proposing this work and making my requests to the staff of *Artists Space*.

4. *Being in a Public Space.*

When any work is open to the public (shown), it is open to physical discourse. Because of this fact, you may add or subtract from this work.

Christopher D'Arcangelo
9/78, New York City

Note: It is with much love that I thank Cathy Weiner for all her help with this work.

1978-79

Sept. 19: Stuart Sherman, *Eleventh Spectacle (the Erotic)*, performance and four short films.

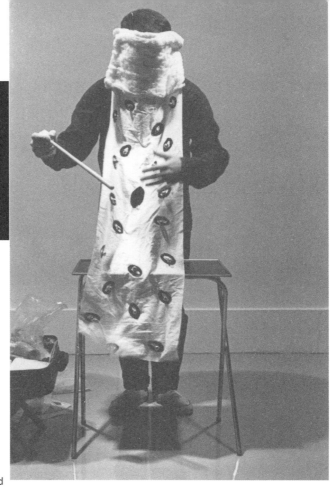

CURATOR

Janelle Reiring I was working at Castelli Gallery when Helene invited me to curate an exhibition of young emerging artists. There wasn't a theme for the show, but it was about artists who were not just concerned about how they presented work but how people saw them and the work. I pretty much knew right away whom I wanted to show. I had always liked Adrian Piper's work. When I first moved to New York, she was one of the really interesting young artists and also the most well known of the bunch. Then she went to Harvard to study philosophy. I wasn't even sure if she was still making art. She showed these photo-text pieces based on her earlier performances. Cindy Sherman showed her film stills and Louise Lawler did a very complex and great piece. She went to the museum at the Aqueduct Racetrack and borrowed an equestrian painting from their collection. During the day, you saw the painting lit, based on the size of the painting from the opposite wall. At night, she projected a light that started out being defined as the same size as the painting, but it projected out through the windows of Artists Space onto the street. It was really an extraordinary piece. Actually, the biggest response was to Cindy's (Sherman) film stills. It was the first time she had shown them. When I saw them in her studio, she had a notebook full of the 8 x 10-inch photos — she picked about eight of them and blew them up to 30 x 40. Chris D'Arcangelo essentially erased himself from the show. In the catalogue and in all the listings where his name would have appeared there's a blank space. In the actual show he had statements about conceptual art on the wall. I liked the idea of having this group show of mostly women and one man. At that time, the lack of women's presence in the art world was pretty strange and it was absolutely felt.

You have to realize how different the times were. First of all, there was only a handful of commercial galleries in New York that showed very contemporary art. And almost none showed very young artists. Once they had shown at a place like Artists Space, there was no place for them to go. Even for the more established artists at Castelli,

with the exception of a couple of really big names, there essentially wasn't a New York market. Support for the conceptualists who showed there all came from Europe. And it wasn't as if I was thinking, "Oh, I'm going to work at Castelli and then I'm going to open a gallery of my own." It didn't seem possible. It almost seemed like the next wave would be agents and people representing artists rather than having a gallery. Then it began to change towards the late 70s. There was a group of collectors interested in work by younger artists. It was a strange thing, you could almost sense it, although there was nothing specific about it. When we opened Metro Pictures, we thought it would take a really long time for anything to happen for these artists and it would be primarily critical support, museum support, and probably support from Europe. It was very lucky this whole thing happened in the 80s. And it had a lot to do with the kind of art people could relate to more. Previously, art had been very dry and very self-referential. But that generation of artists used recognizable images in their work. They had total freedom about what they did. They could paint, make sculpture, take photographs. They could do anything, because they were dealing with materials, references, and images accessible to a much larger public.

Metro Pictures developed over a series of conversations, and the idea for it changed radically. At first we thought maybe I would keep working at Castelli, we'd have a space that would be open at night, maybe in TriBeCa. Over the course of discussions, it became more and more professional and more of a real gallery. When it first opened in 1980, there was Richard Prince, Cindy Sherman, Robert Longo, Laurie Simmons, Walter Robinson, Sherrie Levine, Jack Goldstein, and Thomas Lawson. It was in the space that was the Hawaiian store on Mercer Street, and the parking lot next door was an after-hours club that was torn down.

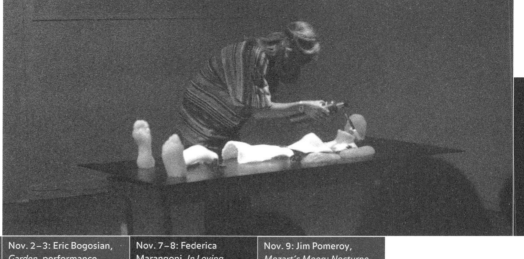

Sept. 23–Oct. 28: Four-person exhibition (Janelle Reiring). Christopher D'Arcangelo, text; Louise Lawler, poster and installation; Adrian Piper, installation; Cindy Sherman, photography. Catalogue with introduction by Janelle Reiring.

↓ Cindy Sherman

Nov. 2–3: Eric Bogosian, *Garden*, performance.

Nov. 7–8: Federica Marangoni, *In Loving Memory of Art*, performance installation.

↑

Nov. 9: Jim Pomeroy, *Mozart's Moog: Nocturne and Apollo Jest*, performance.

Nov. 11–25: Jim Pomeroy, *Making the World Safe for Geometry* and *Projection Piece/Defense Mechanisms*, project room installations.

Nov. 11–Dec. 16: Richards Jarden, *Mats*, pieces woven from matchsticks; Donald Lipski, *Gathering Dust*, installation.

→ Donald Lipski

Dec. 2–16: Peter D'Agostino, *Alpha, Trans, Chung*, photographic installation.

Dec 5: Video screening in conjunction with the publication of book by Peter D'Agostino.

Dec. 19–20: Michael Smith, *Down in the Rec Room* (a comedy featuring *Mike*), performance.

Dec. 21: Mel Andringa, *Babylon/34th Street*, lecture/performance.

↓ Louise Lawler, cover for the catalogue of four-person exhibition, also used as the official logo for Artists Space, Sept., 1978.

Jan. 6–20: R.M. Fischer, *Served Up!*, lamps/sculpture.

Jan. 6–Feb. 10: **Artists Draw** (Donald Sultan). Tom Martin, Auste Peciura, Alan Saret, Patti Smith, Nancy Spero. Catalogue with introduction by Donald Sultan.

ARTIST

Louise Lawler

When I showed an old oil painting in 1978, it was probably more surprising than most things you could do, because everything tried to be incredibly new then. I wanted to show that no matter what you did at Artists Space, you were still showing to its own community of viewers.

There was something very flat footed and open handed about the whole show. The announcement, which was Janelle Reiring's idea, and the way she invited us to participate, was just that: she invited us to be in an exhibition she organized at Artists Space. She wasn't curating it in the normal sense of the word.

Chris D'Arcangelo's participation in the show was to eliminate his name from anything that went outside the gallery. That's why the announcement and catalogue were so strange, because his work was just in the show, not in the catalogue. In a similar vein, I designed a logo for the cover of the catalogue, rather than reproduce something typical of my work. In a way, it was reshowing Artists Space.

Actually, Chris D'Arcangelo and I had spoken quite a bit before the show. We wanted to ask all the artists to agree to just one work, which would be announced as all of our work. We didn't know how we were going to decide whose work or what work it would be, but we met with Cindy to see if she'd agree, and we wrote to Adrian Piper, but never got a response. That was our initial idea for the show. It was interesting but, in the end, it didn't materialize. Since Chris's statement appeared in different rooms, it was more mixed up and harder to distinguish whose work was what. His statement was also in my room so people thought it was part of my work.

I remember sitting on the front steps with Chris reading the review in the *Village Voice*, which negatively said, "These younger artists don't even care if they spill over into each other's room," as if we had all lost integrity. Michael Asher had a fit when Dan Flavin's fluorescences crept in through the doorway, but we didn't seem to care. We were all kind of rip-

offs of other artists' work. They were referring to Adrian, who had done some performances dressed up in smelly clothes which the reviewer saw as a direct reference to Cindy's work. It was as if we hadn't done anything. In response, Chris said, "Well, at least, you're Hans Haacke and I must be Joseph Kosuth." But there wasn't much response to the work in terms of appropriation at that time. It caught on a little later— this was only '78. However, it did start the term. I remember people patted me on the back, "Congratulations, you have a show at Artists Space." But there wasn't anything to be said after that. In a way, we broke the ground for a number of people. It was definitely all in the air. It just hadn't been verbalized in that way yet. There was a real sense of community and mutual involvement at that time. I remember Susan Wyatt telling me there was an artist who wanted to meet me because she liked my work. That's how I met Sherrie Levine. It was interesting to meet someone because they liked your work, not knowing them at all beforehand. In fact, it made me so uncomfortable and I was so afraid of a misunderstanding, that she would like the work for all the wrong reasons, that when we got together to talk to each other I kept saying, "Why don't we go to the movies?" But it turned out okay.

My work consisted of a borrowed painting from the New York Racing Association, which is partially owned by the Jockey Club. That's what made it complicated. They have quite an amazing collection of horse paintings at the Aqueduct Racetrack. I tried to get permission to borrow one, although I wasn't asking them for a specific painting. Instead, it was more a type of painting I wanted, a beautiful horse. I pictured it being in a gold frame, something not to be expected at Artists Space. They were very hesitant to loan me one until I found one guy who really got into it. He actually called me from some board meeting. Meanwhile, I had already picked out this small painting, whereas I had initially wanted something larger, with a big gold frame. But I had to have some kind of relationship to it.

CONTINUED

100

Eric Bogosian Artists Space and the Kitchen were sister spaces in the late 70s. One of the main connections between the two spaces was Cindy Sherman and Robert Longo. Robert worked with me at the Kitchen and Cindy was the receptionist at Artists Space. Around that time, Artists Space did the seminal *Pictures* show and there was this feeling in the air that things were changing. Of course, we were all poor and unknown, but we were very excited about the work we and our friends were doing. For the *Garden* show I built this huge stage out of wood and mesh steel and did a performance on it with some fellow actors and artists, including Michael Zwack, a fellow Artists Space/Kitchen traveler. Later, when I thought I was getting too mainstream, I did another piece at Artists Space which included a warning to potential audience members that it was too harsh. It was. I also performed at an Artists Space benefit during which I took all my clothes off onstage. No one noticed.

LOUISE LAWLER / CONTINUED

In a very corny way, part of the point was to signal that something was going on at Artists Space. I felt it was a very distinct audience of young artists looking at each other's work; and being on the second floor, nobody in the neighborhood, in what wasn't yet called TriBeCa, was too aware of Artists Space. So I rented stage lights. The lights projected through the windows down onto street level. They didn't show up until dark and I left them on until midnight. The light projected onto the Citibank facade opposite Artists Space across the street. When people were in the light, they created big shadows. Then my timer broke and I had to go in every night to turn the lights off. One weekend there was a break-in. I can't remember what the situation was, but there was an insurance problem involving the painting. The painting had been taken off the wall, someone had stolen a jacket and urinated in the corner. Helene called me up the next week to ask me if I knew anything about it. Anyway, that's another story.

Eric Bogosian, *Garden*,
Nov.2-3, 1978, performance.
© Babette Mangolte

Laurie Simmons, untitled, 1977.

Laurie Simmons My pictures were very small, and Helene (Winer) decided it would be great to show them in the hallway. I was really upset about this because it was my first show and I thought, "I can't show in a hallway, I have to show in a gallery." But it turned out to be a spectacular little corridor where everybody stopped and gave the pictures the attention they needed in relation to their scale.

I showed the first little women in bathrooms and kitchens and the black series, which were furniture and postcards pieced together. Rags Watkins saw my work because of Tip (Carroll Dunham). He took my slides back to Artists Space to show Helene, who called me up right away to invite me to show. I had never met her, she just saw the slides and said, "I want to show this work." I wasn't going to show the women in interiors, only the black series. But Helene and Tip talked me into it. So, I almost didn't show those early interiors. I found them embarrassing, but that's the work everybody knows today. They're signature pieces.

TOP and BOTTOM
Protesters and the Black Emergency Coalition demonstrate outside Artists Space at 105 Hudson St.
Photos: Camille Billops, Hatch-Billops Collection, Inc.

Jan. 6 – Feb. 10: Pieter Holstein, *The Waterfall*, installation.

Jan. 6 – Feb. 10: Laurie Simmons, photography.

Jan. 27 – Feb. 10: Ken Feingold, *Place (title to be determined), for a Participant*, installation.

Feb. 16 – Mar. 10: James Casebere, *Life Story no. 1*, photography; Donald (Newman), *The Nigger Drawings*, drawing.

Feb. 16 – Mar. 10: Dennis Adams, *Patricia Hearst – A Second Reading* (extended), installation.

Feb. 16 – Mar. 10: Barbara Levy, photography.

← James Casebere, installation view of photographs.

Mar. 17 – Apr. 28: **Four Artists** (Thomas Lawson). Exchange exhibition of artists associated with New 57 Gallery, Edinburgh, Scotland. At Artists Space: James Birrell, synthesis of film stills; Michael Davey, photography; Gareth Fisher, drawing; Tom Lawson, painting. The exhibition travels to The Art Gallery of Nova Scotia, Canada, August 3 – September 9, 1979. Catalogue with introduction by Thomas Lawson. **Remembrances for Tomorrow**, the other half of the exchange, takes place at New 57 Gallery, Edinburgh, Scotland, July 5 – 25, 1979.

↓

Mar. 17 – 31: **Room 207**, Anthony Thompson, wall installation.

Apr. 7 – 21: **Room 207**, John Gordon, "*In/valid Fragments (simultaneous truths)*", installation.

↑ Installation view, **Artists Draw**, Jan. 6 – Feb. 10, 1978.

Nancy Spero I had been in the women's movement since '69 and then joined AIR Gallery in '72. So in a way, I was an emerging artist, but as you (Claudia Gould) so aptly put it, I was hardly a *young* emerging artist. I was transforming myself by being in New York after Chicago and Paris. I had wrenched myself from all painting to do work on paper, and I was having a very tough time.

I had barely emerged from the antiwar shows I did in New York and the women's shows I did at AIR when Donald Sultan invited me to be in *Artists Draw*. I remember this show very well. I was excited about being in it because it was something outside of AIR. I showed the *War Series*. I was getting a bit of feedback in general at this time. But with my career it's all been retroactive.

This is maybe Pollyanna-ish, but when something like *Artists Draw* happens, it's momentous, even if it didn't have the external impact. Nevertheless, to me these exhibitions early on are extremely important for younger as well as middle-age or whatever-age artists to show their work.

People have a right to say whatever they want to say. But, when you start to censor people's work, then you have to stand outside the institution. You can't do both.

Donald Sultan Helene Winer had seen some work of mine in the CAPS (Creative Artists Public Service grant) finalist show and she really wanted to show it. So, that was how the first little tile pieces were shown at Artists Space. There really weren't other places to show. Artists Space's legacy for young artists was always so powerful because, up until that point, artists were chosen by other artists. We'd always go see who they would pick, which usually was their studio assistant or somebody who painted just like them. Except Chuck Close—he always picked interesting people when he had the chance. When Helene took over, her team decided to try to do something from their point of view. They got some pretty interesting people in there. *Pictures* was a really big deal. It got reviewed in the *New York Times*, which launched a whole flurry of activity, because all the dealers looked for artists in spaces like Artists Space. Just about everybody had been in there. People were coming to see and buy the newest art. My exhibition experience at Artists Space was probably one of the most important I ever had. It was a solid beginning in my life as an artist in New York.

Helene decided it would be interesting if artists curated a show once in a while. So, I put together these people who made beautiful drawings, and the show was called *Artists Draw,* and opened in January 1979. I knew the artists because the art community was smaller then. Alan Saret was such an interesting figure, and his gang drawings were just astonishing. There was Auste Peciura, a woman who had moved to New York from Chicago, who made these fabulous drawings. She became a punk artist. Then there was a guy named Tom Martin who also did beautiful drawings, as well as Patti Smith, the rock musician, and Nancy Spero. I wrote a little piece for it which later led to the *5 Spanish Artists* show in 1985.

The Spanish artists were trying to get out of Spain and become more international. Spain had just opened up after Franco's death and I'd seen some pretty interesting paintings when I was there. So I put together this show and gave all those artists their first exhibition in America. They are still the biggest artists in Spain of that generation.

Howardena Pindell, who was Assistant Curator of Prints at MOMA, had been hammering on Artists Space over the Donald Newman show. So I wrote her a letter saying that as a black woman artist she had every right in the world to hammer on Donald Newman. But as a curator at MOMA she had no business attacking an institution and demanding they censor the work of an artist. She left the museum after that. I think she agreed with me. People have a right to say whatever they want to say. But, when you start to censor people's work, then you have to stand outside the institution. You can't do both. Artists Space had so much trouble for a number of reasons. After Linda Shearer left, the administration was problematic. If you turn an art space into a political action committee you only get politically active people as your support group, and that's a different kind of support. Politics took over Artists Space and it became more of a political, multicultural, and AIDS forum.

Apr. 21–28: **Performance series**.
    Apr. 21: Mitchell Kriegman, *Show and Tell*.
    Apr. 24: Julian Maynard Smith, *Psychoanalysis*.
    Apr. 25: Albano Guatti, *Interval*.
    Apr. 26: Bart Robbett, *The Garden & Standing Up*.
    Apr. 27: Glenys Johnson, *Simulated Performance*.

Apr. 21–28: **Films**.
    Apr. 27: Gerry Wentz, *Sky Break*, 1978; Steve Miller, *Steam*, 1978; Ken Kobland, *Picking Up the Pieces/3 Mistakes*, 1978; Kathleen King, *Untitled (Marriage)*, 1978; Beth B and Scott B, *Letters to Dad*, 1979.
    Apr. 28: James Casebere, *An Udder Orientation*, 1979; Ladd Kessler, *The Sad Poet*, 1979; John Jesurun, *Where are My Legs*, 1978; Vivienne Dick, *She Had Her Gun All Ready*, 1978.

May 5–19: Michael Zwack, *The Levitation of Anna*, installation.

May 5–June 9: William Leavitt, tableau and drawings.

Lucy Lippard When I was in England, I met these artists who were doing a lot of interesting work. I also realized none of us on the Left had any picture of what anybody else was doing, and history was always being lost. So, on the announcement of the exhibition I organized, *Art From the British Left,* I invited anybody interested in starting an archive of socially concerned art to call me. We had a meeting at Printed Matter and at the beginning I announced I did not want to start another organization because I was constantly starting organizations. But when we walked out of the meeting we had started another organization! That is how PAD/D (Political Art Documentation/Distribution) emerged. PAD/D existed from '79 through '87. It was practically the longest living political art group in New York, in my memory anyway. The people in it have since shown in New York, including Mary Kelly, Margaret Harrison, Conrad Atkinson, and Rasheed Araeen. I put Araeen's image on the card.

What I loved about Artists Space when Irving Sandler and Trudie Grace were involved was artists choosing artists. I was excited by it and always felt there should be more exhibitions organized like that. Then I was very unexcited when Helene (Winer) became Director. Not that she wasn't a good person to do it, but I didn't think it should be a curated space. Not that I didn't do stuff there, but it became a different space, another run-of-the-mill space. My tenure on the Board of Directors was '73 to '77. I got off because I went to live in England for a year. I did lose interest in it when it became not an "artists space," so I probably took that excuse to get out. I would still go to all the shows, but it just didn't seem like what it was supposed to be. They had a unique idea to begin with and they dropped the ball.

I got along fine with Helene until *The Nigger Drawings,* which I thought was reprehensible. That was the end of that. I thought she was doing a good job. It was just that one show that I was appalled by. It was a white artist showing abstract charcoal drawings that had absolutely nothing to do with anything, completely contentless. But, he insisted— I can't even remember his name and don't think anybody else can, which is fine—on calling the work *The Nigger Drawings*. It was Howardena Pindell who picked up on it. Howardena worked with other black artists. They founded the Coalition Against Racism in the Arts and raised issues about how much funding black spaces got. In any case, she was the one who rang the bell. She saw it announced someplace, called Artists Space, and asked whether the title really was *The Nigger Drawings* and whether it was a black artist. They didn't know who Howardena was, she just called and got whomever answered the phone. At that point black people were using the word "nigger" a lot, but it was only used "in-house." As a white person, you didn't bloody well go around using the word.

Anyway, the artist finally told us why he called it *The Nigger Drawings*. He said it was because when he was doing charcoal drawings he got the charcoal all over his face. It was the stupidest thing. If he had been dealing with the notion of "nigger" it would have been a little more problematic to censor it. But in this case, he just did it to be a sensationalist, to attract attention, and he got a lot of attention. I remember the protest out in the rain. It was just one day. In fact, I recall Howardena questioning whether we should go ahead with the protest and give this asshole more attention, which is clearly what he wanted anyway. But we decided it was really enough of an object lesson that people should think about it. I thought of it as this liberal artist thing, in which artists think they can do anything without any consequence. Anything goes if you're an artist and something you couldn't say in the subway you can say in an art gallery. On certain levels that works, on others it definitely doesn't. For me, it was a political watershed just to see who stood where on this issue and I refer to it in a piece of my writing.

May 26–June 9: Ken Wade, *Bandage*, installation.

July 5–25: **Rememberances for Tomorrow** (Helene Winer). Exchange exhibition with Artists Space at New 57 Gallery, Edinburgh, Scotland. Sherrie Levine, James Welling, and others.

June 16–July 14: **Art From the British Left** (Lucy Lippard). Photography, books, drawing, photo-text: Rasheed Araeen & the Black Phoenix, Conrad Atkinson, Margaret Harrison, Alexis Hunter, Mary Kelly, Tony Rickaby, Marie Yates. First in a series of socially concerned art exhibitions, which lead to the formation of Political Art Documentation Distribution (PADD).

June 23: Ray Johnson, meeting of the *New York Correspondence School*.

1979–80

Sept. 9–Oct. 15: **10 Artists / Artists Space** (Helene Winer). Exhibition at the Neuberger Museum, Purchase, New York, of work by artists who had their first one-person shows at Artists Space during 1973–75. Laurie Anderson, telephone booth installation; Jonathan Borofsky, painting on ceiling; Scott Burton, table/sculpture; Lois Lane, painting; Thomas Lanigan-Schmidt, installation; Ree Morton, installation and painting; Judy Pfaff, installation; Charles Simonds, sculpture; Barbara Schwartz, painting and sculpture; John Torreano, painting. Catalogue published by the Neuberger Museum, with essays by Irving Sandler and Helene Winer.

Sept. 22–Nov. 10: **Sixth Anniversary Exhibition** (Helene Winer). Exhibition at Artists Space of works by 10 artists who had their first one-person shows at Artists Space during 1973–75. Laurie Anderson, telephone booth installation; Jonathan Borofsky, painting and sculpture; Scott Burton, models; Lois Lane, painting and drawing; Thomas Lanigan-Schmidt, installation; Ree Morton, drawing; Judy Pfaff, drawing; Charles Simonds, documentary photography; Barbara Schwartz, painting and sculpture; John Torreano, painting.

Nov. 14–17: **Films.**
Nov. 14: Beth B and Scott B, *G'Man;* Laura Kennedy and Pat Place, *Strange Samples;* John Lurie, *Hell is You;* Ellen Cooper, Cara Perlman and Kiki Smith, *Poofo.*
Nov. 15: James Nares, *Roma;* Tom Otterness, *Shot Dog Film;* Tim Burns and Lindzee Smith, *Political Transmission.*

Nov. 16: Douglas Hessler and Candace Lenny, *Scene from a Movie;* Eric Mitchell, *Kidnapped;* Cara Perlman, and Jane Sherry, *Topless;* Robert Smith, *Alienation.*
Nov. 17: Willy Lenski, *Relatively Tortured;* Charlie Ahearn, *Deadly Art of Survival;* Ralston Farina, *En Rapport.*

Nov. 27–Dec. 22: Gary Burnley, painting; Martin Cohen, installation; Candace Hill-Montgomery, *Candy Coated*, installation; Louis Stein, installation; Haim Steinbach, installation.

Nov. 24–Dec. 22: Tom Otterness, *Otterness Objects*, sale of multiples.

ARTIST

William Leavitt It was about this city statue, which meant it was also about New York, because L.A. is a desert town. I thought about how East Coast cities have parks with statues. The figure on this statue had become gnomish, like Mr. Magoo riding a horse. I was interested in different kinds of artificial representation. It was just a flat cutout, a painted piece of board. There was an artificial tree. It was rented, but nicely made. It was in part of a room, which had a curtain, a table, and chairs. Everything was more or less realistic and could have been an actual place. There were some drawings, too, sketches for what the scene was like.

While in New York, I ran into a cab driver. He said he played electric piano. So, I asked him to play for the opening. He brought his piano and a friend to sing. It was kind of loose. They played a little lounge music and people sat in the chairs. The idea was to evoke some generic cityscape with mood elements in it, the piano, the lightning. It didn't have to be New York.

Dennis Adams I did a show with some images of Patricia Hearst, which I placed in the space called 10 Windows on Eighth Avenue and 53rd Street. The Hearst family had the cases broken into and took the images out. They were appropriated photographs from the newspaper and there was nothing wrong with that, but they took offense to it. So I immediately had a lot of media attention. Since that show had disappeared, Rags Watkins invited me to do something at Artists Space. I was excited. It was my first opportunity to show work in a semi-official space. I produced a very large installation, an extension of the 10 Windows show, that included 35 photographs and text. I built a room within a room in which these photographs were set end to end along the wall. They went completely around the space — the only break was where you entered. This was the first time I worked with the architecture, conceiving something architecturally. I was not a real builder. The night of the opening it snowed and snowed and snowed. It was the huge storm of February 16, 1979. It was terrible. The feeling was nobody would come. It was also the opening for *The Nigger Drawings* exhibition. But Helene Winer hadn't focused on it, I don't think she even noticed the title on those drawings, although I don't quite remember. But she *was* in a panic over my work. For the opening, I hired two big-armed Pinkerton guards to stand on either side of the doorway as a framing device and to give a little theatrical weight. Apparently, Rags

hadn't told Helene they were coming and when she found out just before the opening, she freaked out. I have no idea why, but she was very upset. She didn't want armed guards coming into Artists Space. But you know, the guards never showed up. I assumed it was because of the snow, but maybe Helene called, I never did know for sure. In any case, we just got drunk, had a good time, and nobody really gave a shit afterwards.

Helene had been afraid something would happen to my work, since it had been publicized all over the newspapers because of the Hearst connection. But a few days after the opening, *The Nigger Drawings* scandal broke out and all of a sudden, the attention went completely to Donald Newman. Nobody mentioned my show, it became invisible — he stole the show. The night before the opening, I met Donald and we had a drink together. He was a nice guy. It was the first time I'd ever laid eyes on him and the last.

Cindy Sherman was the receptionist then. It was the first time I'd ever laid my eyes on her, too. She came into my space and asked if she could help me with the installation. I looked at her and thought she looked very young and very inexperienced. Of course, I was young too. But for some reason I thought, no. Although I do remember thinking she was absolutely the most sincere person I had ever met — I evaluated her in about two seconds. She had a charisma that I strangely remember in this close encounter, which lasted for about 30 seconds. Her hair was blonde and she was very pretty and very charming.

This was not the "political establishment," it was artists and art critics. It was a small group of the art world who never had any great faith in art to begin with. Who didn't seek the truth and didn't equate art with truth.

Dennis Adams, *Patricia Hearst – A Second Reading*, installation, Feb. 16 – Mar. 10, 1979.

→ Announcement card for *The Nigger Drawings*, Feb. 16 – Mar. 10, 1979. (Design by Donald).

ARTISTS SPACE
105 Hudson Street
New York, N.Y. 10013

Committee for the Visual Arts, 1979

DONALD
The Nigger Drawings
February 16 – March 10

Opening:
Friday, February 16, 5-7

ARTIST

Donald Newman It made sense and was consistent with everything else I was doing at the time to just use my first name, Donald. Paul McMahon selected me. At that time, Helene (Winer) really didn't go to studios. Paul was the one. If you read any of the articles there's actually a funny and true anecdote, which is that I spent my first night ever in New York sleeping on Artists Space's floor. When I arrived in New York I had no place to stay, so I went to Artists Space, told them I had gone to Cal Arts, and Paul let me spend the night in the gallery. I had been accepted into the Whitney Independent Study Program. There was a group of people who went from Cal Arts to the Whitney and to Artists Space. Everybody was on the same path at that time. It was very cohesive. Actually, it's funny, 1977 was like it is now, completely dead, a talent void. There was nothing happening. But what little excitement existed was, in fact, at Artists Space. Cindy Sherman, David Salle, Barbara Kruger, Robert Longo, everybody went through there.

The controversy surrounding my exhibition was like most controversies. It had nothing to do with the art. The only thing is, if the art had not been so good, there wouldn't have been a controversy, because it could have been dismissed as some sort of puerile stunt. It was a generational thing. Lucy Lippard, Carl Andre, and that whole crew were on their way out and Salle, me, Sherman, Longo, and everybody else were on their way in with a different aesthetic and approach. *The Nigger Drawings* was the precursor to political correctness, which is basically self-censorship, in the art world. I was attacked by a guy who put bricks on the floor and sold them for $2,000,000, which is absurd, useless, and obscene. Robert Mapplethorpe was not being attacked by anybody in the art world. It wasn't painful to be attacked by the art world, but it was certainly revealing and certainly good to polarize things a little. A lot happened as a result of that show. Helene started Metro Pictures. I obviously got a lot of attention, but so did Artists Space and all the people who had been exhibiting there.

There was a tremendous amount of press, I have a 2-inch stack. I sold all the drawings, Charles Saatchi bought them, and Mary Boone asked me to join her gallery. From a purely art historical perspective the result was interesting. The controversy was mostly played out at a bureaucratic level.

Actually, I did not name the show *The Nigger Drawings*. I have never titled a show in my life. I titled my artwork, of which there were seven drawings called *The Nigger Drawings*. The difference is that the people who wanted to assign culpability to Artists Space said I called the show *The Nigger Drawings*. Their entire case wraps around that. Now, obviously, if Lucy Lippard and Carl Andre call for the censorship of an artist's title, that doesn't look like a good thing. How absurd! This was not the "political establishment," it was artists and art critics. It was a small group of the art world who never had any great faith in art to begin with. Who didn't seek the truth and didn't equate art with truth. I gave the work that title because I wanted one that resonated against the beauty of the work. When Roberta Smith reviewed the show she pointed out nigger is a word most people won't even say. We say cocksucker more than we ever say nigger, right? You just don't say that word. Even when it's bouncing around in your mind, it resonates, especially if you're looking at something beautiful. What was appropriate, shocking, and engaging in '79 is not in '97. A picture of fist-fucking is not that interesting now in the same way the word nigger is not that interesting now. In both cases neither is interesting, because they've been done.

I'm doing figurative painting now. I haven't shown but I'm going to. I was at Artists Space at a very exciting time and I would like to exhibit again, be part of what's happening at the moment. Political correctness in the art world is apparent and still playing itself out. Once people get back to being interested in art, I'll be very interested in exhibiting and participating.

Howardena Pindell What I remember about *The Nigger Drawings* is receiving a phone call from Janet Henry telling me about the title of the show. She said she called Artists Space, asked them why that title, and was told, according to the artist, the drawings are in charcoal and charcoal is black and black is nigger. So, that's what propelled her to call other people. When Janet called, Linda Cathcart was in my studio. I was very upset about it and her reaction was, "It's not important, who cares?" But I felt targeted by that word. Her reaction was nonchalant because she would never be the target of that word. And that's what propelled me to move forward. Lucy Lippard and I made a number of phone calls, it became a chain reaction. A group of us, which included David Hammons and Lowery Sims, gathered at Linda Bryant's gallery on 57th Street. I remember making banners in my studio with David. There was a meeting at Rudolf Baranik's house and a teach-in at Camille Billops's house. I believe we went to Artists Space twice and they had closed down the show. It was a mixed group that went, black and white, artists and critics. The second time we went to Artists Space we got in. Steve Gianakos was yelling and there was a white woman artist who was obviously friends with Helene Winer, who said to us, "Who do you think you are coming down here and telling us what to do? This is a white neighborhood." I was stunned by that. It really hit me about the art world and highlighted why we were there.

Helene was getting Expansion Arts money (NEA) because she had a show from Scotland. Adrian Piper was one of the few black artists they had ever shown. So we were saying to each other, "Scottish artists? This is what they're using Expansion Arts money for?"

I had been living in the New York art world since 1967, and I knew how racist it was. I had seen it from the inside, and as a curator at MOMA, I saw how things functioned there. The racism in the art world has a specific twist to it. You have the art mavens, who are also the big corporate mavens. Now, granted, their corporations are usually all white, but it does not let the art world off the hook to say it reflects the real world when it pushes itself forward as some sacred space or activity, more liberal than other parts of society. There were a lot of very negative things happening when Ronald Reagan became president.

Some good came out of *The Nigger Drawings*. It raised some consciousness about what was happening in the art world, and not just in the art galleries, because everyone saw how sexist and racist they were. They were seeing how the alternative and so-called more liberal venues weren't really all that liberal. So people sensitive to the issue were looking at it with a fresh eye, and that was good. It also pushed me into publishing my point of view, which has helped a number of people. How many artists of color are there across the board? Not just black artists, but Asian artists, and so on? The women artists were really being handled by the Guerrilla Girls, although, in the beginning, they seemed to only handle white women. Later they started looking at artists of color. *The Nigger Drawings* issue galvanized certain individuals to do things differently and address issues head on. It changed my life. It was a catalyst. My work became totally issue oriented, and I started writing about those issues in 1985. It clarified what had been a real problem for me. In fact, I quit MOMA that year, too. I could not tolerate working on the inside of a system that tolerated that sort of thing. One sad side of it—well, I don't know whether it's sad or just a normal residual reaction—is I cannot walk into Artists Space easily. In fact, this has been discussed a number of times, and people still can't go to Artists Space. Someone wanted to use my name for Artists Space and I said, "Absolutely not, cannot do it." No matter what Artists Space does, that memory is still there, certainly in my writing and other people's writing. But, I'm talking to you (Claudia Gould) about it now and that's nice. I can't imagine certain institutions contacting the people they've omitted for years and wanting to discuss it. I don't think Artists Space could get away with omitting the incident from their history. It would be noticed.

Some good came out of The Nigger Drawings. It raised some consciousness about what was happening in the art world, and not just in the art galleries, because everyone saw how sexist and racist they were.

Haim Steinbach, installation. Exhibition Nov. 24 – Dec. 22, 1979.

CURATOR **RoseLee Goldberg** I watched Artists Space closely through the Helene Winer period. She became the Director in 1975, which was a remarkable time. We all looked to Artists Space, especially when I was the gallery curator at the Kitchen from '78 to '80. We were educated for those two to three years by Artists Space. It was one of the few places I would go to see the youngest, newest, most interesting artists who were coming out with work in New York.

There was always a sense that Helene (Winer) was trying to understand the work and critique issues in her programming. That was in the Wooster Street days, before it moved downtown. It was a real magnet then, like the Kitchen. They were the two places to watch. When Artists Space moved down to Hudson Street it was also an interesting moment. It gave a lot of energy to the Fine Arts Building that hadn't been there. We all trudged down to follow it. The rooms really worked very well. They gave it the spirit of an edgy office setting, which perfectly suited them. Somehow, the work seemed to fit right or they made it fit.

In a way, the mystery at Artists Space was also Helene's background, coming from California and being very open to that new generation. She really brought in a much more critical crowd. She would certainly show performance to which I was very much connected. I had given a lecture at Cal Arts in the 70s, and the sense was that she became the early link to that young generation of artists. I truly believe she changed the entire shape and tenor of Artists Space by bringing in this West Coast intellectual world. And it wasn't what we typically knew of the West Coast. Curatorially we were all such free birds. We could be so noninstitutional about how we approached work, which is what was so extraordinary about that period. We had an idea and we just did it—we don't have that now.

ARTIST **Haim Steinbach** I regularly frequented Artists Space because I had my studio in the same building on the third floor, and I felt my work was perfect for that context. I'd been doing installations in my studio for a while. They always consisted of floor to ceiling, about 2 to 3 foot-wide, sometimes 5 foot-wide, strips of wallpaper. One strip butted against the next until it covered the whole wall. Each strip was a different pattern from a different culture. For instance, English pastoral next to Colonial next to a Chinese pattern next to Italian. Then I would put a wooden plank shelf across the different strips of patterned paper, about 4 feet from the wall side to side, on which objects sat. That was the beginning of the work with objects on shelves and the start of the installations.

When Helene offered me a show, it was my first in New York, and it was very important for me. She also let me choose my space. So I took the reception room to make an installation, using the whole space by covering two walls and appropriating Cindy Sherman as part of it. Cindy had her table, basically a minimal white box, on which she had papers and brochures. I changed that white minimal box to blue. Then I built a cabinet-sized white box, which was completely closed, to place against an adjacent wall, on top of which sat a chrome water kettle. It was a way of substituting the minimal white box with another minimal white box and turning Cindy's minimal white box/table into a decorative piece of furniture. Cindy was always inside my installation. She would dress up in office clothing. I had a small musicbox tape in a cassette player that played some very subtle fragments of music I had arranged. Cindy had to live with that for a month.

January **1980** to August **1985**

Linda Shearer interviewed by Valerie Smith

In January 1980, Linda Shearer became Artists Space's Executive Director, where she remained until 1985. She hired Valerie Smith as Curator in the fall of 1981, who stayed until the spring of 1989. Shearer's tenure began at 105 Hudson Street; in July 1984 Artists Space moved to 223 West Broadway. This interview took place on May 10, 1997.

VALERIE SMITH: Let's start from zero. What interested you about Artists Space that made you want to become Director?

LINDA SHEARER: The answer to your question is two-pronged. In 1969, fresh out of college, I started working at the Guggenheim. Soon after, I assisted Diane Waldman, at that time a curator at the Guggenheim, on a new talent show which opened in 1971. Subsequently, in 1977 and 1978, I did two new talent exhibitions sponsored by Exxon. This meant I spent a lot of time in the studios of little-known artists. I realized very quickly I was more interested in and got the most thrill out of working with emerging, rather than established, artists.

When Helene Winer became Director in 1975, she refocused the existing exhibition structure of artists selecting artists by putting together a panel to look at slides from the Unaffiliated Artists File (UAF). It included Helene, Jennifer Bartlett, Bill Wegman, Paul McMahon, Edit deAk, and myself. We had a great time.

When I discovered Helene was leaving in 1980, I thought, oh, this is fabulous, what a perfect opportunity! It seemed entirely natural. I don't think I even formally applied. Clearly, after 11 years at the Guggenheim, this is what really interested me. I'd had a previous involvement with Artists Space. I knew Helene, knew the staff, knew the setup, followed the shows. I had a very comfortable feeling about Artists Space and I was ready to leave the museum.

On the other hand, it was 1980 when Ronald Reagan came into office. He was trying to stop all government support of the arts. So, why was I able to leave a very secure job in a major institution to go to a not very secure job in a not very major institution? It was foolhardy, but it seemed like the right thing to do. And I was excited by it.

VS: What changed at Artists Space after you became Director?

LS: The needs. Artists Space started in 1973. By 1980, it was no longer this by-the-seat-of-your-pants kind of organization. The climate was changing radically and Artists Space was still young. We were at a point where, in order to go on to the next step in its development, we had to aggressively raise money by actively getting more individuals involved. I had to be able to respond to those needs.

I also needed to win over, not a negative feeling, but a sense that, "oh God, it's going to become like an uptown institution and here's this person coming from the Guggenheim who will change it from its funky downtown quality." I was very conscious of not wanting to change that because that was what was so special about it. I had no intention of turning it into an uptown institution. Furthermore, I wouldn't have known how.

There was also the legacy of *The Nigger Drawings* exhibition (1979) that hung over the place. A lot of good community relations needed to be done. So, the job of director automatically jumped to a slightly different level. It had become more administrative and public relations–oriented.

VS: Was the UAF used officially for the first time when you were invited on that panel to select artists for exhibition?

LS: No, I can recall going down to the Wooster Street space for slide viewings before Helene started. With the panel she put together, we went to the studios of artists we thought were interesting and we also looked at all the slides. It was Helene's strategy of taking Artists Space in another direction. And it worked.

vs: I'm thinking of the UAF as a kind of ideological tool. I wonder if this is how you ultimately perceived it? For instance, how did the function of the UAF change from when you, as panelists in the 1970s, were first asked to select artists?

ls: Yes, I think it's fair to say it had an ideological bent. It was definitely a way of promoting Artists Space. Slide registries were everywhere. But the *Selections* exhibition series which we started in 1981 was a way of demonstrating that it was actively used. *Selections* gave the UAF a uniqueness. There was hope, in the sense that just because you put your slides into this deep black hole of a registry, in fact, there was a good chance work would be selected from it. It had been perceived as a dead archive. So we made a conscious effort to turn it around and use it as a promotional tool. But it was more. It was also PR in terms of going out to studios to see artists' work you honestly didn't know.

I was looking at one of the *Selections* catalogues in which we wrote that you, Valerie, had gone to 60 studios. That's incredible! It's amazing, to go to something like 60 studios for one show. That is the grassroots quality of Artists Space. You're potentially delivering something, providing a service for the emerging unestablished artist. It absolutely served a valuable purpose. For example, Simon Watson and Lew Baskerville rigorously went through the UAF looking for artists to show when they were planning to open their gallery. I think they found Deborah Kass. They were always good about promoting it and telling people to use it. So there was a reality attached to the UAF that, in fact, one's slides would see the light of day and potentially get picked up.

vs: Was I the first official Curator of Artists Space?

ls: Yes, because previously Artists Space was based on the idea of artists selecting artists. Then Helene shifted this toward a curatorial direction. But as far as I know, there had never been a curator on staff. The shift was a very deliberate and definite move, which certainly made it more like a museum.

When I arrived, we could have taken any other course. However, at the time, that was the model which seemed to make sense, to hire somebody young, who was in touch with what was going on, who could write, who could be out there in the streets, so to speak, with a critical voice.

vs: You came from a curatorial position. And, as Director of Artists Space, you did a number of shows, but, naturally, not as many as before. How did you feel about this professional change?

ls: I knew I couldn't be a full-time curator, but I really enjoyed the responsibilities that went along with being a director. In fact, when I returned to curatorial work at the Museum of Modern Art in 1985, I really missed the experience of being the director at a place like Artists Space, a smaller institution where you could accomplish more and have greater mobility and activity.

vs: There was some criticism from people who felt that Artists Space became more institutionalized during your administration.

ls: I think it did, just by its very existence. It was inevitable if alternative or artists' spaces were to continue. We were always questioning whether we had run our course, whether we were doing what we set out to do. Was there still a need for Artists Space in the art community? Was there still such a thing as an emerging artist? The general sense was yes, there was.

No matter what, Artists Space wasn't the same as before. There was a lot of soul-searching that went on. This paralleled the enormous growth of the contemporary art world in the 80s. But our idea of Artists Space as a research and development organization for younger artists stayed pretty consistent due to the fact that, like other organizations, we were always concerned with becoming too institutionalized. We struggled over whether we were going in the right direction or whether we should just close up shop. Some places have done that. Not too many, however. Because there's a growth process and you get very attached to what you're doing and how you're functioning. I think we accomplished a lot. I know there's a sense it wasn't nearly as edgy as it once was. But for a lot of people, it was far *too* edgy. You're not going to please everybody by any means.

Do you remember when we did the *New Galleries of the Lower East Side* (1984) show? Suddenly, we were showing all the cool artists who were in commercial galleries on the Lower East Side. And where did that leave us? Somewhere in a middle realm, which was absolutely parallel with our age, our growth, and our development. No doubt about it, we had become like a small museum. The artists, who had been showing in the mid- to late 70s, were becoming extremely successful. As a result, Artists Space had this ready-made history of major artists who had gotten their starts there. It automatically became historical.

I firmly believe there is a place for a noncommercial experience. This is probably the abiding reason, and the passion, which makes Artists Space tick. No matter what, there should be places where artists who aren't necessarily well known are free to experiment and do work that may not be commercially viable. A place to stretch and push themselves as well as push audiences. The difficulty lies in the complexity, because so much of that experimental work is now marketable.

↑ Eric Bogosian, *Advocate,*
performance, Dec. 8-9, 1982
© Babette Mangolte

There was a big shift in 1980. Helene left the nonprofit world and went into the commercial world. Many artists whose work was clearly not about profit, and who existed in the nonprofit world, started to make money. Their work sold, which seemed inconceivable even to the artists themselves. The performance Mike Kelley did at Artists Space on West Broadway could be done at the Whitney now, or at a gallery. It wouldn't need the atmosphere or setting of an "alternative space."

        vs: What were your intentions for the exhibition program when you started? Did you
        have an ideal model?

ls: No. I was more interested in creating an atmosphere. We did a combination of solo shows and group shows. However, we were probably most successful with various installations. The idea of "installation art" is something that was really supported and encouraged in places like Artists Space. We were not alone in this, but we did it very well. The interior architecture, particularly in the old Hudson Street space, inspired that. There was such a range of rooms and spaces in which you could do things. For instance, Michael Byron's installation *For the Nun* (1982) was incredible and amazing in that small back room. And yet, it was possible on West Broadway too. I am thinking of the time Jerry Beck took over the basement. It was wild! It was fabulous!

    What it took was a basic sense of commitment and belief. Half the time we didn't know what the artists were actually going to do. Then the whole "quality" issue was raised. You're going with your gut at that point. That's the way we all operated. We had a clear sense of what was good and what wasn't. In a place like Artists Space, installation work gained a legitimacy because there was a critical substructure to it.

    I remember a number of theme shows you curated, a type which hadn't been done before, and those were good: *A Likely Story*; *Facades, Landscapes, Interiors;* and *Dark Rooms.*

        vs: I initiated the *Dark Rooms* exhibition series and after you left brought back the
        architectural projects to fulfill a need for media artists and architects who didn't have that
        outlet before.

ls: Yes, absolutely. The other thing that was good, which I had forgotten until I glanced through the catalogues, is a lack of ego on the part of the people who ran Artists Space. This is what distinguishes it

↑ Jerry Beck, installation view,
U.S. Projects, May 25–June 29, 1985.

from similar organizations. Because Artists Space has gone through comparatively more directors it's the product of all our personalities. But it's not singular in that sense. It's never been an ego-oriented place, by any means.

For example, with the *US Projects* and the *International Projects* there was a willingness and a drive to have a lot of voices heard, both curatorially and artistically, without being threatened by that in the slightest. To a certain extent, that may have hurt us, in terms of not having a singular vision or identity. But I don't think so. It gave Artists Space an intelligent breadth without spending huge amounts of money. We got curators and artists from other parts of the country to make exhibitions, which, again, provided another kind of outlet.

Our purpose was to give opportunities to artists. But not just a grab bag of any artist who wanted to show. It wasn't a cooperative. In its early days, the opposite was true. The artists selecting artists model was terrific. It worked well. That model served a need, but the need changed. During our phase, it became more like a funky museum.

It was difficult to accommodate the needs and the requirements of every artist. And it was difficult art. But we always tried to provide opportunities that were about experimentation although the results were, perhaps, not always that experimental. Artists Space was always very clear about this. There was never a commercial aspect in any way, shape, or form, even when standard paintings were shown. And still, to this day, I firmly believe all artists should get an honorarium when they show in a museum. They should be paid for providing their services. The idea of respecting artists for their contribution to society was very much at the heart of all artists' spaces. It is an important message that I fear is getting lost in the world at large today.

vs: Yes, unfortunately, this is true and in part tied into the lack of funding. In what ways did the funding for Artists Space affect the exhibition program?

LS: We certainly didn't have a lot of funding. We scrambled for grants for exhibitions and for everything we wanted to do. I can remember once, right when you first started, we were really poor and I felt enormously resentful. After the first year, I thought, we can't possibly survive, we are not even going to make the rent! There were lots of times we had to wait for our paychecks. That's part of the reason people can't last in these jobs. You can't hang on in that way. But then we got a $5,000 grant from the Rubin Foundation that got us through the summer. It was amazing.

We did a lot of aggressive fundraising with individuals and foundations and were very successful with the federal government. But the hardest funding agency of all, and I bet you Susan would echo this, was NYSCA (New York State Council on the Arts). There we were, being grilled by this jerk. And you know we were tough. We were good.

NYSCA has changed, so it may not be the same case today. But their attitude was shaped in part because they had a proprietary interest in Artists Space. They had been the initial funder and they wanted a degree of control. We felt we had to please them. I never felt that with other funders. The Jerome Foundation was wonderfully generous. They only cared that we were supporting, sponsoring, and providing opportunities for unknown artists. Our solicitation of individuals was always on a personal level. They believed in the general concept of Artists Space. They weren't interested in funding specific exhibitions, they just liked the idea of the place.

> vs: Was there a connection between *The Nigger Drawings* (1979) and our difficult relationship with NYSCA, because of the negative residue from that show?

LS: It never went away. The same thing happened at the Guggenheim when they canceled the Hans Haacke exhibition. I worked there then and it was far more complex than people ever realized. But the Guggenheim has never lived that down, just as Artists Space has hardly lived down *The Nigger Drawings*.

Do you remember the piece Eric Bogosian did on Hudson Street, *Advocate,* in 1982? He projected images he got mostly from Amnesty International, so there were scenes of torture and abuse. It was awfully gruesome. But I knew in my heart of hearts it would be okay. It was 8:00 at night in TriBeCa, who was going to attend, who would complain? After all, we were addressing a specific downtown art audience. I really sweated bullets over that performance. And it was absolutely fine. In my naiveté, I had expected Eric not to be so graphic. But of course, why would he, why should he give in to nice behavior? He was right not to.

This was interesting, particularly with the experience of *The Nigger Drawings*, knowing that you've got something potentially controversial. Not potentially! You know it's controversial! But you've made a commitment to the artist. What do you do?

I remember having lots of discussions with a Board member beforehand and we were very concerned. I said, "I can say all I want to Eric, ask him to please take into consideration that we have the history of *The Nigger Drawings* and that if someone takes offense, we could lose funding."

> vs: But you couldn't censor it.

LS: I couldn't, no, and I didn't. I felt that would be totally antithetical to what the place was about. It was my responsibility to make certain he understood the complexity of our situation, which he did. The thing now with *The Nigger Drawings*, and I've talked with Helene a lot about this, was that it was a real eye-opener for everybody. Not just for Helene, but for Artists Space. They probably did the right thing because they had made a commitment to the artist. However, the Board should have been more engaged, more involved. But, again, this situation hadn't happened before. There was no context or previous experience to rely on. I learned a real lesson from that: if you think you've got a problem on your hands, you make sure your Board knows about it, understands the complexity, and supports you. But what's worse? Censoring an artist? You can't do that. That's just as bad. What you have to do is work it through.

> vs: One reason I ask is because, maybe it was after you left, I remember some pressure filtered down from NYSCA to Susan and then to me, that we'd better cover our bases in terms of artists of color.

LS: I don't think that was necessarily a direct result of *The Nigger Drawings*. It was the times. Everyone started to become very conscious of a need for diversity. It was the beginning of a general sense, and an appropriate sense, of the need for affirmative action in the art world. This is one of the objectives, which has suffered a great loss, as we're seeing the NEA get dismantled before our eyes. Hopefully it can still hang in there.

It has to do with accountability. Government agencies can demand an accountability from an organization, so that you must look at yourself critically and demographically. You look at your program, your staff, and your Board to see who's in control, to see there are checks and balances, etc., so that it doesn't become some megalomania or autocratic private world for some individual. That is one of the values of government support.

Again, we felt at times NYSCA was getting far too invasive. There seemed to be more manipulation on the part of their staff. But there was always that legacy for Artists Space. Except for Kenji Fujita, we didn't have people of color on staff. None of this ever happened with the NEA, because the whole peer panel system functioned differently, and it did work.

vs: In retrospect, what would you have changed in the exhibition program or have done differently?

LS: Oh, God! What would you say? Sure, we could have done things differently. And we would certainly be doing it differently if we were doing it now. But I don't feel we missed anything.

vs: Well, I always felt I could have investigated much more. We did a lot. But perhaps not enough. The movement towards multiculturalism had a big effect on me. I remember visiting Fred Wilson at Longwood Gallery in the South Bronx and visiting Giza Daniels-Endesha's studio down the street from there. His work was so strong, I immediately asked him to do a show. I should have looked more in that direction.

LS: Yes, but there's always this fine line between the tenor of the times that you're living in and your own sense of drive. And in the early to mid-80s so much was going on. Take CoLab (Collaborative Projects), for example. They were doing a lot that was ultimately important. Our support of their activities goes back to the very beginning of the institution. Through the Emergency Materials Fund (EMF), we supported all those bizarre projects, which wouldn't have existed otherwise. Were they lasting? Were they great? I don't know, but they were important. Fifty dollars did make a difference. And there was Artists Space helping other exhibitions outside of their walls.

vs: The Board changed when you became the Director. Its function changed.

LS: Yes and no. Donald Droll was President and he was very supportive all along. The Board had curatorial expertise and it had artists' expertise. The importance of the Board was the mandate that it be composed of, at least, 50-percent artists. The artists on the Board have proven to be terrific. Their commitment and sense of responsibility, their belief in the institution, is what has driven it in many ways. Roy Lichtenstein, Mary Miss, Vito Acconci, Cindy Sherman, the number of artists who have believed in the place is a real testimony to its importance. Many of the nonartists on the Board were attracted to being with the artists on the Board. They enjoyed that association.

But what was missing when I got there, which hit me full whammy, was that no one was willing to put money into Artists Space or to raise money. Never having done any fundraising in my life, my biggest challenge was to start fundraising. I actually enjoyed it. But Artists Space never lost its foundation in the artists' community, its basis in reality, and its sense of what the place was about.

For me, the main person on the Board became Katherine Lobell. The fact that she agreed to come on the Board in the first place was terrific. It was a new experience for her. She worked so hard to raise money for Artists Space, and she was successful. It was amazing. She turned us around financially. She believed in the place. And we were a really good team. I credit Katherine with a huge amount because she never wanted to change the organization. She did bring an uptown consciousness to it.

She got a lot of her friends and acquaintances involved and excited about it.

Do you remember when Eric Bogosian performed one of his routines for an Artists Space benefit and mooned the audience? A huge number of people came to a big loft space in the West 30s, which the Guardian Angels were patrolling. The acoustics were very bad, so no one paid attention because they couldn't hear. Eric was clearly getting more and more frustrated, so he mooned them. And he was absolutely right. But no one noticed, and it was Katherine who pulled off the benefit.

vs: Do you feel that Artists Space changed you professionally?

LS: Yes. I really loved it. We had fun. It was low-key, but still very intense. I don't think it ever really stood still. We were always changing, too, and having to keep up. It was never stable. At a certain point, there was a sense of stability, but it was never quiet or easy. It confirmed for me the importance of artists in culture, in society, and in life. That's ideally what the art world should be about. It has to do with a basic respect for artists. And there isn't enough, by any means. That's the tragedy.

I don't like working in atmospheres that are not supportive and congenial, and that was not the case at Artists Space. We were a real team that understood each other and communicated well. For me, it was very positive and constructive, but mostly exhilarating. I'm not saying it wasn't difficult or that there weren't fuck-ups, but that's true everywhere. There was a lot of pressure financially, but we overcame that.

When I decided to leave, I have to say that it was probably time for me to do so. I'd been there five years. We moved into a new space. We were in a new phase. And it was a great opportunity to go to the Modern, although I had said I'd never go back uptown to a big institution again. I later realized that was right. It's constraining. Especially when you're used to a certain professional freedom and independence in running a place. Artists Space was my first experience with that and I wouldn't go back on any point now. Artists Space set a tone for me. And, most importantly, it confirmed the importance of artists.

The place went through some rocky times over the NEA and the David Wojnarowicz incident. It tested the institution. And it *is* an institution. It tested the Board and the staff in extremely tough ways. However, it has remained very true to its underlying mission of serving and providing opportunities for artists, especially those who aren't well known. I go and see almost every show, and the place seems to be thriving.

VS: What do you feel was your contribution to Artists Space?

LS: For better or for worse, I was responsible for its transition just as the 80s peaked, from a small nonprofit gallery and service organization, with limited financial resources, to a more stable "institution." I oversaw its growth to a mature institution that in order to survive and thrive needed more seemingly bureaucratic procedures in place, like board development, benefit parties, umpteen committees, and better personnel benefits. Also, I confirmed a stronger curatorial focus, but always reinforced the fundamental and critical role that artists play in every aspect of the operation.

↑ Michael Byron, *For The Nun*, installation, 1982.

→ Jeff Koons, *Triple Decker*, 1982. **A Likely Story**, Feb. 20–Mar. 27, 1982.

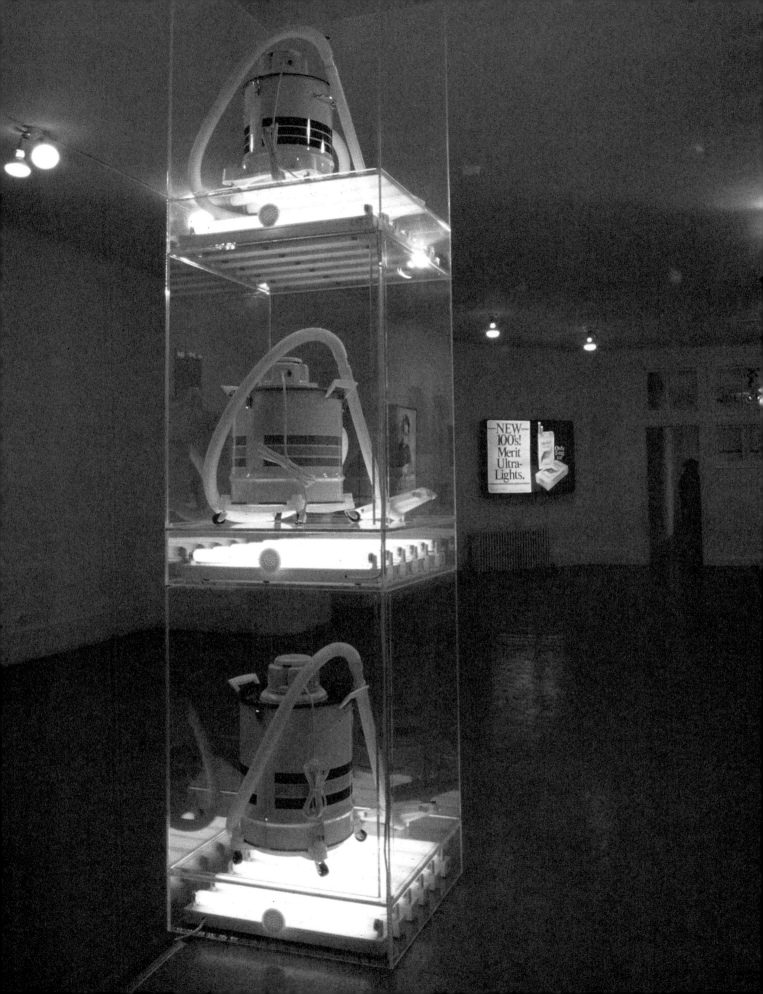

Jan. 5–19: Freya Hansell, installation; Margia Kramer, *Part I: Secret*, floor installation. Accompanied by artist's book, *The Essential Documents: The FBI File on Jean Seberg Part I.*

Jan. 5–Feb. 9: Patricia Caire, *Black and Light Passings*, installation; Ken Goodman, painting; Seth Laderman, photographs.

Jan. 26–Feb. 9: Earl Ripling, theatrical book installation.

Jan. 26–Feb. 9: Ann Wilson, artist, and Cathy Ligon, architect, *Gymnast*, sculpture, libretto pages, painting, work-in-progress, collaborative installation.

1980 JAN–FEB

Silvia Kolbowski My previous exhibitions were self-organized and also in artists' spaces or in storefronts for a period of a month. The first exhibition I did at Artists Space was a project in the hallway. I was very interested in working in that particular context. There was another option, yet I chose the hallway, and used its structure to generate not only the format of the project, but to play with the door opening. It was one of the first exhibitions I had in New York. I remember being left absolutely alone to devise the project. I wasn't asked questions about what I was going to do and nothing was challenged when I brought in the material. I was very happy to work that way. It wasn't as though I had to present the full-blown project for them to approve. They looked at some earlier work of mine and decided they had to show the work that I had done. It was an education in exhibiting as well as an opportunity to exhibit. Their curatorial attitude was specifically laissez-faire.

What Was the Right Answer? is actually a fragment of James Joyce's *Portrait of the Artist as a Young Man,* which deals with a coming of age and sexuality having to do with a young boy's utterances in relation to some quasi-Oedipal situation. In the early 80s, I was much more connected to British film theory and a certain feminist position which involved psychoanalytical readings of images. I was so very young then. My photographs staged two women functioning as models, alternately dressed as a mother and daughter or a father and daughter, always in front of actual doorways. Sometimes the connotations of the photographs were over-sexualized. The piece had something to do with the transfer of sexuality and playing against a strict gender definition. It also played on some tension in the mother-daughter relationship. The third component of the project had photographs of clear masks over the faces, so it definitely picked up on the doorways and hallways. Some of them were doors leading to bathrooms and some to office or storage space, so there was already a narrative of open and closed doors and gendered doors.

Yes, my work was personal in more ways than one. It was geographically personal. Until now I haven't stopped to think about it, but I've done a number of projects since where I chose to occupy an entry or play with the primary and secondary space in the gallery. There was definitely a hierarchy of placement within the galleries at Artists Space. However, I didn't care, it wasn't an issue for me. I found it exciting to work in an empty space.

I guess Artists Space was looking for more space when they moved to West Broadway, but it actually was a major loss. I remember the space on Hudson Street had very interesting windows that looked out onto the street. What often happens with alternative spaces is they have a tendency to move to bigger and more accessible spaces. The problem is the loss of an enormous amount of character and definition. I'm not sure Artists Space ever regained it. There is sometimes a virtue in going out of one's way to a place. When Artists Space was looking around for space, they looked in the Singer Building on Prince and Broadway, but, at the time, they felt it was too out of the way. How quickly things change.

What was a disaster for me wasn't so much *The Fairy Tale* exhibition, but the whole concept of the group show. I was critical of them in general, but it was my failing as well. I did a terrible piece for *The Fairy Tale* show. Shortly after, I stopped showing in group shows because I realized it was bad for my work. From the early 80s on, I attempted to produce somewhat site-specific work, and group shows, particularly in very bland spaces, didn't lend themselves to that. The shows also started to take on the character of large warehouse shows structured around a theme. There was a much bigger influx of artists into the city and out of art schools than when I first started to show a few years earlier. Of course, the exponential growth in galleries and the necessity to reduce risk in commercial spaces, to some extent, precipitated the group show genre, the freelancing of curators, and so on. Perhaps Artists Space became a little too dependent on group shows. Large publicly and privately funded spaces, like Artists Space, were probably motivated more by the desire to cover as much ground and as many artists as possible; the group show is obviously a good format for doing that, but I don't think it always resulted in great shows and it's not the way the space was originally run. It was definitely positive as a space where interesting and maybe noncommercial ideas could be exposed. But the attitude of performing a public service, which became more entrenched later, was not so present in the initial stage. Ironically, that might have been a good thing. It gave the space a certain character which, at the time, was perhaps considered too elitist, too distant or unresponsive. But it was an attitude that allowed them to be extremely selective about what they wanted to do without constantly thinking about gratifying an audience. The original Artists Space showed some work I found somewhat objectionable, and I didn't see eye to eye with all of Helene Winer's ideas and the artists she wanted to support. But it was open enough so somebody like me could show as well as a lot of

CONTINUED

123

Jan: **A Sound Selection: Audio Works by Artists** (Barry Rosen). Traveling exhibition of records, cassettes, and reel to reel tapes by 21 visual artists organized in collaboration with, and presented at, the University of Hartford Art School, Hartford, Connecticut. Vito Acconci, *Three Sounds* (audio tapes from three installations), *Now Do You Believe the Dirty Dogs are Dead?, Monument to the Dead Children*, 1978, and *Decoy for Birds and People*, 1979; Laurie Anderson, *Tiger Park*, 1979, *Born, Never Asked*, 1979, and *The Language of the Future*, 1979; Beth B, *House Calls*, 1978; John Baldessari, *Alfred from Berlin*, 1979; Marge Dean, *Radio Cinema, Sorrento Valley*, 1979; Guy de Cointet, *TSNX C24 VAME*, 1974, *Esphehor Ledet Ko Uluner*, 1973, and *A Few Drawings*, 1975; Bruce Fier, *Score for a Rainbow's End*, 1978, and *Mailgram Series*, 1973-74; Bob

George, *Time Will Tell*, 1978, and *Duet*, 1979; Jack Goldstein, *Untitled (white quarter moon on black label)*, 1979, *Untitled (gold moon crescent on black label)*, 1979, *Untitled (side one green label, side two blue label)*, 1979, *Untitled (side one white label, side two silver label)*, 1979, *Untitled (side one blue band on black label, side two black band on gold label)*, 1979; Allison Knowles, *Onion Skin*, 1978, and *Shoestring*, 1978; Micki McGee, *Her Intestinal Bypass Surgery*, 1979; Jim Pomeroy, *Nocturne III*, 1979; Jim Roche, *Cadillac*, 1973, and *Power Poles*, 1973; Martha Rosler, *What's Your Name Little Girl?*, 1979; Stuart Sherman, *Sounds from Spectacles*, 1978; Michael Smith, *It Starts at Home*, 1980; Mimi Smith, *Color TV News*, 1978, *Shut Up, Goodnight*, 1977; Keith Sonnier, *Air to Air*, 1975; William Wegman, *History of the World*, 1977; Lawrence Weiner, *Having Been Built on

Sand With Another Base (Basis) in Fact, 1978; Reese Williams, *Whirlpool*, 1979.

Although the tour is organized by Artists Space, the show is never presented there (see p. 93, *Audio Works* exhibition Jan. 21–Mar. 4, 1978) The 1980-81 itinerary includes St. Lawrence University, Canton, New York; Contemporary Arts Museum, Houston; Contemporary Arts Center, New Orleans; Aspen Center for the Visual Arts, Aspen; Albuquerque Museum, Albuquerque, New Mexico; and Alberta College of Art Gallery, Alberta, Canada. Catalogue preface by Helene Winer, introduction by Barry Rosen, with statements by the artists.

SILVIA KOLBOWSKI / CONTINUED

other figures I might not have been interested in or supportive of.

When Artists Space's mission shifted to a public service policy, it wasn't about supporting a certain kind of work, it was about supporting as much work as possible. The spectrum of support became much too broad in my opinion. They changed their ideas about what an alternative space should be and should do and who it should answer to, and it coincided with a shift in funding sources and government censorship and perusal. I suspect the first Artists Space was not as concerned with audience response as were the later manifestations of Artists Space. That's always much healthier, but it's probably the reason alternative spaces can no longer stay alive.

ARTIST

Richard Prince

When I first arrived in New York in '74 my friend, Paul McMahon, suggested I look into Artists Space. But I thought it was very amateurish and not what was going on in the galleries, so I never went back. Then Rags Watkins asked me to show in 1977 after seeing a piece I did in a window at Three Lives and Company, the bookstore in the West Village. It was one of the first images I had re-photographed from the advertising section of a magazine. I told him no. I wasn't interested in alternative spaces but in what I then considered real spaces, i.e., commercial galleries. This was a big mistake, of course. I wasn't really aware of Artists Space except for the fact that Paul had worked there, and I only vaguely knew what he was doing. I had never gone to one of their openings. I had a really bad attitude at that time. I just didn't think they were good enough for me. I was giving Rags any excuse not to show. But he kept asking me and I kept trying to convince him no one would like the work or respond to it. So I decided to go with the real alternative, storefront windows, because it was more anonymous as a nonart context and I thought it would work better. I was trying to exist outside the art world. That's the reason I ended up showing at Artists Space so late.

Cindy Sherman and I were not friends until I did a show in February 1980. Previously I had met her and saw her work at the Kitchen. I later learned she had somehow been enlisted by Rags to talk to me. She then arranged a show at Hallwalls. Finally, I told Rags that if he would give me the smallest room in the most obscure corner of Artists Space, I would do it. So he gave me the back room, and I did it. What happened after was really strange. I met Michael Klein. Howard Read came down and wanted the work and Douglas Crimp saw it. All of a sudden, things really changed because of that one little show. I wasn't aware of the *Pictures* show or what other people were doing. I'd been living in the West Village completely isolated and working at Time-Life. All this resisting. I had a very punk attitude, a chip on my shoulder. I thought I was doing something no one else was doing, and therefore it couldn't possibly be incorporated into anything that was going on. No one would like it. It was also a way to protect myself. It was an absolutely nutty, crazy attitude to take. When I became aware, I educated myself and went down to Artists Space to go through the Artists File. Then I met Helene Winer and she said she was thinking of putting together a gallery which she and Janelle Reiring ultimately did. It was that simple.

Feb. 1–16: **Films** (Lindzee Smith).
Feb. 13: Bill Brand, *Split Decision*; John T. Davis, *Shell Shock Rock*; Larry Meltzer and Richard Murphett, *Overland*; Larry Meltzer, *Ballistic Kisses*; Betsy Sussler, *Dreamers of the Absolute*.
Feb. 14: Ericka Beckman, *The Broken Rule*; R. Kuni, Jorge Mendez, Janet Stein, et. al., *God's Police*; Anders Grafstrom, *The Long Island Four*.

Feb. 15: Tim Burns, *Against the Brain*; Vivienne Dick, *Liberty's Booty*; Tina L'Hotsky, *Snake Woman* and untitled short film; Richard Serra and Clara Weyergraf, *Steel Mill/Stahlwerk*.
Feb. 16: Manuel De Landa, *Raw Nerves*; Anthony McCall, Clair Pajaczkowska, Andrew Tyndall, and Jane Weinstock, *Sigmund Freud's Dora*; Michael Oblowitz, *Minus Zero*; Gordon Stevenson, *Ecstatic Stigmatic*.

Feb. 23–Mar. 29: Jeff Balsmeyer, *Giving Peasants Agricultural Advice*, film installation; Silvia Kolbowski, *What Was the Right Answer?*, photo installation; Allan McCollum, painting; Richard Prince, photographs, accompanied by artist's book, *War Pictures*; Jenny Snider, painted drawing.

← Silivia Kolbowski, *What Was the Right Answer?*, installation view.
↓ Richard Prince, photograph.

Apr. 5–May 10: **Seven Toronto Artists** (Ragland Watkins). Susan Britton, photographs; David Buchan, photo-texts; Paul Campbell, photographs; Robin Collyer, photo-texts; Jerry McGrath, sculpture; John Scott, drawing; Shirley Wiitasalo, painting. Catalogue with introductions by Peggy Gale and Ragland Watkins.

Apr. 5–May 10: Bruno Bussman, film installation; Guy de Cointet, *Tell Me*, stage set installation and performance piece.

May 17–June 21: Ed Levine, *Room Construction*, installation; Reese Williams, installation.

I think that the Artists Slide File is an invaluable tool for anybody who wants to know what's going on at any time. It's a very interesting source for the history of art being made here.

1980 MAY-JUNE

May 17–June 21: **Pool Show** (Russell Maltz). Photo and video documentation of projects created by 32 artists in an unused swimming pool at C. W. Post Center, School of the Arts, Greenvale, New York. Roberta Allen, Ann Bar-Tur, Nancy Burson, Jim Clarke, Kevin Clarke, Jon Colburn, Elisa D'Arrigo, Kochi Doktori, Peter Downsborough, Elizabeth Dugdale, John Feckner, Reinhard Gfeller, Mark Golderman, Jane Handzel, Ruth Hardinger, Don Hazlitt, Wopo Holup, Tony King, David Knoebel, Alfred Larsen, Don Leicht, Suzanne Mahlmeister, Russell Maltz, John Mastraccio, Judith Murray, Massimo Pierucci, Lucio Pozzi, Abby Robinson, Ted Stamm, Julius Tobias, William Voorhest, Robert Yasuda, Frank Young. *Pool*, the book, is published by Russell Maltz, 1980.

→ Kevin Clarke

With every new director Artists Space has had a new shape and focus; therefore, I don't think of it as the same institution at all.

ARTIST

Judy Pfaff No one saw my exhibition except students, critics, and those people interested in Laurie Anderson's work. Charles Saatchi also came to some of these events. A year later he actually ended up buying something. Holly Solomon saw the show and immediately asked me to join the gallery and I got a big review in the *Village Voice*. So for me it was as an amazingly fantastic time.

With every new director Artists Space has had a new shape and focus; therefore, I don't think of it as the same institution at all. What's funny is that from an outside point of view, the way Irving Sandler put it together, Artists Space looked undemocratic. What are you going to do? It's all about who you know, who's good friends with whom. But the artists were infinitely more responsible than that. I think they took it very seriously and made serious choices. Your name was on the line, too. Think about who chose Laurie Anderson, Vito Acconci. They're kind of close, but not intimate friends. As a teacher, I see lots of artists. Sometimes I'm on a panel or jury and I've got 20 people, out of which come five artists I think are terrific. Ask the five I've chosen for their five and they'll be so responsible, suddenly, 20,000 slides later. Sometimes the most undemocratic way might be the fairest.

Lisa Austin was the more complicated choice I made for Artists Space. She was in the class I taught at Yale, which also included Ann Hamilton, Jessica Stockholder, and Sean Landers: real stars. She was so earnest and hard on herself, but not a star. I just thought, "Let me do this." It wasn't just a good deed, because she was very interesting. But there are times when, if someone gets a break, it could change the course of things. It doesn't mean they're the most talented. Holly Solomon asked me who I thought was interesting and whom I would want to see in her gallery. The only two artists I ever told Holly to get were Mike Kelley and Ann Hamilton. I also know both these people don't need a break at Artists Space, because it is a different kind of forum than a commercial gallery. I like the fact that for Artists Space I didn't have to choose who I thought was going to be the star.

When I was at Yale, Doreen Gallo was so talented and aggressive; I thought "She's going to make it." I was completely wrong. I don't even know where Doreen is now. She was doing some stuff that was actually grittier than say, Jessica Stockholder. It was somewhere in the vicinity where one would think I would find an affinity. But it was more concretized than anything I would do, more material and base. The last work she did at Yale I thought was going into some very primordial weird shit that scared me. But when she had her show at Artists Space she didn't show that side. I never knew what happened. I thought Jon Kessler was also someone who might have a real shot. Those guys are very prepared for stardom. Lisa was different. She's someone who never got a break and who's still working hard. I thought it was nice timing for her. But I haven't seen her in 15 years. I see a lot of people come and go. It wasn't like she was my good neighbor or anything. She's someone I'm still interested in. She had an original mind. Sometimes it takes a while before it can happen.

↑ Peggy Yunque, *Zorro's Horse*.
Exh: May 9–June 13, 1981.

June 24–26: **Performances**.
June 24: Stuart Sherman, *Twelfth Spectacle (Language)*, performance, film, sound pieces.
June 25: Fernando Doty, *Term: Oil*, performed by Eric Post.
June 26: John Malpede, *Paradigm*, performed with look-alike contest.

July 5–25: **Remembrances for Tomorrow**. New 57 Gallery, Edinburgh, Scotland, (Helene Winer). Second half of the exchange exhibition with Artists Space, including artists associated with Artists Space. Sherrie Levine, Richard Prince, Cindy Sherman, Laurie Simmons, James Welling, photography.

1980–81

Helene Winer resigns and Linda Shearer is hired as Executive Director in January 1980. In 1981, both Cindy Sherman, Program Assistant, and Ragland Watkins, Associate Director, resign, and the staff is restructured. Valerie Smith is hired as Curator, and Susan Wyatt becomes Assistant Director. From 1981 to 1985 the programming of individual and group exhibitions is determined primarily by Linda Shearer and Valerie Smith. The first **Selections** exhibition from the Unaffiliated Artists File is inaugurated.

Sept. 23–Oct. 25: Donald Baechler, installation; Arch Connelly, installation; Nancy Dwyer, drawing; James Goss, painting; James Holl, *Wake Up! It's Time to Go to Work*, installation; Tom Koken, drawing.

↓ James Holl

ARTIST

Allan McCollum Linda Shearer was the one who came up with the idea of using the plaster surrogates as the emblem for the *Hundreds of Drawings* show. That was the first time the surrogates were ever used in any context as emblems for painting, which is what I originally wanted them to be used for. That is one of my favorite memories because I realized there weren't very many people sensitive to my idea. People showed my work, but nobody really followed my train of thought, and I felt Linda must have, at least a little bit. I don't know if I ever talked to her, but she picked up on their functioning as signs and wanted to use them that way. I appreciated it. I remember she was afraid I might not.

What I like is how many times the word "first" comes up in my memory of Artists Space. It's part of their charter. Artists can't already have shown in New York to show at Artists Space and once they've shown at Artists Space they can't show there again. So it's always going to wind up being the "first." Not to mention, of course, the first time I saw lots of other artists' work because it would have been the first time they'd shown. I moved to New York in '75 and my first group show was at Artists Space in December 1977. It was a benefit. Then I had my one-person exhibition there in February 1980. I had a show at 112 Workshop at the same time as the Artists Space show, but Artists Space's opened first. Then I received my first review from that show at Artists Space. It's on my resume. The first time I ever showed a professional photo was at Artists Space in the *35 Artists Return to Artists Space* exhibition in December 1981. I was with Sherrie Levine. God, that goes back! Tim Rollins bought a photo out of that show. It wasn't the first sale I made, but it was my first sale to Tim Rollins. Christo bought my first surrogate—that was really nice.

What I like is how many times the word "first" comes up in my memory of Artists Space. It's part of their charter.

Oct. 28: Joël Hubaut, *K.K. Song Epidemia*, performance. Part of *Une Ideé en l'Air*, works by French artists in galleries throughout New York.

Nov. 1 – Dec. 20: David Kulik, photomicrographs; Frank Majore, Kevin Noble, Ken Pelka, Pat Place, Brian Weil, photography; René Santos, photo-texts (Cindy Sherman).

→ Brian Weil

ARTIST

Carroll Dunham I met Rags Watkins when we were in Cincinnati. Rags had an idea to do a painting show which, in the context of what Artists Space was doing at the time, was an edgy and interesting idea. There wasn't a lot of painting being shown there. It came close to happening a couple of times, but it never came together. When Helene Winer left and Linda Shearer became the Director, Rags again proposed I show my work and Linda was very supportive of the idea.

I showed what I called drawings because they were on sheets of paper and involved a lot of pencil, but they were painted things. It was about two years before I started doing the wood grain. There had been a couple of other situations where one or two of them had been in a big show at P.S. 1 and a few were included in a watercolor show, but they hadn't really been seen. I'd been in New York for almost 10 years working for different artists. The Artists Space show was the first time a lot of people I knew saw what I did. The whole experience was very positive.

At the time I did that show there was certainly no awareness among the people I talked to that an imminent shift was about to happen in the art world. I thought the activity of painting was something pretty marginal. The people I hung out with weren't really doing it and the older artists I knew were coming from a very different direction. So, it came as a big surprise that there were all these other artists, within a year or two of me, who had drawn completely different conclusions about what was interesting to do in painting.

I had been making my work for a while and started to have enough confidence to invite people to my studio. When you put work up in a public place and you know a lot of people will see it who don't know you, it's easier than having it seen in your studio. But it changes something. It's not that I necessarily liked showing so much, but it was always clear if opportunities arose, I wanted to do it. After that I probably went through a reassessment or summarization of what I felt I was doing. I've never really understood what effect exhibiting has on what one does. I know having work seen in these neutral or public places is an important and strange dimension of making art.

The whole structure of the art scene is so different now. There are so many more galleries and levels of galleries and there are so many more artists. Artists Space's mandate is probably more complex now than it was then. Then it was pretty clear, it wasn't a commercially driven situation. Artists could begin to show without dealing with all those other issues. It's harder and harder for a young artist to do that now. I'm sorry it's changed and gotten more complicated and confusing. But, from where we are now, it looked positively simple, straightforward, and pure.

Jan. 17 – Feb. 28: **Architecture: Sequences** (Bernard Tschumi). Philippe Guerrier, photographs, books; Jenny Lowe, etchings and a model; Lorna McNeur, drawings and models; Deborah Oliver, Peter Wilson, drawings. Travels to the Renaissance Society, Chicago, Jan. 10 – Feb. 21, 1982, and to the Gallery at the Old Post Office, Dayton, May 25 – June 17, 1982 (through the Ohio Foundation for the Arts). Catalogue with essay by Bernard Tschumi.

↓ Julie Wachtel, *Chris*, installation. **Selections**, Mar. 14 – Apr. 25, 1981. Photo: David Lubarsky

Jan. 17–Feb. 28: Meryl Chernick, *Don't Make Waves*, film installation; Carroll Dunham, drawing; Tom Rubnitz, painting.

Mar. 4–6: **Slides and Music** (Charlie Ahearn).
Mar. 4: Robert Smith, *AmeriKKKa;* Peter Grass, *Eerie Site on Vision Street*.
Mar. 5: Christof Kolhofer, *Urban Terror;* Nan Goldin, *Motel, Hotel, Brothels & Bars*.
Mar. 6: Charlie A. and Fred, *The Patty Duke Show;* Jack Smith, *Art Crust on Crab Lagoon*.

Mar. 14–Apr. 25: **Selections** from the Unaffiliated Artists File (Linda Shearer). Richard R. Armijo, object and painting; Jay G. Coogan, installation; Kathleen Gilje, painting; Sidney McElhenney, painting; Jeffrey Mendoza, sculpture; Mike Metz, sculpture; Ronald Morosan, sculpture; Andrew Nash, sculpture; Maureen Pustay, painting; Erika Rothenberg, installation; Conrad Vogel, painting; Julie Wachtel, installation; Susan Yelavich, drawing and sculpture. Catalogue with introduction by Linda Shearer and statements by the artists.

ARTIST

Julie Wachtel I just took posters and wheat-pasted them directly onto the wall. The only intervention, aside from putting them in a gallery, was that I cast shadows of spectators by placing a light source in front of them and projecting a shadow, which I just colored in with black magic marker.

I was interested in ideas about desire and absence. In terms of the structure, I wanted an informal strategy that wasn't based on any ideas of composition, just images put next to each other as in a repetition. It was a language of images strung together. Essentially, I continue to do what I did in this early work, which is to deal with an emotional and subjective reaction to imagery. In a way, it's very simple. In this particular piece, there are all sorts of positions of power. There's an image of Mussolini, an authoritarian power figure; Veruschka, who's about sexual power: she's topless and has her hands going down her partly opened jeans; a little girl, orchestrating a kind of seductive power; and John Travolta, who is more an icon for Hollywood success and fame. Before, I was looking at mass media images, but this is the first work that successfully dealt with the images.

I don't want to be corny, but I have totally positive and great memories of Artists Space. Linda Shearer just pulled my work from the Artists Slide File and put me in a show, which was very exciting. She was completely supportive, as were the interns at the time, you (Claudia Gould) and Annie Philbin.

Apr. 28: Adrian Piper, *It's Just Art*, performance.

May 9–June 13: Gary Falk, cutouts and drawing; Brigid Kennedy, *Naked Raid,* installation; Ladd Kessler, *A Fragment from the Wonderful Past*, photo pieces; Peggy Yunque, *Zorro's Horse*, installation.

That's what Artists Space was like back then. They gave untried artists a chance and did all they could to help them look like professionals.

ARTIST

Ladd Kessler My first show in New York was at Artists Space. Nancy Dwyer and Cindy Sherman recommended me to Helene Winer. I made all the units for the installation in the studio. Then I came into the gallery the night before the opening to set up. I worked all night and into the next day and left when the staff arrived at 10 a.m. I went home, fell dead asleep, and missed the opening. While I was asleep Rags had taped over and painted all the brown spaghetti of wires I had left behind. He volunteered hours of his time to make the illusion of my work effective and complete. That's what Artists Space was like back then. They gave untried artists a chance and did all they could to help them look like professionals.

We were all going to clubs a lot in those days, and Robert Longo and Michael Zwack got a bunch of bands to come play at Artists Space. This is my favorite moment at Artists Space. It was historic. Teenage Jesus and the Jerks, The Contortions, Mars, Rhys Chatham. Brian Eno came by, dug it, and came out with the album, *No New York*, which is the definitive no wave album of that period. Unfortunately, the video made of those evenings is lost. Too many drugs in those days.

14.
WE DEFEND EACH OTHER
(YOU CERTAINLY DIDN'T COME TO AN ART PERFORMANCE TO HEAR A LECTURE ON CURRENT EVENTS)
troops

June 24–27: **Emergency: New Films by 13 New York Filmmakers** (Tim Burns). Liza Bear, *Souk El Arba*; Tim Burns, *Trespassed Philippa*; Manuel De Landa, *Magic Mushroom Mountain Home*; Sarah Driver, untitled police film; Bette Gordon, *Variety*; Jim Jarmusch, untitled; Karyn Kay, *149*; Haoui Montaug, *Un Chant Chant Chant d'Amour More More*; James Nares, *Waiting for the Wind*; Kiki Smith, *Pre-Cave*; Lindzee Smith, *No Credit*; Mindy Stephenson, *Drug Bust*; Betsy Sussler, *Horses Have Legs*.

↑ Philippe de Montaut, sets from *Jean Maurice n'est pas Rentre*, film and installation, Sep.19, 1987.

Tim Burns Basically, it was just finishing money. The idea was to give people a camera, some already had Super 8 cameras, or three or four rolls of Super 8 film. It was all Super 8, but there might have been a couple 16 mm movies. Each person was given an artist's fee of $75, that's why it was called *Emergency*. It was at a stage when everything was crashing. It was '81, the last vestiges of the 70s.

I had been in Australia away from the New York film world for two years to make *Against the Brain,* which showed at Bleecker Street. I'd come back to New York to work with Nightshift Theater Group, but I missed the city when it was really happening at Club 57 and another joint in the Village. Tier 3 was around then, too, and the Mudd Club, where I showed *Against the Brain*, when I first got back with it. I was just looking around to see what everyone was doing. And everyone was waiting for money for some project to shoot something. It was just at that point when the new cinema, all the New Wave stuff, had stopped. Jim Jarmusch was working on *Strangers*, that came out a couple of years later. What he ended up doing for *Emergency* was like an environmental mood piece, a long tracking shot through the Lower East Side, which ends up in some tension with this character played by Richard Boes. Liza Bear was finishing something she had been shooting in Africa. Manuel De Landa had a couple of films. He showed *Magic Mountain,* about a Mexican village with a family.

When *Philippa* was screened at Artists Space, people smashed up the furniture. It was a real riot, because, at that stage, it was the first time anyone had shown serious shooting up. Amy Taubin said it was like *The Connection*. It was a music and a drug-crazed thing coming out of the punk 70s. It was supposed to be anti-drugs, but it caused a terrible furor. I had to pull the film out of circulation—it's only been shown four times. When someone in the audience saw someone in the film who shouldn't have been where they were, they smashed up the chairs and caused an enormous amount of damage in the end. There was a very polarized audience. The people who were in my movie caught a lot of shit and I got a lot of shit. In simple terms, I showed people getting high in the most brutal fashion—that's basically what it amounted to.

So it was a very heavy little piece. It was at a point when a lot of people were into the dope, they couldn't control it, and actually became strung out. Many people emerged and submerged. And then AIDS came along and hit them from another angle altogether. The dope wasn't that strong in comparison to what's going on now. The problem was that I shot this movie in and about people around me. Then, when I showed it, it was too compromising to those people who may have or may not have had careers of their own. I could screen it where no one knew anyone, but anywhere close to home it caused all sorts of ramifications later on. In fact, the negative was burned by customs when the film toured Australia. I did a Super 8 tour of New York films in Australia that grew straight out of *Emergency*, which Lindzee Smith traveled with. But that all came to a major disaster.

The situation with my first Artists Space screening in '77, when I showed *Why Cars?—CARnage!*, was you got paid by the minute, $1 a minute. Actually, the film broke down. It was about the performance relationship to Super 8 and everything going wrong all the time: problems occurring in projection,

> *In simple terms, I showed people getting high in the most brutal fashion— that's basically what it amounted to.*

lamps burning out, film caught in the gate and catching on fire. There was a structure and a process, a series of films built up over a period of time. When the projector caught fire, I'd have to rush out into the audience and see how long I could hold them in their seats. I extended the show about two and a half hours. I was forcing people not to leave. And then we had a payoff there at the end. It ran for however long I could keep the audience there. It broke down in the middle, then I would say, "I filmed the gate burning up in the film so when it happens inside the film it looks like the film's stuck in the gate and it's burning." So then it would jam up and start melting with smoke and I'd turn the projector off and run out into the audience. I sang a song, I cried, I went through a series of performances all based around the suicide of this guy who killed himself because he'd lost his license for drunk driving in Melbourne or somewhere and without a car he's nothing. It was like a reality performance. When people started to leave, I turned the film back on and finished it. It was actually an homage to the blackout of 1977 in New York: "When the lights went out the city came face to face with the antagonisms of a society at war with itself." That was from the communist manifesto on the blackout, or something like it.

In a way, the Super 8's were the most successful and interesting for me—to be carrying the projector around and actually perform inside the mechanism of the film. But I could never get back to it.

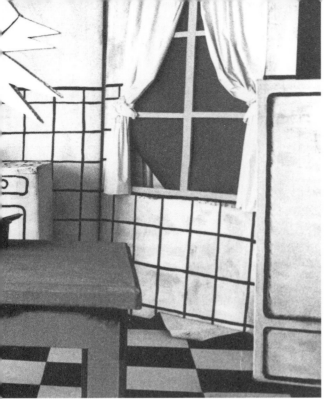

Well, it may have been cool, but Helene was embarrassed by the bleeding-heart liberal aspect of it; although it didn't harm the organization to have that. When Helene arrived all of that ended. There was no longer artists choosing artists, but artists recommending artists.

The thing about Artists Space was that it was somewhat of an open venue. Its mission was to show young artists. So people with a certain level of ambition would approach us. And people who had a coherent and interesting enough body of work would make an exhibition. Otherwise, we would put them in the Artists Slide File. There was something we could do for everybody, which was good. This was one of the great things about that job, you could be a hero. You could give people their first show, then get rid of them and never see them again. You could get credit without having to put up with their day-to-day whining.

While I had this great-sounding job description as a curator, I was actually called Associate Director of Exhibitions. I did two or three studio visits a week for about four years and Helene and I would talk about what I would see; if it made sense to do a show we did it. I also did a lot of the grunt work and all the technical aspects of the exhibitions, which I liked doing. Things like mailing, printing, catalogue stock, installing the show, press services. I felt a tremendous sense of closure from the beginning of a show to when it came down.

I knew Tip (Carroll) Dunham and Laurie Simmons, because they lived in my building. Laurie's was the first show in that hall. Then we started doing shows in a couple of cleared-out storage spaces. In one of them, Christy Rupp once had live geese. That was wackier than something we might have had in the gallery. I knew Dennis Adams from Ohio. He came and showed his work to me at Artists Space. It looked like something to do, so we did it in Room 207. He explained to me that the security guards were part of the whole aesthetic of the thing. So they showed up, but only for the opening. Helene went wacky, she thought it was self-important.

The Nigger Drawings controversy blew up the following Tuesday after the opening. A bunch of people led a march on Artists Space. And Helene, in typical fashion, decided to stonewall them, and didn't open the gallery. Helene doesn't like complications, she'd rather just go away. Then the next day she changed her mind, because it just seemed ridiculous. Of course, there was all the fallout after. We had to deal with a lot of calls. Kitty Carlisle Hart from NYSCA came by, beautifully dressed with her daytime diamonds. I was introduced to Kitty by Susan Wyatt, who said, "This is Rags Watkins, he takes care of the gallery," and Kitty said, "Well it looks lovely," thinking I was the janitor. It was just a big mess.

It was around this time that we really started fundraising. *Pictures*, which was presented by a liquor company, was perhaps the first sponsored exhibition. Then we did a general fundraiser, the first being at the Mudd Club. It became clear we needed to do them because NYSCA was drying up. Essentially Artists Space had been the creature of NYSCA, which was its exclusive funder. The gallery had been a way for NYSCA to channel money directly to artists at a lower level than was possible through them.

Artists Space did not have a fundraising Board. Since Helene was doing the grant writing, she felt she could call the shots on how the organization was run. When she realized she was going to leave, the Board started heating up. Somebody had to take over. This is my memory, which may not be absolutely accurate. Helene tolerated Irving. And Irving, in a professorial way, tolerated Helene like a bad kid. Helene had certain adolescent behaviors—a lot of it was about that. It was unrealistic, organizational ha ha ha. It was really a fun place.

CURATOR

Ragland Watkins The first show I was involved with was *Pictures*. I arrived the same day as the catalogue. It was a good packed opening. I was told not to wear a jacket. We always had wine or liquor and all you had to do was open a bottle and you got a crowd. *Pictures* generated a lot of interest and actually more as it receded into the past. It's greater than any of the individuals in it. There may have been a little tug o' war between Doug Crimp and Helene Winer about who was responsible for what. Ultimately, that was the beginning of their falling out. She felt successful and maybe he didn't feel he was very successful—I don't say it's rational. Anyway, that was my perception of the situation. Helene may have been the source of all these people, because most of them were from Cal Arts. But Doug did the essay and made sense out of it.

Helene was very interesting to talk to. She has a fabulous sense of humor and a very clear sense about what she wants and what she doesn't want. At times it may have been too narrow but, in retrospect, it was part of her great strength. As the Director she was absolutely focused in this very specific direction.

Basically it was Helene and me making decisions, with Helene having the inside track. Artists were attracted to her, gravitated to her. She was cool, but sympathetic at the same time, which is a great combination. But I can tell you, before Helene came Artists Space was not cool.

1981–82

The **U.S. Projects** begins as a series, for which 10 art professionals from around the country each select one artist from their region to do a site-specific installation at Artists Space.

Sept. 19–Oct. 17: Annette Messager, *Les Variétés*, painted photo installation; Philippe de Montaut, sets from *Jean Maurice n'est pas rentre*, film, screenings Sept. 19, 26, Oct. 3, 10, 17; Tom Wolf, painting.

→ Annette Messager, announcement card

Oct. 24–Nov. 21: Seven-person exhibition (Walter Robinson). Ellen Cooper, painting; Jane Dickson, painting; Bobby G, painting; Rebecca Howland, sculpture; Cara Perlman, painting; Kiki Smith, painting; Seton Smith, screens and drawing.

← Bobby G.
Photo: Ann Turyn

Oct. 24–Nov. 21:
U.S. Projects. Meridel Rubenstein, New Mexico, *The Low Riders*, installation (Jean-Edith Weiffenbach).

Oct. 24–Nov. 21: Glenys Johnson, *Wall Drawing*, installation.

ARTIST
Jane Dickson

I was part of a seven-person exhibition at Artists Space organized by Walter Robinson in 1981. Thinking of that show provokes me to remember how many different points in my career Walter has been helpful without making any fuss about it. He included all the artists he felt hadn't yet received the attention they deserved. Walter's like the patron saint and the single-handed bandwagon of the under-recognized. Also, Artists Space was the first place I showed the *Times Squares* paintings, which have taken me a long way since then.

I remember the opening for *Witnesses.* Just the title, *Witnesses: Against Our Vanishing*, reveals it as a show commemorating people who were not sufficiently recognized. It was a really powerful show. I came to the opening with two babies, I had a newborn and a three-and-a-half year old, so I was semi shell-shocked as I was going through the exhibition, thinking maybe this wasn't such a good idea.

I knew Nan Goldin from the Museum School in Boston. It was Nan's coming out party after having been in rehab in Boston. It was important to me on a personal level, as well as politically. It was exciting to be part of that experience and to see Nan recovered and pulling together her political and personal strengths, as well as bringing awareness and attention to everybody else who needed help and hadn't gotten it. She also brought together a whole cross-section of friends like David Wojnarowicz, Linda Yablonsky, and Cookie Mueller.

ARTIST
Annette Messager

The time I spent at Artists Space represents my youth. I was completely unconscious of everything in terms of the future, but they were very happy days of my life. Maybe my show contributed to the development of new work with photos and painting together—it exploded them. I showed two different pieces, *The Vanities* and *The Clues,* which were smaller. They were little signs, like a cross or a circle, and always with a photo of the body, hands, or eyes. I prefer this memory, because *The Vanities* was my fun period. Sometimes a series is important, not because it is a very good series, or that the material is very good, but because you are between two periods. It is important to do this kind of work.

Helene Winer asked me to do the show, but she had just left and Linda Shearer became the Director. It is funny to think that Cindy Sherman was working there at the phone. She was very shy. During this show I met Jack Goldstein and he bought a small piece from me. I remember somebody told me Robert De Niro was leaving his building and I went over to the big picture window in the gallery to see him on Hudson Street. Wim Wenders was at the opening with a French girlfriend whom I knew a little. He was very nice, spoke about the show, and said he liked the work. It was a very American and very New York experience, and, for these reasons, it was important for the development of my work. The problem, though, with this kind of not-so-perfect place, is if you have no recommendation, I am not sure commercial galleries come to see the shows. Although, just after Artists Space, I did a show in Cincinnati with Judy Pfaff.

→ Jim Isermann, *Patio Tempo*, installation. Jan. 9–Feb. 13, 1982.

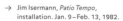

Dec. 4–24: **35 Artists Return to Artists Space: A Benefit Exhibition** (Linda Shearer). Sponsored by 15 New York galleries representing artists who first showed at Artists Space, from its founding in 1973 through 1980. Artists Space receives a contribution for each work sold. Auste, acrylic paint on paper; James Biederman, sculpture; Jonathan Borofsky, installation; Gary Bower, painted vessel; Troy Brauntuch, drawing; Farrell Brickhouse, painting; Gary Burnley, sculpture; Scott Burton, sculpture;

Cynthia Carlson, installation; Charles Clough, painting; R.M. Fischer, lamp; Hermine Ford, painting; Jack Goldstein, painting; Don Gummer, sculpture; Mel Kendrick, sculpture; Lois Lane, painting; Thomas Lawson, painting; Robert Longo, drawing; Allan McCollum, installation; Ree Morton, painting; Matt Mullican, drawing; Judy Pfaff, sculpture; Richard Prince, photograph; Judy Rifka, painting; Walter Robinson, drawing; David Salle, drawing; Thomas Lanigan-Schmidt,

sculpture; Barbara Schwartz, painting; Cindy Sherman, photograph; Laurie Simmons, photograph; Charles Simonds, photomural; Jenny Snider, painting; Donald Sultan, drawing; Anthony Thompson, painting; John Torreano, painting. Catalogue with essay by William Zimmer.

Jan. 9–Feb. 13: Jenny Holzer/Peter Nadin, *Eating Friends*, texts and images on copper plates.

Jan. 9–Feb. 13: Jim Isermann, *Patio Tempo*, installation.

ARTIST

Jenny Holzer I recall quite clearly Louise Lawler had a portrait of a racehorse with a very strong light on it. I thought, "What a very peculiar and great piece," and it made me very curious about her work and about her.

I also have a strong impression of Cindy Sherman out front at the typewriter. I was transfixed by her and because of that, of course, afraid of her. Anything I like I'm afraid of, so I would stand where I could watch her. She looked so good and so strong due in part to the typewriter, which looked that good and that hopeful. I had the feeling she dressed for the part and did it so well, with grace and a sense of humor, that her looks were encouraging, too. I have yet to see a woman dress so appropriately, for any part.

The other image I have is of Mike (Walter) Robinson always hanging around the office talking—he's very oral—having long conversations about how hard it is to find a place to live and that you always have to build it yourself.

Jan. 9–Feb. 13:
U.S. Projects. Jim Sanborn, Washington, D.C., *Invisible Forces*, installation (Howard Fox); Hudson/Buzz Tone Outlet, Cincinnati, Ohio, *No More Magic*, installation (Ruth Meyer).

Feb. 20–Mar. 27: **A Likely Story** (Valerie Smith). Gretchen Bender, photolithographs on metal plates; David Cabrera, photographs; Ronald Jones, installation; Jeff Koons, sculpture; David Robinson, photographs.

→ Ronald Jones

Feb. 20–Mar. 27:
U.S. Projects. Stephen Lapthisophon, Chicago, Illinois, *After All (For R.P.W.)*, installation (Judith Russi Kirshner).

ARTIST

Hudson Artists Space, yeah. Well, it figures most prominently in my late 70s–early 80s calendar. One of those rare serendipitous things: right place, right time. Shit, even if I didn't like the exhibition, there was always the idea. Ideas, ideas, ideas, so many good ideas flowed through that place. It was inspiring.

Through their exhibition program I met a number of artists with whom I have remained friends. Jim Isermann exhibited there at the same time that I did and for the past nine or ten years I have represented his work.

ARTIST / BOARD

Ronald Jones The big difference between what Claudia Gould has to deal with and what Linda Shearer and you (Valerie Smith) had to deal with was the appearance of the East Village and a market structure that supported young artists. Now, with an adjusted marketplace, Artists Space is having one of its nine lives handed back to it. That's very significant, because it had a huge credibility problem for a while. Claudia has made it her goal, first to get it on a good economic footing, which she's managed to do, and now, to bring young artists back to Artists Space. As a Board member that is what I am most interested in doing.

The show I organized, *Customized Terror,* was the first show during Claudia's administration in which artists who have previously shown at Artists Space come back to organize a show. And I think it had roughly the same effect on the young artists I invited as your (Valerie Smith) show, *A Likely Story,* had on me when I first came up. At the risk of sounding nostalgic, when I showed at Artists Space there was no other place where anybody could effectively start, not even Franklin Furnace or White Columns. Artists Space was the only game in town and you (Valerie Smith), Linda, and Helene were able to almost take this for granted. That priviledged position has to be reestablished. Artists Space has a history and a momentum which it never lost. Claudia's just been able to reanimate it in an important way.

I really like the spirit Claudia created bringing in fashion, architecture, and design, so for *Customized Terror* I invited two artists, Brian Tolle and Brian Crockett, and a collective, the graphic design group, Designers Republic. It wasn't necessary they represent or express a theme. I was thinking about *A Likely Story,* when those of us in the show didn't necessarily hang together, but there was a discernible thread. The same thing occurred with *Customized Terror.* There was enough space for the artists to actually show what they can do on some serious level. When the Artists Space newspaper came out, I wrote an essay and asked Jan Avgikos to write one and it gave them all a kick start. The Designers Republic is a business, so they got some attention that came from various angles. But Brian Tolle went immediately into a commercial gallery and Brian Crockett, while he got offers and was in the Whitney Biennial, decided to go solo and he's been able to manage it all on his own. That also struck me as a fairly different approach from the way it was when dinosaurs walked the earth.

Meeting Tom Lawson completely opened up the critical scene for me, because he was so closely associated with Artists Space and the crowd that circulated around it. I think he took on a guru status for everybody because he had such careful insights about them. He was the predominant critical spokesperson for that particular period because he wrote the most intelligent criticism, not only about Artists Space and the artists around Artists Space, but also about that circle of artists as they began to fan out into the real world. This also reflects on Artists Space.

When I asked Tom what I should do, there was really only one option from his point of view, which was to go and see Artists Space. My installation there was a reconstruction of a show at the Green Gallery. I used Douglas Huebler's titles, so his attorney called the morning after the opening and rattled his sword, then we never heard from him again. Preceding *A Likely Story* with Jeff Koons, Gretchen Bender, David Cabrera, and myself, Jenny Holzer and Peter Nadin did an installation, *Eating Friends*. It was an amazing intersection of people. If you just look at those two exhibitions it gives a flavor of what it was like at the time.

My connection with Helene Winer happened three or four years later. I had been writing a lot about the Metro Pictures crowd, principally because of the kind of sensitivity I had experienced at Artists Space and reflected by the fact that Jeff, Gretchen, and Louise (Lawler) had just been there. I was very interested in that particular point of view. But the credit goes to Tom, who told Helene and Janelle Reiring I was also an artist. They came over to my studio and offered me a show. I have to say, I am the Artists Space poster child. I'm like one of Jerry's Kids. Had it not been for you (Valerie Smith) and then Helene…In that sense Artists Space did work, it had an effect, and that's exactly how the Metro Pictures thing fell into place.

Feb. 20 – Mar. 27: Stephen Miller, installation.

↖ Gretchen Bender, *The Pleasure Is Back*, 1982.

Gretchen Bender I wanted to do a scan of these pieces from a series of photo-silkscreens I called *The Pleasure Is Back*. I was taking the appropriation strategies of Sherrie Levine and Richard Prince into what I thought was upping the ante a little. What happens if I reproduce my contemporaries? How would it advertise, an advertisement of art? I was just into a scan rather than a contemplative thing, that was my structure. I wanted this linear look along the wall where your eye would quickly register the arrangement of pieces. You (Valerie Smith) gave Jeff Koons the wall opposite mine in the main gallery. He had a vacuum cleaner in a plexiglass case in the center of the room and a light box with an image of himself as a smiling first grader on the wall. We were able to look in through the big picture window at the end of the gallery and see my work on one wall and his on the other. When Jeff came over to the space he said, "This isn't the way it should be. My work needs to be in the front on both sides." I didn't understand this because I thought it would throw off the whole balance, not just in my work, but in his work, too. So there was a lot of arguing back and forth. And you (Valerie) got caught in the middle wanting to appease Jeff and keep your promise to me. You were in a difficult situation. It was so stressful. I was bewildered because I thought he was not only sabotaging my work, but his own! But then I realized he just wanted people to see his work on both sides of the wall when they looked through the picture window. This was my first show and he was so persistent in his obsessive way.

He said the work had been at Beaubourg (Centre Georges Pompidou) in Paris where the light hit it a certain way, and he needed that light. Now, we're talking about fluorescent light boxes and plexiglass: glowing things. By that time I was

Apr. 1 – 3: **Events** (Valerie Smith).
Reading: Apr. 1: Schuldt, *Life and Death in China (Liu's Dictionary populated)*; Barry Yourgrau, *Man Jumps Out of an Airplane*.

Film and Video: Apr. 2: David Cabrera, *Covers*, *Say When* and untitled; Sharon Greytak, *Sleeping, April 7, 1981*, *Some Pleasure on the Level of the Source*, and *Czechoslovakian Woman*; Sokhi Wagner, *Zone* and *Unrest (a working title)*. Apr. 3: Barbara Broughel, *Princess Grace* and

Count Vestibule, two untitled films, *Genre Lesson #1* and *Genre Lesson #2*, video; John Jesurun, *Last Days of Pompeii* and *Stella Maris*; Jessica Spohn, *Peace Talk* and *Coast to Coast*; Dan Walworth, *House by the River: The Wrong Shape*.

so worn down and frazzled, I went home and just burst into tears. At home Robert (Longo) asked me what was going on, so I told him the whole story. He said it was bullshit and he couldn't believe Jeff was pulling that. What are we talking about, the light in Paris and the light on Hudson Street? Robert was so incensed that he went over to Artists Space and Linda had to step in because we had reached an impasse. But, after a couple of days of trying to reason with him we decided, because Jeff was so persistent, we would rearrange the work the way he wanted, just to see if it would work. And it didn't. So when he saw this he was finally convinced. This was my first exhibition experience. I'd always heard stories about how artists can be so temperamental and difficult. I didn't want to be one of those artists. I was just dying because I was trying to protect the integrity of my idea, but not wanting to be overbearing either. In the end we all went over to McSorley's Bar and finally I felt just fine. In fact, I got a kick out of Jeff! He wasn't a yeller or a screamer. He was the ultimate salesman, just wearing you down.

Jeff Koons I always went to the exhibitions at Artists Space when I was first settling in New York as an artist, and I always enjoyed them. A lot of my friends had already shown there, Richard Prince and others. I was working day and night on my first encased vacuum cleaner pieces, trying to get one finished for a commercial gallery here in New York. It was my triple decker. I just couldn't get the piece finished in time for that show. The day I called this gallery to tell them that the piece wouldn't be finished in time, I could hardly speak. I had lost my voice from working day and night for weeks and weeks. I felt sad because I was at my financial end. I'd invested all my money into the work and I was really down about it. Then you (Valerie Smith) offered to show the work at Artists Space. Even though I had been in other exhibitions prior to Artists Space, Artists Space was my first formal dialogue with the New York art community.

I always appreciated Artists Space for its efforts in the community, giving artists an opportunity to show their work. They've always tried to show cutting-edge work. So people understood I was somebody who wanted to

participate in the community and have a dialogue within art. Showing my encased pieces at Artists Space felt like one of my most important moments. After that, I eventually did go broke and I had to move out of my studio and apartment and go back home. I lived with my parents for a couple of months to save up enough money to rent an apartment again in New York. Then I just let things resonate until I did a show with the basketballs in 1985 at International with Monument. I find myself in the same boat today with the *Celebration* work. A lot of people have never really understood that I always put everything back into the art. So I'm in the same position financially as I was when I was making those encased pieces.

Apr. 10–May 15: **Young Fluxus** (Ken Friedman and Peter Frank with Elizabeth Brown). John Armleder, installation; Don Boyd, installation; Jean Dupuy, constructions; Valery and Rimma Gerlovin, boxes and installation; J. H. Kocman, books; Carla Liss, objects and X-rays; Larry V. Miller, objects; Endre Tot, banner; Peter van Riper, performance and prints; Yoshimasa Wada, sculpture. Catalogue with essays by Ken Friedman and Peter

Frank with Elizabeth Brown. Exhibition travels to the Washington Project for the Arts, Washington, D.C., Sept. 24–Nov. 5, 1982.

Apr.13: Lecture and symposium: *On Fluxus*.

Apr. 10–May 15: **U.S. Projects**. Bruce Charlesworth, Minneapolis, Minnesota, *Lost Dance Steps*, installation with video (Lisa Lyons); Tad Savinar, Portland, Oregon, *Rock*, installation (Mary Beebe).

May 20–22: **Events** (Valerie Smith).

Film:
May 20: Robert Attanasio, *Reagan: Due Process*, film; Richard Baim, *Watch and Wait*, slide show; Keith Sanborn, *The Unseen Hand*, *Kapital*, and *Imitation of Life*, film.

Film and performance:
May 21: Jeff Balsmeyer and Kirby Dick, *Men Who Are Men*, film; Ericka Beckman, *Out of Hand*, film; Ashley Bickerton, *The Love Story of Pythagoras Red Hill*, film.

May 22: Paul McMahon, *Songs*, performance with painted backdrops, *Flattering the Flatterers,* by Nancy Chunn.

→ Paul McMahon and Nancy Chunn

Gilles Jean Giuntini There was a funny incident related to Harm Bouckhaert Gallery. I had gone in there several weeks prior to my show at Artists Space to see if they wanted to look at my work and they said, "No, we're not looking at anybody," and sent me on my way. So I forgot about it. A month and a half later I received a letter from Harm Bouckhaert saying he happened to see my show across the street at Artists Space and wanted to come over to look at my work and talk to me about having a show. I always found that ironic. I never told them about the episode when they shooed me away—that's water under the bridge. It was indicative of what a strong influence Artists Space had. There were so many artists who got their start there and consequently were picked up by galleries. It made people legitimate and it allowed them to be taken a bit more seriously. There were some great shows at Artists Space over the years. The show I had there was pivotal in a lot of ways, not only because it generated solo shows in New York for me, but also in terms of the academic world. Artists Space is very highly respected at the university where I teach, and this helped me get tenure and promoted down the line.

May 29–July 17: **Façades, Landscapes, Interiors** (Valerie Smith). Andrea Evans, Brad Melamed, Aric Obrosey, *Stairway to Suburbia*, installation; Gilles Jean Giuntini, sculpture; Tony Oursler, sets for video; Maggie Saliske, sculpture; Gail Swithenbank, installation.

May 29–July 17:
Primer (for Raymond Williams).
Collaborative installation by **Group
Material (& friends)**, with photographs,
paintings, sculpture, mixed media pieces,
and installations by 30 artists, including
Mario Asaro, Douglas Ashford, Conrad
Atkinson, Futura 2000, Margaret Harrison,
Yolanda Hawkins, Lisa Kahane, Mundy
McLaughlin, Candace Hill Montgomery,
Joseph Nechvatal, Paulette Nenner, Anne

Pitrone, Tim Rollins. Included in the
exhibition are Irish Northern Aid posters,
artifacts from the revolution in Nicaragua,
film stills, magazine pages, and James
Brown records.

← Photo: Anne Turyn

FILMMAKER

Sharon Greytak It was late afternoon. David Springer and I were
in a taxi on the way down to Artists Space and the very first screening
I had in New York . The most vivid image I have of that day is looking
out the windshield of the taxi on the New York urban landscape below
Canal Street where it opens up and there's a horizon. I guess the feeling I had
was that artistically, anything was possible. David and I were grad students.
It was a threshold to a professional thing, when you're no longer a student.
It was a very personal image.

ARTIST

Tim Rollins I'd been involved with the Left wing of the art world
through a group called AMCC. They had meetings at Artists Space on
Wooster Street every Sunday night, or every first Sunday of the month,
for about two years. They were pandemonium sessions, it was great. In the
beginning, Sol LeWitt would be there, Carl Andre would get up and give
speeches, people would just get up. There'd be rip-roaring fights between
Art and Language and *The Fox* folk. Joseph Kosuth was the subject of so much
derision. It was the most amazing education—very exciting. There would
also be May Stevens and Rudolf Baranik. I have good memories of those
meetings. And people were quite hurt, too, because we'd be loud. We
continued to meet when Artists Space moved to Hudson Street, but by then
it began to fizzle out.

Artists are impossible to organize politically for the long term, whether
it's WAC (Women's Action Coalition), or some other group. That's why the
longevity of Group Material is amazing. We got together in 1979 and just
disbanded last year after almost 20 years. Incredible! I left the group,
physically, if not spiritually and intellectually, right after the *Education*
installation at Dia Center for the Arts. That was my swan song. At that time,
I'd finally left the public school system, and thought we had a chance to do
something extraordinary with K.O.S. But it was going to take a superhuman
effort to pull it off, which it did. There's no way it could have happened
had I still been with Group Material. We had different attitudes about what
we wanted to do. I regretted not being in the group, but I didn't regret
not going to those meetings. I felt more a part of it when I left. I talk to Doug
(Ashford), I talk to Julie (Ault). I had felt incredibly guilty because I had
such loyalty to the group. But I felt less guilty about leaving knowing Félix
González-Torres was taking my place. I am like a stubborn little terrier.
I said, "All these groups start and then fall to pieces. Let's get some
longevity here, let's keep it going."

Raymond Williams was the coolest guy on earth. He completely defied
the stereotype of the Marxist-Leftist intellectual. He was replete with
common sense and he had a love ethos about him, he loved people, and he
didn't want to see them hurt. He also didn't have any romantic ideas about
revolution. He had a novel, exuberant, and celebratory notion of what
happiness is all about. That was rare among Marxists. They were saying you
had to wade through rivers of blood in order to achieve a just society. I met
Raymond Williams when he lectured at New York University and he said,
"You know, people don't want to wade through rivers of blood. It's not

necessary." Of course, all his ideas became true,
particularly in Czechoslovakia and the Soviet
Union. I loved his unique and speculative, joyful
and playful approach to knowledge. I loved the
structure of his books. He was such an inspiration.
His book, *Key Words,* is *my* primer. In the early 80s
a lot of young artists who were interested in
politics, culture, and literature read that work. It is
a glossary and social history of words we take for
granted everyday. So, it profoundly lent itself as a
theme for an exhibition using the idea of a work of
art to define a word that is ambiguous in its uses.

It was a collective decision to do the exhibition
around Raymond Williams. I was very excited, but
so was Doug. Everything in Group Material was
collectively decided. No one person could come
up with an idea, it would have to come from the
whole group. Otherwise, it wouldn't fly. However,
this approach did create problems. Individual
members had some great ideas that weren't
executed, because they were one person's idea.

Because of the social nature of the Group
Material projects, many different people,
nonmembers, would participate. We'd hang out
after a day of installing and those people would
be part of the family for that particular project.
If they wanted to stay with the family, they could.
If they didn't, they could leave. It was never a dry
curatorial project. It was more social, and we'd all
have so much fun, that they would want to hang
out with us afterwards. That's what I loved about
Group Material. I met Brad Melamed and Ashley
Bickerton that way. They were showing at Artists
Space at the same time we were, and we talked
forever. Artists Space became an amazing social
setting. I miss that in these spaces today.

Coming to what you could call the mainstream
of alternativeness, Artists Space was alright, but it

CONTINUED

Tim Rollins and the K.O.S.

was almost like crossing the DMZ. Group Material wasn't alternative for the sake of being alternative, it just wanted to do something different. We wanted to do a show at Artists Space because we were invited and it was a wonderful venue, but it was a netherworld between our grassroots funky thing and the more mainstream institutions, which were mainly galleries. We thought we could participate and celebrate Artists Space by working with them and not being puritanical about it. We were also self-critical at the same time, in terms of why we were doing the show in the first place. For instance, why not stay on 13th Street? Why did we respond to the invitation? Why did we want a different audience? We came at it from a very critical stance, critical of ourselves, the space, and of what we were doing. But we also saw it as a wonderful opportunity to do this installation that probably wouldn't have worked in any other venue. I think our doubts came out in the piece. It wasn't a slick exhibition. It was very unusual even for Artists Space. We tried to create an alternative artists' space within the context of Artists Space. We'd done this strategy before, but it was the most successful at Artists Space, at P.S. 1 with the *Timeline* work, and at the Whitney Biennial with *Americana*, in which we did a mini biennial within the Biennial. But the reality is it's very hard for individual work to transcend the context. It's as if you have the most wonderful wine in the world, but it's going to take the form of the vessel it's poured into. This was especially true at the Whitney Biennial, you can't beat it. That's why it's so problematic. So in the *Americana* project we tried to critique it, show an alternative to it, tweak it, but also celebrate it because we participated in it. We're not negative folks. Critique is not necessarily negative. It can be playful and joyous and fun. Raymond Williams had that spirit. He wasn't dour, dry, anti everything, like some Left wing folk we all know so well.

As a participant in AMCC gatherings, I was also a demonstrator in front of Artists Space during *The Nigger Drawings* incident in 1979. It was fun. But after, I questioned whether it was right to have demonstrated and whether AMCC really had an argument. Looking back, we did the right thing, especially since it was only a single afternoon demonstration. We weren't violent or disrespectful, so I felt proud about what we did. People were being far too cavalier about these issues. It wasn't about the drawings. It was about this particular artist and this particular institution using these terms in order to get a rise. It was insensitive and it was time to become more sensitive about what was going on. Who's let in, who's not, and how alternative was alternative? The word was thrown around a lot, and we didn't see anything that could be called truly alternative. It seemed more like a showcase or a clearinghouse for the galleries to take a look at what was going on. There's absolutely nothing wrong with that, but then don't call yourself a radical space, if you're only replicating, in a smaller way, what's happening in the

galleries. So we were looking for alternative, but with a capital "A." Ultimately, it was a wake-up call to say, "It's time to start paying attention to the diversity of artists within New York City." The art world definitely had to do that, but they have only just caught up in the last four or five years.

The Nigger Drawings was a major event and I don't think its importance is really understood. But the incident had a big impact, especially on Janelle Reiring and Helene Winer. And now, they are probably in the avant-garde of the few commercial galleries that have a diverse group of artists. However, early on, Group Material, without a doubt, had the most diverse shows of any group in New York. Of course, we couldn't be compared to El Taller Boricua—next door to the Museo del Barrio—or the Studio Museum in Harlem, where everyone is going to be black. But we had a good mix from the very beginning. It all came out of a sense of quality. We were never into tokenism. We looked at the coolest work around and opened our eyes to what was dynamic. In every case, we had a fantastic coalition of men, women, African Americans, Asian Americans, Latino Americans, gays, lesbians, straight folk. It wasn't a quota system. It was about looking at the work which most dynamically addressed the social theme. We had themes and that was the key to our success. When you really looked and did your research, you'd end up having a fantastic diversity of artists without being a liberal paternalist or maternalist.

But a space's past doesn't determine its future. That's why I don't like Left wing determinist aesthetics. I know a lot of people who did stuff back then and they're doing new stuff now. Even Howardena Pindell did pretty paintings with perfume on them for a while and then she became political. People change and really great spaces are organic. The artists who show at any given space at any given time depends on who's the director or who's on the board of directors. This is all in flux, it's not written in stone. People can't hang on to their

CONTINUED

TIM ROLLINS / CONTINUED

bitterness to the point where their whole identity is linked to it. I have a great right to be bitter, but I'm not. I'm happy! That is why I wasn't opposed to returning to Artists Space to make *Primer (for Raymond Williams)* in 1982 after *The Nigger Drawings* incident. You go through stuff and it gives you power and wisdom. I'm fearless talking about these issues because I have such a deep relationship with the South Bronx community I live in now. I've raised 10 kids of color. Angel's 22 years old, he's like my son. I'm a minister of praise and worship at a black Baptist church in Harlem. So I've gotten a little more fearless when I talk about the real things that need to be talked about. Like, what is the art about and what is the function of a particular space? The function of Artists Space is to 1) give artists their first shows so they can see what they're capable of doing outside their studio, 2) give them confidence, and 3) let the work be seen outside the commercial arena. That's the key. Show it outside the marketplace. Ellen Gallagher's paintings looked really different at Artists Space than they did at the Mary Boone Gallery or at the Larry Gagosian Gallery. The context is completely different. We desperately need a context like Artists Space that is not in the frying pan of commercialism.

The shows in which artists chose other artists were wonderful. I was always curious to see them. One of my best friends now is Renny Molenaar, who was in the same show as Ellen Gallagher, *Artists "Select," Part I* (Nov. 20, 1993 – Jan. 15, 1994). He had rocks wrapped in lace. So I called a friend and said, "You have got to go and see this show!" Artists Space is a place where you can see stuff like that. I wish there were more shows like it. But you can't do every show in the same way because artists are not necessarily the best antennae for what's going on. You do need curators and professionals who see the whole process through. I think that's what I miss. I miss the fact that Artists Space felt to me more like a social space, particularly when Linda Shearer was there. She was like the coolest mom, the whole place was a family. That needs to come back. Maybe that's impossible right now.

We desperately need a context like Artists Space that is not in the frying pan of commercialism.

Michael Byron
The first piece I did at Artists Space was in May of 1982. It was an installation called *For the Nun*, based on an incident that occurred in September of '81. It involved a young novice who had been raped and brutalized, then disfigured by a pair of guys who had been high on freebase cocaine. The tabloids in New York got a hold of the story and it captured the imagination and attention of New York for a while. Later, it became the subject for the Abel Ferrara movie, *The Bad Lieutenant.* I kept a lot of the clippings from the *New York Post* and the *Daily News* about the rape. The incident got a second life in the tabloids when organized crime came into the picture and put a contract out on the rapists.

The piece I did evolved from my studio practice at the time, which was to take home discarded pieces of plywood from the job site I was working at, put them into different configurations, and apply a faux fresco surface. I had constructed a rather large cruciform that was just sitting in the corner of my studio. Then I came across a generic mass-produced religious item, an image of a young nun, which somebody had slashed. Kids were playing with it in front of my apartment building. They were told by their parents to throw it away. At the time, I wasn't entirely conscious of the association with the nun incident that had happened a few months earlier. But when I got it into my studio it began to commune with the cruciform piece, and I started to think about the possibility of making an installation about the young nun. I've always been interested in theater, a tableau or stage approach. I had done a large one several years before in Kansas City and I had been looking for another appropriate subject. This incident certainly had all the drama and the pathos to make an interesting piece. So I began to play around with the idea of creating a room that had votive elements in it. But I also wanted to create an atmosphere of healing, the recovery that the nun would go through, a very silent place, a conflation of a hospital room and a hospital chapel. The chapel consisted of elements that somehow traced the incidents of the attack. The cruciform had a *quatrocento* feel to it, in which the attack was painted on one or more of the panels. The other parts were the slightly altered found image of the nun, a translucent plastic hospital divider suspended from the ceiling, a hospital bed, and a spotlight that shone up through it. My idea was to light it and arrange it in such a way that, upon entering, viewers would get all the emotional information necessary. As they spent time with the votive elements, they would be informed of the specifics of the incident that led to this contemplative room.

Artists Space on Hudson Street had separate rooms that accommodated individual installations while also providing a group setting. The door to my room was an old wooden office door with a translucent glass window on which I had painted *For the Nun.* I was able to create a distinct atmosphere in this room. Without that, I don't think the piece could have been as successful. It was my first solo New York exhibition. It was a big step for me and a great entree into the art world.

In 1986, I went to the picture collection at the New York Public Library to look up an image of a rickshaw. I assumed I would get a stereotypical Asian hand-tinted photograph from the late 19th century. But what I found was a series of photographs published in the 1950s by the South African Tourist Bureau. One of the photographs was of a black South African, dressed in ritual native costume, who was the rickshaw "driver," and a European man taking a picture of him and his passengers, who were also European. The photograph encapsulated the racist imperialist notion of the exotic in a way I had never encountered. I took it home and re-photographed it. It was also around the time Amnesty International made Nelson Mandela's case a cause celebre, and they were putting out as much information about the situation in South Africa as they could. Winnie Mandela was not in prison, but due to

CONTINUED

May 29 – July 17: Michael Byron, *For the Nun*, installation (Valerie Smith).

1982–83

The first **Dark Rooms** exhibition is inaugurated. **Dark Rooms** is an exhibition series of artists using film, video, and slide projections in an installation format. This series responds to the increase in media-based work. Several of the installations over the years are produced by Artists Space. Artists Space begins to host an exhibition of a group of artists working for **Studio in a School**, a nonprofit arts organization that employs professional artists to work on art projects with elementary public school students in New York City.

Sept. 25–Oct. 30: **Selections** from the Unaffiliated Artists File (Linda Shearer). Michael Ballou, sculpture; Robert Carvin, painting; Nancy Chunn, painting; Marcia Dalby, installation; Peter Drake, drawing; Win Knowlton, sculpture; Tony Mascatello, painting; John Miller, drawing; Frank Moore, painting; Ellen Rumm, installation; Leslie Tonkonow, installation. Catalogue introduction by Linda Shearer with statements by the artists.

↓ Michael Ballou

MICHAEL BYRON / CONTINUED

her political activism she had been banned from her homeland and was forced to become nomadic. All of this information on the Mandelas created the feeling of a Greek tragedy. So I took the photograph as a starting point for a piece about them. Originally, I planned to do a piece for each of them. The first one was *House for Winnie Mandela,* which was shown in *Social Spaces.* I made a shanty shack constructed out of 200 suitcases with a corrugated tin roof, about the size of a garden utility shed. There was also a didactic plaque like the kind you often see in front of a site of national interest. In this freestanding plaque was the photograph of the rickshaw scene. It was an homage to the African National Congress struggle as it was embodied at that time by Winnie Mandela. It functioned as a *wattle and daud* monument to her personal struggle and, by extension, the struggle in South Africa to overcome apartheid. Because of its title, the reading of the piece has changed quite a bit over time. So, it brackets that specific time in the political evolution of South African history. I wanted to present the piece in an art context as an aesthetic object as well as for the social issues it represented. *Social Spaces* was perfect.

Both installations I showed at Artists Space depended on having the appropriate venue in which to be seen. Artists Space has always been very responsive; without it, I don't know if I would have done these pieces because I probably wouldn't have shown them. I wouldn't have made *For The Nun* at all without the invitation to participate in the May '82 show. I had installed *House for Winnie Mandela* in my studio hoping to find a venue for it. It took two years to get it out to the public. So I've always appreciated Artists Space's commitment to socially driven, noncommercial environments as part of their program.

↑ Installation view: John Miller and Marcia Dalby.

144

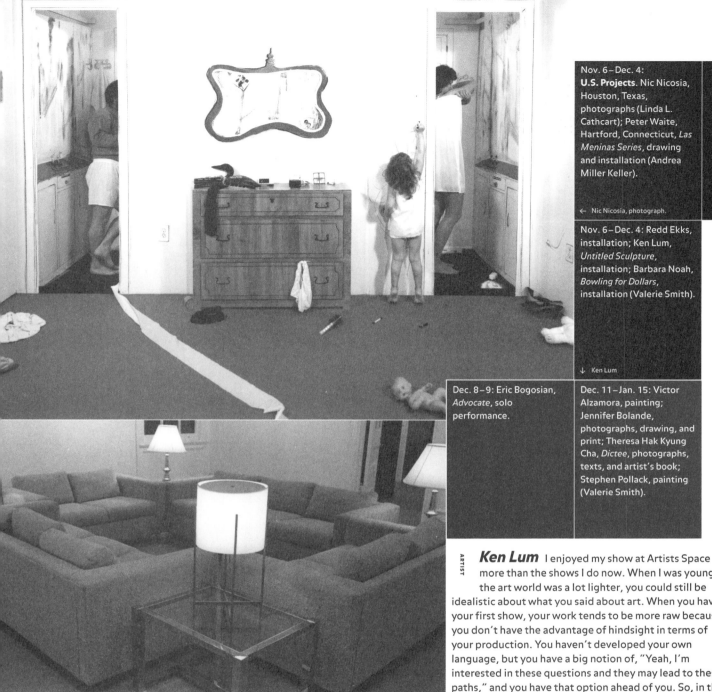

1982 NOV – **1983** JAN

Nov. 6 – Dec. 4:
U.S. Projects. Nic Nicosia,
Houston, Texas,
photographs (Linda L.
Cathcart); Peter Waite,
Hartford, Connecticut, *Las
Meninas Series*, drawing
and installation (Andrea
Miller Keller).

← Nic Nicosia, photograph.

Nov. 6 – Dec. 4: Redd Ekks,
installation; Ken Lum,
Untitled Sculpture,
installation; Barbara Noah,
Bowling for Dollars,
installation (Valerie Smith).

↓ Ken Lum

Dec. 8 – 9: Eric Bogosian,
Advocate, solo
performance.

Dec. 11 – Jan. 15: Victor
Alzamora, painting;
Jennifer Bolande,
photographs, drawing, and
print; Theresa Hak Kyung
Cha, *Dictee*, photographs,
texts, and artist's book;
Stephen Pollack, painting
(Valerie Smith).

ARTIST

Ken Lum I enjoyed my show at Artists Space
more than the shows I do now. When I was younger
the art world was a lot lighter, you could still be
idealistic about what you said about art. When you have
your first show, your work tends to be more raw because
you don't have the advantage of hindsight in terms of
your production. You haven't developed your own
language, but you have a big notion of, "Yeah, I'm
interested in these questions and they may lead to these
paths," and you have that option ahead of you. So, in that
sense, Artists Space was extremely crucial because it was
almost like a cornerstone of a building, a founding block. I don't want to sound nostalgic about it, but the
world seemed more open then. I don't regard art in the same way—it's much more qualified now.

It was the first time I showed in New York. The reception of the piece was small and people would scratch
their heads and ask, "What is this?" I actually liked that because, when I first did a furniture piece, for years
people wouldn't understand it at all. They were intrigued or they thought it wasn't art but ridiculous. They
could even be insulted by it. Later, they came around and everyone wanted a furniture piece. It sounds
paradoxical or contradictory, but once it became accepted and the thing I was invited to do, then somehow, it
lost something for me. In practical terms there was a genuine kind of loss. I guess that's called the problem of
acculturation.

Dec. 11 – Jan. 15: Jürgen Partenheimer, drawing; Stewart Wilson, *Persona Pow! Wow!*, playground.

Dec. 11 – Jan. 15: **U.S. Projects**. Peter Shelton, Los Angeles, California, *Whitehead*, installation (Richard Armstrong).

→

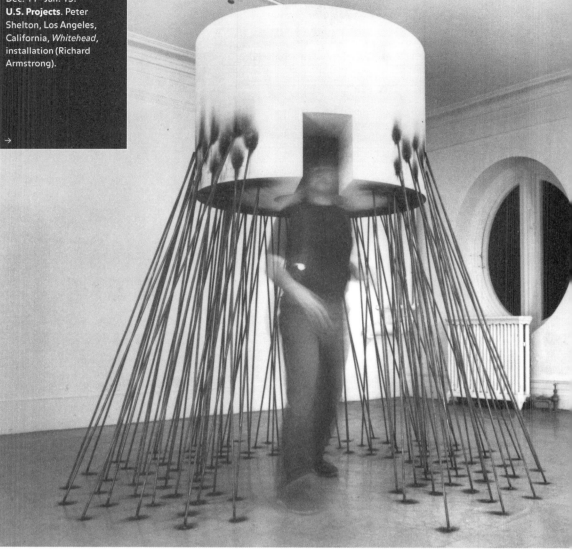

ARTIST

Jennifer Bolande I worked on an exhibition of Super 8 films by artists. It was Helene's (Winer) idea, and I made all the phone calls to arrange for the projectors, and completely organized it. There were maybe 50 artists in a week of film screenings. It was a hot time for Super 8 film. Later Beth and Scott B wound up going into filmmaking in a serious way. There was a whole underground scene of filmmakers. I thought it was really cool to call up all these artists and see how they functioned or how flaky they were. When you're coming out of art school you have no idea what the art world is really like.

I don't remember specifics that inspired my work. It was more the general atmosphere of what people were doing, like Sherrie Levine, Jack Goldstein, or Troy Brauntuch. In particular, the fact that Artists Space wasn't compartmentalized, and different activities were possible. You could be an artist who made films or dance performances. Artwork influences you for such a limited period of time, then you forget about it. It's funny, I can hardly remember any exhibitions, just *Pictures*. It's so subjective.

I was really tuned into Artists Space when I was working there. It was the center of my little universe for the six months I was an intern. Even though alternative spaces had more influence then than they do now, and in the early 80s there were other alternative spaces that were just as viable, in '77 I felt Artists Space was *the* one. It seemed that a lot of really cool people were doing things there. I was always amazed so many people would show up at events. The 70s generation didn't consider me their peer. I was younger. But I was much more focused on that group of people than my own generation. I wasn't looking around for my contemporaries. So when I finally showed at Artists Space, it felt beside the point to me. It is a weird thing you do to yourself. I completely identified with that older work, but I was the next generation, and I do feel they were an audience to me.

Installation view. **A Decade of New Art: Artists Space**,
May 31–June 30, 1984.

WRITER/CURATOR

Linda Cathcart I was not really an active
National Advisory Council member and I didn't go
to any meetings. How it worked was I gave support
from my region. Linda Shearer and Helene Winer
were my friends, I believed in them and the work
they were doing. There weren't so many young
women in professional positions in the art world then.
Linda and I were parallel. I believed in Artists Space and
wanted to support them. Those institutions are always
under siege because they never have enough money, and
people are always questioning them. So I helped them, I
always supplied anything they wanted. When Linda
asked me to do *A Decade of New Art*, my mission was to
select artists who had already shown there. It was a recap
of where they had been so far. But there was something
more defining about it. That kind of exhibition is really
more for the institution. They needed something to mark
the move to West Broadway and they had to have a
balance. When Helene was doing it, she also wanted a
balance with some painters. It wasn't a major moment to
pick four painters and put them together in an exhibition.
That was really the beginning of my involvement and the
beginning of what is now Helene's gallery. The stuff ran
deep at Artists Space. It's not just that people worked
there and graduated and worked somewhere else. They
made continuing threads.

What stands out most in my mind was doing the show
for Nic Nicosia, which was a realization of what I thought
Artists Space was meant to be. I lived in Texas and I was
asked to choose somebody I had seen who hadn't shown
in New York. It was perfect. I thought about Nic and our
long-term friendship. He was one of the first artists to
come to me with slides. I was so impressed with his
photographs that I picked him for a group show in
Houston and then the following year for Artists Space.

He told me he remembered the Artists Space show as one of the most
memorable experiences of his career, like a coming of age. It was
interesting to hear his enthusiasm. He remembered the opening and
everybody there. Everybody was very *there* at Artists Space. A lot. All
the Hallwalls people, who are still connected to me, Helene and Cindy
(Sherman). Nic was a great admirer of Cindy's work and there she was,
the secretary at Artists Space and just beginning to show. Later he
became close friends with Cindy and thinks of himself as part of that
generation of artists even though geographically he wasn't connected
to them. He was connected to them by that show. That seemed to me
pretty much a summation of what Artists Space had been then.

Later, opportunities became available to Nic. The next year he
went on to be in the Whitney Biennial and the Guggenheim New Talent
the year after. Even the review of the Guggenheim show mentioned
having seen his work at Artists Space. Looking at the roster, every
single person who has any talent, who eventually got a gallery, has
been in a show at Artists Space. This is what it was supposed to be
about, to give somebody a chance to stand on their own feet. If they
made it, great. If they had it, good. If they didn't, you had done what
you were supposed to do and Artists Space had done what it was
supposed to do, which was cast this wide net.

Ann Turyn had known me from Hallwalls. She was an artist from
Buffalo and part of the scene there, especially at the CEPA (Center for
Experimental and Perceptual Art) gallery. She's really an intellectual
and literary person. She had this magazine, *Top Stories*, which I always
read, talked to her about, and loved. She said, "Why don't you write
something down?" She was the first person who suggested I write
fiction. I thought, "Well, the catalogues I write are fiction." So I wrote
something. She thought it was great and invited me to give this
reading. It was fun and something I had never done. There was a huge
audience and it was a completely different way of being public. It was
really a stretch for me in a way that so many other things weren't. I
read a story about going to Japan. It felt great to write it, but scary to
read it. When you do enough of these things, you get so you're not
scared anymore.

1983

JAN-FEB

ARTIST

Perry Hoberman *Out of the Picture:
Return of the Invisible Man* was in the first
Dark Rooms show at Artists Space. At the
time, I thought of myself as more of a sculptor. I
was casting about for a narrative to pin this idea
down onto a three-dimensional projection piece. I
decided to use *The Invisible Man* as this privileged
text that was about a character who couldn't be
seen by an audience. This reversed the usual
dynamics of watching a movie where the
characters can be seen by the audience but are
unaware of the audience. Three-D glasses were
available as you entered the room and it was set up
so that once you walked into the room, you were
actually in the way of the projection beams,
casting a shadow. It was all black and white, lasted
about 20 minutes, and ran on a loop. It was the
first big installation piece I'd done in New York.
That show led to whatever I did next, which was
probably at the Kitchen. Then you (Claudia Gould)
invited me to Hallwalls to create the piece again.
That piece was also in the 1985 Whitney Biennial.

*It's to Artists Space's credit
that you continue to uphold
your mandate to work with and
support a younger generation
of artists.*

ARTIST

Stephen Frailey Jim Casebere had put me in *Grand Galop,* but I
actually didn't know him. Opportunities seemed to happen smoothly
and quickly back in those days. The community was really supportive,
but it was also casual. There was a sense of purpose and benevolence. It
certainly wasn't a stressful situation. The way I just described it, it almost
sounds like a relic of the proverbial bygone era. But I was also really green. I
was just a hayseed.

It's to Artists Space's credit that you continue to uphold your mandate to
work with and support a younger generation of artists. It's probably very
tempting to do something more lavish with established artists that would
give you a certain amount of attention. To remain committed to those who
have no name is probably difficult. There is a constant younger community of
artists who arrive in New York and have a consistent need to have their work
shown. It's curious. We get older, we become more savvy, but the younger
generation remains the same.

There was an enormous amount of excitement in the art world in 1983; it
was clear a transition was occurring. Whoever had been thought of as the old
guard wasn't being swept away, but room was being made for a lot of other
people. There was a sense that you arrive in town, you make your work, you
get to know people, and things will take care of themselves. A lot of people
had this feeling of destiny. In retrospect, the 80s was an aberration. It's
possible the artists who are beginning to show their work now may have a
more reasonable and practical point of view.

Feb. 26 – Mar. 26: **Grand Galop** (James Casebere). Ross Anderson, sculpture; Ericka Beckman, installation; Diane Buckler, photographs; Debby Davis, photographs, sculpture; Stephen Frailey, photographs; Biff Henrich, photographs, photomural; Edwin Rath, painting. Catalogue with essay by James Casebere.

1983 FEB–MAR

← Biff Henrich

ARTIST

Biff Henrich Artists Space was one of the very first places I knew about outside of Buffalo which was not a museum. That is always the first impression that sticks with me. Of course, this was largely due to earlier connections Robert Longo and Cindy Sherman had made. Every time I come to New York, I make sure to stop at Artists Space, because a lot of the most interesting work is going to be there some time or another. In my mind, it is part of the routine, part of the inner circle of places and contacts with people. I always find it very accessible to those of us who do not live in New York City. And this fact is a big thing for me.

For *Grand Galop,* I put up a big photo mural in the hallway. The picture was 50 feet long, so I figured you needed to get back to see it. It was the first one of those big murals I had done, and since then I've done about 10. Artists Space gave me the opportunity to do it, to really experiment in the true sense. I didn't have a clue as to whether it would work, but it did. That photographic mural is now in the collection of the Albright-Knox Art Gallery. My personal experience with Artists Space was the greatest. What Jim Casebere wanted to do in *Grand Galop* was include some artists from outside New York City and, in the true spirit of Artists Space, give them some exposure they couldn't get anywhere else. In addition, he wanted to expose the New York public to artists it didn't know about. The exposure thing is a two-way street, people forget that.

Michael Auping had come to Buffalo from Florida. He had previously been in San Francisco and Los Angeles. He wanted to pick one artist from each of these communities for his show, *Colliding: Myth, Fantasy, Nightmare*. Michael is one of the few people who went to the museum world after coming out of an artists' space beginning, and he wanted to acknowledge that in his exhibition. The installation I did for that show was one I never did in any other place. We had a big discussion about it, he wanted me to show my work in a more traditional way. But I said, "No, this is an opportunity!" So I created a work with strobes in a room I painted black to block out the light. The only way to see the images was when the strobes popped on and off. It derived from a bunch of nightmares I had. Dan Walworth thought it was cinematic, I was glad to hear that. My approach to the work was: you're going to New York, the big town, and you want to put on a bigger show, make a bigger effort, have a bigger presence. I probably would not have done the same thing here in Buffalo. The artists who achieve and last are the ones who create opportunities. The art does the work and if the art doesn't do it, then all the promotion and all the posturing isn't going to get it done either.

Feb. 26–Mar. 26:
U.S. Projects. Howard Fried, San Francisco, California, *Sociopath*, installation (Mark Rosenthal).

Apr. 5–7: **Film evenings** (Dan Walworth).
Apr. 5: Doug Eisenstark, *Postcard from Germany…*, 1979-81; Daniele Huillet and Jean-Marie Straub, *Introduction to Arnold Schoenberg's "Accompaniment to a Cinematographic Scene,"* 1973; Susan Kouguell and Ernest Marrero, *One Day Franz Brought Me to His House*, 1982; Leslie Thornton, *Jennifer, Where Are You?*, 1981; Kristin Lovejoy, *Do You See It Now You Don't*, 1983; Dan Walworth, *The Earth Is a Satellite of the Moon*, 1982.
Apr. 6: Yvonne Rainer, *Journeys from Berlin/1971*, 1980.
Apr. 7: David Koff, *Occupied Palestine*, 1982; Nick MacDonald, *Liberal War*, 1972; Kimberly Safford and Fred Taylor, *Los Hijos de Sandino (The Children of Sandino)*, 1980.

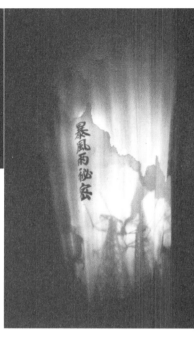

Tim Maul ARTIST The openings were important. As someone who's been around since the early 70s, I think the openings had a sense of focus and urgency with the younger artists that wasn't there before. I was introduced to artists who had real expectations about what the art world could give to them and a real sense of direction. I didn't see this in a lot of locally educated people. In the circle from Buffalo or Cal Arts, there was more of a drive. This set up the 80s. That was completely evident in the openings at Artists Space. I would leave them either really excited or really confused. But Puffy's was very close to Artists Space and people would go there every weekend and drink and dance.

David Cabrera ARTIST *…and his normal reaction of saying oh this is so great, you don't miss me, oh this is great, and that laugh!!!* That was the period of long titles. I put that film program together because, at the time, a lot of people I knew and studied with, students as well as faculty members, were making short films. I thought it was very powerful, very personal work. But, back then, I figured out right away, even though I hadn't been able to articulate it so well, that I had this real focus for facilitating. I wasn't exactly curating, because I was less interested in the role of curator than that of facilitator—helping artists through ideas and getting their work out. It was my first time organizing an exhibition in a formal way. I don't remember the specifics concerning the title at that time, probably because I was less articulate.

But I had these ideas, they were really buried, buried in language, and buried in the academy at Cal Arts. Now that I look back on it, the process, coming out as an artist and as a gay person, was my attempt to find my voice. And this came out in both the titles I've given to shows and in some of the work I've shown, which had these long semi-narrative texts running through them.

Jon Kessler ARTIST In 1980 I had just moved to New York and completed the Whitney Independent Study Program. I knew I needed to bring my work around, but I had no idea how to do it. So I'm at a party for Pat Hamilton and I see this guy who looks familiar. I walk up to him and say, "Did you go to Tyler Hill Camp?" And he says, "Yeah I did, did you?" I had gone there from the time I was 6 years old till I was 12. It was Allan Schwartzman, who had worked at the New Museum. We'd both gone to the same Jewish sleep-away camp. The likelihood of anyone from that camp going into the arts was incredible. So he came over, really liked my work, and called Valerie Smith. There had been a cancellation, so she said, "Next month you're having a show." To have that curatorial spontaneity must have been great. It was great for me too, because literally things changed overnight.

It was not an installation in the reception gallery, but five distinct pieces I had put together during that year. They all utilized handblown glass and played with the idea of using shadows of moving toys. Tom Solomon came over with his parents and Holly Solomon bought a piece. Tom wanted me to show at White Columns, which was set up six months later. He was pissed off because he wanted to be the first to show the work and he felt a bit usurped by Artists Space and me. Valerie called me up a week after the show opened to tell me a piece was in 1,000 pieces on the floor. I'd never really installed work before. Of course, it was the piece that sold and was irreplaceable. My first sale was shit, it was gone.

I met Ashley Bickerton and Michael Byron at my opening. Ashley showed about a month after me at White Columns. I met many of my colleagues that night. I was in college at SUNY, Purchase, when the *10 Artists/Artists Space* show was at the Neuberger Museum. I met all the artists there because they were incredibly accessible and really just hung out. By meeting all of them I felt I was brought into what was really a club, the Artists Space club.

Apr. 9–May 7: Paul Hunter, *Chamber Music*, installation; Jon Kessler, *Dub for Dervishes*, sculpture; Kevin Labadie, *Vulcan's Reign*, installation; Tim Maul and Fred Szymanski, *Broadcast State*, installation; Stephen Whisler, sculpture, drawing (Valerie Smith).

← Jon Kessler

May 10–11: **Film and video**: *and his normal reaction of saying oh this is so great, you don't miss me, oh this is great, and that laugh!!!* (David Cabrera). Howard Better, *One Million B.C.*, *The Only Fear*, 1983, film; Susan Emshwiller, *Teacup Drama*, 1982, film; James Goss, *Amen*, 1982, and *Listen to Me*, 1980, video; Sharon Greytak, *Some Pleasure on the Level of the Source*, 1982, film; Kim Ingraham, *Men Singing*, 1983, and *The Look of Love*, 1982, video; John Owen, *On Smash-up*, 1982, video; Susan Rosenfeld, *Now Playing*, 1983, film; Mitchell (Mitzie) Rothzeid and Mark Stahl, *The Judgment Behind the Accusation May Be Hidden*, 1981, video; Nina Salerno, *Model X*, 1980, video; Mitchell Syrop, *Dizolv*, 1979, and *Watch It. Think It. (Version 1,2,3)*, 1978, film; Rea Tajiri, *Now I'm Turning to Face You*, 1982, video.

May 13: **Top Stories: Reading/Party** (Ann Turyn, editor, *Top Stories*). A benefit hosted by Artists Space and coordinated by Hallwalls, Buffalo, for *Top Stories*, a prose periodical. Readings by 11 writers whose work it has published: Kathy Acker, Constance De Jong, Judith Doyle, Lee Eiferman, Suzanne Johnson, Ursule Molinaro, Linda Neaman, Janet Stein, Lynne Tillman, Ann Turyn, Gail Vachon.

WRITER

Constance De Jong From the very beginning, my serious work has been involved in more than one form: radio, recorded work, and extensions of spoken words. From 1973 to 1974, I adapted the written word for spoken word situations, both recorded and live. For that part of my work, I found an audience and a site at places like Artists Space. At the Kitchen I did one of the first language performances. As a writer, it was more relevant and meaningful to perform at Artists Space than in a place exclusively identified with language, like St. Mark's Church. Some of it was geographic—SoHo and TriBeCa were very young and there was a spirit of building that community, both physically and through art. A lot of us lived in those neighborhoods. There was a regularity of things to do. Places like Artists Space, Franklin Furnace, and 112 Workshop were natural or intimate places for me to go to when the work was very new and very hot. I could perform my output in process, not just my masterpieces. You might think because my work was performed once, not hung for six weeks like a visual artist's, that the commitment was less. It doesn't seem that way when you're the artist.

Recorded, live, or digital work is often diminished or marginalized. People still place the greatest value on the printed word. I have taken my knocks for being the kind of writer I am. Had I not been taken seriously and given the opportunity to present work in different formats in places like Artists Space, where else would it have happened? Lincoln Center didn't want me. A space like Artists Space was about confidence. But it also gave us all an audience: each other. The downside is I wanted to be taken seriously, not just patted on the back and told, "Good girl, you're working, that's fine." I wanted audience feedback and criticism. That was the value of places like Artists Space.

I am not nostalgic but old enough to have a certain history, what you might call openness. At that time, there was a sense that everyone was doing the same thing, that means you (Claudia Gould) and I. There was the building of this physical neighborhood and the building of audience, there was the building of a new independently produced work in dependent alternative spaces, and there was a sense of everyone working. Some people were administrators, some were artists, and some others were musicians. There was a commonality to the input, activity, and work, and a commonness to it.

WRITER

Lynne Tillman Ann Turyn, the publisher and editor of *Top Stories*, had organized an evening of readings. Among others the readers included Kathy Acker and Constance De Jong. Coming from Hallwalls and from SUNY, Buffalo, where people were working with film, text, and gallery art, Ann effected a kind of crossover. There was a whole mix of stuff brought together through *Top Stories*. It was a heady time for a whole generation of artists coming up at that moment. Living downtown, I became friendly with Barbara Kruger and Kiki Smith. Social relationships are very important to the way you see the world.

Jane Dickson was the first artist to ask me to do something with her. She came to me with drawings she had made of a couple living together, a man and a woman. She said, "You live with someone, too. Do you want to write a text about living with somebody?" So I wrote a piece called *Living with Contradictions,* which ultimately became the book of the same title with Jane's drawings and my text. We presented it at Artists Space, interweaving text and image the way they appeared in the book. Jane showed slides of her drawings while I read the text. The *Top Stories* event was a very happy one for me. I've always felt visual culture was as important as literary culture. Although I am at home in the art world, I'm peripheral to it. I became involved in the art world because I was involved in independent film and it led me to more filmmakers, other visual artists, and artists interested in film.

Artists Space hosted a very sad event, the memorial service for Craig Owens, who had died July 4, 1990. The year before, Artists Space had a memorial for Lyn Blumenthal which I had attended with Craig. From the mid-80s on we experienced such a decimation. I was also involved with Nan Goldin's *Witnesses: Against Our Vanishing*. It's interesting to see how a community uses its different spaces and how Artists Space made itself available to the art community. Events like *Witnesses* were very important in terms of being able to console oneself about loss. I believe very intensely that art writing is a deeply social act. So when a space engenders these brief moments, it reflects, and that is an important function.

May 14: Gioia Timpanelli, *Stories*, a storytelling performance from her book *Italian Traveling*.

May 21–July 2: **The Los Angeles – New York Exchange** (Marc Pally and Linda Shearer). Exchange show between Artists Space and LACE (Los Angeles Contemporary Exhibitions): six Los Angeles artists show at Artists Space, six New York artists show at LACE. At Artists Space: Jill Giegerich, sculpture; Victor Henderson, installation; Kim Hubbard, painting; Lari Pittman, painting; Mitchell Syrop, photo texts; Megan Williams, installation.

At LACE, June 8-July 16: Charles Clough, painting; Rebecca Howland, sculpture; Jeff Koons, sculpture; Nachume Miller, painting; Christy Rupp, sculpture; Reese Williams, installation. Catalogue documents both shows, with essays by Susan C. Larsen (Los Angeles) and Roberta Smith (New York) and introduction by Marc Pally and Linda Shearer.

↓   Megan Williams

ARTIST

Lari Pittman The first night I met Linda Shearer, she and Marc Pally proposed the *Los Angeles – New York Exchange* to me, where artists would literally swap spaces: LACE and Artists Space. It was actually the first time I had shown in New York. I immediately liked Linda, she was very disarming, I was very taken by her. She was funny and had a fantastic laugh. If someone can make me laugh, I'm their slave. So I felt very good going into this project.

All group shows are odd groupings. What bonded us together was friendship. We were all on a similar level, in terms of making the work public and putting it in commercial venues or alternative spaces. At the time I felt there was very little context for my work. So the show was both a thrilling moment and an eye-opener for me. On the one hand, it was great to finally recontextualize my work in some other city, to place it in front of another audience. But I was also very aware of being introduced to the machine that New York is and, even then, to a type of xenophobia and provincialism that still characterize New York from my point of view. Its provincialism is both its best and worst asset—it makes it work as an entity. It is also exclusionary; New York doesn't know the rest of the world exists. This was attractive in its centrality but at the same time I was aware of trying to penetrate it. I was definitely not part of that milieu. I felt that very strongly. But it was a good sign, in the sense that within this centrality, which New York was very much enjoying, there was a possibility of contamination. And this contamination was cultural production from elsewhere. I got this feeling through my conversations with some of the artists who had worked in these spaces. Their reactions and observations made me very aware that I was being imported. It was culturally permissible to bash Los Angeles in public, of course—that hasn't stopped.

I've had really good exposure in New York and, in this respect, I'm very thankful for being a mid-career artist, because people either hate the work or like it. There doesn't seem to be much in between. I'm relieved about that. I think consensus is the death of the artist. New York remains a wonderfully contentious environment for my work because people there make a fuss about it. In a way I appreciate this about New York.

ARTIST

Megan Williams Linda Shearer and Marc Pally included me in that very nice group of people. I don't think there was anything duplicated, it was a well-rounded show. I transported this little piece of my life in California to New York. It was in a very dark room with some found work in it. At the time, I had been making, on the spot, what I called "continuous drawing." It was very raw. That kind of risk just doesn't exist anymore in my work. I suppose I've matured past it. But in 1983, the significance of the 70s was still very fresh in our minds. It was where we had come from, it wasn't so overly digested as it is now. I miss that sense of risk taking. Since *Helter Skelter: L.A. Art in the 1990s* (January 26 – April 26, 1992) at the Museum of Contemporary Art in Los Angeles, I no longer wing it by putting up something very spontaneous. But even now, the museums don't have the resources or the support staff that a small alternative space would have had in 1983. In those days, there seemed to be more generosity and an openness that doesn't exist today. Art organizations like Artists Space had to find a way to fundraise differently, and even so there just isn't the experimentation. I regret that. The 80s seemed to change things forever.

The *Los Angeles – New York Exchange* show was about sharing. It was the beginning of a new relationship between Los Angeles and New York. New York has had to accept Los Angeles. But I don't think it really opened up an exchange, because during the 80s there seemed to be this push and pull between the two cities. That's now evolved into what Linda and Marc were trying to generate, a dialogue which truly exists now. A more honest dialogue than it pretended to be in the 80s, which became more about finances.

May 21–July 2: Gioia Timpanelli, *A Mantel with Boxes*, installation.

July 9–25: **Artists from the Studio in a School** (selected in consultation with Donald Droll). Jo-Ann Acey, Susan Austad, Martha Bloom, Thomas Cahill, Michael Filan, Mimi Fortunato, Hannah Gruenberg, Ronald Jackson, Julie Lapping, Jamie Learned, Helene Manzo, Lawrence E. Merenstein, Ellen Meyer, Janice Paul, Dhara Rivera, Anita Saghbazarian, Rochelle Shicoff, Katheryn Sins, Gretchen Treitz.

↑ Fortuyn / O'Brien, *Bon Voyage Voyeur*, installation. **International Projects: Holland.** Feb.25–Mar.24, 1984.

1983–84

During its 10th anniversary season, Artists Space signs a lease for a new location at 223 West Broadway in January 1984, renovates the space in the spring, and moves out of 105 Hudson Street in July. In addition, the organization changes its name legally from Committee for the Visual Arts, Inc., to Artists Space, Inc. Other name changes are: **Unaffiliated Artists File** becomes **Artists File,** and the **Emergency Materials Fund** and **Independent Exhibitions Program** become **Artists Grants**. The computerization of the **Artists File** begins, a process completed in 1985–86. With the support of the **Mark Rothko Foundation**, a series of exhibitions are initiated to present the work of older and mature artists. **International Projects** begins a series inviting four art professionals from outside the United States to select one artist from their country to do site-specific installations at Artists Space.

ARTIST

Irene Fortuyn It was a major moment for us to show at Artists Space as young artists in an international exhibition. New York was really the end of the world for us. Artists Space was still on Hudson Street when we arrived. We were told there would be a space for us to work. It was actually a storage room about 2¹/₂ x 2¹/₂ meters, which is nothing, and full of garbage, without windows. We arrived in the new world with high expectations, facing this garbage bin and no place to sleep, which also was supposed to have been arranged for us. But it was still fantastic. We cleared out the garbage, went around New York, which we were seeing for the first time, found our materials, worked there for three or four weeks, and made this great installation. It was called the *Apple of Paris: A View Over the Ocean* because it was connected with a show we did before in Holland, which we also called *A View Over the Ocean*. It was about ideas on America, archetypical ideas embedded in us without our knowing whether or not they would be true. And we used mythology as a reference — that's the reason for the "Apple of Paris." It was all made of very delicate material, paper and balsa wood.

It was also the beginning of my collaboration with Robert O'Brien. We had some recognition. We met and talked to a lot of people who liked it. In the beginning of an artist's career everything is response. We left with a really good feeling about our work and Artists Space. We came back a year later because we got a studio at P.S. 1. It marked a start. With the first things you do, you don't have the hard feelings you have toward boredom. You're really happy and excited about working. In that sense, Artists Space really fulfilled its promise to us.

ARTIST

Mowry Baden I had a look at the site. It wasn't terribly promising. At that time, Hudson Street was kind of still. It wasn't the domestic street it is now. There were remnants of chandleries and warehouses interspersed with cafeterias and banks. My plan was to put one sculpture out on the sidewalk until people lost interest, then bring out another. I'd hoped that would coincide with some day-to-day cycle. Well, one sculpture was not enough to stop anybody. They're New Yorkers, you know; it takes a lot. I was in despair, completely despondent. I thought this was never going to work. Then I said, "We'll put them all out there!" To my complete relief, it turned out that three sculptures in the street were enough. There were street people who were regulars. One guy, in particular, became a kind of tour guide. A lot of people were proprietary, but that happens with public sculpture. They become the appointed owners, they appoint themselves. Also, there had to be some security, otherwise all that sculpture would have just walked off. Well, I was the security. Artists Space was on the second floor, so everything had to be shuttled up and down into the elevator. I'd bring the stuff down at 10:00 in the morning, stand in the street all day, and take it back upstairs at 6:00. I was there the whole time.

I would hang out at a distance so that my presence didn't contaminate their public experience. I usually hid behind a dumpster down the street where people didn't see me. A couple of times I had to stop vandalism. It was cold and it rained a lot and I wore my foul weather gear. In fact, it was hard work. I just drank a lot of hot coffee. One day, the New York garbage collection came around. They were loading stuff off the curb. It's standard New York practice; people leave out everything from mattresses to tricycles, and Sanitation hauls it away. They reached for my stuff, started to throw it in the dumpster, and had to be stopped. I thought it was funny that they couldn't see the difference. But one of them did remark, "Oh, yeah, hold on, that's art." So one of those guys was hip. That's pretty good. I cut through the barriers there.

Artists Space was terrific, very supportive. They gave me hot soup when I went up there, they were good. Linda Shearer was the Director at the time and she was super. She saw my foul weather gear and wanted to know if I would take her son fishing. I said it would be a lot more fun than standing out on Hudson Street. I think she actually wanted to send him home with me, bring him back to British Columbia, put him on the high seas.

Oct. 1–29: **Selections** from the Unaffiliated Artists File (Donald Droll, Board President of Artists Space; Trudie Grace, first Executive Director; Irving Sandler, first Board President; Linda Shearer. Each curator selects three artists from the File: Romany Eveleigh, drawing; Jane Kaplowitz, drawing; Colin Thomson, painting (Droll); Claudia Fitch, sculpture;

Barbara Friedman, painting; Gary Perkins, sculpture and projection (Grace); Fred Guyot, sculpture; George Palumbo, sculpture; Michael Torlen, painting (Sandler); Mark Innerst, painting; Amanda Kyser, installation; Bob Smith, boxes (Shearer). Catalogue with statements by the artists.

Nov. 5–Dec. 3: **Three Artists Select Three Artists**. Artists who have shown at Artists Space each select one artist: Robert Guillot, furniture (Scott Burton); Ron Janowich, painting, drawing (Hermine Ford); Doreen Gallo, construction (Judy Pfaff).

Nov. 5–Dec. 3: Ernst Benkert, *Meshes, Crosses, Bars*, 1976-83, drawing (Gary Burnley, Donald Droll, Linda Shearer). First in a series of three one-person exhibitions sponsored by the Mark Rothko Foundation to present work by older and mature artists. Brochure with essay by Joseph Masheck with statement by the artist.

Nov. 5–Dec. 3: **International Projects**. Andy Patton, Toronto, Canada, *The Architecture of Privacy*, painting (Tim Guest). Brochure with essay by Tim Guest.

ARTIST

Annette Lemieux I was David Salle's assistant when he called to ask if I'd like to show at Artists Space. I chose two very large paintings. One was called *National*, which consisted of two canvases representing a flag with a small cross, and beside it was a bust on a pedestal. The second painting, *Manna,* was from 1983, and had a big M with the word "Manna." I also showed smaller drawings, gouaches on paper from 1983 and 1984. They were little icons with images of broken bones. That period was very important for me because I was recovering from an accident where I was run over and it physically forced me to make smaller, more manageable work. I had to come up with other ways of expressing my ideas. That's when I realized I could use photographs, found objects, and painting. The accident made me use materials I had not been involved with before; it sped up the process. That is clear in *National,* where I was trying to break out of the rectangle by adding a small cross to the canvas and a piece of sculpture next to the painting.

Dec. 10–Jan. 14: Hundreds of Drawings. Benefit exhibition in which every artist who has shown at Artists Space is invited to submit one small work for sale to benefit Artists Space (artists choose to donate 50 percent or 100 percent of proceeds). Dennis Adams, Olga Adorno, Victor Alzamora, Ross Anderson, Mel Andringa, Jackie Apple, Ida Applebroog, Robert Appleton, Richard R. Armijo, Dianne Arndt, Mario Asaro, Douglas Ashford, Robert Attanasio, Julie Ault, Auste, Alice Aycock, Donald Baechler, Richard Baim, John Baldessari, Michael Ballou, Paula Barr, Ann Bar-Tur, Ericka Beckman, Gretchen Bender, Ernst Benkert, Diane Bertolo, Ashley Bickerton, James Biederman, Cathy Billian, Timothy Binkley, Dara Birnbaum, Dike Blair, Marc Blane, Jennifer Bolande, Jonathan Borofsky, Gary Bower, Don Boyd, Troy Brauntuch, Farrell Brickhouse, Barbara Broughel, Diane Buckler, Gary Burnley, Nancy Burson, Scott Burton, Michael Byron, David Cabrera, Patricia Caire, Andrea Callard, Cynthia Carlson, Robert Carvin, James Casebere, Bruce Charlesworth, Louisa Chase, Rhys Chatham, Meryl Chernick, Nancy Chunn, Charles Clough, J.B. Cobb, Martin Cohen, Jon Colburn, Paul Colin, James Collins, Arch Connelly, Jay G. Coogan, Ellen Cooper, David Crum, Robin (Lee) Crutchfield, Roger Cutforth, Dorit Cypis, Marcia Dalby, Elsa D'Arrigo, Michael Davey, Debby Davis, Scott Davis, Tom DeBiaso, Margaret Dewys, Jane Dickson, Kochi Doktori, Peter Drake, Carroll Dunham, Fontaine Dunn, Jean Dupuy, Nancy Dwyer, Martha Edelheit, Barbara Ess, Andrea Evans, Romany Eveleigh, Lauren Ewing, Gary Falk, Ralston Farina, Ken Feingold, John Fekner, R.M. Fischer, Gareth Fisher, Claudia Fitch, Hermine Ford, Stephen Frailey, Deborah Freedman, Barbara Friedman, Bobby G, Doreen Gallo, Valery Gerlovin, Jill Giegerich, Kathleen Gilje, Gilles Jean Giuntini, Joan Lee Goldberg, Eunice Goldin, Nan Goldin, Jack Goldstein, Ken Goodman, James Goss, Cie Goulet, Dan Graham, Peter Grass, George Green, Colin Greenly, Sharon Greytak, Albano Guatti, Robert Guillot, Don Gummer, Fred Gutzeit, Jane Handzel, Freya Hansell, Ruth Hardinger, Michael Harvey, Martha Haslanger, Don Hazlitt, Susan Heinemen, Biff Henrich, Victor Henderson, Candace Hill-Montgomery, Perry Hoberman, James Holl, Pieter Holstein, Jenny Holzer, Rebecca Howland, Joel Hubaut, Kim Hubbard, Hudson, Tannis Hugill, Paul Hunter, Mark Innerst, Jim Isermann, Ron Janowich, Richards Jarden, John Jesurun, Glenys Johnson, Poppy Johnson, Suzanne Johnson, Ronald Jones, Brigid Kennedy, Jon Kessler, Ladd Kessler, Rick Klauber, David Knoebel, Win Knowlton, Ken Kobland, Silvia Kolbowski, Tom Koken, Jeff Koons, Margia Kramer, Jill Kroesen, Barbara Kruger, Amanda Kyser, Eliot Lable, Kevin Labadie, Seth Laderman, Thomas Lanigan-Schmidt, Stephen Lapthisophon, Louise Lawler, Thomas Lawson, William Leavitt, Susan Leites, Marilyn Lenkowsky, Willy Lenski, Les Levine, Sherrie Levine, Barbara Levy, Marsha Liberty, Donald Lipski, Barbara Liss, Inverna Lockpez, Robert Longo, Ken Lum, Frank Majore, Russell Maltz, Tony Mascatello, Tim Maul, Michael McClard, Allan McCollum, Sidney McElhenney, Mundy McLaughlin, Paul McMahon, Brad Melamed, John Mendelsohn, Jeffrey Mendoza, Mike Metz, Henrietta Michelson-Bagley, Martica Miguens, John Miller, Stephen Miller, Byoung Ok Min, Mary Miss, Haoui Montaug, Frank Moore, Gerry Morehead, Robert Morgan, Ron Morosan, Ree Morton, Matt Mullican, Antonio Muntadas, Judith Murray, Gwynn Murrill, Peter Nadin, James Nares, Andrew Nash, Joseph Nechvatal, Joe Neill, Paulette Nenner, Nic Nicosia, Kevin Noble, Richard Nonas, Mary Obering, Aric Obrosey, Dennis Oppenheim, Tom Otterness, Jurgen Partenheimer, Andy Patton, Ken Pelka, Gary Perkins, Cara Perlman, Ellen Phelan, Virginia Piersol, Pat Place, Stephen Pollack, Lucio Pozzi, Richard Prince, Tom Radloff, Yvonne Rainer, Edwin Rath, Tony Rickaby, Judy Rifka, Thor Rinden, Bart Robbett, Joyce Robins, Abby Robinson, Walter Robinson, Tim Rollins/Roy Rogers/Jose Carlos (Tim Rollins + K.O.S.), Erika Rothenberg, Meridel Rubenstein, Tom Rubnitz, Ellen Rumm, Christy Rupp, Aldona Sabalis, Livio Saganic, Maggie Saliske, Jim Sanborn, René Santos, Michel Sauer, Tad Savinar, Carolee Schneemann, Mira Schor, Schuldt, Barbara Schwartz, Joanne Seltzer, Peter Shelton, Cindy Sherman, Stuart Sherman, Laurie Simmons, Teri Slotkin/Cavanagh/Lisa Kahane/Warren, Bob Smith, Michael Smith, Mimi Smith, Philip Smith, Jenny Snider, Nancy Spero, Jessica Spohn, Ted Stamm, Carole Clark Stein, Lewis Stein, Haim Steinbach, Donald Sultan, James S. Sutter, Mitchell Syrop, Susanna Tanger, Valery Taylor, Anthony Thompson, Colin Thomson, Ann Thornycroft, Bart Thrall, Gioia Timpanelli, Ted Titolo, Leslie Tonkonow, Marvin Torffield, John Torreano, Francesc Torres, Paul Tschinkel, Bernard Tschumi, Peter van Riper, Meryl Vladimer, Conrad Vogel, Gail von der Lippe, Julie Wachtel, Ken Wade, Peter Waite, Cid Collins Walker, Alida Walsh, Dan Walworth, Jeff Way, William Wegman, Lawrence Weiner, Stephen Whisler, William White, Megan Williams, Reese Williams, Peter L. Wilson, Stuart Wilson, Tom Wolf, Ann-Sargent Wooster, Robert Yasuda, Susan Yelavich, Frank Young, Barry Yourgrau, Yunque, Chris Zeller, John Zorn, Michael Zwack.

← Allan McCollum, *Untitled*, photo for **Hundreds of Drawings** poster.

We had some recognition. We met and talked to a lot of people who liked it. In the beginning of an artist's career everything is response. We left with a really good feeling about our work and Artists Space.

Jan. 21–Feb. 18: **Reconstruction Project**. Benefit exhibition for *Artists' Call Against U.S. Intervention in Central America*. 20 women artists reconstruct an ancient Mayan codex (Sabra Moore): Emma Amos, Camille Billops, Frances Buschke, Josely Carvalho, Catherine Correa, Chris Costan, Colleen Cutschall, Sharon Gilbert, Kathy Grove, Marina Gutierrez, Virginia Jaramillo, Kazuko, Sabra Moore, Helen Oji, Catalina Parra, Linda Peer, Liliana Porter, Jaune Quick-To-See Smith, Nancy Spero, Holly Zox.

Jan. 21–Feb. 18: **New Galleries of the Lower East Side** (Helene Winer). Group exhibition of work in all media from 17 galleries on the Lower East Side. Participating galleries: C.A.S.H., Christminster Fine Art, Civilian Warfare, East 7th Street Gallery, Executive Gallery, 51 X, Fun Gallery, Tracey Garet, International with Monument, Gracie Mansion, Nature Morte, The New Math Gallery, Oggi Domani, Pat Hearn, Piezo Electric, P.P.O.W, Sharpe Gallery. Artists in the exhibition: Stephen Aljian, Alan Belcher, Paul Benney, Zeke Berman, Ellen Berkenblit, Keiko Bonk, Tom Brazelton, Barry Bridgwood, Nancy Brooks Brody, Chris Chevins, Craig Coleman, Rich Colicchio, Michael Collins, George Condo, Gregory A. Crane, Mark Dean, Jimmy de Sana, Futura 2000, Robert Garratt, Dana Garrett, Judith Glantzman, Arthur Gonzalez, Rodney Alan Greenblat, Kathleen Grove, Richard Hambleton, Kiely Jenkins, Sermin Kardestuncer, Elizabeth Koury, Stephen Lack, Leora Laor, Robert Loughlin, Paul Marcus, Frank Moore, Peter Nagy, Michael Ottersen, Steven Parrino, Rick Prol, Hope Sandrow, Michael Sangaris, Bruno Schmidt, Peter Schuyff, Huck Snyder, Ahbe Sulit, Frederick Sutherland, Meyer Vaisman, Oliver Wasow, Dondi White, David Wojnarowicz, Robert Yarber, Zephyr, Rhonda Zwillinger. Brochure with essay by Helene Winer.

Jan. 21–Feb. 18: **International Projects**. Didier Vermeiren, Brussels, Belgium, sculpture (Jan Debbaut). Brochure with essay by Alain Vanderhofstadt and statement by the artist.

Feb. 25–Mar. 24: **Three Artists Select Three Artists**. Jolie Stahl, painting (Rebecca Howland); Larry Johnson, photographs (Richard Prince); Annette Lemieux, painting, drawing (David Salle).

↗ Annette Lemieux

Feb. 25–Mar. 24: Sally Hazelet Drummond, painting (Gary Burnley, Donald Droll, Linda Shearer). Second in the series of exhibitions sponsored by the Mark Rothko Foundation. Brochure with essay by Irving Sandler and statement by the artist.

Feb. 25–Mar. 24: **International Projects.** Irene Fortuyn/Robert O'Brien, Amsterdam, Holland, *Bon Voyage Voyeur, A View Over the Ocean*, installation (Paul Groot) accompanied by artists' book, *Thoughts About Perseus About Sculpture About Light About Space About Spatiality Signature Heroism Dialogue Bon Voyage Voyeur*. Brochure with essay by Paul Groot translated by Fortuyn/O'Brien.

Mar. 29: **Events: Reading** (Reese Williams). Peter Nadin, Richard Prince, Reese Williams.

Mar. 30–31: **Film: Berlin/Super 8: The Architecture of Division**, film series (Keith Sanborn).
Mar. 30: Christoph Doering, *3302*; Die Todliche Doris, *Das Leben des Sid Vicious (The Life of Sid Vicious)*; Thomas Kiesel, *Incendio Italiano*; Monike Funke Stern, *Speed*; R.S. Wolkenstein, *Der Tanz Mechanikk (The Dance Mechanic)*; Yana Yo, *Gehindieknieunddrehdichnichtum (Benddownanddon'tturnaround)*; Antje Fels, *WasfürGeister (What Kinds of Ghosts?)*.
Mar. 31: Axel Brand and Anette Maschmann, *Computer Bild (Computer Image)*; Walter Gramming, *Hammer und Sichel (Hammer and Sickle)*; Andrea Hillen, *Revue Film (Spectacle Film)*; Knut Hoffmeister, *Berlin/Alamo*; Horst Markgraf, *Norma L*; Roza Spak, *Handlich (Handleable)*; Teufelsbergproduktion, *Sinnfilm II (Sensefilm II)*.

ARTIST

Ashley Bickerton In '84 I was thinking a lot about Orwell. My friend, Tom Zimmer, wrote a mad piece of clanking polysyllabics to accompany the work I showed. You (Valerie Smith) referred to it as coming out fully dressed. I really liked that analogy. I guess it was 14 years ago now. It was Jack Goldstein's influence. Great big dense chunks of cubical texts that you could hit with a sledgehammer. I am not sure I could actually read it, but it really was English.

It is hard to talk about Jack Goldstein without getting into a literary description of madness. The isolation of two people locked away in Brooklyn in their fucking megalomaniacal world where they tell each other they're the only things that are relevant to anything, completely out there, but creating some kind of energy feeding on itself like a great pustulating hair follicle. Delusion of madness on both sides. Isolation. It fed on isolation. When you want to create an internal energy, you create an external paranoia. We were together in fascism.

You came first, darling. You're everybody's first. I remember the social milieu. Whole groups of Cal Arts students madly hanging around Artists Space frequenting every opening until they got a show there and then they disappeared. When it became apparent that they got their show, or when it became apparent they weren't going to, they just faded out. That's why there was always a crowd there. It was like lining up for a discotheque.

Mar. 31–May 5: Mowry Baden, viewer-activated sculpture (Gary Burnley, Donald Droll, Linda Shearer). Exhibition sponsored by the Mark Rothko Foundation. Baden and sculptures were on the sidewalk outside Artists Space.
Mar. 31–Apr. 14. Photo and video documentation
Apr. 17–May 5. Brochure with essay by Gary Goss.

↓ Mowry Baden

Apr. 7–May 5: Ashley Bickerton, painting; Robert Hammond, installation; Justen Ladda, *Man Adjusting a TV Set*, installation (Valerie Smith).

← Justen Ladda

Apr. 7–May 5:
International Projects.
Doriana Chiarini, Bologna, Italy, sculpture (Germano Celant). Brochure with essay by Germano Celant.

ARTIST

Justen Ladda I went out one night and brought in all this junk I had found in some dumpsters to use for the installation. I dug out an entire kitchen, a television, a carpet, an old bed, and a table. I was very pleased because that stuff was really from the garbage. Then I set it all up in the room and started working with the lights. People have a prejudice towards black light because they associate it with cheapo tricks or decoration in discotheques. Unfortunately, this gives black lights a bad connotation, but there is something about them that is truly fascinating. Black light energizes the paint. Fluorescent colors come alive, they activate the light source. The beauty of black lights is that they don't cast any shadows. Many people who came to my installation didn't realize I had actually painted an image of the TV screen over all the objects in the room. People thought there was a clear piece of plastic hanging in the space that the image was painted on. So they all tried to touch what they thought was a screen. When I saw people doing this I knew the piece worked.

ARTIST

Peter Halley The *Selections* show I participated in was quite meaty. My memory of it is that there were other interesting artists in it as well who also went on to do other things. On a curatorial level, it was pretty impressive selecting, because sometimes you're in these group shows and you don't feel so good about a lot of the other work.
Before I came to New York somebody gave me a catalogue of the *Pictures* exhibition. It was a big thing for me in terms of understanding the new dialogue that was about to emerge in the 80s. Yet I didn't quite understand it; I remember staring at Sherrie Levine's *Lincoln* and trying to figure out what it was all about. The whole nature of the show was so different from anything I was used to that it definitely caught my attention.

When I first came to New York in 1980, Artists Space was on Hudson Street. The work I saw there and its nature as an institution had the biggest impact on me. Also, the space on Hudson Street has to be one of my all-time favorite exhibition spaces, because it was a labyrinth, and the feeling of being in a set of abandoned offices was quite theatrical and dramatic. Each room worked well to allow individual artists to present their work.

I honestly believe that Helene Winer is one of the great curators of the post-war era. She shepherded in the 80s in terms of appropriation and neoconceptualism and, of course, the use of photography. People may not remember that she was a Director at Artists Space. It was an extraordinary *kunsthalle* under her, and one of the few times a nonprofit space led the way in establishing a whole new artistic vision.

Tony Oursler, set for video.
Façades, Landscapes, Interiors, May 29 - July 17, 1982.

223 West Broadway, May 1984.

May 31–June 30: **A Decade of New Art: Artists Space** (Linda L. Cathcart). Tenth anniversary retrospective of work by 65 artists who have shown at Artists Space, installed at 105 Hudson and 223 West Broadway. Ericka Beckman, Gretchen Bender, Dara Birnbaum, Eric Bogosian, Jonathan Borofsky, Troy Brauntuch, Michael Brewster, Gary Burnley, Scott Burton, Michael Byron, Cynthia Carlson, James Casebere, Louisa Chase, Charles Clough, Arch Connelly, Marcia Dalby, Carroll Dunham, Nancy Dwyer, William Fares, R. M. Fischer, Hermine Ford, Stephen Frailey, Bobby G, Jack Goldstein, Don Gummer, David Haxton, Biff Henrich, Jenny Holzer, Rebecca Howland, Mel Kendrick, Jon Kessler, Jeff Koons, Barbara Kruger, Thomas Lanigan-Schmidt, Thomas Lawson, John Lees, Sherrie Levine, Robert Longo, Ree Morton, Matt Mullican, Nic Nicosia, Kevin Noble, Tom Otterness, Ken Pelka, Judy Pfaff, Ellen Phelan, Adrian Piper, Jim Pomeroy, Richard Prince, Walter Robinson, Tim Rollins, Ellen Rumm, Christy Rupp, David Salle, Cindy Sherman, Laurie Simmons, Charles Simonds, Michael Smith, Philip Smith, Ted Stamm, Donald Sultan, John Torreano, Roger Welch, Peggy Yunque, Michael Zwack. Catalogue with essay by Linda L. Cathcart.

Alfredo Jaar

ARTIST/BOARD

I had just finished studying architecture and filmmaking in Chile. It was during the dictatorship of General Pinochet, and I was simply suffocating. I had a French education, so I was on my way to Paris. Most intellectuals in Chile and Latin American spoke either French, German, or Italian, and of course, Spanish. At that time we didn't look to the U.S. as a place to go because we always saw it as this capitalist monster in the North. We had this history of repression from the U.S. Nevertheless, I had this fascination for New York, which I had visited in '77, and wanted to return for three months. I just wanted to see what was going on and then continue to Europe. Instead, I moved to New York in February '82 and have stayed ever since. It took a year to figure out the galleries. Coming from Chile, the East Village was a little scary. I didn't have much respect for what was going on there. It was lively and stimulating, but my work didn't fit in. I had worked for Site for many years, so I developed a quiet architectural practice and slowly started to understand how things worked. Putting my slides in the Artists File was one of the first steps I took. When Valerie Smith called it was just unbelievable. I was very young and had been in New York only two years.

I did a very fragile installation about democracy. It was a big plexiglass box with a silkscreened text on top and hundreds of eggs and neon tubing inside. I was mimicking the incubation of democracy or the incubation of some monster. It was the Reagan years and beginning to get tough. At the same time, because extremes touch each other, there was an opening for this type of work. There was also a big photographic piece on one of the walls, an appropriated ad from the Getty Foundation. I recently looked at the catalogue and reread my statement. I can't believe I said those things! It says something like, "My responsibility is to define my work's relationship to society in the real world. I would like to be in that privileged group of creative professionals who have the opportunity to make all of us think. To think about the total destruction of mankind. To think about the widening gap between the developed countries and the Third World. To think about the ideological media idiotization of our lives. To think about the urgent need for social change. To think about, oh yes, the pursuit of happiness. To think is only the first step, the second is action." It was 1984 and I was a nobody attacking the Getty! I felt confident Artists Space would back me up. So I just went for it.

The Artists Space Board meetings were only about making suggestions. The staff listened to us, but didn't necessarily implement our thoughts. At first, I found it very interesting and fascinating and thought it was the right way to go. But as time went by, nothing came out of these discussions. So I felt a gap was starting to open between the mission and what was finally happening in the institution. I was confused about the mission of the Board. It was very frightening and very sad to see what was happening. The art world changed. There was no money and people were asking, "What the hell are we doing with an alternative space? What does it mean today?" I left at that moment. It's amazing now, working with such a small budget, that you (Claudia Gould) have been able to do the programs you have done and with such visibility. In that sense, Artists Space is a generous institution. It has all my respect and admiration. It's like my home and my family — it's very important to me.

Mel Ziegler

ARTIST

An architect friend was having a hard time drawing this building. He didn't like what he was working on, so he drew a palm tree in front of it. I gave him a hard time about drawing a landscape in front of the building because he couldn't get the building to work. We talked about this for a long time. Out of that discussion came *Instant Landscape,* this idea you could alter something depending upon the landscape and the things placed in front of it. This was right after the project Kate (Ericson) and I did called *Unplanted Landscape.*

We were living in Manhattan and wanted to continue working on suburban projects. So we went out to Long Island and came across a tract home that had been there since the 50s. It had no landscaping, no shrubbery or trees, just grass. The couple had pulled it all out because they didn't like what was there. We proposed to landscape the plot in front of the house, with the rootballs remaining in burlap, for about a month. That project was a precursor to *Instant Landscape* for Artists Space. *Instant Landscape* was the third of three truck projects we did in New York City, but the only and last time I worked on a project without Kate.

I remember it was down to the wire to try and get permits through Artists Space. They had never done anything like this before, so it was almost impossible for the insurance company. I had to go to the Department of Transportation and get the permit because the truck was going to be parked on the street. Finally, we went back to the Lower Manhattan Cultural Council, who gave us the permit, and Artists Space bought the insurance through them. It was a 40-foot flatbed trailer with

CONTINUED

1984–85

Sept. 29–Oct. 27: **Five Artists** (Will Insley). Taka Amano, drawing and models; Nina Kayem, painting; Alan Steele, sculpture; Paul Stimson, painting; Marybeth Welch, installation. Brochure with essay by Will Insley and statements by the artists.

Nov. 3–Dec. 1: **Selections** from the Artists File (Valerie Smith). Douglas Ashford, photo-text; Jessica Diamond, drawing; Kate Ericson, installation; Peter Halley, painting; Amy Hauft, installation; Alfredo Jaar, installation; Hilary Kliros, sculpture; Barbara Lattanzi, installation; Charles San Clementi, installation; Anthony Silvestrini, photographs; Charles Yuen, painting; Michelle Zalopany, drawing; Mel Ziegler, outdoor installation.

Catalogue with introduction by Valerie Smith and statements by the artists.

← OPPOSITE PAGE: Alfredo Jaar

↓ Mel Ziegler, *Instant Landscape*.
Photo: Pelka/Noble

MEL ZIEGLER / CONTINUED

80 ornamental juniper trees in their rootballs cabled down onto the truck. That was the basis of the project. I was a little nervous because it was outside and vandalism is a big problem in the city; I always suspect something will happen. I think one tree was stolen, and that was toward the end of the exhibition. But I decided I would catch the person if they came back. So I ended up standing inside Artists Space looking outside the door the whole night. Early one morning I found Andy Spence painting over dollar signs and a statement saying "tree murderer for big art bucks" sprayed all over the front door of Artists Space. It was ironic because I was probably going to lose money on the project, and I watered the trees every other morning, because I wanted to sell them to be planted at the end of the project. I got out a hose and made sure they were kept alive. One day watering the trees, someone in the building across the street yelled, "Tree murderer!" from a window. We never could find out exactly where it was coming from.

One of the nicest things that came out of it was meeting Mary Miss for the first time. I was out there photographing the project and this woman came up to me and said, "Do you know who did this?" I had always been a great admirer of her work. She introduced herself and we became good friends and always kept in touch. It was a nice way to meet somebody and start a friendship.

Dec. 8–Jan. 12: **Forced Sentiment** (Robert Longo). Peter Coates, painted wood relief; Anne Doran, painted wood relief; Steven Koivisto, painting; Kevin Larmon, painting; Joel Otterson, sculpture; Steven Parrino, painting; Anne Surprenant, painting. Catalogue with essay by Tricia Collins and Richard Milazzo, preface by Robert Longo.

Dec. 15: Curator's tour by Robert Longo.

1985 JAN–APR

Jan. 26–Feb. 23: **Dark Rooms** (Valerie Smith). Judith Barry, *In the Shadow of the City...vamp r y...*, slide and film installation; Eva Brandl, *The Golden Gates*, slide installation; James Carpenter, *Shaking*, film installation; Jon Rubin, *Alice Underwater*, film installation. Brochure documents this exhibition and the 1983 **Dark Rooms,** with introduction by Valerie Smith and essay by John Hanhardt.

Feb.9: Curator's tour by Valerie Smith.

↓ Judith Barry
    Photo: Kenji Fujita

Mar. 9 - Apr. 6: Bert Carpenter, painting and drawing; Charles Harbutt, photographs; Duane Zaloudek, drawing installation (Gary Burnley, Donald Droll, Linda Shearer). Exhibition sponsored by the Mark Rothko Foundation. Three brochures: Carpenter essay by Jane Necol; Harbutt essay by Andy Grundberg and Julia Scully; Zaloudek essay by Claire Copley.

Mar. 23: **Get It in Writing: An Evening of Readings** (John Miller). Dennis Cooper, Mike Kelley, John Miller, Benjamin Weissman, and Dana Duff.

Mar. 30: **Marathon slide show,** an all-day slide presentation of all artists in the Artists File, with Linda Shearer and Valerie Smith.

Apr. 13 – May 31: **Five Spanish Artists** (Donald Sultan). Miquel Barceló, Miguel Angel Campano, Menchu Lamas, Ferrán García Sevilla, José-María Sicilia. Gallery talk, Apr. 20. Catalogue with introduction by Donald Sultan and essays by Ramón Tío Bellido, Juan Manuel Bonet, Marga Paz, Kevin Power, Francisco Rivas, and Francisco Calvo Serraller.

May 9 – 11: **Super-8 Solar System** (Peggy Ahwesh/Steven Gallagher).

May 9: Joe Gibbons, *Living in the World, parts 1 & 2,* 1983-85; Lewis Klahr, *Picture Books for Adults;* 1982-85; Margie Strosser, *Autobiography in Three Acts,* 1982.

May 10: Janet Callahan, *Pre-War Criminal,* 1984, and *Survival of the Fittest,* 1985; J. Foley, *Boy/Boy,* 1983, and other films; Richard Kern, selections from *Manhattan Love Suicides,* 1984-85; Max Henry, *Liberace,* 1984; Patty Wallace, *Honcho,* 1984, and *Honcho,* 1985.

May 11: Peggy Ahwesh, *Learning the Hard Way,* 1985; Barbara Broughel, *Abstract Realism, numbers 1 & 2,* 1984-85; Direct Art Productions (Sid Gilbert/Fabio Roberti/Michael Wolfe), *Bloody Stump,* 1983, *A Portrait of the Man,* 1984, *Good Lovin Guitar Man,* 1984, and *Heterosexual Love,* 1984; Stephen Gallagher, *A Common Bond,* 1985; Paul Sharits, *Brancusi's Sculpture Ensemble at Tirgu Jiu,* 1984.

ARTIST

Judith Barry When I first came to New York I felt I had to start over, because I'd already had a lot of shows in San Francisco yet I was completely unknown here. I was also trying to change my work from performance and single channel videotapes to installation. I remember being excited when I finally talked you (Valerie Smith) into giving me a show. You were the only one remotely interested in letting me do an installation, which was a big transition for me. It was my first real installation.

On one side was Jon Rubin with this fabulous piece about Alice in Wonderland with the history of film and projections. On the other was James Carpenter with his great piece of little projectors about leaves, and I was in between them. I was so excited to be doing an installation in a gallery. But I remember having conversations with both of them and they each said to me that they were leaving, starting over in different areas, and I could have their equipment. James took me aside and said, "I'm not going to be doing this anymore, I think this is the very last of these installation pieces in a gallery." It was a funny moment, like passing the torch. Especially with James, he implied, "Now it's your turn to do this for a while." He really did want to give me his old projectors, which was very sweet, but I didn't take them in the end, because I felt he should keep them for symbolic reasons, if nothing else. There was a parallel between my starting over at Artists Space and, simultaneously, Jon and James starting over in another way. I hadn't quite realized that situation, but I'm constantly starting over. It is one of the things that Artists Space provided.

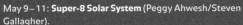

May 14–15: **Memory Jam: A Retrospective of Films and Performances at Artists Space, 1973–1985** (Regina Cornwell). Films screened at the Collective for Living Cinema, New York.

May 14: Vito Acconci, *Three Relationship Studies (Manipulations, Imitations, Shadow Box)*, 1970; John Baldessari, *Title*, 1971; Nancy Graves, *Izy Boukir*, 1970; Dan Graham, *Sunset to Sunrise*, 1969; Mary Miss, *Cut-Off*, 1974; Richard Serra/Clara Weyergraf, *Steelmill/Stahlwerk*, 1979.

May 15: Beth B and Scott B, *Letters to Dad*, 1979; Tim Burns, *Thus Went Philippa*, 1983; Manuel De Landa, *Ism Ism*, 1978; Jack Goldstein, *The Chair*, 1975, *The Knife*, 1975, *Shane*, 1975, and *Metro-Goldwyn-Mayer*, 1975; David Haxton, *Cube and Room Drawings*, 1976-77; Ken Kobland, *Vestibule*, 1978; Stuart Sherman, *Globes*, 1978, *Scotty and Stuart*, 1978, *Skating*, 1978, and *Baseball/TV*, 1979.

May 16–18: **Memory Jam: A Retrospective of Films and Performances at Artists Space, 1975–1985** (Edit deAk and RoseLee Goldberg). Performances at Artists Space.
May 16: Matt Mullican, *The List* and other works, 1973-81; Robin Winters, *Relax*, 1985.
May 17: Paul McMahon, *Song Paintings*, 1982, *Potato Jokes*, 1984-85, *Songs*, 1978-1985, and *Mild Style*, 1984, video; Michael Smith, *Minimal Movement Message and/or Minimal Message Movement*, 1975, excerpts from *Down in the Rec Room*, 1978, excerpts from *Selected Routines*, 1980–85, *Baby IKKI*, 1975, and *Go For It Mike*, video.
May 18: Jill Kroesen, *Lowell Jerkman Story*, 1981; Robert Longo, *Sound Distance of a Good Man*, 1977.

← Michael Smith with Harry Kipper, *Baby IKKI*, 1985.
© Paula Court

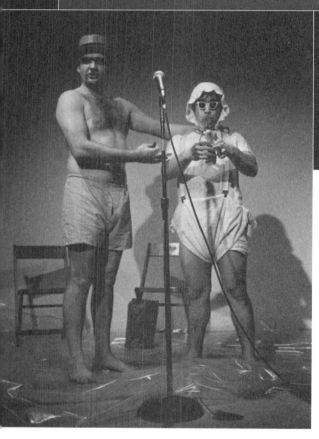

Mary Miss When Artists Space started in 1973, a lot of us were trying to find alternative ways of interacting with the art world, whether it was trying to do work outside the usual gallery structure or whether it was finding other kinds of galleries. Helene Winer brought me on the Board when it was on Hudson Street. Actually, we hardly had Board meetings. There was this study then which looked at Artists Space and critiqued it from within. We interviewed a lot of people and spent a lot of time talking about it. I thought Helene's programming was too homogeneous. She successfully developed a group of artists and a type of work which she went on to support in a larger way. She made a big contribution.

My interests were elsewhere. I really liked the complexity, richness, and interaction of many different types of work—different fields overlapping, dancers, artists, and poets. I was less interested in this very discrete thing on the wall. But, you know, it wasn't a big deal. It's not as if there were Board meetings where people were saying, "Oh, Helene, this can't go on!" She was doing her thing. There was very little Board interference. I worked a lot with Linda Shearer. Linda operated very differently than Helene. She had Board meetings and asked for people's opinions whenever issues started to come up. All of a sudden, during Linda's time, it really grew up as an organization.

As a Board member, I felt it was important to have artists' voices present in the organization. That's what I liked about Artists Space, as opposed to just a curatorial voice or a benefactor's voice. I felt it was important for artists to give something back to the community, to be supportive, to be engaged and talk about issues, rather than just be the bad boy or bad girl— a stereotypical artist off doing your own thing.

When Artists Space started there was such a sense of empowerment. Artists could affect things, they could take their work out of the usual structure, and engage with the culture and society in different ways. It's hard to describe the sense of idealism or the way we thought, but we were very serious about it. As I said the evening I was honored at your benefit, it is very shocking to find, 25 or 30 years later, that artists have become so vilified. It's almost as if the opposite has happened from what we expected at that early point. It makes you aware you can't be so secure in your optimism. People say, "Oh, the pendulum will swing back the other way." But in the meantime, here we are stuck with a fairly difficult funding situation. I still think Artists Space represents something important. Although many people have dismissed the idealism that came forth in the late 60s and early 70s, I'm not willing to. I still think that period made a very important contribution. More than ever, artists act as though they have to do what everybody else tells them to do. But the notion of having some independence of movement and sense of empowerment is extremely important.

May 25–June 29: **U.S. Projects**. Jerry Beck, Boston, mixed media (Kathy Halbreich); Anita David, Chicago, *Talking to a Man, 1983,* installation (Anne Rorimer); Audrey Glassman, Minneapolis, photographs (Marge Goldwater); Sherry Markovitz, Seattle, *From Dust to Dust and In Between,* installation (Anne Focke); and Patricia Thornley, Atlanta, installation (Alan Sondheim). Catalogue with essays by Anne Focke, Marge Goldwater, Kathy Halbreich, Anne Rorimer, and Alan Sondheim.

June 8: Gallery talk in conjunction with **U.S. Projects**.

July 13–Aug. 3: **Artists from the Studio in a School** (selected in consultation with Patterson Sims). Jo-Ann Acey, Susan Austad, Gail Bach, Noah Baen, Lisa Bateman, Olivia Beens, Rick Bleier, Corliss Block, Thomas Cahill, Valerie Constantino, Lorraine Fiddle, Beth Hausman, Julie Lapping, Helene Manzo, Lawrence E. Merenstein, Marilyn Reynolds, James Richards, Greg Russell, Mary Ann Rose, Anita Saghbazarian, Marcy Snapp, John Stevenson, Robin Sulkes, Gretchen Treitz, Alice Turkel, Dennis Whitehouse, Stewart Wilson, Oscar Yacila.

ARTIST / WRITER

John Miller *Get It in Writing* was experiential. There was Mike Kelley, Dennis Cooper, and Benjamin Weissman which, in retrospect, was a very good lineup. It came about through Mike, whom I had met in 1978, and Benjamin, whom I knew from Cal Arts. I knew Dennis Cooper through Benjamin and Beyond Baroque. These days, Beyond Baroque (a literary arts center in Venice, California) isn't as central to the Los Angeles art scene as it was when I was in school. The ties were strong, all of us had done something there. So the reading was a natural extension of the Beyond Baroque scene. Beyond Baroque had a strong overlap between writing and visual art. Much more so than in New York, where the poetry and visual art scenes were more separate. Those fields are both bigger in New York. Also, there was a specific Los Angeles sensibility that had affinities to literature and literary criticism, which were my particular interests, in the vein of the book project, *Cave Canem,* which I did with Dan Walworth. That night we were all there: early, nervous, and fretting. You (Valerie Smith) waltzed in at the last minute and Dennis looked at us as if to say, "What are you guys all bent out of shape for?" Dennis was offhand about it. For him, reading in a visual arts venue wasn't so important. And Benjamin read something having to do with recollections of his mother. It was at a time when he was just hitting his stride as a writer.

There was a Los Angeles version of Pop, with which I may have shared some things. It's about looking at very vernacular subjects in a really unidealized way. Very violent and in part a reaction to violence. In a way, Dennis's stories are always the same. There's always a bodily transgression, but also an interesting juxtaposition between milieu and what's at work in the story. In Benjamin's writing, the story often happens through vivid pictorial details, characteristic of different things like class-based identity (although he would never put it in that literary correct language, I'm sure). And he relates that to personal interaction and degradation, which is what his stories are all about. My work is always hopping back and forth between an apocalyptic nightmarish quality because of the brown impasto signifying there's an everyday normality. Part of the point is the structure between the two. One is contained in the other, the operation of the everyday can fluctuate the terms of the apocalypse. In the drawings I showed earlier on at Artists Space, the accent was on everydayness. I wanted the pictures not to close the conventional avant-gardist challenge to the viewer. But a year or two ago I showed some slides in Chris Williams's class and he said it was funny seeing them because everybody now regards them as punky and somehow dangerous. When I showed them out in Los Angeles, there was a fairly well-known director who likened them to Raymond Carver. I was happy it was a literary allusion.

1985–86

In 1985 Linda Shearer resigns and Susan Wyatt becomes Executive Director. For the 1985–86 season, programming is determined by Susan Wyatt and Valerie Smith, Curator. A formal video program is initiated to run concurrently with exhibitions, and Dan Walworth is hired as the Film/Video Curator in 1986.

Sept. 19: Preview and curator's talk with Kay Larson.

Sept. 21–Oct. 19: **Selections** from the Artists File (Kay Larson). Dorothy Cochran, prints; Nicholas DeLucia, photographs; Roger Freeman, photographs; Robin Hill, sculpture; Steven Kasher, photo installation; Julian Lethbridge, painting; Thor Rinden, painting; Jacques Roch, painting; Jessica Stockholder, installation; Peter White, painting; Tad Wiley, sculpture; Philip Zimmerman, drawing. Catalogue with essay by Kay Larson and statements by the artists.

Sept. 28: **Marathon slide show**, an all-day slide presentation of all artists in the Artists File with Linda Shearer and Valerie Smith.

Oct. 20: East Village insider's tour by Deborah Sharpe, Sharpe Gallery.

Oct. 24–26: **Film** (Linda Dubler, Atlanta; David James, Los Angeles; Julia Lesage, Chicago).
Oct. 24 (David James): Paul Arthur, *The Cliffs the Silk City Detour*, 1985; Kit Hellman, *Hollywood Series #1, Erratic, Hollywood Series #2,* and *An Afternoon Walk*, 1984; Corey Kaplan, *The Monster Frankenstein,* 1985; Andrew Karp, *The Juche Idea,* 1984; Buddy Kilchesty, *The Singing Cell,* 1981; Susan Rosenfeld, *Now Playing,* 1983; Craig Schlattman, *Bag,* 1985; Richard Serra, *Nightfall,* 1982, and *Framed,* 1984; Barbara McCullough, *Water Ritual #1: An Urban Rite of Purification,* 1979; Iverson White, *Dark Exodus.*
Oct. 25 (Julia Lesage): Sharon Couzin, *Salve,* 1981; Jo Anne Elam, *Lie Back and Enjoy It,* 1982; Chick Kleinhans, *It's Not Made by Great Men,* 1981; David Obermeyer, *Snapshot/Portrait Film,* 1980; Jean Sousa, *Swish,* 1982; Coleen Sullivan, *Buffalo One, Buffalo Two...,* 1985; Bill Stamets, *Major Speaks to Group,* 1983; Bill Stamets, *China President Visits Chicagoland,* 1985.
Oct. 26 (Linda Dubler): Lee Sokol, *Aqui Se Lo Halla (Here You Will Find It),* 1983; Nancy Yasecko, *Growing Up with Rockets,* 1985.

Nov. 2–27: **Four Artists** (Elizabeth Murray). Margrit Lewczuk, painting; Lizbeth Marano, sculpture; Dona Nelson, painting; Jenny Snider, painting. Brochure with introduction by Elizabeth Murray.

Nov. 9: Curator's talk with Elizabeth Murray.

ARTIST/CURATOR

Kathryn High

In 1985, Artists Space had a video curator and was showing video regularly. So was the Kitchen, but there weren't many venues. That's why it was incredible that Artists Space did this program and actually had a curator who looked at work regularly and put on shows. It was definitely a place people went to all the time to see work.

I was so happy to have a space where there was just video being shown. I liked the couch in the basement and going down there to watch stuff. It was quiet and isolated, which allowed me to concentrate on whatever was being screened. I appreciated the separate space set aside for this. Often, it ends up being in the basement, which is not the most ideal place, but I was happy it was something full time.

Dan Walworth, and later Micki McGee, paid attention to themes coming up in artists' work—and not just artists with big names. They paid attention to how people expressed themselves with the medium and what it meant to use video as a tool. They kept abreast of recent developments. As a curator and an artist, I admired their selections and the programs they put together. If we looked at those programs today, they would still hold up. One thing that's always been impressive about Artists Space's shows is you either got other connections out of them or a discussion about the work, but just showing the work wasn't the only focus. It was a bigger event.

ARTIST/BOARD

Hermine Ford

It was my first one-person show in New York. It was a very distinct body of work for me of abstract horizontal paintings divided into four rectangular areas. They were more methodical than my work later became because there was something different going on in each section. I loved that show. A lot of people saw and responded to it, and it carried me a long way. Watching other artists exhibit their work at Artists Space over the years, I've seen how it's always been a major experience for them, too. It works for both young emerging artists and older under-recognized artists.

Shirley Jaffe's exhibition, sponsored by the Mark Rothko Foundation, was one of the last shows to which I felt a personal connection. She is a middle-aged artist, born in America, yet she lived in Paris for many years. It was an exhibition I hadn't thought of, but I immediately realized it was a great idea. She had shown at Fourcade in Paris and had no opportunity to show in New York. It was wonderful for Shirley, she was completely thrilled. That's interesting, because artists are usually extremely unaware of their exhibition's impact or lack thereof. I have seen Shirley at regular intervals all through these years and I keep telling her—but she doesn't believe me—that I constantly run into particularly young women artists, at least a full generation behind me, who say, "Shirley Jaffe, I know her work." And I ask, "How do you know it?" and they say, "The first time I ever saw her work was at Artists Space." Young women are keenly interested in middle-aged women artists and follow them very carefully. I love that.

I was exhausted from Artists Space when I left the Board. We had been through such a turmoil. I maintained, as far as I know, good relationships with everybody involved. But it was so draining, so intense, with everything we went through. So I haven't been really involved with Artists Space for the last few years. But I am thrilled that it's survived.

Nov. 2–27: Video: What Does _She_ Want (Lyn Blumenthal). Laurie Anderson, _O Superman_, 1981; Nancy Angelo/Candace Compton, _Nun and Deviant_, 1976; Max Almy, _Modern Love_, 1979; Lynda Benglis, _Female Sensibility_, 1974; Maxi Cohen, _The Edge of Life_, 1984; Cara DeVito, _Ama L'uomo Tuo_, 1974; Hermine Freed, _Art Herstory_, 1977; Julie Gustafson, _The Politics of Intimacy_, 1983; Kathy High, _Not Black and White_, 1985; Calvin Klein, _Shari_, 1984; Barbara Latham, _Consuming Passion_, 1983; Ardele Lister, _Split_, 1981; L'Oreal, commercial; Branda Miller, _Unset Blvd._, 1985; Sheri Millner, _Womb with a View_, 1983; Susan Mogul, _Take Off_, 1974; Paper Tiger Television, _Ynestra King Reads Seventeen_, 1983; Candace Reckinger, _Impossible Love_, 1974; Martha Rosler, _Losing: A Conversation with Parents_, 1977; Jesse Rosser, _Love Cannibal_, 1980; Saturday Night Live, _The Planet of the Men vs. the Planet of the Women_, 1983, producer Dick Ebersol, Lorimar Productions.

Dec. 4–5: Art Breaks, benefit premiere of Music Television Network (MTV) artists' videos and exhibition: Jean Michel Basquiat, Jonathan Borofsky, Charles Clough, Luigi Ontani, Richard Prince, Richard Tuttle.

Dec. 14–Jan. 18: Split/Vision (Robert Mapplethorpe and Laurie Simmons). Alan Belcher, installation; Jerald Frampton, photography; Laurie Neaman, photography; Lydia Panas, installation; Julie Wachtel, poster piece (Simmons); Peter Berlin, painted photography; Paul Blanca, photography; George Dureau, photography; Mark Morrisroe, photography; Jean-Marc Prouveur, photo pieces (Mapplethorpe). Catalogue with essay by Andy Grundberg.
Jan. 11: Curators' talk with Mapplethorpe and Simmons.

ARTIST/CURATOR

Carole Ann Klonarides

Back in the early 80s there were not too many alternative spaces that showed video on a regular basis. Susan Wyatt approached Lyn Blumenthal, Director of the Video Data Bank in Chicago, and me to help create a regular program of videos.

Artists Space then created a little video viewing area down in their basement where Lyn did the first show. When I organized my exhibition, I thought it would be interesting to help the audience come to terms with video, not just as a creative tool, but show how artists used the television lens and how the media not only influenced their work, but supplemented it. I began to see the history of the representation of artists through film and television, which creates the myth of the artist. I changed the adage of Andy Warhol, "Everyone will be famous for 15 minutes," to "Everyone will be famous for 30 seconds," which is the time of a commercial spot. During one year I collected about seven hours of off-the-air coverage of artists on talk shows, on news shows, and on TV shows, sitcoms, etc., in addition to some unavailable films. At that time VCRs were a new phenomenon, people were just beginning to tape programs on TV. _Famous for 30 Seconds_ was the depiction of artists represented through the medium of film.

MICA TV has always worked with artists to create a video equivalent of their ideas within their work. Michael Owens, my partner in MICA TV, and I created these little spots. We also incorporated, within the program, other artists and critics who do the same thing. Artists like Joan Loch, who did 30-second spots of John Cage and Laurie Anderson, as well as some interviews with artists and writers. The seven-hour program was so well received that several years later the Whitney Museum approached me to include an edited version for their _Image World_ exhibition.

Susan was very willing to create an ambiance in the video viewing room. We papered it with _ArtNews_ covers and other depictions of artists in the media. It created a discussion about how artists were beginning to reinvent themselves through the eyes of media masters. Of course, Artists Space was the perfect context to curate _Famous for 30 Seconds,_ because it had always been about artists selecting other artists and using their own community to recreate themselves.

Dec. 14–Jan. 18: Seth Weinhardt, _Immanent Madness_, film installation.

Jan. 25–Feb. 22: Six Sculptors (Valerie Smith). William Harvey, Lisa Hoke, Steven Schiff, Ritsuko Taho, B. Wurtz, Yuriko Yamaguchi. Brochure with essay by Valerie Smith. Feb.1: Curator's talk with Valerie Smith.

Nan Goldin Until the mid-80s, I was always really late for my shows—editing them in the cab on the way there. Before *The Ballad of Sexual Dependency,* I did all these small slide shows, and then about 1983 they started to develop into *The Ballad.* I showed *Motel, Hotel, Brothels and Bars* when Artists Space was on Hudson Street. *Motel, Hotel* came from a popular rap song. It was the CoLab period and the whole ambience in those days was everybody just hanging out—life didn't have the same kind of pressure. I'm sure there was a big market, but I didn't know anything about it. We had our own alternative reality to the art world. We were busy in the late 70s and early 80s, Vivienne Dick, Bette Gordon, Robert Cooney, Kiki Smith, Cara Perlman, Jane Dickson, and myself—it was all that scene. There were a number of these places, OP Screening Room, Artists Space, ABC No Rio, and communal events where the audience was made up of mostly the artists in the show, who were all friends.

I recall Susan Wyatt calling me in Boston and then she took all the credit for the *Witnesses* show, acting like she curated the show to the press. It was the first show I had ever curated. But in all the media hoopla there was hardly a word about the fact that I had curated the show or that it was my idea. It was my curatorial debut, and I really wanted to hear from other curators. Elizabeth Sussman told me later she based her 1993 Whitney Biennial on *Witnesses: Against Our Vanishing.*

I thought about the show for a year, consulting with my friends. During this conceptual period Mark Morrisroe died. Vittorio Scarpati died. Cookie Mueller died the day the show opened. I was living in Boston at the time, just out of detox, and I wanted to make amends to my community. I had been really strung out for a few years, so I missed the 80s. I was there for everyone, but not as much as I wanted to be for the people who were sick. I thought of a number of issues I wanted to deal with and I decided to talk about AIDS. It was my service to my community, because it was the most pressing issue in our lives. It was the only thing really crucial to me. Anyway, instead of making it theoretical, which I'm incapable of, I decided to just select my friends, the same people who are in my photos and have inspired my work. Friends living with AIDS, friends who had lost their lovers, friends who had lost their family, and some of the most important people to me who had already died, like Peter Hujar. So I told Susan I wanted to do a show about AIDS. I had three or four different ideas and she encouraged me to do the AIDS show.

Then I needed to come up with people to write a text. Again, I asked friends. I wanted Marvin Heiferman to write something, but he said he was too busy or didn't feel it was right, but that David (Wojnarowicz) would be perfect. I'd known David since 1980, but we hadn't really worked closely together. He wrote this incredible piece, it was amazingly powerful. And we were in constant contact from that point on. He called and read me the piece and, at the same time, sent it to Susan. She immediately started trying to censor it. So, right from the start I was in an adversarial position with Susan, because of my loyalty and love for David. At first she took out "fucking." Then she asked him to remove the part about the fat cannibal and Cardinal O'Connor and also the section about dousing Jesse Helms on fire. I learned a lot from David. I learned never to allow anyone to censor me. David taught me pretty quickly that you don't make those kinds of compromises. He was adamant about never compromising one step. He took out one "fucking" from the text and refused to remove any more. I said there was no way I could do the catalogue without his text. It was the most brilliant piece written about AIDS, and still is. The fact that he wrote it for *Witnesses* was a great honor. So, Susan called Mr. Frohnmayer and sent him a copy of the text. So began David's torment by the Right wing, including the Christian Coalition, for the rest of his life. David and I were really proud that in 1989 words could still have that effect, to the extent that people would want to censor them. You know, if Susan had left it alone, they probably never would have seen it.

Frohnmayer came to Artists Space and there was a refusal to compromise, so the $10,000 NEA grant was taken away. It had more to do with the text than the exhibition. Susan also allowed them to go through the material I'd chosen to approve or disapprove it for the show. But I didn't censor anything. I don't recall if they actually had any problem with the material, except for the memorial piece using Mark's (Morrisroe) bloody sheets by the artist Ramsey McPhillips. It horrified them.

My whole life and work have been about inclusion rather than exclusion. I wanted to include as many friends as I could. And the negativeness in the whole affair had to do with Artists Space's administration, basically Susan Wyatt. It had to do with the attempted censorship of David's text. Leonard Bernstein refused the Congressional Medal of Honor in support of my show. And he refused to go to lunch at the Bushes' (Mrs. and former President George Bush). As a result, we got the money back. It was completely shocking to me because, although I had been reviewed in the back page arts section of the *New York Times,* I had never been on the front page of newspapers. I had journalists calling me from 6:00 a.m. until 11:00 p.m. at night—I felt inadequate to talk about it. I felt David should really talk. I was confused. I had Susan pulling me in one direction, telling me to encourage David to censor the work so everything would be much easier. I completely supported David. I just didn't feel prepared. They'd say, "This is your 15 minutes of fame, if you don't say anything now no one will ever want to hear from you again." I was interviewed for TV in Boston and it was going to be on the local news station, but the Berlin Wall came down that day. However, the good that came out of it was that it brought the community together. The bad part was it was very stressful for David. The media went on a feeding frenzy after him. Susan was convinced journalists and the media would look at the show, or so she said. In fact, it is unlikely they would have seen the show or read the text. Whether it would have had the same power in the community, if all of that hadn't happened, I guess not. It would have had an audience, because I'd included so many people and they had so many friends; it would have been a big opening nevertheless. Opening night, *Witnesses* had around 15,000 people and demonstrations all over the place. So on that level it was good. We took on the NEA and we won.

Jan. 25–Feb. 22: **Video: Famous for 30 Seconds: Artists in the Media** (Carole Ann Klonarides, edited by Jeffrey Turtletaub). Michel Auder, *Portrait of an Artist at Work: Cindy Sherman*, 1984; Barry Blinderman/Shalom Gorewitz, *Conversation with Robert Longo*, 1984; Chris Burden, *Three Commercials with Explanation: Crawling Through Glass, Poem for L.A. (Science has Failed Heat is Life, Time Kills), Chris Burden Promo*, 1973–76; Stefaan de Costere/Chris Dercon, *Why We Men Love Technology So Much*, 1985, with Jack Goldstein, Paul Virilio, Klaus von Bruch, produced by Claude Blondeel for BRT; Circle Fine Art Galleries, *The Light Sculpture of Bill Parker*, 1984; Jaime Davidovich, *SoHo TV Presents: The Live! Show*, 1982, with John Torreano, Paul McMahon, René the Best Artist; Tracy Egan/Art McFarland, *EyeWitness News Channel 7, Jenny Holzer—Sign on a Truck*, 1984; Suzan Etkin/Don Munroe, *Andy Warhol's TV—Kenny Scharf and Keith Haring*, 1983, *Body Prints*, 1985, *Andy Warhol's Fifteen Minutes with Charlie Clough*, 1984, *Andy Warhol's TV—On Tour with Michael Smith and William Wegman*, 1982, *Andy Warhol's TV—James Brown*, 1983, and *Andy Warhol's TV—RoseLee Goldberg interviews Cindy Sherman and Molissa Fenley*, 1982; *Fantasy, L.A., Keith Haring*, 1982; Louise Greenfield, Sally Simmons, and Michael Hirst, *Richard Hambleton's Night Life*, 1983; Jeannette Ingberman and Papo Colo, *EXIT IN 3-A fiction documentary*, 1985, about Jerry Kearns, Elaine Lustig Cohen, Hunt Slonem; Japan News, Tokyo, *Keith Haring*, 1983; Carole Ann Klonarides/Michael Owen (MICA-TV), *R.M. Fischer—An Industrial*, 1983, *Richard Prince—Editions*, 1982, *Laurie Simmons—A Teaser*, 1982, and *Cindy Sherman—An Interview*, 1981; Carole Ann Klonarides/Jeffrey Turtletaub, *Hollywood Stereotypes—The Way They Weren't*, 1985; Late Night with David Letterman, *Man Ray and William Wegman*, 1982; Joan Logue, *René and Georgette Magritte*, 1984, *30 Second Spots—TV Commercials for Artists: John Cage, Meredith Monk, Arnie Zane and Bill T. Jones, Maryanne Amacher, Robert Ashley, Charlemagne Palestine, Simone Forti, Carlos Santes, Spalding Gray, Richard Teitelbaum, Philip Glass, Laurie Anderson*, 1982; Aaron Spelling/Douglas S. Cramer, producer, ABC, *Love Boat* (with Andy Warhol), 1985; Branda Miller, *Andy Warhol/Leroy Neiman Opening Party November 14, 1981*, 1981; Music Television Network (MTV), Marcy Brafman, creative director, *ArtBreaks—Jean Michel Basquiat*, 1985, *ArtBreaks—Charles Clough*, 1985, and *ArtBreaks—Richard Prince*, 1985; Charles Osgood/Dan Rather, Channel 2 News (CBS), *Keith Haring*, 1982; Ripley's Believe It or Not! and Rolanda Watts, News 4 New York, *Eric Staller*, 1985; Saturday Night Live, film by Gary Weiss of William Wegman and Man Ray, 1975; Edin Velez, *Oblique Strategist, Too*, 1982, with Brian Eno.

BOARD

Richard Armstrong I moved to New York in 1973 and Artists Space was a place I frequented. I had a romantic idea about it from its inception. I certainly remember some very early shows of Judy Pfaff and Ellen Phelan. Their exhibitions marked the beginning of my knowing artists who showed. So when Linda Shearer asked me to be on the Board of Artists Space in 1984, it was especially meaningful for me.

After we moved over to West Broadway, it felt like a very public and thriving place again. In particular, there was this sense of affluence on the land and cash in the wind. There was a very organic art market where people needed entrees and there were a number of entrees available to them. In some ways, it made the job more difficult for Artists Space. So it became more institutionalized, only, to the degree that by then there were so many more ways for an artist to get into the art world, it may not have seemed quite as pressing trying to get a show. I always thought it had a wonderful identity, which it never lost. Even in the rough times, the scope of the ambition of the people who worked there was sufficient to guarantee a wide variety of people would be brought into the system. That only changed after Susan (Wyatt) left. And I left right then myself. I was not enthusiastic about her successor.

The principal culprit of the whole *Witnesses: Against Our Vanishing* episode was John Frohnmayer. He mishandled it. He had a very Pollyanna approach. Of course, he had no understanding at all about what the artists' aspirations were. But then, he had a very peculiar and parochial analysis of the threats coming down the pike. He tried to bring them to us and threaten us. There's no preparation for that kind of crisis. And particularly when you're dealing with people who have lived inside a long cocoon of idealism. He came to be a peacemaker and his motivation may have been genuine, but instead, he rubbed terrible pepper into people's eyes. I remember a particular meeting we had on West Broadway where we sat around in a circle and he made one gaff after another, and many different voices from the Board spoke back to him forcefully. It was very upsetting. It reminded me of the protests of the late 60s. Our responses weren't really measured and I'm afraid the pressure succeeded in dividing people. There will always be a division when you've got 20 different egomaniacs sitting around the room. That division contributed to Susan's leaving. There was a Newtonian reaction, a shock, then an aftershock. People started feeling she wouldn't come back to Artists Space. Instead, she was going to become a pioneer in resisting censorship. I felt it was a worthy cause but ultimately, not central to Artists Space's existence. So it was a huge unbridgeable chasm. I was trying to be a loyal puppy, but I had grave doubts about the whole thing. I was in a peculiar position of wanting to be tremendously loyal to the cause but not really having any conviction about content. But you don't get to pick your fights. When you think of the accumulated honorable actions and, in some instances, great foresightedness, it adds up to a tremendously worthy enterprise.

Feb. 27–Mar. 1: **Foreign Relations**. Three evenings of poetry readings, films, and video (Catherine Benamou, Dan Walworth, Valerie Smith).

Feb. 27 (Central America and the Caribbean): Raymond Cajuste, Collis Davis, *Voyage of Dreams*, 1983, film; Pedro Rivera, Susan Zeig, *Manos a la Obra: The Story of Operation Bootstrap*, 1983, film; Roberto Vargas, reading. Discussion with filmmakers.

Feb. 28 (Africa): José Cardoso, *They Dare Cross Our Border*, 1981, film; Trinh T. Minh-ha, *Naked Spaces: Living is Round*, 1985, film; Mfundi Vundla, reading. Discussion with Trinh T. Minh-ha.

ARTIST

Michael Paha Frankly, when I showed at Artists Space, it was like a tree falling in the woods. It was so early in my career, I didn't think it was weird I was showing with only guys because I thought, "Hey, I've got an opportunity to be in an exhibition in New York!" It didn't matter which gallery or who was in it. When I got there, I was asked whether I could do an installation for $500 and I said, "Sure." Then I found out that's how much it costs to breathe in New York. I spent the money just on the glass. But I managed like I always do. Honorariums are like seed money, I usually put my own money into it. Sometimes it's better, other times it's not.

Artists Space was exciting. I did an installation in two weeks and it was one of the first I had done outside of college. I wasn't well versed in making installations. Two weeks was a difficult task for me. I was very naive, but also very psyched about it. The day before the opening, I worked all the way through the night and the next day until 4:30 in order to finish up. I ordered all of the insects from Carolina Biological Supply. They were shipped from Burlington, North Carolina, to Artists Space. We got a discount because Artists Space was nonprofit. We had the passalid beetles. It was a difficult situation in the terrarium, because the beetles started committing suicide, jumping into the water containers and they were unable to get out. Actually, for the length of space they had, it was incidental that one would fall in. It's so noticeable when something like that happens. But it became a learning experience. It gave me an opportunity to be less functional and literal and more abstract in the idea. There was a broken window and a fishing rod in the installation, which was something I wanted to play with. I had done this piece at ArtpArk which was all about feeding and observing, but I wasn't able to get to the metaphor I was interested in. The Artists Space opportunity gave me a chance to develop the site specificity of the work. I'm the kind of person who doesn't go in the studio and live there. I work for projects and do installations, a lot of which are site specific. I didn't quite know exactly where I would go with my installation when I got to Artists Space. I sent parts out to New York and thought I'd have something on the walls. But how it would work, the heights, etc., is all about being in the space. It was a challenge because I thought I understood the situation, but realized there was a whole new set of rules.

It was a difficult situation in the terrarium, because the beetles started committing suicide, jumping into the water containers and they were unable to get out.

Mar. 1 (The Middle East): Edward Said, *In the Shadow of the West*, 1984, video; Ilan Ziv, *The Hundred Years War: Personal Notes* (Part I), 1983, video. Discussion with Edward Said.

Mar. 8–Apr. 5: **Recent Art from Chicago** (Susanne Ghez). Don Baum, sculpture; Bill Benway, painting; Neraldo De La Paz, sculpture; Deven Golden, *The Death of Pompey*, installation; Joseph Hilton, painting; Wesley Kimler, painting; David Kroll, painting; Paul La Mantia, painting; Jim Lutes, painting; Ken Warneke, painting and sculpture; Michael Paha, installation. Catalogue with essay by James Yood and statements by the artists.

Mar. 8: Talk with Susanne Ghez.

← Michael Paha

Apr. 12-May 10: Tony Labat, *Social Disease*; Larry Miller, *Two Possibilities*, video installations (Tony Oursler).

Apr. 12–May 10: **Moderns in Mind** (Valerie Smith). American surrealists: Gordon Onslow-Ford, painting; Gerome Kamrowski, sculpture and installation; Lee Mullican, painting and sculpture. Exhibition sponsored by the Mark Rothko Foundation. Catalogue with essays by Susan M. Maurer, Dan Cameron, Susan Larsen, Evan M. Maurer, and Martica Sawin and foreword by Valerie Smith.

Apr. 26: Curator's talk with Valerie Smith.

→ Lee Mullican

May 16: **Performances/Readings: The Critics Voices Volume IV** (Douglas Blau). Tape by Brian Cullman, images by Douglas Blau, slide show with music; Marvin Heiferman, *On Press Releases*; Gary Indiana, *The Times*; Paul McMahon, *The Sohoiad of Junius Secundus (AD MCMLXXXIV)*; Jeff Perrone, *Re: Boy Do I Love Art or What?*

May 24–June 28: **From Here to Eternity: Fact and Fiction in Recent Architectural Projects** (Valerie Smith). Conceptual and theoretical drawings, models and diagrams of architectural projects: Douglas Darden, Elizabeth Diller/Ricardo Scofidio, Donna Goodman, Laurie Hawkinson/Henry Smith-Miller, Michael Kalil, Kenneth Kaplan/Ted Krueger/Christopher Scholz, Mark West. Catalogue with introduction by Valerie Smith, essay by Beatriz Colomina, and statements by the artists. June 7: Curator's talk with Valerie Smith.

May 24–June 28: Wyn Geleynse, film installation (Valerie Smith).

June 14: Open house for newly computerized Artists File.

ARTIST

Lee Mullican Yeah, *Moderns in Mind*, good title! The preparation was getting Gordon (Onslow-Ford) really involved. He wasn't sure at the beginning if he wanted to do it or not. He hemmed and hawed and finally I said, "Gordon, we're going to do it! There's just no way out of this. It's a chance for us to show together in New York!" It was a rare opportunity. Of course, your (Valerie Smith) enthusiasm also had a great deal to do with it. I had known the space from seeing Matt (Mullican) perform there. It was very effective. The exhibition gave me a chance to show my paintings and a lot of the bronzes for the first time. And Gordon had prepared many ideas which he followed through on. It gave us a chance, as California artists, to be seen in New York, and that was really important. So many people showed up for the opening from the Bay Area whom I'd completely forgotten. I just couldn't believe it. So it was an exciting and real event for us because we had not shown in New York for quite some time.

1986-87

Sept. 2–13: **Artists from the Studio in a School** (Selected in conjunction with Patterson Sims). Jo-Anne Acey, Susan Austad, Gail Bach, Noah Baen, Olivia Beens, Rick Bleier, Corliss Blick, Thomas Cahill, Valerie Constantino, Anne Dohna, Lorraine Fiddle, Valerie Hammond, Beth Hausman, Shelley Krapes, Julie Lapping, Helene Manzo, Joan Mullen, Marilyn Reynolds, Mary Ann Rose, Daniel Rosenbaum, Anita Saghbazarian, Marcey Snapp, John Stevenson, Robin Sulkes, Radiah Sumler, Gretchen Treitz, Alice Turkel, Barbara Valenta, Gerry Wagoner, Stewart Wilson, Oscar Yacila.

Sept. 18–Oct. 18: **Selections** from the Artists File (Valerie Smith). Hanno Ahrens, sculpture; Polly Apfelbaum, sculpture; Mo Bahc, installation and drawing; Moira Dryer, painting; Shelagh Keeley, books and drawing; Andy Moses, painting; Tom Radloff, painting; Bonnie Rychlak, sculpture; David Winter, installation and drawing. Catalogue with foreword by Susan Wyatt and introduction by Valerie Smith. Sept. 27: Curator's talk with Valerie Smith.

ARTIST

Mark Dion The organizers of the exhibition *The Fairy Tale* were a group of people who were in the Whitney Independent Study Program before me. The exhibition was quite ambitious, with a well-researched and put-together catalogue. It was my second or third exhibition, but really my first exhibition in a very public space in the United States. It was incredibly important to me. It took a lot of work and I took it very seriously. I had just done the Whitney Independent Study Program exhibition and a project with Four Walls when Adam Simon was running it in Hoboken. That was the total extent of my experience.

I was still very much sitting on the fence about whether I was going to continue to be an artist or not. It was important to do an exhibition like that in my home town and to learn how it brings a lot of people together. And it was interesting to be in an exhibition with experienced artists, people whose work I followed and respected. There were, for example, Vito Acconci and Silvia Kolbowski, as well as Andrea Fraser, Gregg Bordowitz, and all my peers. It was the first moment I felt like an artist and part of the art community rather than the student community. I would meet people whom I knew a little and whose work I knew. For instance, Haim Steinbach came up to me and said, "Oh, I saw your show. It was really interesting and it relates to something I did at Artists Space some time before." Suddenly, I felt I was out there, I was one of the gang. It was a very important transition point. It was also about the importance of feeling part of the continuity of artists. There were people whom I respected, who had a very strong

relationship to Artists Space, especially in the beginning of their careers. People I'd studied with, like Tom Lawson, Barbara Kruger, and others like Matt Mullican. These are people whom I identified with and people whom I learned a lot from, either as teachers or as other artists. Suddenly I was one of those people who had done something at Artists Space, too. So I began to think of myself as existing within that continuity. Not as a consumer of ideas, but as a producer of ideas and work. And it was very powerful.

The Fairy Tale exhibition helped me formulate a lot of my aesthetics, because I was forced into a situation where I had to produce work. It was a time when the art being produced was extremely slick, and I was interested in going in the opposite direction, partly because I had to. I was utterly broke. On the other hand, art without a lavish production budget was an interesting aesthetic position. The project I did was very much related to the commodity critiques of other more established artists, but I was trying to bring those ideas to a living space, rather than just have the stuff coolly presented. In the piece I created a subjective character who lived inside this room we could visit or have a slice-of-life view into. For this young genderless child I created a sickening toy universe, equipped with a video entirely based around the Smurfs.

I tried to address our obsessions with collecting and how they begin early in life. I also related collecting to consuming, in a more normal sense of one acting in the economy obsessively, and how these desires are created in us. The video was terse and didactic, functioning very much like a lot of my work at the time. On video, I had re-edited a Smurf program, replacing the original voice-over with one of alleged dissident Smurfs who'd taken over the news station. They had programmed in an audio critique of Smurf society from a variety of different positions, feminist, Marxist, trying to understand the economic impact of the international toy industry where toys are made, how they're distributed, and how they're advertised. I took an ethnographic position, examining Smurfs as though they were a real society. Then I examined Smurfs as a commodity and the statistics about how toys function. Smurfs are very important because they exist in a global economy in a way that very few toys had up to that point. You had toys identified with a place, but you could buy Smurfs in Buenos Aires, Copenhagen, Kuala Lumpur, or San Diego. They were truly international toys and there was something very unique about that. That's much more common now. However, they are toys that had a very strange generation because they weren't as coordinated as they are now. Smurf was maybe the first in which the toy came first and the cartoon later. Then all of these other products were generated: the cereals, the books, the clothes. It was a model for licensing in such a way that you couldn't figure out what had been originally invented.

At the time of the exhibition, I wasn't feeling particularly good about the art world. I wasn't sure it was a place I really wanted to be. The superfluity in art made the art world seem like a place where you couldn't really say that much. It helped a lot to be able to show my work with a group of peers with whom I felt very aligned. More or less after this I started working with Ashley

CONTINUED

1986 OCT - NOV

Oct. 30–Nov. 26: **The Fairy Tale: Politics, Desire, and Everyday Life** (Curt Belshe, Ana Busto, Sarah Drury, Hilary Kliros, Lise Prown, Steven Schiff). Vito Acconci, sculpture; Ericka Beckman, photographs; Curt Belshe/Lise Prown, installation/construction; Gregg Bordowitz, sound piece; Chris Bratton/Annie Goldson, installation with video; Ana Busto, photo pieces; James Casebere, light box; Mark Dion, installation; Andrea Fraser, gallery talk and tour; Félix González-Torres, installation;

Perry Hoberman, installation; Julia Kidd, photo-assemblage; Mary Kelly, drawing and text; Hilary Kliros, sculpture with slide projections and sound; Silvia Kolbowski, photo-texts; Louise Lawler, photo-texts; Robin Michals, painting; Aimee Rankin, box with kinetic sculpture; Juan Sanchez, painting and drawing; Steven Schiff, sculpture/installation with sound. An issue of *New Observations* (45) is published in the spring of 1987 with the exhibition organizers

as guest editors. Jean Fisher, Fredric Jameson, and Jack Zipes's essays are reprinted from Artists Space's publication along with essays by Vito Acconci, Betsy Hearne, Didi Heller, Martin Winn, and excerpts from Andrea Fraser's gallery talk. Catalogue with essays by Jean Fisher, Fredric Jameson, and Jack Zipes, introduction by Curt Belshe, Ana Busto, Sarah Drury, Hilary Kliros, Lise Prown, and Steven Schiff.

Nov. 1: Gallery talk by Jack Zipes.

Nov. 8, 15, 22: Gallery tour by Andrea Fraser.

← Mark Dion

MARK DION / CONTINUED

Bickerton. He was very engaged with this hype, and there was a lot of money floating around. But working with him I learned, in fact, that here was a guy who worked seven days a week from 10 o'clock in the morning to 11 o'clock at night and actually had quite a bit of integrity as an artist. Those superfluous things were not driving him, they were marginal to his practice, he was working regardless. So that convinced me the position of an artist was still one which could be maintained in a reasonably effective and engaged way. And it was true for a lot of people who were around then. But I was very young and naive and not entirely sure of what it meant to be an artist. I needed to see close-up examples of how people managed and be able to examine the different available positions. Of course, you don't see this when you're that young, and I didn't have a drive for it. I wasn't in the game for

success or power, whatever that means. I was interested in working with ideas, and I realized that's, in fact, what most people want. But I needed to see this firsthand. By having the exhibition, working with Ashley, and being more centrally involved, I became a participant rather than an observer. It was a big step.

Oct. 30–Nov. 26: **Video** in conjunction with **The Fairy Tale: Politics, Desire, and Everyday Life** (Dan Walworth). Norman Cowie, *Lying in State*, 1986; Sarah Drury, *Columbus Discovers America*, 1986; Jacqueline Frazier, *Curly Locks and the Three Brothers*, 1985; Joan Jonas, *Upside Down and Backwards*, 1979; Ardele Lister, *So Where's My Prince Already*, 1973–76; Bruce and Norman Yonemoto, *Kappa*, 1986; Jay Ward Productions, *Fractured Fairy Tales* (*Rapunzel*) and *Fractured Fairy Tales* (*Tom Thumb*).

Nov. 1–2: **Film** in conjunction with **The Fairy Tale: Politics, Desire, and Everyday Life** (Robin Dickie and Dan Walworth). Screened at the Collective for Living Cinema, New York.
Nov. 1: Ericka Beckman, *Cinderella*, 1986; The London Women's Film Group, *Rapunzel Let Down Your Hair*, 1978.
Nov. 2: Lotte Reiniger, *The Frog Prince*, 1954; Roberto Rossellini, *The Machine to Kill Bad People*, 1948.

ARTIST

Andrea Fraser I moved to New York in '81. I knew some of Artists Space's history because I had worked for Tom Lawson and studied with Craig Owens. But it was mostly from Tom that I understood Artists Space was really important.

My talk for Artists Space was the second gallery performance I had done. The first was at the New Museum. So I saw myself as already working within the framework of institutional critique. But there was something very funny about trying to do that at an artists' space. I will always remember asking Susan Wyatt about Artists Space's educational programs and tours and whether there was a docent program. She said "No, there's none of that! The only tours are the ones I do or the curators do." So there I was, all gung ho to come in and critique the institution and the thing was, Artists Space was already established as a critique of art institutions. It was very funny and an interesting position for me. It had to do with my place in that history, for example, how institutional critique, which started in the late 60s and early 70s, had spawned particular artistic practices, artists' organizations, and alternative organizations. But when I got around to it, I found myself trying to bring that practice back to this very same organization, which had been established as a rejection of the museums and established institutions.

It was a funny tour. Consequently, maybe now, I will be able to reflect more on it. I might study how alternative spaces and artist-run organizations have become institutionalized and what processes that entails. Is it a problem for those organizations or is it currently a condition of becoming more effective? For my tour, I didn't try to approach those questions. Instead I focused on the theme of the exhibition, fairy tales, and my interpretation of it in light of the then-recent debates on pornography in '86. It was when the Meese Commission on Pornography was active. I did the tour in the fall, after that summer's Hardwick Decision of the Supreme Court, which upheld the state's right to criminalize homosexual sodomy. I had just turned 21 in September and was very interested and concerned about how children and minors—I still identified myself as a minor in certain ways—were identified with women in the discourse around pornography and sex laws of the Right. The traditional line and the rationale for restricting pornography is to protect children—obviously this is still going on today with the Internet. In the discourse of the Meese Commission and the McKinnon-Dworkin Ordinance, women were identified with children in that they had to be protected from sexuality.

The Artists Space performance and the first one at the New Museum were preaching to the converted. That's what happens when you try to do that type of critique in an organization that's already self-critical and established to serve a constituency of which you're part. That was my community, which was the funny thing about it. The aspect about the tour which could have gotten a bit beyond all that had to do with my age and status because I wasn't Jane Castleton in that tour. That's the only tour I did, one of the early ones, where I was Suzy Rogers. I said, "My name is Suzy, free, white, and 21." So I was coming out as a 21-year-old and trying to deal with it. Maybe not for anyone else, but for me that was important because I was always lying about my age.

Dec. 5: **Performance**: Mike Kelley with Sonic Youth and Molly Cleator, *Plato's Cave, Rothko's Chapel, Lincoln's Profile*. The artist's book, *Plato's Cave, Rothko's Chapel, Lincoln's Profile* by Mike Kelley is published by New City Editions, Venice, California, in association with Artists Space.

Dec. 11–Jan. 24: **Contained Attitudes** (Saskia Bos). Group exhibition of young European artists who have not shown previously in New York: Jan Van Oost, sculpture, Belgium; Alain Séchas, sculpture, assemblage, France; Meuser, installation, West Germany; Ton Zwerver, sculpture, photographs, Holland. Catalogue with essays by Saskia Bos and Chris Dercon.

Dec. 11 – Jan. 24: **Video** in conjunction with **Contained Attitudes** (Chris Dercon). Alain Bourges, *Lumière et Circonstances (Part I)*, 1986; Studio's Independent Theatre, *Absolute Art*, 1985, and *Souvenirs of the Heart*, 1986; Koen Theys, *Song of My Country (Part I, Reingold)*, 1986; Graham Young, *Nil by Mouth*, 1983, and *Accidents of the Home (Epilogue*, 1983*, Holiday Insurances*, 1985, *Indoor Games*, 1986*, Gas Fires*, 1984). Catalogue with essays by Saskia Bos and Chris Dercon.

→ Graham Young

Feb. 5 – Mar. 14: **Dark Rooms** (Valerie Smith and Dan Walworth). Anne Bray, *Man on First and Third*, slide installation; Kendall Buster, film installation; John Knecht, *I'm Glad to the Brink of Fear*, video installation; Charles Long, *Gnomons' Land*, film installation; Carolee Schneemann, *War Mop*, video installation. Brochure with essay by Dan Walworth.

ARTIST

Mike Kelley *Plato's Cave, Rothko's Chapel, Lincoln's Profile* was a big project and very complicated. It was a lot of work. It was my biggest projection because we had a light person and we had to build a stage. We did three or four days of rehearsals with Sonic Youth, Molly Cleator, and Adam Rudolf. They were pretty well-known new musicians. Molly was my foil. It broke down into two parts. The monologue was broken into pseudo-dialogue, so it was theatrical. She had a very big part in it. It was like an abstract version of *Who's Afraid of Virginia Woolf?* There was a giant didgeridoo that Ad Rudolf played. It flipped and came down the model ramp. I think Molly sat on it. My memory of it is terrible because when I'm working on those things I really blank out. I just remember it was arduous. We had a very heavy rehearsal schedule and the technical things were done last minute. In addition, I was trying to produce a book and it was complicated. There was a very good crew helping, but it was so involved and so fast, I don't have any memory of it beyond this kind of whirlwind of a production. I haven't done anything like that since. It was my last serious performance. I've collaborated and designed them but that's the last one I performed in. I have no plans for doing another.

I knew Sonic Youth through Kim Gordon from Los Angeles. I decided I wanted to do a piece which played with the notion of rock theatrics, even though Sonic Youth mostly didn't play. It was a fairly structural piece that went in and out of different models. I was doing a couple of things at once: playing, breaking a monologue into pseudo-dialogue, and vacillating between different theatrical modes—monologues, theatricals, and something like rock theatrics. It was a fairly formal deconstructive kind of project. The title has nothing to do with anything. It really wasn't about those subjects at all. It was just a way to generate subject matter. It could be ordered, it was arbitrary. I wanted to set up something that was dramatic, so I decided to break it into a male/female thing to create sexual tension. I don't think the text had anything to do with that, it was more about how it was presented. It played with presentational form. It gave a soap opera feel or a dramatic feel. I was thinking about something like *Who's Afraid of Virginia Woolf?,* where there's this heterosexual drama. They're just fighting all the time or talking through all this tension, dramatic tension, but when I thought back on it, I couldn't remember anything of what they were arguing about, it wasn't important. In that piece there was a poetic component to the text

determined by these arbitrary three possessive forms. There were various ways of presenting that, either by this charged dramatic interaction or by a poetic recitation, sometimes presented more like a song mode. And then there was the play. Sonic Youth did incidental music and sound effects. They functioned like a kabuki orchestra. But at one point, they did play a piece of a song that I danced to, a type of go-go boy thing. At the end, they did a big rock crescendo. But for the rest of it, they never played music, they did ambient sound. For example, if I dropped something, they would make a big explosion. For most of the piece you didn't see them, they played behind a closed curtain. The curtain would open and close at various points, and they would direct the action in front or behind the curtain on the model ramp or on the stage. It was more like the way an orchestra functions in a play.

What was great about it was that all this spectacle stuff was going on in New York then. People were doing these really big things, mostly at BAM (Brooklyn Academy of Music). But those venues weren't interested in my work at all. They wouldn't touch this structural work. I've never done anything with BAM. Intermittently they send me a letter where they always turn down my proposals. So it was great that I could do this at Artists Space, because it was about that kind of spectacle. It's so cool that they put all this work into mounting such a complicated thing, and it's probably one of the biggest events they ever did. It wasn't cheap to do, either. It struck me at the time that it was done somewhat in opposition to this mentality of BAM's.

Feb. 5 – Mar. 14: Video: TV Sandino (Annie Goldson and Carlos Pavam of Xchange TV). Program of broadcast television from Nicaragua. Martha Wallner and Miriam Loaisiga, *Con Guerra o Sin Guerra (With or Without War)*, 1987; Miguel Necochea for the Ministry of the Interior, *Nieve (Snow)*, 1986, and *Operacion Oro (Operation Gold)*, 1985; Sistema Sandinista de Television, *Aqui en Esta Esquina (Here on This Corner)*, 1983, and *Resumen Anual 86 (News Synopsis 1986)*; Lucero Millán, *Golpes de la Corazón (Blows of the Heart)*, 1983, and *La Virgen Que Suda (The Sweating Virgin)*, 1983; César Rodrigues for Sistema Sandinista de Television, *Cabildo de Mujeres: Nuestra Opción para el Futuro (Women's Town Hall: Our Option for the Future)*, 1986; public service announcements. Catalogue with introduction by Annie Goldson and Carlos Pavam, essays by Michèle Mattelart and Joel Kovel.

Feb. 14: Curator's talk with Dan Walworth.

FILMMAKER/CURATOR

Keith Sanborn There was one interesting blunder I made in the organization of *Underexposed,* a film series I curated with Andy Moses in 1987. MOMA had a print of an obscure Belgian film from the 1920s by Charles Dekeukeliere, *Histoire de Détective.* It's almost entirely in French with a very Warholian spirit to it. Unmatched historically, as far as I know. I knew the negatives were at the Belgium Film Archive. So I trotted out my French and wrote a letter to the director, Jacques Ledoux, telling him we were doing this screening and didn't have a lot of money, and asking him would there be any 16 mm prints of the film to lend for the screening? Little did I know that Ledoux was actually the head of the International Film Archive Union! He was very nice and wrote me back immediately to say he'd be happy to send the print; however, the rule of the International Film Archive Union states that if a print exists in the host country you must ask them first. Well, I *had* asked MOMA. Theirs was a unique print, the only one they had, and they wouldn't give it to us. Ledoux knew we were in a hurry and had already taken the liberty of making a request for us. He said it was a formality and if they weren't willing to do it, then he would send us a print. So in pure naiveté, we basically embarrassed MOMA into giving us the print and learned a technique for extracting what you want from recalcitrant film archives.

In the organization of *Underexposed,* Andy Moses and I had our first and only meeting with Jack Smith. It was quite a strange encounter in his apartment, somewhere on First Avenue between Houston and First Streets. At that time, *Flaming Creatures* was not accessible, so we put it out of our minds and did not consider it for screening. We ended up showing *Blonde Cobra,* which has a problematic authorship because somebody else shot the footage. The footage is really Jack Smith's, and there's a lot of audio of Jack Smith, but it was all put together by Ken Jacobs. Although the film is usually attributed to Ken Jacobs and he certainly had a role in it, it is probably the best film record of anything Jack Smith has done, because I think his other films were not rediscovered. There is an incredible story about *Flaming Creatures.* It was basically resurrected by Jerry Tartaglia, who had been one of Tony Conrad's students at Antioch College. He was working in a film lab and someone pointed to a pile of film reels saying, "This stuff's been here forever, throw it out." So he went through some of it and sure enough, there was the original negative for *Flaming Creatures!* He had seen it in Tony's class. Of course, he returned it to Jack. It would have otherwise been headed for the dumpster.

Roger Jacoby is also an under-recognized filmmaker. Probably his most notorious film is *How to Be a Homosexual.* People would come to the screening expecting fist-fucking and what they got was this incredible hand-processed technique. In Part II of the series, also hand processed, Roger examines some of his lesions, which by then had started to show up. So it is a very intense film. It's one of the first, if you want to label it by genre, AIDS films, but in more of an artistic context. It was not exactly didactic, that is in a direct way, but very rich and extremely challenging visually.

Feb. 5 – Mar. 14: Architecture Project (Elizabeth Diller). Hani Rashid, *Kursaal for an Evacuee,* architectural installation. Brochure with introduction by Elizabeth Diller and statement by the architect.

Feb. 14: Curator's talk with Valerie Smith.

We also showed the Otto Muehl films. I remember I had to introduce them, so I wrote a little text which I memorized, but it was a challenge. Basically, I wanted to let people know that they might find the material somewhat offensive without insulting the filmmaker or completely diminishing the shock value. So I gave the standard disclaimer that the work contained some sexually explicit imagery. In one film, *Leda,* there is a goose or a swan on downers and a woman making love to it. At the end of the movie they cut the goose's head off and she starts masturbating with it. But it wasn't so much the masturbation that people were upset by, nor the scenes of shitting or pissing or anything else that got them angry. Rather, much to my surprise, it was the fact that they killed this animal. I had approached that screening with some trepidation, because not more than a year before, the film had been shown by Craig Baldwin in San Francisco and during a screening someone pulled the plug on the projector. There are a lot of available films out there that, for all practical purposes, you might only see once in your life, if you can just extract them from the right sources.

My interests are on this weird edge between the experimental film world and the fine arts world. So I thought it would be an amazing opportunity to create a tiny little bit of seepage between those two which are otherwise completely, hermetically sealed off from each other.

Mar. 26–May 2: **Abstraction in Process** (Roberta Smith). Fontaine Dunn, painting; Robert Hall, painted constructions; Benje LaRico, painted constructions; Stephen Spretnjak, sculpture and drawing. Catalogue with essay by Roberta Smith.

Mar. 26–May 2: **Video: Buying In and Selling Out: Dealing with the Forms of Broadcast Television** (Dan Walworth). Caterina Borelli, *Passeggiate Romano (Walking through Rome,* 1985; Tony Cokes, *Face Fear and Fascination,* 1984; John Gurrin, *Sunstroke,* 1984; Reginald Hudlin, *Reggie's World of Soul,* 1985; Nora Ligorano and Marshall Reese, *The Touch,* 1986; Paper Tiger Television, *Leonard Henny—How Nations Televise Each Other, or Ronald Gone Dutch,* 1985; Shelly Silver, *Meet the People,* 1986.

May 15–16: **Video, Reading, and Films on the Philippines: Marcos, the Mountains and Mao** (Dan Walworth).
May 15: Jeffrey Chester, Charles Drucker, *Philippines: The Price of Power,* 1986, film; Kidlat Tahimik, *Perfumed Nightmare,* 1978, film.
May 16: Jon Alpert, Maryann DeLeo, Rochit Tañedo, *The Philippines: Life, Death and the Revolution,* 1986, video; Jessica Hagedorn, reading.

Elizabeth Diller In the mid-80s, there was a moment when little organizations like Artists Space became interested in the intersection of architecture with visual arts, public art, and architectural theory. It was a hot moment in New York when there was a lot of discourse around architecture and dissident practices. Architects were all of a sudden recognized and put into a dialogue with visual and performing artists, and we took advantage of this. We met Beatriz Colomina for the first time during the show, *From Here to Eternity*. She's an historian of architecture with architectural training and was invited to write an essay for the catalogue. Our first conversation was about Duchamp and how he influenced our work, so we were exchanging ideas around an artist.

We met Hani Rashid in Milan where he was working on the Triennale with Daniel Libeskind. We were doing an installation just next door, separated by a couple of works by Duchamp. This was a very large exhibition, with 20 installations and 2200 pieces of art and artifacts pertaining to domesticity from museums all over the world. At that point, very few architects had decided to make an alternative practice. Even then, Hani was much more independent. It was clear he would be getting out from under the wing of Daniel. My selecting him to show was just an opportunity for him to do that. The other thing I remember is how incredibly pissed I was that he didn't show up for his own opening. I was absolutely furious. He probably had been up all night, but so are all of us when we do shows. Probably he was terrified. He put everything into that installation. We always go through this when we have an opening—all of the horror scenarios in our brains. We think of all the people there, all the things that could go wrong, and all of the ways that our work could be abhorred. It's incredibly intimidating to get past the inertia of going. When you finally get there, of course, you want to bask in the glory, it completely changes. Maybe it was the terror of the first time with Hani. Nevertheless, I was there representing him and looking at my watch, thinking, "What the fuck is going on here?"

We did have a terrific appreciation for Artists Space, not simply because it was so significant in terms of our exposure, but because it was there for architecture, a forum when there were very few. There was respect for architecture as something other than a profession. At that time, architecture had a bad name. There are still very few people who have a vision about it— Valerie Smith, Susan Wyatt, and you (Claudia Gould). On the other hand, there aren't many architects who have devoted their work to independent research and can engage in a dialogue about contemporary issues. Most architects are involved in the economics and the politics of architecture. If they realized the many ways it dissects a culture, they would understand how much power architecture actually has. This is the way Ric (Scofidio) and I think about our own work. The relationships between bodies and buildings and programs and signs are very complex, and architects only inherited those conditions; they didn't produce them. They are continually redefined and/or sustained in their former definition. Any architect who thinks that architecture is just a structural discipline doesn't understand the complexities of architecture. Very often this is why we feel alienated from architects and architecture. I have more of a dialogue with artists, cultural theorists, and writers because they're not phobic about the reaction between their work and a contemporary culture. Architects very often are. They think that making interesting forms is where it's at—this is our big problem with formalism.

Douglas Blau As the budding travel writer that I was at the time, I had written a piece on Robert Beton for *Real Life* in '81 and Brian Wallis wanted to reprint it for *Tourist Attractions*. The reading event coincided with the publication and I remember not wanting to read my own writing, but to do something else. So I brought my friend, the music and travel writer Brian Cullman, with me and together we did this very silly stand-up routine where we read various entries, he one then me, all from the dictionary of imaginary places. When we thought that we had done enough and everybody had been chuckled out, we called it a day and said good-bye. The best part of that whole program was Constance De Jong reading something so wonderfully, it was utter magic.

We did the fourth and final *The Critic's Voices* at Artists Space. The first three were performed at White Columns. Paul McMahon got dressed up in a toga and recited in rhyming couplets *The SoHoiad* by Robert Hughes. Hughes found out about the performance and called Paul and they had a long conversation in advance. I think Hughes wanted to know whether or not he was going to be parodied or treated like Homer. Gary Indiana read a Pauline Kael piece. Jeff Perrone read Cookie Mueller. We also had a slide show. It was a strange night.

ARCHITECT/CURATOR

WRITER/CURATOR

182

May 21–June 27: Calvert Coggeshall, painting; Frederick Hammersley, painting (Richard Armstrong, Hermine Ford, Irving Sandler, Valerie Smith, Susan Wyatt). Exhibition sponsored by the Mark Rothko Foundation. Catalogue with essays by Hedda Sterne on Coggeshall and Merle Schipper on Hammersley.

May 23: Talk by Frederick Hammersley.

→ Hani Rashid, *Kursaal for an Evacuee*.
Architecture Project,
Feb. 5–Mar. 14, 1987.

May 21–June 27: **Video: Heterogeneity and Alienation** (Bérénice Reynaud). Nan Goldin, *The Ballad of Sexual Dependency*, 1987; Louis Hock, *The Mexican Tapes: The Winner's Circle-La Migra*, 1986; Mako Idemitsu, *Yoji, What's Wrong With You?*, 1986; Ram Loevy, *Between the River and the Sea*, 1983; Chip Lord, Branda Miller, and Antonio Muntadas, *Media Hostages*, 1985, including Chip Lord, *Future Language*, Branda Miller, *Unset Boulevard*, and Antonio Muntadas, *SSS*; Candace Reckinger, *Impossible Love*, 1983; Michael Rouse, *Tanabe*, 1984; Stuart Sherman, *Berlin West / Andere Richtungen*, 1987; Leslie Thornton, *There Was an Unseen Cloud Moving*, 1987. Brochure with essay by Bérénice Reynaud.

Hani Rashid

ARCHITECT/CURATOR

I met Liz Diller when I worked on the Milan Triennale in 1986. I had just finished school and I was collaborating with my former teacher, Daniel Libeskind, on an installation piece. Liz Diller and Ricardo Scofidio were next door doing an installation. She saw me in there every day for nine weeks, building this thing. Because of the amount of effort I was putting into that piece, she probably thought I would be a strong candidate to have my own show.

A *kursaal* is an anachronistic term in English, but it still holds in German, which is something between a beach house, a pagoda, and a pavilion. It's a word that encompasses a number of these other typologies for a building: it's a kind of kiosk or small building. Usually, it's thought of more as an escape or retreat or tranquil recluse. The evacuee was an idea I got from the press about someone who had lived in Central Park for years and was found out. This person symbolized homelessness and shelter, issues still pertinent today. At that time, I thought this person made a convenient and interesting allegory for the poets or artists living within a society but at the same time reclusive, needing detachment from reality, and cocooning themselves within the metropolis. I found it intriguing that there is a notion of homelessness which encompasses insanity or madness. Another notion is an elevated sense of being, a piece of mind. I became fascinated with a story about a guy found in South Dakota who lived for 15 years under a bridge over a canyon. For years people had sightings of this small figure climbing this immense trestle. Finally, one day someone discovered his shelter filled with nothing but newspapers, a toaster oven, and a TV set. He had hooked his cables into the electric power lines over the bridge and was feeding off of the power system of the city. At the same time, he was absolutely invisible to everybody. They called him the Spiderman. They never found him, but they did take apart his house and put it back where it had come from, the local dump. My project was related to Dubuffet's journeys through France, looking for the art recluses and of the insane in asylums, "art brut." My idea was not exactly to resurrect or glorify that approach, rather to enter into that state of mind, to build an installation that allowed people, for one moment, to walk into a strange world within the metropolis with a sense of these dynamics swarming around.

This is when I first started working with Lise Anne Couture. She was an integral part of the project, but we were not yet officially partners, she was still in school. We formed the partnership right after that. We basically began a process of deconstructing New York City, then rehousing it into another space. This was before it was fashionable to deconstruct, nevertheless it was in the air. We took a printout of the *New York Times* business section and lined the space with stock exchange market reports pasted upside down. They were just strange hermetic hieroglyphs. I had no idea what those numbers meant. It was a crazy process; I was fanatical about getting the pigment into the paper so it would have this stonelike yellowish gold color. So a bunch of Cooper Union students came and with Liz's help they hand-rubbed the pigment on the wall. There was a lot of wall space to cover and we had no idea it would take us all night. In addition, a series of structures were built in: an abstracted trestle bridge, a TV embedded in a concrete icon that became a church-place to meditate, a weaving machine so one could imagine making one's own clothes. It strangely resembled the meeting of medieval machinery and a modern landscape of implements like toasters, TVs, etc. Then it all came together in the space. In the end, it looked and felt more like a tomb than a house —they are not that far apart, somehow.

It was the first time I experienced a place where I felt excited and thrilled at the prospect of being able to fervently impress my ideas in the public realm without being looked at as an oddball.

May 21 – June 27: **Architecture Project**. Ian and Lynn Bader, drawing, models, objects, photo-documentation (Patricia C. Phillips). Brochure with essay by Patricia C. Phillips.

June 25 – 26: **Readings: Tourist Attractions** (Ann Turyn and Brian Wallis) Writings by each reader from *Top Stories*, issue #25 – 26.

June 25: Douglas Blau and Brian Cullman, Cheryl Clarke, Constance De Jong, Gary Indiana, Suzanne Jackson, Micki McGee, Jane Warrick.

June 26: Linda L. Cathcart, Susan Daitch, Robert Fiengo, Caryl Jones-Sylvester, Judy Linn, Glenn O'Brien, Sekou Sundiata, Lynne Tillman.

1987 – 88

Sept. 8 – 19: **Artists from the Studio in a School** (selected in consultation with Patterson Sims). Jo-Ann Acey, Susan Austad, Gail Bach, Noah Baen, Olivia Beens, Rick Bleier, Sandra Bloodworth, Thomas Cahill, Ann Dohna, Lorraine Fiddle, Janice Gabriel, Shelley Krapes, Julie Lapping, William Lucero, Helene Manzo, Joan Mullen, Vernita Nemec, Marilyn Reynolds, MaryAnn Rose, Daniel Rosenbaum, John Stevenson, Robin Sulkes, Radiah Sumler, Barbara Valenta, David Vereano, Gerry Wagoner, Stewart Wilson, Oscar Yacila.

Oct. 1 – 31: **Selections** from the Artists File (Kellie Jones). Lillian Ball, sculpture; Marina Cappelletto, painting; David Gesualdi, painting; Cynthia Hawkins, painting; Lisa Mann, light boxes; Stefani Mar, installation; Hunter Reynolds, installation; Cari Rosmarin, painting; Carol Sun, painting; Félix González-Torres, objects and photo-texts; Fred Wilson, installation. Catalogue with essay by Kellie Jones.

WRITER/CURATOR

Patricia C. Phillips Because of the heterogeneity of my interests, constantly crossing between art and public art, architecture and design, Artists Space was always this wonderful kind of magnet where I could go regularly to encounter an incredible circulation of ideas or, at times, just the unruly simultaneity of seemingly competing or contrasting ideas. It was an important place in terms of the development of my thinking about criticism and the role criticism plays within art and public culture. Artists Space has been extraordinarily inclusive and investigative in terms of its mission, which has drawn me to it over the years.

The viability of places like Artists Space at this point in history is a very interesting and perplexing issue, not unique to Artists Space by any means. How do you develop some sort of alternative to ensure that it persists and endures while avoiding those kinds of processes and methodologies that start to institutionalize the practice? Quite frankly, the kind of zeal and excitement I felt at Artists Space 15 years ago is not the same today. But I'm different, too. I have a lot more history I bring to the space now and to my understanding and encounter of it. I am still not that confident about the receptiveness and continued viability of the commercial system to support truly searching and untested work. There are those moments that can happen in conjunction with a commercial gallery, but I'm not so sure that what seems possible, at this very moment, is something we can depend on and will reliably be there for young and emerging artists. So I continue to advocate for places like Artists Space and Storefront for Art and Architecture because they pursue objectives and a mission beyond those of most commercial galleries. Artists Space is, of course, about showing art, but it's also about all kinds of other activities and events, from informal discussion and dialogue to symposia. And again, the commercial system is not taking on the pedagogical or educational dimensions an alternative space can.

When you visit a commercial gallery it's still, it's serene, the work is there and you may talk with a friend about it. But often it is a very solitary experience. This is not the case in a place like Artists Space that encourages and, to some extent, compels participation and dialogue. It's not only because of the art, but all the other attendant activities that happen in an alternative space. I'm still optimistic or idealistic enough to feel that's absolutely indispensable. I have been influenced a lot by being a teacher and having worked with art and architecture students for the past 15 years. You start to look for art organizations that, in a different way, can support the inquiry or educational objectives you may be involved with as a teacher. It's great to have Artists Space to send your students to. The model of more established artists creating situations and possibilities for emerging artists to do and show work, to try untested ideas, is something very wonderful and generous. But there's also something of great critical interest. I'm always interested in what other artists are looking at, whether it's what's happening in other disciplines or finding out the artists other artists look at. I like that. There's a sense of family or role and responsibility in terms of the construction of the future. The future is inscribed by all kinds of forces that are often beyond just the interest and possibilities of ideas or experimentation. Experimentation is important, indispensable. At times, it can be accommodated in the commercial situation, but that's not always the most congenial environment for it.

Oct. 1–31: **Video: Floating Values: A Survey of Gendered Investigations** (Chris Hill). Vito Acconci, *Undertone*, 1972; Max Almy, *Modern Times*, 1979; Lynda Benglis, *Female Sensibility*, 1973; Lyn Blumenthal, *Doublecross*, 1986; Ayoka Chenzira, *Secret Sound Screaming*, 1986; Phyllis Christopher, *Say Bye Bye*, 1986; Valie Export, *Korperaktionen (Body Actions): Homo Meter II*, 1974, *Asemie Die Unfahigkeit Sich Durch Mienenspiel Ausdrucken Zu Konnen (The Inability of Expressing Oneself through Plays on Appearances)*, 1973, *Hyperbulie*, 1973, *Body Politics*, 1974, *Remote Remote*, 1972, and *A Perfect Pair*, 1986; Hermine Freed, *Art Herstory*, 1974; Richard Fung, *Chinese Characters*, 1986; Annie Goldson, *Tender Detachment*, 1986; Joan Jonas, *Vertical Roll*, 1972; Owen Land, *Noli Me Tangere*, 1983; Pier Marton, *Are We and/or Do We Like Men*, 1986; Martha Rosler, *Vital Statistics of a Citizen, Simply Obtained*, 1977; Alan Sondheim and Kathy Acker, *The Blue Tapes*, 1983; Lisa Steele, *The Gloria Tapes*, 1979, excerpts from *Tunnel of Love* and *Court Date*; Bruce and Norman Yonemoto, *Vault*, 1984; Julie Zando, *I Like Girls for Friends*, 1987.

↓ Valie Export
  Photo: Chris Hill

CURATOR

Kellie Jones When I organized a *Selections* show for Artists Space, it was traumatic. Not for me, but for many African American artists because of the whole history and protest of *The Nigger Drawings* show at Artists Space. Because of this, a lot of people said, "Oh, you can never do anything for Artists Space, remember they did *The Nigger Drawings* thing!" I was in college during *The Nigger Drawings* and I missed the whole controversy. It wasn't even at all on my radar screen. But I did hear about it, researched it, and talked to people to figure out what the controversy was. *Selections* was about healing a wound — for a lot of people, for the institution, as well as the black artists' community of a certain generation. Of course, younger people weren't really aware of it. But certainly there were enough people around who had protested and had been through it and felt the sting. I looked back over the introduction I wrote for the *Selections* catalogue. I referred to it obliquely. It was hard as a younger writer. At the time, I didn't really want to mention it very specifically. In retrospect, if I had, my intro wouldn't have been so cryptic, but really very clear that I was referring to that show and trying to make a statement to put the whole thing to rest. As it is, I think what I said was about trying to have a more diverse art community. I definitely would have said, "In February 1979, *The Nigger Drawings* happened, this was the response on both sides, it was unfortunate. But *Selections* takes a step toward healing that wound." I would have been very specific. In the essay I do talk about diversity, which I think was important. Hindsight is always 20/20. I did what I felt was the right thing to do at that moment. Now we have an artist like Kara Walker and black people can be flipped out by that, in a different way. There are many issues on diversity in the art world that are still questioned, but like anything, times change, the discussion changes, and issues change.

The main point was to make a statement through the institution about racism and segregation in the art world, try always to combat that in the show, and try to make shows that reflect what the world really is like. There are producers all over the world making objects that

don't necessarily fit into the very narrow prescription of what Art, with a capitol A, is supposed to be. Looking back on *Selections* makes me see this certainly has been my approach to curating in the last 10 years. Some shows I do will have only people of color, but most often they try to be integrated in some way. If I have integrated group shows, I also try to write solo pieces that highlight artists who may not have had that kind of attention.

Selections was the first time I got to work with Félix González-Torres. It was the most amazing studio visit I ever had, probably ever will have. I went to his small studio on Grove Street and I said, "This isn't a studio. Where is the art?" Then we proceeded to sit and talk for two hours about all manner of things. He showed me not one piece of art, not one! And I still put him in the show based on slides. He didn't have anything else to show me. I'll always remember that day as being the quintessential conceptual art studio visit where you don't see any art. I always liked Félix from that time on.

I would not have had an opportunity to be a curator without places like Artists Space. They allow young curators to try things. It's a shame that this country doesn't have any respect for the innovation of young artists, young spaces, or anything that isn't the Metropolitan Museum of Art or the National Gallery. If there's any way I can be helpful to change what's going on, then that's what I want to do. Artists Space is part of the art world, it would be awful if it were lost.

Nov. 6–9: **Underexposed: A Selected History of Neglected Films** (Andy Moses and Keith Sanborn). Brochure with introduction by Andy Moses and essay by Keith Sanborn.
Nov. 6: **The Body and the Mind**: Kenneth Anger, *Fireworks*; The Fleischer Brothers, *Bimbo's Initiation*; Ken Jacobs, Bob Fleischer, and Jack Smith, *Blonde Cobra*; Roger Jacoby, *Kunst Life I-VI*; George Méliès, *The*

Melomaniac, The Inn Where No Man Rests; Otto Muehl, *Materialaktionsfilme*; Carolee Schneemann, *Fuses*; Ann Severson, *Near the Big Chakra*.
Nov. 7: **Dectective Work**: Charles Dekeukeliere, *Histoire de Détective*; Sergei M. Eisenstein, *Bezhin Meadow;* Maurice Lemaître, *Un Soir au Cinema* and *Pour Faire un Film*; Christopher Maclaine, *The End*; Chris Marker,

The Koumiko Mystery.
Nov. 8: **A Woman Possessed**: Maya Deren, *The Haitian Footage*.
Nov. 9: **More Detective Work**: Don Levy, *Herostratus*. Screening at the Public Theater, New York.

ARTIST

Félix González-Torres

Artists Space's function is very relevant right now, because it's one of the few places where young, new artists can show in a professional environment. Their work gets respect and the proper presentation, including catalogues and announcement cards, which is hard to get when you are just starting. You can take these things for granted, but it really is tough in the beginning. Artists Space is a very democratic space. You don't have to come from money to show there. People from different backgrounds can feel very comfortable at Artists Space.

One of the other reasons I like Artists Space so much is the Artists Grants, because if you are a young artist, $200 can mean doing the project or not doing it. It may not sound like a lot but, believe me, when I was struggling it really made a difference. And for a number of my friends who are video artists, $200 pushed them into production. Another service is the Artists Slide File. I know it works, because it worked for me and for my friends. My first gallery show came from the Artists Slide File. So I am a living witness. I'd never gone around with slides to galleries because that's like panhandling. The Artists Space Slide File is one of the few I feel has some integrity.

As for the exhibition program, I thought the Michael Asher show was one of the best I had seen around in a long, long time, and only a place like Artists Space would take a venture that is so uncommercial. I was also especially impressed by *Min Joong Art,* the Korean show—where else can you see that kind of work? What was smart too was the idea of renting out the video programs for private viewing. It takes into consideration the new social situation, in which almost everyone has a VCR at home. Twenty years from now people are going to say that was a big change in the gallery situation.

ARTIST/BOARD

Fred Wilson

Selections was important because it marked a transition in my work. Certainly, at that time, Artists Space was a very important place to exhibit in New York. I don't know what other artists thought, but I really wanted important work to be there. The majority of objects I had been making had been large outdoor pieces. I had done a couple of indoor installations, but I knew I wanted to do something else, so I took the opportunity to do it at Artists Space.

I decided to create this platform that could not be walked on but included objects on top that would inform the space. It was a transitional piece between the first large platform pieces and what I'm doing now, the museum. I was searching for a context within which to juxtapose objects. This island setting was it. I was very happy with the piece because it pushed me farther than I had gone. I always knew I was going to do this, I just never had. It was very different work from what I had done in the past. Afterward I did one or two other pieces like it and then I moved into just using the objects. So it was a seminal piece. There were flowers in the piece and I was told they would be changed when necessary. I hadn't thought anybody would do that, so I was quite pleased. I'm a little naive about the art world in some ways, not having been involved with galleries to a great degree other than running them myself. I appreciate the willingness to present the work the way you want it to be presented and that people take you seriously enough to go along with it.

I hadn't been on any boards prior to Artists Space, but I felt it was an extremely organized operation, like a well-oiled machine. Until the crisis of *Witnesses: Against Our Vanishing,* I hadn't realized the importance of the artists on the Board. A majority artist Board is the ideological rudder of the institution. And in that situation it was important to maintain the course. There was a lot of animosity toward Artists Space for a number of years, or at least grumblings, that came to a head long before I was on the Board or ever showed at Artists Space. Obviously, by being on the Board, I tried to make sure people of color were at least considered in the dialogue. I don't remember at what point Artists Space began to be better about that but I tried to bring it into the context of what they do. In small ways, I tried to broaden their consciousness and get them to think globally. Everybody was very nice; it never was a contentious situation. However, I felt I was as close as I was going to get to corporate culture. It's funny to think of Artists Space as being corporate, but what struck me was how they looked at the small art community, the upper end of the art community, as opposed to everyone else. Also, how they looked at the structures of other social environments and what they thought about and what they didn't think about. It was very congenial within the Board, but they were not particularly open. Ideas would be bantered around, but they never took hold in any major way. By the time I came on the Board there was some acknowledgment that change was needed, because money was being held back; they realized they had to do something. Inviting Kellie Jones to organize a show was part of it. I was on the NEA and NYSCA panels prior to being on Artists Space's Board and I realized how all the spaces revolted against the new rules—the fact that they had to become more aware.

← Fred Wilson, installation
Selections, Oct.1-31, 1987.

Nov. 12–Dec. 23: **We the People** (Jimmie Durham and Jean Fisher). Group exhibition of Native American artists: Pena Bonita, photo installation; Jimmie Durham, installation; Harry Fonseca, painting; Marsha Gomez, sculpture; Tom Huff, sculpture; G. Peter Jemison, drawing and paper pieces; Jean LaMarr, mural; Alan Michelson, installation; Joe Nevaquaya, painting; Jolene Rickard, photographs; Susana Santos, painting; Kay Walkingstick, painting; Richard Ray (Whitman), photo-texts. Catalogue with essays by Jimmie Durham, Jean Fisher, and Paul Smith, and an introduction to the video program by Emelia Seubert.

1987 NOV – DEC

← Jimmie Durham

↓ Ute Indian Tribe Audio Visual, *The Ute Bear Dance Story*, video, 1986.

ARTIST/CURATOR

Dan Walworth One of the coolest things we did at Artists Space was that trip we made to Tijuana. We called somebody from Border Art Workshop and they said, "Well, come on down!" David (Avalos) took us on a tour of Tijuana first. It was the most astounding moment to see everybody get ready to cross the border. We went to this spot, it was like a big soccer field, and at the end of it was a fence. Everybody was just hanging out in the field and there were tortilla salesmen hanging out there with their little umbrella stands and everything. It was not quite like a carnival, but a big city. The "theater of the border" was the phrase. And as soon as it got dark everybody just took off and ran across— it just seemed very strange. At the same time it was so calm. I guess a lot of these people were going to get arrested and returned.

Foreign Relations was a film show that had a sold-out crowd the night Edward Said came to read. We were one of the few places to program political work. Susan (Wyatt), despite her Republican upbringing—or very conservative Democratic upbringing, was very open to that, coming at it from a civil liberties point of view, as was Linda Shearer. It didn't require a lot of pushing or begging and cajoling. Everybody was very open to it.

I remember one evening when we had invited the commissioner for literature for the government of Nicaragua, Roberto Vargas. It was an evening of readings and film screenings. Jessica Hagedorn was there, the commissioner, who happened to be in town, and some others. It worked out that he would come and read a couple of poems and talk to us a little bit about Nicaragua. But it was so embarrassing, because here's this guy working for a whole government and we had like nine people show up.

One of the first out-and-out political shows we did was Annie Goldson's *TV Sandino*. The Sandinistas were a big deal back then and it was very popular. For a while we were programming shows that dealt with America's involvement in foreign countries, introducing people to what was going on in these other places through videotapes. It was like a cultural exchange except we never gave them anything except money. We gave them a fair amount of money, considering. We paid probably better than any other institution in New York at the time.

Uprising: Videotapes on the Palestinian Resistance, organized by Elia Suleiman, was similar to the *Foreign Relations* show that we did. But with this exhibition we got involved with a lot of brew. There was a great deal of back and forth and it showed in New York pretty much without a lot of comment. It got its normal pick in the *Village Voice*. But in Boston at the ICA (Institute for Contemporary Art) there was this furor because they insisted on running it with an Israeli show so it would be a balanced program. Elia and I decided we didn't want that. We thought it was kind of insulting. It was during the Intifada, around 1989.

Nov. 12–Dec. 23: **Video** in conjunction with **We the People** (Emelia Seubert and Dan Walworth). Chris Spotted Eagle, *Do Indians Shave?*, 1972; Arlene Bowman, *Navaho Talking Picture*, 1986; Asiba Tupahache, *A Tragedy and a Trial*, 1986; Victor Masayesva, Jr., *Hopiit 1981*, 1981; The Ute Indian Tribe Audio-Visual, *The Ute Bear Dance Story*, 1986; Gerald Vizenor, Rick Weise, and Gail Johnson, *Harold of Orange*, 1983.

Jan. 8–9: **In the Streets: Protest Films from the 60s and 80s** (Dan Walworth).
Jan. 8: *Pig Power*, 1969, newsreel; Larry Brose, *An Individual Desires Solution*, 1985; Harriet Hirshorn, Colleen MacDonald, Sandy Silverman, and Donna Stein, *You Can't Die From Sleeping*, 1986; Chris Marker, *Paris in the Month of May*, 1968; Mary Ann Tolman, *How We Live*, 1987.
Jan. 9: *Chicago Convention Challenge*, 1968, newsreel; *The Case Against Lincoln Center*, 1968, newsreel; Andrea Kirsch, *Fair Doctrine*, 1987; Youth International Party, *Yippie*, 1968.

Chris Hill CURATOR We're now in a time where video programs are being phased out, because it's a little more difficult to get local support for video, as compared to painting or photography exhibitions. Before, there wasn't a lot of emphasis on bringing in numbers of people paying admission. This is a problem for video now. Film tends to draw bigger audiences because historically it's been around longer, and it has a different visibility in terms of a general audience. But the period when video was respected as a relatively new art form and discourse was very important. People were getting paid to pay attention to only video, as opposed to curating video as an adjunct to film or some other agenda. The programs that came out of Artists Space were significant because the curators had diverse agendas. But not in the sense that resonates at the moment, which tends to be more like cultural diversity and multiculturalism. They had a broad interest in media strategy which was formally inventive as well as socially aware, but inventive in a more cultural hacking way, like culture jamming. And there are many kinds of interventions. As curators, Dan Walworth and Micki McGee saw themselves as both active and intervening within culture.

This retrospective is an important opportunity to look back at the last 25 years and consider the role of artist-run centers and public funding as it has shaped and supported an art discourse. It is essential to establish a space and resource for alternative culture. And it is particularly relevant for video because of its position vis-à-vis television, especially American television, which tends not to support much more than something designed to create a market. I'm sitting here, in eastern Europe, talking to students about the importance of maintaining some kind of local stage as it's being flooded by American television. They're pretty gaga with German money and American television, so it's a struggle. These spaces, but Artists Space in particular, were extremely important for video because of the very broad articulate framework that Dan and Micki brought to their work. This is especially true now when you look at centers that have survived the

last six years but have phased out video programs or their video curatorial or programmer jobs. There may be video programs in a lot of these spaces, but often the video is not being programmed by somebody full time, rather by film programmers or visual arts programmers. However, the video field did thrive over the last 15 years, when there was enough support for full-time curators.

In the early 80s, cultural theory started to play a very important role in media, which was different than its role in painting. The possibility of there being an alternative stage for media arts was particularly important for video because of its relationship to mainstream television and film. Television is not an alternative stage, with only a few exceptions. I certainly believe that public access and public television is important. But by and large, these are not the kind of educated and articulate audiences that you get at artist-run spaces. Such audiences are important for the development of the field to the extent that artist-run spaces were allowed to be experimental sites in the 80s, places for research and development. Often, those audiences are other groups of artists. Especially in the last five or six years, the importance of an audience of makers has unfortunately been lost and superseded by ticket sales.

Micki and Dan were unusually attentive to people programming and making video outside of New York. I benefitted from their approach. They invited me to program the *Floating Values* show. They were willing to take chances. As a curator, I learned a lot from their programs. And in turn, I invited Dan to Buffalo to show his tape about Palestine. Buffalo was often respected as an audience and as an interesting site by people who were working in New York. Living outside New York City, it was very important for us to participate in the discourse.

Floating Values was first screened at Hallwalls in February of '87 and at Artists Space in October '87. It was a survey, which afforded me an opportunity to do a lot of research. I talked to some people about what they had seen in the 70s that was important to them. For example, some people mentioned *The Blues Tape* with Kathy Acker and Alan Sondheim. She seduces him the whole time he is talking. Finally, he completely loses it. When I heard about it I called Kathy Acker, who was living in London, and she said, "Oh my God, I have no idea where a copy of that tape is, if you find it, you can show it." So I contacted Alan, who had a copy his father was keeping. It was an open reel tape. And he said, "I'll send it to you, if it doesn't work just toss it in the garbage." We tried it and it just stuck to the heads. But Tony Conrad happened to have some manual that discussed how to save audio tape open reel, so we saved the tape. We rubbed silicone into it and burnished it over the heads and made it run. Then we made a 3/4-inch copy and showed it. It's an important document.

Jean Fisher In the mid-80s there was hardly any work by contemporary Native American artists visible in the mainstream. There wasn't, as Edgar Heap of Birds would put it, a "beads and trinkets." That is to say, a type of postconceptual critical artwork. It was that critical proponent in certain artists' work that Jimmie Durham was very interested in. In any case, this is work that was marginalized at the time. Matt's Gallery in London included a few of the artists like Edgar and Joe Overstreet; and Kenkeleba House used to show these artists. Otherwise, now and then, one would crop up at the Native American Community House, but that was more of a trading post than a gallery. We were after a mainstream venue and, I have to say, Artists Space understood the idea of the project and agreed to stage it as soon as we put it together. I always respected Artists Space for this because it was the mid-80s and before multiculturalism became a fashionable idea. At the time there was very little debate around those issues but a lot around primitivism, which was always an historical debate. However, we wanted to deal with contemporary artists and their situation.

We organized the exhibition as a division of labor. The theme and the selection of artists was more appropriate for Jimmie to do. I handled the administrative work when he needed it and the negotiations with Artists Space. Jimmie's idea of the show was very interesting. From his point of view it was us, meaning Native American Indians, looking at them looking at us. He originally wanted all the artists to do a specific project around this idea. In the end this proved impractical because, at the time, there were very few artists who had the financial resources. Ultimately, some artists came up with a specific project, but others sent in any work they had. So, it was a mixture of work. Dan Walworth organized the Native American film and video program, which was very important. He negotiated with the film department of the Museum of the American Indian.

The exhibition took place during the year of the bicentennial of the writing of the American Constitution. So in our discussions for the title of the show we decided on *We the People*. The phrase "we the people" appears to be borrowed from the Iroquois. Two spaces were organized, one to look vaguely like an ethnographic display, very formal with vitrines, and the other was to be something more exuberant, colorful, and delightful. We painted the plinth a kind of Indian red color which was a rather risky thing to do.

It was one of the best-attended shows at Artists Space, but it had almost no coverage from the art press. It had a small article by Lucy Lippard, but then she was the obvious person to review it. She didn't place the review in a mainstream journal, but in an already marginalized journal. The other review appeared in the British magazine *Artscribe*, but it was clearly by someone who had never been to see the show, because all his reference points were taken from the little catalogue that Artists Space made. For example, no mention of

CONTINUED

Alan Michelson I had been taken away from my family clan and nation and was in the process of escaping when I decided to make various personal moves toward the recovery of my identity. I was trying to find my way back. This meant dumping unnecessary burdens and acquiring a certain knowledge through contacts I was in the process of making and expanding. But I actually had to use the knowledge and tools I already had from growing up in a non-Indian environment. Art tools such as painting helped me to deal with some of this more personal material that was also public. And the knowledge gained through a particular cultural and emotional experience to find my way back to a different one: a birthright that was interfered with. I encountered people along the way: Jerry Beck, who was an influence, and Jimmie Durham. He spoke at Mass Art (Massachusetts College of Art, Boston). I was bowled over by what he said. Jimmie is a very powerful speaker. I approached him after the talk and told him where I was coming from. I didn't know what to expect, but he seemed to have an understanding of my situation and a way of framing it that I had never considered. It was an enormous relief to me. The gist of it was that I wasn't alone. Thirty percent of American Indians were being removed from their families and tribal situations and placed in these other situations. From feeling like somebody who had a private and rare situation, I realized that there was a context. Even if it was the context of being nobody, it was a context. So that was very powerful. The political spin he put on it was also very powerful and congruent with my own politics, which were always underdog stuff.

When I was invited to show in *We the People*, I expressed certain reservations about my authenticity as a "Native American" artist, which they just laughed at and were very kind about. So I took the plunge. But I didn't want to show painting even though their decision to include me may have been based on seeing slides of my previous paintings. I was able to propose an installation and they accepted it despite the fact I had no track record in that field. It was a very important show for me for those reasons. I was looking at the history of the assimilation of my own people, the Iroquois Six Nations people. I traced some of the sources of what had befallen them. I was digging in these history books, reading about Jesuit relations, discussions by priests of the savages and their susceptibilities to finding God, etc. I was interested in one culture trying to dominate and force certain kinds of material on another while not being able to see the contradictions in taking this high moral tone.

In some ways my art has really been about displacement for a long time. I used the emotional grounding of my personal experiences to explore historical displacements and losses. My non-Indian family prepared me very well for that. I received a thorough education that was not only self-referential but enabled me to analyze it, to look at things I needed to explore both as an artist and as an independent researcher.

Jan. 14–Feb. 13: **Video: Other Versions (Perversions)** (Dan Walworth). Remo Balcells and Lee Warren, *The Grooming Tool*, 1986; Tony Conrad, *An Immense Majority*, 1987, and *In Line*, 1986; Robert Huff, *The Asshole is a Tense Hole*, 1985; Hilja Keading, *I am, 1986,* and *Yes/No*, 1985; Tony Labat, *Lost in the Translation*, 1984, and *Mayami: Between Cut and Action*, 1986; Paula Levine, *Mirror/Mirror*, 1987; Mark Verabioff, *Crossing the 49th*, 1985. Catalogue with essays by Martin Winn and Dan Walworth.

↑ Tony Labat

Jan. 14–Feb. 13: **Social Spaces** (Valerie Smith). Perry Bard, *Lower Level*, installation with sound; Michael Byron, *House for Winnie Mandela*, installation; Stephen Glassman, kinetic sculpture and large-scale performance props; Ann Hamilton, installation; Henry Jesionka, installation. Catalogue with introduction by Valerie Smith.

↗ OPPOSITE PAGE: Ann Hamilton

↓ Michael Byron
   Photo: Scott Hyde

Jean LaMarr's huge mural. Whether you liked it or not, you could hardly ignore the fact that it was there. That was the only art press we got, which must have been very disappointing for Artists Space. This was the end of 1987. Had we staged the show three years later there would have been a lot of interest. But it is true, everyone had overdosed on multiculturalism. The debate got very tired and ragged at the edges.

Because we had already organized the first exhibition, *Ni' Go Tiunh A Doh Ka* (*We are Always Turning Around... On Purpose*) at SUNY Old Westbury (Amalie A. Wallace Gallery, April 8–May 8, 1986), we were, even at that time, well aware of the whole Christian ghettoization of Native Americans and promoting ethnicity. We never really wanted to do that. The point was to show critical work. Before we approached the artists about what the show could be, we thought it ought to be different kinds of voices, a multi-ethnic position type show. But we decided against that because the issues around Native Americans were, in many respects, so specific. To have added critical issues of other groups would have confused and diluted the issues we wanted to present. Ultimately, all the artists had different experiences, which were inconsistent with each other because of their different backgrounds. One could not generalize, and this was the interesting point. One can get Native American work into mainstream galleries, but it still remains the ghetto. In order to follow the trajectory of treating Native American artists the way mainstream artists are treated, the next step was to organize individual exhibitions of Native American artists. Which is what I did.

ARTIST

Ann Hamilton The Artists Space project was very much a learning piece.

The particular circumstances of time and distance raised many process and maintenance questions related to working at a distance from the installation space. I was living and teaching in California at the time and a lot of the early and critical decisions had to be made with an understanding of the space based on photographs and floor plans. Some people are probably better at it than I am, but I find without an initial physical experience, it is impossible to feel the volume or sense the presence of a space. It is difficult to understand how I am to work with or against it, to gauge how much or how little a space needs. Some modifications and changes can be made during the actual installation, but by then the basic structure is already in place and it is difficult to backtrack. Some of the weaker aspects of the piece at Artists Space helped me better understand how more time in direct relationship with a space is crucial in working with its felt quality, rather than indirect information. Since then, what's clear to me is the importance to transform, but not deny, the space and architecture where I make the work.

On another level, scheduling the performer and replenishing the ashes where she sat made the ongoing maintenance of the Artists Space installation the challenge it continues to be in my new work. The needs of the project force a collaboration with the institution which can be enormously satisfying but also an enormous strain on friends and staff. The nature of the work's relationship to the institution never ceases to be a question. When the piece was installed and changed for the museum in Santa Barbara where it was later exhibited, I had a chance to spend many weekend hours up to my chin in paper ashes. After being mistaken for a mannequin for the hundredth time, I began to resolve for myself how there may be life within the work, but the work is not the life, and to see ways to introduce another gesture.

From the light-box image at Artists Space to the video image, which later faced it across the space in Santa Barbara, I began to understand where that gesture already was in the work. I saw how the physical processes my hands and body go through to make something are as much a work's meaning as the final image or object itself. The large black and white transparency of my torso holding a huge steaming bowl of dead flowers became the illumination for the room. The effort of holding the weight and heat could be seen in my straining neck and shoulders. I began to think about how that gesture, more than the pinned and collected insects, the fermentation bottles, or the magnetic stirrer, spoke to the way objects of our fascination are suffocated rather than nourished by human tending and the exaggerated scale of our consumption. Trusting "how" a gesture is made more than "what" is made began to signal an important change in the work.

Feb. 25–Apr. 2: **Colliding: Myth, Fantasy, Nightmare** (Michael Auping).Carlos Alfonzo, painting and ceramic plates; Biff Henrich, photo installation; Cherie Raciti, sculpture; Jeff Rubio, painting and drawing; M. Louise Stanley, painting and drawing. Catalogue with essay by Michael Auping.

Feb. 25–Apr. 2: **Video: Unacceptable Appetites** (Micki McGee). BBD&O, *Campbell's Soup Commercial* and *Crystal Light Commercial*, 1987; Cecelia Conduit, *Possibly in Michigan*, 1983; Marge Dean, *Autobiography of a Fat Girl*, 1979; Vanalyne Green, *Trick or Drink*, 1983; Todd Haynes and Cynthia Schneider, *Superstar: The Karen Carpenter Story*, 1987; Kathryn High, *Not Black and White*, 1984; Ketchum Communications, *Beef Industry Council Commercial*, 1987; Barbara Latham, *Consuming Passions*, 1983; Suzanne Lacy, *Learn Where the Meat Comes From*, 1976; Jeanine Mellinger, *White Food and Chocolate*, 1984; Peter Mitchell, *It Takes a Lot of Milk to Make a Country Strong*, 1987; Linda Montano, *Anorexia Nervosa (excerpt #1 and excerpt #2)*, 1981; Ogilvy & Mather, *Fibertrim Commercial*, 1985; Martha Rosler, *Losing: A Conversation with the Parents*, 1977; Jason Simon, *Production Notes: Fast Food for Thought (Schlitz excerpt and Mars excerpt)*, 1987; Sarah Tuft, *Don't Make Me Up*, 1986; Young and Rubicam, *Diet Dr. Pepper Commercial*, 1987. Brochure with essay by Micki McGee.

↑ Kathryn High

Stan Allen There was a certain moment during the late 70s right up to the end of the 80s when there was a lot of uncertainty in architecture about exactly what its own disciplinary boundaries were. For instance, what possible connections architecture might make to film, to art practices, to philosophy, or the role of theory. So it was a very wide open period. I have strong memories of my first year in New York and seeing Bernard Tschumi's *Architectural Manifestoes* show at Artists Space on Hudson Street. I was a student and the notion that one could do this kind of speculative work, that it could be part of an architect's practice, was very significant for me. It gave us permission to do a certain kind of work. Then, some years later, to be in the position to organize and be included in one of these shows underscores the importance of Artists Space's role. At that time, we were working through what exactly it meant for an architect to exhibit his or her work in a gallery. You could argue that the one thing actually not present in the gallery is the architecture, so it has to be something other than the architecture: drawings, models, statements, etc. Rather than simply accepting those surrogates for what they are, we tried to make the condition of the surrogate more explicit and thematic in the work.

The climate in the architecture world has shifted a little. Now there's less interest in open, speculative work, in part because it has been done and now people build on it. So many architects from the *London Project* are involved in—I don't want to necessarily say—a more conventional architecture, but we're all interested in getting things built. I don't see that as turning our back on speculative work but recognizing it as one phase that's been necessary to work through in order to move on to practice with a slightly different approach.

Those early years were so exciting because the conventions for doing architecture shows in a gallery hadn't yet been established. People like Elizabeth Diller and Bernard Tschumi were very instrumental in that way. However, it is slightly unfortunate that now there's a kind of model in place for what it means to do an architecture exhibition. It probably includes installation to some extent. Some architecture shows I see now are a little disappointing because they just plug into an available formula. Whereas in those early years there was a sense that people were really trying to figure it out and ask these questions. Part of the current feeling is that the most interesting challenges for architects are in practice, and not necessarily in this world of exhibition and galleries. It should be both. The last time I did an installation gallery show was in Germany in '92. I always said if I was asked to do a show again I would propose that whatever change I made in the gallery would have to be permanent. That may be why no one has asked me to do something.

Apr. 14–May 14: **The London Project** (organized by participating architects). Architectural exhibition by 10 architects from New York and London: Stan Allen/Marc Hacker, *Scoring the City: The Hollargraph*, model, diagrams; Karen Bausman /Patricia Pillette, *Greenwich*, installation with models; Neil M. Denari, *The Philosophy of Impossibility. Science: Architecture,* model and diagrams; Leslie Gill, *Fictive Interpretation of London,* etching; Jesse Reiser/Nanako Umemoto, *Globe Theater,* books, drawing, sculpture; Alastair Standing, *200 (A.W.A.L.) 2000. The Story of the Wall,* drawing; Marek Walczak, *London,* drawing. Accompanied by the book, *The London Project,* co-published by Princeton Architectural Press and Artists Space with a foreword by John Hejduk, essays by Patricia C. Phillips, statements and texts by the architects, and an afterword by K. Michael Hays.

↓ Jesse Reiser and Nanako Umemoto

Apr. 1–May 14: **Too Black, Too Strong!** (Reginald Woolery). Video program and works on paper: Mary Easter, *Some People,* 1988; Phillip Mallory-Jones, *What Goes Around, Comes Around,* 1986, *The Trouble I've Seen,* 1976, and *Extra Rooms,* 1980; Albert Marshall, *Suppositions on History,* 1985; Barbara McCullough, *Shopping Bag Spirits and Freeway Fetishes: Reflections on Ritual Space,* 1984; Daniel Tisdale, slide installation; LaMonte Westmoreland, collage; Reginald Woolery, collage. Program notes with introduction by Reginald Woolery and essay by Deirdre A. Scott.

June 2–July 2: Michael Asher, untitled architectural installation; James Coleman, *Seeing for Oneself,* 1987–88, narrative slide show with music and voiceover (Valerie Smith). Catalogue with introduction by Valerie Smith and essays by Anne Rorimer, John Vinci, and Jean Fisher.

↓ Michael Asher

June 2–July 15: **Video: Telling Tales** (Dan Walworth). Jan Baracz, *The Touch,* 1987; Constance De Jong and Tony Oursler, *Joyride TM,* 1988; Paulette Phillips and Geoffrey Shea, *Work,* 1987; Jim Shaw, *The Andersons,* 1986; Orinne J. T. Takagi, *Community Plot,* 1984.

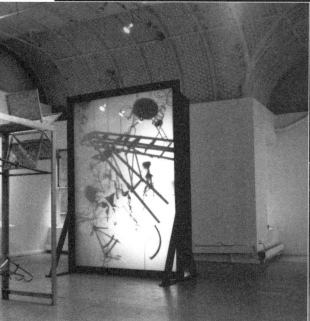

ARCHITECT

Leslie Gill Artists Space became an education in how to proceed with group projects and work in the nonprofit world. Personally, it was an interesting experience. Working with you (Valerie Smith) and Susan Wyatt was one of the most ethical situations I had encountered. I really appreciated that because Karen (Bausman) and I have been involved in a few projects with nonprofits where, in the end, we felt we had not been treated well. In terms of my development, it was a way of looking at a granting experience and a group dynamic that allowed me to see how architects and artists think very differently about their work. The process of getting grants and writing up the proposals pointed out how differently artists and architects develop their work and perceive their financial standing. I learned a lot from Artists Space. They were very generous with information, where other institutions would try to make it functionary.

→ James Coleman, *Seeing for Oneself,* 1987-88.

Susan Wyatt interviewed by Evelyn B. Leong

Susan Wyatt was the Executive Director of Artists Space from 1985 to 1991. I met with Wyatt in late December 1993 to discuss issues such as alternative arts spaces, public arts funding, and freedom of expression. All of these issues have been extremely important to Wyatt, who has been an outspoken and active advocate for the arts. During the late 1980s, controversies developed over legislation which tried to label what type of art could be deemed obscene and therefore, be refused government funding. In 1989, during heated debates over censorship and obscenity in the arts, Artists Space and the National Endowment for the Arts (NEA) became embroiled in controversy over the exhibition Witnesses: Against Our Vanishing, *a show about sexuality, AIDS, death, and memory. This interview was originally published as "An Interview with Susan Wyatt" by Evelyn B. Leong in* Gulf Coast: a Journal of Literature and Fine Arts, *vol. VI, no. 2, Summer 1994.*

EVELYN LEONG: Let's begin with some background on your tenure at Artists Space and the history of the organization itself. How long were you there?

SUSAN WYATT: I was at Artists Space for 17 years. I actually started as a student intern when I was at Sarah Lawrence College. After I graduated, I started working there part-time doing odd jobs while I was looking for something else. It gradually became a real job.

EL: When you took over as Director in 1985, what was your vision? What did you want for Artists Space?

SW: At the time, I didn't have one. People were always asking and people still want to know. I don't think I totally buy into that concept. What I wanted to do at Artists Space was to continue some of the things we had always been doing. It had less to do with my vision and more to do with what was going on in the art world. I wanted to be responsive to what was going on in the community. One of the things that I did was to increase the publications in an attempt to document the shows. We started organizing international shows. Between 1985 and 1988, there was so much focus on younger artists and commercial galleries. It was a time when 22-year-old artists were having solo shows in those galleries. For us to be a showcase for younger artists' work and provide one-person exhibitions for younger artists in New York didn't mean too much. We also started a series of exhibitions of artists from around the country who were chosen by curators from other parts of the country. Part of that was because we didn't have a staff that could travel. It was a way to utilize curators from different regions who would not normally have the opportunity to do a show in New York and who would be knowledgeable about artists working in that area.

Regarding international shows, one of the major shows I put on was an Eastern European exhibition entitled *Metaphysical Visions/Middle Europe* **which took two years to plan. It was just before the breakup of the Soviet Union and during a time when Eastern Europe was very closed off. Valerie Smith, who was Artists Space's curator at the time, had a very particular interest and a desire to learn more. It took two years for us to get the funding, but it wasn't so much the funding that made it difficult, though at the time, it seemed insane to take on such a thing. We actually were able to raise the funds. Valerie went over and traveled around to figure out what we could do. In some countries, it was easier for her to have meaningful contact with the artist community than others, but overall she had a very difficult time. Once she came up with a concept and some of the artists, we had to figure out a way to get them and their work out. I think there were seven or eight artists in the show and all of them came to New York for the show. It was, for some, the first time they had left their countries. Yugoslavia was easy to arrange. It was a very different place then. But with the Czech artists we had a lot of difficulty getting them out. One of them was "unofficial" and that was very tricky but we managed to do it. Getting the work out physically was also very difficult although in the case of the Polish artists, most of them created work on**

site. The kind of work the Polish artists were doing involved materials like dirt, scrap wood—materials that one could duplicate very easily here. We did several international shows.

The international exhibitions were a way for us to carve out a different niche in New York. Besides the NEA, we could get funding from the foreign governments involved and from certain foundations. We were able to get money for the Eastern European show because there had been nothing like it in New York before. When you're working at a place like Artists Space, you need to make the resources and the mission come together somehow. You can't do things when you can't find funding for them. But you can't do things just because the funding is available either.

EL: For you, what is the major difference between alternative spaces and museums?

SW: I think a major difference is the focus. It wasn't so much going into a studio and looking at all the work and making an interpretive judgment or thinking thematically. Partly because of the type of artists we were dealing with, in most cases, it was the first time they were showing. We wanted to present an opportunity where they had choices and could control how the work was presented. Rather than mediating between the art and the public, the idea was to present the work in a more direct way.

For instance, I think the New Museum of Contemporary Art in New York City has more of a focus on the curator. Our focus at Artists Space was more on the artist. My predecessor, Linda Shearer, had a good way of putting it. She would say, "We curate artists, not the art," We wanted to take leaps of faith and we did, many times. I'm sure museums also do that but for us the point was not about putting together a perfect exhibition. It was much more about experimentation.

EL: Is Artists Space the only alternative space to have a slide registry?

SW: There are other slide registries but I think it's one of the most effective. The registry has been a part of Artists Space from about its second year. By the 1980s, it became more utilized after Linda Shearer selected from the slide file for her first exhibition which then started an annual series of exhibitions which we called *Selections*. It was a way to highlight the file and for us to have a nonthematic presentation of eight to twelve younger artists' work.

Artists Space has always had a service component. In fact, when it started, it never really intended to be an exhibition space. Artists Space started with the idea of assisting artists. The primary focus was on financially supporting artists and the first program was called the Emergency Materials Fund. This program made small grants to artists who were having shows in other nonprofits (colleges, libraries, galleries). If they needed basic costs for shipping, insurance, framing, etc., we gave them grants. The grants were not intended as sole sponsors. Artists who show in nonprofit spaces have to bear so much of the burden of exhibiting. The program was set up to help ease that burden.

EL: What was the original intent of the founders of Artists Space?

SW: In 1973 the two founders, Trudie Grace and Irving Sandler, had a series of meetings with artists and asked them what kinds of things were important and what they needed. What kept coming up over and over again was the need for exhibition space which was free from political and commercial considerations. And that's how the exhibitions began.

EL: So, I assume you carefully watched other alternative organizations.

SW: Oh, you have to. To survive, an organization has to develop its own identity so you have to have a sense of what others are up to. It's interesting, though, because the first year I was at Artists Space and probably up through the 1970s, we had very little interaction with the other alternative spaces. There really wasn't any vehicle for that. One of the reasons the National Association of Artists Organizations (NAAO) was founded was to try to foster, not just locally but nationally, what these places were about and to advocate for them. It's hard because so many organizations are struggling and there's so little money. It's as though you're swimming out there in the ocean and you don't see the other swimmers. So NAAO was important; it helped us to see the other swimmers.

In some parts of the country, there is only one alternative space in that city and it has to serve the whole broad range of constituencies. That's a very different kind of role than a place like Artists Space in New York. If you don't have a variety of commercial galleries in a city and you're not dealing with an active art market, a different kind of program would make a lot more sense. I think the sad thing now, because of the decline in funding, is that some of the bigger alternative spaces have really suffered. The Washington Project for the Arts (WPA) and Los Angeles Contemporary Exhibitions (LACE) in Los Angeles have had severe cutbacks and cannot do the types of shows they did six or seven years ago. You want to have diversity; you want to have both the Metropolitan Museum of Art and the Walker Art Center. Even the major museums are suffering from budget cuts.

Some people feel that alternative spaces should exist when they are relevant, then die. The attitude is that another will come along. I can understand that argument but I don't agree with it. I think that will happen anyway but I don't think it's a thing to foster. Also, it is just so hard to put together an organization and get it established and stabilized. There have been so few new alternative spaces lately. It's so much more difficult to start them in this climate.

In 1989, Senator Jesse Helms, for which the Helms Amendment is named, fought to curb federal financing of art deemed obscene, and a modified version of his bill was passed into law that Fall. Organizers of exhibitions of photographs by Robert Mapplethorpe and Andres Serrano both suffered as a result of this legislation. Susan Wyatt had been speaking out against what she saw as blacklisting. Wyatt was very concerned about the fact that when the Helms law passed, the Institute of Contemporary Art (ICA) in Philadelphia and the Southeastern Center for Contemporary Art (SECCA) in Winston-Salem, North Carolina, which had received a combined $45,000 from the NEA, were singled out by Congress and that the NEA received a symbolic $45,000 cut to its budget as punishment for the grants. The two organizations had been put on a list, requiring them to provide detailed justification to a Congressional Committee in order to receive an NEA grant. Wyatt suggested that if SECCA and the ICA were on a blacklist, all exhibition spaces should be on a blacklist. Wyatt also suggested that arts organizations call the NEA, ask about some of the work that they were showing, and ask about the law and its language. [1] *For these suggestions, Wyatt received both support and criticism. Some agreed that a blacklist was being established and Wyatt added that blacklists were only powerful if they were small; a large list would lose its power.*

While Wyatt was Director of Artists Space, the organization became involved in a difficult controversy with the NEA and the Helms Amendment over an exhibition entitled Witnesses: Against Our Vanishing *(November 1989-January 1990). Artists Space received a $10,000 grant from the NEA for the exhibition; however, that grant was later rescinded, then reinstated, after much controversy. I asked Wyatt about the origins of the show and about the controversy that followed.*

SW: Artists Space hadn't done a photography exhibition for quite some time and so we invited the photographer Nan Goldin to organize a show for Fall 1989. As time passed, it did cross my mind that *Witnesses*, which was going to be primarily photography, dealt with the subject of gay sexuality and that it might be questioned or a problem in some way.

That summer of 1989, it became increasingly clear that photography was a hot issue. It seemed to a lot of people, including myself, that part of the problem with photography was that many people could not understand that photography was an art. I believe I talked to the Executive Committee of the Board of Artists Space at some point that summer about the potential for controversy. Talking to the Board about upcoming shows was something I did on a routine basis anyhow. I didn't want any kind of controversy to come up or have any weird vibes out there in the community without the Board having some knowledge of it so that they wouldn't be caught off guard.

> **EL:** One of the pivotal pieces in the *Witnesses* exhibition was actually in the accompanying catalogue, and I remember it provoked the most concern. The artist, David Wojnarowicz, wrote an essay entitled "Post Cards From America: X-Rays From Hell," which is a very personal account of his experience with AIDS. Tell me about that.

SW: Nan Goldin and Connie Butler (who replaced Valerie Smith as curator) had been working together on the exhibition and catalogue. Nan wanted several artists to participate in the catalogue, including David Wojnarowicz and Cookie Mueller. Cookie was very sick with AIDS and couldn't write anything but we figured out a way for her to participate.

Just before I left to go to the NAAO conference in October, Connie Butler received a copy of David Wojnarowicz's text for the catalogue. She wrote me a note which said that I might want to read this. I read David's essay and I felt that this essay was something I needed to run by our Board. We had never even published words like "fuck" or "shit" in any of our catalogues. Beverly Wolff, who is a lawyer, had recently joined the Board at Artists Space, and it seemed like an opportunity to utilize this new Board member who could help us with legal matters. I asked Connie to have Beverly look over the text. Since I'm not a lawyer, I didn't know about libel laws. I didn't know if the public figures mentioned—Cardinal O'Connor, Jesse Helms, William Dannemeyer—might sue. It was a totally new experience for me to deal with these issues. So I asked Connie to get the text to Beverly in preparation for an Executive Committee meeting. It was something I knew I wanted to advise Artists Space's Executive Committee about and to also talk about what we wanted to say to the whole Board about the show. There is no question in my mind that we would go ahead with the show and I knew that there might be some controversy. I had known that even before David's text came up. It was just a way of being prepared.

When I got back from the NAAO conference, Beverly and I talked about the text and some of the NEA issues. Both of us were very interested in the question about the constitutionality of the Helms law. We talked about the grant and about the pros and cons of giving the grant back which she had

1   Part of the wording of the Helms Amendment prohibits the NEA from being used to "promote, disseminate or produce materials considered obscene, including sadomasochism, homo-eroticism, the sexual exploitation of children or individuals engaged in sex acts" and that grant proposals will be denied "which, when taken as a whole, do not have serious literary, artistic, political or scientific value."

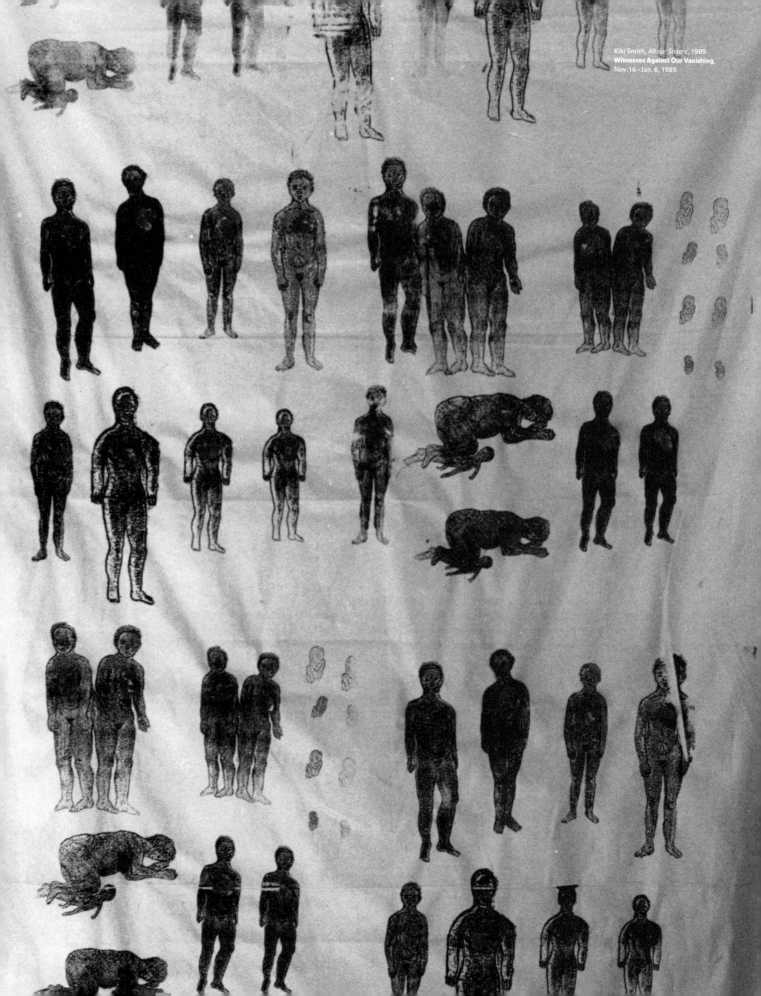

posed to me as an option. And I had argued with her very strongly against doing any such thing. It was more a theoretical discussion than anything else. One of the things she said was that she couldn't assure me that the text was not libelous. The implication, the sense I got from her, was that it might not be libelous but that she couldn't guarantee that Cardinal O'Connor's or Jesse Helms's lawyers might not think that it was nor that we would be protected from a lawsuit. She recommended that I call David and ask him to remove the names and to discuss them generically as government officials. I was under a lot of pressure, and I called David. I don't think I got into any of the specifics but I did say that we had some concerns and that I wanted to talk to him about the text. We talked about it a little bit. He was extremely forceful about wanting to keep the text exactly the way it was. It was a difficult conversation and I can't recall many other situations I had like that at Artists Space but I felt that I had to talk to him about the essay.

Once I talked to him and had hung up the telephone, I realized that there was no way in hell that we could press him for changes in the text, nor did I want us to. I called Beverly and told her that we had to publish the text the way it was and asked her what we needed to do to protect ourselves legally. Beverly wanted David to sign a legal waiver, which was actually very standard, and we discussed the fact that we had no contracts with any catalogue writers or artists. That was something we discussed changing. She also suggested that we have a disclaimer in the catalogue. That seemed feasible. In the more theoretical discussion when we discussed our options, Beverly and I had talked about the idea of taking the catalogue out of the scope of the grant. Our catalogues generally cost $6,000 or $7,000. We had received a small grant from a corporation that wanted to be anonymous and we had applied for money from the Robert Mapplethorpe Foundation which granted us $5,000. So when I met with the Executive Committee, one of the things I talked about was possibly allocating this $5,000 grant from the Mapplethorpe Foundation to the publication of the catalogue.

I called the NEA the day before the Executive Committee meeting and spoke to David Bancroft who supervises Special Exhibitions grants, which is the type of grant we had been awarded. I asked him about the possibility of changing the scope of the grant and I told him a little bit about the show. I wanted them to know that it was possible that some of the works were sexually explicit. One of the reasons I did that was because I was concerned about an incident that occurred during the controversy over the summer regarding the Andres Serrano and Robert Mapplethorpe grants.[2] Hugh Southern, who was then the Acting Chairman of the NEA, wrote a letter to members of Congress basically saying that he was personally offended by Serrano's work.[3] I was horrified by that and I didn't want the NEA to write anything like that about the Artists Space show. Part of my thinking was that if we removed the catalogue from the grant, we would remove the most potentially contentious artwork involved and the one where the NEA would probably have to be the most apologetic. And I didn't want them to be apologetic in any way about this grant or this exhibition. I made several statements at the time which were quoted in various news articles that I wanted the NEA to stand up for the show. In his book,[4] John E. Frohnmayer, the then new Chairman of the NEA, said he didn't understand what I meant by those statements. What I was thinking about was Southern's letter. I didn't want them to be apologetic so by shifting the money, my thought was that it would allow the NEA to be supportive and not cast aspersions on the work in the show. From a practical and political point of view, to remove the catalogue would make the grant more defensible. This wasn't necessarily my point of view, but I was trying to protect our artists and the organization. I was really horrified by the way Mapplethorpe and Serrano had been attacked. During a visit with a colleague in the Fall to see Senator D'Amato, my colleague had gone through the Congressional record and made a list of adjectives that had been used to describe Serrano and Mapplethorpe. I remember her reading that list in our meeting with Senator D'Amato. I was amazed by the degree of hostility and ridicule these two legitimate artists received. I didn't want any artist showing at Artists Space to be dragged through the mud in that way. I knew Andres Serrano and that it had been an extremely difficult time for him. I didn't want that to happen to David Wojnarowicz or anyone else.

    EL: How did the Board respond to your suggestion of taking the catalogue out of the NEA grant?

SW: Prior to the meeting, I looked into the possibility of making that shift, and I was told that it could be done. David Bancroft advised me on the type of letter to write to the NEA. I posed it to the Executive Committee and they agreed. The Mapplethorpe Foundation grant was to be used in any way we wanted for the exhibition. I discussed this with Bancroft and he said we didn't need to say anything about the show, just that we had raised the money for the catalogue. He told me to request a change in the budget. It was very straightforward and simple.

But when I re-read the award letter, I realized that it wasn't just a question of changing the budget. In the letter, the grant included the exhibition *and* the accompanying catalogue. At the time, it was known that Senator Helms was going through NEA files, so I called Bancroft back, and I asked him about

2 An exhibition of photographs by the late Robert Mapplethorpe was scheduled to open at the Corcoran Gallery of Art in Washington, D.C., during the summer of 1989. While the exhibition did receive a grant from the NEA, due to the debates in Congress over homoerotic art and obscene art, the Director of the Corcoran, Christina Orr-Cahall, decided to cancel the exhibition.

3 The artwork in question was a piece by Andres Serrano entitled *Piss Christ* (1987), a photograph of a plastic crucifix submerged in urine.

4 *Leaving Town Alive: Confessions of an Art Warrior.*

the possibility of getting a new letter because I was concerned about Helms reviewing the Artists Space file some time in the future and claiming that the NEA had funded a catalogue personally attacking him. Bancroft explained that the same language was used in every letter whether there was a catalogue or not. This would ensure the NEA getting credit for any publication. I also asked him if the NEA wanted to be credited as a funder of the show. I wanted to ask about this specifically because I had been thinking about the funder who had asked to be anonymous. One of the things I noticed while looking over the list of conditions for grants from the NEA was that they suggested receiving a credit line, but it was not required. Bancroft referred me to Ana Steele who, at the time, was in the Chairman's office. In the meantime, he told me he would check into my question about changing the text of the letter so that "accompanying catalogue" could be removed. I also called Steele before the Executive Committee meeting but she told me that she couldn't give me any advice. So, the Executive Committee basically left the credit issue up to me. It seemed ridiculous not to credit the NEA and as they hadn't asked to have their name removed, there was no justification for my hiding their involvement so I went ahead and put the credit on the announcement card which went out to 10,000 people.

In the meantime, John E. Frohnmayer had just begun his tenure as NEA Chairman and as he had been unable to attend the NAAO conference, he offered to meet with Charlotte Murphy, the Director of NAAO, who invited me and Inverna Lockpez, the Director of International Arts Relations (INTAR) in New York City, to also attend. I was also planning to go to the National Council[5] meeting which was scheduled for early November. I wanted to follow up on possible cuts to the Visual Arts Program and to hear the National Council discuss the Helms language.

Anyhow, I went down to Washington the day before the meeting with Frohnmayer. I reconnected with Bancroft about changing our award letter and he advised me to send a letter requesting the change and that it would not be a problem for NEA to issue a new award letter. I told him that I had gone ahead and credited the NEA on the announcement card. We agreed that I should let Ana Steele know. I called Celeste Dado, the Assistant Director at Artists Space, and asked her to draft this letter and get it out because Bancroft had okayed the change.

Meanwhile, Charlotte, Inverna, and I went to meet with Frohnmayer. When we got there we were told that he would be half an hour late and we should wait. So with half an hour to kill, I called Steele and told her everything—letter, credit, etc. She said she wanted to advise me that the Chairman had been briefed about our show and that she thought he might raise it in our meeting. Charlotte, Inverna, and I had carefully planned what we wanted to say to Frohnmayer. I didn't want the *"Witnesses"* show, something I considered a completely separate issue, to take up NAAO's time with the Chairman. I told Steele that I was concerned about that and although I would be happy to talk to him about it if he wanted, we were there to discuss NAAO matters. She said she could try to get a message to Frohnmayer but she couldn't guarantee it. By that time, I was fairly panicked. I had never met this man so it was off-putting. Anyhow, we ended up having a very nice meeting and covered all the topics Charlotte, Inverna, and I had planned. One of the things we discussed included arranging a tour or town meeting in New York for Frohnmayer and he was very positive about that. When we got up to leave, he said "Susan, I need to speak to you privately." Charlotte and Inverna looked shocked, and they left. I stayed. We had a perfectly straightforward conversation. I brought him up-to-date about the show and went over all the details that I had gone over with Bancroft. He asked me a few questions about the show and asked if it was still possible to put a disclaimer in the catalogue for the NEA. Since we were already putting in a disclaimer on behalf of Artists Space, it seemed odd for me to say no. It had taken us a little time to figure out what Artists Space had wanted to say so I told him I did not know what a disclaimer for the NEA should say. He asked if he supplied us with the text, would we include it. I said yes. He said that Andrew Oliver Jr., the Acting Director of the NEA's Museum Programs, would be coming to New York and would like to visit Artists Space to see the work for the show. I explained to him that we had not yet collected all the work since the show was not to open for another month but that we would make an effort to get what we could together. He said that was fine, to let Oliver see whatever he could and also to let him read the catalogue text. That was the whole discussion. He never gave me any indication that the NEA might withdraw the grant. He was clearly concerned about the grant but my understanding was that Oliver would come and no action would occur until after his visit.

I went back to New York and collected what we could for Oliver's visit. There were some people who criticized me for allowing Oliver to come. Some of my colleagues thought I shouldn't have allowed him to.

EL: Are these people other arts administrators?

SW: Yes, one is a director of another alternative space. I said, "You mean you would have said no to a visit from a funder?" I had nothing to hide. If the NEA had a problem with the work, let them say so. I

5 The National Council for the Arts advises the NEA.

Feds shift, give AIDS show grant

JOAN SHEPARD

hattan Cultural Affairs Editor

AIDS Art May Put Helms To a Test

NEA Reconsidering Support for N.Y. Show

AIDS Art

NEA, From C1

sial art. "In order for the NEA not have a controversy on its hands wi out having any opportunity to get p pared for it, I decided to contact NEA.

"I also felt that I kind of wanted in a bit argues with NEA about the issue of censorsh said Wyatt. "I wanted to offer them opportunity, as it were, to kind of st up for the show, to take credit for fact they funded it."

Wyatt said the show, "Witness Against Our Vanishing," cost $30,0

Cardin

Frohr

The Endowment vs. the

New York Art Exhibition
To Test Federal Restrictions

CLASH OVER AIDS EXHIBIT

Ho gallery fears Fed backlash

Story on page 5

Space director Susan Wyatt talks to reporters

NEA Halts Grant for Show Displaying AIDS Artwork

NEA Gallery Still in Standoff

Art for AIDS sake h

rts?

So ho gallery ars backlash

MARZULLI

Ope ns Thursda

...to... aitan... ...ort...o...t...
... one...en...
...nalist materials. Frohnmayer said.

The show is set to open
next week.

"It is very much to the gai-
lence ex... ...et the ...ted
N... ...o... ...h the an-
... ...how... ...ibit...
said

Wyatt said she altered the
N... to the show's content
because she was concerned
Helms "might not particularly like the artwork."

Returning the grant would
set a bad precedent, said
Manhattan artist David Woj-

Nonprofit Gallery in TriBeCa
Finds Itself at Storm's Center

ARTS AGENCY GIVES BACK

Wrong to Rescind Art Grant

Amei Wallach

Endowment not withdraw its sponsor- "masochism," and "homoeroticism."
ship on the basis of perceived

10G GRANT TO AIDS SHOW

By ANDREA PEYSER

Offensive art exhibit

Ex-NEA Head Requests Session of Arts Advisers

■ **Arts:** On-going crisis prompts unusual request. Committee of authors stalls amid sensitivity to political, sexual content.

By ALLAN PARACHINI
TIMES STAFF WRITER

rts: Anger and Concern

ayer Says He'll Seek End of Art-Grant Law

Helms with gasoline and setting him

feds trying to yank gallery's grant

S show
testing
curb on
ds for art

NEA Chief Defends Grant Cut

Decision Based on Art, Not Politics, He Says

When Art Is 'Too Political'

admit that it was nervous-making. We thought carefully about who should be there. It was decided that Nan Goldin not be there for the meeting itself but that she should be in the gallery or stop by to just say hello. Connie, the curator, and Celeste, who wrote the government grants, and I were there. No Board members. Since Beverly and I had talked about some of the current pornography laws, I had shown her some of the photographs. There was one image which she advised me could potentially be problematic. It was a Peter Hujar photograph of a nude baby, and she expressed concern because of the child pornography laws. That was the only image she thought might be problematic. She advised us to try to contact the parents of the child and get a letter on file indicating that they had given permission for this photograph to be taken. We tried to track them down.

EL: Was that photograph included in what you showed Oliver?

SW: Yes. I don't remember if he said anything about it although I doubt it. We did everything we were supposed to do. In fact, I attended a seminar which Beverly and another lawyer, Barbara Hoffman, had given at MOMA for arts organizations about some of the recent changes in the child pornography laws among other things. It was quite amazing what things one had to do to comply with the law. We never were able to track down the parents of the baby in the Hujar photograph.

EL: How was Oliver's site visit?

SW: Oliver came on a Tuesday morning, looked at the work, and was very pleasant. He acted very unsurprised by everything. The catalogue at that point was too long for him to sit and read so I made him a copy of the galley. I explained Mr. Frohnmayer's interest in a disclaimer and told him that we needed him to get back to us promptly as we had a deadline. He already knew about the NEA credit on the announcement card. Oliver said that he would read the catalogue, report back to Frohnmayer and that we would hear from them. This was also the week that I was planning to go down to Washington for the National Council meetings. Meanwhile, Elizabeth Hess of the *Village Voice* had already contacted me about the show. She wanted to do a pre-review.

That afternoon, Frohnmayer called. He knew that the announcement cards and press releases had gone out. He asked if there would be copies of releases that we would distribute later. When I said yes, he asked us to put a disclaimer on the press release and any other material. I was confused but I said yes. I didn't want to get into any kind of argument with him. I wanted to hear what he had to say, hang up and then figure out what to do. He read me the disclaimer which I recognized as being out of the legislation. It said something like "the findings, recommendations, and opinions included herein do not reflect the views of the NEA." He basically instructed me to remove the name of the NEA from the show—from the press releases, walls of the exhibition, the catalogue—and told me the disclaimer should be posted on every publication and anywhere else appropriate. But it seemed contradictory to put up a disclaimer without a credit. It was as strange as posting a sign like "the Pope doesn't agree with this…" It made sense to have a disclaimer alongside the acknowledgment of support but not separated. I didn't know how I was to answer the question about whether the show was funded by the NEA. I told him that there was press interest in the show. He said to have them call him directly. It just seemed very strange and I didn't want to get into any heavy discussion so I got off the phone. There was no way in the world I was going to say to Elizabeth Hess when she asked if the show was funded by the NEA, "you better call John Frohnmayer to find out." It just didn't make sense. On top of that, what about our receptionist who sits near the entrance of the gallery? Here's this show about AIDS and sexuality and it's also full of photography and it's funded in part by the Robert Mapplethorpe Foundation and it has this disclaimer about the NEA. She was going to be asked this question about whether the show was funded by the NEA by most every visitor. It wasn't clear to me what kind of answer she could give.

In our conversation, Frohnmayer said nothing about taking the grant back. Oliver had acted so calm. But I guess he was shocked by the work or at least that's what I heard later. I called Beverly and some other Board members to try to figure out what would make sense. I finally decided that I would try to call Oliver, which I did. I reached Nancy Pressly instead, the second in command in the Museum Program, who was as perplexed as I was after I explained Frohnmayer's request. I thought about it that night and talked to other Board members but they, too, were confused. I thought that I would try to point out to Frohnmayer that his request didn't make any sense unless the disclaimer was accompanied by credit. I also thought the disclaimer was awkward and would likely raise more questions and cause more notice. When I spoke with Oliver the next morning and told him that I was seriously considering calling Frohnmayer back, he said he didn't want to discourage me from calling Frohnmayer but that he did not think he would change his mind. I consulted with Board members and thought more about it that day. Eventually we decided that I would rewrite the disclaimer with less strange language and call Frohnmayer with the proposal that we would be willing to put up a disclaimer if we could credit the NEA. I wanted to point out the absurdity of his instruction. Beverly had warned me before I called him that if I brought up anything about giving the money back, that he would pounce on it so I should be careful. She was right. I was very careful about what I said to him.

When I spoke to him, Frohnmayer wasn't very pleasant and essentially said that he thought that I was calling to give the grant back. I said no, that I wasn't and told him my proposal. I told him that if he wanted to ask us for the grant back, I would convey that to my Board. He started to try to press me to give the grant back, so I got off the phone. A few minutes later, Beverly called to say that she was getting calls from the Legal Counsel's office at the NEA. I told her what Frohnmayer had said. She called the NEA back and tried to explain our point of view and tried to make clear that if there was a way the NEA could force us to give the grant back, that was what they would have to do but to expect us to voluntarily give it back wouldn't work.

Beverly received a draft of a letter by fax that the NEA was going to give to me, essentially asking for the grant back. They knew that I was going to Washington, D.C., for the Council meeting the next day. I managed to get a torn copy of the draft before catching the last shuttle to Washington. Beverly told me that when I arrived for the meeting at nine a.m., I should look for Art Warren who was the NEA's legal counsel and that their letter would be waiting for me to pick up. So that's what I understood. But when I showed up at nine the next morning, the first person to approach me was Allan Parachini, the prime reporter on this story, who was writing for the *Los Angeles Times*. He said that he understood that I had a letter from the Chairman requesting our grant back for our AIDS show. I was flabbergasted. I wanted to know who told him about such a letter and he said the press person at the NEA had. I hadn't gotten any letter so I told him his information was wrong. I connected with Art Warren and Julie Davis, a special assistant to the Chairman who later became legal counsel. Frohnmayer had recently issued a statement telling grantees that if they had questions about the new Helms law to call his office and they would work with them to resolve any problems. I told Davis that I had advocated that policy at the NAAO conference but that if someone asked me now if they should do that, I didn't think I would say yes. She agreed that I had a good point.

I was given a copy of the letter in draft form, and I had a fairly long meeting that afternoon with Warren about the draft. I asked for all the legal grant requirements and I tried to understand exactly what was involved with the termination of grants. I asked for all the legal papers which he said he would get me the next day. We went over the draft line by line. I asked over and over again if we were being asked to voluntarily give the grant back, to voluntarily put the disclaimer up. I wanted to know what their reason was for asking us to give the grant back. I was just trying to get as much information as I could. I also wanted to keep the fact that I had this letter completely confidential. I didn't want it coming out in the press. I had seen what had happened at the Corcoran with its Board and what had happened with Christina Orr-Cahall over the Mapplethorpe exhibition; half the Board thought canceling the show was the right thing to do and the other half thought it was the wrong thing to do and both factions had talked to the press. I didn't want my Board to be divided—half saying we should give the grant back and half saying we should not give the grant back. I wanted to have as strong a statement as possible from Artists Space and I felt that if it came out in public too soon, I didn't know where all the shoes would drop. The staff had voted unanimously as I left for Washington that we should not give the grant back. I didn't want to see the organization ripped apart. I wanted to make sure everyone knew what was going on before it became a public event. I asked them to please instruct Parachini and I was assured of confidentiality. I really had no direct dialogue with Frohnmayer that day although all the accounts say that I did. He came up to me before I got the letter and basically shook my hand. It was an indication of respect and that we had agreed to disagree.

The whole event was very strange. I felt like every eye in the room was watching and that Frohnmayer was watching my every move. I was told that the letter was completely confidential and I could tell the press when I wanted. They had told no one and they had corrected Parachini. I also tried to convince them not to give me the letter. If they wanted Artists Space to give this grant back, I would convey that to my Board. They didn't need to write it in a letter. By that point, we were in the process of setting up an emergency Board meeting that was scheduled for the middle of the next week. I also volunteered to Julie Davis to remain in Washington to talk more to Frohnmayer. Although the National Council Meeting would be meeting on Sunday, I explained that I could meet with them on Sunday afternoon or I would even be willing to stay until Monday and meet then. I just wanted to have as much dialogue with them as I could and to get as many reasons as I could. I managed to put off Parachini by agreeing to have lunch with him the next day.

I didn't tell anyone that I had the letter. It was burning a hole in my briefcase. The only people I told were Beverly and Carolyn Alexander, our Board President. I had also been in touch with the Artists Space staff including Connie Butler who kept in touch with Nan. I was not in touch with David Wojnarowicz directly but I did want to keep him apprised. Richard Elovich was a very close friend of David's and was, at that time, running an organization called Movement Research which also gets NEA money. After my last conversation with David, he was very angry with me. I didn't feel that it was productive to have that much direct dialogue with him. I did speak to Elovich several times that weekend. I thought he would understand what I was dealing with. I also knew that he would be in touch with David and keep him informed. We were trying to keep it all together; I didn't want it to fall apart in an ugly way. I wanted Artists Space to take a really strong stand. We also had finally sent the letter requesting to make the change in the award letter and the budget.

Shortly after Warren handed me Frohnmayer's actual letter asking for the grant back, I mentioned the letter which Artists Space had just sent requesting the change in the scope of the grant. He said it hadn't arrived so I told him to expect it. During all those discussions I had that entire weekend, no one said anything about not allowing that change nor was there any disagreement. Unfortunately, later that did occur. In Frohnmayer's book, *Leaving Town Alive: Confessions of An Art Warrior*, he said he knew nothing about my letter requesting the removal of the catalogue from the grant. What they tried to do later, when it all became public, was to use the catalogue as an excuse for killing the grant. That was exactly what I had tried to prevent. The NEA knew about the change we wanted to make in the scope of the grant. I waited all that time to ensure we could get permission. Bancroft assured me we had that permission.

I had lunch with Allan Parachini the next day. Parachini told me, before I agreed to meet him, that he was going to do a story in the *Los Angeles Times* which would appear Monday no matter what. I decided it was better to talk to him generally about the show, to explain what Artists Space was about and also to explain my concerns about the Helms amendment, rather than have him publish a story without the background. It had been on my mind that even though our grant was from 1989, Frohnmayer used the 1990 language as his primary reason for taking the grant back. Actually, he said in his letter that it was for political reasons that he was asking for the grant back. At least, that's my interpretation. Parachini said Joe Slye, who was then head of the press office at the NEA, had told him that I had gotten a letter from the Chairman and that was why he asked me about it. I assumed that the NEA had corrected him.

EL: Do you believe that?

SW: I don't know. I think Slye did tell Parachini in the beginning. I don't know why I was told by the NEA that Frohnmayer's letter was confidential. I don't really think Frohnmayer was lying. I think they were trying to be confidential. They told me the next day that while it was strictly confidential, they had sent it to three people on Capitol Hill which didn't surprise me. I assumed they sent it to Representative Sidney R. Yates (D-Illinois) who helped defeat the Helms Amendment in its original form, Representative Pat Williams, and Senator Claiborne Pell, both of whom head reauthorization committees for the NEA.

I decided it was better to meet with Parachini because I thought it would be better to tell him directly about Artists Space and *Witnesses*. I wanted to tell him about Day Without Art, that *Witnesses* was not just some isolated, wild, and crazy show about AIDS. It was part of a national event. I wanted to be somewhat vague so the NEA could change its mind, so that it wouldn't be locked into a hard and fast position. That was one of the reasons I suggested that they not put their request in a letter because I figured that once they did, it would be harder for them to switch back. I wanted to allow as much possibility for change in the situation. Parachini seemed excited about the show and clearly thought he had a big story. I asked him to fax me a copy of his article as I was planning to stay in Washington, D.C., until Monday for the possibility of meeting with Frohnmayer.

I spent Saturday and Sunday talking to Board members and on Monday, I met with Art Warren, Julie Davis, and John Frohnmayer. I told Frohnmayer about our Eastern European show, about official and unofficial art. I tried to suggest that there was a tremendous amount of sympathy for *Witnesses* and he should talk to the NEA staff. I asked for specific reasons for his requesting the grant back and he said that there were three. First, that the nature of the show had changed and had become political rather than artistic. Secondly, that portions of the catalogue were inflammatory and that he believed strongly in respect for individuals. He said because the catalogue attacked specific individuals, it violated his principles. Thirdly, there was a particular photograph of an erect penis which he called the "masturbation" photograph. He objected to that photograph. We talked for about an hour and a half.

I was to return to New York that afternoon and an emergency Board meeting was scheduled for a few days later. I told Frohnmayer that we would be back in touch after our Board met. I don't regret anything that I said even though I was quite direct. He seemed to be someone who was willing to listen. And as long as he was willing to meet and talk with me, I thought it was best to lay things out as clearly as I could.

He was still very interested in a meeting with artists in New York City.[6] I wanted to continue the dialogue with him. It wasn't very often I had the chance to meet with an NEA Chairman and I wanted to utilize this opportunity. Also, if there was anything I could do to argue for the NEA, I would do it. At his confirmation hearings, Frohnmayer was asked if the NEA got enough money and he said no; I thought that was great. I wanted to reinforce the positive things that he was trying to do. But, if Artists Space had to choose between the good of public funding and the good of artists, there was no question that artists had to take precedence. I was lucky because Artists Space had a very clear and strong mandate about its priorities. I wanted to find a strategy that would allow the NEA to fund the show, be supportive of it, and be clear about what it was funding and not be apologetic. It was very hard to think that this situation could cause organizations like Artists Space to have to give up on public funding. I didn't want that to happen.

EL: What was your reaction to Allan Parachini's article?

SW: I was very upset when I read it. First of all, he mentioned a lunch that Charlotte, Wendy Luers,[7] and I had which made it seem as though there was some sort of conspiracy. He used a quote from me about how these issues didn't just affect small institutions that dealt with emerging artists, but that they affected all arts organizations. I said something about the Metropolitan Museum of Art and the Museum of Modern Art (MOMA). So he quoted this thing about the Met and included Wendy Luers in that passage. I was terribly upset about that. He also said that I had received a letter from the Chairman. I never told him that I had the letter. One of the things I told Art Warren was that I would not tell anyone about the letter but when I did, the NEA would be informed. I didn't want Frohnmayer to think that I went ahead and told Parachini without letting the NEA know. I called Parachini immediately and asked him if I had told him about the letter. He said no and I asked him if he would tell that to Frohnmayer but he refused. He said it would lead to a series of questions that he did not want to answer. I immediately called Frohnmayer and spoke to Julie Davis who had just received a fax of the article but hadn't finished reading it. I did reach Wendy Luers later in the day. I wanted her to hear about the article from me. She was extremely kind.

But I am suspicious about the article; whoever leaked the story was trying to set up this situation in a particular way. There were specific details which no one would have known except someone who was extremely well informed about our negotiations. It had to be someone who was very closely involved and who had access to details about the grant and our negotiations. Also, Artists Space was described in a certain way to set up a particular image, an image which was not flattering and would make it politically difficult for the NEA to give us the grant.

EL: What finally happened?

SW: The Board and the staff all agreed that we would not voluntarily give the grant back and I drafted a short letter to Frohnmayer which told him what our position was. Meanwhile, to keep the artists in the show informed, we set up a meeting with everyone to go over the situation. Connie and Celeste organized this meeting with the artists. Because I was busy trying to rally as many prominent, important politicians and others with influence to understand the issues and be supportive of us, I wasn't able to be as attentive to the artists as I would have liked.

I was also trying to get the other arts involved. Visual arts, especially contemporary visual arts, is so misunderstood. I couldn't understand why other disciplines didn't see how this affected them. For instance, why hadn't PEN spoken out on these issues earlier? I spoke to Frohnmayer about that to some degree and I remember telling him that it was fortunate *Witnesses* was about AIDS because there was a lot of sympathy for this issue. I felt that the artwork would speak for itself. It seemed to me that there was a possibility to help change people's perceptions. This might help red-flag questions about legislation and make people question what was going on and try to advocate against restrictions. This issue might get more people involved since this wasn't just a visual arts or a photography issue.

Anyway, when the NEA and Artists Space released to the press Frohnmayer's letter and our response, all hell broke loose. It was on the front page of the *New York Times*. It was like a war. I kept in touch with Frohnmayer and Julie Davis. It was my understanding that Frohnmayer's letter to me asked for what is called "termination by convenience." We had said no, so Frohnmayer told the press that the matter would be turned over to the Justice Department. We didn't know what that meant. At that point, Beverly Wolff was trying to get us a lawyer who would look at our case for a first amendment lawsuit and to see what legal grounds we had. Beverly advised me that if we did file a lawsuit, it would be a several-year proposition and a lot of our resources would go into that lawsuit. We really had to think about our priorities. I thought the best thing to do was to get people together to speak out against this termination of our grant. There was a lot going on. For example, the Visual Artists Organizations' panel was happening, which is the panel that makes decisions once a year about artists organizations all across

6   This meeting took place at Artists Space at the height of the controversy, the day before Mr. Frohnmayer returned the grant.

7   Wendy Luers is a member of the National Council for the Arts. Mrs. Luers is also married to William Luers, President of the Metropolitan Museum of Art.

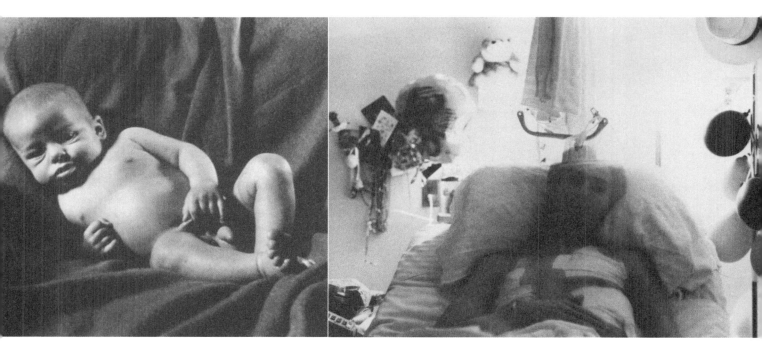

the country. A lot of panelists were calling me and saying that they didn't know whether or not to go ahead and serve. I was very upset at the idea that some of them would resign. I was afraid that if some or all of them resigned, there would be no grants in that category. I was worried that the whole field would be defunded. I asked them all to go to the panel, to make decisions, raise the issues and talk to Frohnmayer about the issues but have their panel meeting. Some of the articles accused me of trying to lobby panel members. That wasn't what happened. Rather, panelists were calling me and I didn't want them to quit. I was afraid the NEA would fall apart from within. I had invested so much of my life in this field and I did not want to see it screw itself.

At this point, I was trying to find out who the recipients of the National Medal for the Arts were because a White House ceremony was scheduled for the next week. Leonard Bernstein's manager called to say that Bernstein was interested in possibly refusing his medal. Rather than refusing the medal, I thought it would be better for the medalists to show up at the White House and make a statement in support of free expression. I had this fantasy about a unanimous statement, that the medalists would say something to the President. Bernstein's manager wanted to read the catalogue text and by that point, I figured out what to say to these requests. I pointed out the absurdity of reading the text because the catalogue was not funded by the NEA so what difference would it make? Also, I pointed out that we believed in free speech in this country so no matter what the text said, it could be published and available. I told Bernstein's manager that this was our position and if Mr. Bernstein wanted to read the text upon understanding that we found no reason for him to do so, then to let me know. I never heard back. I also suggested that Mr. Bernstein show up to the medal ceremony and make a statement rather than refuse the medal. But Leonard Bernstein did refuse his medal and it was a wonderful, powerful statement. It saved us. It turned the tide and it hit Barbara and George Bush right in the face. I think this gesture had a lot to do with our getting the grant back. And it also made a lot of people think about what was happening to free expression and about the issue of AIDS. Robert Motherwell, who was also a national medal recipient, wanted to give us a contribution to replace the $10,000. I had to explain that we were refusing those kinds of contributions. We wanted and needed money, but we did not want to drop our claim to the grant. Mr. Motherwell ended up giving us an unrestricted gift of $10,000.

On November 16, 1989, the day Witnesses opened, Frohnmayer, in the face of a great deal of public and political support for Artists Space, announced that the grant had been reinstated. Cookie Mueller died the day before the show opened, and Mark Morrisroe had also just died. Both artists were in the show and they were close friends of Nan Goldin's. Because several artists did not want their works to be photographed for fear that their work might be manipulated by the media, Artists Space had to work out logistics regarding how to handle the media. I asked Wyatt about the exhibition's opening and the final outcome of her experience with Witnesses.

SW: This was an extremely emotionally charged time. Several artists were nervous about their works being photographed. A poignant example was a very beautiful portrait of David Wojnarowicz taken by the late Peter Hujar which David did not want in the show. David did not come to the opening, I think, partly because he was angry with me and because Artists Space had removed the catalogue from the grant. He had an idea that we could refuse to accept the grant back but there was no way we could. David was also afraid of being physically attacked if he were identified. At a reading scheduled during the show, he read with a mask on. He was also afraid that an NEA grant for a retrospective of his work which was to open in Illinois a few months later might be jeopardized. He didn't want his text to be quoted out of context and he was very concerned about the copyright issues. He didn't want his text leaked to the press before the show opened. I didn't realize it until later that one error I may have made was to give that text to Andrew Oliver. I shouldn't have done that, I guess. Someone at the *New York Post* managed to get David's home number and after several conversations, David decided to trust this reporter and quoted some of his text which then appeared in a very damaging story in the *Post*. David was extremely upset and angry that this reporter had tricked him. David and I had a lot of discussions and I have a tremendous amount of respect and affection for him, though he was angry at me. I learned a lot from him. I was very sad when he died in 1992. But I'm not sorry that I asked him those questions about the text and the possibility of change. If I hadn't had that conversation, I never would have understood how strongly he felt. My understanding of the depth of his feelings allowed me to be much more forceful in my defense of that text. I never would have understood how much it meant to him if I had not questioned him. I'm sorry he could never understand that. I will always be grateful for my interaction with him. Up to that point in my life, I don't think I really understood that kind of anger or that kind of fear; I don't even think I do now. I have a somewhat better understanding because of some of the things I've learned in the last few years about human hypocrisy. Anyhow, David and I had very different world views and I think it was very hard for him to trust someone like me.

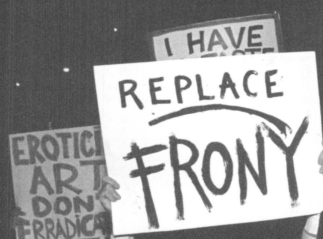

OBSCENE
ART?

I HA
NO TASTE

NO
TAXATION
WITHOUT
ARTISTIC
REPRESENTATI

FASCIS
BEGIN
WITH
CENSORSH

READ MY LIPS

HELMS
impedes
THE 1st
AMENDMENT

I HAVE
ASTE

KEEP 1st
AMENDMENT
STOP HELMS

HAND
OFF

REPLACE
FRONY

EROTIC
ART
DON
ERRADICA
IT!

SMARI

Pe

Through it all, I have to say that this incident did get a lot of people involved in the issue and spurred action. That was great. People in different disciplines started to realize that these restrictions affected them. So, that was all really important. On Day Without Art at the Museum of Modern Art, Leonard Bernstein played the piano and David Wojnarowicz appeared without a mask and read from his text. Seeing David without a mask in that very public situation—knowing that his voice and words were resonating far and wide that day—made me very happy. A few weeks later, Hujar's picture of him was on the front page of the *Village Voice*. So there were a lot of good things that came out of it. But it had a big effect on Artists Space. That part of it is very sad, all the stresses and strains which hurt the organization.

I remember going to a local NAAO meeting, although I don't remember whether it was before or after the show opened. It was not a warm and cozy meeting. A lot of people had questions about what I did and were angry at me. It's very odd when in your own community, you get these strange vibes but then everywhere else you go, you're treated like a celebrity. It's hard not to be bitter about it. I'm still sort of recuperating from it, I guess. I have continued to be extremely active on arts advocacy, but I've learned that people make up their minds about who you are and if you do something they don't expect, it's hard for them to deal with it.

EL: Why did you leave Artists Space? What were your thoughts about it?

SW: I left for a number of reasons. I had been at Artists Space 17 years and had been its Director for six years. I felt I had accomplished the things I wanted. I had expanded the exhibition program, established an effective and influential video program, increased its artists services, greatly increased its visibility and expanded its funding base. Partly because of the *Witnesses* event, I had become very interested in arts advocacy. That event opened new arenas to me, and I wanted to participate in them. I was invited to speak at a variety of events across the country and that meant I was constantly on the go. In addition to running Artists Space, keeping up with these opportunities to advance dialogue on issues which were increasingly important to me, I was trying to follow up on the access the event gave me to legislators and others with influence. It was exciting but very exhausting. I finally realized I needed a break, to assess what I was doing and where I was going.

The effects of *Witnesses* had also caused me a great deal of personal strain. It caused tensions in relationships among staff and Board members at Artists Space and among the community of my peers. Those pressures were very draining and caused me pain. I found I disagreed with some Artists Space Board members on certain issues, and I felt my productivity as the organization's leader was affected by these conflicts. I saw many different avenues through which I could pursue my career, avenues which had been opened due to my accomplishments at Artists Space and through my arts advocacy work. I discovered skills and interests I had not realized I possessed. So it was a combination of factors and it was bittersweet.

Witnesses changed my life and it touched many others. I will always remember it with great pride. Though it brought pain with it, I would do it over again just the way I did at the time. Its effects on the harmonious staff and Board relationships at Artists Space and among my peers are the one thing I wish I could have prevented. But realisitically, they were inevitable. Growth is always painful as is learning. I grew a great deal and learned a lot. I realized it was time to move on.

September **1985** to June **1991**

1988–89

At the end of the 1988–89 season Curator Valerie Smith resigns and Connie Butler is hired in early 1989. Dan Walworth, the Film and Video Curator, resigns in 1989 and Micki McGee is hired. In 1988–89 a new program is added, titled the **Project** series, which is devoted to presenting installations or solo exhibits of work by individual artists. Thereafter, for each of its six exhibition slots per season, Artists Space organizes a group exhibition, an individual **Project**, and a video program.

Sept. 6–17: **Artists from the Studio in a School** (selected in consultation with Patterson Sims). Jo-Ann Acey, Lynne Aubert, Susan Austad, Noah Baen, Olivia Beens, Rick Bleier, Rhea Burden, Kim Bush, Thomas Cahill, Anne Dohna, Janice Gabriel, Andrea Gardner, Elizabeth Grajales, Valerie Hammond, Robin Holder, Shelley Krapes, Iris Kufert, Helene Manzo, David Newton, Heather Nicol, Valis Oliver, Marilyn Reynolds, Barbara Valenta, David Vereano, Gerry Wagoner, Oscar Yacila.

Sept. 29–Nov. 5: **Min Joong Art: A New Cultural Movement from Korea** (Wankyung Sung and Huyk Um). Group exhibition: Choi Byung Soo, banner exhibited on facade of Artists Space for **Min Joong** opening and during the exhibition at the Cathedral of St. John the Divine, New York; Durung (an anonymous group of artists formed in 1982), scrolls; Boksoo Jung, drawing and cutout pieces; Yongtai Kim, photo installation; Kwangju Visual Art Research Institute, painting and banners; Jonggu Lee, painting; Ocksang Lim, mural; Jungki Min, lithographs; Yoon Oh, woodcut; Buldong Park, photography; People's Art School, woodblock print; The Photo Collective for Social Movement, documentary photographs; Chang Song, painting. Catalogue with essays by Lucy Lippard, Kwang Hyun Shim, Wankyung Sung, and Huyk Um.

→ OPPOSITE PAGE: Min Joong, banner exhibited on façade of Artists Space.

ARTIST

Zoe Leonard *Selections* stands out in my memory because it was one of the first times I showed somewhere I felt was really serious. At that time in my life it was a big deal for me. The way it happened was great. I was out on a walk with a friend, Kathy Quinilin, who stopped at Artists Space to drop off her slides. She explained the Artists Slide File to me and I was wowed: I thought it was a smart thing. So I made slides, dropped them off the next week, and I never expected anything to come of it. Immediately, I get this phone call, inviting me to be in a show. I was completely floored! I had a really good but emotional experience. I had hardly shown my photographs at all and had this accumulation of years of work. It was a group show and I could only hang three. Nevertheless, it was really good for me. In some ways it was a cathartic experience, because I felt I was taken seriously outside of the interesting, but rather narrow, confines of the East Village art world, which in a lot of ways was about personalities, not about work.

What perhaps affected me more was *Witnesses: Against Our Vanishing,* the exhibition Nan Goldin curated. It was an incredible show because there was no hesitation between life and art. All of us, those of us who were HIV-positive, those of us who were HIV-negative, were experiencing in our lives the overwhelming reality of the AIDS crisis. We were drowning in it. So it was great to see a show that was not in hindsight. It was right there, about that very minute. I remember a similar time, regarding Susan Sontag's book, *AIDS and Its Metaphors.* I was so angry with her because I didn't understand how she could be right in the middle of it, watching her friends die, going to hospitals, and write about this subject with such intellectual distance. But *Witnesses* felt like another piece of my day. Ramsey McPhillips included an unbelievable piece he'd done in the hospital. There was a letter and blood, words and bloody sheets or a hospital gown. It was so angry, so palpable, it broke this idea of the patient no longer being angry, lying very still, eating Jell-O. This man was so full of rage and a desire to live. I was moved. In conjunction with the show, David Wojnarowicz did an incredible reading. He wore a mask, that big Ronald Reagan mask he would wear sometimes, and did this knockout reading. It was one of the last times I saw him perform.

Video in conjunction with **Min Joong Art: A New Cultural Movement from Korea** (Our Film Yard Collective and Dan Walworth). Christine Choi and J.T. Takagi for Third World Newsreel, *Homes Apart,* 1988, (excerpt from a work-in-progress); Younhee Jang, *For the Hero,* 1987, Sang; Kyeidong Community and Dongwon Kim, *The Sang Kyeidong Olympics,* 1987; Toa Film Collective and Sangbin Lee, *Kukmin Jang (Funeral Ceremonies),* 1988; Toa Film Collective, *Agriculture is the Foundation of the Nation,* 1988; University Film Alliance, *We Can Never Be Divided,* 1988.

Sept. 29–Nov. 5: **Project**: *I Miss the Revolution,* Bolek Greczynski, installation (Valerie Smith). Artist-in-residence at Creedmoor Psychiatric Center, Greczynski established the Living Museum to work with patients/artists on an installation entitled *The Battlefields Project. I Miss the Revolution* is a collaborative installation by Greczynski and the crew of *The Battlefields Project.* Greczynski has a concurrent installation at the Grey Art Gallery, New York, entitled *Body Fluids of the French Revolution.* Brochure published in collaboration with the Grey Art Gallery, with essays by Tom Finkelpearl, Anthony Heilbut, and Janos Marton.

↑ Installation view. **The AIDS Crisis Is Not Over,** Nov. 17–Jan. 7, 1988. Photo: Peter McClennan

Oct. 15–16: **Cultural Politics Between the First and Third Worlds** (Dan Walworth). Collective for Living Cinema, New York. Film program in conjunction with **Min Joong Art: A New Cultural Movement from Korea**

Oct. 15: **Films:** Jin Che, *Discarded Umbrella*, 1985; Dongho Han, Sungjin Jung, and Jeagu Lee, *Mother*, 1987; Dongho Han, Hyunhwa Hong, Sungjin Jung, Misun Kim, and Youngjong Kim, *Pass Over the Fence*, 1987; Donghong Jang, Jeagu Lee, Myungja Lee, and Jungock Oh, *The Day We Expect*, 1987 and *Yellow Flag*, 1987.

Oct. 16: **Panel discussion:** Hal Foster, Lucy Lippard, Wankyung Sung. Dan Walworth, moderator.

Nov. 17–Jan. 7: **Selections** from the Artists File (Valerie Smith). Ronald Baron, sculpture; Barbara Broughel, sculpture and drawing; Giza Daniels-Endesha, installation; Howard Halle, sculpture; Deborah Heidel, sculpture; Jim Hodges, sculpture; Lars Klove, sculpture; Zoe Leonard, photography; Whitfield Lovell, drawing; Yong Soon Min, installation; George Moore, painting; Judy Palaferro, drawing; Craig Pleasants, sculpture; Pamela Wye, drawing. Catalogue with essay by Valerie Smith.

↑ Jim Hodges
Photo: Peter McClennan

↓ Giza Daniels-Endesha
Photo: Peter McClennan

Nov. 17–Jan. 7: **Video: The AIDS Crisis Is Not Over** (Gregg Bordowitz). Gregg Bordowitz and Jean Carlomusto, *Ain't No Justice*, 1988, *PWA Power*, 1988, *Seize Control of the FDA*, 1988, and *WORK YOUR BODY—options for people who are HIV positive*, 1988; Jean Carlomusto, *The Helms Amendment*, 1988; Adam Jassuk and Bob Huff, *We Are Not Republicans*, 1988; Bob Huff, *We're Desperate. Get Used to It*, 1988, and *AIDS News: A Demonstration*, 1988; Carol Leigh, *Just Say No*, 1988; Carol Leigh a.k.a. Scarlot Harlot, *Safe Sex Slut*, 1988, *Pope Don't Preach*, 1988, and *Bad Laws*, 1988; Carol Leigh a.k.a. Scarlot Harlot and the Sisters of Perpetual Indulgence, *The Star Spangled Banner*, 1988; Testing the Limits Collective, *Testing the Limits*, 1988. Brochure with essay by Gregg Bordowitz.

ARTIST/CURATOR

Gregg Bordowitz *The AIDS Crisis Is Not Over* was important within the early history of ACT UP because it allowed me and a number of other people to use the early AIDS video work as an emerging body rather than just a bunch of tapes. It gave us an opportunity to work with the category, AIDS video, and now it has been recognized. I did not single-handedly bring this about. Dan Walworth's invitation to curate it meant he was alert to something new and emerging, and I was in the middle of it along with several other people.

The accompanying panel I organized enabled a bunch of ACT UP people to articulate the relationships between media politics and ACT UP. The panel was significant because it was the meeting of the art crowd and the AIDS activists crowd. A lot of the activists from ACT UP came to hear the conversation on the role of art in the emerging political movement.

The work I saw at Artists Space that was very important to me and related to what we did with the AIDS video was the program Dan organized on activist films from the early 70s. I remember seeing the Black Panther movie and a movie made by the yippies on the 1968 riot in Chicago at the Democratic National Convention. Seeing that video had an enormous influence on me, and I was motivated to become involved in media and video work that represented the efforts of AIDS activists and furthered that cause. It was affirming. I was certainly aware of historical activist work throughout the 20th century and recently the work of the Black Liberation. But I had never seen those specific works before. In the context of the mid-80s, it emphasized what I was setting out to do. It set me on fire. In addition, the *Foreign Relations* program, in which the British television series *The Arabs* was screened and at which Edward Said spoke, also left its mark. It was a great event and important in developing my understanding of the way in which representation affects people's lives.

Nov. 19: **Panel discussion. AIDS Activism: Media as Direct Action** (Gregg Bordowitz). Panel discussion with Jean Carlomusto, Douglas Crimp, Avram Finkelstein, Ray Navarro. Gregg Bordowitz, moderator.

Nov. 17–Jan. 7: **Project**: Purvis Young, *Me and My Mink*, painting and books (Cesar Trasobares). Brochure with essay by Cesar Trasobares.

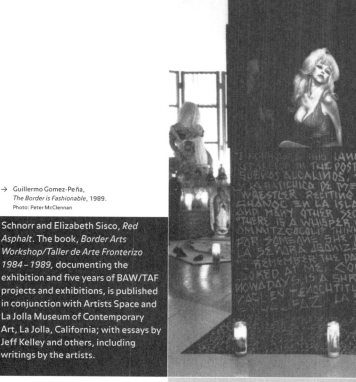

→ Guillermo Gomez-Peña,
The Border is Fashionable, 1989.
Photo: Peter McClennan

Jan. 19–Feb. 18: **Vidas Perdidas/Lost Lives: Border Art Workshop/Taller de Arte Fronterizo** (organized by participating artists). Multimedia installation dealing with the United States/Mexico border: Guillermo Gomez-Peña, *The Border is Fashionable*, with commissioned velvet paintings by Beth Ruiz and Miguel Mariscal, and Cholo, calligraphy by Victor Orozco Ochoa;

Emily Hicks and Rocio Weiss, *Santa Frida Appears to the Wrestler Bride*, with David Forbes, collaborator; Berta Jottar, *Unprepared to Lose Your Soul*; Richard A. Lou, *Undocumented Family*; Victor Orozco Ochoa, *Chicanosauruz*, with Vidal Aquirre and Julian "Chiquilin" Ortega, collaborators; Robert Sanchez, *Encinitas Gardens*, with flowers by Julian "Chiquilin" Ortega; Michael

Schnorr and Elizabeth Sisco, *Red Asphalt*. The book, *Border Arts Workshop/Taller de Arte Fronterizo 1984–1989*, documenting the exhibition and five years of BAW/TAF projects and exhibitions, is published in conjunction with Artists Space and La Jolla Museum of Contemporary Art, La Jolla, California; with essays by Jeff Kelley and others, including writings by the artists.

ARTIST

Guillermo Gomez-Peña

In the mid-80s BAW/TAF (Border Art Workshop/Taller de Arte Fronterizo), as community-minded experimental artists, were treated to the opening of a brand-new art world. Interdisciplinary collectives were sprawling everywhere: the Guerrilla Girls and Grand Fury were in New York, the LAPD (Los Angeles Poverty Department) and ASCO (a Chicano performance art group) in Los Angeles. On the other hand, the BAW/TAF were operating on a particular front: the U.S./Mexico border and hard-core immigration politics. We were all part of that whole milieu and political energy. The art world became a laboratory to develop radical ideas, but the main objectives existed outside the realm of art. It was the zeitgeist of the times.

My recollection is that up to that point, BAW/TAF had chosen to operate regionally. The work we had been doing was mainly in California. If any of us left the area, it was only to do solo work. So when the Artists Space show happened, it was one of the highlights in the life of BAW/TAF. It became a seminal experience, because it launched the Workshop nationally. From that moment on our visibility increased month after month as invitations started coming in from all over. Everyone was seriously interested in our ideas of the artist as a binational diplomat, social thinker, and media pirate. The media became an important context for the work. We staged many performances strictly for the media. We had many adventures across the country and later on in Europe, when the Workshop was invited to participate in the 1990 Venice Biennale. The golden era of the group was precisely during the years between 1988 and 1990. Then, as with most utopian cultural projects, the Workshop split up after being crowned an art superstar. There was this collective decision to disband and everyone but one stubborn member—of course the only white male at the time—left. He started a new BAW/TAF, but I lost track of him.

Chicanos have learned to survive and operate in culturally hostile environments. We have become quite savvy at presenting and distributing ideas in multiple contexts. In my books I have written extensively about the notion of multicontextuality, of being an insider/outsider, a border crosser between and among unlikely cultural contexts and communities. And I have written about the ethical and political challenges that this fluid position entails. We understand the maximum we can aspire to is to be insider/outsiders or partial insiders and we use this condition to our advantage. The art world only gets to see what we do with our right hand, so to speak, but not what we do with the other. It was precisely during the BAW/TAF days that Chicanos began to shed separatist notions about identity. We were into coalition politics and we developed strong ties with African American, gay, and feminist collectives. The very composition of our group was multiracial and binational. The idea was also not to discriminate and to perform in Chicano community centers as well as alternative white institutions, in the streets as well as in big museums. This hybrid praxis is still in my work. One day I am at the Corcoran Gallery of Art or the Walker Art Center, the next I am in a youth center in East L.A. or in a National Public Radio (NPR) radio studio. Because what I have to say to each community is different. I perform multiple roles on multiple fronts.

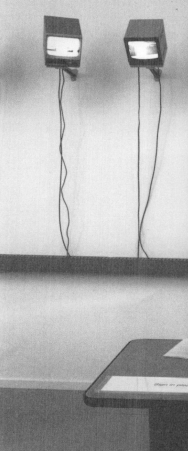

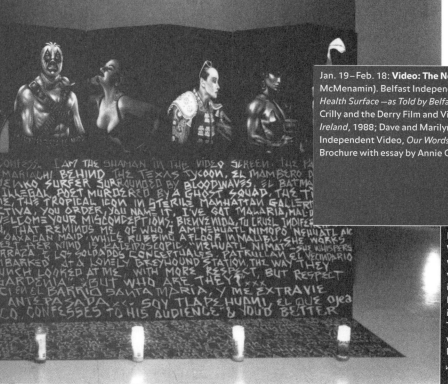

Jan. 19–Feb. 18: **Video: The North of Ireland** (Brendan McMenamin). Belfast Independent Video, *Under the Health Surface —as Told by Belfast Women,* 1986; Anne Crilly and the Derry Film and Video Collective, *Mother Ireland,* 1988; Dave and Marilyn Hyndman with Belfast Independent Video, *Our Words Jump to Life,* 1988. Brochure with essay by Annie Goldson.

Jan. 19–Feb. 18: **Project**: Michael Sorkin, *Model City,* architectural installation (Valerie Smith). Brochure with essay by Michael Sorkin.

Mar. 2–Apr. 1: **Dark Rooms** (Valerie Smith and Dan Walworth). Stephen Barry, *Palladium,* kinetic sculpture with film projection; Luis Nicolau, *The Treason of Judas,* video installation; Julia Scher, *Security by Julia II,* installation with security cameras, monitors, and guards; H. Shearer, *rage...or whatever moves you,* video installation; Jana Sterbak, *Attitudes,* installation; Patricia Thornley, slide, film, and sound installation. Brochure with introduction and notes by Valerie Smith and Dan Walworth.

↙ Julia Scher
Photo: Kenji Fujita

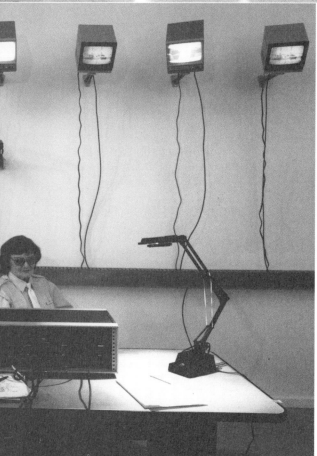

ARTIST

Robert Sanchez One of the most important aspects of the BAW/TAF show at Artists Space was the catalogue. It was a five-year overview of our projects that had been done up to that point. It is an important document. It was also interesting to meet people who knew of our work and came out to see the show, since it was our first project in New York. Our exhibitions had been focused primarily here on the West Coast, especially San Diego, because of its relevance to the border region and the fact that the group itself was focused mainly on issues of immigration, border cultures, and the whole dynamic surrounding the U.S./Mexican border.

The group talked a lot beforehand about traveling these ideas to Artists Space. We discussed how the information might be seen by what we thought was an audience with very little awareness of the deeper complex issues going on here concerning immigration and the media analysis of border issues. And it would be an audience, like most other audiences outside this region, that probably had received its information from the media. The large turnout surprised us. Thanks to Artists Space, the publicity was very effective because we ended up doing some live radio interviews. There were a lot of contacts made with the media in terms of reviews of the show that came out before, after, and during the exhibition itself. That's one of the things that propelled the group into a higher profile just within the art world. The overriding objectives throughout had to do with trying to project a voice through the media that stemmed from the group's ideas, and to create dialogue and debate that would focus on border issues. It was important because once we started getting that press out of New York, whether it was the *Village Voice,* the *New York Times,* or other publications, we also started getting individuals and institutions interested, such as Capp Street in San Francisco. We got a lot of response from people who had read things about the group, more specifically about the issues from the show at Artists Space.

Organizing shows that used the term "border" was problematic for our group, because often the focus would not be on issues specific to U.S./Mexican immigration with which we were dealing. They were more a metaphorical use of the term "border" that could deal with gender and sexuality. So there were two issues we were struggling with: how to keep focused on the issues with which we were closely aligned and also deal with the museums and gallery exhibitions of "border shows" that weren't specifically about what we were presenting.

Mar. 2–Apr. 1: **Video: Signs of Fiction** (Sharon Greytak). Rohesia Hamilton Metcalfe, *After the Paint Has Dried,* 1986; Lynn Kirby, *Sharon and the Birds on the Way to the Wedding,* 1987; Jon Moritsugu, *Der Elvis,* 1987; Pola Rapaport, *Tooth and Mask,* 1987; Margot Starr Kernan, *Still Stories: Watching, Hiding, and Breaking and Entering,* 1988; Ela Troyano and Uzi Parnes, *Loisada Lusts,* 1987; Jack Walsh, *Present Tense,* 1987. Brochure with essay by Sharon Greytak.

Mar. 2–Apr. 1: **Project**: Laurie Palmer, *Winter Flush: A Temporary Garden,* botanical installation (Judith Russi Kirshner). Brochure with essay by Judith Russi Kirshner.

Apr. 13–May 13: Shirley Jaffe, painting; Murray Reich, painting (Richard Armstrong, Hermine Ford, Irving Sandler, Valerie Smith, Susan Wyatt). Sponsored by the Mark Rothko Foundation. Brochure with essay on Jaffe by Meyer Raphael Rubenstein; brochure with essay on Reich by Elizabeth Frank.

Apr. 13–May 13: **Video: Document and Dream** (Dan Walworth). Shu Lea Cheang, *Color Schemes,* 1989; John Heyn and Jeffrey Krulik, *Heavy Metal Parking Lot,* 1986; Jonathan Horowitz, *Making Pharoah's Red Flag Video,* 1988; Laura Kipnis, *A Man's Woman,* 1988; Stashu Kybartas, *Danny,* 1987; Robert Morin, *My Life is for the Rest of My Life (Ma Vie c'est pour le Restant de mes Jours),* 1980, and *The Thief Lives in Hell (Le Voleur Vit en Enfer),*

1980; Jayce Salloum, *Episode 1: So. Cal.,* 1988; Keith Sanborn, *A Public Appearance and a Statement,* 1987; Julie Zando, *Hey Bud,* 1987. Brochure with essay by Dan Walworth.

BOARD

Philip Aarons

I was first introduced to Artists Space when teaching an arts administration course at Columbia University. Judith Lyczko, the Development Director of Artists Space, was one of my students. After a session on real estate contracts and leases, she came up and said they had a problem with their own lease. They weren't thinking of moving, but they were being forced to move from Hudson Street. I helped them negotiate the lease on West Broadway. I was asked to join the Board as a result of being helpful during that particular time. They were also facing a significant deficit, maybe as a result of the expenses of the move. I was able to use a connection I had with a friend whose family foundation gave them a significant amount of money, and this cleaned up the deficit for that particular year.

The division of staff and board responsibility evolved a great deal at this point in the organization's history. Linda Shearer was very interested in the curatorial side of the organization and had a wonderful sense of what she wanted to do. She also had a great and direct affinity with a lot of the artists. At the same time, particularly with Susan Wyatt on the administrative side, there was a clear sense of what the Board had to do, even though it was going to remain 50 percent artists and 50 percent nonartists. The feeling was that the nonartists had to take a greater responsibility for the fundraising requirements of the organization, which they did. The Board became a little more involved in the financial side of things, making sure the budgets worked, were balanced, and updated. The Board also made sure we knew where we were financially, that we were planning appropriately year to year and quarter to quarter and not getting into significant budget deficits, which had plagued the organization as NYSCA funding dried up. If you go back and listen to Irving Sandler, you'll understand their vision of alternative: laid-back, artist-run, artists choosing artists, and uninterested in a commercial space. By the time Linda was there, that really wasn't what was happening. The organization had some real stature. They wanted to do catalogues—like any institution that grows, it wasn't simply a group of people getting together and putting on their own shows.

An appropriate way to look at *Witnesses: Against Our Vanishing* is that the Board ultimately made the decision to back Susan. It was Susan's mission to take the stand she did, particularly as it evolved into a highly public and visible position. In the beginning there was a fair amount of debate among Board members. Does it really pay to piss off the NEA? Was this the right strategy? Did it really matter? Were we sort of foolhardy in our firm stand? Once everybody sorted it out, they said, "Yes, this is an important issue. We shouldn't compromise. That's what Artists Space is all about." I was a frequent advocate of that position within the Board. But the Board had to be constantly reminded that when some issues are important enough they go beyond institutional survival, particularly for an organization like Artists Space. Sometimes you have to do things that may threaten the longevity of the organization. If we don't take those stands, no one else will, certainly the Metropolitan Museum of Art isn't going to. However, there were definitely people on the Board who had different feelings. They felt there could be more compromise on our part, that this wasn't an issue worth fighting about. There were ways in which language could be changed or disclaimers could be added to satisfy certain people and not take this fight to the edge. These ideas were not voiced once the decision was made to support Susan, nor were these positions held to the detriment of getting the organization focused on meeting the crisis. It then became a very serious crisis.

I was very upset with the Board's poor treatment of Carlos Gutierrez-Solana. At the beginning, the Board chose someone who was going to present to them everything he ultimately *did* present to them, both positive and negative. One thing I felt strongly about and said was, "Carlos is going to be someone who will be constantly challenging you. That's the way he lives, it's the way he thinks, it's the way he behaves. You can't expect to have an easy go of it because he's really ready, that's his personality. If you don't think you're up to that, then let's not hire him." No one should have been surprised. Then to take that and say, "Well, he's not what we want, he's too challenging, he's too difficult, he's not careful enough with money. He is an interesting guy, but it's less pleasant to go to Board meetings and he's always saying, 'you should raise the money, not me.'"

I finally left the Board because I had been there 11 years and that was enough. The organization was in good hands when you (Claudia Gould) arrived.

Apr. 13–May 13: **Project**: Barbara Steinman, *Of a Space, Solitary/Of a Sound, Mute*, video installation (Bruce Ferguson). Brochure with essay by Bruce Ferguson.

May 19–20: **Films-In-Progress: Coming Soon** (Leslie Thornton and Dan Walworth).
May 19: Mark Daniels, *Under the Rose*, excerpts from dailies on videotape with a live reading; Andrew Horn and Jim Neu, *House of Dragons*, screenplay-in-progress performed live with slides; Deborah Meehan, *Truer than Truth*, excerpt from workprint on videotape; Linda Peckham, *Murdered in Our Beds* (working title), excerpt from workprint on videotape.
May 20: Lincoln Shlensky, *Denuncias*, rough cut on videotape.

May 25–July 1: **Metaphysical Visions: Middle Europe** (Valerie Smith). Group exhibition of work by artists from Czechoslovakia, Hungary, Poland, and Yugoslavia: Mrđjan Bajić, sculpture; Mirosław Bałka, sculpture installation; Jiří David, painting installation; El Kazovszkij, installation; Željko Kipke, painting; Jiří Kovanda, painting; Mariusz Kruk, sculpture installation; Piotr Kurka, sculpture. Catalogue with essay by Valerie Smith and statements by the artists.

↓ Installation view
Photo: Peter McClennan

May 25–July 1: **Deconstruction, Quotation & Subversion: Video from Yugoslavia** (Kathy Rae Huffman). Brenda Beban, Hrvoje Horvatić, *For You in Me and Me in Them to be One (Ja u njima u meni da budu sasvim jedno)*, 1989; Hristo Pop Dučev, Aleksandar Stankovski, and Zlatko Trajkovski, *Closeness*, 1987; Goran Gajić and Zoran Pezo, *Merry Television: Mirko and Slavko (Vesela Televizija: Mirko i Slavko)*, 1985; Marina Gržinić and Aina Šmid, *The Girl with an Orange (Deklica z Oranzo)*, 1987, *Axis of Life (Os življenja)*, 1987; Jurij Korenc, *Radio Student: 20 Years of Media Fights (Radio Študent: 20 let medijskih bojev)*, 1989; Mare Kovačić, *The American Dream*, 1986; Dalibor Martinis, *Liquid Ice (Tekući led)*, 1988; Mladen Materić, *Dance of the 80s (Ples osamdesetih)*, 1984; Milan Peca Nikolić, *Kosovo: 600 Years Later (Kocobo: 600 godina poslije)*, 1989; TV Gallery: Milan Peca Nikolić and Dragica Vukovic, *Essays on Modern Art (Ogledi iz moderne umetnosti)*, 1987; Retrovizija: Peter Vezjak, *Laibach: Sympathy for the Devil*, 1988; Igor Riđanović, *TV Test*, 1988; Miha Vipotnik, *Baptized Under Mount Triglav (Krst pod Triglavom)*, 1987. Catalogue with essays by Kathy Rae Huffman and Biljana Tomić.

ARTIST/BOARD

Kiki Smith Walter Robinson organized this show of four women and one male artist at Artists Space because most of the women in CoLab essentially had no representation, either in commercial galleries or alternative spaces. And a lot of men were picked up quickly. It took another five years until I got a one-person show. During that time, my work changed a great deal before it was presentable and made sense. It was a generous activity on Walter's part to organize this. It was humbling.

During *Witnesses: Against Our Vanishing* I felt negation. But the artists were verbally adept and could articulate the problems in the relationship between the government and art, AIDS and representation. David Wojnarowicz and I were very good friends in the early 80s. By the time *Witnesses* opened our friendship was, not over, but something like over, so it was a good opportunity for me to reconnect. The exhibition was organized under quite adverse circumstances. David was personally attacked and it took tremendous energy, but he was someone capable of doing it. As a writer and an artist he rose to the challenge. There are few artists who had the verbal skills he had.

I liked going to see movies at Artists Space when it was on Hudson Street. It was nice to be included in a film screening there. The show got a review that said I should leave art-making to my father. I was making pictures of cats which I probably will return to now. I've gone back to what I did 20 years earlier. Mostly I liked going to see films and Mike Kelley's performance. I liked Artists Space during that period more as an art consumer than as a participant. I remember *Art-Rite* organized an event at Artists Space a long time ago and it was through that event that I met Walter. In general, Artists Space introduced me to the artists and the work of my generation. So it was useful to me.

1989 – 90

Sept. 5 – 16: **Artists from the Studio in a School** (selected in consultation with Ileen Sheppard). Jo-Ann Acey, Lynne Aubert, Noah Baen, Olivia Beens, Rick Bleier, Kabuya Bowens, Kim Bush, Thomas Cahill, Anne Dohna, Anona Evans, Joan Giordano, Gwen-Lin Goo, Elizabeth Grajales, Julie Healy, Carol Heft, Neddi Heller, Robin Holder, Iris Kufert, Mark LaRiviere, Lynn Margileth, Yelena Matulic, Maureen Mullen, Heather Nicol, Antonia Perez, Lyn Riccardo, Skyler Switzer-Kohler, Barbara Valenta.

Sept. 28 – Nov. 4: **Selections** from the Artists File (Connie Butler). Michael James Asente, sculpture; Tina Aufiero, sculpture; Willie Cole, sculpture; Esperanza Cortés, painting; Taka Kawachi, painting; Eric Rhein, sculpture; Teddy Schapiro, painting; Sean Scherer, installation; Katherine Sherwood, painting; Jo Yarrington, installation. Catalogue with essay by Connie Butler.

ARTIST/BOARD

Elizabeth Murray I have never shown at Artists Space. When it started in 1973, I was a young emerging artist and didn't know anybody or any of the people who might have selected at Artists Space. I honestly didn't even think about it. I did not feel left out because it never occurred to me somebody would ask me to show my work in that situation. I remember seeing Judy Pfaff's work and Ellen Phelan's. I saw all the shows and I loved them because a lot of my friends showed there for the first time.

Women were starting to show, and their shows were powerful. It was one of the first moments in the art world not created by the New York School. The women who were showing were independent artists. It was another generation of women coming up and very different in feeling from the women of the Abstract Expressionist — New York School. There's no question those women paved the way, however flawed their paving may have been. It was tough and they suffered. It was a time when you had to be male-identified. They were living inside a culture where it would really be hard to imagine those women doing anything else. It has so much to do with the class you're born into and the time in which you manage to reach a maturity.

I wanted to show four women. It was important to me at that point, because there was this whole new advent of macho art coming in. David Salle, Julian Schnabel, and Anselm Kiefer had taken over. It was the peak. And I'm telling you, it was weird out there. Talk about weird politics going down. The problem with it was that people were talking out of both sides of their mouths. The money thing was getting horrendous and a lot of women were being blanketed by the huge influx of all these guys. Of course, at the same time, there were other things going on, but not as apparent. Cindy Sherman was starting to make a big impression on people, as were Laurie Simmons and Barbara Kruger. Susan Rothenberg was also very strong at that moment. But there were all these other women working away, young and old, who were getting passed over by this huge "guy" locomotive. The point is, Artists Space was still a forum for showing work not being seen, for bringing up other issues.

I had no relationship with Artists Space before *Four Artists,* which I organized in 1985. I came on the Board in 1990 just as the whole thing became intensely political and then started to fall apart. As a Board, I felt we handled the issues that came up during *Witnesses: Against Our Vanishing* very well. The Board was very supportive of Susan Wyatt. When the Jesse Helms moment started to happen, my private feeling was that this was huge and people were playing different angles, but I didn't really know who was playing what. I had just started on the Board and I wasn't interested in doing anything other than working as an artist who had feelings and thoughts about certain things. Part of it was so overblown. There were a lot of histrionics, which just didn't make sense to me, in terms of the real art involved in the show and the basic purpose of Artists Space. It was such an intense time, confronting the whole issue of what an artist means in society and the politics that were going on.

I was on the search committee for the new director and I thought almost everybody who applied would have been interesting. Everybody was just closing their eyes hoping the big crash really wasn't going to be as terrible and as devastating as it was. It was as if the slate had gotten wiped clean and we were just kidding ourselves. The choice made wasn't a choice of looking five years ahead. We just didn't know what was really going to go down in terms of money. Within a few years, everybody realized a big mistake had been made. Not so much in regard to Carlos Gutierrez-Solana, but in regard to what the economic future could be.

The money situation now is more like it was in the 70s in terms of very small budgets. This is better for artists, but tough for organizations. It's important to fight for every penny you can get. I've come full circle in my thinking about what the government should be doing. This may sound very stupid to you (Claudia Gould), but I used to feel very strongly that the government shouldn't be involved with art at all, that they just screwed it up. In the 80s when the Robert Mapplethorpe and Andres Serrano incidents happened, I felt they shouldn't be involved with individual artists. Then when I started to go to Washington, D.C., with other artists and talked to people in the government, my eyes were opened to these grassroots organizations that were going to completely fold without this money. It made me realize how much we need the money. I'm beginning to look around and see individual artists need the money, too. But I don't know who should come first, I don't think there's a way to say that.

Artists Space is still doing the same thing, and it's going to be around for a long, long time because the issue will always be: "What is our mission?" To me, it was very simple. The mission was to show young unaffiliated artists and give them a way to have an outing. It hasn't changed. It's doing a job that's always going to be necessary. But you don't get a lot of attention for showing unknowns because it's a mixed bag. When you (Claudia) read me the names of the first artists who showed at Artists Space 50 percent of them maybe became well known and the other 50 percent you don't even recognize. That's just a chance you take. Yet that's what's exciting about it. It's a trial-and-error process that galleries can't take— it's not their job. When you give young artists a chance to show their work in public, it's a huge support. It's enormous, it's wonderful. I still think Artists Space is one of the most important organizations around.

220

Sept. 28 – Nov. 4: **Extended Definitions: Video Experiments in Perception** (Cara Mertes). Nancy Buchanan, *Sightlines*, 1988; Jonathan Giles, *Sentence Completion*, 1988; Alexander Hahn, *Viewers of Optics*, 1987; Lynn Hershman, *Confessions of a Chameleon*, 1985; Gary Hill, *Incidence of Catastrophe*, 1988; Andrew Neumann, *Phenomenology (parts a,b,c)*, 1988; Scott Rankin, *This and That*, 1988; Norie Sato, *Reservoir, 1988*. Brochure with essay by Cara Mertes.

Sept. 28 – Nov. 4: **Project**: Don Stinson, *Perspective: The State of Existing in Space Before the Eye*, drawing (Herbert Muschamp). Brochure with essay by Herbert Muschamp.

Mirosław Bałka I never had a fascination with America. So the exhibition at Artists Space was just about making the show. New York was very hot and we spent most of the time sitting in this hot apartment looking at this program on television about how to paint. We sent Piotr (Kurka) out to get a few beers and with Mariusz (Kruk) we sat in front of the television, drinking beer in our underwear.

I remember very well these powerful works of Mariusz's. That was his best period. And the idea that if you cut the egg with the ax it would split in two halves. It was part of the work. It was very brave at that time. I still remember the chair with the string. During the opening everybody stepped on it and the chair collapsed. It was very good energy; those were masterpieces of Mariusz's in that show!

I remember when Mrđjan Bajić went to the bank to get the money. On the Polish black exchange market we earned a lot of money from that show. We brought all the money back and didn't spend it in restaurants, so we had money for at least a few months of work. One week's per diem was enough to live on for half a year in Poland. Also, Artists Space paid for our transportation and accommodations. It was the difference between official exchanges. As I remember, the fact that none of us had sold anything was a good indication of the times. When we arrived in New York we were poor guys. I had to go to Norway to paint houses and Piotr painted racing cars, he was more ambitious. Mariusz and Piotr had Czech girlfriends. After the exhibition, Piotr even gave his sculpture to a Czech lover he knew in New York. Now, that's a real story, Jerzy Skolimowski could make a short movie from this. There was no future. You didn't know what you were going to do the next day. Or how you would manage to survive as a human being let alone as an artist. I didn't think at all. But that was the situation when we were free, free and naked. It was funny when you think of it from the perspective of time, it was a great time in some ways.

Nov. 16 – Jan. 6: **Witnesses: Against Our Vanishing** (Nan Goldin). Group exhibition exploring the influence of AIDS on aesthetics, culture, and sexuality: David Armstrong, photography; Tom Chesley, painting; Dorit Cypis, installation; Philip-Lorca diCorcia, photography; Jane Dickson, drawing; Clarence Elie-Rivera, photography; Darrel Ellis, drawing; Allen Frame, photography; Peter Hujar, photography; Greer Lankton, assemblage; Siobhan Liddell, painting; Ramsey McPhillips, installation/assemblage; Mark Morrisroe, photography; James Nares, painting; Perico Pastor, drawing; Margo Pelletier, drawing; Vittorio Scarpati, drawing; Jo Shane, assemblage; Kiki Smith, silkscreen prints; Janet Stein, assemblage; Tabboo! Stephen Tashjian, painting; Shellburne Thurber, photography; Ken Tisa, painting; David Wojnarowicz, photography. Catalogue with essays by Nan Goldin, David Wojnarowicz, Linda Yablonsky, and Cookie Mueller, with additional statements by the artists.

I remember how I installed my work upstairs and you (Valerie Smith) were not happy so I had to show my work downstairs, which finally was good. There was ash and one man sitting with a pile of salt beside him, and there was a fence. At that time, the work was not good for the New York situation. Fashion is what people were looking for. If this work were to be shown now, it would receive more interest than it did 10 years ago. At that time I was already fed up with figures, but I had to show them because I was invited to the show at the last minute and I didn't have any other work finished. I was already leaving figurative work. Making them started to become boring for me.

The work I did at that time wasn't ending or beginning. With work there is never a wall, it's always the open space and the problem of the distances in the space, of perspective. You are closer to some things and farther away from others. So the border exists in distances in some way and you still find movement to this border. It's just a big landscape and a working landscape. When you leave something it becomes smaller and something else becomes bigger. When you enter this place it's like a game. You're just walking between oases.

Nov. 28–29: **Witnesses: Against Our Vanishing** (Nan Goldin and Barbara Barg). Two evenings of readings with proceeds donated to ACT UP (AIDS Coalition to Unleash Power).
Nov. 28: Barbara Barg, Max Blagg, Richard Elovich, Jim Fouratt, John Giorno, Gary Indiana, Sylvére Lotringer, Sharon Niest (reading Cookie Mueller), Achy Obejas, Lynne Tillman.
Nov. 29: Bruce Balboni, Richard Hell, Bob Holman, Ridy Kikel, Eileen Myles, Rene Ricard, Sarah Schulman, Fiona Templeton, David Wojnarowicz, Linda Yablonsky.

Nov. 16–Jan. 6: **Uprising: Videotapes on the Palestinian Resistance** (Elia Suleiman and Dan Walworth). Norman Cowie, Ahmed Damian, and Dan Walworth, *Nazareth in August*, 1986; Mai Masri and Jean Chamoun, *War Generation: Beirut*, 1988; Gilles Dinnematin, *Does the Cactus Have a Soul?*, 1987; Georges Khleifi and Ziad Fahoum, *The Stone Throwers*, 1989; Amos Gitai, *House*, 1980; Mona Hatoum, *Measures of Distance*, 1988, and *Eyes Skinned*, 1988; Rashid Mashrawi, *The Shelter*, 1989; Jayce Salloum and Elia Suleiman, *Intifada: Speaking for Oneself*, 1989. Catalogue with an essay by Hanan Mikhail-Ashrawi and an interview with Elia Suleiman and Georges Khleifi by Dan Walworth.

Roberta Smith
True to its word, Artists Space provides "alternatives"; they constantly bring to our attention things that for one reason or another are being missed.
They remind us that there are other things going on than what is presented by more established institutions. Generally the role of the alternative space is to catch what falls through the cracks, between larger public institutions and commercial ventures such as art galleries; there is a kind of art on a certain scale that doesn't get shown in New York's major museums. I remember seeing Jon Borofsky's and Scott Burton's work for the first time at the 155 Wooster Street space. Artists Space's involvement through Helene Winer with the various kinds of photo work is also particularly memorable to me.
It may be that their involvement has now shifted to the area of video or architectural installation. But they still find alternative things to do, even though there is a lot of competition from the galleries, which have become more active since the 80s and are really ferreting out artists. At Artists Space there is always work that is getting the attention it deserves; in some ways it is remarkably like it always was.

Nov. 16–Jan. 6: **Project:** Benito Huerta, *Attempted: Not Known*, sculpture, drawing, hand-colored book (Marilyn A. Zeitlin). Brochure with an essay by Marilyn A. Zeitlin.

Valerie Smith
I was hired by Linda Shearer in the Fall of 1981. I believe I was the first official Artists Space Curator. As a professional curator herself Linda was very generous to a novice, and I will always remember that. Linda gave me an enormous amount of responsibility. Basically, she let me have a hand at everything: curating exhibitions, of course, but also film, events, projects, as well as choosing people to curate outside exhibitions. The program was very much a mix between shows we organized individually and thinking with Linda about people who would be appropriate to curate projects. In the beginning I hadn't quite realized what it meant to be a curator at Artists Space. It was a hesitant start, but Linda trusted me totally and that curatorial freedom continued when Susan Wyatt became Director. It's very hard to come by a job like that now. I was lucky.

We did some amazing shows on Hudson Street. On the recommendation of Jenny Holzer, I went to Michael Byron's studio on 13th Street and Avenue B or C and at the time that was really out there. It was a tiny little apartment and a huge painting, a story of his family, took up one wall. It was very raw and it impressed me. Later at Artists Space he did *For the Nun*, a great project in the last room to the left down the hallway. It was about a nun who had been raped. You opened the door and, with caution, walked in—it was very moving. Those back rooms always had memorable projects.

A Likely Story tied a number of artists together who had like minds. With the exception of Jeff Koons, these artists seemed to take an intellectual distance from their subject matter to make art historical or cultural references. *A Likely Story* was just a way of putting somewhat similar but perhaps unlikely aesthetic positions together. Jeff Koons showed his sparkling stacked Hoovers. He also put up a photograph of himself as a young boy with crayons— the quintessential young artist. In many ways that photo was more telling than the vacuum cleaners, which became so famous.

In *Facades, Landscapes, Interiors* Tony Oursler did three little landscape installations. One was a small mound in the middle of the large gallery with a TV monitor and an oil rig. His tapes with the funny finger puppets picking through these industrial landscapes were quite well known. But I was more interested in seeing the installations, the production behind the videos, and what he could do with them. Again, that was another exhibition, incorporating a diverse group of work around a loose theme. Many of those tentative exhibitions were like pieces of a puzzle; they only make sense when the puzzle is complete and there's time to look back.

One of the more successful series of exhibitions was *Dark Rooms*, which I schemed up and Hartley Shearer titled. *Dark Rooms* fullfilled an incredible need to give primary exhibition space to multi-media projects, which had previously been relegated to the margins of what was considered important to show in the art world, and

CONTINUED

for obvious reasons. *Dark Rooms* helped pave the way for media installations both in the galleries and later in the museums. Judith Barry's *In the Shadow of the City… Vamp r y….* project was a perfect example of where this kind of work was going. And because media work has a long history, one of the first *Dark Rooms* was a little sampling of early work in this field to Judith Barry, who represented the latest development.

The idea for James Coleman and Michael Asher had to do with the baroque and the classical, the narrative and nonnarrative, approaching the conceptual practice from radically different points of view. It was an unusual coupling, but they are approximately of the same generation, so it made sense to put them together, and it worked.

The problem I often found with Artists Space was when I planned an exhibition I couldn't include artists who had previously shown there, even though they may have fit perfectly or made the necessary connection between generations and sensibilities. Occasionally we made exceptions with very noncommercial work. But for the most part we stuck to the mandate, so it was always a little frustrating. On the other hand, it kept me looking, constantly looking. Titling exhibitions was also a challenge, because it meant finding the common ingredient, which often was not completely baked, so there was always a little fiction and fudging going on. The bonding element usually comes after the concept has been realized, but by then it's too late because you've done it. So a museum comes along, picks up the idea, and refines it. Artists Space was the guinea pig.

Conceptual or theoretical architecture was another aspect of the program I felt was important, but it hadn't up to that time in the art world been covered in any consistant way by any gallery. For a while, Artists Space had somewhat forgotten architecture after the Bernard Tschumi exhibitions. There was a gap of several years until it became very clear we had to do something. Storefront for Art and Architecture was doing some very interesting projects, but Storefront was the only other outlet, except for Max Protetch, who showed established architects and designers. That need started the architecture project series and, in addition, every other year we did a major architectural show. So we began to show some way-out work like Hani Rashid's *Kursaal* and *From Here to Eternity,* which, for better or worse, was another umbrella title for bizarre theoretical ideas spanning the material to the spiritual or cosmic worlds in construction.

When I arrived, the *U.S. Projects* series was already in place. Linda drew up a list of curators she knew would pick a good cross-section of interesting artists. It was enormously successful, because it was a way to engage expert eyes familiar with their local art scenes to invite artists from around the nation to come and do wonderful and quirky projects. In the early days we didn't have money for me to gallivant all across the country. So this was a perfect way of tapping into what was new in North America. *International Projects* was the outcome of a successful *U.S. Projects*. Several of the curators for those projects were hip European names I came up with through my connections to artists who had worked over there . These smaller *International Projects* evolved into larger European shows. We asked Saskia Bos of de Appel Foundation, Amsterdam, to curate an exhibition, and later I traveled to Eastern Europe to research *Metaphysical Visions*. At that time nobody in the U.S. was interested in going there let alone in organizing a show of artists from those countries.

Toward the mid-80s, we had another important focus, which was the great video program Dan Walworth curated. Dan and I started doing the *Dark Rooms* shows together. It was during this time that Artists Space's attention veered toward the left, especially in terms of the video program, film evenings, and events. It was important for us to get other points of view. I partially attribute this new consciousness to Dan, who introduced a lot of new material and video artists to Artists Space. At the same time the exhibition program in general slowly became more politically aware. It made sense to encourage Jean Fisher and Jimmie Durham to organize *We the People* and it made sense to encourage Wankyung Sung and Hyuk Um to organize *Min Joong Art,* especially in the 80s when an entire segment of the art world was mainly thinking about their wallets. However, one of my best memories and the most fun I had as a curator was driving down to Tijuana with Dan and a bunch of friends. We stopped in San Diego to meet some members of the Border Art Workshop/Taller de Arte Fronterizo with whom we were going to do a show. They took us to the border in the desert where we witnessed the absurdity of the border as we ate tapas and watched the sun set. It was mind-blowing…a great trip, a great memory, a wild show.

In the mid-80s, the word was we weren't representing enough artists of color. I took that pressure as a positive challenge, because we had sunk a bit into a comfortable programming without quite realizing it—we weren't reaching out enough. It was a strong nudge from NYSCA which made me go out and do some serious research. African American artists especially were not knocking on Artists Space's door. In order to address these gaps in our programming I got in touch with people like Fred Wilson, who was curating shows at the Longwood Art Gallery. I asked him whom I should talk to and who was interesting. Fred was very generous and receptive. Through him I met Giza Daniels-Endesha, a young rebel, who did this great totemic cum votive installation with layers of political and historical references: lynching, Tawana Brawley, and other current events. He was squatting with other artists in an abandoned building in the South Bronx. I went up to meet with him and it was immediately clear he would do something great.

I learned so much working at Artists Space during those fat years in the 80s. It definitely influenced the work I did later. It was a challenge and I grew up with Artists Space. But after eight years I was overdue and it was time to let someone else have a crack at it. I am an ardent believer in rotating curators and directors.

NOVEMBER **1991** TO DECEMBER **1993**

Spring Benefit, April 27, 1993.

Carlos Gutierrez-Solana
interviewed by Amy Wanggaard

Carlos Gutierrez-Solana was Executive Director of Artists Space from November 1991 to December 1993. He hired Amy Wanggaard in 1992, and she stayed at Artists Space until 1995. Gutierrez-Solana began his tenure on 223 West Broadway and moved to 38 Greene Street in October 1993. This interview took place on April 3, 1997.

AMY WANGGAARD: You started at Artists Space in November of 1991, but you had known Artists Space for a long time as the director of the Visual Artists Program at the New York State Council on the Arts (NYSCA). In this regard, I was reading through an essay in *A Decade of New Art,* 1984, by Linda Cathcart. She wrote that when Artists Space began, it was filling a void, for there were no places for artists to show.

CARLOS GUTIERREZ-SOLANA: Yes, what Linda wrote was true. But the fact is, White Columns was the first. It was originally called 112 Workshop on 112 Greene Street.[1] Artists did what they wanted to do. It seemed totally unstructured. It was absolutely great. Some of the best work I've seen was done there. Then Artists Space came along as its institutional cousin, in the sense that it was engendered and supported by the state. At the time, any place that supported artists was great. So a lot of people did stuff there as well. It was filling a void, as Linda wrote.

AW: The AIDS FORUM was one of the first programs you implemented at Artists Space. How did you decide the issue was important enough to organize a forum? And how did it work?

CGS: There were multiple reasons. I cared a great deal about it. I felt the whole issue was burning in everyone's minds, or bodies. I don't know if the Board ever knew this or whether it was important for them to know, but I am HIV- positive. So it was a personal issue as well. I also realized that there were so many people involved and affected by this, that it needed a forum.

AW: Artists Space was housing the Visual AIDS Slide Registry in the Artists File.

CGS: Yes, and, for A Day Without Art, Artists Space had already booked Robert Farber's *Every 10 Minutes.* It was a gorgeous piece. Sadly, Robert is dead now.

The AIDS FORUM was the result of a dinner conversation I had with Carolyn Alexander and an artist friend, Frank Moore. It was also about the frustrations I felt coming into a new place as Director, and not having much room to schedule for half a year or more. I said, "Well, Frank, can you do something, if I give you the space?"

AW: What did he say?

CGS: He said "Yes!" Frank (Moore) and Marc Happel created the first AIDS FORUM, *Honor Their Dignity*, which ran from November 1991 through January 1992. It was an incredible shrine.

From then on, it was all word of mouth. We had no money to advertise, but we didn't intend to advertise. It was not going to be another "program initiative." Although I tried to get funding for the FORUM project and for publishing a catalogue, unfortunately that never happened.

I felt the AIDS FORUM had to be done. It was that simple. I wanted to tell everyone at Artists Space that we could do projects which were different, didn't cost much money, and still respected artists. We always paid the artist. It was never much, usually 55 or 75 bucks. But we always paid them.

1   112 Workshop on 112 Greene Street, New York City, was founded by Gordon Matta-Clark and Jeffery Lew in 1969. It changed its name to White Columns in 1979.

↑ Carlos Gutierrez-Solana and Pat Oleszko,
Spring Benefit, April 27, 1993.

AW: The AIDS FORUM changed every couple of weeks and didn't take the entire length of the gallery.

CGS: There was no interruption to the AIDS FORUM—that was the most incredible thing. And that's why it was set up where it was. First of all, I hated the idea of having the gift shop in the front space where you first come in, even though I realize we all need to earn revenue. As far as I'm concerned, AIDS is still a burning issue. That's why the FORUM needed to be up front, as a constant reminder.

It all started because I thought A Day Without Art was a very nice and wonderful thing. In fact, I really loved Robert Farber's piece, *Every 10 Minutes* (1991) but, I felt it wasn't enough. I still think we should have A Day Without Art all the time—always reminding people that this issue is not dead.

In the process of organizing the AIDS FORUM, we discovered there were tons of people who had something to say about it. It's interesting that it ended. At the same time, it was such a pivotal program, it was picked up by other institutions throughout the country. There has been something ongoing somewhere ever since.

The AIDS issue aside, the FORUM was just another means of letting artists express themselves in a way that is not pure product and doesn't have to do with normal operations.

Curatorially, it was totally democratic. It was first-come, first-served. Artists were booked as long as their proposed work had something to do with AIDS.

AW: What if work came up that you didn't like? How did you deal with that?

CGS: It didn't matter.

AW: You didn't care?

CGS: No. If it had to do with AIDS, they got booked. That was the whole idea. It wasn't about art criteria. It was about responding to a crisis. We presented 25 AIDS FORUMs over two years. They changed overnight. Artists understood that. Everyone did their best. They were responsible for doing their work in the space and removing it. Then the next person would install their work. They briefly coexisted when changing presentations. The AIDS FORUM was always ongoing.

AW: What direction did you want to take Artists Space?

CGS: I believe the reason I was offered this job was to diversify the program. I thought, from a curatorial point of view, Artists Space had gotten too rarified, too conceptually oriented or pseudo-conceptually oriented.

In my opinion, Artists Space had reached a point where it was too regimented. They had these pretentious curatorial shows above ground that were pseudo-intellectual and totally unrelated to anything that was going on. As far as I could see, they had nothing to do with anything. And then, all these other artists from the File were being relegated to the most horrible galleries downstairs called the "Underground."

My philosophy was to debunk all that crap. Take everything, put it in a mixer, and have it come out wherever it comes. Wherever it's most appropriate for work to be, that's where it was going to be.

I felt that Artists Space had gotten very distant from people. That it was no longer a forum for artists, but a forum for curators who wanted to use it as a stepping stone. This is all very personal, but, I thought the shows were alienating in their attitudes about art and artists. I wanted to bring Artists Space back to the artists.

AW: How did you do that?

CGS: I don't know if I did that. Well no, that's not true. I know we did that. In the two years I was at Artists Space, I listened to everyone I worked with. I dealt with prior obligations, and tried to alter them to fit our new role and mission. I did that by creating different spaces and contrasting shows, by programmatically juxtaposing a variety of genres and disciplines. I wanted to create an environment where people experience art as they do in real life. Artists Space always aspired to be a multicultural center. I felt this was a worthwhile mission. But it's gotta be more than just pretending. So, I wanted to make a real multicultural center.

AW: What did you do?

CGS: I invited dancers and drag queens, black writers and gay photographers. I also invited painters of every gender and genre, as well as performance artists, clay artists, fabric artists, and even a few conceptual artists.

In my mind, Artists Space was never supposed to have been the end-all of the art world. It was the beginning of the art world for many of these people. It always had been.

Cindy Sherman was a secretary at Artists Space. She was allowed to do all her personifications while she was working. So, what's wrong with having James Godwin do his own personifications? It was a new generation and different from mine. I was always very conscious of that. I thought I was good for running the place, but, not *right* for running the place.

AW: Why not? What do you mean?

CGS: I thought, at this point in my life, all the people who worked with me had more talent and energy than myself. I mean, go on… I'm 40-some years old. It's true.

There have always been great people. Like Denise Fasanello. Like you, Amy. Like Charles Wright. Like Gary Nickard. All of you had ideas and something to say about what the place should be and what the art world is. I think I maneuvered it pretty well. But it was still about the artists. It wasn't about me, nor about us. And it also wasn't about the people on the Board.

AW: One of the things you did at Artists Space was the Four Walls show, *Rope/Radio/Return of the Repressed*. Connie Butler began to talk to Four Walls, before you started as Director.

CGS: It was one of the greatest shows we ever did. My thanks to Connie for starting the ball rolling.

AW: What was that show about?

CGS: It was about the spirit of Artists Space. Basically, we called up people from the Artists File, and artists chose. We were only the conduit. We pretty much did whatever they wanted. However, we set some parameters and they stuck by them.

AW: The Four Walls show was a three-part show. The first, *The Rope Show* (1992), started in the Artists File.

CGS: Then there was *The Radio Show* (1992) and *The Return of the Repressed* (1992). They were all kooky shows. They weren't "great art" shows, although a lot of the work was interesting and full of high energy. I don't think Artists Space was or should be about making "great art" shows. The Four Walls shows were about creating opportunities for artists and empowering them to some degree, which is always what Artists Space is supposed to do.

Amy Sillman, Mike Ballou, and Adam Simon selected three artists. Then they visited the artists' studios and selected work for the show. Independent of each other, those three selectees came back to the Artists File to select three other artists. And it kept going on like that.

I feel it's important to say that the three original selectors were not included in any of the exhibitions. It was hard for them, but we insisted on it. Unfortunately, it's not something that's perceived as a conflict of interest anymore, at Artists Space or anywhere for that matter.

AW: Tell me about the benefit.

CGS: I insisted on having my first benefit at Artists Space.

AW: That's true. It hadn't been at Artists Space for years.

CGS: It was a wonderful benefit. It was hard for me, because I never got to eat. But dinners were at 28 restaurants all over SoHo and TriBeCa. The restaurants donated everything. We had very little expenses.

AW: I remember, you went around on a motorcycle. You visited every single site.

CGS: That's right. I stopped in, and greeted and thanked our guests. Even though they enticed me to stay there was no time, I had to quickly move on to the next restaurant.

AW: Then we all went back to Artists Space where there was a huge party.

CGS: It was a big thing. It was cheap. You might not remember, but for that benefit we commissioned artists from the Artists File, again, and anybody who wanted to, to make drawings on very long (17 feet or longer) sheets of paper, which we supplied. Lots of different styles hanging one next to another. It was a gorgeous collage, and an apt metaphor for our programming approach.

AW: Then the drawings were raffled off. It was a lot of work. But it raised a whole lot of money for Artists Space. This was important, because, at the time, we didn't have any money—we were struggling, financially.

CGS: Oh, let's not get into that.

AW: Yes, we gotta get into that. It was an important thing that was going on. It was 1991-1992 and there was no money. Doing a benefit was important, because it reinvigorated interest in the space.

CGS: More people came to Artists Space in two years than they had in the previous five years. From the time I was hired, I believed the Board wanted me to turn Artists Space into a truly multicultural, multidisciplinary space. And I had my own ideas of what that was about.

AW: What were your ideas?

CGS: I don't think it was just lip service. I think it was about doing it, about being a cultural center. If the organization Other Countries: Black Gay Voices in the Age of AIDS wanted to have a reading, we'd do it. If we wanted to do the AIDS FORUM, we'd do it. If sculptor Petah Coyne and choreographer Irene Hultman wanted to do a collaborative performance, we'd do it. That was my idea. The biggest problem I had was convincing the staff we had to do all this day and night.

AW: One other thing you knew was, in order to survive, Artists Space needed money. And in order to have money, not only did we need to write grants and get grants, we needed to find more of a grassroots way to make money.

So, in your first year at Artists Space, the major step you made was to mount the exhibition, *Putt-Modernism* (1992). Where did you first hear about that idea?

CGS: When I came to Artists Space, I had chats with everyone on the staff. I pried into everyone's thoughts about what they were doing, what they could be doing, what they wanted to be doing, and what they thought they should have been doing. At the end of my interview with Ken Buhler, I asked, "Well, anything else?" Then I guess he felt emboldened. And he said, "Well, there is this thing I always wanted to do." It's true. I can remember that to this day. I can see his face. He was like, "Well, you know, I don't know, shucks." I said, "Well, what for Chrissakes?" And he said, "Well, I always thought it would be kind of cool if artists did a miniature golf course."

I don't know what clicked in my mind, but I said, "That's a great idea!" He looked at me like I had gone nuts, gone bananas. He never had that kind of response from anyone. And I said, "Let's do it."

AW: So what happened?

CGS: We did it. I said, "Okay, let's get a bunch of artist Board members together to see what they think of this idea." Not even ask them, just talk about it. "We're doing this thing, and what do you think? Do you wanna be in it?" They all did.

Everyone had to make a miniature golf hole. This is the kind of thing I'm about. It's as silly as you can get. It was a fundraising ploy. It came out of a genuine idea, a dream Ken had and it was a genuine and serious show in many ways. Ken should always be given credit for this piece, which is still traveling.

AW: It started in 1992 and, five years later, continues today as a fundraiser for Artists Space. At the opening on August 1st, we had a huge party for the show, which was up for two months.

CGS: Some 30,000 to 40,000 people came through in those two months alone. That's more than all the people who ever came to Artists Space in its 10 or 20 years...

AW: They all came through to play golf?

CGS: No, they came through to see the exhibit, and play golf. Everything is an artist's work. It was serious. It's the only miniature golf course in the nation that deals with homelessness, with AIDS, with the Gulf War—with serious issues. And it was a lot of fun to play. I made par every time.

AW: In your second year at Artists Space, you programmed a whole host of shows. You introduced *Ping Chong*: A *Facility for the Channeling and Containment of Undesirable Elements* (1992), Ping Chong's first visual installation in New York. You showed *Artists from Studio in a School* in a regular exhibition slot, rather than a quick one-week run as we had always done. You continued *A New World Order* (1992). That was an obligation you needed to keep. You brought in an artist from upstate New York, Susie Brandt, who presented a beautiful, gorgeous show. I loved it. The blanket show.

You did *Activated Walls* (1993). You presented a Cuban media event with film, video, and readings organized by Carl George and Jack Waters. Then, *Doug and Mike's Adult Entertainment* (1993). You worked with Carol Sun, an Asian American artist, who showed paintings. You presented the work of Tony Bechara, Carmen Herrera, Tom Murrin, and Mac Wells in an exhibition sponsored by the Mark Rothko Foundation.

Those were shows you felt were important. At that point, you were going on with your vision of Artists Space. What did you think needed to happen?

CGS: Well, listen to the list you just read. That's the most diverse program schedule I have ever heard from any institution in New York. That's what I thought should happen—we should be doing everything.

Look, think of it like this: when I tried to get Artists Space back on top, I had to do everything in my power. I actually believed that. I believed I was hired to do multicultural and multidisciplinary programs and I was always trying to figure out how we could do it and what we could do to bring in all kinds of different people, without bursting us.

Artists Space was my life. It wasn't about Artists Space. It was about creating a situation I believed was appropriate for artists, such as the fashion and performance evening, *The Celebrity Ribbon Cavalcade* (1992), to benefit Visual AIDS.

The greatest thing to do, next to a great entrance, is a great exit. I brought this up to the Board, and I thought we should consider it. I already felt this way before I got to Artists Space. I was asked to come to Artists Space because they wanted some soul perhaps, and a little color—a little tinge of tan, as it were. I mean this exactly the way I said it. They also wanted to keep their grants coming through the government. I'm a vain person. I'm a strong man. I think I can do a lot of things. So I came on board and

did a lot of things. But I also believed that, if we couldn't sustain it, we should proudly step aside and let others do it.

I think the staff, who decided to stay on after I arrived, was great. They believed. They cared about something I had, to some extent, lost faith in. I had to learn to respect their belief, to care for it. That's why I believed in making something out of this space. I thought it was doable. I think we did something worthwhile when we were there.

> **AW**: At one point you wanted to buy a three-million-dollar building. What did you think could happen in a new building? How could Artists Space financially sustain going into a venture like that? We were totally strapped. What did you want the Board to do?

CGS: I wanted the Board to think about the long-term viability of this organization, if there was to be one. The fact is, they had never thought of the long term in this organization. That's why they could not deal with such a building.

> **AW**: What would have happened in that space?

CGS: I was trying to take Artists Space to another level, to make it become more self-reliant and less dependent on grants. I believed it should be more responsible for its existence, more financially in control of its destiny and less reliant on the erratic, often capricious, kindness of funding organizations. I believed, in order to survive and thrive in the 90s, nonprofits needed to become entrepreneurial. The building represented a sacrifice and a risk. But, in the long run, it would have afforded Artists Space independence from the inefficient tyranny of grant writing—independence it sorely needed to uncompromisingly focus on serving artists. But the Board didn't want to take the risk.

> **AW**: We did decide, at that time, to move Artists Space, which was approximately 10 years after its last move. We settled on 38 Greene Street in SoHo, the center of the commercial art world. You chose the space. You thought it would be the space in which Artists Space could operate. Why did Artists Space move then?

CGS: The Board wanted to. Also, we had some issues with the TriBeCa landlord, with visitor accessibility, and I hated the place we were in. It was, for my purposes, one of the most awful places, in terms of spatial flexibility and the like. We did a lot of good things with the staff, offices, reorganizing the exhibition space. But it was hideous. I never thought it was a good space for what we were trying to do.

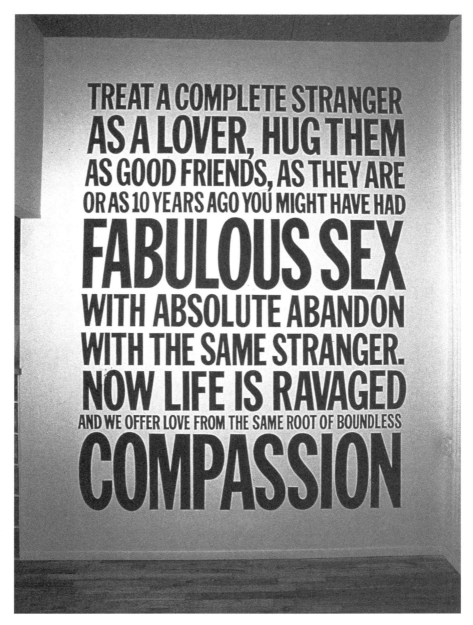

↑ **AIDS Forum:** John Giorno, *Fabulous Sex / Compassion*,
text installation, Nov. 20–Dec. 24, 1994.
Photo: Patty Wallace

All photographs this page from
Spring Benefit April 27, 1993

AW: The last show you organized was a three-part *Artists "Select,"* for Artists Space's 20th anniversary, mounted at 38 Greene Street. It was a series where we went back to the original way of putting together shows. You selected the artists who had shown there before. It was a diverse group. A multicultural group.

CGS: The whole point of our 20th-anniversary exhibitions was to let artists select whom they wanted. I thought Artists Space needed to reexamine itself. It was important to try and figure out what we were doing. I wanted to know. I'd never been there. I mean I had been there, but from a different perspective. My staff made me realize we were doing what we should be doing. I wanted to be able to turn over the whole place to younger people. But I realized that wouldn't happen.

I don't know if you remember, but a long time ago I said, "Amy, I shouldn't be running this place." I really believed in alternative spaces. But I believed to be alternative, they should be run by the people who are closest to them, who are closest to the street, who are down there.

The fact is that people are making art. We all look at it. And that's it. I don't have any hidden agendas. I didn't have agendas then, when I was running Artists Space, and I don't have agendas now. I just wanted to let the most people do the most.

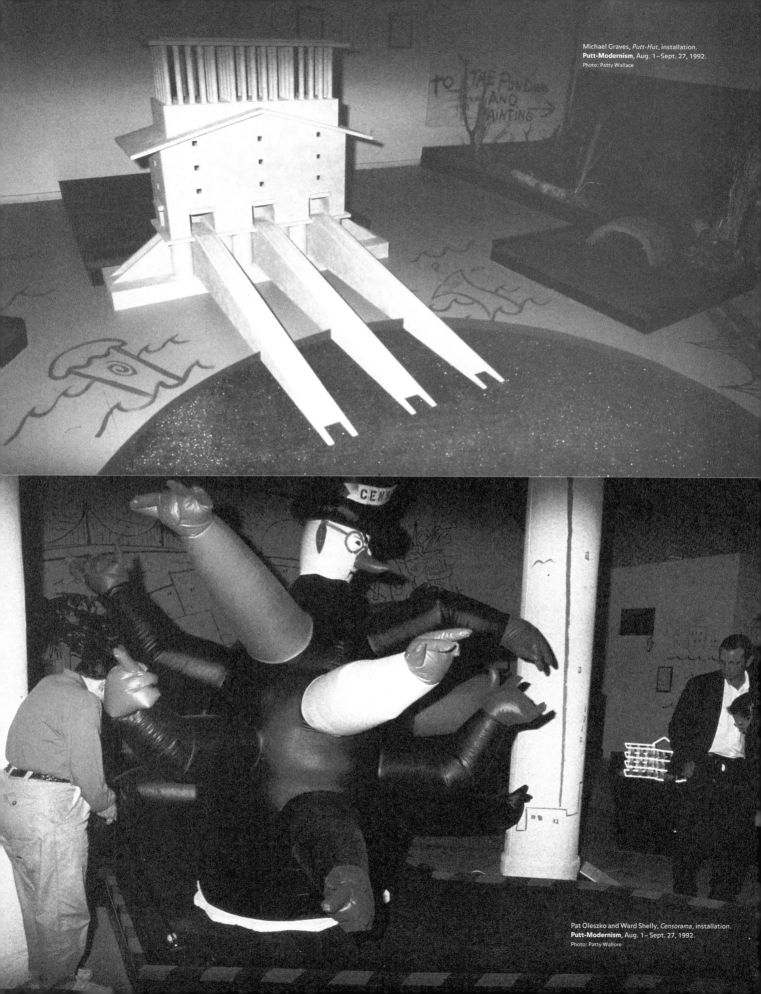

Michael Graves, *Putt-Hut*, installation.
Putt-Modernism, Aug. 1 – Sept. 27, 1992.
Photo: Patty Wallace

Pat Oleszko and Ward Shelly, *Censorama*, installation.
Putt-Modernism, Aug. 1 – Sept. 27, 1992.
Photo: Patty Wallore

Jan. 18–Feb. 24: **Paraculture** (Sally Couacaud). Group exhibition by Australian artists: Gordon Bennett, painting; Janet Burchill, installation; Fiona Foley, drawing; Matthÿs Gerber, painting; Jeff Gibson, photographs; Tim Johnson, painting; Narelle Jubelin, objects; Lindy Lee, painting. Catalogue with essays by Sally Couacaud, Keith Broadfoot & Rex Butler, Ross Gibson, and Meaghan Morris.

Jan. 18–Feb. 24: **Project**: Fred Tomaselli, *Diurnal Experiments and Nocturnal Investigations*, installation (Connie Butler). Brochure with essay by Connie Butler.

↓ Installation view.

Jan. 18–Feb. 24: **Video: In Search of Paradise (Or, Anywhere But Here)** (Steve Fagin and Bill Horrigan). Screened simultaneously at Artists Space and Los Angeles Contemporary Exhibitions (LACE): Leslie Thornton, *Peggy and Fred in Kansas*, 1988; Mike Anderson, *Old Antelope Lake*, 1966; Annette Barbier, *Women's Movements*, 1989; Gloria Ribé, *From Here, From This Side*, 1988; Dan Boord, *The Nature Theatre of Oklahoma*, 1985; Terese Svoboda, *Komodo*, 1986; Alexander Kluge,*The African Lady, or Love with a Fatal Outcome*, 1988; Peter Thompson, *Universal Hotel*, 1986. Catalogue with excerpt from the script of Steve Fagin's *The Machine That Killed Bad People* and essay by Bill Horrigan, produced in association with LACE.

Mar. 8–Apr. 7: Ed Clark, painting; Carol Haerer, painting; Ted Kurahara, painting (Connie Butler). Sponsored by the Mark Rothko Foundation. Catalogue with essays by Connie Butler, Kellie Jones, and John Yau.

Mar. 8–Apr. 7: **Project**: Les LeVeque, *Some Questions Concerning Technology*, video sculpture (John Knecht). Brochure with essay by John Knecht.

↑ Les LeVeque, video sculpture.
© Peter McClennan

Beverly Wolff I knew Linda Shearer, we had served together on the Board of VLA (Volunteer Lawyers for the Arts), and she recommended I get involved with Artists Space. As it happened, the *Witnesses* problem immediately occurred upon my joining the Board. So it turned out not to be a bad move to add a lawyer to the team, and it was certainly something I wanted to do.

The first question was whether the NEA was going to give us the grant at all. They wanted us to put a disclaimer on the walls. So at that point, we were looking at two things. One, whether or not we should make a disclaimer; two, whether they had said they weren't going to give us the money. In fact, I believe they weren't going to pay us the grant money they had already awarded us. The NEA, as with all government entities, is governed by this very arcane Administrative Procedure Acts. Susan Wyatt and I walked through the legal issues. Early on we decided we needed a litigator to tell us what our chances and options were. Through my connections at VLA I was able to get Ron Rauchberg, who agreed to take on the case pro bono. He met first with Susan and then with the Board to chart our various options. However, we realized the legal remedies available to us were greatly limited. We decided the better way to go was to raise a public outcry. It seemed more effective and Susan was really good at doing it. She brought important people together in a series of meetings, first in New York, then in Washington, D.C. For example, Congressman Pat Williams from Montana, who was very involved in arts funding at the time, came to New York and met with people. It paid off in the end. The NEA decided to give us the money and then they asked for it back. We said we wouldn't give it back. They finally agreed we could keep it, but not to support the catalogue. This was not a great solution, but not a bad one. Later, we had problems from the religious right, who must have sent some people to the gallery. They made claims that we were possibly violating New York or federal pornography statutes. The claims were particularly aimed at our video displays. So we then looked at whether or not we had to legally place a disclaimer in the video gallery. During the same time, we already had a statement saying the materials might be sensitive to minors. Some museums do it—we don't at MOMA. It's a very tough topic: whether or not to have a statement. It's interesting how many people, who are very much for freedom of expression, draw limits when it comes to what children can see.

It was one of those moments when a lot of Board members felt there was something to be active about. It was important and we were all being battered by it. We had town meetings to talk about the issues. Everybody came together around the situation with a very good spirit. I believe David Wojnarowicz wanted us to say we didn't want the money and to give it back. He wanted Artists Space to take a much more empowered position and to break with the government by saying we don't need you. But Artists Space did the right thing. It's very easy today to sit here and say, "Gee, we should have done what David wanted because no one gets funding from the NEA anymore." That would have been a great thing. At the time, I don't think any of us understood how serious and fragile the funding issues were, how wrapped up they were with *Witnesses*. It was very hard for everybody to really believe one incident like this was going to cause the funding to be wiped out totally for individual spaces and artists. We thought the importance of government funding was greater than making a statement. In retrospect, if we had known they were going to do this, of course we should have

CONTINUED

Mar. 8–Apr. 7: Stone's Throw: Television from Cuba, Island in Goliath's Sea (Dee Dee Halleck and Monica Melamid). Collection of Cuban media projects from broadcast television and independent experimental producers, including the premiere of *Export TV: Anatomy of an Electronic Invasion*, a documentary on TV Marti about the plan to broadcast United States Information Agency (USIA) news programming and United States–produced Spanish language television on Cuban airwaves: *Los Abuelos Se Rebelan (The Grandparents Rebel)*, *Policía en Accion (Police in Action)*, *Ritmo Oriental (Eastern Rhythm)*, *Cuando Yo Sea Grande… (When I Grow Up…)*, *Arco Iris Musical (Musical Rainbow)*, *Don Minimo*, *¡Hola, Mar! (Hi There, Ocean!)*, *Circulo Infantil (Day Care Center)*, *Calabacita (Lullaby)*, *Septima Familia (Seventh Family)*, *Esquina Caliente (Hot Corner)*, *La Mar Sera Rizada (The Sea Will Be Turbulent)*, *¡Oh, Melancolia! (Oh, Melancholy!)*, *El Espectador (The Spectator)*, *No Por Que Me Dice Fidel Castro (Not Because Fidel Castro Told Me)*, *Puntos De Vista (Points of View)*, *Verdicto En l'Habana (Verdict in Havana)*. Catalogue with essays by Dee Dee Halleck, Camilio Hernández, Jean Franco, Reynaldo González, and Laurien Alexandre.

BEVERLEY WOLFF / CONTINUED

walked away from it. We got more money than most other arts organizations in New York, but it was very important to Artists Space. So it was a difficult position to take.

Susan was spending more time in Washington, D.C. She was very directed toward continuing the advocacy role and evolved into a fabulous advocate for this cause. We got some special grants, of which the most memorable were from Agnes Gund, Arne Glimcher, and the Art Dealers Association. All in all, *Witnesses* was probably a good thing for Artists Space. We handled it well and got through it. At that point Susan had been at Artists Space 17 years; it was probably time for her to move on.

I really don't have much to say about Carlos Gutierrez-Solana. I did not connect with him in any way. Carlos was impatient about the lack of Board participation. He thought it was up to the Board to solve the financial problems of the organization. Maybe it was. But unfortunately, it wasn't realistic at Artists Space. His vision of the institution was far greater than our financial reach. He wanted us to buy a building and have money for it. For a while, he thought he could pull it off. I don't know if Phil Aarons thought that, too. I was very disappointed, Phil was a great Board member, but he dropped off because he suddenly realized we weren't going to have the money, and he was not somebody who was going to help with that.

Interestingly enough, my relationship with Susan was better than it was with Carlos. We're now almost 10 years away from *Witnesses*. When Susan left and we were looking for a new director, some of us may have thought, unrealistically, we had a chance to become something bigger and better than we had been. Now we're all very happy we still exist and have found a way to maintain ourselves. But at the time, there was the view that, with this new publicity and presence in the world, we could move to another space and have greater recognition. There was the hope that maybe we could move up to the status of The Drawing Center.

Carlos really politicized the art being shown at Artists Space. Suddenly political art took over, and it was very pointed. There was too much of it, no curatorial voice. He had terrible battles with the curators and got rid of them. He polarized the program as a political outlet for his issues. The Board was very concerned when he took over the curating. His answer was, "I don't have the money for the curators, I don't have this or that." I have always thought it was up to the artist Board members and Board members like Irving Sandler, not me, to make those decisions. I never presumed to talk about the curatorial vision, but it bothered me. In retrospect, Artists Space is a much better place now.

Apr. 19–May 19: Mike Henderson, painting, drawing, installation (Connie Butler). Catalogue with essay by Connie Butler.

Apr. 19–May 19: Beverly Semmes, sculpture installation (Connie Butler). Catalogue with essay by Connie Butler.

Apr. 19–May 19: Project: Ralph Paquin and Ann Stoddard, *Erawa – Era Was*, installation (Dana Friis-Hansen). Brochure with essay by Dana Friis-Hansen.

↓ Installation view.

Apr. 19–May 19: Video: Joint Ventures (Ernest Larsen). The Black Cat Collective, *Many Faces of Paper*, 1989; Michael Balser and Andy Fabo, *Blood Risk*, 1990; Lisa Steele and Kim Tomczak, *White Dawn*, 1988, and *Private Eyes*, 1987; Sherry Millner and Ernest Larsen, *Out of the Mouth of Babes*, 1987; Annie Goldson and Chris Bratton, *Counter-Terror*, 1990; Can Candan, Dylan Nolfi, and David Wadsworth, *Boycott Coke*, 1990; Gregg Bordowitz and Jean Carlomusto, *Current Flow*, 1989, *Midnight Snack*, 1989, and *Something Fierce*, 1989; Charles Brack, Gregg Bordowitz, and Jean Carlomusto, *Car Service*, 1989; David Bronstein, Gregg Bordowitz, and Jean Carlomusto, *Vogueing*, 1990; Phil Zwickler and David Wojnarowicz, *Fear of Disclosure*, 1989. Brochure with essay by Ernest Larsen.

May 25–26: **Film and Video: Coming Attractions: New Narratives on Race and Sexuality** (Roddy Bogawa). Second annual presentation of film and video works-in-progress.
May 25: Roddy Bogawa, *Some Divine Wind*; Shu Lea Cheang, *Those Fluttering Objects of Desire*; Larry Carty, *Don't Believe the Hype*; Paper Tiger TV (Kelly Anderson and Simone Farkhondeh), *Hamid Naficy Reads Images of Iranians in the American Media*.
May 26: Peggy Ahwesh, *In Plato's Cave*; Moyra Davey, *Hell Notes*; Jennifer Montgomery, *Age 12: Love With a Little L*; Testing the Limits Collective, *Voices From the Front*.

May 31–June 30: **Recycling L.A.** (Barbara Goldstein). Group exhibition by emerging architects from Los Angeles: Janek Bielski, *Urban Mission*; Ron Golan, Eric A. Kahn, and Russell N. Thomsen (Central Office of Architecture), *Miracle Mile Remodel*; Sheila Klein and Norman Millar, *Beverly's Ring*; Heather Kurze, Kathleen A. Lindstrom, and Paige Norris, *Pico & La Brea Hiring Site*; Charles D. Lee and Elizabeth Wang-Lee, *Ribbon Park*; Warren Wagner and William Edward Webb, *Santa Monica Stone Garden*. Newspaper with essay by Barbara Goldstein and statements by the architects.

May 31–June 30: **Video: Disarming Genres** (Micki McGee). Kaucyila Brooke and Jane Cottis, *Dry Kisses Only*, 1990; John Greyson, *The Kipling Trilogy*, 1984–85; Rea Tajiri, *The Hitchcock Trilogy*, 1987; Norman Cowie, *Lying in State*, 1990; Tony Ramos, *About Media*, 1977; Chip Lord, *Not Top Gun*, 1989; Joan Braderman, *Joan Does Dynasty*, 1986. Brochure with essay by Micki McGee.

May 31–June 30: **Project:** *LOOP 2: Cultures Converge*, film installation (A.T.W. [Around the World], an international artists network): François Alacoque, Canada; Mercedes Barros, Brazil; Vinzenz Brinkmann and Jarg M. Geismar, West Germany; Terry Chan, Hong Kong; Jagoda Przybylak and Janusz Bakowski, Poland; Eva Schicker, Switzerland; Kiko Takagi, Japan. Brochure with essay by Micki McGee.

↑ Ming Fay, sculpture.
Selections: Alijira & Artists Space
Sept. 27–Nov. 3, 1990.
Photo: Peter McClennan

1990–91

In 1990–91 a new ongoing series, **Underground,** is added to the exhibition program. **Underground** is devoted to individual installations by artists selected from the Artists File by in-house staff. During this season, Artists Space also reduces the number of exhibition slots from six to five.

Sept. 4–15: **Artists from the Studio in a School.** Jo-Ann Acey, Christine Autumn, Noah Baen, Olivia Beens, Kabuya Bowens, Tim Casey, Kenneth Cole, Lisa Corrine Davis, Anne Dohna, Gwen-Lin Goo, Linda Gottesfeld, Elizabeth Grajales, Valerie Hammond, Beth Hausman, Julia Healy, Elana Herzog, Robin Holder, Shelley Krapes, Mark LaRiviere, Patrice Lorenz, Lynn Margileth, Gail Molnar, Maureen Mullen, Heather Nicol, Cathy Ramey, Stacy Rawlings, Timothy Roeschlein, Daniel Rosenbaum, Ruth Sauer, Skylar Switzer-Kohler, Barbara Valenta, Barbara Verrochi, Neel Webber.

ARTIST

Beverly Semmes My Artists Space show happened very fast, there wasn't a time lag between planning it and doing it, which was amazing. A lot of institutions can't move that quickly. It was refreshing, because I had been working on some pieces for over a year and seeing them in a space other than my studio was very important in terms of doing the next thing. After a day of installing, I thought of my show differently. I could never get a mental grasp on that front room at Artists Space while I was in my studio. So I brought work to the gallery that I didn't show.
I had wanted to make the pink feather coat the centerpiece. But it didn't fit once I got it there. I had thought that front room would be like a set design for a performance I was going to do about sewing the coat. I imagined a path one would take walking into the show. It had a lot to do with defining a place. Later, that sense of place was integrated into the costume pieces. During those years I was using wheat, hay, and straw, and thinking about space in a certain way. I couldn't imagine approaching a commercial gallery with those materials and ideas. The laboratory setting of Artists Space on West Broadway was good. Many artists could move through it. It seemed like such a big space compared to other SoHo galleries. There were endless nooks. And there was a certain charm in being off the beaten track.

The Artists Space brochure became immensely important to me, more than I realized at the time. The fact that people read your (Connie Butler) essay years later made it a significant document of that early moment. It is a nice idea to have a record of the work that lives beyond the exhibition, especially since it was work I took apart at the end of the show. If someone were to write about the work now, they wouldn't think about it in the same way. It's important it was done when it was.

Since the NEA crisis in 1989 which surrounded *Witnesses: Against Our Vanishing,* there's been an undercurrent feeling that artists' spaces are threatened. There is almost a sadness around them because of the change in politics and the constant bombardment from the Right wing, which wants to see art funding demolished. It is always hanging over our heads. I've often felt it was the end for certain spaces. When people get used to looking at artwork in beautiful environments, it becomes harder to look at it in a more funky space. That's got to be a pressure. But sometimes the rawness of alternative spaces can be refreshing after the slickness of commercial ones.

Sept. 27–Nov. 3: **Selections: Aljira & Artists Space** (Carl E. Hazlewood). Group exhibition chosen from the Artists File designed to highlight the recent decision to expand the File's scope to include New Jersey artists: James Andrew Brown, sculpture; Cicely Cottingham, painting; Ming Fay, sculpture; Paul Gardère, assemblage; Renée Green, installation; Zhang Hongtu, painting; Barbara Klein, drawing; Franc Palaia, photo-pieces; John Salvest, assemblage; Rafael Sanchez, photographs and painting; Dui Seid, sculpture. Catalogue with essay by Carl E. Hazlewood.

↓ Renée Green, installation.
Photo: Peter McClennan

ARTIST / CURATOR

Ernest Larsen The idea for *Joint Ventures* came out of my interest in the dynamics of collaboration, how artists work together. Most of the video work was political. There was a problem because the video venue was down in the basement of Artists Space, a relatively wide open space with a big monitor. When it became clear I was going to include some pretty sexually explicit work, I think Susan Wyatt complained. She was a little worried about it. I don't think it came up directly as an issue because I never talked to her directly about it. Nevertheless I was firm about including those tapes. They were one of the most interesting collaborative works done at that time. The problem was worked out by changing the space. When you came down the stairs, what had been an open space immediately to your right was now a six-foot-high wall to protect vagrant eyes from this video. An ambiguous disclaimer was posted stating that some of the work was sexually explicit. This was after the onslaught of NEA protest. It seemed a case of unfortunate self-censorship. I complained but put up with it because it didn't really change anything as far as I was concerned. In the end, it worked out all right. Of course, nobody complained about the tapes. The unfortunate fact with a lot of "catch as catch can" video is the small audience. You'd be lucky to have a complaint in order to get some attention. It's too bad I didn't create a fictional offended person! That's one way for video work to get some media attention. Art discourse, criticism, is not exactly highly developed, but video discourse is pathetic.

Sept. 27–Nov. 3: **Teaching TV** (Chris Bratton). A survey of video projects promoting media literacy.

Program I: Representing School. Students of Cooper Contemporary School, Minneapolis, with Nancy Norwood, *Video Alphabet* and *Cooper Rules: The Box*; students of Film in the Cities, Minneapolis, *The Case of the Disappearing Homework*; students of I.S. 291, New York, with Albert Webber, *The Fight, the Chase, the Agreement, and the Maze*; Jonelle, I.S. 291, New York, with Albert Webber, *Untitled Excerpt*; David McGuirl of Youth Vision, Providence, Rhode Island, *Quiet Desperation*; students of the Creative Learning Community School, New York, with Betsy Newman, *Bloody Mary* and *Mayhem in the Mirror*; students of Alta Loma High School, California, *Images of SADBOYS*; students of Madison High School, Boston, with Branda Miller, *Talkin' bout Droppin' Out*; students of Jefferson High School Humanities Program, Los Angeles, with Gina Lamb, *Textbook Mystery: Oral History*.

Program II: The Forms of Experience: Speaking through Mass Culture. Daniel Gonzalez, I-EYE-I Video Workshop, Henry Street Settlement, New York, with Branda Miller, *The Birth of a Candy Bar*; students at Longfellow School, Portland, Maine, with Huey (James Coleman), *Fun Glasses*; students of the Exploring Media Program at the Bronx Museum of Art, New York, with Alonzo Speight, *Lunchroom Wars*; Scott Potelle, Lawrence High School, Fairfield, Maine, *Insanity Unleashed*; Chris Weiner, Long Prairie High School, Minnesota, *The Second Week of Deer Camp, My Book?* (with David Bengston); Natasha Campbell, the Exploring Media Program at the Bronx Museum of Art, New York, with Alonzo Speight, *Lady C*; Oriela Monteza, Middle College High School, New York, *Rock Talk*; students of the Candace Street Free Arts Program, Providence, Rhode Island, *No Fresh Words*; Chen Rowher, Dearborn High School, Michigan, with Russ Gibb, *Bordersong*; Lula Triggs, VIDKIDCO, Long Beach Museum of Art, California, *Mr. Big + Bad, Parts 1 and 2*; Benjamin Gutierrez, VIDKIDCO, *Street Art, A Reminiscence by Melecio Contreras*; students of King Middle School, Portland, Maine, with Huey (James Coleman), *Spirits and Ghosts, True Stories From Asia*; students of Teen Aid High School, New York, with Joan Jubela, *Flatbush Avenue*.

Program III: The World Television Makes: Critical Work on Media. Excerpts from in-school media programs at the Carver Creative and Performing Arts Center, Montgomery, Alabama; Hope High School, Providence, Rhode Island; and the Boston Film and Video Foundation's Taft Middle School Media Project: students at Hutchinson Park Elementary, Minnetonka, Minnesota, with Lou Ann Dresson and Kay Voight, *Video Tricks*; John Holechek, Apple Valley High School, Minnesota, *TV to the Max*; Daniel Gonzalez, I-EYE-I Video Workshop, Henry Street Settlement, New York, with Branda Miller, *The Birth of a Candy Bar*; students of Through Our Eyes Video and History Project, Bronx Satellite Academy, New York, with Pam Sporn and Paper Tiger TV, *Torn Between Colors*; students of Rise & Shine Productions, New York, with George Sosa, *Media Zone*; students of Through Our Eyes Video and History Project, Bronx Satellite Academy, New York, with Pam Sporn, *The Road to Mississippi: Reclaiming Our History*; Southwest Alternate Media Project, Houston, *Video Adventures*; Mark McCullough, Old Orchard Beach High School, Maine, *Static*.

Program IV: Other Schools: Student Producers in the Community. Students at the Educational Video Center, New York, *2371 Second Avenue, An East Harlem Story*; Nema Brewer of Appalshop, Whitesburg, Kentucky, *Mountain Haint Tales*; students of Rise & Shine Productions, New York, with Cyrille Phipps and Dorrie Brooks, *Whose Park Is This?*; students at Roxbury Boys and Girls Club, Massachusetts, *Stop the Violence*; students of the JFK Library Corps, Boston, *Homelessness and Us*; students at the Educational Video Center, New York, *Trash Thy Neighbor*; students at the Thomas Jefferson High School Humanities Program, Los Angeles, *Just Say No…Narcotics Barricade*; students at the Bilquist School and The Northwest Film and Video Center, Portland, Oregon, *Outward Bound*.

Sept. 27–Nov. 3: **Project**:
Joel Katz, *History Lessons*,
video installation (Micki
McGee). Brochure with
essay by Micki McGee.

→

Sept. 27–Nov. 3:
Underground:
Paul Ramirez-Jones,
AMANAPLANACANALPANAMA,
sculpture installation.
Selected by Connie Butler.

↓ Detail

Nov. 9: **Panel discussion.** In
conjunction with **Teaching
TV,** selected screenings
and presentations by video
students and teachers.
Panelists include Steve
Goodman, Gina Lamb,
Branda Miller, Alonzo
Speight, and Pam Sporn.

Nov. 10: Premiere of *The
Bus Stops Here*, video by
Julie Zando and Jo Anstey,
and screening of selected
works from **Body
Language: Studies in
Female Expression.**
Brochure with essay by
Julie Zando.

Nov. 15–Jan. 5: **Post–Boys & Girls: Nine Painters** (Ken
Aptekar). Group exhibition exploring gender issues in
painting: Ken Aptekar, Greg Davidek, Nancy Davidson,
Greg Drasler, Lee Gordon, Margo Machida, Holly Morse,
Lillian Mulero, Millie Wilson. Catalogue with introduction
by Ken Aptekar and essays by Carol Zemel, Michael
Kimmel, Renée Green, and James Saslow.

Nov. 15–Jan. 5: **Video: Body Language: Studies in Female Expression** (Julie Zando).
Videos by women artists: Julie Zando and Jo Anstey, *The Bus Stops Here*, 1990; Joelle de
la Casiniere, *La Grimoire Magnetique*, 1983; Mindy Faber, *Identity Crisis*, 1989; Ilse
Gassinger and Anna Steininger, *Die Evidenz Des Kalkuels*, 1987; Ilse Gassinger, *Exposed*,
1989; Gwendolyn, *Prowling by Night*, 1990; Barbara Lattanzi, *Soma*, 1989; Mara
Mattaschka, *Kugelkopf*, 1985; Azian Nurudin, *The Headhunters of Borneo—A Recollection*,
1989; Sherry Kromer Shapiro, *Am I My Mother's Keeper?*, 1989; Shelly Silver, *We*, 1990;
Leslie Singer, *Laurie Sings Iggy*, 1987. Brochure with essay by Julie Zando.

Nov. 15 – Jan. 5: **Project**: Robert Gero, *(Energeia)*, sculpture (Buzz Spector). Brochure with essay by Buzz Spector.

Nov. 15 – Jan. 5: **Underground**: Gail Rothschild, installation.

Dec. 1: **A Day Without Art** (Connie Butler and Micki McGee). Artists Space closes its regular exhibitions to present a one-day video program and installation investigating the body and body politic in relation to medical, ethical, and social conditions of AIDS treatment. Installation by Hillary Leone; video artists include Carl Michael George, Gwendolyn, Marlon Riggs, and Ellen Spiro.

ARTIST

Renée Green I was in a group exhibition in 1990 organized by Willie Cole at Aljira in Newark, New Jersey. However, my connection with Artists Space goes back to Hudson Street when I visited it as a student and had my slides in the Artists File. But writing the essays for the *Post – Boys & Girls* show that Ken Aptekar organized was the first contribution I made there. The first essay I wrote was fairly long and historical. I tried to trace various relationships to feminism and think critically about various forms of production. I wrote about *The Difference Show* that was at the New Museum in 1984. I wanted to give a historical reference to the choices people make in terms of media. For example, how painting was questioned for a long time and how various people had explored sexual difference. I wrote about this in relation to the paintings in the show and asked, "Why painting?" I made a reference to the 1936 essay by Walter Benjamin, "The Work of Art In the Age Of Mechanical Reproduction," on which my title was based. I didn't want to write specifically on the work of each artist, but to raise questions about different theoretical approaches to painting and other ideas.

Ken asked me if I could write something more personal, but I was having a lot of problems with that as a mode. The question of where I located my subjectivity was being asked of me a lot at the time. I ended up writing a first-person narrative, but kept wanting to make it into a story about a persona. I suppose you could say it was me, although whatever that means is still ambiguous. Originally I was invited because Ken wanted to include me as a painter, but I was moving away from painting as a designation. My work didn't really fit into the category. So a strange mixture of things happened. This was the year after the NEA controversy, so it was appropriate that Ken should do a show about gender and raise these questions.

A few years before, Dia had had a series of discussions on contemporary culture. I wrote an essay which opened with a conversation I had there with a painter about being able to continue working. In what way, what form, what audience? All these different questions came up and all these painters were wondering what to do. This show had references to sex in the family and other things that pushed the prohibitions raised in the NEA debates. But I remember the reception to that show was weird. There was a negative response in the *New York Times,* which is not necessarily surprising. I felt ambivalent about it and that came through in the essay. But as a show it came off. It looked good and what was attempted was interesting.

My contact with Artists Space began when I was a student at SVA (the School of Visual Arts). That was also my first contact with P.S. 1, Franklin Furnace, and Printed Matter. Around 1980, the venues for interesting critical work and activities involving experimentation seemed limited. Younger people seemed to gravitate to these spaces as well as to clubs such as Hurrah's or CBGB's. At that time there was a big division between commercial galleries CONTINUED

Jan. 17 – Mar. 2: **Reframing the Family** (Connie Butler and Micki McGee). Group exhibition exploring the mythology of the American family. Esther Bubley, photography; Deborah Coito, photography; Daniel Canogar, assemblage; Lou Draper, photography; Hanh Thi Pham, photography; Richard Hill, photography; Doug Ischar, installation; Zoya Kocur, photography; Vince Leo, installation; Kathleen MacQueen, installation; Celia Alvarez Munoz, installation; Allan Sekula, photography; Linn Underhill, photography; Carrie Mae Weems, photography. Catalogue with essays by Connie Butler, Micki McGee, and Barbara Ehrenreich.

→ Installation view.
Photo: Peter McClennan

Jan. 17 – Mar. 2: **Video** in conjunction with **Reframing the Family** (Micki McGee). Beth B and Ida Applebroog, *Belladonna*, 1989; Cara DeVito, *Always Love Your Man*, 1975; Richard Fung, *The Way to My Father's Village*, 1988; Vanalyne Green, *A Spy in the House That Ruth Built*, 1989; Mako Idemitsu, *Yoji, What's Wrong With You?*, 1987; Jan Mathew, *Let's Not Pretend*, 1990; Cara Mertes, *The Natural Order*, 1991; Sherry Millner, *Scenes from the Micro-War*, 1985; Martha Rosler, *Born to be Sold: Martha Rosler Reads the Strange Case of Baby $M*, 1988; Mary Ellen Strom, *Shut Up and Listen,* 1990.

Jan. 17 – Mar. 2: **Project**: Kathe Burkhart and Chrysanne Stathacos, *Abortion Project*, installation (Connie Butler). The project mirrors Simone de Beauvoir's *Manifeste* in which signatures were gathered of women who had abortions. Exhibition travels to Real Art Ways, Hartford, Connecticut, Oct. 11 – Nov. 9, 1991; Hallwalls, Buffalo, New York; New Langton Arts, San Francisco, California.

Feb. 1 and 8: **Film: Reframing the Family** (Cara Mertes and Micki McGee). Two evenings of screenings at Anthology Film Archives, New York.
Feb. 1: Jane Campion, *Peel,* 1991; Billy Woodberry, *Bless Their Little Hearts,* 1984.
Feb. 8: Mary Hestand, *He Was Once,* 1989; Peggy Ahwesh, *From Romance to Ritual,* 1986; Camille Billops and James Hatch, *Suzanne, Suzanne,* 1982; Martin Arnold, *Piece Touchee*, 1990.

Feb. 15 and 22: **Readings: Reframing the Family** (Deborah Artman). Two evenings of fiction and narrative readings. Dorothy Barnhouse, Laurie Carlos, Tim Connor, Jessica Hagedorn, Howard Kaplan, Karen Latuchie, Robbie McCauley, Laura Miller, Letty Cottin Pogrebin, Mark Richard, and John Weir.

Jan. 17 – Mar. 2: **Underground**: François Morelli, *The Body Politic*, installation.

RENÉE GREEN / CONTINUED

and alternative spaces. As a young artist, it seemed more likely you would be able to start with Artists Space. It developed a reputation for being a place to find whatever was next. But it was also a social space. That's how I recall it anyway. There were discussions, events, and meetings that I'd go to. In retrospect it was a strange time. There were different trends in the early 80s, pattern painting and neo-expressionism among them. At least at Artists Space you could see divergent styles.

It was important for me to follow the work that came out of the *Pictures* exhibition. I had heard about the artists who were in the show from a teacher's assistant at SVA. I was trying to keep up, so I went to check it out, not completely comprehending what exactly was going on. I also remember being with a bunch of people standing around watching the Berlin Wall come down on TV at Artists Space. I always just stopped by, looked in, and talked to people. It was a gathering place. During the 80s, the commercial scene was alienating. I associate Artists Space with getting out of school, Reagan coming into office, voting for the first time, and going to events more on the fringes. Gradually Artists Space changed and became more institutionalized. I first showed in 1981 at The Drawing Center. It, too, has changed considerably.

What sustained me during the 80s was alternative venues. I also spent a lot of time at clubs, at CBGB's, and saw performances at 8 B.C. and Neither/Nor, which had bizarre performances that sometimes filtered into an Artists Space area. Hierarchically, that would be the next rung, the more publicized venue. Commercial galleries with fringe scene connections started to organize these events, too. The appeal of working with Pat Hearn was her knowledge of these events and performances. It happened gradually, but there was a moment when the alternative spaces and going to hardcore gigs didn't seem to have the same importance they once did. It was a combination of things — the NEA situation, changes in the way people were working, and the acceptance of younger, more experimental gallerists by the art establishment. There wasn't the same community of people — it was another generation working in funky gallery situations with international connections. There was a search for other markets and audiences that exploded beyond the alternative space situation. That is absolutely what happened in my case, because the next year I started to work with people in other countries. And that came out of having shown at the Clocktower and P.S. 1 in 1990 and then later in some commercial galleries, including the Pat Hearn Gallery.

Mar. 10: **Remapping Boundaries: Video Art and Popular Culture** (Liz Kotz). Evening screening of selected works from the video program with personal appearances by the artists at the Collective for Living Cinema, New York: Dale Hoyt, *The Complete Anne Frank*, 1986; Robert and Donald Kinney, *Stephen*, 1991; Abigail Child, *Swamp*, 1991.

Mar. 14–May 4: **Remapping Boundaries: Video Art and Popular Culture** (Liz Kotz). Video program: Cecilia Dougherty, *Grapefruit*, 1989; Robert and Donald Kinney, *Stephen*, 1991; Azian Nurudin, *What Do Pop Art, Pop Music, Pornography and Politics Have to Do With Real Life?*, 1990; Leslie Singer, *Hot Rox*, 1988; Abigail Child, *Swamp*, 1991; Dale Hoyt, *The Complete Anne Frank*, 1986. Brochure with essay by Liz Kotz.

Mar. 14–May 4: **Western Agenda** (Connie Butler). Group exhibition of large-scale sculpture installations: Deborah Garwood, Ava Gerber, Page Houser, Rita McBride, John Monti, David Schafer. Catalogue with essay by Connie Butler and statements by the artists.

← Installation view. (L) Rita McBride and (R) Ava Gerber.

Mar. 14–May 4: **Underground**: William White, *Boxes*, sculptural installation.

Mar. 14–May 4: **Project**: Jim Rittimann, *Reconstructions*, assemblages (Chris Bruce). Catalogue with essay by Chris Bruce.

ARTIST / BOARD

Cindy Sherman I feel a definite allegiance to Artists Space. They wanted more artists on the Board, and I was gung ho for that. I don't like the idea of going to a lot of meetings and being on committees. I would love to be that kind of Board member who doesn't go, but I would feel too guilty brushing off Artists Space—just being a name on a list. I wish other artists like Dave Salle were more involved. It pisses me off that people like him reach a level of success and then don't contribute, don't put back. Some people probably think Artists Space had its day and it's not relevant anymore. They could be right. I don't know. But it seems the pendulum is swinging back and now is a really ripe time for places like Artists Space, despite the fact funding isn't as easy to get as it was when I was a Board member 10 years ago. Since Claudia Gould's been involved the Board meetings are a lot less torturous than they used to be. In the past, listening to people talk about numbers for the budget, I would sit there and pray I wouldn't fall asleep or pretend to read something just to keep my mind active. It's not so much more interesting or fascinating now, maybe it's just my being a little older, relating to the crises of having to raise money, that makes meetings seem a bit more engaging. The easiest thing for me to do for Artists Space is to be generous with my work, which is the easiest thing for any artist to do. I'm more impressed with people like Carolyn Alexander, who are able to lead Board members and steer us out of problems. She's more of an important figure for the Board. She and Virginia Cowles hold it together. My role as an artist Board member is different. But I don't see it as having more of an impact because I've given more. I would feel too guilty to say, "Well, yeah, I've had enough now, I'm going to leave."

...it seems the pendulum is swinging back and now is a really ripe time for places like Artists Space, despite the fact funding isn't as easy to get as it was when I was a Board member 10 years ago.

May 10–11: **Coming Attractions: Documentary and Narrative Films in Progress** (Barry Ellsworth). Third annual presentation of works-in-progress, with appearances by the artists.
May 10: Irene Sosa, *Woman as Protagonist: The Art of Nancy Spero*; Sabine Krayenbuhl, *The Twins*; Camila Motta, *Sylvia: Story of a Kidnapping*; Yvette Pineyro, *Chico O'Farrill*.
May 11: Kelvin Zachary Phillip, *Love In Brief*; Laura Larson, *Dodge City*; Mary Anne Toman, *The Female Offender*; Tom Kalin, *Swoon*.

May 16–June 29: **Art's Mouth** (Connie Butler). Chelo Amezcua, drawing; Prophet William J. Blackmon, painting; Freddie Brice, painting; Ray Hamilton, drawing; Bessie Harvey, dolls; Asterios Matakos, assemblage; Phillip Travers, drawing. Exhibition sponsored by the Mark Rothko Foundation. Catalogue with introduction by Gregory Amenoff, essay by Connie Butler, and statements by the artists.

→ Kathe Burkhart and Chrysanne Stathacos, *Abortion Project*, installation view. **Project**, Jan. 17– Mar. 2 1991.
Photo: Peter McClennan

ARTIST

Chrysanne Stathacos The *Abortion Project* came out of a discussion I had with Kathe Burkhart, a painter and conceptual feminist artist. We talked about how men were joining forces with AIDS issues and getting attention. But women's issues, especially abortion and general feminist art issues, were nonexistent. At that time, abortion rights were under attack. We decided to do a project together, which was the beginning of our friendship.

It was pre WAC (Women's Action Coalition), pre the *Bad Girls* show at the New Museum (Part I, January 14–February 27, 1994; Part II, March 5–April 10, 1994), by many years. There were no women's shows anywhere. We were in a void. As we worked together the project evolved into a wall installation of collected signatures, which Kathe instigated. It became a doubling of memory, of looking back at the start, *Manifesto 343,* where women were strong and public about their rights to their bodies. Women's rights and feminism are very closely aligned to being an artist. As an independent woman artist, you are working from a feminist basis. Sometimes, very successful women artists deny their feminism because they are scared of the word. Feminism is not a dirty word. I'm proud to say I'm a feminist, and Kathe would say the same thing. The whole issue is that at the end of the 80s there was nothing around. The only political shows you saw dealt with AIDS and male bonding.

It began at Artists Space, and the group show was at Simon Watson's gallery. That's an important connection, because that show was one of the first all-women shows. It had Sue Williams, Nan Goldin, everybody. Unfortunately, at Artists Space we opened the night the Gulf War started. It cast a shadow in a weird way. When the *Abortion Project* opened for the second time at Real Art Ways in Hartford, Connecticut, there was the Anita Hill case. The third time, we had protesters at Hallwalls in Buffalo. At New Langton Arts, there was an S&M parade in San Francisco, but that's a little different.

The *Abortion Project* is a conceptual public arts project. It was loud and about the community. The signing and naming became very important and inspired other similar projects. We collected signatures in snow storms and effectively reached past the art community. It was on TV in Buffalo. People would discuss their experiences. This project could not have happened within the traditional gallery system at that time because women artists were not being seen. Things are better now, but the prejudices still exist. Everyone thinks they don't, but they do if you look at the number of male artists versus female artists, whether it's at biennials or any other big show, in galleries, or auctions. It's better but it's not equal.

ARTIST

Rita McBride The impetus for *General Growth* came from ideas I have about the parasitic relationship between architecture and art and the elements that define architecture like walls, pillars, floors, and sculpture. This piece was in reaction to Michael Asher's work, which I have mythologized. On Artists Space's walls Asher attached additional wall space. The walls of sheetrock originally went up to 10 feet, leaving 4 feet of unarticulated space above, where it was impossible to show work. Asher's idea was that these walls were more sculptural than architectural. I like the fact that the shape of my piece, *General Growth*, was determined by the amount of drywall footage Asher added. It was a fairly large but simple piece of drywall and wood construction in an oval shape that attached itself by the use of black leather weight-lifting belts that strapped around the column. It added more wall space, but not where art could inhabit, so it was dysfunctional in terms of architecture for art. You could look through to the interior structure, which was somehow important to me. It was shockingly big, but it often seemed to disappear when it appeared to look like a wall. During the opening, people put their coats next to it and their drinking cups along the edge. This pleased me because then it didn't inhabit that space of monumental sculpture—it was somewhere in between. CONTINUED

May 16–June 29: **Video Witnesses: Festival of New Journalism** (Barbara Lattanzi). Selections from the first annual festival originating at Hallwalls, Buffalo, and part of The Touring Video Exhibition Program, Video Data Bank. Chittenden Community TV, *MAC-V*, 1985/87, *The Housing Show*, 1987; Jim Hartel, *Flag Burning Ceremony*, 1990; Lisa Rudman, *American Junk*, 1990; Colin Jessop and José Martinez, *The Underground Voices of the Panamanian People*, 1990; Riad Bahhur and Tom Hayes, *The Killing of a Palestinian*, 1988; Charles Steiner, *Nothing to Lose: A Polish Odyssey*, 1989; Gina Latinovich, *Dead from the Effects*, 1987; Black Cat Collective, *Many Faces of Paper*, 1989; Ira Manhoff, *Showdown in Atlanta*, 1989; Tony Cokes, *Black Celebration*, 1988. Catalogue with essay by Barbara Lattanzi.

May 23: **Video Witnesses: Festival of New Journalism** (Chris Hill). Selections from the second annual festival, originating at Hallwalls, Buffalo: Nell Lundy, *No Rights Implied*, 1990; Carol Leigh, *Die Yuppie Scum*, 1989; California Prostitutes Project, *CALPEP*; 1990; Buffalo Artists Against Repression and Censorship, *Disorderly Conduct*, 1990; Media Against Censorship, *Mac Attack!!* (work-in-progress), 1990; Art Jones, *Know Your Enemy*, 1990. Presentation by Chris Hill.

May 16–June 29: **Project:** Deborah Small, *Our Bodice, Our Selves*, installation (Madeleine Grynsztejn). Brochure with essay by Madeleine Grynsztejn.

May 16–June 29: **Underground:** Vivian Selbo, *Uncontaining*, installation.

← Installation view

Artists Space was one of the few public forums where work was viewed in an unstructured way. It was my dream to show in these places where artists go before they show in galleries and became defined by an attitude and atmosphere.

RITA MCBRIDE / CONTINUED

Artists Space was one of the few public forums where work was viewed in an unstructured way. It was my dream to show in these places where artists go before they show in galleries and become defined by an attitude and atmosphere. That's the beauty of a place for exploration and where fantasy projects are realized. But budget problems make them a strange support without support. However, conflict and contradiction informs work: You're allowed to dream as largely and as strangely as possible, but the realization constantly comes up short. That's a valuable lesson for artists, curators, and institutions.

Alternative spaces are incredible and need a lot more support than they're getting. I'd like to see them go back to their original freshness. There should be a rapid turnover, with the whole staff and Board changing every two years. If the same people stay for too long they get burned out and it becomes very incestuous, very nepotistic. The staleness with which LACE was operating meant it could never realize its function. It's okay once in a while to choose an older, underexposed artist, but that should be the rare case. In addition, paying artists is so important, even if it's a token. There's supposed to be a collaborative aspect to these spaces. It's the best part about them, where new specific projects are realized with the help of the staff, funding, and the space. But it's ridiculous when everyone is getting paid except the artist. I believe these spaces should exist and become really strong. They serve a very important function. They're accessible and they give young artists their first shows. That's what these places do. The actual physical space isn't that important, it could be anywhere. It's more about the idea of a nonprofit place, which is pro-artists — a haven for artists.

I was affected by the NEA controversy at Artists Space, specifically with my show. A lot of energy was transferred from support and exhibitions to a highly politicized debate. That was too big a task. It wasn't wrong for Artists Space to get political, but it didn't have the resources to function both ways. Compromises were the result. Susan Wyatt was very passionate about NEA censorship and cared very little about us small little artists there. Obviously, she felt her funding was going to be in jeopardy, but it shouldn't be in Artists Space's charter to take the lead in those areas. They have to concentrate on artists' production, even more so now that art-making is rapidly lessening. Would it have been a stronger move if Susan had concentrated on producing an incredible exhibition program instead of fighting it out in the political arena? I don't know. Showing great work is ultimately what these places are for. There are tons of mistakes, pain, and anguish over work. But there are so many lessons to be learned. When I started my career, everybody looked at the alternative spaces. I'm sad to report that's not the case anymore. Somehow, Artists Space feels like it's run by an old bunch of people, even though it's changed. It isn't the word on the street that it was before. There were so many bad shows in a row — it happens to everyone. But instead of correctly supporting those shows, they tried to do infrastructure work. There was so much infrastructure damage that it became the focus and, of course, the shows suffered.

1991–92

In July 1991, Susan Wyatt resigns and Celeste Dado takes over as the Acting Executive Director. In November 1991, the Board hires Carlos Gutierrez-Solana to become the new Executive Director. Connie Butler resigns as Curator and Micki McGee resigns as Film/Video Curator in February 1992. Charles Wright is hired as Curator/Program Coordinator. In addition, **The Underground** and **Project** series are discontinued. Instead, Gutierrez-Solana implements changes to diversify programming, reflecting a vision of Artists Space as a community-based arts center. For instance, the **AIDS FORUM** is initiated as an ongoing program dealing with issues on AIDS, where artists are invited to display their work on a first-come, first-show basis for three-week intervals.

Sept. 3–14: Artists from the Studio in a School. Jo-Ann Acey, Ed Askew, Susan Austad, Kimberly Bush, Nancy Coates, Noel Copeland, Louise Fischer Cozzi, Lisa Corinne Davis, Anne Dohna, Elise Engler, Camilla Fallon, Gwen-Lin Goo, Linda Gottesfeld, Tony Gray, Valerie Hammond, Julia Healy, Elana Herzog, Lisa Jacobson, Willie Kasuli, Maria Katzman, Mark LaRiviere, Marcia Lyons, Lynn Margileth, Diane Matyas, Maureen Mullen, Heather Nicol, Beverly O'Mara, Antonia Perez, Christopher Priore, Cathy Ramey, Timothy Roeschlein, Daniel Rosenbaum, Susan Hong Sammons, Hilda Shen, Rochelle Shicoff, Barbara Spiller, Patricia Sullivan, Barbara Valenta, Barbara Verrochi, Cleve Webber, Neel Webber, and Steve White.

Sept. 26–Nov. 9: Warp and Woof: Comfort and Dissent (Connie Butler). Exhibition of mixed media works and installations by emerging artists addressing sexual politics, worship, and war. Janine Antoni, Xenobia Bailey, John Bermudes, Natalie Bookchin, Simon Grennan & Christopher Sperandio, Sowon Kwon, Kim Lee Kahn, Dinh Le, Jason Reed, Caroline Stikker, and Andrea Zittel. Catalogue with essay by Connie Butler.

↗ Andrea Zittel, mixed media installation.
  Photo: Peter McClennan

↓ Janine Antoni, *Viewer's Red*, (detail).
  © Janine Antoni

ARTIST

Janine Antoni I first heard about Artists Space from Tom Lawson, who was my teacher at RISD (Rhode Island School of Design). He told us about showing there with Cindy Sherman, Robert Longo, and Ron Jones, and how Metro Pictures later came to be.

When I left school I knew that I could send slides to nonprofits and people would actually look at them as opposed to commercial galleries. Looking back on my arrival in New York City, I realize how important relationships are. Several of us moved from RISD together. We shared studios, got each other jobs and shows. We helped each other make art and think about it. Having a community has been esssential to my creative process. Paul Ramirez-Jones was the first one of us to get a show at Artists Space. Later Andrea Zittel and I exhibited our work in a group show there.

When Connie Butler approached me, I was working with makeup and was very excited to do this new piece. I made maybe a hundred lipsticks by hand. I mixed the colors and assigned each lipstick to an everyday activity. Every time I did that activity I changed the color of my lipstick. So I carried a cosmetic case around with me, which had one lipstick for making art, one for eating breakfast, and a lipstick for when I menstruated. It became a diary of my life. Looking at all the little palettes I made, you could understand something of my life; for instance, you would know that I saw a particular person a lot if a certain color lipstick was almost used up. You could basically measure my life through lipstick.

I was also researching names of lipsticks in cosmetic stores. I got interested in how you could really tell something about our culture by looking at lipstick. There were crazy names like Network Burgundy, Million Dollar Red, and Sassy Pink. Then I tried to personalize the lipstick by applying it to my own life. I also exhibited this little cigar box with lipstick for the future. They are wish-fulfillment lipsticks—lipsticks to wear when I have a baby or if I get into the Whitney Biennial, or whatever.

I made this trench coat called *Undercover* to carry these lipsticks around with me. When you opened it up like a flasher's coat, it was lined with lipsticks. Then I manufactured a lipstick especially for Artists Space which was bright red—called *Viewers Red*—for people to wear for viewing art. I made a little cosmetics display with a mirror at the front desk, where the lipstick was sold for $20. People wore it during and after the show or whenever they wanted to look at art.

I made maybe a hundred lipsticks by hand. I mixed the colors and assigned each lipstick to an everyday activity.

Sept. 26–Nov. 9: **Film and Video: Urban Space/The City as Place** (Molly Hankwitz). Exhibition addressing urban renewal, gentrification, and housing issues: C-Hundred Film Corporation; public service announcements; Jem Cohen, *This is a History of New York (The Golden Dark Age of Reason)*, 1988; RENEW (Peter Gillespie, Hank Lindhardt, Jon Rubin), 1991, excerpt; Nancy Salzer & Pablo Frasconi, *The Survival of a Small City*, 1987; Christine Noschese, *Metropolitan Avenue*, 1985; Michael Penland, *American Dreaming*, 1990; Jason Simon, *The March of Time*, 1985; Marcia Wilson, *The Squatter Blues*, 1990. Brochure with essay by Molly Hankwitz.

Sept. 26–Nov. 9: **Project**: Lewis deSoto, *The Language of Paradise*, multimedia installation (Lawrence Rinder). Based on the cosmology of the artist's patrilineal ancestors, the Cahuilla People. Brochure with essay by Lawrence Rinder.

CURATOR

Connie Butler I was surprised Artists Space was interested in somebody who had been working in the Midwest rather than in New York. But I think that was one of the reasons I was hired: I was from the outside, without connections and preconceived ideas about the community. It was an exciting time to be at Artists Space, because the exhibition budget was as big as it had ever been. It was at the height of its financial growth, but it was also at the height of its institutionalization.

My first show was a *Selections* exhibition, which enabled me to make a million studio visits right away and get to know the city really well. I responded to some of the more quirky work I was seeing, and a couple of those artists continue to be interesting.

I also enjoyed the *Project* series. It was important because some very interesting artists came through that series as they had before my time at Artists Space. But the more significant shows were the curatorial collaborations I did with Micki McGee, the media Curator, in which many different media were involved. For example, *Reframing the Family* was probably the best and most important show. The idea was to select an initial group of artists, who in turn selected artists they had influenced or who had influenced them regarding issues of family. There was a generational metaphor built into the show, which I liked very much. The curatorial process was controlled, yet open at the same time. It was also successful, because we programmed a series of fiction readings and film and video screenings that built into the curatorial process. Personally, that was the moment I began to question what it meant to do curatorial work and how one could investigate different strategies of organizing an exhibition.

Reframing the Family was organized during the Gulf War and had far-reaching cultural ramifications in terms of defining the American family. In addition, it had a big influence on shows that came after it. Like the photography show, *Terrors and Pleasures of Domestic Comfort*, at MOMA (September 26–December 31, 1991). It was a footnote for a lot of exhibitions which then explored those themes. Those issues were in the air, but I always thought of Artists Space as a place where those kinds of ideas land first, are experimented with first. Not that we always had to be the first ones, but it was often the case. And often they were tried in the toughest way at Artists Space, which made me feel proud. When that happened we were being successful, we had a finger on the pulse of what artists were thinking about and the issues they were looking at.

One of the best, most meaningful series at Artists Space was *Dark Rooms,* which you (Valerie Smith) started, because it highlighted this work that still has so little platform. Now media installations are more prominent. Those were definitely projects that wouldn't have happened anywhere else. The 1992 show *Working* was really an extension of *Dark Rooms*, we just called it something else, because we thought *Dark Rooms* started to ghettoize the work a little. It was

basically media installations about labor.

By the time I was at Artists Space, there seemed to be less overt pressure to present different curatorial points of view than there may have been earlier. Although we did get direct feedback from NYSCA to include more artists of color on the Board or in the shows. It just made my job a bit more labor intensive. I needed to do more looking to incorporate into my vision different kinds of cultural approaches to making work, of which I had no previous knowledge. I felt a responsibility to educate myself more, which I hadn't before I came to Artists Space. It was the first time I was in that position, and now I see this as just part of what I had to do as a curator. It was great training.

I was already involved in questioning authorial/curatorial voices and practices anyway, so when Carlos (Gutierrez-Solana) came in filled with rhetoric about how we shouldn't have a single vision and we shouldn't have curators, I fell for it. Prior to his arrival we actually worked very hard not to make it about one voice in any way. But in the end, he wanted to get rid of us so *he* could be the one with the single vision. Essentially he wanted to eliminate our jobs. He didn't want to have curators anymore. It was his philosophy. In no uncertain terms he told us we had to rethink how we would operate there—become his slave or leave— because our jobs were going to be radically changed from what they had been. We talked a lot back and forth and, to his credit, he tried to allow us to have a place there afterwards. He didn't fire us, but made it impossible for us to find any room. Micki left first. I tried to hang in there, but it became absolutely unworkable, because Carlos wanted to have the final say on everything. His vision for what the place should be was very different. He wanted to focus on AIDS-related work, a lot of performance, almost to the exclusion of everything else. That's fair. I also thought Artists Space was ripe for a change. In a way it had to go over a cliff, but it's just too bad it was at the expense of the entire staff. It didn't become financial until later, after we left. I would have loved to stay. It was the best job I ever had and maybe will ever have. It was fantastic. The ability to respond to work so quickly. God, you could see something and within eight weeks you could do something about it if you wanted. And the amount of work you could deal with, too, because of the mandate of not doing solo shows. You don't have this anywhere else.

CONTINUED

Sept. 26–Nov. 9:
Underground: José Gabriel Fernandez, untitled installation.

Nov. 21–Jan. 11: **Working** (Connie Butler and Micki McGee). Exhibition of media installations investigating the vicissitudes of power and projections: Deborah Bright with Nancy Gonchar, *Lost Histories/Chicago Stories,* 1990; Gavin Flint, *Gaijin/Stripper,* 1990–91; Carol Jacobsen, *Night Voices,* 1990–91; Stashu Kybartas, *King Anthracite,* 1990–91; Sherry Millner, *Protective Coloration,* 1991; Leslie Sharpe, *Double Trouble, The Sequel,* 1991. Brochure with statements by the artists.

→ Stashu Kybartas, *King Anthracite.*

Nov. 21–Jan. 11:
Underground: Joan Giroux and Eric Heist, untitled installation.

CONNIE BUTLER / CONTINUED

Artists Space got me into this good Protestant habit of constantly looking at work. I felt it was my duty to go out there. I still think it's very important. I had come from institutions where the solo retrospective was de rigueur. So when I arrived at Artists Space, I was terrified by the idea of doing all these group shows and having to dream up these themes every six weeks. Now, I'm no longer scared. It freed me up and I'm able to think in more broad, cultural terms, like an editor. That's been very helpful and has made for more interesting work.

Obviously there have been moments when Artists Space almost closed, and people have said, "Maybe it should close and reopen." It's an interesting moment for places like Artists Space because they are forced to redefine themselves, due to the work museums and galleries are doing. I think they're totally essential. I notice it here in Los Angeles, where there's a huge lack of places that will show work ahead of when it will be seen anywhere else. It's not so much an alternative to the market in market terms anymore. It's not simply about showing more controversial work or work not supported by galleries. Rather it's about making room for a more intellectually engaging atmosphere, where people can take their time, establish a dialogue between the work, between artists, which only happens with a freedom that doesn't exist in bigger institutions. I began to feel Artists Space was a way to work in New York without all the pressures that exist in other institutions, like galleries or museums, which are totally dead in the water. It's parallel to the mainstream, but outside of it.

I was at Artists Space from spring of '89 to spring of '92. Shortly after I arrived the *Witnesses* exhibition exploded. It was the first time I had ever been politically engaged on any level. It changed me and the way I look at work forever. It was an amazing moment in the art community, because of how the community galvanized around Artists Space, both for and against. I had never been through so much media attention. The exhibition went from 15 visitors a day to 50 an hour. It was just incredible to feel the pressure from the media and see how artists' work got taken out of context and distorted. To try to defend against that was very interesting. David Wojnarowicz's writing and images were taken out of context by Jesse Helms or somebody, who distributed on the floor of the Senate xeroxes of parts of his images. We felt so helpless in the face of that. We wanted to defend David, to articulate his work in the best way possible, but felt really attacked by the Right and the people who were on the opposing side. We tried to be clear and make the correct decision at a moment when there was so much pressure on the organization. In some cases I don't think we did make the right decisions. Whatever decisions we made changed the organization forever in many ways.

Tremendous damage was caused by the attacks of the far Right on the arts. It produced a truly insidious long-term effect in the broadest terms. Nobody ever talks about what happens to institutions that go through moments like the *Witnesses* incident. On the one hand, Artists Space needed to go through some change. The staff talked in Board meetings and internally about what we were and should be doing. Should we be educating more, reaching out more, and trying to engage this huge audience we had found? On the other hand, the pressure caused a paranoia within the organization, everybody looked for a fall guy. How could we fix it? And they fixated on

Susan (Wyatt), because she had been the public standard bearer throughout *Witnesses*. She may have made some wrong decisions, but she did an amazing job as public spokesperson. She really rose to the occasion and grew a lot with the experience. It took her interests in a different direction, to Washington, D.C., and advocacy work, and it did take her away from Artists Space to some extent. But nobody cut her any slack, including the staff. Nobody could figure out a way to let her do advocacy work and be the Director.

Susan made the wrong decision when she called the NEA, ostensibly to warn them about the catalogue and she offered them the option of putting the money on the show instead of the catalogue. She believed she called so they wouldn't be broadsided. But some part of her also called them to see what would happen, to turn it into a test case. That was the part of Susan who was waking up and interested in advocacy and wanting to be a rabble rouser. Then the NEA withdrew the grant. I remember when Celeste Dado, Susan, and I were standing in Celeste's office desperately trying to figure out what to do. There were 85,000 press people on the phone. The artists, including Nan (Goldin), were hysterical. Once everything started to snowball, we made our decisions as clearly as possible. At the time, in separating the catalogue from government funding, we thought we were protecting the catalogue, so it could still exist as part of the show. It seemed as if this was a way to preserve everything but Nan chose to see it as censorship. I'm not sure. I like Nan a lot, but she was very difficult and unfair. Susan was concerned about David's text in the catalogue but from the start she decided to publish it as David wanted it. They phoned each other back and forth. She learned from him, grew to respect him and his integrity. Their conversations made a huge impression on her. I was acting as the middle person through a lot of this because David would just lose it on the phone with me about something Susan had said. So I heard a lot of it. She was fanning the fire a little bit. We all felt that had she not brought the text or the show to the NEA's attention they wouldn't have reacted. But she really believed she did it for this other reason. In the end she tried to go with David and be as supportive as she could. David had a profound impact on her life, and on all of us.

Nov. 21–Jan. 11: AIDS FORUM: Frank Moore and Marc Happel, *Honor Their Dignity*, mixed media installation.

Nov. 30: Media event: Robert Farber, *Every Ten Minutes*, audio installation.

↓ © Harvey Weiss

Jan. 16–18: New Year, New Work (Micki McGee). Three nights of new films and videotapes:
Jan. 16: Jeanne C. Finley, *Involuntary Conversion*; Les LeVeque & Diane Nerwen, *Light Sweet Crude*, *The Warden Threw a Party*; Paper Tiger TV, *Global Dissent*; Sherry Millner and Ernest Larsen, *The Desert Bush*.
Jan. 17: Kathy Brew, *Mixed Messages*; Barbara Lattanzi & the Media Coalition for Reproductive Rights, *A Bed-Time Story*; Cathy Cook, *The Match that Started my Fire*.
Jan. 18: Jonathan Robinson, *sight unseen: a travelog*; William Jones, *Massillon*.

Feb. 13–Mar. 21: Jared FitzGerald, Nickzad Nodjoumi, Gilda Pervin, Kendall Shaw (Connie Butler and Carlos Gutierrez-Solana). Four solo shows of work selected from the Artists File: FitzGerald, painting; Nodjoumi, painting; Pervin, mixed media work; Shaw, mixed media installation. Brochure. With an introduction by Connie Butler and Micki McGee.

Feb. 13–Mar. 21: Japan:Outside/Inside/In Between (Micki McGee with Yumi Saijo). Three-part video program investigating representations of Japan. Catalogue with essay by Micki McGee0.

Part 1: Outside Looking In. Work by Western video artists about Japan: Louis Alvarez and Andrew Kolker, *The Japanese Version*, 1990; Peter Callas, *Kinema No Yoru (Film Night)*, 1986; John Goss, *OUT Takes*, 1989; Gary Hill, *Ura Aru (The Backside Exists)*, 1988; Steina and Woody Vasulka, *In the Land of the Elevator Girls,* 1990; Edin Velez, *The Meaning of the Interval*, 1987; Bill Viola, *Hatsu Yume (First Dream)*, 1981.

Elizabeth Enders I first went to Artists Space on Hudson Street when Linda Shearer was Director. I was curious about an institution that was committed to helping artists. I was getting a master's in painting at New York University when Katherine Lobell asked me to join the Board and become chair of the Events Committee in 1985.

During *Witnesses*, the Board was very committed to artists speaking out and the crucial importance of government support for the arts. A lot of us were writing letters for continued support and getting involved in that way. When John Frohnmayer came up to defend his position, there was a press conference at Artists Space. I really thought he was trying to be supportive in some way, but didn't know how. His position was, "You can speak, but the government doesn't have to support it." There was a very determined conservative element. Artists Space was on the front line, but the events that happened would have happened anyway. Art was the scapegoat.

Carlos Gutierrez-Solana brought in a new perspective and opened up Artists Space to more artists. There were a lot of voices that hadn't been heard that should be heard, which made me very pleased. It is the responsibility of a Board member to do everything possible to make sure the institution is healthy, support it, and make the right decisions. I was very concerned about the debt and what we as Board members could do about it.

I particularly loved the Artists Committee meetings. There were all sorts of ideas about what could be done to help artists. The artists were exceedingly enthusiastic and energetic, but with staff problems it wasn't always possible to follow through.

Feb. 13–Mar. 21: **AIDS FORUM**: Robert Bordo, painting.

Apr. 9–May 23: **Rope/ Radio/ Return of the Repressed** (Mike Ballou, Amy Sillman, and Adam Simon). Three-part exhibition series organized in cooperation with Four Walls. Foldout with notes by Mike Ballou, Amy Sillman, and Adam Simon.

Apr. 9–25: **The Rope Show** (Mike Ballou, Amy Sillman, and Adam Simon, Four Walls). Group exhibition conceived as a curatorial experiment. Each of the three organizers picks an unfamiliar artist from the Artists File; each of these three selected artists then chooses an artist from

the Artists File, applying the same criteria; ultimately, three strands or "ropes" of six artists comprise the resulting exhibition of 18 artists: (Rope 1) Nicholas Arbatsky, Dara Silverman, Jeanette Martone, Tetsu Okuhara, Suzanne Bocanegra, Helen Oji; (Rope 2) Teresa Schmittroth, Constance van Rolleghen, Prudencio Irazabal, Eva Mantell, Susan Daboll, Michael Alexis; (Rope 3) Craig Kalpakjian, Didier Canaux, Michael Merchant, Itty Neuhaus, Anne McDonald, and Barbara Shinn.

↓ →

Apr. 9–25: **Japan: Outside/Inside/In Between. Part 2: An Inside View** (Micki McGee with Yumi Saijo). Second part of the three-part series featuring work of video artists living in Japan: Mako Idemitsu, *Kiyoko's Situation*, 1989; Visual Brains (Sei Kazama and Hatsune Ohtsu), *De-Sign, Volumes 1-3*, 1989; *De-Sign 1: Kunren*, 1989, *De-Sign 2: 5-7-5 Hi-Cook*, 1990, *De-Sign 3: Stand-Drift*, 1990; Osamu Nagata, *The Other Side*, 1990; Yoshitaka Shimano, *TV Drama*, 1987; Junji Kojima, *Trance Verge*, 1991; Dumb Type, *Ph*, 1991; Hiroshi Araki, *Mechanic and Angel*, 1990; Akihiro Higuchi, *Cue*, 1990; Jun Ariyoshi, *Self Image*, 1991.

Apr. 9–25: **AIDS FORUM**: Ricardo Zulueta, *In Memoriam*, photo-based sculpture installation.

Apr. 9–May 23: Eileen Neff, *The Mountain A Bed And A Chair*, installation (Judith Tannenbaum). Brochure with essay by Judith Tannenbaum.

May 1: **Private/Public** (co-directed by Allen Frame and Madeleine Barchevska, co-presented with Creative Time, Inc., in conjunction with TriBeCa Open House). Evening of selected scenes from agitprop public performances in New York City, including Madeleine Barchevska, Allen Frame, Linda Maldonado, Angela Salgado, Antonio Valente, and Philip Walker.

Micki McGee Ernest Larson organized a program on the collaborative modes of working in film and video production — collaborative authorship. There were tapes from Gay Men's Health Crisis, and safer sex videotapes, which were extremely explicit. We spent lots and lots of hours trying to figure out how best to screen this work. Ultimately it came down to just showing the tapes. But it was very touchy and complicated for the Board and for Susan (Wyatt), because of the prior controversy that came out of the *Witnesses* show.

There's no way of talking about the experience of working at Artists Space without also discussing the fact that three weeks after I started the NEA withdrew their grant for *Witnesses*. The organization was never the same. It was a disaster, because a full-time staff of four and another four or five part-timers were coping with 500 to 1,000 phone calls a day with three phone lines. It was really crazy. People worked enormous hours to manage the traffic flow because, suddenly, Artists Space was on the front page of the *New York Times*. And instantly the place was no longer a small institution. People imagined it as a very large and very important institution. When, point of

fact, it continued to be a very small organization with a very small staff and a very modest budget by the standards of major institutions. Artists Space suddenly had to rally all kinds of resources to defend its position, to defend the Executive Director's position, and to defend the work that was being shown. It was very trying, and ultimately those fights are really about destroying institutions—undermining the places where ideas are allowed to come and be supported. When I was a guest curator at Artists Space, it was wide open to ideas. What kind of an exhibition would you like to do? What are you thinking about? What is interesting? You'd propose something and a couple of months later you'd find out, "Yes, we'd like to do the show, let's talk about how to do it." That's very threatening to the dominant culture, to have an organization that supports people's ideas and thinking in a nontraditional way. That type of support for grassroots thinking is very challenging to other cultural interests. So an attack like the one mounted at the NEA against Artists Space made it one of the key hot points, but it was also very destructive to the institution. I thought I would be at Artists Space for 10 years because I loved the institution. But it was not the same after a month or two. Not much could have happened differently. It was very unfortunate.

Connie (Butler) and I talked about exhibitions we could do together. We decided to challenge the Right's ownership to the notion of family with the exhibition, *Reframing the Family*. We thought the idea was extremely timely and would generate a lot of interesting press. We dealt with alternative notions of the family and how it isn't, strictly speaking, a nuclear family but all kinds of community and social structures that support people's development. CONTINUED

MICKI McGEE / CONTINUED

Not very many people came to the opening and we wondered what was going on. Then we went downstairs, turned the video program off and turned the television set on to discover that the bombing of Baghdad had started. Everyone was completely horrified, very, very upset. People went on their various ways home to try and figure out why we were going to war. We thought this would be our opportunity to respond to this attack — this cultural war on institutions like Artists Space — by taking a different perspective than the Right's high ground with a concept like the family. But there was a lot more on people's minds than the family.

I left after two and a half years, because in January of 1992, Carlos Gutierrez-Solana had a meeting with Connie Butler and me to tell us he had no more use for curators. He'd spoken with the Board and they were not comfortable with the idea of laying us off because Celeste Dado, Connie, and I had all rolled up our sleeves and kept the place running for a six-month period, possibly longer, when there was no executive director and no development staff in place. We were writing grants and doing all the development work, night and day, keeping the place going. So the Board wasn't thrilled with the idea of Carlos's letting us go. But he didn't think curators were a valuable asset to the institution. It was a new ball game and Carlos had a very strong notion of what he wanted to do, not only as Executive Director but as Artistic Director. If you're the Artistic Director, what do you need a curator for? In a sense, it was almost a performing arts more than a visual arts notion of the institution.

The day before we went away for vacation he told us he didn't need any more curators. We were so shocked. He said the Board had told him he had to keep us on staff, but he wasn't sure what our jobs would be and we would not have any curatorial role to play as far as he was concerned. It was very funny. We were not given any job description or any sense of what we were supposed to be doing. And we had a whole batch of programs in the works. I had a huge three-part exhibition of Japanese videos. One section was Japanese videos by Japanese video makers. Another was videotapes about Japan by American video makers, and the last series of tapes was about people who are both Japanese and American — people who sit in between the two cultures. That exhibition wasn't done yet, but it was near and dear to my heart. So before I left I made an agreement with Carlos to finish that show. It was quite tempestuous getting the exhibition finished and getting him to pay the artists, etc. And I felt good I had completed it before I left. But it was certainly not a smooth transition for any of us. Connie was a brave soul and stayed awhile longer. Carlos replaced us with Charles Wright, who described his role to me as being a kind of exhibition coordinator, to facilitate other people's curatorial plans. So that was the direction it went with Carlos.

Carlos did some great things. He got Ken Buhler to do the miniature golf show which was a stroke of genius — a brilliant idea. And I don't know if that would have happened if he hadn't been of the mind that curators were dispensable. So there was actually a good side to his plan. Carlos objected to a kind of professionalism in curators. He thought of us as parasites of artists rather than as people supporting artists.

That was an unfortunate shift for Artists Space. Previously, when people left, they had an ongoing relationship with Artists Space. A lot of talent walked away when Susan (Wyatt) left. They were gone, and not drawn on as resources for the gallery, and that is a sad transition for any organization, because you end up losing intellectual capital and institutional memory.

1992 MAY

May 3: **The Radio Show**. Media event broadcast on WFMU 91.1 FM from 7 to 11 p.m. A live radio program featuring artists discussing designs for unrealized art projects, with on-site interviews at Artists Space. The listening audience is also encouraged to call in and participate with descriptions of their own similar endeavors. Concurrently, a one-day presentation is mounted in the gallery of designs, schemes, and plans for unrealized projects by more than 50 artists.

May 7–23: **The Neurotic Art Show II: The Return of the Repressed**. Open telephone call-in show focusing on the theme of neurosis, featuring small works by the first 200 artist-callers who are affiliated either with the Artists File or with Four Walls.

May 8–9: **Video: The Talking Cure**. Premiere of new work presented in conjunction with **The Neurotic Art Show II: The Return of the Repressed** (Jason Simon). Tania Cypriano, *Ex-Voto*; Andrea Fraser, *May I Help You*; Wendy Geller, *Stories for the Garden: Evolution*; and Joe Gibbons, *Sabotaging Spring* and *Elegy*. Foldout with notes by the organizers.

May 10: **Panel discussion** in conjunction with **The Neurotic Art Show II: The Return of the Repressed.** Led by three psychoanalysts and one psychoanalyst/art historian; panelists include Donald Moss, Paola Mieli, David Lichtenstein, and Ellen Handler Spitz.

May 7–23: **Japan: Outside/Inside/In Between.**
Part 3: Individuals, In Between (Micki McGee with Yumi
Saijo). Janice Tanaka, *Memories from the Department of
Amnesia*, 1989; Rea Tajiri, *History and Memory*, 1991;
Allan Berliner, *Intimate Stranger*, 1991; Gavin Flint, *Drift*,
1991; Ruth Lounsbury, *Halving the Bones*, 1992; Shigeko
Kubota, *Video Girls and Video Song for Navaho Sky*, 1973.

May 7–23: **AIDS FORUM**:
Sue Llewellyn, *To Dario*,
paintings.

May 24–25: **Beauty and the Beast: A Collaborative
Project**. Petah Coyne and Irene Hultman, performance
and installation. Performers include Elizabeth Caron,
Irene Hultman, Jim Kempster, Bob Loncar,
Rachel Lynch-John, Jo McKendrie, Chrysa Parkinson,
and Cheng Chien Yu.

May 26–July 11:
**Beauty and the Beast:
A Collaborative Project**.
Petah Coyne
and Irene Hultman,
installation/set. Produced
in conjunction with the
earlier performance.

→ © Barbara Yoshida

Mike Ballou You (Connie Butler) approached Four Walls to do an
exhibition at Artists Space before Carlos Gutierrez-Solana was Director.
We decided the show would reflect the site and situation of Artists
Space. We thought about what that was and came up with three shows:
The Rope Show, which is the core of Artists Space — the Artists File,
The Return of the Repressed, and *The Radio Show*. The process involved three
people who reviewed all the slides. We had eight generations of artists, so 24
artists altogether. That was the structure. It was really just to show how the
Slide File worked. It was artists choosing artists. *The Radio Show* expressed
the site of the exhibition. We had overlapping rings of audience: at the radio
station, in air space, and on the telephone at Artists Space. And then all three
overlapped around the topic of an unrealizable project. *The Return of the
Repressed* was a neurotic show which dealt with authority and artists'
expectations of an audience. We were free-falling with all the shows. We
wanted to maintain the spirit and format of Four Walls, which is about
exchange. Normally, the format would be an exhibition and a panel. For *The
Rope Show* we had a reception and everybody met each other and talked
about how these connections were actually formed. *The Radio Show* was in
a talk show format. There was a panel at the radio station and people were
interviewed at Artists Space, which Carlos didn't appreciate at all. All
enjoyable projects have their own spin life afterward. The skill of the shrinks
on the panel in turning the questions on the audience paid off quite well.
There was a time when some people wanted to question the role of the
curator, play around with what it meant, but being a curator or organizer
is not a bad thing to be.

It would be interesting to see if alternative spaces could come up with
strategies that aren't just about display, but more about integrating artists in
a modern cultural fabric, such as asking artists to consult on various subjects
instead of just producing objects. Galleries need to do the same thing. At this
point, there's no economic basis to support the art world the way we know it
because the buying base is so small. I'm by no means advocating the abolition
of commercial galleries. They're central to what we need because they

present rarefied objects. But they're going to have
to think in broader terms to support that.

It is fairly open at Four Walls, and we purposely
destroy ourselves as we develop. This past year,
we have moved away from the strict
panel/exhibition format because certain means of
exhibiting only attract the same people. Instead,
we are trying to set up projects in clubs and other
places to include people you wouldn't expect.
It's the hardest thing to do, but it has allowed
more people to participate and has produced a
cross-pollination.

The NEA problem at Artists Space affected
everyone one way or another, because it was in our
community. It could have been avoided. It
politicized a lot of art. It made not only the NEA
but NYFA and NYSCA very cautious about funding
something that wasn't truly institutionalized.

Being an artist who runs a space has changed
my work in a lot of ways. I don't make a body of
work anymore. I work from project to project. It's
also allowed me to experience a lot of
collaboration, which has been terrific, and to see
what it's like on the other side of the fence, how
much work it takes to put together an exhibition.
I'm not as myopic as I used to be.

June 4–22: **AIDS FORUM**: Robert Boyd, *Heart of Glass*, mixed media installation.

June 11–July 11: **A New World Order: Part I: Choice Histories: Framing Abortion** (Connie Butler). Group installation about reproductive rights in the U.S. by REPOHistory, a collective of artists: Ayisha Abraham, Todd Ayoung, Betty Beaumont, Curt Belshe, Sam Binkley, Marie-Annick Brown, Regina Corritore, Jim Costanzo, Ed Eisenberg, Betti-Sue Hertz, Joyce Kim, Tom Klein, Hilary Kliros, Lisa Maya Knauer, Janet Koenig, Carin Kuoni, Irene Ledwith, Flash Light, Kara Lynch, Sabra Moore, Mark O'Brien, Jayne Pagnucco, Lise Prown, Megan Pugh, Leela Ramotar, Michael Richards, Robin Schweder, Greg Sholette, Sylvia Sukop, Tess Timoney, Sarah Vogwill, Darin Wacs, and Dan Wiley. Artists' book published by REPOHistory with essays by Connie Butler and Tess Timoney.

June 11–July 11: **Video: Choice Histories.** Ana Maria Garcia, *La Operacion (The Operation)*; ReproVision, *Access Denied*; Irene Schonwit and Carol Downer, *No Going Back.*

June 11–July 11: **Video: HerStories in Color** (Tony Cokes). Linda Gibson, *Flag*; Yun-ah Hong, *Memory/all echo*; Shikha Jhingan, *Once This Land Was Ours*; Indu Krishnan, *Knowing Her Place*; Kara Lynch, *An Attempt to Get Some Knowledge from an Institution of Higher Education*; Tracey Moffatt, *Nice Colored Girls*; Pratibha Parmar, *Emergence*; Gloria Ribe, *From Here, From This Side*; Valerie Soe, *New Year.*

June 23–July 11: **AIDS FORUM:** Robert Giard, *Tribute to Joe Beam*, black and white photographs.

June 26: **Dear Joe, Dare Dreams (Tribute to Joe Beam)**. Evening of readings by members of Other Countries: Black Gay Men Writing, a group dedicated to documenting and communicating experiences of gay men of African heritage. The evening is based on responses to Joseph Beam's death that were published in Boston's *Gay Community News*. Readers: Guy-Mark Foster, Colin Robinson, and Allen Wright.

CURATOR

Ken Buhler When I was involved in Artists Space, Connie Butler was curating. She is a professional and at MOCA (Museum of Contemporary Art, Los Angeles) now. So the shows had a bit more of an organized and thematic flavor. I blended in very well, because I have a background working with museum shows. But there was a lot of questioning about what Artists Space's role was, which continued the whole time I worked there. I remember Robert Storr, Stephen Westfall, and a bunch of prominent people in the art world down in that basement meeting room talking about what Artists Space's role would be for the 90s. I don't think anything very conclusive was drawn. But the one point that came up repeatedly was the difference between Artists Space's role of showing non-commercially viable work and the East Village evolution and aftermath, which produced a willingness of galleries to show just about anything. The result was Artists Space could no longer claim the territory of just serving the needs of noncommercial artists. Of course, there are still artists who can't get shown any other way. All sides were represented at that meeting. Some people said Artists Space had run its course, it should never have become an institution. But others claimed there were still artists out there who hadn't been shown. Connie had a great job, because New York is full of young artists wanting to show their work, and she had the pick of them all. I recently moved to Brooklyn and know everyone out there, because they almost all showed at Artists Space. Connie put them in shows and they have since achieved quite a lot of success: Fred Tomaselli, Janine Antoni, Andrea Zittel, Jason Reed, and Joe Amron, who used to volunteer to paint signs for Artists Space and now has Pierogi 2000**.**

Having survived my first fundraiser, I knew an Artists Space fundraiser was like every other: some good food, some music, you go out and shake your booty a little, and you go home with a multiple. It seemed so amazingly boring, especially for Artists Space. So sitting at my desk the day after, I suddenly said to Lynn McCary and Laura Miller, "I know what we're doing for a fundraiser next year, *Putt-Modernism!*" This was something I'd thought about before. It was just such a powerful idea, I thought no one would be able to say no. I swore Lynn and Laura to secrecy, because I thought if Exit Art or Art in General heard of it they'd surely do it. But when I told Susan (Wyatt),

it was in one ear and out the other. Her mind was on other things. Clearly it had to be heard by the right person, and that turned out to be Carlos (Gutierrez-Solana). I could see the lightbulb flashing above his head when I told him. He was so into it and had so much belief in me. It wouldn't have happened without him. He trusted me to guide this thing despite the fact that we had no idea whether it would make a dime or not. That's the other great leap of faith. He liked it enough as a concept exhibition that if it completely failed, it would still have been worth doing.

Putt-Modernism defined a lot of things Carlos wanted from Artists Space. He really did believe in trying to bring in a bigger audience. As soon as the press release went out people were calling and wanting exclusives. When it opened in August, Carlos and I would talk every day on the phone, "How many people came in today?" "Really?" We kept expecting the numbers to go down, but they kept going up and up and up.

I became more obsessed with *Putt-Modernism* as it developed. I had it bad. Fundraising was my excuse. It's been five years now and a week doesn't go by without someone telling me they still remember that exhibition. The other day it was a real estate developer! Miniature golf is the perfect concept for an exhibition, a fantasy world full of architectural and sculptural potentials, where you let artists go wild and see what they come up with. Well, they all put out for it in a big way, and it left an impression.

1992 – 93

The 1992–93 season opens with **Putt-Modernism**. As of 1998, the show continues to travel to venues across the country. Artists Space is closed from August through September 1993 in preparation for its move from West Broadway to its present location at 38 Greene Street. **Arts Benefit All Coalition Alternative (ABACA)** is founded as a collaboration between five not-for-profit organizations located in downtown Manhattan (Art in General,

Artists Space, Franklin Furnace, The Drawing Center, and Lower Manhattan Cultural Council) and Satellite Academy, an alternative public high school on the Lower East Side for under-served students from throughout New York City.

1992 AUG–NOV

Aug. 1–Sept. 27: **Putt-Modernism**. Viewer-interactive 18-hole miniature golf installation by 22 artists (Ken Buhler and Carlos Gutierrez-Solana). Gregory Amenoff, Dina Bursztyn, Mel Chin, Chris Clarke, John Diebboll, Elizabeth Enders, Frank Gehry, Michael Graves, Barry Holden, Jenny Holzer, Elizabeth Murray, Pat Oleszko & Ward Shelley, Alison Saar, Cindy Sherman, Sandy Skoglund, Joan Snyder, John Torreano, Fred Wilson, Nina Yankowitz. Catalogue with essay by Ken Buhler and statements by the artists.

→ Gregory Amenoff, installation view

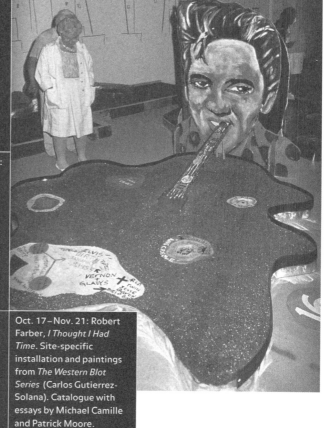

Oct. 14: **Paper as Ceremony: Dieu Donné Papermill Lecture Series**. Six-part lecture series exploring ritualistic uses of paper. Carol Thompson, *Words, Patterns, and Paper: Islamic Sacred Writing in the Art of West Africa*.

Oct. 17–31: **AIDS FORUM**: Merle Temkin, *For My Brother (1940–1992)*, window screen embroidery.

Oct. 17–Nov. 21: **Ping Chong: A Facility for the Channeling and Containment of Undesirable Elements** (Carlos Gutierrez-Solana). Site-specific installation and video retrospective of artist's work accompanied by a series of performances by Ping Chong and Company. Video works include *Paris*, 1982, *Plage Concrete*, 1988, and *I Will Not Be Sad in this World*, 1992. Foldout with essay by Katy Kline and artist's statement.

Oct. 22–24 and 29–31: **Undesirable Elements**. Performance by Ping Chong and Company: Cochise Anderson, Eva Gasteazoro, Emerald Trinket Monsod, Hiromi Sakamoto, Tania Salmen, Regine Anna Seckinger, and Olga Shuhan.

Oct. 17–Nov. 21: Robert Farber, *I Thought I Had Time*. Site-specific installation and paintings from *The Western Blot Series* (Carlos Gutierrez-Solana). Catalogue with essays by Michael Camille and Patrick Moore.

Oct. 17–Nov. 21: **A New World Order II: Remapping Tales of Desire** (Connie Butler). Installation by Karen Atkinson and Associates recreating a travel agency bureau to explore descriptions and depictions of women's bodies used in the language of discovery and travel. Atkinson also collaborates with critic and art historian Andrea Liss to produce a guidebook titled *Remapping Tales of Desire: Writing Across the Abyss*. Kim Abeles, Pamila Bailey, Sylvia Bowyer, Chrono, Robbert Flick, Nancy Floyd, Michelle Hirschhorn, Vinzula Kara, Kerr & Malley, Ernie Lafky, Tom Lawson, Joseph Luttrell, Daniel J. Martinez, Andy Mennick, Leo Morton, Rachel Murray, Mark Niblock, Laura Paley, Laura Parker, Jonathan Parker, Susan Rankaitis, Sandra Rowe, Lisa Shoyer, Monique Van Genderson. Artists' book.

Nov. 3–21: **AIDS FORUM**: Danny Dries, *Generic Memorial (for Wm. Schwedler, 1942–1982)*, mixed media sculpture.

Nov. 11: **Paper as Ceremony: Dieu Donné Papermill Lecture Series**. Dorothy Field, on paper in Asian cultural life.

Dec. 1: **The Celebrity Ribbon Cavalcade** (co-produced by Marc Happel and Carlos Gutierrez-Solana). Fashion show and performance evening hosted by Charles Busch to benefit Visual AIDS. Guest performers: Jerri Allyn, Penny Arcade & Dancers, Brother Tongue Collective, David Ehrich, Ellen Fisher, Marga Gomez, Katy K, John Kelly, Frank Maya, Reno, Jim Self & Patrick Rawlins, Robert Sherman, Gary Schiro, Sons & Daughters; models (House of Field): Afro-Dite, Mistress Formica, Miss Guy, Miss Lulu, Perfidia, Miss Robbie Martin; The Buschmen: B.J. Engler, Dominic Falcione, Eric Goldstein; models: Lindsay Archoud, Darryl Brantley, Betsy Davis, Mary V. Davis, Psychotic Eve, Robert Ferris, Stephen Hammel, Garry Hayes, Bryant Hoven, Peter Iorizzo, Derek Jackson, Scott Jackson, Joe Joyce, Kelly, Sheila McCain, David McWeeney, Gerard Mignone, Doug Ruva, Susan Song, Stephen Winter.

Dec. 9: **Paper As Ceremony: Dieu Donné Papermill Lecture Series**. Miguel Angel Cossio, *Traditions: Paper in Mexican Ceremonial Life*.

Dec. 12–Jan. 9: **AIDS FORUM**: Thomas Lanigan-Schmidt, *Weep Not for Me But for Your Children (Lazarus and The Jibard: Epos)*, mixed media installation.

Dec. 12–Jan. 30: **Divine Comedies**. John deFazio, painting, ceramic crematory urns, and collage (Carlos Gutierrez-Solana). Artist's book.

Dec. 12–Jan. 30: Sighting the Gallery. Joel Saunders and Scott Sherk, architectural installation. Brochure with essay by Joel Saunders and Scott Sherk.

Dec. 12–Jan. 16: Artists from the Studio in a School (Carlos Gutierrez-Solana). Jo-Ann Acey, Susan Austad, Olivia Beens, Daniel Bergman, Kabuya Bowens, Andrea Callard, Tim Casey, Braden Clary, Nancy Coates, Greg Decker, Catherine De Vuono, Larry Dobens, Anne Dohna, Maria Dominquez, Susan Dunkerley, Elise Engler, Gail Flanery, Angela Fremont, Linda Gottesfeld, Tony Gray, Jimmy James Greene, Valerie Hammond, Julia Healy, Barbara Hertel, Elana Herzog, Miranda Hunt, William Kasuli, Maria Katzman, Mark LaRiviere, Patrice Lorenz, Lynn Margileth, Gail Molnar, Maureen Mullen, Antonia Perez, Cathy Ramey, Mary Anne Rose, Timothy Roeschlein, Daniel Rosenbaum, Maddy Rosenberg, Hilda Shen, Barbara Spiller, Patricia Sullivan, Marsha Trattner, Barbara Valenta, Carlos Velazquez, Barbara Verrochi, Neel Webber, Stephen White.

.

Jan. 12–30: AIDS FORUM: Gary Pletsch, *parAIDS*, clay.

Jan. 13: Paper as Ceremony: Dieu Donné Papermill Lecture Series. Wen Yi Hou, *Paper Visions from China*.

Jan. 20–24: Kyle de Camp, *Ladyland*, performance.

Jan. 27–30: Alyson Pou, *To Us at Twilight…*, performance.

Feb. 10: Paper as Ceremony: Dieu Donné Papermill Lecture Series. Elaine Koretsky, *The Gold Beaters of Mandalay*.

Feb. 18–Mar. 6: AIDS FORUM: Dui Seid, *AIDS/Service*, sculpture.

Feb. 18–Apr. 3: Susie Brandt, *Blankets*, mixed media blankets (Carlos Gutierrez-Solana). Brochure.

Feb. 18–Apr. 3: A New World Order III: The Curio Shop (Connie Butler). Group exhibition by GODZILLA, the Asian American Arts Network, a New York–based national network of Asian American artists, writers, and curators working to create increased opportunities for Asian American artists. John Allen, Tomie Arai, Mo Bahc, John Brekke, Barry Chann, Jean Chiang, Andrew Chin, Mel Chin, Sung Ho Choi, Ken Chu, Y. David Chung, Kimiko Hahn, Skowmon Hastanan, Zhang Hongtu, Arlan Huang, Dorothy Imagire, Michi Itami, Guy Jean, William Jung, Betty Kano, Byron Kim, Alexander Ku, Nina Kuo, Sowon Kwon, Bing Lee, Colin Lee, Lanie Lee, Walter Lew, Janet Lin, Munio T. Makuuchi, Dean-E Mei, Kazuko, Helen Oji, Selime Okuyan, Paul Pfeiffer, An Ngoc Pham, Debi Ray-Chaudhuri, Dawn Saito, Kerri Sakamoto, Samoa, Kit-Yin Snyder, Jeremy Spear, Carol Sun, Mitsuo Toshida, Rumiko Tsuda, Martin Wong, Lynne Yamamoto, Mimi Young, Garson Yu, Charles Yuen, Susan L. Yung, Sanda Zan Oo.

Catalogue with essays by Pamela Lee, Lawrence Chua, and Margo Machida, and introductory note by Kerri Sakamoto.

Feb. 19: Performance/ readings: Home on De Range. (Jessica Hagedorn and Helen Oji, co-producers). In conjunction with **A New World Order III: The Curio Shop**. Performers: Kimiko Hahn, Walter Lew, Dawn Saito, and Samoa.

↑ Godzilla, entrance installation

Feb. 18–Apr. 3: Jerry Phillips, *It Should Have Been the Happiest Moment of My Life*, drawings (Carlos Gutierrez-Solana). Brochure.

Mar. 9–13: **Paper as Ceremony: Dieu Donné Papermill Lecture Series**. Carter Hodgekin, exhibition of works on paper in conjunction with the artist's lecture.

Mar. 10: Carter Hodgekin, *Paper as Metaphor: Pulp, Place, and Impermanence*.

Mar. 9–Apr. 3: **AIDS FORUM**: Harvey Weiss, *Wailing Wall*, paper collage installation.

Mar. 16–Apr. 3: **Rage and Desire** (Michael Lee). Group exhibition of artists featured in *Sojourner: Black Gay Voices in the Age of AIDS* publication, produced by Other Countries: Black Gay Men Writing. Warren K. Bradley, *Shame*, *Fear in the Age of AIDS*; Michael Cummings, *Here To Dare*, *California Dreaming*, *Images of the Night*, *Steven Biko*; Thomas Harris, *Black Body*; Michael Lee, *Keeping David Alive*, *Je Ne Regret Rien*, *My Ambivalent Lover*; Anthony Kenneth Marshall, *Fruit*, *Vogue a Self Portrait*, *Ray*; Don Reid, *The Conversation*, *Untitled*, *The Outcast*; Marlon Riggs, *Fear of Disclosure*; Robert Sims,

Sistas in the Hood, *Visionaries*, *Healing*; Julio Dicent Taillepierre, *Then Now…For Each Other I*, *Then Now…For Each Other II*; Robert Vazquea-Pacheco, *The Spirit of God Moves over the Waters*; Steve Williams, *Rage*.

Mar. 16: **Readings.** *Sojourner: Black Gay Voices in the Age of AIDS*.

Apr. 13–May 15: **Activated Walls** (Carlos Gutierrez-Solana). Group exhibition of artists from the Artists File commissioned to make work directly on the walls: Chuck Agro, Jesus Aguilar, Joe Amrhein, Arlyne Bayer, Pam Butler, Kristy Chu, Robert Clarke, Christopher Estridge, Bruce Eves, Frank Farmer, Stephen Ford, Alvaro Garcia, Matthew Haberstroh, Janet Henry, Susan Lee, Julio Mateo, Matt Miller, Kathryn Myers, John Rosis, John Sapp, Mark Smith, Michael Smith, Doug Skinner, Deborah Whitney.

May 12–14: Doug Skinner and Michael Smith, *Doug and Mike's Adult Entertainment*, performance.

↓ Photo: Patty Wallace

Apr. 13–May 15: **AIDS FORUM**: Bruce Eves, *INTERROGATION!*, text/photo installation.	May 6: **Films, Video, and Reading. Media Event: Cuba: Facts, Fiction, and Film** (Carl George and Jack Waters). Works from and about contemporary Cuba by Kelly Anderson, Ivan Arocha, Carl George, Ramirez Hernandez; Jaime Manrique reads a memoir of Reinaldo Arenas.	May 29–June 19: **AIDS FORUM**: Bradley Wester with Eric Latzky, *STILL SITTING?*, collaborative installation.	May 29–July 10: *Artists Space Multiples*, group exhibition.	June 3–July 10: Carol Sun, *The China Mary Series*, paintings (Carlos Gutierrez-Solana). Brochure with essay by Kerri Sakamoto.

1993 APR – JULY

ARTIST

Ellen Gallagher I'm mostly interested in readability and the idea of black abstraction, work whose meanings are primarily experiential and nonverbal, which includes Miles Davis, Derrick May, and Bert Williams. Culturally, Americans have been able to engage with abstraction through music. But when you get into objects, there's still a denial. I find that fascinating, which is also why I'm interested in the minstrel show. It's the first public acknowledgment of African American culture and, of course, it would have to be a coon show. These shows are early American abstractions — the disembodied voice and meaning, the eyes and lips. I was always struck by the way a Burt Williams recording gave you really strong feelings, but feelings that are impossible to describe — to put into language. Bert Williams was trained as a Shakespearean actor. He was a fair-skinned black, tall, handsome, and erudite, yet in the early part of the 20th century, the only way he could get theater work was to black up. He had to invent a world within the limits of a coon show. But to hear a recording of him singing, speaking this coon dialect in a Shakespearean accent, is so moving. There's nothing like hearing this horrible text, in a fake British accent, to draw attention to the disruption. He was able to take this given script, and by changing the timing and pitch he inserted a humanity; instead of just illustrating along with it, he busted it. And people were able to engage a disembodied voice with all this information locked inside. American culture is intimate with the black voice. That's what our whole musical tradition is based on, these secret intimacies, but our culture never acknowledges the black body. It always has to be cruelly distorted.

I feel my work is completely about a female African American experience. My work has a lot of sexual content, but that's rarely spoken about. That's the affinity I feel toward Kiki Smith. She is able to engage the work intimately. People often try to lock the work of black artists into emblematic meanings. I want access to the idiosyncrasies of experience, for example, to Celtic death heads and Irish burial tombs. When I speak about building idiosyncratic meanings, it's about having a complex relationship to history. The work is still coming from my experience. However, I'm not particularly interested in an overall gestalt picture. There is so much history unaccounted for in our day-to-day language. When you reveal information, such as the way cartoons have their origins in the minstrel show, in the vaudeville structure, and the way race is masked and revealed in these cartoon animals, there is such a "present" as well as a "history" that the fact and origin of the sign, although not irrelevant, is certainly not the sum meaning.

While my experience is different, as an African American and as a woman, I do share a context with an older generation of women artists, rather than a particular line of working. But my history and my source material is not primarily located within the art world or in visual art produced by black or women artists. It's been my relationship to their writing where I have found the most affinity. I remember seeing the 1993 Whitney Biennial and thinking everyone was toeing the line. There didn't seem to be much space for artists of color and women artists to have complex moral visions. There was a sense

I feel my work is completely about a female African American experience. My work has a lot of sexual content, but that's rarely spoken about.

that you had to morally open these doors. Often the objects weren't as interesting as the language artists developed around the work. The reason for this is because no one else was willing to talk about their work and they knew it. They came into the practice from a conceptual space where they knew they had to be both the practitioner and the translator. So to locate their work solely in an object is historically incorrect, because their work is a practice of discourse that should be taken as concrete. They were their own critics. They had to be, no one else would talk about it, no one else could.

38 Greene Street, October 1993.
Photo: Corine Cherepak

© Johanna Fiore

June 3–July 10: Margaret Nielsen, *Idiosyncratic Landscapes*, paintings (Thomas Rhoads). Brochure with essay by Thomas Rhoads.

June 3–July 10: **Tony Bechara, Carmen Herrera, Tom Murrin, Mac Wells** (Carlos Gutierrez-Solana). Tony Bechara, painting; Carmen Herrera, painting; Tom Murrin (Alien Comic), masks and performance; Mac Wells, painting. Exhibition sponsored by the Mark Rothko Foundation. Catalogue.

June 18, 19, 25, 26: Tom Murrin/Alien Comic, *Report from the Interior*, performance.

June 22–July 10: **AIDS FORUM**: Laura Migliorino, *The Language of AIDS*, mixed media installation.

1993–94

In October 1993, Artists Space relocates from West Broadway to its present location at 38 Greene Street. In December 1993, Carlos Guiterrez-Solana resigns, and in January 1994, Claudia Gould is hired as the Executive Director. Gary Nickard, previously Program Director becomes Curator in February 1994 and resigns in July 1994. In honor of the 20th anniversary of Artists Space, the exhibition season is dedicated primarily to a three-part **Artists "Select"** show, which recreates the curatorial method used from 1973 to 1976, whereby established artists select emerging and under-recognized artists.

Oct. 23–Feb. 27: **Putt-Modernism** (Ken Buhler and Carlos Gutierrez-Solana) is represented at the South Street Seaport/Fulton Market Building.

Nov. 20–Jan. 15: **Project:** Mark Alice Durant and Jeanne C. Finley, *Training of a Fragile Memory*, collaborative installation: photography, video, and text (Gary Nickard). Artists' book.

Nov. 20–Jan. 15: **Artists "Select," Part I**. First in a three-part series of group exhibitions in which established artists select emerging and under-recognized artists: Kristine Yuki Aono (Margo Machida), Jeffrey Barron (Carl Hazlewood), Connie Beckley (Tiffany Bell), Michael Bergt (Paul Cadmus), Elizabeth Burke (Mary Beth Edelson), Renée Cox (Lyle Ashton Harris), Kevin DeForest (Barbara Ess), James Elaine (Edgar Franceshi), Andrew Fenner (Lynda Benglis), Leslie Fry (Perry Bard), Ellen Gallagher (Kiki Smith), Ava Gerber (Cecilia Vicuna), Diana Rodrigues Gil (Celia Alvarez Muñoz), Cynthia Hawkins (Elizabeth Murray), Robin Kahn (Mike and Doug Starn), Craig Kalpakjian (Andrea Zittel), Richard Kern (Beth B), David Krueger (Cindy Sherman), Kuozhong Lee (Stefani Mar), Joe Letitia (Chuck Close), Maria Lino (Luis Cruz Azaceta), Niki Logis (Mark Rappaport), Loring McAlpin (Frank Moore), Renny Molenaar (Kukuli Velarde), Senga Nengudi (Lorraine O'Grady), David Sandlin (Elizabeth Enders), Jane Sherry (Tom Otterness), Janet Stein (Nan Goldin), Ellen Sullivan (John Torreano), Holly Sumner (Donald Sultan), Eva Sutton (Nancy Dwyer), Merrill Wagner (Dorothea Rockburne), Tony Wong (Li-Lan), Charles Yuen (Helen Oji).

↗ Facing page top, installation view, Renée Cox. Photo: Patty Wallace

Nov. 20–Dec. 24: **AIDS FORUM**: John Giorno, *Fabulous Sex/Compassion*, text installation.

Dec. 3–18: **First Annual Night of 1,000 Drawings.** Open call to artists to donate small works on paper. A drawings exhibition and benefit sale.

Jan. 4–22: **AIDS FORUM**: Tom Strider, installation.

Feb. 1: **Artists Space—Fact or Fiction**. Open forum Town Meeting organized by Artists Space Board members Catherine Woodard and Brian Goldberg to function as a two-way question and answer session.

→ Photo: Gary Nickard

Jan. 3–Feb. 19:
Satellite exhibit:
Angela Fremont, *What's a Mother to Do?*, painting (Denise Fasanello). Exhibited at Dance Theatre Workshop.

Jan. 25–Feb. 12: **AIDS FORUM**: Carl Tandatnick, *USAIDS*, silkscreen paintings.

Jan. 26–Mar. 19: **Artists "Select," Part II**. Second in a three-part series of group exhibitions in which established artists select emerging and under-recognized artists: Lisa Austin (Judy Pfaff), Helene Aylon (Dotty Attie), Michael Bennett (Swon Kwon), Amir Bey (Marilyn Nance), Michael Burke (Tony Bechara), Michael Daube (Sandy Skoglund), Jim Drobnick (Rudolf Baranik), Wendy Geller (Jason Simon), Doug Hammett (Mike Kelley), Janet Henry (Lanie Lee), T. Osa Hidalgo (Catherine Saalfield), Judy Jashinsky (Steed Taylor), Sam Korsak (Alice Aycock), David Knudsvig (Jennifer Bartlett), Michael Levine (Jerri Allyn), Siobhan Liddell (Polly Apfelbaum), Anthony Margarucci (Sydney Blum), Doreen McCarthy (Matt Mullican), Sherry Millner (Yvonne Rainer), Garry Nichols (Judy Rifka), Ivy Parsons (Sylvia deSwann), Jenny Polak (May Stevens), Carl Robert Pope Jr. (Willie Birch), Jennifer Reeves (Peggy Ahwesh), Liisa Roberts (Liliana Porter), Richè Rodriguez (Juan Sanchez), Stephanie Rowden (Mary Hambleton), Ana Tiscornia & Alberto Lastreto (Rimer Cardillo), Brian Tripp (James Luña), Jeannie Weissglass (Nancy Grossman), Tad Wiley (Marisol), and Barbara Zucker (Shirley Jaffe).

Tuesday Night at the Movies
Feb. 8: Liisa Roberts, film
Feb. 18: Jennifer Reeves, film
Mar. 15: T. Osa Hidalgo, video

↓ Installation view.
Photo: Patty Wallace

Benita-Immanuel Grosser, Yoga sessions, Sept. 10 – Oct. 12, 1996.
A Strategy Hinted At: New Conceptual Artists, Sept. 6 – Oct. 26, 1996.
© Benita-Immanuel Grosser

JANUARY **1994** TO PRESENT

Claudia Gould
interviewed by Denise Fasanello
and Ronald Jones

Claudia Gould has served as Executive Director of Artists Space, at 38 Greene Street, since January 1994. Ronald Jones, an artist who first showed at Artists Space in February 1982, became a Board member in 1995. Denise Fasanello is an artist who began working at Artists Space as an intern. In the summer of 1992 she became the Artists File coordinator, and then Curator, from September 1994 until January 1996. This interview took place on April 5, 1997.

RONALD JONES: The first question I want to ask is, how would you describe the topography of contemporary culture from your perspective as Director of Artists Space approaching its 25th season?

CLAUDIA GOULD: You must be kidding, Ron—but let me think about this for a minute. Artists Space cannot be separated from the world, so what you want to ask me is, what is the layout of culture at the end of the 20th century from the minute perspective of the contemporary art world?

RJ: That's another way to put it.

CG: The other day on C Span there was a program on the 20th-century novel with Joseph Heller, Kurt Vonnegut, and William Styron. The writers were asked the question, "What has changed about the novel in this century?" Vonnegut, who was elliptic, finally said something like this: "Earlier in this century the novelist wrote about fantastical characters and places that a normal person would reasonably never expect to go. Now this is no longer true. Today people can go anywhere and travel is accessible to most everyone. So our stories do not have the same mystery, they cannot hold the same aura. As writers we are not as useful." This made me think about the Internet. Now, one can sit anywhere in the world and pull up the current exhibitions at most museums. Also, the Internet is full of international news and information. You don't have to move at all to "see" the latest show in a New York museum, or know what is going on in the most remote parts of the globe.

↑ **evans**and**wong**, fashion show and performance of spring 1995 collection, Oct. 22, 1994.

Therefore, the topography of 20th-century culture is speed. The urge to speed is the desire to be in several places at once. We are also face to face with the experience industry, not only in Hollywood and Disney World, but also in the art world. We no longer tell people about art, we tell them about the experience of art. A perfect example of this would be Mariko Mori's three-dimensional, odorous video at the 1997 Venice Biennale.

The situation at Artists Space is very open. You can do anything if you have the know-how and the correct tools. Money is always a factor. But money has never encumbered artists, nor has it prevented Artists Space from presenting good work.

RJ: I will ask this question another way: Do you think your specific interests in fashion, architecture, and multimedia differentiate you from past directors?

CG: No, past directors covered this as well. I am not inventing anything new for Artists Space. Our public may not be aware that Helene Winer began presenting paper architecture in 1978 with Bernard Tschumi's exhibition *Architectural Manifestoes*. When Susan Wyatt was Director, Curator Valerie Smith also did a number of architecture exhibitions. Now I am just expanding on that history to include all of design, which encompasses architecture, graphics, fashion, and product design.

My first year, we hosted a fashion show with evansand**wong. It was great! The place was packed with 300 people and I was very pleased so many showed up for this free event. It really was a performance.**

DENISE FASANELLO: *DressCode* was presented as a fashion show and as a sculptural installation with text. Have you ever been interested in artists who reference fashion?

CG: Not as subject matter for artists. But I am interested in style and fashion. I go to Comme des Garçons, Yohji Yamamoto, and Issey Miyake like I would go to a commercial gallery or a museum. I follow fashion as I do contemporary art. I give it equal importance. I love to look at the clothing by Lucio Fontana and Sonia Delaunay. These artists made clothing for people to wear, not fashion as art. The only exception to this would be my admiration for the early work of Judith Shea or the current work of Charles Ledray.

RJ: How do those areas overlap at Artists Space?

CG: Artists Space has always been a crossroads for many disciplines. First of all, young artists bring all of this to Artists Space. Because they have their ear to the ground, I am able to keep up with what's happening in the streets and the clubs just by going to work every day. For instance, the video and performance artist Kristin Lucas, who first showed at Artists Space in 1996, has a very distinct style. Her hair is usually blue or yellow. When she wore the color orange, she predated, by two years, the surplus on the streets. The minute she walks into the room she shines. Most importantly, she is probably one of the more interesting younger artists working with technology today.

RJ: Maybe you're one of the first directors who has genuinely come with those interests in place. The distinct effect this must have on Artists Space is different from your predecessors.

CG: I suppose that's true. I made a big point of bringing back the architecture programs. The Squat Theatre project was very important in that the nightlife at Artists Space was re-ignited. Last season we began collaborating with Harvestworks to do more music events, and this year we are working with new bands. To inaugurate our 25th anniversary, we will work with Laurie Anderson. Artists Space did some very memorable evenings of music in the late 70s and early 80s—Arto Lindsay and the Lounge Lizards, Mike Kelley and Sonic Youth performed together. *Tellus*[1] recorded that performance at Artists Space for their 1986 issue. We did a lot of evening events with young bands and filmmakers that were really great. We plan to continue this and it is something I look forward to.

DF: Since you've been Director, is there one show to which you feel particularly close?

CG: Bringing back the artist-selected shows is very close to me. It's great fun to set the stage for the year by inviting the artists to curate. You never know what you are going to get, and this is terribly interesting. I was planning *A History of Squat Theatre* (1996) before I came to Artists Space. The Squat project, like the artist-curated projects, has that great unknown attached to it, which I love. Another important component for us that I really believe in and feel close to is the *Open Video Calls*.

DF: What are your thoughts about Artists Space at present?

CG: I am conscious of what Artists Space is now. Former directors gain a perspective and a breath, which is impossible when you are the director. I am naturally more self-critical, more sensitive, and, probably, more self-conscious. But I am very pleased to see that the work we have done for the past few years is paying off. I feel we are in a good place, both financially and artistically.

DF: I appreciate what you just said. I have a different perspective on Artists Space now than I did almost two years ago. On my way over today, I told Ron I felt Artists Space was in a better position than it had been in a very long time.

CG: I feel it as well, especially in the artists we are showing and in the student interns working with us. There is a community.

DF: Artists Space was my introduction to the art world as well as critical to my development. I met most of my friends and colleagues through Artists Space. Rechanneling the curatorial energy through artists has been a good idea for the organization. However, what's ultimately important is the emerging artist, not the recognized artist/curator.

CG: Yes, the emerging artist is especially important.

DF: That feeling has to be on the street, too. That's beginning to happen.

CG: When everything changes so quickly, the most important step is to keep up. Again, speed is the issue here. A few months ago Valerie Smith said to our (former) Curator, Pip Day, "You have to be out there Pip! And you've got to get the artists before others do, before the gallery across the street gets them." That is a lot of pressure.

In the late spring of this year, a student of Ron's sent in his slides. I liked the work, but Pip was not so interested. This summer Gavin Brown gave the student a show. The competition is enormous. We used to be one of the only kids in town doing this. Now, some of the young commercial galleries seem like

1 *Tellus* is an audio magazine published by Harvestworks and founded by Claudia Gould, Joseph Nechvatal, and Carol Parkinson in 1981.

alternative spaces. The topography of the art world has expanded and changed so much since 1973, and even since the 80s, that Artists Space cannot be concerned with the same issues it once was. Nevertheless, in 25 years, we have adapted without losing sight of our original mission.

DF: It's true. For the most part, the mission has not changed, and because of that there were times when our job was about crisis management.

CG: It took me about a year to figure things out, because it was crisis management well into 1995. The bulk of a $200,000 debt cleared later that year. At roughly the same time, Artists Space started changing curatorially. *Customized Terror* (1995), the show you, Ron, organized with The Designers Republic, Bryan Crockett, and Brian Tolle, was a turning point and one of the more interesting shows since I have been here. I still think about it.

DF: Some of our shows develop a myth. I think this one will, too. Unfortunately, the timing for *Customized Terror* was not good. We were just climbing out of a financial black hole and the community had barely begun to notice what was happening at Artists Space.

RJ: My first advice to any young artist was to "go to Artists Space, take your slides to Artists Space." But four or five years ago, they just rolled their eyes at me. Did the community shift away from Artists Space?

DF: At one point, it made more sense to organize something on one's own than to go to Artists Space.

CG: Irving Sandler has also said that most of the shows at Artists Space never get noticed. By the same token, it is not our function to produce stars. Our function is to encourage young people to use Artists Space as a testing ground, to succeed or, perhaps, fail. Failing is not a negative issue for Artists Space.

RJ: That's the beauty of Artists Space.

DF: Right. But do you feel there's even more pressure now not to fail because everyone is competing for funding? 10 or 20 years ago, it was easier to put up a show and wait to see what happened.

CG: I don't feel pressure about failing in our exhibition program or anything else I do here. The only real pressure I had was being able to pay the general operating support, and that daily anxiety disappeared in late 1995. Lately, I feel pressure because we are doing too much in regard to the 25th anniversary and this book. But, I did have one goal this Fall, which was to get reviewed by the *New York Times*. We got mini reviews for the *Permutations* (1997) and *Digital Mapping: Architecture as Media* (1998) exhibitions, and full reviews for *Lines of Loss* (1997) and *Abstraction in Process II* (1998). This made me very happy because we had not received a review from them in over three years!

The exhibitions are about trying to make a point, to do the best we can and move forward. It is trial and error in many instances. I like that sense of the unknown and experimentation for myself and for Artists Space. If we had to close our door because of lack of funds, then I would feel the loss and failure. However, I would not be solely responsible. Alternative spaces are precarious animals, especially today. When the Board of Directors hired me, I distinctly remember that they said, "We will give you a year to see how things go and if you cannot make a go of it, then we should consider closing." I felt a tremendous amount of pressure the first year. We had a gigantic debt and had lost the support of the young artists' community. We had lost our identity. I did not want to become the Director who closed down Artists Space! Nothing was more of a motivation to succeed. But, for the first 18 months, it was always in the back of my mind.

RJ: Under the current circumstances, how has the funding structure dictated curatorial issues for Artists Space?

CG: It doesn't.

DF: You don't think it does? I thought it did.

CG: I don't think the shows would be different if we had loads of money. The difference would show in our increased generosity toward artists and maybe we would commission artwork. We could also have more support staff to relieve the tremendous stress on everyone.

DF: Do funders want to know exactly what you will show? How does this institutionalize Artists Space?

CG: In my gut and in my heart I'm really anti-establishment. My staff knows I hate the concept of institutionalization. I am constantly being pushed by this, probably from funders more than anyone else. But funders understand who we are, and if they don't we explain it to them.

RJ: Do you decide what you want to do first and then go find the money?

CG: Yes. No one has ever said, "Here's some money, go do a show." The exception was the Mark Rothko Foundation, who gave us a major grant in 1986 to do a series of shows presenting the work of older under-recognized artists.

↑ Vanity Fair photo shoot for Feb. 1999 issue, Nov. 16, 1998.

266

DF: Let's talk about the bigger picture. How has the funding structure changed since Artists Space was solely funded by NYSCA (New York State Council on the Arts)?

CG: It was a gradual weaning from NYSCA, and now from the NEA. We became a line item at the DCA (City of New York Department of Cultural Affairs) in 1986; that has decreased some, but it is steady. *(see graph on page 338)*

DF: My impression was that, 25 years ago, the purpose of Artists Space was to provide an open forum for work not commercially viable. Now that the political climate has changed in regard to art funding and education in this country, what do you feel are the advantages and disadvantages of being not-for-profit?

CG: The advantages are easy. More freedom, your standard freedom, more choices, but less money. The disturbing issue regarding the NEA and censorship is that Artists Space and other alternatives are asked to self-censor if they accept government money. This kind of thinking is similar to the commercial system or private sector, which exercises extreme caution lest they offend a client. As if the NEA or the general American public are our clients! It is very dangerous for the government to be involved with this. We have had freedom for a long time. You cannot be both, nonprofit and commercial. When we curate a show at Artists Space, it does not even enter our consciousness that artwork is salable. There would be no point for Artists Space to exist if we were for profit and had to think about these issues.

RJ: Do you think Artists Space currently exhibits a democratic cross section of what's going on in the culture? Or is it more programmatic, by virtue of who's the director and who's the curator?

CG: Yes and no. I have a very specific taste and style—this is not democratic at all. However, the program at Artists Space is diverse, probably more so than other alternative spaces, despite our individual styles and tastes. Sixty percent of our shows are selected by artists that I invite. I make it a big point to invite a cross section of people: Peter Eisenman, Andrée Putman, Willie Cole, Hani Rashid, Alessandro Mendini, Tom Lawson, Greg Lynn, Gabriel Orozco, Tony Oursler, and Gary Simmons, and Frank Moore, who in turn invited Sur Rodney (Sur) and Geoff Hendricks. Pip and I are curating shows and taking recommendations from many people with whom we speak. We also have the Artists File, which we all use. We have *Open Video Call,* which has become very popular and more diverse than we had hoped for. I don't know how more open we could get, except to let it be a free for all without any curatorial control. We are extremely democratic and as far reaching as we can be.

In Helene Winer's era, the program was much less democratic, but her focus was very particular. Artists Space really benefitted from this focus. She created an identity for herself and for the institution. But I don't believe it was democratic. One cannot disregard the time when she was here, the artists who came on the scene, and the influence they had. Artists like Laurie Simmons, Cindy Sherman, Richard Prince, Robert Longo, Jack Goldstein, Louise Lawler, Sherrie Levine. Helene was at the beginning of a movement.

RJ: I have often observed that gallerists or curators and directors of museums or alternative spaces are at least as creative as the artists they show. Helene was creative in one way, you and Denise in another. Having that as a premise, what is your ambition for Artists Space?

CG: I have one objective, to make Artists Space once again a viable and respected place for artists to show. My ambition is to find a way to return to artists, to keep our constituency. When I was an intern at Artists Space (1980-81), there was a vital community, not only among interns (Annie Philbin and I were interns together), but among the artists who showed and who came to the shows. I am beginning to see this liveliness again, and it is very satisfying. I feel Artists Space's power. It is with the young artists, who really don't know where to go. We are a place open to them.

RJ: How much effect did the atrophy of disposable income in the 80s and the collapse of the East Village revitalize the mission of Artists Space?

CG: In some ways the emergence of the East Village art scene usurped our mission, made institutions like Artists Space seem irrelevant. Commercial galleries were looking and acting like alternative spaces. Artists who showed there were mostly young and emerging. But some were more established, like Haim Steinbach, Julie Wachtel, Gretchen Bender, and Jeff Koons. They all passed through Artists Space in the late 1970s and early 1980s. It was certainly cooler to show and sell your work in the East Village than to show in a big group exhibition at a place like Artists Space. The art community in the East Village was very exhilarating.

Money was flowing through Artists Space, the budget was up to one million dollars. Artists Space was becoming a mini museum, but it wasn't necessarily more interesting. This is what money can do.

Artists Space board of directors and staff, March 3, 1998
© Tim Miller

Claudia Gould and Laurie Anderson,
Spring Benefit, April 11, 1996.
© Johanna Fiore

Dinner after benefit screening of Cindy Sherman's film *Office Killer* at Angel Orensanz Foundation, December 2, 1997.

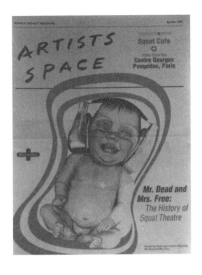  

My challenge is to get more money for Artists Space, to develop the endowment, but without losing the look and feel of the organization. For me the "look" of Artists Space is very important. Taking the daily struggle away, stabilizing Artists Space should not make it more institutionalized. We need to be true to ourselves and I feel there can and should be a balance here. We should not lose sight of who we are and what we do best, which is to serve artists in our exhibitions, our Artists File, and now, our grant program. In the 1980s, the East Village looked like an alternative space and the alternative space looked like a museum. Everyone was wearing one another's hats.

> **RJ:** It's true, many of the galleries appropriated the mission of Artists Space. In a way, Artists Space and those early galleries passed like ships in the night. How would you compare the difference between the mission of Artists Space in 1987 and its mission now?

CG: Again, the mission of Artists Space hasn't fundamentally changed, it has simply stretched. We are less institutionalized than we were in 1987. Our budget is less than half of what it was then. It's safe to say we are more like we were in the mid-70s than in the mid-80s, more grassroots because of economics. I don't think of it as a negative shift—as a matter of fact, it is good. In a strange way, this situation has saved us, made us more honest.

> **RJ:** From where you sit today, what was beneficial about Artists Space's historical trajectory: the embattlement that Susan Wyatt suffered, the scrutiny of federal agencies, of Congress, and then the budget reductions?

CG: There is no doubt that the controversy surrounding the exhibition *Witnesses: Against Our Vanishing* (1989) was historic and interesting for the organization as a whole. I have some private thoughts about the entire sequence of events and how Artists Space handled aspects of it, but in retrospect, the episode was important. It shaped many things we still struggle with today — for instance, with our government and the NEA. It is another notch on our timeline.

> **DF:** I wonder if you feel the weight and richness of Artists Space's history to be burdensome, in the sense that you feel competitive with it?

CG: In the beginning, I did. The glory days were long gone. I feel very free now, despite the constant struggle and juggling of money. I am able to look to the future without losing touch with the day to day. However, I am envious of the spontaneity with which they did shows in the past because of the unconditional support of NYSCA, the NEA, and the DCA.

Rags Watkins told me the story about the first time he saw the work of Laurie Simmons. Carroll Dunham showed Rags slides of Laurie's work. He then showed them to Helene Winer. A month later, Laurie had a one-person show at Artists Space. I love this immediacy. Other people have told similar stories.

> **RJ:** If Helene's tenure is marked by the construction of *Pictures*, Linda's by multiculturalism and greater amounts of money flowing through the institution, Susan's by this embattled relationship with the government, and Carlos's by a commitment to the AIDS FORUM and an intensification of multiculturalism, what's yours? Is it the recovery of an earlier mission?

← Selection of **Artists Space** Newspapers
Photo: Amy Sung

CG: Recovery? We are recovering on a daily basis. As with any recuperation, it's a little tenuous. You're not quite sure, until you're in the clear and looking back, just how things really are. It is easy to say what each director was marked by. Let's wait until I leave to evaluate my tenure. In the meantime, I can say we have reinfused Artists Space with new energy. Starting the Artists Space newspaper has helped.

> **DF:** The newspaper is the positive result of assessing what the institution needed and what artists wanted in terms of information. It was fabulous that catalogues were produced for almost every show, but they were not free. The newspaper is an announcement card, catalogue, and information sheet, all for free.

> **RJ:** As the present Director, you have a privileged and historical perspective. Where is Artists Space?

CG: Now that we're working on our 25th-anniversary book, I'm able to see clearly the amazing history of contemporary art and culture Artists Space has produced. And I mean art with a big A.

But it is a 25-year history of specifically, though not exclusively, New York contemporary art. When you look through the pages of our book, you will see that. It is very satisfying to review Artists Space and say, without a doubt, we have contributed to the history of contemporary art. I read the more recent interviews of artists who just showed here and they are okay, clearly young and happy to have had a show. They are very different than the interviews of the artists who showed here 10 or 20 years ago. If Cindy Sherman was 25 years old now, she would sound just like them. Time and perspective are amazing.

> **RJ:** So, do you feel you have helped shape it?

CG: Absolutely! It is an incredible feeling. I'm not so sure any alternative space can say that the way Artists Space can.

> **RJ:** And where do you think it will be 25 years from now?

CG: Outer space, between Jupiter and Venus! People are always asking me about the future, the future, the future!

Well, I've never thought about my personal future, nor my professional future. I have always lived in the present and never had a plan. But, for the first time, I am able to think in the present about the future. It has to do with having goals and working toward them.

From a financial point of view, the future is very important. When we were not financially stable, my life was dramatically altered. But, on the artistic level, I like to keep the schedule more open. I am not a fortune-teller, so I cannot say where we will be in the future, but a dream would be to have an endowment that could cover the salaries and rent. This would be ideal. We could concentrate on only raising money for programs. If this was the case, we would potentially have more programs and we could give more money to the artists for their projects.

> **DF:** When you start asking, "Where will we be curatorially in 25 years?," you neglect what is happening now. However, don't you feel anyone running a nonprofit must face a certain amount of career anxiety and financial instability?

CG: Yes. I have been working in nonprofits for 21 years. You get used to it. I can't imagine working in the commercial sector. I am envious of their freedom with money, but it is tied to other constraints I would not be able to deal with. Artists Space is different now than when I first arrived in 1994. If I made payroll or rent one week, I wouldn't know whether I could make the next. I had no idea where I was going to get the money.

I distinctly remember March 1994. We had a benefit coming up in a few weeks, but we did not have payroll the next day. I kept hoping money would arrive in the mail for the benefit, so the staff could get paid. By the end of the day, I called all my friends who I knew were coming to the benefit and I sent an intern around town to pick up their donations, just to make payroll. So when NYSCA was bothering me about our 'long-range plan,' I would just laugh at them. I was simply trying to get through the following day, the following week seemed like an eternity, forget about next year, that was impossible. I was just trying to survive in the contemporary art community.

We were very surprised to find out at the end of 1994 that we were denied NYSCA funding for the 1995 fiscal year. As a result we began doing honorary benefit dinners that January, in addition to our spring benefit. While NYSCA support was partially reinstated for the 1996 season, you have to remember that in 1989 Artists Space was receiving $350,000 from the government. Today we receive approximately $30,000, so we continue to struggle for government support. This December we organized a benefit screening and dinner for Cindy Sherman's film *Office Killer,* and five months later it's our spring benefit again. The dinners carry a great deal of goodwill and are fun, but they are also an extremely draining way to fundraise. Writing one government grant and receiving $25,000 is, naturally, easier than inviting 100 people to pay $250 for a special dinner.

RJ: Jane Alexander spoke about building art communities as a political tool. How can that have meaning for you?

CG: Well, we are an art community. We have built an art community. Artists Space has been doing it for 25 years! It doesn't really have much meaning. Arts organizations across the country, whether they are in the theater, dance, or visual arts communities, are doing it. She's saying this so the Senate understands what she's talking about. It's just a tool for her.

RJ: So Claudia, go back to the future for a second. Realistically understanding money as a problem, describe the best possible conditions in which Artists Space could provide creative incubation for the community.

CG: I think being as curatorially open as possible is very important. We are starting a mini project space in November 1998 that will change every four weeks. The space is intended to be more flexible. If we see something in an artist's studio, we can show it a month later. This is exciting to us. The grant program to artists is being revised in the fall of 1998. Naturally, I would like to be able to put more money into this program to make the pot larger. Giving money away is always popular with artists. Bringing back this program is very important to me. This was something that was inconceivable four years ago.

RJ: You have brought artists back to Artists Space as the hub of the art community. Having accomplished this in some measurable way, do you think Artists Space should begin to expand its role? For example, you were invited to propose a project for the 1997 and 1999 Venice Biennale. Would you sponsor traveling exhibitions?

CG: Classic Artists Space shows definitely should not travel. It is so against my idea of what the place should be. It would be silly for us to tour an exhibition of young artists showing for the first time. After a while, it wouldn't look fresh, and that must be maintained at all times.

RJ: This morning I pulled up the NEA's Web site. One could choose from the topics Visual Arts on a Shoestring, Giving and Volunteering in the Arts, Pro Bono / Pro Arts, and the fourth one, How to Have Fun Helping an Arts Organization Run Their Business.

CG: Visual Arts on a Shoestring. Been there, done that. Giving and Volunteering in the Arts. Been there, done that. Pro Bono, Pro Arts. Been there, done that. How to Have Fun. Been there, done that. Helping Arts Organizations. Been there, done that. Honing your business skills. That's a joke. How to work under extraordinary pressure, still keep a smile on your face, and get up the next day and want to be there again.

Mr. Dead & Mrs. Free: A History of Squat Theatre (1969–1991),
Installation view, Mar. 30–Jul. 13, 1996.
Photo: Bill Orcutt

Brian Crockett, sculpture.
Customized Terror, May 20–July 15, 1995.

Installation view, **Mr. Dead & Mrs. Free: A History of Squat Theatre
(1969–1991)**, Mar .30–Jul. 13, 1996.
Photo: Bill Orcutt

Marina Rosenfeld, *Performance for Turntable Orchestra*
during opening for **Hot Coffee**, Jan. 18, 1996.
Photo: Sara Pierson

Feb. 15–Mar. 15: **AIDS FORUM**: Steed Taylor, *Untitled*, painting.

Mar. 1: **Tuesday Night at the Movies**: Jayce Salloum and Walid Ra'ad, *Talaeen a Junuub (Up to the South)*, world premiere of a new video work (Gary Nickard).

Mar. 8–26: **AIDS FORUM**: Robert Lukasik, *Symbolic Gestures: Icons for the Age of AIDS*, drawing.

→ Detail photo, right

Mar. 8: **Tuesday Night at the Movies**: *Silent Dissent*, a documentary-in-progress by Open Dialogue a 50-member group of "dissident" scientists, about their efforts to disclose unreported controversies in AIDS research.

Mar. 30–May 21: **Artists "Select," Part III**. Third in a three-part series of group exhibitions in which established artists select emerging and under-recognized artists: Ceclie Abish (Mary Kelly), Janice Bridgers (Jessica Diamond), Tim Burns (Bette Gordon), Charles Burwell (Candida Alvarez), Seoungho Cho (Peter Campus), Rogelio López Cuenca (Antonio Muntadas), Daze (Martin Wong), Douglas Dibble (Andrew Ginzel), Max Estenger (Ricardo Zulueta), Amanda Fin (Donna Dennis), Maria Elena Gonzalez (Ernesto Pujol), Doug Henders (John Schlesinger), Tony Jannetti (Ping Chong), Jennifer Kotter (Ida Applebroog), Jerry Kwan (Ming Fay), Agosto Machado (Thomas Lanigan-Schmidt), Howard McCalebb (Betti Sue Hertz), Editha Mesina (John Coplands), Trena Noval (Carrie Mae Weems), Nicky Paraiso (Laurie Carlos), Michael Phillips (Jack Sonenberg), Robert Reynolds (Brian Goldberg), Andrea Robbins & Max Becher (Martha Rosler), Kathleen Schimert (Matthew Barney), Shelly Smith (Timothy Binkley), Lou Storey (Greta Gunderson), Patricia Sullivan (Hermine Ford), Rigoberto Torres (John Ahearn), John Townsend (Ursula von Rydingsvard), Richard Tsao (Nina Kuo), Marguerite van Cook (Rebecca Howland), Kukuli Velarde (Marina Alvarez), Coop von Osten (Erika Beckman), and Grace Williams (Alyson Pou).

↙ Seougho Cho, video installation. Photo: Patty Wallace

Mar. 29–Apr. 16: **AIDS FORUM**: Glen Sacks, *Miracle House*, drawing.

Apr. 5–May 17: **Tuesday Night at the Movies**: *BANNED!* (Alan Law). Selection of international films screened on video which have at one time been censored in the United States.
Apr. 5: *Ecstasy*, 1933, Czechoslovakia, directed by Gustav Machaty.
Apr. 12: *La Ronde*, 1950, France, directed by Max Ophuls.
Apr. 26: *The Lovers*, 1958, France, directed by Louis Malle.
May 3: *The Virgin Spring*, 1960, Sweden, directed by Ingmar Bergman.
May 10: *Never on Sunday*, 1960, Greece, directed by Jules Dassin.
May 17: *Last Tango in Paris*, 1973, Italy, directed by Bernardo Bertolucci.

Apr. 19–May 7: **AIDS FORUM**: Larry Jens Anderson, *Untitled*, painting.

May 10–28: **AIDS FORUM**: Jennifer Sloan, *The Four Humors, an AIDS Piece*, sculpture.

May 31–June 18: **AIDS FORUM**: Kenneth Sean Golden, *A Queer Kind a House*, prints.

↑ Photo: Patty Wallace

June 11–July 30: A Terrible Beauty: Images of Conflict in Ireland (Gary Nickard). Exhibition of photographs documenting the past 25 years of war in Northern Ireland, by Donna De Cesare, Philip Jones-Griffiths, Axel Grünewald, Ed Kashi, Oistín Mac Bride, Don McCullin, Chris Steele-Perkins, Dana Tynan. Sponsored by the Mark Rothko Foundation. Catalogue with essay by Gary Nickard.

Video: A Terrible Beauty: Images of Conflict in Ireland.
June 14: Art MacCaig, *Irish Ways*; Chris Bratton and Annie Goldson, *Counterterror*; Sinn Fein Information, *The Funeral of Larry Marley.*
June 21: Derry Film and Video, *Behind the Mask*; Art MacCaig, *Against Her Majesty.*

June 11–July 30: **Project:** Barbara Zucker, *For Beauty's Sake*, sculpture (Denise Fasanello).

June 21–July 9: **AIDS FORUM:** Robert Blanchon, *Carcharodon carcharias*, mixed media installation.

July 12–July 30: **AIDS FORUM:** Cynthia Mandansky, *Elizabeth*, prints and sculpture.

1994–95

Denise Fasanello former Artists File Coordinator is hired as Curator in September 1994. The *Artists Space Newspaper* is launched. The eight-page publication serves as an invitation/catalogue and a general information sheet on Artists Space. The *Artists Space Newspaper* is produced five times a year and sent out free to the mailing list. The **Project** space is dedicated to architecture/design and film/video projects. The spring/summer months are dedicated to film and video festivals and the **Open Video Call**, in which artists sign up on a first-come, first-served basis to present their work. In January 1995 the **Artists File** is renamed **the Irving Sandler Artists File.**

Sept. 10–Oct. 22: **Selections.** Mixed media exhibition selected from the Artists File (Claudia Gould with Debi Sonzogni): Elena Berriolo, Binda Colebrook, Betsy Kaufman, Aric Obrosey, Shirin Neshat, Todd Slaughter, and Richard Thomas. Newspaper introduction by Claudia Gould.

Sept. 10–Oct. 22: **Project:** evansandwong, *DressCode*, installation (Denise Fasanello). Newspaper.

Oct. 22: evansandwong *Somebodies: Fairies, Queens, Emperors, and their New Clothes*: New Spring 1995 "Collection," fashion show and performance.

↑ Todd Slaughter, installation view.
Photo: Patty Wallace

→ © liselovanderheijden

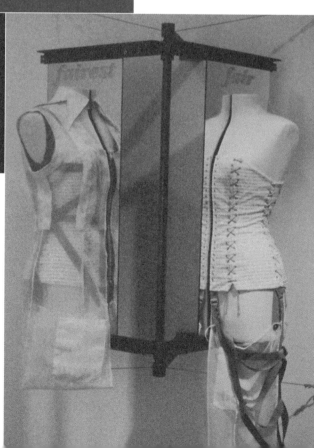

ARTIST

Binda Colebrook I came to the Town Meeting in February 1994 with my brother. It was great to be given the opportunity to say something. At that time I asked if the Artists File was actually used for selecting work, having just put my slides in the file – this was of interest to me. A few months later Claudia Gould and Debi Sonzogni made a studio visit. It felt like a more democratic system than the general way galleries seem to work. It was a very satisfying positive experience and empowering.

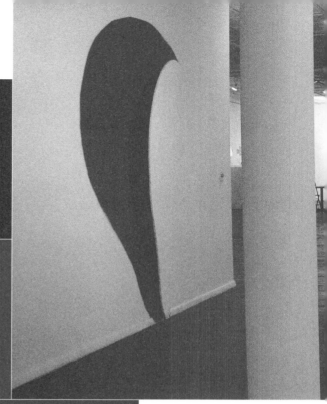

1994 OCT - 1995 JAN

Oct. 29 – Jan. 7: **Conceptual Art from the Bay Area** (Claudia Gould and Gary Nickard). Sited installations by Tom Marioni and David Ireland as well as historical video documentation of important conceptual work by Terry Fox, Howard Fried, Lynn Hershman, David Ireland, Tom Marioni, Linda Montano, and Bonnie Sherk. Newspaper with statements by the artists.

→ Installation view, David Ireland and Tom Marioni.
Photo: Patty Wallace

Oct. 29 – Jan. 7: **Money Commission Project** (Holly Brubach). Commissions from the *New York Times Magazine* of new designs for U.S. currency by Tucker Viemeister, J. Abbott Miller and Ellen Lupton, Karen Bausman, Todd Oldham, and Barbara Bloom. Designs are published in the October 30, 1994 issue of the *New York Times Magazine*. Newspaper with article by Holly Brubach.

Oct. 29 – Jan. 7: **Project: Six Moons Over Oaxaca** (Jerri Allyn). Artist-exchange exhibition of silkscreened, hand-etched, letter-pressed and offset printed postcards concerning the topic of premature death, created by 12 artists from North America and Mexico. In New York: Jerri Allyn, Robert Christie, Tennesse Dixon Rice, Isabel Dominguez, Penny Hall, Sarah Luddy, Rosemary Passentino; in Oaxaca: Gerardo de la Barrera, Miriam Ladrón de Guevara, Abelardo Lopez, Cecilio Sánchez, and Filemón Santiago. Newspaper with statements by the artists.

Nov. 5: **Symposium: Six Moons Over Oaxaca** at Artists Space and El Museo del Barrio. Jerri Allyn, Gerardo de la Barrera, Julia Herzberg, Susana Torruella-Leval, Tomás Ybarra-Frausto, Victor Zamudio-Taylor, C. Ondine Chavoya, and Gian Seminara. Screening of film by Llordes Portillo and Susana Muñoz.

DESIGNER

Victor Wong *DressCode* was an installation and fashion show based on three fashion collections we'd done. We took one exemplary piece from each of the collections and created an installation putting the clothing in a *scene* to explain it. Not only is the object on display, but it's conceived for the viewer in context. It was actually our third fashion show and third collection. We'd presented collections in Paris and London, but it was the first time we did it in New York. We saw the first three collections as a triptych.

Claudia Gould had an idea for a *Project* space and she started asking different artists and designers whom they thought were interesting new voices. It was through Diller/ Scofidio and Todd Williams and Billy Tsien that Claudia found out about us. She was talking about multidisciplines, which is one of our interests. We gave her an architecture, fashion, and graphic design show all in one. Our exhibition at Artists Space helped us synthesize our ideas and make them cohesive. In addition, it was our first exhibition, and it helped being able to show our work to the public in that particular forum, a gallery space. Now we wouldn't rule out any site in which to present our work. Strangely enough, we ended up meeting a lot of people in France who had seen the show at Artists Space. We recognized their names in the show's guest book.

We see more exhibition spaces in New York than in Paris that are willing to show cross-disciplinary work. Paris is still very segregated, and you've got to hold your turf and prove yourself for a couple of years. But Artists Space was great, because we're always trying to reach a different audience and find other ways for people to look at our work. If you show design in an art forum, it changes the way you understand design, and it also changes the way you understand art.

Dec. 1: Day Without Art.
Memorial in conjunction with **Six Moons Over Oaxaca** in honor of the 6th International Day of Action and Mourning in response to the AIDS crisis.

Dec. 10–23:
Second Annual Night of 1,000 Drawings.
Open call to artists to donate small works on paper. A drawings exhibition and benefit sale.

Dec. 21–Jan. 27:
Satellite exhibit:
Sue Johnson, *Evolutionary Paths*, painting (Debi Sonzogni). Selected from the Artists File and exhibited at Dance Theatre Workshop.

Jan. 19: Benefit dinner in honor of Irving Sandler.

1994 DEC – 1995 JAN

↓ © Raimund Kummer

Jan. 28–Apr. 6: **Project**: Osvaldo Romberg, *Las Americas: The Return of Martin Steel*, installation (Dominique Nahas). Newspaper essay by Dominique Nahas.

Apr. 18–May 4: **Sit Down and Watch It** (Michel Auder). Film and video component of a mini festival devoted to media and literature and presented concurrently with **Authors in Search of a Publisher: Literature Program**. **Video**: Joel Bartolomeo, Rachel Feinstein, Aki Fujiyoshi, George Kuchar, Marie Legros, Alix Pearlstein, Doug Skinner, and Michael Smith. **Screenings**: (artists select artists):

Luther Price (Ericka Beckman), Richard Kern (Beth B), Bertha Jottar (Jason Simon), Pelle Lowe (Erika Beckman), Peter Celli (Tony Oursler), Lana Lin (Peggy Ahwesh), Karen Redgreene (Stephen Vitiello), John Brattin (Stephen Vitiello), Ruben Ortiz-Torres (Juan Guardiola), and Jesse Lerner (Juan Guardiola).

Authors in Search of a Publisher: **Literature Program** (Gillian McCain). Second half of a mini festival of media and literature. **Readings**: Apr. 19: Christian X. Hunter, Michele Madigan Somerville, Sharon Mesmer.

Apr. 26: Chris Simenuk, Linda Yablonsky, Jose Padua.

May 3: Mike DeCapite, Janice Johnson, Carl Watson.

↓ Photo: Patty Wallace

ARTIST

Shirin Neshat There's no question the commercial world has very little contact with the community. There's an obvious sense of arrogance and isolation because they're afraid of being bombarded by artists. That is why they are so distant. As a result, the nonprofits are able to recognize interesting new work at the earliest stages. In general, if issues surface in New York like AIDS or multiculturalism, the alternative spaces are the first ones to respond by organizing shows that deal with them. At the same time, the definition of what alternative spaces are or should be has changed. That's another challenge: how do you redefine your mission in order to remain contemporary? It's not just a financial problem— the demands are different. The audience has changed, generations of people are changing, and we feel we're still able to generate ideas that are keeping up with the times. We are all questioning ourselves. I believe there's a demand for alternative spaces, probably more so now.

↑ Shirin Neshat, photographs. **Selections**, Sept. 10–Oct. 22, 1994. Photo: Patty Wallace

BOARD

Richard Shebairo I was fortunate enough to have my tenure as Treasurer coincide with yours as Director, since you (Claudia Gould) are such a bulldog about finances. You really pulled the finances together. So I didn't really do all that much. My contributions are relatively minor. One great saving aspect of everything of late is the sale of the Theodoros Stamos house. All of a sudden, we're in a position to look to the future instead of feeling we're on this horrible treadmill that keeps getting faster and faster each year. Since you've taken over it's been difficult, but we've managed to cut where we had to cut and, if anything, we're running too tight a ship, certainly in light of our present position. The only thing I can say, which is going against the tide, is that we need to loosen the purse strings, rather than keep the pressure on. I feel confident that you're under control in this.

A TRIBUTE to Irving Sandler
January 19, 1995

May 4: **Open Video Call.** Guest viewer Michel Auder. First-come, first-show for artists to present five to ten minutes of videotape: Jesse Nieuwenhuis, *Ethics & Force VII*; Ron Rocheieall, *Doris' Daydream*; Eva Mantell, *Things You Could Do*, Laura Parnes, *Embarrassing Childhood Memories Combined with a Description of an Atomic Chain Reaction*; Debbi Sutton, *True Stories/Other Voices*; Glenn Downing, *Blue Gum/U.S. Of A*; Alicia Porcel de

Peralta, *Your Body is of Her Body*; Ann Korman, *Hot Fudge, Ice Queen, Footage*; Austin Thomas; Annie Wright, *Killer Babe*; Lisa DiLillo, *Rep*; Tatiana Parcero, *Life Lines*; Lee Williams, *Love, Drugs and Food*.

May 20 – July 15: **Customized Terror** (Ronald Jones). Group exhibition of installations and sculptures by artists and designers whose work attempts to redefine political art: Bryan Crockett, sculpture; Brian Tolle, mixed media; The Designers Republic, banners and stickers. Newspaper essays by Ronald Jones and Jan Avgikos.

↓ Front desk.
Photo: Bill Orcutt

May 20 – July 15: **Project: Satellite Choice: Young Curators Explore Diversity**, group exhibition of small works and video by artists, curated by students from the ABACA Visual Thinking program at the Satellite Academy. Student Curators: Christopher Braithwaite, Rayshan Clyde, La Tanya Martin, Dominick Martinez, Eduardo "Wingy" Mercado, Eddie Rivera, Tawana Taylor, Nelibel Santana, Efrain Serrano. Artists: Kabuya Bowens, prints;

Olga Hubard; Rejin Leys, prints, drawings, and collage; William L. Pope, video and performance; Ela Shah, architectural structures; Gordon Simpson; and Danny Tisdale, installation. Newspaper.

HERE

May 23: **Special event: The Sky's the Limit: Live Performances by Artists with Disabilities** (organized by the National Multiple Sclerosis Society in conjunction with CREATIVE/WILL, artists with MS, at Grey Art Gallery and Study Center, New York University). Live taping of audio arts program that is broadcast on the public radio show, "Disability & Health Today," with Dr. Bob Enteen. Kevin Brown, poet; John Farris, short-story writer;

Molissa Fenley, dancer/choreographer; Odris Gomez, singer, songwriter; Anita Hollander, actress, singer, songwriter; Jesse Jane Lewis, performance artist; Cathy Weis, videographer.

June 2–3: **Special event**: Diane Torr, *Drag Kings and Subjects*.
June 2: *The Politics and Practices of Cross-Dressing*, lecture.
June 3: *King for a Night: Walk Like a Man, Talk Like a Man*, workshop on cross-dressing.

ARTIST

Bryan Crockett

Ronald Jones and I had a student-professor relationship that spawned this event at Artists Space. It was my first opportunity to show in New York, so I was completely ecstatic. Actually, I remember being not so impressed by a couple of the shows at Artists Space when I was at Cooper Union from 1988 to 1992. But I was very excited that Ron was organizing the show and that Brian Tolle, whose work I really admire, was also included. Designers Republic was an interesting addition to the mix. I'm always curious about how seemingly incompatible art goes together. Confusing barriers can be set up in the relationship between different artists' work and different forms of production. Nobody had an idea how that relationship would work in our show.

Artists Space was my New York debut of the balloon work. I'd previously shown it for my thesis at Yale where I had inflated the balloons entirely with my lungs. By the time I'd reached Artists Space, I'd learned a thing or two. My strongest memory of Artists Space is working with the balloons on site. I had never worked with different sizes and shapes before. I remember the annoying balloons would occasionally burst and pop and the noise of the installation took over the entire space. Everyone was incredibly patient with all the blasts, although their nerves were probably strung out by the end. The balloon work wasn't fully synthesized yet. The maintenance called for a lot more attention than I had anticipated, so I ended up going once a week to monitor my construction. I remember going into the back room to inflate new balloons and people from the press came in from time to time. I'd try to talk to them about the installation, but balloons kept blowing up in their faces. Someone from *Hot Wired* magazine came in a bit reserved and didn't really

want to talk to me, but I forced myself upon him and ended up blowing this humongous balloon just as he came in the room. It made it into the article he wrote.

I also showed the cat/rat, which was a small standing naked animal, and I included an alligator, which required a little assistance up the stairs, a little more than I had imagined. What sticks out in my mind is the absurdity of it all, carrying this alligator like a coffin and resting every 10 or 15 steps to look down the stairs and see this huge smile on its face.

The Irving Sandler Artists File begins to accept photo CDs; by the end of the season, slides are no longer submitted to the file. The Website (http://www.avsi.com/artistsspace) is initiated in September 1995. It includes visual and textual information on both main gallery and project space exhibitions as well as general information on Artists Space: mission, funders, staff, Artists File, multiples, and intern/volunteer information. Each show remains on the site, forming an archive of the exhibitions as the site is updated. Denise Fasanello resigns in January 1996, at which time Anastasia Aukeman is hired as Curator.

Sept. 16–Oct. 28: **Somatogenics** (Laurie Simmons, Cindy Sherman, and Sarah Charlesworth). Group exhibition of photography, video, and sculpture focusing on the body. Sarah Buffum, Inez Van Lamsweerde, Marie Legros, Sterck and Rozo, Adrienne Urbanski, Charles White. Newspaper with statements by the artists.

Installation view. **Customized Terror**, Brian Tolle, mixed-media; The Designers Republic, banners.
Photo: Bill Orcutt

→ Inez Van Lamsweerde.
Photo: Bill Orcutt

ARCHITECT

Greg Lynn There's a generational break happening in architecture that's very generously sponsored by people like Peter Eisenman. So I would think he understands not only my work, but realizes it is informed by young architects internationally. Peter wouldn't say my work was exemplary of that generation, but very connected with it. We're talking about why Peter would pick me, but it's related to why I picked somebody like Ben van Berkel. Right now I'm in the middle of a group of five to ten architects who are working on similar themes. What's great about Peter is that throughout his career his signature has been to continually reinvent himself. That's also common to other people close to Peter. People like Frank Gehry or Philip Johnson didn't mature the way most architects mature; they constantly moved. In age and experience there's a huge gap between us, but in terms of sensibility, research, or experimentation, Peter's one of those architects who feels as much an affinity with the younger generation as he does with architects from his own.

Architects have a big problem when it comes to exhibiting their work. I have been involved in enough shows with other architects before Artists Space to know that the difficulty is, when viewers go to an architecture show they're not sure what they're supposed to see. People think architects make buildings, they go to a building to see architecture. Often when they go to a gallery they expect to see tiny buildings and models, like what you see all the time at MOMA. I thought about how architects exhibit their process and conceptual thinking. To do that, I decided not to show anything resembling a building. Instead, I made a spatial atmosphere in Artists Space where videotapes and models were shown. Consciously, I didn't want those videotapes and models to be finished products or miniature buildings in terms of models. They were meant as conceptual diagrams. In my desire to resist experiencing a building, I didn't put any drawings in the show. I relied heavily on computer animation to generate the projects. If I were to do it again, I would provide a bit more drawn information.

The show at Artists Space opened up a lot of dialogue with a few painters with whom I've found an affinity. I have even started to exhibit with them. The response of the artists was deep and direct, they connected with the work in a deep way. It has opened up connections I wouldn't have had access to otherwise. And it also communicated well with the larger audience. Architects can't explain what they do, so it's very difficult to interact with an architect except on the level of an opinion about a building—certainly not about process.

The architectural community was honestly confused about what they were visiting. Basically, they acknowledged the concept of the show, but didn't want to accept it as architecture. They said the models were too small to be understood as buildings. So if I had included a few clues, some plans and sections, architects could have better engaged in the show. The great thing about Artists Space is that it's not an architecture gallery. The most important aspect of the show was not that it publicized my work to other architects but that it opened up a dialogue with other disciplines represented at Artists Space.

When I picked Ben van Berkel, he wasn't known in the United States and he wasn't familiar with Artists Space. I told him it wasn't Storefront for Art and Architecture and it wasn't MOMA. It's more like Storefront, but Storefront's primary audience is architects. I said his responsibility was to connect architecture to a larger audience without defaulting to a show of buildings. That's not easy. He's very interested in the art world and knows a lot about art. In every conversation with Ben, he talks about how he wants to run his office like Warhol's Factory. In the Netherlands architects are so highly respected culturally. Everybody on the street can tell you about their favorite architect and they know what's going on. It's not like that in the U.S. There's no interest, familiarity, or support. I think Ben expected he would be showing to an educated community, an audience knowledgeable about architecture. It took him some time to figure out that he had to do something different than he would have done in the Netherlands.

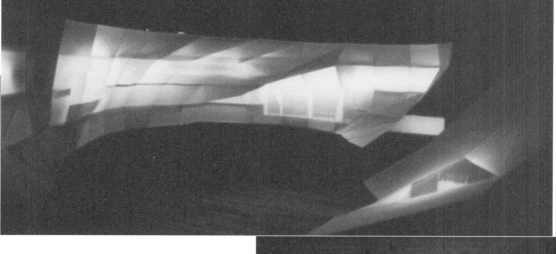

Sept. 16-Oct. 28: **Project**: Greg Lynn, multimedia architectural installation (Peter Eisenman). Newspaper introduction by Peter Eisenman.

Sept. 26: Peter Eisenman talks with Greg Lynn.

→ © Greg Lynn

ARTIST/CURATOR

Denise Fasanello I worked with Connie Butler as a student intern, while I was a junior at Cooper Union. I helped her one or two days a week on a specific project, *Selections*. When Susan Wyatt left and Artists Space was without a director, I continued. I ran the Artists Slide File and later I was hired to work as Gary Nickard's assistant. I helped Artists Space make that gigantic move to SoHo and then stayed on with you (Claudia Gould).

I received the most seriously amazing education from looking at all those slides. I'd never seen anything like it before in my life. I saw real New York artists working, not artists you'd have to see through the gallery or museum system to know about. And I got to meet them. It's crazy to think about the work I was interested in as an intern compared to what I wound up interested in by the time I became Curator.

The administration was much bigger when I first started with Susan. Carlos (Gutierrez-Solana) scaled it down a bit. It wasn't until you (Claudia) tapered it to an even smaller team of four that I understood what was happening administratively with the debt and mounting deficit you inherited. That's also when I got the chance to seriously roll up my sleeves and work. When I became Curator, it was the first time I actually went out to look at art. That was Artists Space's biggest mistake— not since Connie Butler had anyone actively gone out into the community and looked at artwork. Shows were done differently by Carlos. He hardly made studio visits. This was one of the responsibilities you (Claudia) insisted on implementing right away. By the time I left our biggest complaint was that we were bogged down with administrative crisis after crisis and couldn't get out to look at more work, which is really what we were supposed to be doing.

I was Curator for only one year. It was certainly a phenomenal period. I became really good at balancing 50 million things at once. The *evans*and*wong* exhibition and fashion show was the first project I was responsible for organizing. Then it was great starting up the film and video series. I remember when we started to think about the idea for *Open Video Call* and having artists do the selecting. When we started to ask artists to select, it seemed so unfair to have the media artists come in for a day and push the other art aside. So we extended the downtime between shows and had nothing in the gallery but a couple of chairs for video viewing. It was really great. This became signature style for us.

When I first started at Artists Space the look and the feel of it was so different. Connie was a real curator. By the end of the 1980s, the shows were almost too museumlike. I thought, "Well, that's fun and all, but times are changing and it just doesn't seem hip anymore to do exhibitions like that." If Artists Space was supposed to be supportive at the beginning stages of someone's career, well then hell! We should be able to do whatever we want! Such as ask Michel Auder to pick a handful of weird quirky videos, some well known and some not known at all, change the physical space to make it look like a lounge, and have it up for only a couple of weeks; let's have none of these institutionalized exhibitions! Those steps were really important. But NYSCA was thinking, "You have to have a video program on women of color,

who live in wherever," etc. I just wasn't interested in exhibitions like that. They always pushed us to be more institutionalized. But the feel of the space is so important. Now Artists Space is more true to itself. To come into a space and always see something different is really important. The show Gary Simmons and Tony Oursler did felt like a great Artists Space show. The idea of drawing and video is very interesting and new. The Artists Space newspaper is also great. That was the other problem Artists Space had— getting out all the information it had to say. There had been a lack of consistency and continuity in the look of the space, which started to pull together after you (Claudia) came.

I have many close friends— artists and other curators— whom I met through Artists Space. It has helped me find a community. As an artist, Artists Space certainly taught me how to go about being in the art world, which is not an easy thing. At the Town Meeting in February 1994, Robert Atkins said Artists Space really killed itself with its own democracy. It neutralized itself and became about quantity rather than quality. That always echoes in my heart. If you say something changed with alternative spaces, it shouldn't be that it is now about running an orphanage, but about running a contemporary space with good work. You're not going to get everybody in there, but you're going to get more than most, and failing is part of the whole picture. That's truly the mission of Artists Space.

OPPOSITE PAGE
Anne Marie Jugnet, installation.
Photo: Bill Orcutt

Nov. 11–Jan. 6: **Anne Marie Jugnet** (Jérôme Sans), site-specific installation of projections and video. Newspaper essay by Jérôme Sans.

Nov. 11–Jan. 6: **Project:** Vincent Beaurin (Andrée Putman), installation of sculptural furniture pieces and working drawings. Introduction in Newspaper by Andrée Putman.

Dec. 7–23: **Third Annual Night of 1,000 Drawings.** Open call to artists to donate small works on paper. A drawings exhibition and benefit sale.

Jan. 20–Mar. 16: **Project: Exhibit A: Design/Writing/Research** (Claudia Gould). Design exhibition by Design/Writing/Research, a studio directed by J. Abbott Miller and Ellen Lupton, examining dimensional type through the centuries. Newspaper.

Jan. 20–Mar. 16: **Unnaturally Yours** (Willie Cole). Group exhibition of work selected from the Artists File that incorporates the elements (earth, air, water, and fire) as points of departure for personal investigations. Alejandro Berlin, Nicole Carstens, Daniel O. Georges, Ben Jones, Wendy Lewis, Peter Whitney. Newspaper with statements by the artists.

← Alejandro Berlin, sculpture.
Photo: Bill Orcutt

ARTIST/CURATOR

Willie Cole I'd been to some exhibitions at Artists Space and I was in the Artists Slide File, but I hadn't had much contact. I was spending more time running a nonprofit space in Newark during the 80s than trying to show my work. My studio was in New Jersey and I could never get anybody to come. I had a dealer but it was financial, not an exhibition relationship. Fortunately, when I got a residency at the Studio Museum in Harlem, my studio mate, Renée Green, knew a lot of people in New York. Fred Wilson visited Renée and saw my work, which he recommended to you (Connie Butler). My Franklin Furnace show may have come before Artists Space, but it was an installation and performance as opposed to an object show. The one good thing about Artists Space was nobody knew me. I could stand back and observe people watching the work. I enjoyed that.

I did get a direct impact from Artists Space. Carolyn Alexander told me she saw my work there. Two years later we got together. Artists Space also led to a show at P.S. 1. I always thought the strategy was to show at all the nonprofit spaces to find a dealer. Artists Space gave me a lot of confidence. The Tony Shafrazi Gallery had a big interest in my work. All of these events made my Artists Space show in 1989 very important to me.

My New Jersey perspective makes me see things differently. I've always been a bit outside the art scene. Because of the clout of New York there's no space for failure. Spaces for failure and experimentation should be in alternative spaces. In the show I curated at Artists Space, *Unnaturally Yours,* there was an artist who did a cannibal piece with hot dogs. It lasted about one hour. The mechanism started melting and he felt badly and was so stressed out during the show he could hardly speak at the opening. He broke down. I told him Artists Space is a place where you can show something that you feel good about and work out all the kinks. It doesn't have to be a gold exhibition. There are some alternative spaces that are not so high profile as Artists Space, where artists can be a little less stressed. Maybe that stress comes from New York. When I was invited to show in a nonprofit space in Newark I didn't know what I was going to do, but I knew it would not be something I normally do. Rather, it would be something with which I could test the market.

I'm still a Board member at Artists Space. The first year I went to almost every meeting. This year I've only been to one. All the Board members seem to know the same people. So they drop a lot of names and mention who has money and who doesn't and I'm outside of all that. But I did enjoy curating a show at Artists Space. I'd like to do it again. That's where I felt involved.

DESIGNER

J. Abbott Miller My show was a good opportunity to deal with design issues in a context free of commercial constraints. It wasn't like being an artist for a day. It was about having design material seen in a context that lightened its practical functions. There was some confusion, even among designers, in the automatic assumption that, "Oh, Abbott wants to be an artist." I'm interested in how the gallery context puts a different pressure on what's being seen. It meant I could show work that, in some sense, was disengaged from being on a poster or selling something or having a client. I also did a little book about the material in the Artists Space show. It was very successful as a publishing venture in a way that surprised me. When you (Claudia Gould) mentioned the relationship to architecture, I realized no one in graphic design really does projects. But, it's almost paper architecture. It's a hell of a lot more interesting to be a graphic design student or a young graphic designer than it is to be a young architect. The odds against producing your vision of the world as an architect are much greater. We have a practice of design akin to art practices, in that we're pursuing a certain set of interests which touch upon design, design history, and design theory, but it's also our medium. So we're working on both, back and forth, being able to comment directly or verbally on design, but also just dealing with design issues in their physical form.

Mar. 30 – July 13: **Mr. Dead & Mrs. Free: A History of Squat Theatre (1969–1991)** (Eva Buchmuller, Claudia Gould, and Anna Koós). Exhibition of original sets, props, films, and videos of avant-garde theater group which originated in Hungary and was subsequently based in New York: *Pig Child Fire!*, 1977; *Andy Warhol's Last Love*, 1978; *Dreamland Burns*, 1986; and *L Train to Eldorado*, 1989. The project space becomes the Squat Theatre where film and video are screened; the main gallery recreates the Squat Café where the history of Squat is recorded in photographs. Evening events occur throughout the duration of the show. Newspaper with inroduction by Claudia Gould. Catalogue written and compiled from Squat Theatre archives by Eva Buchmuller and Anna Koós, with introduction/acknowledgments by Claudia Gould. Essays by Alisa Solomon and Andras Halasz.

Eva Buchmuller
© Johanna Fiore

Edit deAk and Vito Acconci

↑ Arto Lindsay performing during
Spring Benefit, April 11, 1996.
© Johanna Fiore

↑ Diego Cortez and Joseph Kosuth
Spring Benefit, April 11, 1996.
© Johanna Fiore

ARTIST

Alejandro Berlin At one point I was close to Artists Space because I volunteered there. That's when I met Willie Cole, who put me in his show *Unnaturally Yours*.

In the exhibition, I included *Artificial Spring*, which is a lung activated by a bellow and made with balloons that inflate and deflate. *Art Talk* is a rubber tongue on a canvas, flapping at the sound of a recorded voice saying, "Blah, blah, blah." I also had a small latex heart in the shape of a strawberry, palpating and moving around with the noise of an actual heartbeat.

My perception of Artists Space is still that most artists would give an arm and a leg to get a show there.

CURATOR

Eva Buchmuller The exhibition for Squat Theatre was a summarizing and a reminiscing of that historical time. It was also about pacifying the past. I thought of it as last rites, but it was not at all sad and there was no nostalgia, which was very important.

The point of Squat Theatre and why we existed at all had to do with a life project. It was a way of turning your entire life into something artful or something that fooled everybody else. The Artists Space project was everything I wanted it to be. I have sometimes thought that maybe we should have planned even more programs and researched them more extensively. The way we put it together was a little too fast. However, the book is great. We succeeded in doing it as big and rich as possible, without being posh or sentimental. It's something that remains after the show is over, and more importantly, it's an historical document on Squat.

Mar. 30–July 13: **Project:** Squat Café, photographs and videos of Squat Theatre performances. Newspaper.

Apr. 2: **Open Video Call.** Guest viewer Christine Van Assche. First-come, first-show for artists to present five to ten minutes of videotape: Yung-Te Wu; Kathleen MacKenzie, *Ritual*, *Journey*; Lisa Shafir, *Sometimes I just can't Sleep*; Seung-Jae Jo, *Dear*; Sang-Joon Ahn, *2Me #1, #2, #3, Into the*; Yeon Jae Kim, *A Fish*; Ann Meredith, Adam Ames, five videos; Attanasio and Giannelli, *Not From Concentrate*; Nurit Newman, *Complex Princess*; Neil Goldberg, *Hallelujah Anyway, She's A Talker*; Lynn Mullins, excerpts from four videos, *Bed*; Catherine Bull, *Moonraker*; Michael Ross, three videos; Mark Verabioff, *Malethrall, Lashout*; Jennifer Rawlison, *Reflections*; Kristin Lucas, *Watch Out for Invisible Ghosts*; Ron Littke, *Faith*; Richard Gordon; Diana Stone; Taryn Fitzgerald, *In the Heart of the Belly*; Ann Rosen Korman, *Dating the Tube Toy*; Jeremy Slater; De-Chuen Wu; Dora Rose; Lisa Andrews, *Sightseeing Tours*; Roni Givigliano, *Atlantis*; Mercedes Vicente; Mark Zero, *Time Part #1*.

← Neil Goldberg, *Hallelujah Anyway*, 1995, video still.
→ Adam Ames, *Tear*, 1995, video still.

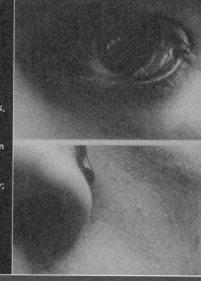

Apr. 3–July 13: **Video.** Group screening of ten video artists from two major shows, **Points de vue (Images d'europe)** (Christine Van Assche, Stéphanie Moisdon, Dirk de Wit), 1994, and **X/Y Feminin-Masculin, le sexe de l'art** (Christine Van Assche, Stéphanie Moisdon, Nicolas Tremley), 1995, at Centre Georges Pompidou, Paris. From **Points de vue**: Johan Grimonprez, *Where is your Helicopter?*; Alison Murray, *Kissy Suzucky Suck* and *Pantyhead*; Imogen Stidworthy, *Intimate*; and Stephanie Smith, *Untitled (Tissue)*. From **X/Y**: Act-Up Paris, *Prevention* and *Hécatombe*; Sadie Benning, *It Wasn't Love*; Marie-Ange Guilleminot, *Mes Poupés*; Lucy Gunning, *Climbing Around My Room, The Football Players*; Pipilotti Rist, *I'm not the Girl who Misses Much*; and Gillian Wearing, *Confess All on Video. Don't Worry You will be in Disguise. Intrigued? Call Gillian… .*

ARTIST

Adam Ames

April 1995 was the first *Open Video Call* I was in. The first couple were very good. People showed works in progress and finished works. Personally, it had a big effect on my career. Out of the Artists Space *Open Video Call,* my video, along with Kristin Lucas's, was sent to a curator at the New York Film Festival, Lincoln Center and consequently we were both included there. Since I'd only been making video for two and a half years, it was especially wonderful to have an opportunity to show it to people who are not only established in the art world but forerunners in the field, like Barbara London and John Hanhardt.

The first video in the *Open Video Call* of June 1997 was a woman who taped her performance. It went on for an hour, but the length made for a boring setup and everyone was restless after 10 minutes. It was turned off because of the time limit. So that set a tone at the beginning. But the next tape, oh, man! That naked guy! I was there with my mom and her boyfriend, and the guy proceeded to lift his legs over his head and start touching himself. That evening we talked about whether or not that should have been included. My mom gets very absolutist when she feels

strongly about things and she said, "He shouldn't have been in it. It was horrible and it tainted all the other work that was up there." But it's an open call, and we're supposed to be open to anyone. Therefore, we can't tell someone not to submit something or even not to play something. Ideologically, I probably fall somewhere in the middle. Yes, it's open, but there was something about this that made me feel he did it to thumb his nose at the whole process, whether it was the art world or Artists Space or people in the audience. It was smug and self-righteous in its pornographic stance, which is a perfectly fine posture for art or anything. If someone had told me this would happen, I would have thought, "Great, he got a rise out of the audience or bothered some people." It's very tough to get a reaction or a response from audiences today. That's actually something I am interested in. I also want people to respond to the characters I play or the acts I perform. However, I want to do it in a way that's a little tougher, by mediating the work through stylization, for instance, or cropping and framing. I get a reaction by making people understand it's manipulated and artificial. I emphasize this and then have them respond anyway. What this guy did was too simplistic, it was a potshot.

Open Video Calls are also important for their screening deadline. You know the tapes are going to be seen by a certain group of people who come to Artists Space at a certain time. It is fabulous that Artists Space is open to video in the first place—a lot of places aren't. Because it's open, there's great stuff and there's mixed stuff. I've participated in four of them. With the exception of the naked guy, everything has been accepted very eagerly and enthusiastically.

Apr. 30–May 23: **Film, video, reading, and performance**. Original Squat Theatre performers and artist friends of Squat select emerging readers, videographers, filmmakers, and performers to present new work.

Apr. 30: Michelle Har Kim, poetry reading; Anna Koós, *3% of Knowledge*, essay film; Rebecca Moore and band, performance.

May 2: Kristin Lucas, *Cable Xcess*, video (Perry Hoberman); Bureau of Inverse Technology, *Suicide Box*, video; Panoptical Motor: Caspar Stracke and Julie Murray with Bradley Eros, Ikue Mori, and Komiko Kimoto, video (Peggy Ahwesh); Fridolin Schönwiese, *Cosmodrom*, film.

May 7: Bern Nix and trio (Eva Buchmuller); Robert Frank, *Hunter*, film with Stephan Balint; Jenõ Menyhàrt, performance.

May 9: Steve Doughton, *Ferrum 5000*, film (Ann Magnuson); Mica TV: Diane Nerwen and Les LeVeque, video; Gary Lucas, music, (John Cale).

May 14: Vito Acconci, reading; Peter Haury, video (Joseph Kosuth); 3 girl bands: Odes, Bliss, and Blood; B. Blush, music (Ralph McKay); Ramm Ellzee, performance (Eva Buchmuller and Anna Koós).

May 16: Midnight movies in prime time: Peggy Ahwesh, *The Family Crisis*; Vivian Dick with Lydia Lunch and Pat Place, *She Had Her Gun All Ready*; M. Henry Jones, *Soul City*; Julie Murray, *Anathema*; Robert Frank, outtakes and home movies; Marc Ribot, performance

May 21: Ari Marcopoulos, short films and videos (Jim Jarmusch); Tom Jarmusch, *Friends*, video; Birgit Staudt and Joerg Soechting, *Marc Ribot—Descent into Baldness*, video; Zeena Parkins, solo electric harp.

May 23: Aki Fujiyoshi, made-for-TV sculptures (Joseph Kosuth and Cornelia Lauf); Elliott Sharp, solo performances for Christian Marclay's music-box guitar and his own doubleneck bass guitar.

↙ Odes, May 14, 1996.
Photo: Anastasia Aukeman

June 6: **Reading and lecture**: Barry Yourgrau, new stories; Andras Halasz, *Cinematism*, lecture.

June 8, 15: **Film**. A screening of original Squat Theatre movies selected by Eva Buchmuller and Anna Koós.

June 13: **Reading and film**. Susan Daitch and Catherine Texier, new works; Chris Kraus, *Gravity & Grace*, new film.

ARTIST

Neil Goldberg My first experience with Artists Space was in April 1996, when I was in an *Open Video Call*. It was a stampede of video makers who were each given 10 minutes on a first-come first-served basis to show their work to a roomful of high-endurance video spectators. I remember it lasted about four hours. That evening of videos initiated a number of critical dialogues which were alternatively exhilarating, tedious, gorgeous, frustrating, and which continue to this day. Artists Space has provided a venue to present and discuss my work with fellow artists, critics, and curators. It has also provided a bridge to other institutions and exhibition opportunities. Artists Space seems singular among nonprofit spaces in bringing museum-level curators to see the work of emerging artists. I wonder how this relationship can be formalized, enlarged, and carried out past an artist's emergence into the art world? More importantly, Artists Space has provided a sense of continuity, a feeling that my work is being followed through time, addressed, goaded, criticized, and cultivated. As an artist I have neither felt coddled nor disregarded but simply taken at my word and engaged.

June 20: **Open Video Call.** Guest viewers John Hanhardt and Louise Neri. First-come, first-show for artists to present five to ten minutes of videotape: Tina LaPorta, *Camera work*; Rachel Schreider, *This is Not Erotica*; Les LeVeque, *The Free Space of the Commodity*; Diane Nerwen, *Under the Skin Game*; Kevin Hart, *Untitled*; Ann Korman, *Ice Queen/He Loves Me*; John and Allesandro, *Mean Room, Big Top, My Daddy Do To*; Barbara Pollack, *Game Boy*; Adam Ames, selected videos; Mike Sale; Ellen Cantor; Barbara Rosenthal, *Whispering Confession*; Bill Creston, *Cripple*; Catherine Cullen, *Shape of Desire, Adventures of a Lemon*; Laurie Halsey Brown, *A Forest of Forgotten Words*; Amy Jenkins, *Closures, Bathtub, House and Bedrooms*; Helen Rousakis, *Untitled Garlic 1-2-3*; Gabriella Simon, Anna Kiraly, *Next Please!*; Aki Fujiyoshi; Richard Gordon, *Untitled*; Neil Goldberg, *Hallelujah Anyway 1-2-3*; Nurit Newman, *Complex Princess*; Jessica Goodyear, *Jesica Piscis*; Kevin Kelley, *Supernatural Premiere*; Perry Bard, *The Kitchen Tapes*; Ethan Crenson, *Fission*; Jolie Guy, *Figure and Ground*; Lauren Berkowitz, Lisa Andrew, *Sightseeing Tour*; Roni Giviglino, *Times Square*; Maria Jose Lessa, *The Empty Arena*; Jamie Dolinko, *VIP, Ben Lisa Roberta*; Lisa Dilillo, *What is the Circumference of Your Belly Button*; Reynald Reynolds, *History of the Future*; Arleen Schloss, *Windows of Change/Chance*; Taryn FitzGerald, *In Your Quiet Little Way*; Lynn Shelton, *In the Bleak Midwinter, Secrets of the Flesh*; Mariana Jaroslavsky, *Tres Pinyols 7'25", Las Naranjas Del Sueño 1'25"*; Doron, *Art Around the Park*; Aimeé Margolis, *Amy Hill Bridge*; Larry Shea, *Quest*; Mlho Suzuki, *Untitled*.

1996–97

The **Artists (web)Space** is initiated in November 1996, featuring a new artist every month. Artists who submit works on photo CDs to the **Irving Sandler Artists File** are curated on the **(web)Space**; the works are chosen from the expanding digital file. Each artist is profiled with a statement, 10 works, a resumé, and biography. The Website continues to present the bimonthly newspaper. Thread Waxing Space joins ABACA to replace Franklin Furnace who left during the season. Anastasia Aukeman resigns in January 1997, and Pip Day is hired as Curator in February 1997.

Sept. 6–Oct. 26: **A Strategy Hinted At: New Conceptual Artists** (Anastasia Aukeman): Steven Carter, Brigitte Engler, Aki Fujiyoshi, Neil Goldberg, Benita-Immanuel Grosser, Orit Raff, Mike Sale, and Michael Zahn. Newspaper essays by Anastasia Aukeman and Peter Halley. Sept. 10–Oct. 12: Free beginner yoga sessions by Benita-Immanuel Grosser.

Sept. 28: **Meet the Artists**. Discussion.

Oct. 5: **Neo-Conceptual Video** by artists in the exhibition.

↓ Photo: Bill Orcutt

Sept. 6–Oct. 26: **Project**: Angie Eng, *Safety Belt*, video installation (Anastasia Aukeman). Newspaper essay by Anastasia Aukeman.

Sept. 6: **Video and performance**: Benton Bainbridge, Naval Cassidy, Angie Eng, and Nancy Meli Walker, *The Pool*, live video performance.

Sept. 28: **Meet the Artists**. Discussion.

ARTIST

Kristin Lucas I was a student in New York, so I went around and looked at different spaces all the time, and I knew about Artists Space. Perry Hoberman was teaching a computer animation class I took at Cooper Union. I was very interested in Perry's work because he was always into alternative spaces, setting up pieces which would only be around for a day or two or just an evening. He always put so much work into it. I liked that he was using technology and was critical of it at the same time. I'd never met anyone who had such a grasp for the material.

Perry invited me to show in the Squat Café during the *History of Squat Theatre* exhibition. I did not have anything so he really encouraged me to make something. It led to a big spree of all nighters from which I made my first video, *Cable Excess*, which related to Artists Space's open screening nights. The show wasn't until May, but there was an *Open Video Call* before that, so I made another video for it. I was so excited to finally be producing work again. When it was screened, it got a great reaction. Lots of people came. And then the program grew tremendously, from maybe 12 the first year to 50 the next. We were up all night watching them. You (Claudia Gould) called me to screen another video the night someone from the Whitney Museum came. I tried to get an entirely new video together but couldn't. However, I was able to bring in material, which I hadn't finished editing. A lot of people were showing excerpts of work or work in progress.

Then Anastasia Aukeman recommended me to Gavin Smith, and I was selected for the New York Film Festival, Lincoln Center. Artists Space did a good job promoting me. Because of Artists Space, I ended up in the New York Video Festival and the Whitney Biennial. Graham Leggat from MOMA was another person who came. He looked at my tapes after the recommendation you gave them and decided to work with me. When I showed at the second *Open Video Call,* I already had a following. It was so great.

I'm interested in working with the space and doing an alternative project like performance, because I can engage the audience on a totally different level. I can add a dimension to the work. The performance I did for Artists Space is about my relationship to an audience and about myself as a multimedia artist. It's about the competition I have when I'm in a space with a monitor and challenging the relationship to that hypnotic box. I want to refocus the attention onto the body so it provides a presence, my physicality, in the space. For *Station to Station* I submitted drawings and some things from my portfolio to Gary Simmons and Tony Oursler. The performance related to video because I was doing a live mix and editing the video while performing. The wall drawing provided the background for the performance. It was a sound piece and a sketch for the videos. In it I was dealing with technology and the pervasiveness of media in our culture.

<table>
<tr><td>

1996 OCT – 1997 JAN

</td><td>

Oct. 28: **Political Advertisment (1952–1996)**. Premiere screening of a video anthology of 12 years of presidential campaign ads, edited by Antonio Muntadas and Marshall Reese.

</td><td>

Nov.: **Artists(web)Space**: Jeremy Stanbridge.

</td><td>

Nov. 9 – Jan. 4: **A Living Testament of the Blood Fairies** (Geoffrey Hendricks, Frank Moore, and Sur Rodney (Sur). Text-based work on fairytales, cartoons, myths, and rituals by artists with HIV/AIDS who have been served by the Archive Project of Visual AIDS: Robert Blanchon, Brian Buczak, Valerie Caris, Joe De Hoyos, Robert Farber, Copy Berg, Rebecca Guberman, Elliott Linwood, David Nelson, Mike Parker, Jorge Veras, and Martin Wong. Newspaper with statements by the artists.

Dec. 7: **Meet the Artists:** Discussion with curators.

</td></tr>
</table>

ARTIST

Michael Zahn

Anastasia Aukeman and I talked about different aspects of how painting and information relate to one another and about deconstructed environments as screen reality or actual space. Artists Space has a reputation for showing groundbreaking work by emerging artists and organizing shows of impact, some immediate, others not. The most important show everybody knows about is *Pictures*.

It's pretty obvious now that context generates content in innumerable ways. That's indicative of postmodernity in general. But all these questions about choice and framing and rationale are as routinely overdetermined as are all definitions about medium. In *A Strategy Hinted At: New Conceptual Artists,* Anastasia was trying to examine the legacies of both the minimal and conceptual movements, with one being the logical development of the other. She wanted to show the way they placed the linguistic experience at the center of their investigation of the material world.

Many artists in this show dealt with the weird question of dematerialization. What attracted me at the beginning of my career was all the endgame questions about painting and the death of painting that nobody really seems to care about anymore. My practice definitely relates to painting, and I made it clear to Anastasia I didn't want to present work that was two-dimensional, which meant having two walls that intersect to form another. Artists Space allowed me to pursue something conceivably salable but definitely not portable. It was a question whether or not it was painting, sculpture, or some quasi-architectural intervention. If it wasn't portable, then it certainly wasn't an original piece. And this, in turn, raised more questions about presence and absence and pattern and sequence and other temporal issues. Once I started working in the space, things just emptied out more and more. I wanted to keep it very lean and spare, to have a stylized formality like a Japanese garden. It was a total thrill to have a yoga class in the next room.

CURATOR

Anastasia Aukeman

A recurring theme of my job at Artists Space was working with fantastic artists on their shows. Right off the bat I worked with Willie Cole, who was installing *Unnaturally Yours*. Then there was Frank Moore, Geoff Hendricks, Sur Rodney (Sur), Tony Oursler, and Gary Simmons. And also the Squat Theatre people, Eva Buchmuller and Anna Koós, who are both amazing and have boundless energy. Their show was *Mr. Dead & Mrs. Free: A History of Squat Theatre.*

Looking back at the slides of the performances from the early 70s, it seemed like an idyllic time for Artists Space, so I made it one of my goals as Curator to revive the evening events. Whether curating shows myself or working with another curator, I wanted to have nonstop evening events. *Squat Theatre* launched it. We had musicians, poets, and performances every Tuesday and Thursday night for three months. It was a very bonding experience, working on the schedule with Eva Buchmuller and Anna Koós. I got to know people like Elliott Sharp and Ralph McKay. The project was so huge, I was floundering a little and Ralph called to offer his assistance. He became my right-hand person. He knows everyone, and connected me to musicians and to performance and film people. He's the organizer of the Nantucket Film Festival and introduced me to the people from the New York Film Festival at Lincoln Center, who organize the film and video summer series. That connection resulted in getting Adam Ames, Kristin Lucas, and the Bureau of Inverse Technology to come to Artists Space to see the videos and the films, and subsequently they were invited to be in the Lincoln Center film festival. So Ralph was a great find, he was there 100 percent. These events needed a lot of prep work, installing monitors, setting up sound systems for these bands. He did essentially all of that or found me people who could because I didn't know how to set up microphones and equipment. He did everything gratis and was there for almost every night. It was very labor intensive.

It was in Squat's spirit to do performances and poetry readings, they did it routinely. It just happened to coalesce with what I saw as something Artists Space needed. And it was an opportunity for Eva and Anna to reinvite filmmakers who had been part of Squat Theatre to return and screen their films such as Robert Frank and his *Hunter*. Vito Acconci was connected with Squat Theatre. Mark Rebo, Peggy Ahwesh, Jim Jarmusch, half of the programming consisted of friends of Squat Theatre. When we invited people to select other people it got really interesting. We extended the exhibition another month. I invited Susan Daitch and Catherine Texier to read, simply because I was interested in their work, and then it became a little looser and more organic. My first show was based around the idea of neo-conceptualism. I had seen the term neo-conceptualism used in *Artforum* and thought, "Let's explore what conceptualism is now." CONTINUED

Nov. 9–Jan. 4: **Project:** Jeff Francis, wigs (Cindy Sherman). Newspaper introduction by Cindy Sherman.

Nov.14: **Discussion.** Terence Dixon, *Artists in 'Cyberia': Protecting Art on the Internet*; W. E. Scott Hoot, *Estate Planning for Artists Living with HIV/AIDS.*

Dec.: **Artists(web)Space:** Inka Essenhigh.

Dec. 4: **Fourth Annual Night of 1,000 Drawings.** Open call to artists to donate small works on paper. A drawings exhibition and benefit sale.

A Living Testament of the Blood Fairies, Nov. 9, 1996–Jan. 4, 1997.

← Copy Berg, *Faxed Journal Drawings,* 1996, installation.
Photo: Bill Orcutt

↓ Elliott Linwood, *Initiation,* 1993.

↘ Photo: Bill Orcutt

Jan.: **Artists(web)Space:** Jean-Marie Martin.

ANASTASIA AUKEMAN / CONTINUED

The show was a shining moment during my time at Artists Space because it was selected as the worst show of the season by *Artforum*. Initially, I was stunned and hurt because I had gone to such lengths to get them a nice press shot. Jan Avgikos wrote this snotty review about what a vapid show it was. But it's one of my guidelines as a curator: if it gives one pause enough to write a venomous review, there must be something there. The whole Hairy Hoo School in Chicago is based on that. That was my high point. So, thank you, Jan Avgikos.

It was followed by the *Living Testament of the Blood Fairies,* curated by Frank Moore, Geoff Hendricks, and Sur Rodney (Sur), which was just incredibly moving. They were so thoughtful and so much fun to hang out with. That show was probably the most satisfying for me to put together. Initially, I was apprehensive about the idea of putting only artists who are HIV positive in the exhibition. But in the course of putting the show together I got a chance to ask Frank what that meant about artistic integrity and curatorial vision, where that fits in when you're narrowing

your group down to artists who have AIDS. Frank had thought quite a bit about it and this opened up a really interesting dialogue for me. I frequently gave guided tours of the exhibition to graduate students or high school classes. The reactions from the audience was consistently, "Wow, these are people just like me." It's very cliché and trite, but it gave a human face to AIDS.

We published in our newspaper the event *Meet the Artists*. On a given Sunday, the artists would come to the exhibition and the public could hear what they had to say. Each time, it was amazing. People would be passing through town or come purposefully to hear this. Inevitably we got a group that grew as the artists talked. Some people would say, "What the hell do you think you're doing, this is garbage!" Then the artists could defend themselves. Or they asked more penetrating questions and got involved in a real dialogue. Again, *Meet the Artists* was a way of bringing back the old Artists Space where it really was just a bunch of people sitting around hashing out issues, which is lacking in the art world now. Today there's no center and there's no community. So I made a point to include as a component of every exhibition a *Meet the Artists,* and evening activities in between.

Benefit dinner in honor of Richard Armstrong
and Mary Miss, January 10, 1997.
Anastasia Aukeman and Richard Armstrong.

Ben van Berkel, *Mobile Forces*, installation.
Project: Apr. 12 – May 24, 1997.
Photo: Bill Orcutt

Station 1

John Bratlin
Maura Jasper
Les LeVeque

Benefit dinner in honor of Richard Armstrong
and Mary Miss, January 10, 1997.
Mary Miss.

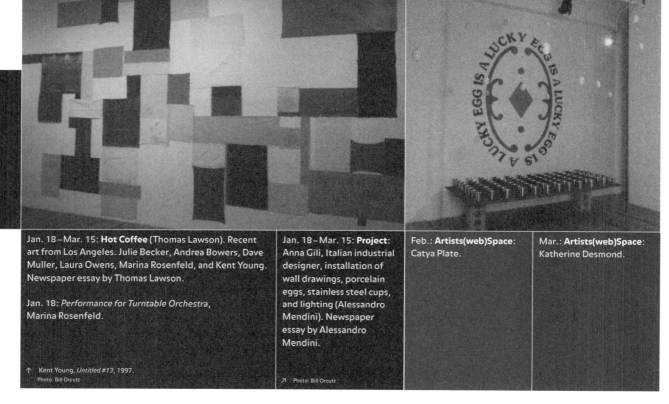

Jan. 18–Mar. 15: **Hot Coffee** (Thomas Lawson). Recent art from Los Angeles. Julie Becker, Andrea Bowers, Dave Muller, Laura Owens, Marina Rosenfeld, and Kent Young. Newspaper essay by Thomas Lawson.

Jan. 18: *Performance for Turntable Orchestra*, Marina Rosenfeld.

↑   Kent Young, *Untitled #13*, 1997.
    Photo: Bill Orcutt

Jan. 18–Mar. 15: **Project**: Anna Gili, Italian industrial designer, installation of wall drawings, porcelain eggs, stainless steel cups, and lighting (Alessandro Mendini). Newspaper essay by Alessandro Mendini.

↗   Photo: Bill Orcutt

Feb.: **Artists(web)Space**: Catya Plate.

Mar.: **Artists(web)Space**: Katherine Desmond.

ARTIST / CURATOR

Tom Lawson My show at the Hudson Street space was called *In Camera*. It was four boxes and a wall drawing installed in Room 207, a small place down the back corridor, where you could try things. They were tiny things, 10 inches high, made of wood and painted black, with peepholes. You looked in to see a space fractured with mirrors. Some had little figures in them, some were more abstract and hard to define spaces. They were great scenes with a funhouse of mirrors and a shoot-out. No one knew what or who they were shooting, if it was a reflection or an actual target. The drawing was theoretically a projection of one of those images right onto the wall. The idea was to look into this little hole and see this little space, and out through the space there would be the drawing on the wall.

One of the great things about alternative spaces at that time was you could do something that basically only your friends saw. It was out of your studio, but not completely out in the world. If you had an idea, you just talked to Paul McMahon, and two or three weeks later you showed something for one or two weeks. It's very important for young artists to try things where they can really fuck up. That's one of the saddest things about the situation now, there's all this pressure, it's make or break.

In the last 20 years of alternative spaces there has been a loss in the generational connection. Back in the 70s it was all about younger people, youth culture. Now, these spaces have grown older, are more established, and there's a loss. On the other hand, there's also a gain, people know how to do things, they don't have to reinvent the wheel every time. There's an established way of getting things done, making sure people know about the show, disseminating the information, the depth of the archive.

I was on a panel at LACE just before coming out to New York to set up *Hot Coffee*. They had a show commemorating BLISS, one of the newer, noninstitutional alternative spaces in Los Angeles. It's just someone's living room and occasionally they do a show. The panel was on the future of alternative spaces. I was struck by how alternative spaces were originally about trying to find a way for artists to live and make art that would make sense in a new situation, not just produce expensive objects. This future space would be more complex and our support would be more complex. We lost that in the 80s. The market boom took over. At this conference the younger people didn't want to think about working collaboratively or cooperatively. They didn't understand what that meant. But it's important. We need to keep the system running and available because, eventually, when they want it, it won't be there.

I am from a small town in a small country. It's very difficult to be an artist in a small place and very difficult to be a young artist. It's easier once you've done something, then you can go back. So I went to New York, but I didn't have a very clear idea of what that meant. I didn't even know how to show. Today's students understand all that. Within six months of my arrival in New York from Edinburgh, I met Paul at Artists Space on Wooster Street. I had a Saturday job sitting in a gallery on Wooster Street. The phone rang and it was this guy who wanted me to keep an eye on this chair and make sure it wasn't stolen. It was a Scott Burton bronze chair and the idea was to install it on the street. I got to talking to Paul. He was doing what I was doing, but at a more interesting place. When they moved down to Hudson Street I got to know Helene Winer. She had these Friday afternoon get-togethers. It wasn't exactly formal. If you were nearby, you might drop over to Artists Space and hang out in Helene's office at the end of the week. They were mostly just hilarious afternoons, Paul was the funniest person. He's a riot. Cindy Sherman was there, of course, and David Salle, Barbara Bloom, Sherrie Levine, Jim Welling, and all that crowd. Richard Prince came in a little later on and Robert Longo was around. All those Buffalo people came in together. Matt Mullican would sometimes be there. They were just cut-ups, hanging around gossiping and making fun of things, talking about art ideas.

Susan Morgan and I started *Real Life* magazine, which was made possible by Artists Space, who conduited grants to us from the NEA and from NYSCA until

CONTINUED

Apr.: **Artists(web)Space**: Greg Geffner.

Apr. 12–May 24: **Project**: Ben van Berkel, *Mobile Forces*, site-specific installation exploring the role diagrams play in the architectural design process (Greg Lynn). Newspaper essay by Greg Lynn.

Apr. 12–May 24: **Station to Station** (Tony Oursler and Gary Simmons). Exhibition of single channel video, drawing, and wall pieces by nine artists exploring the relationship between the processes of making video and thinking: John Brattin, Dan Cooney, Ethan Crenson, Sam Easterson, Scott Gregory, Maura Jasper, Ann Kugler, Les LeVeque, and Kristin Lucas. Newspaper conversation between Tony Oursler and Gary Simmons.

Apr. 17: **Performance**: Kristin Lucas, *"a common object has special powers…"*

Apr. 19: **Meet the Artists**. Discussion.

May: **Artists(web)Space**: Eveline Mooibroek.

June: **Artists(web)Space**: Susan Otto.

↑ Sam Easterson, drawings and notes.
Photo: Bill Orcutt

TOM LAWSON / CONTINUED

we moved to Los Angeles in 1991. In a funny way, *Real Life* came out of those Friday afternoon sessions at Artists Space.

It was always about where could we show and what were we going to do next. It didn't seem as though the art world at that time was all that interested in discussing young or new ideas. The big magazines obviously didn't want to. *Avalanche* had closed down. *Art-Rite* was failing or losing energy and didn't seem to publish very often. There was a gap and we talked about how someone should do a magazine. At some point during one of those discussions I thought, "Well, no one's going to do it unless someone does it." Susan and I were together back then and she was a writer, so it was great to have someone who could find people to write. It was one of the hard things about putting together an artist's magazine. Once we got money from NYSCA we paid $100 to the writers. We published 23 in total. We raised the money and did preliminary work in 1978 and the first issue came out in 1979. Some years were busier than others and some numbers were double issues. I remember going up to Buffalo to print the first issue, it was so much cheaper there. Cindy and Robert had a friend who had a print shop and would do a deal for us. But the thought of going to Buffalo in the dead of winter on a Greyhound bus was crazy.

In 1979 I was invited to curate a Scottish artists show. It was a mix: some painting, some sculpture, some photographic conceptual art. The artists in the show were all friends of mine from the art college I'd gone to, the University of St. Andrews, in Edinburgh. They had all come over to New York and were waiting for their work to arrive—there

It's very important for young artists to try things where they can really fuck up. That's one of the saddest things about the situation now, there's all this pressure, it's make or break.

was some hold-up in customs. Finally we got a call and had to go down to the World Trade Center for the work to clear because there was an issue about some photographs. My friends are all my size, big guys, and we had on big overcoats. We entered this office and a completely blasé New York secretary looks up and says, "Yeah?" We tell her we're here from Artists Space and she turns to her intercom and says, "Four men from outer space."

I get real pleasure out of thinking, talking, and handling art. It's a blast to make and move images and to try to do things without moving images. I had been thinking about how interesting younger artists are in Los Angeles. It has probably always been fairly interesting because of its great art schools and its ongoing and rolling alternative scene, which is a little less organized and institutional than the older style alternative spaces. There's a lot of activity, and I was beginning to see something happening there, which inspired me to want to do a show or write an article—something. So, when you (Claudia Gould) invited me to organize a show at Artists Space, it was great, just perfect. I actually had a bigger show in mind, of the new painting ideas developing in Los Angeles. But *Hot Coffee* was a way to test this. It allowed me to throw something together to see if it made any sense or if it was just something I liked and had a response to. I still don't know if I can articulate it, but I do think the show came together more coherently than I could have hoped for. It was a mix of very private and very public work. It was about mass media with the Hollywood issue in the background and it was about everyday life, the sublime and the ridiculous all wrapped into one. It had to do with the Southern California experience, where there's tons of space but you're in your room for weeks. It's very flattering that Jerry Saltz related *Hot Coffee* to the *Pictures* show. I was just pointing to some new developments. But there might well be something fairly important happening in Los Angeles. If *Hot Coffee* proves to be an early sign of that, all the better.

June 7 – July 19: Tampering with the Reel (Pip Day). Mini festival of film and video by emerging artists Andrew Bordwin, Mark Lewis, Stom Sogo, Jalal Toufic, and Erika Yeomans. Newspaper essay by Pip Day

→ Andrew Bordwin, *CM2: Decisions Kept*, installation. Photo: Bill Orcutt

June 7 – July 19: Project Space: Artists Select Series. Two-week exhibition of video projects by emerging artists selected by established video artists. Presented in conjunction with **Tampering with the Reel**. Newspaper.
June 7 – 21: Connie Walsh (Marina Abramovic).
June 7: Evening screening: Connie Walsh, *Fondly Fruit, Transition* and *Body Bag*.
June 24 – July 5: Carola Dertnig (Alix Pearlstein)
July 8 – 19: Liza Johnson (Judith Barry)
July 8: Evening screening: Liza Johnson, *Good Sister/Bad Sister*, 1996, single channel; Rita Gonzalez, *Electronic Bodies*, 1996 (Liza Johnson).

June 9, 26, and July 10: Open Video Call. Evening screenings of five to ten minutes of videotape on a first-come, first-show basis. Video presented in conjunction with **Tampering with the Reel**.

June 9: Guest viewers Stephen Vitiello and Cheryl Donegan: Thelma Mathis, *Victoria's Secret Life*; Pete Silvia, *X. Artist*; Marcello Mazzella; Liz Bougatsos, excerpts from *Gun Dilemma, Fallacies of Food, Milk and Honey*; Milenka Berengolo, *W(hole)*, excerpts; Corinne Cherepak, footage from *Serve Yourself*, photo/video installation; Adam Ames, *Dudley*; Seth Kirby, *A Cigarette Before Unrest*; Kari French, *Beyond the Surreal World of the Barbie Dolls*; Eddie Pardovani, *Hot Pursuit*; Aimeé Margolis, *2 Poems*; Wendy Klemperer, Chris Schavo, *Courtship of Rambo and Smileyface, My Pretty Pony, Summertime*;

Tom Jarmusch, Fabienne Gautier, *Left Aside*; Lynn Mullins, *Untitled*, part of installation *Seams Made Visible*.

June 26: Guest viewers Gavin Smith and Bob Paris: Corinne Cherepak, *Serve Yourself, Self Portrait Series*; Ethan Crenson, *Fission*; Lucretia Knapp, *Casting Stones*; Choon-Jin Lee, *Halloween*; Marcello Mazzella, *Elicon Silicon*; Joe Sola, *Machine*; Liz Bougatsos, *Fallacies of Food, Gun Dilemma*; Christina Cobb, three excerpts; Shang Shang, *Octopus Chair, Powpaw*; Domenica Bucalo, *Naked Swimmers*; Gardner Post, Emergency Broadcast Network, *Instructional Music Videos for the 21st Century*; Bleiz, *Professor Potamus*.

July 10: Guest viewers Barbara London and Kristin Lucas: Carola Dertnig, *Dancing with Remote*; Kim Connerton, Eiko Sakai, *Mediatation*; Adam Ames, *Rant*; Andrew Bordwin, *CM2: Interior, CM2: Exterior*; Johanna MacArthur, *Ant*; Seppo Renvall and Alli Sarolarner, *Greetings to Mum, Dancing Shortly I & II, Nonstoppampam*; Robert Lawrence, *3 scripts for Performance*; Lynn Tondrick, *Northeast Corridor*; Dahn Hiuni, *Interview*; Marcello Mazzella, *Elicon Silicon*; Mau Ceppi, *Panoramic Voltage*; Ali Maino and Josh Cicerone, *Josie, Wrinkle*; Myriam Varela, *Chicken Habitat*; Amy Jenkins, *Closures*; Joe Sola, *Machine*; Corinne Cherepak, *Bathing with Chopin*.

ARTIST/CURATOR

Frank Moore I have a vague recollection that Donald Droll stimulated or provoked my inclusion in the *Selections* show. Or he may have suggested me to someone who did because Donald had been turned on to me by the painter Jim Bishop, who put me in a show at P.S. 1.

At that time I was dealing with format, making shaped paintings. Then I thought about what was coming off on the inside of the paintings and I cut big holes in them. But it wasn't simply a formal problem. I worked representationally, trying to hook painting up to some meaning. It was a period when we were all young and going in and out of relationships more rapidly than we do now. It was a metaphor for finding yourself in a relationship with someone who's not really committed. You might be in an embrace, but their mind might be somewhere completely different. I was experimenting and Artists Space provided a forum to think about the work from different points of view in a more objective surrounding, stripped of personal reference. There's a whole bubbling ferment of young and older artists who haven't yet achieved a certain level essential for success. It's clear how valuable these opportunities are. Some people go through the system quickly and graduate. Others stay for a longer time.

It's hard to imagine I would have done something different for *A Living Testament of the Blood Fairies* show. I really enjoyed all the wonderful encounters, like working with Joe De Hoyas, who is so young, earnest, intense, and wasn't getting any play in the fine art arena. The show made a huge difference for him. It also was a major event in Rebecca Guberman's life. Seeing the impact was moving for me. It takes me back to an earlier level of excitement and passion. One can get so jaded here. It all seemed to fall so beautifully into place, including the funding. There were so many people trying to help make it work, even coming from beyond the grave. It was a difficult period in my life in terms of my health. But in the end it was great, especially because Geoff Hendricks and Sur Rodney (Sur) were magic to work with.

June 12: **Performance**: *Collective Clubhouse Project*, experimental film and 'musik' by Adrian Goycoolea, Bruce McClure, Alex Mendizabal, Stom Sogo, and others.

July: **Artists(web)Space**: Marco Breuer.

July 9: **An Evening of New Music** (Carol Parkinson). Electronically altered sounds, live processed music, and interactive video by Lisa Karrer, David Simons, Annie Gosfield, Roger Kleier, Paul Geluso, Leopanar Witlarge, Daniel Carter, Tom Beyer, Dafna Naphtali, and VJ Lo$$Vega$.

Aug.: **Artists(web)Space**: Joe McKay.

↑ Carola Dertnig, *Dancing with Remote*, video still. **Open Video Call**, July 10, 1997

↓ Karen Kimmel, *Savor*, installation and performance. **Project**, Sept. 11–Nov. 1, 1997.
© Karen Kimmel

1997–98

In September 1997, Artists Space establishes an endowment fund and cash reserve from the proceeds of the sale of a building it inherited in 1985 from the Mark Rothko Foundation and from an anonymous member of the Board. In April the Website address is changed to www.artistsspace.org. The Lower Manhattan Cultural Council leaves ABACA.

Sept. – Oct:
Artists(web)Space: Marcello Mazzella.

Sept. 11 – Nov. 1: **Project**: Karen Kimmel, *Savor*, installation and three performances incorporating design and architecture (Pip Day). Newspaper with artist interview by Pip Day.

Sept. 11, Oct. 2, 23: **Performance**: Karen Kimmel.

Sept. 27: **Artist Talk**.

ARCHITECT

Ben van Berkel Greg Lynn and I met a few years ago in Holland. We developed a particular pull and push game, where we used each other's ideas and developed them in our individual work.

I had seen Greg's show so I knew about Artists Space. I like this specific method of working in which one architect invites the next for a show. What struck me was the nonthematic approach, which was inspirational and quite unusual for an architect. It was wonderful to have an exhibition on the topic of working together on a diagram. We made a plane of consistency, which we called "wallpaper," on the wall of the gallery, and emphasized the diagram as a generator to greatly enlarge the projects alongside reference material, showing very small pictures of the buildings themselves. Also interesting was the specific mediation technique of working with digital prints on very traditional material. It gave them a double effect throughout the whole space.

Most architectural exhibitions today have this finished look. Architects like to control too much. They have their particular photographers and they keep most of the work in their pocket. I remember we all had a very interesting dialogue about how Greg and I could structure this project in order to bring in elements from 1987 to the present and still have it look fresh. Although the structure was linear, the eye didn't read it that way. What we did was literally pull together the work, which referred to the thinking process. The whole idea coalesced when we decided to be honest and show everything. This lightheartedness and bubbling material that went in all directions made the exhibition very casual, which was nice.

This lightheartedness and bubbling material that went in all directions made the exhibition very casual, which was nice.

Sept. 11–Nov. 1: **Permutations** (Pip Day and Debra Singer): David Arnold, Candice Breitz, Nina Katchadourian, David Lindberg. Newspaper with essay by Pip Day and Debra Singer.

Sept. 11: **Performance:** David Arnold.

Sept. 27: **Artists Talk.**

↙ (TOP) Nina Katchadourian, *Surface Spoils: Concrete Music from Europe*, 1997.

↙ (BOTTOM) David Arnold, *Helicopters*, 1997 (detail).
Photos: Bill Orcutt

Sept. 18: **Open Video Call.** First-come, first-show for artists to present five to ten minutes of videotape: Richard Gordon, *Transference*; Shawn Reddy, *Water Skier*; Marcello Mazzella, *Robot/Me, Labor Day 10001001*; Taryn FitzGerald, *Knead*; Yael Bartana, *Shtime, Ant-Bulb*.

Nov.–Dec.:
Artists(web)Space:
Steve Robinson.

Nov. 14–Jan. 10:
Project: *Present Tense: The Architecture of George Ranalli* (Michael Sorkin), drawings and models. Newspaper with essay by Michael Sorkin.

← Photo: Bill Orcutt

ARTIST

Karen Kimmel *Savor* was a different audience and a different way of working for me. It was an opportunity to consider what my art could be, given the architectural parameters within the space. It was the first time I had done three performances in a single piece. I was concerned about it, but that was the risk. Artists Space really worked with me to help attract an audience to respond to that situation. It made a big difference because the piece naturally comes to life when there are people. I was surprised to find that when you put art on a pedestal, even though it's quasi-functional, it becomes intimidating to people. I learned a lot from that experience, in terms of what is approachable and what's not. I also learned how the dynamic of individuals activating an object opens up possibilities, lowers intimidation levels, and lets people in. I don't know if the installation was completely successful when it wasn't activated. I wanted people to walk through it, sit on it, and experience it. But you don't ride something without permission, so it plays with those ideas. On the whole, it was successful because I learned where I want to take it next time.

ARTIST

David Arnold *Permutations* was the first "official" exhibition I had after I got out of graduate school at Columbia University. It was a "testing out" for me. My earlier work was a lot rougher, more brutal, especially the heavily performance-based stuff. For Artists Space I thought about the fact that the work would be installed for two months. I made some good decisions and some bad decisions. But it's the first time I've had to make them based on the length of time the work would be in a gallery and the fact that people are going to come look at it who don't know me from a hot rock. What they see at Artists Space they compare to the work they see in the billion art galleries surrounding Artists Space. My work, then, is placed in a context I have to be very aware of. I know they have just gone to the Jack Tilton Gallery or Deitch Projects and they're next coming here. On the other hand, even though my work is really out there in the world, it's also a little more forgiving at Artists Space. It's not as if it were my first solo show where if I had really screwed up it would be like taking a baseball bat to my head. When the art world viewers come and don't like something or don't think someone is quite there yet, they realize this is the artist's first output and the mistakes made here are part of learning about what it's like to show. Your career's not over. But you're only going to be in one show at Artists Space, and it's exciting because it is where so many people have gotten their start. It was also nice to have some control over what pieces were shown in *Permutations*. There was discussion and there were links between the other work in the show.

Nov. 14 – Jan. 10: **Lines of Loss** (Gabriel Orozco). Exhibition of contemporary Mexican artists with works ranging from sound installations to video, kinetic sculpture, and architectural interventions: Gabriel Kuri, Damian Ortega, Manuel Rocha, Mauricio Rocha, Guillermo Santamarina. Newspaper with essay by Gabriel Orozco.

Nov. 14: **Performance:** Guillermo Santamarina.

↘ Guillermo Santamarina.
Photo: Pip Day

Gabriel Kuri, sculpture.
Photo: Bill Orcutt

Dec. 9: **Fifth Annual Night of 1,000 Drawings.** Open call to artists to donate small works on paper. A drawings exhibition and benefit sale.

Jan. – Feb.: **Artists(web)Space:** Blanche Dolmatch.

Jan. 24 – Mar. 14: **Abstraction in Process II** (Claudia Gould and Irving Sandler). Abstract painters Elizabeth Cooper, Lori Ellison, Ian Hughes, Andrew Kennedy. Newspaper with introductions by Claudia Gould and Irving Sandler and statements by the artists. (Part I, curated by Roberta Smith, was shown Mar. 26 – May 2, 1987).

Jan. 24: **Artists Talk** with selector.

↓ Andrew Kennedy, installation view.
Photo: Bill Orcutt

Jan. 24–Mar. 14: **Project**: Elke Lehmann, *4(to)5*, (Dennis Adams) installation with enclosed rats. Newspaper introduction by Dennis Adams.

Jan. 24: **Artist Talk** with selector.

← Photo: Bill Orcutt

1998 JAN–MAR

All photographs from Benefit screening and dinner of Cindy Sherman's film *Office Killer*, Dec. 2, 1997.

All photographs from
Spring Benefit April 11, 1996.

1998 FEBRUARY

Feb. 10: **Open Video Call.** Guest viewers Gavin Smith, Bob Paris, and Marina Rosenfeld). First-come, first-show for artists to present five to ten minutes of videotape: Pet Silvia, *What Ain't Art*; Scott Fulmer, *Monologue*; So Yong Kim, *She Dog*, *Three Actions*; Anne Gardiner, *Look Up and Smile*; Elyce Semenec, *Free Falling*, *Surrender (love)*; Stephanie Rothenberg, *Untitled*; Rose Miasaki, *Inner Dive*, *Untitled*; Richard Gordon, *3-D*; Susan Ingraham, *Perlop*; Rich Sullivan, *Tourist*; Andrew Bordwin and Adam Ames, *The Night I Showed at Lincoln Center*; Grant Harris, *Infospace*, Kiomi Kawaski, *Untitled*.

Installation view. **Digital Mapping: Architecture as Media**

ARTIST / BOARD

Tony Oursler
I was mostly showing videos in '82. I had done a bunch of installation pieces that were like the piece we showed in *Façades, Landscapes, and Interiors*. There were three parts to it, mostly a card, paper, and an electronics combination. The piece was a TV inside an oil derrick, it would faintly receive broadcast signals. There were some lights that plugged in, too. I had shown something at the Kitchen before that when I was in school, but this was the first installation I showed in Manhattan. It was based on my work *Son of Oil*, which connects a lot of the mythology around oil production and petrochemicals. It was a very conspiratorial piece. There was an electric light built into this jar of burning petroleum jelly so it kept warming up and oozing out onto this painted surface—it was really foul. I don't remember the reaction, I just remember it was a great thing to do. That was the whole thing for me, finally to get to show these pieces. Although they had high-tech stuff built into them, they were very ephemeral, just paper and paint. They weren't really meant to be preserved.

When Dan Walworth took the helm of the video department at Artists Space it was interesting, because he's a super scholarly guy, but not without a sense of humor. He's also an artist in his own right, so he had great energy to bring to the place. I think it was a renaissance time for Artists Space in terms of media. Dan was championing work he was into, and it was great to see Artists Space still cranking at a time when everyone was only paying attention to money. It was already 1988 and having Dan there was cool because he had more of a Marxist attitude in a period of heavy economics in the art world. However, people like myself were not participating in that financial high in any way, shape, or form. It was an incredibly depressing era in New York, so I left. I moved to Boston to teach because I couldn't make a living in New York. Dan did very interesting programming, which flew in the face of what was happening. One of the great things about Artists Space was, by definition, they were more interested in ideas than in economics. I had a lot of strong feelings about that, having studied conceptual art and so forth. A lot of the

models for my production and my whole outlook on what could happen in the art world revolved around alternative spaces. There was this circuit where people who were making things completely outside the economic zone could work. There was Hallwalls in Buffalo, LACE in Los Angeles, and a myriad of places in San Francisco. In a way that was how Tony Labatt's work seemed to make a lot of sense for Artists Space, because he was also coming from that point of view in San Francisco.

The artists in *Station to Station* were, of course, Gary's (Simmons) choices and my students and acquaintances from Boston, New York, Minneapolis, and all around. We got names from various sources and dug into it that way. But basically we did everything collaboratively. I felt if either of us had a problem with somebody, they would be out. I've done some curating over the years in different places and I know a lot about how much you can ask and how much you can expect from people and how to bypass awkward situations that might come up. So we worked carefully with the artists in terms of trying to find work that fit in with what we were after. It was a process, a way of documenting process with these artists because rather than do a theme show, like an illustration, we wanted to have the work be first. More of a parallel to the way life is, you don't see things in a beam, you see things in sequence. What we wanted to do, as artists, was to figure out a way to highlight an artistic process that unified everybody. First we got the artists we were interested in and then we started to find aspects in their work that made sense as a group. We approached it as an exploration. We also kept in mind Artists Space's great history of showing relatively unknown people, and this was a chance to introduce them to the throngs.

I definitely learned something about my own work by doing this curatorial project. Number one, Gary is so astute when it comes to certain image-making. I learned a lot from him. Number two, just seeing so many artists' work, we could have done three shows. I've got lists. I felt it was an extension of teaching. That ties into early experiences I had with John Baldessari as a teacher, and also recommending someone to someone else at the Kitchen. There is a history that operates for me and it's one reason I wanted to get involved with Artists Space: to give a little bit of something back. I guess that's why we all do it. There's a great history of people doing that benevolent work for Artists Space. I've been a Board member for about a year. My involvement is financial as well as curatorial. I've also done an edition for Artists Space, the *Talking Photograph*.

The tenor of the time is so different. Now there's a youth culture engine that's currently really intense in the art world. It seems like younger artists are economically a higher priority. A lot of people feel that what happens in one of the commercial galleries across the street is maybe more interesting than what happens at Artists Space. Another reason I wanted to join the Board has to do with politics. There could be a space that operates in between the economic world. You could have a space where artists invent things, develop their work, and show their work, where it's truly outside the economic engine. I've had this argument with well-known critics and other artists: some gallerists believe if something is good or interesting it will automatically translate into the economic world, that it can be exhibited and

CONTINUED

TONY OURSLER / CONTINUED

will work through that system on its own merit. I don't necessarily agree. Maybe I'm wrong, maybe it is true. But once you're in the system and able to function within it, it's convenient to say everything can. I'm not sure. It's important that places like Artists Space exist, but they have to exist on a radical level, on a parallel to that structure, but not on a close parallel, because then there's a problem. If it truly can be done in the gallery across the street, then it doesn't have any business being shown at Artists Space. There may be enough small, commercially based exhibition spaces to make Artists Space appear from another era, but, we all agree, the jury's not in.

Mar. 28–May 23: **Digital Mapping: Architecture as Media** (Hani Rashid). Four young international architects: John Cleater, Ridzwa Fathan, Patrick Keane, and Marie Sester. Newspaper with essay by Hani Rashid.

Apr. 4: **Artists Talk:** John Cleater and Patrick Keane with curator.

1998 MAR–MAY

↙ Ridzwa Fathan.
Photo: Bill Orcutt

ARTIST

Andrew Bordwin Being new to getting my work out and showing it in different places, I see Artists Space as occupying a very important niche in the art world. It's divorced from the commerce of art and the necessity that selling work imposes upon the day-to-day business conducted in a gallery. Instead, the emphasis is on the curator's vision and the focus is on showing good art.

There's a much needed bridge between the world of the university, specifically art school and academia in general, and the world of the gallery. Artists Space makes that connection in such a way that artists have new ideas and fresh approaches to work, which makes for a higher caliber and greater focus than what you find at your average critique on any given day in class. In addition, it doesn't have any constraining obligation to the dollar bill. I like selling my work and I want a house in the country. But the question is, when does one discuss this during the process of making or showing art? I like it to be the last thing considered, not the first. In many instances, I'm finding it to be the first thing.

A direct effect to come out of *Tampering with the Reel* was my commitment to realizing an idea I've had for some time. My piece was incredibly labor intensive. So much work went into it, trips back and forth from here to Massachusetts where I did the editing and shooting. I really had to focus on what this tape was going to be about and resolve all these issues. I might not have gone through with it had it not been for the show.

Now that I have several other ideas for installation pieces, I am just going to go ahead and make them, because wanting to is enough. That's all that matters. It's of inestimable value to see an idea realized. That doesn't always happen.

← Installation view.

Mar. 28, Apr. 18, May 2, 16: **Performance**: Anne Gardiner, *Through the Tulips* and *The Red Red Rose*, installation and performance series. Newspaper essay by Anne Gardiner.

Apr. 4: **Artist Talk.**

May–June: **Artists(web)Space**: Benji Whalen.

June 4–July 17: **SCOPE: Summer Video Festival** (Pip Day). Selections from an international call for entries, rotating every two weeks. Newspaper.

June 4–17: **SCOPE 1:** Adam Ames, *(not)hole*, 1998; Perry Bard, *My Little Box of Nazis*, 1997; Lynn Cazabon, *White Boy*, 1998; Martin Christel and Inge Lechner, *Untitled*, and *Horizontal Dancing*, 1997; Dan Cooney, *Blowing, Sucking, Breathing*, 1998; Carola Dertnig, *Dancing with Remotes Rehearsal*, 1998; Edy Ferguson, *Earth People* and *Metropolitan Life*, 1998; Peter Freund, *Foreign Film*, 1998;

Nancy Golden, *Soul Murder* and *Gerry Goodbye*, 1998; Yasmyn Karhof, *Not Waving but Drowning*, 1998; So Yong Kim, *She Dog*,1998; Harold Klemm and Theo Lipfert, *Make Sure Our Address Shows Through the Window*, 1997; Debra Bosio Riley, *Silent Orange Movie*, 1998; Lise Skou, *TV-Surveillance No. 2*; Franck and Oliver Turpin, *Siamoiserie II*; Type A, *Dance*, 1998; Mara Zoltners, *Duet* and *Descending Odalisque*, 1997.

June 4–July 17: **Project**: Concurrent with **SCOPE: Summer Video Festival**: Marjatta Oja, video installation; Nicolás Guagnini and Karin Schneider, collaborative documentary film (Liisa Roberts).

ARTIST

Anne Gardiner Artists Space is not restricted to a particular type of work or too focused on one idea. This seems to run across the board in terms of the work shown there, revealing an expansive vision still lacking in a lot of places, even other alternative spaces. If an institution is performance, but also architecturally based, it doesn't fit a category. There still may be a fear of spaces that aren't clearly defined.

CURATOR

Pip Day I started at Artists Space about six months after finishing my master's at the Center for Curatorial Studies at Bard College. It was a funny time because I had just spent two years thinking really hard about the role of the institution in contemporary art. The idea of working at an alternative space was appealing to me as it seemed there would be a lot of flexibility rethinking structures. Sinking my teeth into Artists Space, I realized it wasn't quite as idyllic as I had imagined. There was very little money, a tiny staff, and hardly any time for serious thinking and discourse about what the space needed. There was definitely a "poorhouse" stance taken at Artists Space—the sting of the poverty and debt incurred before Claudia's (Gould) time was still apparent. Although she had been tremendously successful in pulling the space back into financial shape, the staff and the programs still suffered. I regretted being so overextended that I couldn't spend more time on what I saw as this huge and very exciting potential for developing the space. Nevertheless, drywall had to be hung, walls painted, and lighting done. I had some great moments with artists during installations—some bizarre conversations have come out of paint fumes, exhaustion, and nervous energy. And I developed some great friendships.

The hairiest show to put together, but also one of the most fun, was *Digital Mapping: Architecture as Media*. Working with Hani Rashid was fabulous. Hani was enthusiastic, smart, and thoughtful about what he wanted to do with the show. I had very little knowledge of architecture so it was great to see him bring in some really experimental young architects and take some risks. Each architect made a project specifically for the show; some were successful, some less so, but all of them were interesting.

And like true architects, they waited for the *charrette* before finishing their installations. Ridzwa Fathan breezed in from Malaysia with a team of friends to help him and finally installed his last projector at 6:30 the night of the opening—which started at 6:00. He mistakenly threw out his master (and only) copy of his video the night before. It was missing in action for many hours, until finally it was found in the garbage the next day at about 7 a.m.

Concurrently there was Anne Gardiner's installation/performance in the Project Space—another crazy and great piece, really scary, where we peeled the paper off the plexiglass entrance to the space an hour into the opening party. We had some bizarre late-night moments during that installation, with the music for her piece, "Tiptoe Through the Tulips" and the theme song from *Rosemary's Baby,* echoing throughout the gallery. Although those installations were really draining, I had amazing contact with the artists.

I learned a lot from *Station to Station*. Tony Oursler and Gary Simmons were really clear about opening up the curatorial possibilities. They kept it very casual—monitors and VCRs were put on top of the boxes they came in, tapes on top of the

CONTINUED

310

June 6: Video screening (Marjatta Oja). Four Finnish artists: Tiina Reunanen, *Allison*; Nina Bjorkman, *Experiment with Black and White*; Kari Yli-Annala, *The Nests of Wind*; TV Program "A-Studio," *A document of Minna Heikinaho*.

June 11: Open Video Call. Guest viewer Thelma Goldin. First-come, first-show for artists to present five to ten minutes of videotape: Fabrice Guyot, *Le Bar Ideal*; Kim Lonnerton, *Portrait of the Artist as a Young Woman*; Nathalie Van Doxell, *Come Take a Bath in the Bathtub Where T-paulin Bath*; Marcia Antabi, *Hanah (SOB A PELE)*; Reverend Jen, *The Whitney Le Blanc Story*; Norm Francoeur, *Untitled*; Matias Aguilar, *Baaadlad of Papaya Unguinea*; Pet Silvia, *Original Sin*; Carola Dertnig, *Dancing with Remotes*; Dan Cooney, *Popping* and *Spitting*; Richard Gordon, *Transference*; Kevin Hart, *Untitled*; Nicola Benizzi and Michael Dvorkin, *Untitled*.

June 18: SCOPE 2: Opening reception and screening. Koya Abe, *Thank You Chinatown*, 1998; Dexter Buell, *Treadmill/Zootrope #1 (wipeout)*, and *Sleep/No Sleep*, 1997; Dan Cooney, *Spraying*, 1998; Roger Cremers, *Propositional Attitudes*, 1997; Ethan Crenson, *Addendum (to the video Fission)*, 1997; Michael Patrick Dee, *Signal*, 1998; Carola Dertnig, *Byketrouble*, 1998; Brendan Earley, *Room II "Eye,"* 1998; Sam Easterton, *A Sheep in Wolf's Clothing*, 1998; Neil Goldberg, *Still Point*, 1998; Bradley Rust Gray, *"mom (working),"* 1998; Liselot van der Heijden, *Chess*, 1997; Laura Herman, *Ryan*, 1997; Runa Islam, *Turn (Gaze of Orpheus)*, 1998; Jason Clay Lewis, *Skin Flaying (Coyote)*, 1998; Jillian McDonald, *Wonderful World of Peafowl: Courtship of the Peacunt*, 1998; Sarah Pierce, *The Remorse of Synchronic Spaces: part two*, 1998; Txuspo Poyo, *Safe*, 1998; Matthew Scott, *Adrenaline*, 1997; Lisa Shafir, *dream*, 1998; Miho Suzuki, *Keep Smiling: 11 Minutes of Bowing*, 1998; Fiona Tan, *Linnaeus' Flower Clock*, 1998; Kristin Tripp, *Surface Tension*, 1998; Sheralyn Woon, *Again*, 1998.

June 25: Open Video Call. Guest viewer Chrissie Iles. First-come, first-show for artists to present five to ten minutes of videotape: Michael Portnoy, *Evianese Gesamtcyntsjerk*; Joe Sola, *Annotation* and *Machine*; Carola Dertnig, *Dancing with Remote(s) 1,2,3*; Miho Suzuki, *Practice*; Christine Tripp, *Untitled* and *Untitled*; Richard Gordon, *Transference*; Jennifer Unruh, *Parastesis/Memory/Untitled*; Greg Leshé, *Tail-spin Slightly Elevated* and *Personal Radar*; Carrie Stewart, *Spinning*; Lois Burkett, *DogGONE*; Nurit Newman and Neil Goldberg, *Out of this World*; *Hallelujah Anyway No.1*, and *12 x 155*, Phyllis B. Lehrer, *The Emotional Banquet* and *Archetypical Room*; Soomin Ham, *Blue Threshold*; Karl Frederick Haendel, *Kids Don't Play with Guns*; Constant, *Untitled*; Carrie Dashow, *Untitled*; Type A, *Untitled*; So Kim, *Untitled*; Rohesia Hamilton Metcalfe, *If Spring, Then Hope and Also Winter*.

PIP DAY / CONTINUED

VCRs. And couches and armchairs were set up around the space. People actually stayed whole afternoons, eating lunch, looking at tapes, and popping them in and out as they chose. It was strangely empowering to be able to do that. And not a single tape was ever missing.

My first show at Artists Space was the summer film/video festival *Tampering with the Reel,* which was a very conceptual show that grew out of my graduate studies. It included single channel video, film, video installation, and a lot of experimental evening programming, as well as a series of *Open Video Calls.* The *Open Video Calls* were so "Artists Space" — artists arrived and signed up to show work on a first-come, first-served basis. There were some terrific videos, and some not so great. Art professionals like Barbara London, Stephen Vitiello, and Gavin Smith were incredibly generous with their comments and suggestions following the screenings. Gavin was great at opening up a discussion about the work. He gave constructive criticism and asked probing questions.

The following fall I co-curated *Permutations* with Debra Singer. It was the first collaboration I had worked on and I really loved it. Debra and I shared the outlook that a group show should open up relationships between artists. We tried not to lay too constricting a theoretical framework on the exhibition, while maintaining a certain complexity in the thinking behind it. We opted to show only four artists in order to give each a lot of space and to get a feel for the artists' concerns. That same fall I also invited Karen Kimmel to do an installation, *Savor,* in the Project Space. In both shows there was work that involved performance and objects in ways that were very interesting, if slightly difficult for the audience to follow. I was tired of seeing big, easy group shows of emerging artists whose work was reduced to being squeezed into big, awful exhibitions. These artists were dealing with complex and difficult ideas and I wanted to challenge them to do something tough, which would make the audience work at it a bit. Karen did an installation that was activated three times during the show. The rest of the six weeks it was in what she called its "passive" mode. Like Dave Arnold's helicopter launch pad in *Permutations* and Anne Gardiner's later performance/installation, Karen's piece perplexed the audience because they weren't sure if they were seeing the remnants of something they had missed, or if it was really "ART." I think that confusion was very healthy.

I arrived at Artists Space open to letting the place tell me what it needed and what it was capable of. I spent a lot of time talking to artists and other people about Artists Space. My main goal outside of exhibition programming was to work on establishing an infrastructure that not only provided services for artists, but also created a network for a younger generation — my generation — of artists, arts professionals, and writers. This is a long-term and slow endeavor for which I had only begun to lay the seeds. I started organizing afternoons where I invited one to five

CONTINUED

June 26: **Nearly the Solstice Party** (David West). Music and performance by Flux Information Sciences (Tristan Bechet, Sebastien Brault), The Reverend Jen, The Spitters (Mark Ashwill, Liza Price, D.D. Dorzillier), Hall of Fame (Theo Angeil, Samara Lubelski, Dan Brown), The Unband, DJ Carlo McCormick.

July – Aug.:
Artists(web)Space:
Jody Rhone.

Opening: *Scope* June 4, 1998.
Photo: Pip Day

July 1: **SCOPE 3:** Opening reception and screening. Emmanuelle Antille, *Reflecting Parts*, 1998; Adriana Arenas, *Discernable Proportions*, 1997; Celia Ayneto, *Passages #5*, 1998; Lois Burkett, *dogGONE*, 1997; Guillermo Cifuentes, *First Lesson*, 1998; Sue de Beer, *loser*, 1997; Rory Donaldson, *Viral Devaluation*, 1998; Anne Gardiner, *Look Up and Smile*, 1998; Richard Gordon, *Transference*, 1997; Stephen Hutchinson, *Seventy Nine*, 1997; Malcolm Jamieson, *Here We Go Again*; George Kimmerling, *This is My Body*, 1998; Matthias Kohler, *a city—a portrait of the anonymous city*, 1997; Mayumi Lake, *Mimicking Ritual #18*, 1997/1998; Gary Lindgren, *Sea*, 1998; Johanna MacArthur, *The Word Was God*, 1997; Cari Machet, *Heaven*, 1997; Audrey Marlhens, *What I Tell You Three Times is True*, 1998; Gloria Marti, *Where you get that nose from, Lily? Got it from my father, silly*, 1998; Megan Michalak, *Event-Horizon*, 1998; Lynn Mullins, *Oasiswall*, 1998; The Poool, *Zero Travels*, 1997; Jennifer Reeder, *My Little Pretty*, 1998; Reynold Reynolds and Patrick Jolley, *Seven Days Til Sunday*, 1998; Mark Shepard, *FYU*, 1998; Lise Skou, *TV Surveillance No. 3*, 1998; William L. Stancil, *Pool*, 1998; Kerry Tribe, *3 Minute Snapshots*, 1998; Pia Wergius, *Season*, 1998; Erika Yeomans, *Hardhead Flair*, 1998.

PIP DAY / CONTINUED

artists and curators to get together and talk about what they were working on. It got people talking to each other. It's surprising that a lot of young curators and writers don't feel they have access to meeting young artists and vice versa. I figured Artists Space was the perfect rendezvous. Given the time and resources I would have loved to set up a number of more formal panels, which I would have interspersed with smaller informal groupings. It's important to develop a sense of community within the generation of emerging artists, especially in a city like New York, where it is easy to get lost. This is definitely something I will continue after Artists Space. Looking back on my recent tenure there, I think it's a shame the life of the space outside the exhibitions themselves—outside of the bare-bone necessities—isn't more of a priority. It has always been such an important part of what Artists Space is.

The idea of a second Project Space was in response to the need to pick up the pace at Artists Space. I did a lot of studio visits and saw a lot of great work, so there was a certain frustration in not being able to simply invite someone who is doing interesting work to have a show in say, two months' time. Project Space 2 allows for the spontaneity of saying, "You're doing good work, let's show this project, this work-in-progress" without too much deliberation on the curator's part or the artist's. The budget is minimal, and the shows rotate on a monthly basis (as opposed to every two months or so for the rest of the exhibitions). More artists have the chance to show, and the focus on New York–based artists will give something of an indication of what's going on out there—what artists are thinking about, what issues are pressing, and what developments are occurring in the emerging scene. Artists Space, at its best, should act as a barometer and a showcase for these kinds of explorations.

BOARD

Carolyn Alexander

Linda Shearer came to speak to Brooke Alexander and me about one of us joining the Board. There wasn't any particular relationship between Artists Space and our gallery, except Brooke and I had a reputation for contributing time and energy to organizations. In fact, Linda had to run it by both NYSCA and the NEA to ask whether it was appropriate to have a dealer on the Board. I was very enthusiastic about Linda—her energy and her excitement were irresistible. Richard Armstrong and I were new Board members at the same time. I joined just after the move into the West Broadway space and very shortly afterward Linda decided to go to MOMA. When I arrived, it was definitely an organization that was very stable financially and very secure curatorially. It had an amazing track record through its days on Wooster and Hudson Streets. In the first few years, my main role was fundraising with other dealers, which is something that doesn't exist anymore. We had enormous support from art dealers at that time.

Witnesses: Against Our Vanishing changed the whole atmosphere. It was probably the biggest crisis the organization has ever gone through. Artists Space came under a depth of scrutiny it had never undergone before and the effects of that went on for years and years. That was the beginning of decreased support from NYSCA and the NEA. The Board was very supportive of Susan Wyatt. Instead of just being the person who took over from Linda, this was the moment when Susan came into her own. In retrospect, it probably could have been handled differently. It wasn't the right situation for Artists Space to have such a bloody battle. At the time, I was a little wary of the way the press jumped on it. Susan was interviewed on the radio and on television, but I don't know if it was the best way to go for the organization. It snowballed. In retrospect, we allowed it to get out of control: I didn't have the experience with the press or government agencies to be the Board member to make the strong move to stop it.

Susan subsequently left and Carlos Gutierrez-Solana was hired. Carlos was extremely energetic and full of ideas. He wasn't dismayed by what Artists Space had been through. He had worked for years running the Visual Arts program at NYSCA, so we thought that would be helpful. And he did make things happen. He opened up the program at Artists Space. And it was a very different kind of program, which we thought would be good for the organization at that particular moment. Again, maybe it was a situation of the Board not being as closely involved as we should have, because Carlos also took over the role of curator. CONTINUED

1998–99

25th Anniversary Season
Please note 1998–99 schedule as of October 1998.
Laurie Anderson inaugurates the 25th anniversary season with an exhibition. Two major New York City institutions salute Artists Space during this season. Artist talks take place at the Museum of Modern Art; the Solomon R. Guggenheim Museum's magazine commissions a piece devoted to Artists Space. A second smaller and more flexible gallery, **Project Space 2** opens to exhibit the work of artists selected by the in-house Curator and/or guests, the exhibitions rotate monthly. The small grant program for artists creating projects outside of Artists Space is reinstated and renamed the **Independent Project Grants** (IPG). Pip Day resigns as Curator in July 1998 and Jenelle Porter is hired in September 1998.

1998 SEP–NOV

CAROLYN ALEXANDER / CONTINUED

Artists Space had been operating at almost $1,000,000. One of our big problems right after Susan left was to make the staff face up to the fact that this could not continue. It was a very bad moment for funding. We had a debt and realized we would then have to run at a budget more like $400,000 to $500,000. It's always hard for a staff to accept, but Carlos said he could absolutely do it. And he *could* do it. That's one reason why he didn't have a curator, but he did have a lot of extra people on the administrative side. It was probably set up more like his department at NYSCA.

One thing we all felt was that Artists Space had become what we called too institutionalized. What Carlos brought to it was a faster turnover; the immediacy was wonderful and it was lively. *Putt-Modernism* was Ken Buhler's idea. Carlos saw its potential and ran with it. The *AIDS Forum* was also wonderful. But after a while, the program became too narrow. Carlos was not a good fundraiser. He was very uncomfortable around wealthy white America. The way he worked with the Board was not very good because he focused only on a couple of us with whom he felt comfortable. Susan, on the other hand, had a great talent for keeping the Board together. Carlos did not. So suddenly it was fractious, but animated. Carlos did get the budget down and managed to reorganize and see Artists Space through the move, but not without big financial problems for the organization.

The role of a Board in these organizations is difficult. You ask us to have oversight, you ask us to be responsible. On the other hand, you want your director and your curators, who are usually a lot younger and more involved in the day-to-day art world than Board members, to feel that they can offer ideas freely. Once you hire them, you try to let them follow through on their ideas. Our Board members have objected to shows quite loudly and clearly, particularly during Carlos's time. Toward the end of his era, the constituency had become very narrow and curatorially it got very mushy and fell apart. Something had to be done. After Carlos had left and before hiring you (Claudia Gould), the Board seriously considered whether Artists Space should vote itself out of existence. After we made our decision not to, the other big thing we talked about was getting the curatorial side back on track again. This was one of the strong points the Board was looking for when we hired you. In spite of going slightly off track, Artists Space is now back in a very vital place for younger artists.

In organizations like Artists Space, the curator and director should not stay forever. Curators should be there for three to five years, directors, at the most, five to eight years. And the maximum time anyone should remain on the Board is six years.

My biggest contribution as a Board member is being a voice of experience and having a role in advising on difficult situations, whether they are financial, philosophical, or just giving guidance about where the organization should be or whether it is an appropriate action to take or an appropriate person to ask for help. It is helpful for arts organizations to have a dealer on their Board because they bring their contacts from the collecting and museum worlds. The hardest thing, apart from financial crises, which all these organizations go through, is taking the organization through a transition, particularly of the director.

Sept. 19–Nov. 7: **Laurie Anderson:** *Whirlwind.* (Claudia Gould) Exhibition commemorates Anderson's early association with Artists Space in 1973. Works include *Whirlwind*, 1996, a three-dimensional viewer-activated audio installation; *Small Handphone Table*, 1978; *Windbook*, 1974; *Hearring*, 1997; *Tilt*, 1994; *Self Playing Violin*, 1974; *Viophonograph*, 1975; *Tape Bow Violin*, 1977; *Digital Violin*, 1984; *Four Songs for Analog and Digital Violins*, 1977–1984; *Neon Bow*, 1986; *Dummy with 1/6 Suzuki* 1992; *Solid Body Lead*, 1986. Newspaper with introduction and artist interview by Claudia Gould.

September 19: Performance on ice, 6:15, 6:45, 7:15, and 7:45.
↑

313

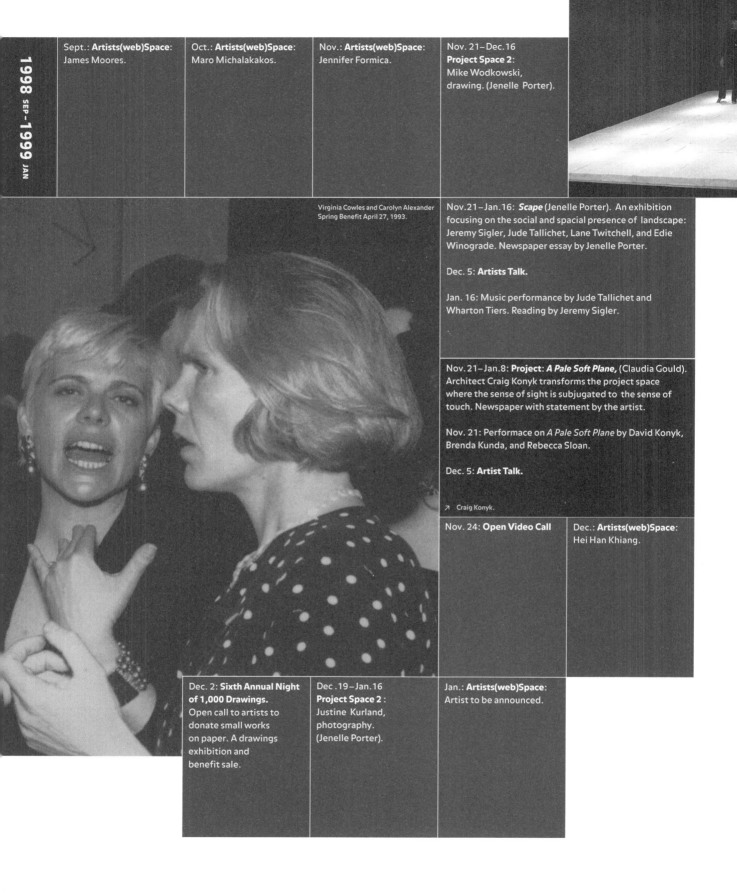

Sept.: **Artists(web)Space**: James Moores.

Oct.: **Artists(web)Space**: Maro Michalakakos.

Nov.: **Artists(web)Space**: Jennifer Formica.

Nov. 21–Dec.16
Project Space 2:
Mike Wodkowski,
drawing. (Jenelle Porter).

Virginia Cowles and Carolyn Alexander
Spring Benefit April 27, 1993.

Nov.21–Jan.16: *Scape* (Jenelle Porter). An exhibition focusing on the social and spacial presence of landscape: Jeremy Sigler, Jude Tallichet, Lane Twitchell, and Edie Winograde. Newspaper essay by Jenelle Porter.

Dec. 5: **Artists Talk.**

Jan. 16: Music performance by Jude Tallichet and Wharton Tiers. Reading by Jeremy Sigler.

Nov. 21–Jan.8: **Project:** *A Pale Soft Plane,* (Claudia Gould). Architect Craig Konyk transforms the project space where the sense of sight is subjugated to the sense of touch. Newspaper with statement by the artist.

Nov. 21: Performace on *A Pale Soft Plane* by David Konyk, Brenda Kunda, and Rebecca Sloan.

Dec. 5: **Artist Talk.**

↗ Craig Konyk.

Nov. 24: **Open Video Call**

Dec.: **Artists(web)Space**: Hei Han Khiang.

Dec. 2: **Sixth Annual Night of 1,000 Drawings.** Open call to artists to donate small works on paper. A drawings exhibition and benefit sale.

Dec .19–Jan.16
Project Space 2 :
Justine Kurland,
photography.
(Jenelle Porter).

Jan.: **Artists(web)Space**: Artist to be announced.

Feb.: **Artists(web)Space**: Artist to be announced.

Feb. 20–Mar. 12: **Project Space 2**: Denise Fasanello (Claudia Gould)

Feb. 20–April 3: Group exhibition of emerging artists to be announced (Nan Goldin). Newspaper.

Feb. 20–April 3: **Project:** (Bryan Crockett) Randall Peacock. Newspaper.

Mar.9: Artists Talk at the Museum of Modern Art in celebration of our 25th anniversary: Vito Acconci, Janine Antoni, Elizabeth Diller, Jeff Koons, and Sonic Youth (Claudia Gould) moderated by Robert Storr.

Mar.: **Artists(web)Space**: Artist to be announced.

Mar. 17–April 3: **Project Space 2:** (Jenelle Porter) Artist to be announced.

Apr.: **Artists(web)Space**: Artist to be announced.

Apr. 17–May 7: **Project Space 2:** (Ellen Gallagher) Artist to be announced

Apr. 17–May 29: Group exhibition (Chuck Close, Elizabeth Murray, and Kiki Smith). An exhibition of emerging and under-recognized artists to be announced . Newspaper.

Apr.–May: **Project:** *Chimeric Architectures.* (Bernard Tschumi) An exhibition exploring the idea of organic hybridity in architecture.Susan Kolatan and William MacDonald. Newspaper introduction by Bernard Tschumi.

May: **Artists(web)Space**: Artist to be announced.

May 12-29: **Project Space 2:** (Claudia Gould) Artist to be announced.

June: **Artists(web)Space**: Artist to be announced.

June 12-July 17: **Project Space 2:** (Jenelle Porter) Artist to be announced.

June 12–July 17: **Film and Video Festival** (Jenelle Porter). A series of evening music and video events presented by various DJs and VJs. Artists to be announced. Newspaper.

June 12–July 17: **Project: Subway to the Outside** (Claudia Gould) Jeanne van Heeswijk, Dutch artist and curator examines and challenges accepted notions of appropriate exhibition and work space . The project began in November with a series of ongoing off-site events by the artist and seven other colleagues. Newspaper.

BOARD

Virginia Cowles My involvement in Artists Space began in 1986 with Carolyn Alexander and Katherine Lobell. Katherine asked me if I could get involved in the Events Committee in order to bring younger people into the organization. I chaired the Events Committee for two or three years, then I was asked to join the Board during the time of *Witnesses: Against Our Vanishing*. I saw how the community reaction to the exhibition put Artists Space in the minds of people on another level. We'd always been cutting edge, but not that well known. It's been fascinating to see the evolution from Susan Wyatt's era, when she was so much a part of the organization, through Carlos Gutierrez-Solana, who took it in a completely different direction, and now with you (Claudia Gould) as you take the organization back toward Artists Space's original mission. It's nice to see it come full circle.

Witnesses energized the Board and made them stand up and take a look at the organization they were serving. When Artists Space got on the front page of the *New York Times* and on the MacNeil/Lehrer Report, a lot of members became very excited and interested. They got it and knew where they needed to go. As a new Board member who had been very quiet, it got me involved awfully quickly. It was fascinating to see Artists Space involved in a political issue and making a statement for the art world against censorship. The reaction to *Witnesses: Against Our Vanishing* was very positive within the New York art community and beyond.

The move from TriBeCa to SoHo was very good for the organization—you had to really make an effort to go to TriBeCa. Alternative spaces are very necessary, more so now than they were in the 80s and the early 90s. Commercial galleries are not willing to take chances on young emerging artists because they need to pay their rent. It's that simple. Alternative spaces may be going back to where they were when they began. It is essential there be vehicles to show young new art, although it's very difficult to survive with cutbacks in government and corporate funding.

In retrospect, I would think a little harder about joining the Board of an alternative space again. It's definitely much more difficult than I imagined, but it's also more exciting. If you want to be involved in the art world and the first to see and be part of something new, it's definitely the way to go. Unfortunately, you won't have the luxury of just enjoying the artistic part of it. It's more business. You have to think, "If I join this Board, do I have the financial connections, can I really help in that way?" If you're not sure you want to do that, then you shouldn't. I'd rather be asked to join the Board for a more creative reason. But I understand the necessity and I do have access and I am able to help the organization financially. Another nice part about Artists Space is that you can, like the artist, start as an intern as you (Claudia) have done, and make a career for yourself. That's what Artists Space is about.

Nearly the Solstice Party.
The Spitters, performance, June 26, 1998.
Photo: Pip Day

Nearly the Solstice Party, June 26, 1998.
Photo: Pip Day

Laurie Anderson, *Whirlwind*, 1996
Whirlwind, Sept. 19–Nov. 7, 1998
Photo: Bill Orcutt

Key to Chronology

ABACA
Arts Benefit All
Coalition Alternative

ACT UP
AIDS Coalition to Unleash Power

Aljira
Aljira, a Center for Contemporary
Art, Newark, New Jersey

AMCC
Artists Meeting for
Cultural Change

ASCO
Chicano performance group,
Los Angeles

BAW/TAF
Border Art Workshop/
Taller d'Arte Frontierzo, San Diego

Cal Arts
California Institute of the Arts

CAPS
Creative Artists Public Service
program

CETA
Comprehension Employment
Training Act

CoLab
Collaborative Projects

DCA
Downtown Cultural Association

Dia
Dia Center for the Arts

DWR
Design/Writing/Research

ICA
Institute for Contemporary Art
Boston.

INTAR
International Arts Relations

K.O.S.
Kids of Survival

LACE
Los Angeles Contemporary Exhibitions

MOCA
Museum of Contemporary Art,
Los Angeles

MOMA
Museum of Modern Art,
New York City

NAAO
National Association
of Artists Organizations

NEA
National Endowment for the Arts

NYSCA
New York State Council on the Arts

NYFA
New York Foundation for the Arts

PAD/D
Political Art Documentation
and Distribution

P.S. 1
P.S. 1, Contemporary Art Center,
Long Island City, New York

RISD
Rhode Island School of Design

SECCA
Southeast Center for Contemporary
Art

SUNY
State University of New York

SVA
School of Visual Arts, New York City

VLA
Volunteer Lawyers for the Arts

WAC
Women's Action Coalition

WPA
Washington Project for the Arts

History of the Irving Sandler Artists File

In 1974, Artists Space launched what has since become one of the largest artists' registries in the country. First established as the "Unaffiliated Artists File," the registry was conceived as another way to assist under-recognized and emerging artists and to serve as a resource for curators from Artists Space and elsewhere. Throughout its history, Artists Space has regularly organized group exhibitions, titled *Selections*, in which curators or already established artists select artists registered in the File.

The "Unaffiliated Artists File" — renamed simply the "Artists File" in 1983 — was composed solely of unaffiliated, New York – based artists. In 1990, the File was expanded to include New Jersey artists; today, while New York – area artists are most heavily represented, many of the File's more than 3,000 artists are located all over the world. Registration in the Artists File is a free service open to all artists who are not represented by a commercial gallery. The File is also used free of charge by members of the public, most commonly curators (both independent and affiliated), artists, commercial galleries, collectors, students, and other nonprofit exhibition spaces. In 1995, the File was officially renamed the "Irving Sandler Artists File" in honor of the numerous and continuing contributions made by Artists Space's founder and first Board President, Irving Sandler.

Since 1986, the File has existed as a computerized database. The database format allows users to perform focused searches for artists and artwork according to specific criteria (such as media, materials, or style), as well as ensuring the safekeeping of the ever-growing number of artists' records. During the 1994 – 95 season, a grant from the Reed Foundation enabled Artists Space to continue the process of digitizing the File by augmenting the slide files with Kodak photo CDs. The photo CDs create a digitized archive of artists' images, and will also provide for a smooth transition to an online database — the next step for the Irving Sandler Artists File. In the future, a File accessible via the Internet will give registered artists more exposure than ever before, and will allow our users to search the database, browse the images, and research the work from any location.

In the fall of 1996, Artists Space took another step toward this goal with the initiation of a website designed by Avalanche Systems. The site is yet another way for Artists Space to reach its audience, providing information about exhibitions and programming. It also features a virtual exhibition of work selected monthly from the File, the *Artists(web)Space*.

The Irving Sandler Artists File has been a significant resource for unaffiliated artists for 25 years, and has served as a model for similar registries around the country, in the Caribbean, Eastern Europe, and Australia. As Artists Space moves toward the next century, the File will continue to embrace new technologies in order to provide emerging and under-recognized artists with the greatest possible exposure.

↑　Unaffiliated Artists File, 1974-1986.　　　　↑　Unaffiliated Artists File, digitized in 1986.

History of the Emergency Materials Fund,
the Independent Exhibitions Program, 1973–1991,
and the Independent Project Grants, 1998–present.

Artists Space was founded in 1973 in response to the professional needs of an ever-growing number of younger, emerging artists. Of the programs administered by the Committee of the Visual Arts through Artists Space, the exhibition opportunities afforded by the gallery space are perhaps the best known. But the less visible grant programs, which made small funds directly available to unaffiliated artists for 18 years, resulted in the successful presentation of more than 1,000 exhibitions in that period. The Emergency Materials Fund (EMF) assisted artists with the presentation of their work at an established nonprofit venue, while the Independent Exhibitions Program (IEP) served to support the needs of artists who were involved in the creation, production, and presentation of work in unconventional contexts outside of the existing institutional structure. The singular accessibility of these small financial awards was intended to directly aid artists who were actively pursuing one of these two distinct paths. As a result, the activity generated by those grants included some of the most experimental and challenging art produced in that period.

The Emergency Materials Fund was established in 1973 with funding from the New York State Council on the Arts and supplemented in 1974 with funds from the National Endowment for the Arts. EMF grants were available to artists who had already been selected or scheduled for exhibition at a nonprofit venue — a museum, an alternative gallery space, a university library or gallery, and so forth. These grants of $75 to $150 each were intended to cover the basic presentation costs associated with the exhibition that could not be absorbed by the host venue. Elements such as transportation, framing, equipment rental, or material, often essential to the professional presentation of an artist's work, could be prohibitive in light of the limited resources of many not-for-profit venues. By covering a portion of these costs, the EMF grants enabled a significant number of artists to improve the quality of presentation for exhibition of their work — an important consideration in the early stages of an artist's career.

By 1976, it had become apparent that an increasing number of artists were attempting to present their work in decidedly unorthodox contexts. In recognition of this shift, the Independent Exhibitions Program was established as a means of assisting unaffiliated artists working on projects and exhibitions independent of institutional sponsorship. Through the IEP, grants of up to $150 for individuals (up to $400 for a group of artists) were available on a first-come, first-served basis for projects that made use of unconventional locales: open studios, exhibitions in temporary spaces, street works and events, and publications were among the sorts of projects commonly proposed. The IEP funds supported the work of artists who were interested in exploring nontraditional methods of presentation by defraying expenses such as printing fees for announcements, posters, or press releases, insurance, space preparation, transportation, and mailing fees. By subsidizing these costs, the IEP permitted artists to retain control over the exhibition and presentation of their work and to operate successfully outside the existing market-driven structure. Both the EMF and IEP grants were discontinued in 1991 due to lack of financial support.

Independent Project Grants

This new granting program was initiated in the Fall of 1998, at the beginning of Artists Space's 25th anniversary year. The Independent Project Grants builds on both previous grant efforts by providing direct financial assistance to unaffiliated artists for the public presentation of their work in noncommerical, noninstitutional venues within the five boroughs of New York City. IPG grants are available to both individual artists and groups, to help organize and produce self-initiated exhibitions, performances, site-specific works, Internet projects, film and video screenings, and other art events and projects. Like the Independent Exhibitions Program grants of the 1970s and 80s, these grants are intended to encourage and enable artists to find and/or create new situations, new means, and new methods for presenting their work.

Twenty grants of $500 each are awarded on a lottery basis three times a year; these basic funds may assist artists in meeting such costs as press releases, framing, announcements, posters, space rental, installation fees, shipping, film editing, etc. In keeping with the spirit of the IPG, grant applications are simple and concise, comprising a short summary of the project, a brief description of expected expenses, and a list of participating artists. All eligible applications are entered into the random lottery pool from which grant recipients are chosen.

↑ Independent Exhibition Program grant recipient,
Eggs on End: Standing on Ceremony,
Spring Equinox Celebration, Jeannette Park, NYC,
Mar. 20, 1980.
© 1980 Sarah Jenkins

↑ Emergency Materials Fund grant recipient
Robin Winters, *Idea Warehouse*, 1975.
Photo: Lizbeth Marano

↑ Independent Exhibition Program grant recipients
Artists Magazines: Judith Aminoff, *Cover*; Dick Miller,
Spanner; Daniel Freeman, *Dumb*; Tom Lawson, *Reallife*;
Alex J. Hirka, *Smegma #3*, 1979–1980.
Photo: Anne Turyn

Board History

Staff History

Special thanks to Artists Space's invaluable team of volunteers, interns, and all the part-time staff who were not included in this abbreviated staff history.

Trudie Grace, Director,
May 1973–September 1975

PART TIME

Edit deAk, Administrative Assistant,
Assistant Director, 1974–1975

Helene Winer, Director,
October 1975–January 1980

FULL TIME

Paul McMahon, Assistant Director,
October 1975–July 1977

Patrick O'Connell, Program Assistant,
February 1976–August 1977

Ragland Watkins, Associate Director,
Exhibitions, September 1977–August 1981

Susan Wyatt, Program Administrator,
1975–1977; Associate Director, Services,
1977–July 1981

PART TIME

Linda Kraut, CETA Artist, 1979–1980

David Salle, Development Consultant,
1975–1976

Cindy Sherman, Program Assistant,
September 1977–1978; Program
Coordinator, 1978–1981

Susan Wyatt, Administrative Assistant,
1975

Michael Zwack, CETA Artist,
1977–1978

Linda Shearer, Executive Director,
January 1980–August 1985

FULL TIME

Valerie Smith, Curator,
September 1981–June 1989

Ragland Watkins, Associate Director,
Exhibitions, September 1977–August 1981

Susan Wyatt, Associate Director,
Services,1977–July 1981; Assistant
Director, 1981–1983; Director, 1983–1985

PART TIME

Frank Farmer, Installation Coordinator,
September 1981–January 1984

Kenji Fujita, Program Assistant,
September 1981–August 1982; Program
Coordinator, September 1982–August
1984; Production Coordinator, September
1984–August 1985

James Kraft, Pro-bono Consultant,
1981–1982

Linda Kraut, CETA Artist, 1979–1980

Nancy McDermott, Development
Consultant, 1981–1982

Cindy Sherman, Program Coordinator,
1978–1981

Andrew Spence, Registrar/Preparator,
March 1984–June 1989

Kathleen Sweeney, Office Manager,
1983–1985

Janice Vrana, Administrative Assistant,
1984–1985

Susan Wyatt, Executive Director,
September 1985–June 1991

FULL TIME

Anne Bergeron, Development Director,
November 1989–May 1991

Connie Butler, Curator,
March 1989–April 1992

Celeste Dado, Executive Assistant,
November 1985–December 1987;
Assistant Director, January 1988–December
1990; Associate Director, January 1991–
March 1992

David Rogan Hazard, Preparator/
Registrar, June 1989–October 1990

Lynn Herbert, Programs and Publicity
Coordinator, December 1987–July 1989

Lyda Pola, Office Manager, May–October
1985; Artists File Coordinator, October
1985–December 1988

Valerie Smith, Curator,
September 1981–June 1989

Hendrika ter Elst, Artists File
Coordinator, February 1989–1992

Deborah Whitney, Development/
Finance Assistant, May 1990–August 1992

Lauren Wisbauer, Administrative
Assistant, April 1986–December 1987

PART TIME

Thelma Adams, Development
Consultant, 1990–1991

Rhea Anastas, Program
Assistant/Development Assistant,
January–June 1990

Kenneth Buhler, Registrar/Preparator,
October 1990–May 1994

Kenji Fujita, Design Coordinator,
September 1985–May 1988

Stacy Godlesky, Office Manager,
November 1985–April 1992

Barbara Hertel, Photo Archivist,
November 1988–April 1989

Stacy Jamar, Administrative Assistant,
March–December 1989

Anna Kustera, Development Assistant,
February 1988–March 1990

Judith Lyczko, Development Consultant,
1981–1982; Development Director,
1982–1986

Lynn McCary, Administrative Assistant,
January 1989–June 1991

Micki McGee, Film and Video Curator,
September 1989–March 1992

Laura Miller, Design Coordinator,
September 1988–April 1991

Andrea Pedersen, Development
Director, November 1986–October 1989;
Benefit Coordinator, January 1989–
May 1990

Roberta Sklar, Public Affairs Consultant,
November 1990

Andrew Spence, Registrar/Preparator,
March 1984–June 1989

Jane Tennan, Development Consultant,
1990–1991

Patricia Thornley, Publications
Coordinator, September 1989–March 1991

Daniel Walworth, Film and Video
Curator, November 1986–October 1989

Jenelle Porter

Matt Isaac

Elizabeth Hires

Lisa Metcalf

Carlos Gutierrez-Solana, Executive Director, November 1991–December 1993

FULL TIME

Lori Blount, Development Director, January 1992–February 1994

Connie Butler, Curator, March 1989–April 1992

Celeste Dado, Associate Director January 1990–March 1992

Denise Fasanello, Program Associate/Artists File Coordinator, June 1992–August 1994

Gary Nickard, Programs Coordinator, October 1992–July 1993; Programs Director, July 1993–February 1994

Hendrika ter Elst, Artists File Coordinator, February 1989–1992

Amy Wanggaard, Development/Finance Associate, September–November 1991; Executive Associate, May 1992– December 1993

Deborah Whitney, Development/Finance Assistant, May 1990–August 1992

Charles A. Wright, Jr., Exhibitions Coordinator, March 1992–September 1992

PART TIME

Thelma Adams, Development Consultant, 1990–1991

Kenneth Buhler, Registrar/Preparator, October 1990–May 1994

Allen Kleinman, Development Associate, October 1992–April 1994

Lynn McCary, Administrative Assistant, January 1989–June 1991

Micki McGee, Film and Video Curator, September 1989–March 1992

Peter Siegel, Director of Finance and Management, February 1992–September 1993

Patricia Thornley, Publications Coordinator, September 1989–March 1991

Peter Whitney, *Putt-Modernism* Tour Coordinator, July 1992–December 1993

↑ End of the year staff and intern party on the *Pioneer*, July 30, 1998.
Photo: Amy Sung

Claudia Gould, Executive Director, January 1994–present

FULL TIME

Anastasia Aukeman, Curator, January 1996–January 1997

Lori Blount, Development Director, January 1992–February 1994

Pip Day, Curator, February 1997– July 1998

Denise Fasanello, Programs Associate/Artists File Coordinator; June 1992–August 1994; Curator, September 1994–January 1996

Elizabeth Hires, Artists File Coordinator/Development Associate, November 1997–October 1998; Development Associate, October 1998– present

Tara Mc Dowell, Assistant to the Director, June 1998–present

Elizabeth Metcalf, Development Director, March 1996–July 1997; Assistant Director, July 1997–present

Gary Nickard, Programs Director, July 1993–February 1994; Curator, February 1994–June 1994

Michael Poehlman, Assistant to the Director, February 1996–January 1997

Jenelle Porter, Curator, September 1998–present

Patrice Regan, Development Director, July 1994–January 1996

Sara Reisman, Assistant to the Director, March 1997–June 1998

Austin Thomas, Assistant to the Director, October 1995–October 1996

Amy Wanggaard, Assistant to the Director, January 1994–October 1995

PART TIME

Kenneth Buhler, Registrar/Preparator, October 1990–May 1994

Pamela Butler, Finance Associate, September 1992–June 1993; Bookkeeper, November 1993–June 1994

Burton Greenhouse/ Checks & Balances NY, Inc., February 1995–present

Allen Kleinman, Development Associate, October 1992–April 1994

David Krueger, Artists File Coordinator, April 1995–January 1996

Xanda McCagg, Intern Coordinator, January 1996–July 1997

Sara Pierce, Artists File Coordinator/Development Associate, January–July 1997

Judith M. Ruiz, Bookeeper/Accountant, July 1994–October 1995

Matthew Isaac, Artisits File Coordinator, September 1998–present

→ Artists Space staff, March 3, 1998.
L TO R: Elizabeth Metcalf, Elizabeth Hires, Pip Day, Sara Reisman, Claudia Gould.
© Tim Miller

↓ Stacy Watson and Matt Isaac

↘ Tara Mc Dowell

Publications History

Throughout most of its history Artists Space produced a publication to accompany each exhibition. These catalogues, brochures, and newspapers feature reproductions of the artists' work as well as critical essays and statements by curators, artists, and commissioned writers.

Pictures
September 24 –
October 29, 1977.
Essay by Douglas Crimp and acknowledgments by Helene Winer.
CATALOGUE WITH BLACK AND WHITE REPRODUCTIONS. 32 PAGES.

New Art Auction and Exhibition
December 10, 1977 –
January 7, 1978.
CATALOGUE WITH REPRODUCTIONS. 38 PAGES.

Bernard Tschumi: Architectural Manifestoes
April 8 – 29, 1978.
Preface by Helene Winer and statement by the architect.
CATALOGUE WITH BLACK AND WHITE REPRODUCTIONS. 20 PAGES.

Traditions / Five Painters
May 13 – June 10, 1978.
Essay by Linda L. Cathcart and acknowledgments by Helene Winer.
CATALOGUE WITH BLACK AND WHITE REPRODUCTIONS. 16 PAGES.

four-person untitled exhibition
September 23 –
October 28, 1978.
Introduction by Janelle Reiring and statement by Adrian Piper.
CATALOGUE WITH BLACK AND WHITE REPRODUCTIONS. 10 PAGES.

Artists Draw
January 6 –
February 10, 1979.
Introduction by Donald Sultan and acknowledgments by Helene Winer.
CATALOGUE WITH BLACK AND WHITE REPRODUCTIONS. 16 PAGES.

Four Artists
March 17 – April 28, 1979.
Introduction by Thomas Lawson and acknowledgments by Helene Winer.
CATALOGUE WITH BLACK AND WHITE REPRODUCTIONS. 24 PAGES.

10 Artists/Artists Space
September 9 –
October 15, 1979.
Acknowledgments by Suzanne Delehanty, Irving Sandler, and Helene Winer.
CATALOGUE WITH BLACK AND WHITE REPRODUCTIONS. 30 PAGES.

A Sound Selection: Audio Works by Artists
January 1980.
Produced to accompany the traveling version of this show, based on *Audio Works*, presented at Artists Space in 1978. Essay by Barry Rosen, statements by the artists, and acknowledgments by Helene Winer.
CATALOGUE. 24 PAGES.

Seven Toronto Artists
April 5 – May 10, 1980.
Introductions by Ragland Watkins and Peggy Gale and acknowledgments by Helene Winer.
CATALOGUE WITH BLACK AND WHITE REPRODUCTIONS. 22 PAGES.

Architecture/Sequences
January 17 –
February 28, 1981.
Preface and essay by Bernard Tschumi and acknowledgments by Linda Shearer.
CATALOGUE WITH BLACK AND WHITE REPRODUCTIONS. 20 PAGES.

Selections
March 14 – April 25, 1981.
Acknowledgments by Linda Shearer.
CATALOGUE WITH BLACK AND WHITE REPRODUCTIONS. 20 PAGES.

35 Artists Return to Artists Space: A Benefit Exhibition
December 4 – 24, 1981.
Introduction by William Zimmer and acknowledgments by Linda Shearer.
CATALOGUE WITH BLACK AND WHITE REPRODUCTIONS. 28 PAGES.

Artists Space: Emergency Materials Fund – Independent Exhibitions Program, 1973 – 1981
1982.
Acknowledgments by Linda Shearer.
CATALOGUE DESCRIBING THE GRANTS PROGRAMS WITH A LIST OF RECIPIENTS AND BLACK AND WHITE REPRODUCTIONS. 18 PAGES.

Young Fluxus
April 10 – May 15, 1982.
Essays by Peter Frank and Ken Friedman with acknowledgements by Linda Shearer.
CATALOGUE WITH BLACK AND WHITE REPRODUCTIONS. 32 PAGES.

Selections
September 25 –
October 30, 1982.
Introduction and acknowledgments by Linda Shearer with statements by the artists.
CATALOGUE WITH BLACK AND WHITE REPRODUCTIONS. 20 PAGES.

Grand Galop
February 26 –
March 26, 1983.
Essay by James Casebere and acknowledgments by Linda Shearer.
CATALOGUE WITH BLACK AND WHITE REPRODUCTIONS. 20 PAGES.

The Los Angeles – New York Exchange
May 21 – July 2, 1983.
Essays by Susan C. Larsen (Los Angeles) and Roberta Smith (New York), introduction and acknowledgments by Marc Pally and Linda Shearer.
CATALOGUE WITH BLACK AND WHITE REPRODUCTIONS, DOCUMENTS BOTH EXHIBITIONS. 32 PAGES.

Selections
October 1 – 29, 1983.
Statements by the artists and acknowledgments by Linda Shearer.
CATALOGUE WITH BLACK AND WHITE REPRODUCTIONS. 18 PAGES.

Ernst Benkert
November 5 –
December 3, 1983.
Essay by Joseph Masheck, statement by the artist, and acknowledgments by Linda Shearer.
BROCHURE WITH BLACK AND WHITE REPRODUCTIONS.

International Projects: Canada – Andy Patton
November 5 –
December 3, 1983.
Essay by Tim Guest and acknowledgments by Linda Shearer.
BROCHURE WITH BLACK AND WHITE REPRODUCTIONS.

International Projects: Belgium – Didier Vermeiren
January 21 – February 18, 1984.
Essay by Alain Vanderhofstadt (translated by Felix Adrien d'Haeseleer), statement by the artist, and acknowledgments by Linda Shearer.
BROCHURE WITH BLACK AND WHITE REPRODUCTIONS.

New Galleries of the Lower East Side
January 21 –
February 18, 1984.
Statement by Helene Winer and acknowledgments by Linda Shearer.
BROCHURE WITH BLACK AND WHITE REPRODUCTIONS.

International Projects: Holland – Irene Fortuyn/Robert O'Brien *February 25 – March 24, 1984.* Essay by Paul Groot (translated by Fortuyn/O'Brien) and acknowledgments by Linda Shearer. BROCHURE WITH BLACK AND WHITE REPRODUCTIONS.	**Sally Hazelet Drummond** *February 25 – March 24, 1984.* Essay by Irving Sandler, statement by the artist, and acknowledgments by Linda Shearer. BROCHURE WITH BLACK AND WHITE REPRODUCTIONS.	**Mowry Baden** *March 31 – May 5, 1984.* Essay by Gary Goss and acknowledgments by Linda Shearer. BROCHURE WITH BLACK AND WHITE REPRODUCTIONS.	**International Projects: Italy – Doriana Chiarini** *April 7 – May 5, 1984.* Essay by Germano Celant and acknowledgments by Linda Shearer. BROCHURE WITH BLACK AND WHITE REPRODUCTIONS.	**A Decade of New Art** *May 31 – June 30, 1984.* Essay by Linda Cathcart and acknowledgments by Linda Shearer. CATALOGUE WITH BLACK AND WHITE REPRODUCTIONS. 80 PAGES.
Five Artists *September 29 – October 27, 1984.* Introduction by Will Insley and acknowledgments by Linda Shearer. BROCHURE WITH BLACK AND WHITE REPRODUCTIONS.	**Selections** *November 3 – December 1, 1984.* Introduction by Valerie Smith, statements by the artists, and acknowledgments by Linda Shearer. CATALOGUE WITH BLACK AND WHITE REPRODUCTIONS. 12 PAGES.	**Forced Sentiment** *December 8, 1984 – January 12, 1985.* Preface by Robert Longo, essay by Tricia Collins and Richard Milazzo, and acknowledgments by Linda Shearer. CATALOGUE WITH BLACK AND WHITE REPRODUCTIONS. 28 PAGES.	**Dark Rooms** *January 26 – February 23, 1985.* Essay by John Hanhardt, introduction by Valerie Smith, and acknowledgments by Linda Shearer. Also documents earlier *Dark Rooms* exhibition, January 22 – February 19, 1983. BROCHURE WITH BLACK AND WHITE REPRODUCTIONS.	**Bert Carpenter** *March 9 – April 6, 1985.* Excerpted interview with the artist by Jane Necol and acknowledgments by Linda Shearer. BROCHURE WITH COLOR AND BLACK AND WHITE REPRODUCTIONS.
Charles Harbutt *March 9 – April 6, 1985.* Essay by Andy Grundberg and Julia Scully, statement by the artist, and acknowledgments by Linda Shearer. BROCHURE WITH BLACK AND WHITE REPRODUCTIONS.	**Duane Zaloudek** *March 9 – April 6, 1985.* Essay by Claire Copley and acknowledgments by Linda Shearer. BROCHURE WITH BLACK AND WHITE REPRODUCTIONS.	**Five Spanish Artists** *April 13 – May 31, 1985.* Introduction by Donald Sultan and preface by Carmen Giménez. Essays by Francisco Calvo Serraller, Ramón Tío Bellido, Juan Manuel Bonet, Kevin Power, Marga Paz, and Francisco Rivas. Acknowledgments by Linda Shearer. CATALOGUE WITH COLOR AND BLACK AND WHITE REPRODUCTIONS. 104 PAGES.		**U.S. Projects** *May 25 – June 29, 1985.* Statements by the selectors (Kathy Halbreich, Anne Rorimer, Marge Goldwater, Anne Focke, and Alan Sondheim) and acknowledgments by Linda Shearer. CATALOGUE WITH BLACK AND WHITE REPRODUCTIONS. 32 PAGES.
Selections *September 21 – October 19, 1985.* Introduction by Kay Larson and acknowledgments by Susan Wyatt. CATALOGUE WITH BLACK AND WHITE REPRODUCTIONS. 12 PAGES.	**Four Artists** *November 2 – 27, 1985.* Introduction by Elizabeth Murray and acknowledgments by Susan Wyatt. BROCHURE WITH BLACK AND WHITE REPRODUCTIONS.	**Split/Vision** *December 14, 1985 – January 18, 1986.* Essay by Andy Grundberg and acknowledgments by Susan Wyatt. CATALOGUE WITH BLACK AND WHITE REPRODUCTIONS. 28 PAGES.	**Six Sculptors** *January 25 – February 22, 1986.* Introduction by Valerie Smith and acknowledgments by Susan Wyatt. BROCHURE WITH BLACK AND WHITE REPRODUCTIONS.	**Recent Art from Chicago** *March 8 – April 5, 1986.* Essay by James Yood, statements by the artists, and acknowledgments by Susan Wyatt. CATALOGUE WITH BLACK AND WHITE REPRODUCTIONS. 32 PAGES.
Moderns in Mind *April 12 – May 10, 1986.* Essays by Evan M. Maurer, Susan M. Maurer, Susan C. Larsen, Martica Sawin, and Dan Cameron. Foreword by Valerie Smith and acknowledgments by Susan Wyatt. CATALOGUE WITH BLACK AND WHITE REPRODUCTIONS. 38 PAGES.	**From Here to Eternity: Fact and Fiction in Recent Architectural Projects** *May 24 – June 28, 1986.* Essay by Beatriz Colomina, statements by the artists, introduction by Valerie Smith, and acknowledgments by Susan Wyatt. CATALOGUE WITH BLACK AND WHITE REPRODUCTIONS. 28 PAGES.		**Selections** *September 18 – October 18, 1986.* Introduction by Valerie Smith and foreword by Susan Wyatt. CATALOGUE WITH BLACK AND WHITE REPRODUCTIONS. 30 PAGES.	THE LOS ANGELES NEW YORK EXCHANGE

The Fairy Tale: Politics, Desire, and Everyday Life
October 30 – November 26, 1986.
Introduction by Curt Belshe, Ana Busto, Sarah Drury, Hilary Kliros, Lise Prown, and Steven Schiff.
Essays by Jean Fisher, Fredric Jameson, and Jack Zipes.
Acknowledgments by Susan Wyatt.
CATALOGUE. 24 PAGES.

Contained Attitudes
December 11, 1986 – January 24, 1987.
Essays by Saskia Bos and Chris Dercon and acknowledgments by Susan Wyatt.
CATALOGUE WITH BLACK AND WHITE REPRODUCTIONS. 22 PAGES.

Dark Rooms
February 5 – March 14, 1987.
Essay by Dan Walworth and acknowledgments by Susan Wyatt.
BROCHURE WITH BLACK AND WHITE REPRODUCTIONS.

TV Sandino
February 5 – March 14, 1987.
Essays by Michèle Mattelart (translated by Bérénice Reynaud) and Joel Kovel, introduction by Annie Goldson and Carlos Pavam, and acknowledgments by Susan Wyatt.
CATALOGUE WITH BLACK AND WHITE REPRODUCTIONS. 14 PAGES.

Hani Rashid:
Kursaal for a Evacuee
February 5 – March 14, 1987.
Introduction by Elizabeth Diller and acknowledgments by Valerie Smith and Susan Wyatt.
BROCHURE WITH BLACK AND WHITE REPRODUCTIONS.

Abstraction in Process
March 26 – May 2, 1987.
Essay by Roberta Smith and acknowledgments by Susan Wyatt.
CATALOGUE WITH COLOR AND BLACK AND WHITE REPRODUCTIONS. 24 PAGES.

Recent Paintings:
Calvert Coggeshall and Frederick Hammersley
May 21 – June 27, 1987.
Essays by Hedda Sterne and Merle Schipper.
Acknowledgments by Susan Wyatt.
CATALOGUE WITH COLOR REPRODUCTIONS. 16 PAGES.

Lynn & Ian Bader
May 21 – June 27, 1987.
Essay by Patricia C. Phillips and acknowledgments by Susan Wyatt.
BROCHURE WITH BLACK AND WHITE REPRODUCTIONS.

Heterogeneity and Alienation
May 21 – June 27, 1987.
Essay by Bérénice Reynaud and acknowledgments by Susan Wyatt.
BROCHURE WITH BLACK AND WHITE REPRODUCTIONS.

Selections
October 1 – 31, 1987.
Introduction by Kellie Jones and acknowledgments by Susan Wyatt.
CATALOGUE WITH BLACK AND WHITE REPRODUCTIONS. 32 PAGES.

Underexposed: A Selected History of Neglected Films
November 6 – 9, 1987.
Introduction by Andy Moses, essay by Keith Sanborn, and acknowledgments by Susan Wyatt and Dan Walworth.
BROCHURE WITH BLACK AND WHITE REPRODUCTIONS.

We the People
November 12 – December 23, 1987.
Essays by Jimmie Durham, Jean Fisher, Emelia Seubert, and Paul Smith.
Acknowledgments by Susan Wyatt.
CATALOGUE WITH BLACK AND WHITE REPRODUCTIONS. 36 PAGES.

Social Spaces/ Other Versions (Perversions)
January 14 – February 13, 1988.
Introduction by Valerie Smith, essays by Martin Winn and Dan Walworth.
Acknowledgments by Susan Wyatt.
CATALOGUE WITH BLACK AND WHITE REPRODUCTIONS. 20 PAGES.

Colliding: Myth, Fantasy, Nightmare
February 25 – April 2, 1988.
Introduction by Michael Auping and acknowledgments by Susan Wyatt.
CATALOGUE WITH BLACK AND WHITE REPRODUCTIONS.

Unacceptable Appetites
February 25 – April 2, 1988.
Essay by Micki McGee and acknowledgments by Susan Wyatt and Dan Walworth.
BROCHURE WITH BLACK AND WHITE REPRODUCTIONS.

The London Project
April 14 – May 14 1988.
Foreword by John Hejduk, essay by Patricia C. Phillips, statements and texts by the architects, and afterword by Michael Hays.
BOOK, PUBLISHED BY PRINCETON ARCHITECTURAL PRESS AND ARTISTS SPACE, WITH BLACK AND WHITE REPRODUCTIONS. 96 PAGES.

Michael Asher/ James Coleman
June 2 – July 2, 1988.
Essays by Anne Rorimer, John Vinci, and Jean Fisher, notes by Valerie Smith, and acknowledgments by Susan Wyatt.
CATALOGUE WITH BLACK AND WHITE REPRODUCTIONS. 32 PAGES.

Min Joong Art:
A New Cultural Movement from Korea
September 29 – November 5, 1988.
Essays by Kwang Hyun Shim, Wankyung Sung, Lucy Lippard, and Hyuk Um, and acknowledgments by Susan Wyatt.
CATALOGUE WITH BLACK AND WHITE REPRODUCTIONS. 32 PAGES.

I Miss the Revolution
September 29 – November 5, 1988.
Essays by Tom Finkelpearl, Anthony Heilbut, and Janos Marton, and acknowledgments by Susan Wyatt and Thomas Sokolowski.
BROCHURE PUBLISHED IN COLLABORATION WITH THE GREY ART GALLERY, NEW YORK.

Selections
November 17, 1988 – January 7, 1989.
Essay by Valerie Smith and acknowledgments by Susan Wyatt.
CATALOGUE WITH BLACK AND WHITE REPRODUCTIONS. 44 PAGES.

The AIDS Crisis Is Not Over
November 17, 1988 – January 7, 1989.
Essay by Gregg Bordowitz and acknowledgments by Susan Wyatt and Dan Walworth.
BROCHURE WITH BLACK AND WHITE REPRODUCTIONS.

Purvis Young:
Me and My Mink
November 17, 1988 – January 7, 1989.
Essay by Cesar Trasobares and acknowledgments by Susan Wyatt.
BROCHURE.

Border Art Workshop – Taller de Arte Fronterizo:
Vidas Perdidas/Lost Lives
January 19 – February 18, 1989.
Essays by Shifra Goldman, Jeff Kelley, and Michael Schnorr. Contributions by BAW/TAF artists. Acknowledgments by Susan Wyatt and La Jolla Museum of Contemporary Art. Co-published by Artists Space and La Jolla Museum of Contemporary Art, La Jolla, California.
BOOK WITH BLACK AND WHITE REPRODUCTIONS. 94 PAGES.

The North of Ireland
January 19 – February 18, 1989.
Essay by Annie Goldson and acknowledgments by Susan Wyatt and Dan Walworth.
BROCHURE WITH BLACK AND WHITE REPRODUCTIONS.

Michael Sorkin: Model City
January 19 – February 18, 1989.
Essay by Michael Sorkin and acknowledgments by Susan Wyatt and Valerie Smith.
BROCHURE WITH ONE BLACK AND WHITE REPRODUCTION.

Dark Rooms
March 2 – April 1, 1989.
Acknowledgments and essay by Dan Walworth and Valerie Smith.
BROCHURE WITH BLACK AND WHITE REPRODUCTIONS.

Signs of Fiction
March 2 – April 1, 1989.
Essay by Sharon Greytak and acknowledgments by Susan Wyatt and Dan Walworth.
BROCHURE WITH BLACK AND WHITE REPRODUCTIONS.

Laurie Palmer —
Winter Flush:
A Temporary Garden
March 2 – April 1, 1989.
Essay by Judith Russi Kirshner and acknowledgments by Susan Wyatt.
BROCHURE.

Shirley Jaffe
April 13 – May 13, 1989.
Essay by Meyer Raphael Rubinstein and acknowledgments by Susan Wyatt.
BROCHURE WITH COLOR REPRODUCTIONS.

Murray Reich
April 13 – May 13, 1989.
Essay by Elizabeth Frank and acknowledgments by Susan Wyatt.
BROCHURE WITH COLOR REPRODUCTIONS.

Document and Dream
April 13 – May 13, 1989.
Essay by Dan Walworth and acknowledgments by Susan Wyatt.
BROCHURE WITH BLACK AND WHITE REPRODUCTIONS.

Of a Place, Solitary/
Of a Sound, Mute
April 13 – May 13, 1989.
Essay by Bruce W. Ferguson and acknowledgments by Susan Wyatt.
BROCHURE WITH BLACK AND WHITE REPRODUCTIONS.

Metaphysical Visions: Middle Europe/Deconstruction,
Quotation & Subversion: Video from Yugoslavia
May 25 – July 1, 1989.
Essays by Kathy Rae Huffman, Valerie Smith, Biljana Tomić and statements by the artists (translated by Ivan Vejvoda and Jelena Mesić). Acknowledgments by Susan Wyatt and Valerie Smith.
CATALOGUE WITH BLACK AND WHITE REPRODUCTIONS. 32 PAGES.

Selections
September 28 – November 4, 1989.
Notes by Connie Butler and acknowledgments by Susan Wyatt.
CATALOGUE WITH BLACK AND WHITE REPRODUCTIONS. 32 PAGES.

Extended Definitions:
Video Experiments
in Perception
September 28 – November 4, 1989.
Essay by Cara Mertes and acknowledgments by Dan Walworth and Susan Wyatt.
BROCHURE WITH BLACK AND WHITE REPRODUCTIONS.

Don Stinson — Perspective:
The State of Existing in
Space Before the Eye
September 28 – November 4, 1989.
Essay by Herbert Muschamp and acknowledgments by Susan Wyatt.
BROCHURE WITH BLACK AND WHITE REPRODUCTIONS.

Witnesses: Against Our Vanishing
November 16, 1989 – January 6, 1990.
Essays by Nan Goldin, David Wojnarowicz, Linda Yablonsky, and Cookie Mueller. Acknowledgments by Susan Wyatt and statements by the artists.
CATALOGUE WITH BLACK AND WHITE REPRODUCTIONS. 32 PAGES.

Benito Huerta —
Attempted: Not Known
November 16, 1989 – January 6, 1990.
Essay by Marilyn A. Zeitlin and acknowledgments by Susan Wyatt.
BROCHURE WITH BLACK AND WHITE REPRODUCTIONS.

Uprising: Videotapes on the Palestinian Resistance
November 16, 1989 – January 6, 1990.
Essay by Hanan Mikhail-Ashrawi. Interview by Dan Walworth with Elia Suleiman and Georges Khleifi. Acknowledgments by Susan Wyatt and Micki McGee.
CATALOGUE WITH BLACK AND WHITE REPRODUCTIONS. 16 PAGES.

Paraculture
January 18 – February 24, 1990.
Foreword by Sally Couacaud, Susan Wyatt, & Connie Butler. Essays by S. Couacaud, Keith Broadfoot & Rex Butler, Ross Gibson, & Meaghan Morris.
CATALOGUE WITH COLOR AND BLACK AND WHITE REPRODUCTIONS. 44 PAGES.

Fred Tomaselli:
Diurnal Experiments and
Nocturnal Investigations
January 18 – February 24, 1990.
Essay by Connie Butler and acknowledgments by Susan Wyatt.
BROCHURE WITH BLACK AND WHITE REPRODUCTIONS.

In Search of Paradise/Or, Anywhere But Here
January 18 – February 24, 1990.
Excerpt from the script *The Machine That Killed Bad People* by Steve Fagin. Essay by Bill Horrigan. Acknowledgments by Susan Wyatt, Micki McGee, Laurie Garris, and Adriene Jenik. Produced in association with Los Angeles Contemporary Exhibitions (LACE).
CATALOGUE WITH BLACK AND WHITE REPRODUCTIONS.

Ed Clark/Carol Haerer/Ted Kurahara
March 8 – April 7, 1990.
Essays by Connie Butler, Kellie Jones, and John Yau. Acknowledgments by Susan Wyatt.
CATALOGUE WITH COLOR REPRODUCTIONS.

Les LeVeque: Some Questions Concerning Technology
March 8 – April 7, 1990.
Essay by John Knecht and acknowledgments by Susan Wyatt and Micki McGee.
BROCHURE WITH BLACK AND WHITE REPRODUCTIONS.

Stone's Throw: Television from Cuba, Island in Goliath's Sea
March 8 – April 7, 1990.
Essays by Camilio Hernández, Jean Franco, Reynaldo González, and Laurien Alexandre. Introduction by Dee Dee Halleck. Acknowledgments by Susan Wyatt and Micki McGee.
CATALOGUE WITH BLACK AND WHITE REPRODUCTIONS.

Beverly Semmes
April 19 – May 19, 1990.
Essay by Connie Butler and acknowledgments by Susan Wyatt.
BROCHURE WITH BLACK AND WHITE REPRODUCTIONS.

Mike Henderson
April 19 – May 19, 1990.
Essay by Connie Butler and acknowledgments by Susan Wyatt.
BROCHURE WITH BLACK AND WHITE REPRODUCTIONS.

Erawa – Era Was: An Installation by Ralph Paquin and Ann Stoddard
April 19 – May 19, 1990.
Essay by Dana Friis-Hansen and acknowledgments by Susan Wyatt.
BROCHURE WITH BLACK AND WHITE REPRODUCTIONS.

Joint Ventures
April 19 – May 19, 1990.
Essay by Ernest Larsen and acknowledgments by Susan Wyatt and Micki McGee.
BROCHURE WITH BLACK AND WHITE REPRODUCTIONS.

Recycling L.A.
May 31 – June 30, 1990.
Introduction by Barbara Goldstein, statements by the architects, and acknowledgments by Susan Wyatt.
NEWSPAPER WITH BLACK AND WHITE REPRODUCTIONS.

Disarming Genres
May 31 – June 30, 1990.
Essay by Micki McGee and acknowledgments by Susan Wyatt.
BROCHURE WITH BLACK AND WHITE REPRODUCTIONS.

LOOP 2: Cultures Converge
May 31 – June 30, 1990.
Essay by Micki McGee and acknowledgments by Susan Wyatt.
BROCHURE WITH BLACK AND WHITE REPRODUCTIONS.

Selections: Aljira & Artists Space
September 27 – November 3, 1990.
Notes by Carl E. Hazlewood and acknowledgments by Susan Wyatt.
CATALOGUE WITH BLACK AND WHITE REPRODUCTIONS.

Joel Katz: History Lessons
September 27 – November 3, 1990.
Essay by Micki McGee and acknowledgments by Susan Wyatt.
BROCHURE WITH BLACK AND WHITE REPRODUCTIONS.

Post – Boys & Girls: Nine Painters
November 15, 1990 – January 5, 1991.
Essays by Carol Zemel, Michael Kimmel, Renée Green, and James Saslow. Introduction by Ken Aptekar and acknowledgments by Susan Wyatt.
CATALOGUE WITH BLACK & WHITE REPRODUCTIONS. 32 PAGES.

Body Language: Studies in Female Expression
November 15, 1990 – January 5, 1991.
Essay by Julie Zando and acknowledgments by Susan Wyatt and Micki McGee.
BROCHURE WITH BLACK AND WHITE REPRODUCTIONS.

Robert Gero: (Energeia)
November 15, 1990 – January 5, 1991.
Essay by Buzz Spector and acknowledgments by Connie Butler and Susan Wyatt.
BROCHURE WITH BLACK AND WHITE REPRODUCTIONS.

Reframing the Family
January 17 – March 2, 1991.
Essays by Connie Butler, Barbara Ehrenreich, and Micki McGee. Acknowledgments by Susan Wyatt.
CATALOGUE WITH BLACK AND WHITE REPRODUCTIONS. 32 PAGES.

Daniel Canogar, Kathleen MacQueen, Zoya Kocur
January 1991.
Artists' book produced in conjunction with *Reframing the Family*.

Remapping Boundaries
March 14 – May 4, 1991.
Essay by Liz Kotz and acknowledgments by Susan Wyatt and Micki McGee.
BROCHURE WITH BLACK AND WHITE REPRODUCTIONS.

Jim Rittimann: Reconstructions
March 14 – May 4, 1991.
Essay by Chris Bruce and acknowledgments by Susan Wyatt.
BROCHURE WITH BLACK AND WHITE REPRODUCTIONS.

Western Agenda
March 14 – May 4, 1991.
Essay by Connie Butler and acknowledgments by Susan Wyatt and Connie Butler.
CATALOGUE WITH BLACK AND WHITE REPRODUCTIONS. 24 PAGES.

Art's Mouth
May 16 – June 29, 1991.
Essay by Connie Butler, statements by the artists, introduction by Gregory Amenoff, and acknowledgments by Susan Wyatt and Connie Butler.
CATALOGUE WITH BLACK AND WHITE REPRODUCTIONS.

Video—Video Witness: Festival of New Journalism *May 16–June 29, 1991.* Essay by Barbara Lattanzi. CATALOGUE WITH BLACK AND WHITE REPRODUCTIONS. 16 PAGES.	**Deborah Small: Our Bodice, Our Selves** *May 16–June 29, 1991.* Essay by Madeleine Grynsztejn and acknowledgments by Susan Wyatt and Connie Butler. BROCHURE WITH BLACK AND WHITE REPRODUCTIONS.	**Warp and Woof: Comfort and Dissent** September 26– November 9, 1991. Essay by Connie Butler and acknowledgments by Celeste Dado and Connie Butler. CATALOGUE WITH BLACK AND WHITE REPRODUCTIONS. 24 PAGES.	**Urban Space/ The City as Place** *September 26– November 9, 1991.* Essay by Molly Hankwitz and acknowledgments by Celeste Dado and Micki McGee. BROCHURE.	**Lewis deSoto: The Language of Paradise** September 26– November 9, 1991. Essay by Lawrence Rinder and acknowledgments by Celeste Dado and Connie Butler. BROCHURE WITH BLACK AND WHITE REPRODUCTIONS.
Working *November 21, 1991– January 11, 1992.* Acknowledgments by Connie Butler and Micki McGee and statements by the artists. BROCHURE WITH BLACK AND WHITE REPRODUCTIONS.	**Jared FitzGerald, Nickzad Nodjoumi, Gilda Pervin, Kendall Shaw** *February 13– March 21, 1992.* Acknowledgments by Carlos Gutierrez-Solana and Connie Butler. BROCHURE WITH COLOR REPRODUCTIONS.	**JAPAN: Outside/Inside/In Between** *Part 1: February 13– March 21, 1992. Part 2: April 9–25, 1992. Part 3: May 7–23, 1992.* Essay and acknowledgments by Micki McGee. CATALOGUE WITH BLACK AND WHITE REPRODUCTIONS.	**Rope/Radio/ Return of the Repressed** *April 9–May 23, 1992.* Acknowledgments by Carlos Gutierrez-Solana and Mike Ballou, Amy Sillman, and Adam Simon of Four Walls. BROCHURE.	**The Mountain, A Bed, and A Chair** *April 9–May 23, 1992.* Essay by Judith Tannenbaum and acknowledgments by Carlos Gutierrez-Solana. BROCHURE WITH BLACK AND WHITE REPRODUCTIONS.
Choice Histories: Framing Abortion *June 11–July 11, 1992.* An artists' book produced by REPOHistory in conjunction with the exhibition *A New World Order—Part 1.* Essays by Connie Butler and Tess Timoney. BLACK AND WHITE REPRODUCTIONS.	**HerStories in Color** *June 11–July 11, 1992.* Introduction and acknowledgments by Tony Cokes. BROCHURE.	**Putt-Modernism** *August 1– September 27, 1992.* Acknowledgments by Carlos Gutierrez-Solana, Ken Buhler, and Stephanie French. Essay by Ken Buhler with statements by the artists. CATALOGUE WITH COLOR REPRODUCTIONS.	**Ping Chong: A Facility for the Channeling and Containment of Undesirable Elements** *October 17– November 21, 1992.* Statement by the artist, essay by Katy Kline, and acknowledgments by Carlos Gutierrez-Solana. BROCHURE WITH BLACK AND WHITE REPRODUCTIONS.	**Robert Farber: I Thought I Had Time— From The Western Blot Series** *October 17– November 21, 1992.* Essays by Michael Camille and Patrick Moore. Acknowledgments by Carlos Gutierrez-Solana. CATALOGUE WITH COLOR REPRODUCTIONS.
Remapping Tales of Desire: Writing across the abyss *October 17–November 21, 1992.* Text by Karen Atkinson and Andrea Liss. Artists' "guidebook" produced by Side Street Press in conjunction with the exhibition *A New World Order—Part II.* BLACK AND WITH REPRODUCTIONS. 36 PAGES.		**John deFazio: Divine Comedies** *December 12, 1992– January 30, 1993.* Artist's book printed on newsprint. Statement by the artist and acknowledgments by Carlos Gutierrez-Solana. BLACK AND WHITE REPRODUCTIONS.	**Joel Sanders and Scott Sherk: Sighting the Gallery** *December 12, 1992– January 30, 1993.* Statement by the artists and acknowledgments by Carlos Gutierrez-Solana. BROCHURE WITH BLACK AND WHITE REPRODUCTIONS.	**Susie Brandt: Blankets** *February 18–April 3, 1993.* Acknowledgments by Carlos Gutierrez-Solana. BROCHURE WITH BLACK AND WHITE REPRODUCTIONS.
Jerry Phillips: It Should Have Been the Happiest Moment of My Life *February 18–April 3, 1993* Statement by the artist and acknowledgments by Carlos Gutierrez-Solana. BROCHURE WITH BLACK AND WHITE REPRODUCTIONS.	**A New World Order— Part III: GODZILLA: The Curio Shop** *February 18–April 3, 1993.* Statements by the artists and acknowledgments by Carlos Gutierrez-Solana. CATALOGUE WITH BLACK AND WHITE REPRODUCTIONS.	**Margaret Nielsen: Idiosyncratic Landscapes** *June 3–July 10, 1993.* Essay by Thomas Rhoads and acknowledgments by Carlos Gutierrez-Solana. BROCHURE WITH COLOR AND BLACK AND WHITE REPRODUCTIONS.	**Carol Sun: The China Mary Series** *June 3–July 10, 1993.* Essay by Kerri Sakamoto and acknowledgments by Carlos Gutierrez-Solana. BROCHURE WITH COLOR REPRODUCTIONS.	**Tony Bechara, Carmen Herrera, Tom Murrin, Mac Wells** *June 3–July 10, 1993.* Acknowledgments by Carlos Gutierrez-Solana. CATALOGUE WITH COLOR AND BLACK AND WHITE REPRODUCTIONS. 22 PAGES.

The Training of a Fragile Memory
November 20, 1993 – January 15, 1994.
Artists' book by Mark Alice Durant and Jeanne C. Finley.
PUBLICATION WITH BLACK AND WHITE REPRODUCTIONS.

A Terrible Beauty: Images of Conflict in Ireland
June 11 – July 30, 1994.
Essay by Gary Nickard and acknowledgments by Claudia Gould.
CATALOGUE WITH BLACK AND WHITE REPRODUCTIONS.

Artists Space Newspaper
Sept/Oct 1994, no. 1/vol. 1.
Introduction for *Selections* by Claudia Gould, statements by the artists. Introduction for *DressCode* by Denise Fasanello.
NEWSPRINT WITH BLACK AND WHITE REPRODUCTIONS.

Artists Space Newspaper
Nov/Jan 1994 – 95, no. 2/vol. 1.
Introduction for *Conceptual Art from the Bay Area* with statements by the artists. Introduction for *Six Moons Over Oaxaca*, statements by Jerri Allyn. Introduction for the *Money Commission Project* by Holly Brubbach.
NEWSPRINT WITH BLACK AND WHITE REPRODUCTIONS.

Artists Space Newspaper
Jan/March 1995, no. 3/vol. 1.
Essay for *Las Americas or The Return of Martin Steel* by Dominique Nahas. Introduction for *Raimund Kummer* by Claudia Gould.
NEWSPRINT WITH BLACK AND WHITE REPRODUCTIONS.

Artists Space Newspaper
April/July 1995, no. 4/vol. 1.
Introduction for *Satellite Choices*. Essays for *Customized Terror* by Ronald Jones and Jan Avgikos.
NEWSPRINT WITH BLACK AND WHITE REPRODUCTIONS.

Artists Space Newspaper
Sept/Oct 1995, no. 1/vol. 2.
Introduction for *Greg Lynn* by Peter Eisenman. Introduction for *Somatogenics* with statements by the artists.
NEWSPRINT WITH BLACK AND WHITE REPRODUCTIONS.

Artists Space Newspaper
Nov/Jan 1995 – 96, no. 2/vol. 2.
Essay for *Anne Marie Jugnet* by Jérôme Sans. Introduction for *Vincent Beaurin* by Andrée Putman.
NEWSPRINT WITH BLACK AND WHITE REPRODUCTIONS.

Artists Space Newspaper
Jan/April 1996, no. 3/vol. 2.
Introduction for *Unnaturally Yours* with statements by the artists. Introduction for *Exhibit A: Design/Writing/ Research*.
NEWSPRINT WITH BLACK AND WHITE REPRODUCTIONS.

Squat Theatre 1996
March 30 – July 13, 1996.
Produced in conjunction with the exhibition *Mr. Dead & Mrs. Free: A History of Squat Theatre (1969 – 1991)*.
Written and compiled by Eva Buchmuller and Anna Koós. Introduction by Alisa Solomon and Andras Halasz. Acknowledgments by Claudia Gould.
CATALOGUE WITH BLACK AND WHITE REPRODUCTIONS. 232 PAGES.

Artists Space Newspaper
April/May 1996, no. 4/vol. 2.
Introduction for *Mr. Dead & Mrs. Free* with history of Squat Theatre.
NEWSPRINT WITH BLACK AND WHITE REPRODUCTIONS.

Artists Space Newspaper
Sept/Oct 1996, no. 1/vol. 3.
Essay for *Angie Eng: Safety Belt* by Anastasia Aukeman. Essays for *A Strategy Hinted At* by Anastasia Aukeman and Peter Halley.
NEWSPRINT WITH BLACK AND WHITE REPRODUCTIONS.

Artists Space Newspaper
Nov/Jan 1996 – 97, no. 2/vol. 3.
Introduction for *Jeff Francis* by Cindy Sherman. Essay for *Blood Fairies* by Frank Moore, Geoff Hendricks, and Sur Rodney (Sur) with statements by the artists.
NEWSPRINT WITH BLACK AND WHITE REPRODUCTIONS.

Artists Space Newspaper
Jan/March 1997, no. 3/vol. 3.
Introduction for *Anna Gili* by Alessandro Mendini. Essay for *Hot Coffee* by Thomas Lawson.
NEWSPRINT WITH BLACK AND WHITE REPRODUCTIONS.

Artists Space Newspaper
April/May 1997, no. 4/vol. 3.
Introduction for *Ben van Berkel* by Greg Lynn. Conversation about *Station to Station* by Tony Oursler and Gary Simmons.
NEWSPRINT WITH BLACK AND WHITE REPRODUCTIONS.

Artists Space Newspaper
June/July 1997, no. 5/vol. 3.
Introduction for *Tampering with the Reel* by Pip Day.
NEWSPRINT WITH BLACK AND WHITE REPRODUCTIONS.

Artists Space Newspaper
Sept/Oct 1997, no. 1/vol. 4.
Essay for *Permutations* by Pip Day and Debra Singer. Interview with Karen Kimmel by Pip Day.
NEWSPRINT WITH BLACK AND WHITE REPRODUCTIONS.

Artists Space Newspaper
Nov/Jan 1997 – 98, no. 2/vol. 4.
Essay for *Lines of Loss* by Gabriel Orozco. Essay for *Present Tense: George Ranalli* by Michael Sorkin.
NEWSPRINT WITH BLACK AND WHITE REPRODUCTIONS.

Artists Space Newspaper
Jan/March 1998, no. 3/vol. 4.
Introductions for *Abstraction in Process* by Irving Sandler and Claudia Gould with statements by the artists. Introduction for *Elke Lehmann: 4(to)5* by Dennis Adams.
NEWSPRINT WITH BLACK AND WHITE REPRODUCTIONS.

Artists Space Newspaper
March/May 1998, no.4/vol. 4.
Essay for *Digital Mapping* by Hani Rashid. Statement by the artist for *Anne Gardiner: Through the Tulips & The Red Red Rose*.
NEWSPRINT WITH BLACK AND WHITE REPRODUCTIONS.

Artists Space Newspaper
June/July 1998, no. 5, vol. 4.
Scope: Summer Video Festival by Pip Day.
NEWSPRINT WITH BLACK AND WHITE REPRODUCTIONS.

Artists Space Newspaper
Sept/Nov 1998, no. 1, vol. 5.
Introduction for *Laurie Anderson: Whirlwind* by Claudia Gould. Interview with Laurie Anderson by Claudia Gould.
NEWSPRINT WITH BLACK AND WHITE REPRODUCTIONS.

United Graffiti Artists 1975
September 9 – 27, 1975.
Essays by Hugo Martinez and Peter Schjeldahl. Accompanied exhibition at Artists Space.

Published by United Graffiti Writers, Inc.
CATALOGUE WITH COLOR AND BLACK AND WHITE REPRODUCTIONS.

History of Benefit Artists' Multiples

Over the years Artists Space has worked with a number of well-established artists to create a collection of limited edition artists' multiples. Two or three new editions are produced each season, usually in conjunction with the annual Spring Benefit. The proceeds from the sale of these multiples continue to serve as an important source of funds for programs.

Dimensions are in inches; height precedes width precedes depth. Editions of the works are in parentheses. Asterisks (*) indicate artists whose work was not produced in connection with the annual Benefit.

1973 Hans Namuth* *Fifty-Two Artists*, 1973 Black and white photographic portfolio, 11 x 14	**1979** Roy Lichtenstein *Untitled*, 1979 Serigraph on silk shirt (100)	**1983** Cindy Sherman *Emerging Artist*, 1983 T-shirt	**1984** Steve Gianakos *Moving*, 1984 Color lithograph, 31 1/2 x 47 3/4 (40)	Stewart Wilson *Personas*, 1984 One-of-a-kind 3-inch-high figures costumed in fabrics, furs, foils, and feathers accompanied by their signed and numbered color portraits
1985 Richard Bosman *Untitled*, 1985 T-shirt	Laurie Simmons *Party Picture*, 1985 Color photograph, 11 x 14 (50)	**1986** R.M. Fischer *Night Writer*, 1986 Brass, steel, plastic, marble, electric light, 15 x 7 x 7 (75)	Robert Longo* *Arena Brains*, 1986 Color lithograph, 44 x 29 (75) →	
Tom Otterness *Untitled*, 1986 Bronze, 3 x 3 1/2 x 1 1/2 (13) 	Cindy Sherman* *Untitled*, 1986 C-print, 20 x 24 (75) →			John Torreano *Jewel*, 1986 T-shirt
	1987 Jon Kessler *CAPSULE*, 1987 Mixed-media table piece, 3 x 9 x 11 (30)	Sherrie Levine *After Walker Evans*, 1987 Black and white photograph and frame, 8 x 10 (15)	Tim Rollins + K.O.S. *Amerika*, 1987 T-shirt	**1988** John Baldessari *Aligned Trumpeting*, 1988 Color lithograph, 22 x 30 (50)
Ashley Bickerton *GOOD/BAD*, 1988 T-shirt	Nancy Dwyer *Why Y (?)*, 1988 Polished cast hydrocal, 5 x 4 3/4 x 5 1/4 (30)	**1989** Richard Artschwager* *Klock*, 1989 Mixed media, 7 1/4 x 42 3/4 x 3 3/4 (25)	Barbara Bloom *The Titanic (POSH: Port Out, Starboard Home)*, 1989 Commemorative champagne bottle in wooden box, 5 x 15 x 5 (33)	Matt Mullican *Untitled*, 1989 Oil on canvas, 24 x 24 (20)

Nancy Spero *Goddess and Centaur*, 1989 T-shirt	**Carrie Mae Weems** *Jim, if you choose to accept, the mission is to land on your own two feet*, 1988–89 Gelatin silver print, image: 15 1/2 x 15 1/2, sheet: 20 x 16 (50)	**1990** **David Ireland** *Dumb Balls…*, 1990 Yellow concrete balls, palm-size	**Louise Lawler** *Who Says, Who Shows, Who Counts*, 1990 Three wine glasses on glass shelf, 8 1/2 x 14 x 4 1/4 (50)	**Annette Lemieux** *Artificial Heart on Sleeve*, 1990 Gelatin silver print, 23 1/4 x 20 (50)
William Wegman *Untitled*, 1990 T-shirt	**1991** **Joseph Kosuth** *Untitled*, 1991 T-shirt	**Cindy Sherman*** *Untitled*, 1990–91 C-print, 16 x 20"(125)	**Lorna Simpson** *C-Rations,* 1991 Black and white photograph, image 19 x 42 (50) ↓	**Kiki Smith** *Untitled*, 1991 Fired enamel on glass with shelf, 18 x 18 (50) →
	1992 **Jenny Holzer** *"Truism" Golf Ball*, 1992 Single golf ball in four colors: light blue, pink, yellow, orange; six *"Truisms"* printed with black ink (unlimited edition) ←	**Mike Kelley** *Untitled*, 1992 Silkscreen on wood and leather, 32 1/4 x 5 1/2 x 3/4 (50) ↓	**Mary Kelly** *Follow Me*, 1992 T-shirt	**Tom Otterness** *Lovers*, 1992 Bronze with silver nitrate patina, 4 1/4 x 4 1/4 (irregular) (25)
1993 **Rob Clarke** *Putt-Modernism,*1993 T-shirt	**John Diebboll** *Untitled* (for *Putt-Modernism* exhibition), 1993 T-shirt		**Cindy Sherman** *Untitled Secretary*, 1978/93 Sepia-toned black and white photograph, 11 x 14" (125)	

		1994 **Willie Cole** *A.R.T.* *(in the new world order)*, 1994 Oilstick on blackboard, 18 x 24 (48)	
Andres Serrano *Klansman (Knighthawk Edition of Georgia, V)*, 1990 Cibachrome print, 24 x 30 (50)	**Sue Williams** *I Have No Inner Life, So Sue Me*, 1993 T-shirt **Sue Williams** *Women's Heads*, 1993 T-shirt		**John Giorno** *Fabulous Sex*, 1994 T-shirt (Partial proceeds from the sale of this T-shirt benefit the AIDS Treatment Project)

		1995 **Elizabeth Enders** *Leopard, from the Book of Going Forth by Day*, 1995 T-shirt	
Annette Messager *Protection*, 1994 Mixed media with photograph, 20 x 20 (40) ←	**Richard Prince** *Oedipus Schmedipus*, 1994 Screenprint on T-shirt stretched over canvas, white with lacquer frame, 25 3/8 x 19 1/2 (26)		**evansandwong** *Untitled*, 1995 T-shirt

Robert Mangold *Untitled*, 1995 Etching with aquatint, 24 x 30"(50)	**Andrea Zittel** *Perfected Pillow,* 1995 Black and green velvet single bed with pillow, both fringed, bed 80 x 40, pillow 18 x 36 (39)	**1996** **Diller + Scofidio** *Untitled(+/-)*, 1996 T-shirt	**Tony Oursler** *Untitled (Talking Photograph)*, 1996 Color photograph mounted on plastic frame with 10- second audio recording, four batteries, inside custom box, 6 x 7 x 1/2 (100)	**Kiki Smith** *Ginzer and the Birds*, 1996 Black and white lithograph with collage and Gampi silk tissue on paper, 16 x 24 (50)
1997 **Ellen Gallagher** *Untitled*, 1997 Lithograph and watercolor on Misu paper, 25 x 19 1/2 (20)				**Nan Goldin** *Suzanne and Philippe on the train, Long Island*, *1985* Cibachrome print, 16 x 20 (100)
1998 **Louise Bourgeois** *Jitterbug*, 1998 Lithograph, 18 x 24 (50) →				**Mona Hatoum** *Birds of a Feather*, 1997 Chromogenic color print, 10 x 12 (50)

Government Support

City of New York, Department of Cultural Affairs
    Cultural Challenge Program
    Materials for the Arts
    Program Services
Institute of Museum Services
    General Operating Support
National Alliance of Media Arts Centers
National Endowment for the Arts
    Advancement Program
    Heritage and Preservation Program
    Inter-Arts Program
    Media Arts Program
    Museum Program
    Visual Arts Program
New York Council for the Humanities
New York State Council on the Arts
    Architecture, Planning, and Design Program
    Electronic Media and Film Program
        (formerly separate funding from the Film Program
        and the Media Program)
    Literature Program
    Museum Aid Program
    Visual Artists Program (formerly the Visual Arts Program)
Re-grant funds and services from:
    Film Speakers Bureau
    Locus
    Media Bureau
    M.E.R.C. (Media Equipment Resource Center)
    Poets & Writers, Inc.
    Publishing Center for Cultural Resources
    Technical Assistance Fund

Foreign Government Support

Association Francais d'Action Artistique
Australian Council
The British Council
Canadian Consulate General
City of Rotterdam
Commissariat aux Relations Internationales de la
    Communaute Francaise de Belgique
Consulate General of the Federal Republic of Germany
Consulate General of the Netherlands
Consulate General of Spain
Italian Trade Commission
The Ministry of the Flemish Community
The Netherlands – American Community Association Inc.
New South Wales Ministry for the Arts
P.E.A.C.E. (Programa Español de Accion Cultural
en el Exterior)
The Scottish Arts Council
The United States – Spanish Joint Committee for Cultural
    and Educational Cooperation

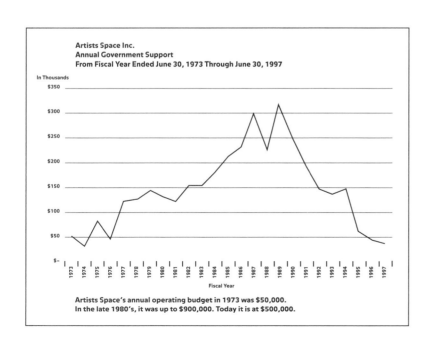

Artists Space Inc.
Annual Government Support
From Fiscal Year Ended June 30, 1973 Through June 30, 1997

In Thousands

Artists Space's annual operating budget in 1973 was $50,000.
In the late 1980's, it was up to $900,000. Today it is at $500,000.

Foundations

*Grants begin at $150 through fiscal year 1991
and $1,000 from fiscal 1992 through fiscal 1998.*

Harriett Ames Charitable Trust
Art Matters Inc.
Avery Arts Foundation
J.M.R. Barker Foundation
The David Bermant Foundation: Color, Light, Motion
Bohen Foundation
Louis A. Bradbury Fund
Edward R. Broida Trust
Florence V. Burden Foundation
Charina Foundation
Robert Sterling Clark Foundation, Inc.
Cowles Charitable Trust
Geraldine R. Dodge Foundation Inc.
The Dover Fund
Downe Foundation
Estate Project for Artists with AIDS
Experimental Television Center
Robert D. Farber Foundation
I. J. Feldman Foundation
Foundation for Contemporary Performance Arts
Fan Fox and Leslie R. Samuels Foundation
The Howard Gilman Foundation
Stephen A. and Diana L. Goldberg Foundation, Inc.
Herman Goldman Foundation
The Horace W. Goldsmith Foundation
Graham Foundation for Advanced Studies in the Fine Arts
The Greenwall Foundation
Heathcote Art Foundation, Inc.
Jerome Foundation
Jewish Communal Fund
The Jewish Community Foundation of Metrowest, New Jersey
W. Alton Jones Foundation, Inc.
Alfred Jurzykowski Foundation
The J. M. Kaplan Fund
Seymour Knox Foundation
Lannan Foundation
The Lauder Foundation
The Dorothea L. Leonhardt Foundation
The Joe and Emily Lowe Foundation, Inc.
The Robert Mapplethorpe Foundation, Inc.
Mariposa Foundation

The Penny McCall Foundation
The Menemsha Fund
Joyce Mertz-Gilmore Foundation
Mex-Am Cultural Foundation
Mexican Cultural Institute
The Monterey Fund
Motherwell Foundation, Inc.
The Netherland – America Foundation
The New York Community Trust
The Norton Family Foundation
Open Society Fund, Inc.
The Overbrook Foundation
Betty Parsons Foundation
The Reed Foundation, Inc.
Larry Rivers Foundation
The Rockefeller Foundation
Saul Rosen Foundation
Arthur Ross Foundation
Mark Rothko Foundation
Samuel Rubin Foundation
May and Samuel Rudin Family Foundation, Inc.
Sandpiper Foundation
Silver Mountain Foundation for the Arts
Smorgon Family Charitable Foundation
Nate B. and Frances Spingold Foundation, Inc.
Stern Foundation
Stimuleringsfonds voor Architectuur
The Surdna Foundation, Inc.
TASAP Trust
Thayer Family Fund
Roy and Niuta Titus Foundation
The Veronese Foundation
Vinmont Foundation Inc.
Lila Wallace – Reader's Digest Fund
The Walter Foundation
The Andy Warhol Foundation for the Visual Arts, Inc.
Ealan Wingate Foundation
Wray Charitable Trust

One Anonymous Foundation

Corporations

*Grants begin at $500 through fiscal year 1991
and $1,000 from fiscal 1992 through fiscal 1998.*

Agnes B
American Can Company Foundation
The American Express Company
Art Dealers Association of America
AT & T Foundation
Boeringer Ingelheim Pharmaceuticals
Brooke Alexander, Inc.
CBS Foundation
Chase Manhattan Bank N.A.
Citibank
Comme des Garcons
Consolidated Edison Company of New York, Inc.
Cuervo 1800
D&R Realty Corporation
Daimler-Benz of North America
Equitable Real Estate Group, Inc.
Etant-Donnes
Exxon Corporation
First Boston Corporation
Fleetwood Litho and Letter Corporation
General Atlantic Corporation
Grand Marnier

The Grand Street Foundation, Inc.
I.B.M. Corporation
I. M. Pei & Partners
J. P. Morgan
Lehman Brothers Kuhn Loeb
Lunn Ltd.
Management Consultants for the Arts
Merrill Lynch & Co. Foundation, Inc.
Miu Miu
Mobil Foundation, Inc.
National Distillers and Chemical Corporation
Pace Gallery of New York
PaineWebber
Payson Enterprises, Inc.
Perry Ellis
Philip Morris Companies Inc.
R. H. Macy & Co., Inc.
Skidmore Owings & Merrill
Smorgon Consolidated Industries
Times Mirror
U.S. Trust Company of N.Y. Foundation
Warner Communications

Galleries

*Gallery Dealers in Support of Artists Space was initiated in 1985
and ran through 1993. Annual contributions ranged from $250 to $1,500.
Unless otherwise noted, all galleries cited were located in New York .*

Acquavella Contemporary Art
Brooke Alexander
Pamela Auchincloss Gallery
Massimo Audiello Gallery
Baskerville + Watson
BlumHelman Gallery
Mary Boone Gallery
Grace Borgenicht Gallery
Laura L. Carpenter (Dallas)
Leo Castelli Gallery
James Corcoran Gallery (Santa Monica)
Charles Cowles Gallery
Crown Point Press
Maxwell Davidson Gallery
John Davis Gallery
Marisa del Re Gallery
Dolan/Maxwell (New York and Philadelphia)
Andre Emmerich Gallery
Fawbush Gallery
Ronald Feldman Fine Arts
Germans van Eck
Barbara Gladstone Gallery
James Goodman Gallery
Marian Goodman Gallery
Scott Hanson Gallery
Pat Hearn Gallery
Arnold Herstand & Company

Nancy Hoffman Gallery
Rhona Hoffman Gallery (Chicago)
Ikkan Art International
Kent Fine Art
Phyllis Kind Gallery
Barbara Krakow Gallery (Boston)
Carlo Lamagna Gallery
Lang & O'Hara Gallery
Galerie Lelong
Luhring, Augustine, and Hodes Gallery
Metro Pictures
McNeil Gallery (Philadelphia)
Robert Miller Gallery
Victoria Munroe Gallery
Pace Gallery of New York
Anne Plumb Gallery Inc.
Rubin Spangle Gallery
Mary Ryan Gallery
Tony Shafrazi Gallery
Jack Shainman Gallery
Holly Solomon Gallery
Bernice Steinbaum Gallery
Stux Gallery
Edward Thorp Gallery
Barbara Toll Fine Arts
Zabriskie Gallery

Benefit Contributors

Benefits continue to be the primary vehicle through which individuals contribute to Artists Space. The following is a list of benefit donors of $1,000 and more through 1998.

Philip E. and Shelley Fox Aarons
Caroline and Stephen Adler
Agnes B
Brooke Alexander
Carolyn Alexander
Stephen and Ann Ames
R. T. and Generosa Ammon
Artforum
ARTnews
Milton and Sally M. Avery
Josh Baer
Anne Bass
Dianne Benson
Richard Berge
Elaine Berger
Gretchen and John Berggruen
Catherine Woodard and Nelson Blitz, Jr.
The Bohen Foundation
Ted Bonin
Livio M. Borghese
Frederic Brandt
Edward R. Broida
Peggy and Ralph Burnet
Blake Byrne
Dr. and Mrs. Robert E. Carroll
Joanne Cassullo
Leo Castelli
Frances Chaves
Christo and Jeanne-Claude
Eileen and Michael Cohen
William N. Copley
Kenneth A. Cowin
Charles Cowles
Jan Cowles
Virginia Cowles and Michael Schroth
Douglas S. Cramer Foundation
Caroline Cronson
Linda and Ronald F. Daitz
Elaine and Werner Dannheisser
Agnes De Fleurieu
Jeffrey Deitch
Frank DeVito
Beth and James DeWoody
Hester Diamond
The Downe Foundation
Edward R. Downe, Jr.
Donald Droll
Vivian L. and Justin S. Ebersman
Kenneth L. Edlow
Richard Ekstract

Diana and Fred Elghanayan
Carolyn Enders
Elizabeth and Anthony Enders
Mrs. John F. Enders
The Equitable
Frank Kolbert and Frank Farmer
Sue and Stuart Feld
Andrea Feldman
Fleetwood Litho & Letter Corporation
Susan and Arthur Fleischer, Jr.
Foundation for Contemporary
    Performance Arts, Inc.
Rebecca and David Friendly
Gagosian Gallery
Carol and Arthur A. Goldberg
Susan and Jerry Goldman
Bill Goldstein
Nancy Graves
Mr. and Mrs. Robert E. Grimes
Michael Groholski
Don Gummer and Meryl Streep
Agnes Gund and Daniel Shapiro
Alvin D. Hall
Joe Helman
John F. Hennessy, Jr.
John F. Hennessy III
Frederick B. Henry
Rhona Hoffman Gallery
Benjamin D. Holloway
Susan and Michael Hort
Bryan Hunt
Arthur P. and Gail Pincus Jacobs
Richard H. Jenrette
Howard B. Johnson
Richard Kahan
Sidney and Elizabeth Kahn
Ursula Kalish
Dr. and Mrs. Michael Kalisman
Alex Katz
Mr. and Mrs. Stephen Kellen
Jim Kempner
Mr. and Mrs. Pentti Kouri
James Kraft
Martin Kunz
Phyllis and Edward Kwalwasser
Benjamin Lambert
Emily Fisher Landau
Mr. and Mrs. Ronald S. Lauder
Raymond J. Learsy
Gail LeBoff and Michael Bradley

Phyllis and Gerald LeBoff
Ann Tenenbaum and Thomas H. Lee
The Dorothea L. Leonhardt Foundation
Donna and Jonathan Levinson
Frances and Sydney Lewis
Dorothy and Roy Lichtenstein
Ellen and Arthur Liman
Lintas: Worldwide
Harriet and Lester Lipton
Vera G. List
Carl D. Lobell
Katherine S. Lobell
Lawrence Luhring
Luhring, Augustine, and Hodes
Herbert C. Lust III
Ninah and Michael Lynne
Anne MacDonald
Joel and Sherry Mallin
Robert and Sylvia Plimack Mangold
Donald B. Marron
Margo Dolan and Peter Maxwell
Kari McCabe and Nate McBride
Penny and David B. McCall
Donald McKinney
Meryl and Robert Meltzer
Sara Meltzer
Michael and Mimi Mendelson
Ronay and Richard Menschel
Jane and Robert Meyerhoff
Deborah Millman
Galeria Montenay
Mr. and Mrs. George K. Moss
Elizabeth Murray
Needham Harper Worldwide, Inc.
New York Stock Exchange
Wilson and Eliot Nolen
Peter and Eileen Norton
Obelisk Gallery
Claes Oldenburg
Janice Oresman
PaineWebber
Philip Morris Companies Inc.
Sandy and Robert Pittman
Nancy and Joel Portnoy
Galeria Joan Prats
Prestige Art Ltd.
Bill Previdi
Mr. and Mrs. Eugene C. Rainis
Robert Rauschenberg
Martin J. Raynes

Reader's Digest
Dan Redmond
Jon Reed
Judy Rifka
Jose Cobo Romero
Arthur G. Rosen
Abraham and Lillian Rosenberg
    Foundation, Inc.
James Rosenquist and Mimi Thompson
Samuel and May Rudin Foundation, Inc.
Barbara and Ira Sahlman
Elizabeth B. Schaffner
Schoeman, Marsh, Updike & Welt
Christopher and Hannelore Schwabacher
Stanley J. Sehler
Richard Serra and Clara Weyergraf
Joel Shapiro and Ellen Phelan
Mr. and Mrs. Robert F. Shapiro
Richard Shebairo
Mr. and Mrs. Eric P. Sheinberg
Cindy Sherman and Michel Auder
Sidney Singer
Mr. and Mrs. Alan B. Slifka
Nancy and Arnold Smoller
Ruth Cummings Sorenson
Patricia and David Specter
Emily and Jerry I. Spiegel
Betsy and Robert Stang
Peter R. Stern
John L. Stewart
Walter Sudol
Mr. and Mrs. Edward F. Swenson, Jr.
Mr. and Mrs. A. Alfred Taubman
Mr. and Mrs. Robert S. Taubman
William S. Taubman
Catherine Vance Thompson
Jane Timken
Roy and Niuta Titus Foundation
Emily Todd
Katherine Wade
Jane and Marty Weinberg
Cheryl and Henry Welt
Angela Westwater
Helene Winer
Anna Wintour
Ann A. and F. Mark Wyatt
Mr. and Mrs. Masahiko Yanagi

Three anonymous contributors

Index

Numbers in **boldface** are longer quotes; numbers in *italics* are photos

A

A.T.W. (Around the World), 236
Aarons, Philip, **218**, 235
ABACA (Arts Benefit All Coalition Alternative) 252, 284
Abe, Koya, 311
Abeles, Kim 253
Abish, Cecile, 276
A. Project (Abortion Project), 240, 242
Abraham, Ayisha, 251
Abramovic, Marina, 298
Abstraction in Process (1986), 182, 330
Abstraction in Process II, 266, 302, 303, 334
Acconci, Vito, 22, 25, 28, 33, **35**, *35*, 38, 39, 47, *47*, 53, 72, 87, 88, 93, 119, 124, 126, 168, 177, 185, *288*, 290, 293, 315
Acey, Jo-Ann, 155, 169, 176, 184, 214, 220, 236, 244, 254
Acker, Kathy, 39, 33, 95, 153, 85, 188
Activated Walls, 229, 255, *224–255*
Act-Up Paris, 289
Adams, Dennis, 104, **108**, *108*, 135, 157, 334
Admiral, Richard, 68
Adorno, Olga, 157
Afro-Dite, 253
Agee, Mia, 71
Agnoli, Kathleen, 92
Agostini, Peter, 28
Agro, Chuck, 255
Aguilar, Jesus, 255
Ahearn, Charlie, **49**, 82, 88, *89*, 95, 96, 107, (Charlie A.) 131
Ahearn, John, 84, 276
Ahn, Sang-Joon, 289
Ahrens, Hanno, 176
Ahwesh, Peggy, 167, 236, 240, 261, 280, 290, 293
AIDS Activism, 216
AIDS Crisis Is Not Over, The, 214, 215, 330
AIDS FORUM, 226–27, *231*, 244, 247, *247*, 248, 250–56, 250, 270, 276, 277, 313
AIDS/Service, 254
Alacoque, François, 236
Alex, Michael, 248
Alexander, Brooke, 312
Alexander, Carolyn, 9, 12, 203, 226, 241, 287, 310, **312–13**, *314*, 315
Alexander, Jane, 272
Alexandre, Laurien, 235, 332
Alfonzo, Carlos, 192
Alien Comic, 260
Aljian, Stephen, 158
Allen, John, 254
Allen, Roberta, 126
Allen, Stan, **192**, 193
Alloway, Lawrence, 23, 34, 35, *47*
Allyn, Jerri, 253, 261, 278, 334
Almy, Max, 171, 185
Alpert, Jon, 182
Alta Loma High School, 237
Alvarez, Candida, 276
Alvarez, Louis, 247
Alvarez, Marina, 276
Alzamora, Victor, 145, 157
Amacher, Maryanne, 173
AMANAPLANACANALPANAMA, 238
Amar, Maurice, 46
Ambitious Lovers, The, 82
Amenoff, Gregory, 30, 242, 252, 332

Ames, Adam, *289*, **289**, 290, 292, 298, 308, 310
Amezcua, Chelo, 242
Amos, Emma, 158
Amrhein, Joe, 255
Amron, Jon, 251
Anderson, Beth, 82
Anderson, Chochise, 252
Anderson, Kelly, 236, 256
Anderson, Larry Jens, 276
Anderson, Laurie, 13, 25, 28, **33**, *33*, 35, 38, *43*, 47, 53, 85, 88, 91, 93, 107, 124, 126, 171, 173, 265, *268*, 313, *313*, *318–19*, 334
Anderson, Mike, 234
Anderson, Ross, 149
Anderson, Ruth, 45
Andre, Carl, 28, 46, 72, 73, 93, 109, 141
Andrew, Lisa, 290
Andrews, Benny, 65
Andringa, Mel, 100, *100*, 157
Angeil, Theo, 312
Angelo, Nancy, 171
Anger, Kenneth, 186
Anstey, Jo, 238
Ant Farm, 93
Antabi, Marcia, 311
Antille, Emmanuelle, 312
Antin, Eleanor, 33
Antoni, Janine, **244**, *244*, 251, 315
Aono, Kristine Yuki, 260
Apfelbaum, Polly, 176, 261
Apple Valley High School, 237
Apple, Jacki, 45, 78, 93, 157
Applebroog, Ida Horowitz, 84, 157, 240, 276
Appleton, Robert, 96, 157
Aptekar, Ken, 238, 239, 332
Aquirre, Vidal, 216
Araeen, Rasheed, 106, 107
Arai, Tomie, 254
Araki, Hiroshi, 248
Arbatsky, Nicholas, 248
Arcade, Penny, 253
Architectural Manifestoes, 95, *95*, 192, 181, 182, *183*, 184, 264, 328
Architecture Project, (2/87) 181; (5/87) 184; (1–2/89) 217
Architecture: Sequences, 95, 328
Archoud, Lindsay, 253
Arenas, Adriana, 312
Arenas, Reinaldo, 256
Ariyoshi, Jun, 248
Arlen, Nancy, 96
Armijo, Richard R., 131, 157
Armleder, John, 140
Armstrong, David, 251
Armstrong, Richard, 30, 146, **173**, 183, 218, *294*, *295*, 296, 312
Arndt, Dianne, 47, 157
Arnold, David, 300, *300*, **301**, 311
Arnold, Martin, 240
Arocha, Ivan, 256
Aron, Donn, 47, 78, 88
Art & Language, 140
Art and Class, 72, 73, *73*
Art Breaks, 171
Art From the British Left, 106, *106–7*, 107
Artforum, 23, 29
Art-Rite, 33, 47
Art's Mouth, 242, 333
Arthur, Paul, 170
Artists "Select," 143, 232, 261, *261*, 276, *276*, 298

Artists as Filmmakers, 23, 40; (2/74), 29; (11–12/74), 45; (3/75), 47
Artists Draw, 100, *104–105*, 105, 328
Artists Film series, 68, (1/76), 69; (1–3/76), 72; (3/76), 73; (4–5/76), 74; (11/76), 80; (12/76), 82; (3–4/78), 95
Artists from the Studio in a School, 144, 155, 169, 176, 184, 214, 220, 229, 236, 244, 254
Artists Space – Fact or Fiction, 260, *260*
Artists Space Multiples, 256
Artists Space Newspaper, 277
Artists(web)Space, 291–93, 296, 297, 299–302, 310, 312, 314, 315
Artman, Deborah, 240
ArtpArkArt III, 95
Artschwager, Richard, 31, 335
Asaro, Mario, 141, 157
Asente, Michael James, 220
Asher, Michael, 100, 193, *193*, 223, 242, 330
Ashford, Douglas, 141, 157, 163
Ashley, Robert, 173
Ashwill, Mark, 312
Askew, Ed, 244
Atkins, Robert, 286
Atkinson, Conrad, 106, 107, 141
Atkinson, Karen, 253, 333
Attanasio and Gianelli, 289
Attanasio, Robert, 74, 140, 157
Attempted: Not Known, 222, 331
Attie, Dotty, 261
Aubert, Lynne, 214, 220
Auder, Michel, 173, 280, 284, 286
Audio Works, 93, *93*
Aufiero, Tina, 220
Aukeman, Anastasia, 285, 289–91, **292–93**, *294*, 334
Ault, Julie, 141, 157
Auping, Michael, 149, 192, 330
Austad, Susan, 155, 169, 176, 184, 214, 244, 254
Austin, Lisa, 126, 261
Authors in Search of a Publisher, 280
Autumn, Lindsay, 236
Avalos, David, 187
Avgikos, Jan, 138, 284, 334
Aycock, Alice, 84, 157, 261
Aylon, Helene, 261
Ayneto, Celia, 312
Ayoung, Todd, 251

B

B, Beth, 49, **92**, 93, 95, 106, 107, 124, 146, 168, 240, 260, 280
B (Billingsley), Scott, 49, 74, 87, 88, 95, 106, 107, 146, 168
Bach, Gail, 169, 176, 184
Baden, Mowry, **155**, 159, *159*, 329
Bader, Ian and Lynn, 184, 330
Baechler, Donald, 127, 157
Baen, Noah, 169, 176, 184, 214, 220, 236
Bagley, Henrietta, 48
Bahc, Mo, 176, 254
Bahhur, Riad, 243
Bailey, Pamila, 253
Bailey, Zenobia, 244
Baim, Richard, 140, 148, 157
Bainbridge, Benton, 291
Bajic, Mrdjan, 221

Bakowski, Janusz, 236
Balboni, Bruce, 222
Balcells, Remo, 190
Baldessari, John, 93–95, 124, 157, 168, 335
Baldwin, Carl, 46
Baldwin, Craig, 181
Balint, Stephan, 290
Ball, Lillian, 184
Ballou, Michael, 144, *144*, 157, 228, 248, **250**, *250*, 333
Balser, Michael, 235
Balsmeyer, Jeff, 125, 140
Bancroft, David, 198, 199, 204
Bands, 71, 82, *82*, 96
Bankowsky, Jack, 10
Bannard, Darby, 48
Baracz, Jan, 193
Baraka, Amiri, 73
Baranik, Rudolf, 23, 34, 46, 65, 72, 110, 141, 261
Barbier, Annette, 234
Barceló, Miquel, 167
Barchevska, Madeleine, 248
Bard, Perry, 190, 260, 290, 310
Barden, Jim, 46
Barg, Barbara, 222
Bark, Jared, 88
Barney, Matthew, 276
Barnhouse, Dorothy, 240
Baron, Ronald, 215
Barr, Paula, 34, 157
Barron, Jeffrey, 260
Barros, Mercedes, 236
Barry, Judith, 166, *166–67*, **167**, 223, 298
Barry, Robert, 93
Barry, Stephen, 217
Bartlett, Jennifer, 30, 33, 40, 56, 72–74, 114, 261
Bartolomeo, Joel, 280
Bar-Tur, Ann, 126, 157
Baskerville, Lew, 115
Basquiat, Jean Michel, 171, 173
Bateman, Lisa, 169
Batona, Yael, 301
Battlefields, Project, 214
Baum, Don, 175
Bausman, Karen, 193, 277
Baxandall, Lee, 73
Bayer, Arlyne, 255
BBD&O, 192
Beal, Jack, 34
Bear, Liza, 47, 93, 134
Bearden, Romare, 22, 28
Beaulieu, John, 48
Beaumont, Betty, 251
Beaurin, Vincent, 287, 334
Beauty and the Beast, 250, *250*
Beban, Brenda, 219
Bechara, Tony, 229, 260, 261, 334
Becher, Max, 276
Bechet, Tristan, 312
Beck, Jerry, 116, *117*, 169, 189
Becker, Julie, 296
Beckley, Connie, 69, 93, 260
Beckman, Ericka, 88, 95, 125, 140, 149, 157, 162, 177, 178, 276, 280
Beckman, Laurel, 93
Beebe, Mary, 140
Beens, Olivia, 169, 176, 184, 214, 220, 236, 254
Behrman, David, 45
Belcher, Alan, 158, 171
Belfast Independent Video, 217
Bell, Tiffany, 260
Bellido, Ramón Tio, 167, 329
Belshe, Curt, 177, 251, 330
Benamou, Catherine, 174

Bender, Gretchen, **139**, *139*, 157, 162, 267
Benglis, Lynda, 23, 34, 72, 171, 185, 260
Bengston, David, 237
Benizzi, Nicola, 311
Benjamin, Walter, 239
Benkert, Ernst, 156, 157, 328
Bennett, Gordon, 234
Bennett, Michael, 261
Benney, Paul, 158
Benning, Sadie, 289
Benom, Ronald, 93
Benway, Bill, 175
Berengolo, Milenka, 298
Berg, Copy, 292, *292*
Bergman, Daniel, 254
Bergman, Ingmar, 276
Bergt, Michael, 260
Berkavitz, Lauren, 290
Berkenblit, Ellen, 158, *287*, 288
Berlin, Alejandro, 287, **288**
Berlin, Peter, 171
Berlin/Super 8: The Architecture of Division, 158
Berliner, Allan, 250
Berman, Zeke, 158
Bermudes, John, 244
Berns, Ben, 28
Bernstein, Leonard, 172, 206, 210
Berriolo, Elena, 277
Bertei, Adele, 96
Bertolo, Diane, 80, 84, 157
Bertolucci, Bernardo, 276
Beton, Robert, 182
Better, Howard, 153
Beuchat, Carmen, 30, 45
Bey, Amir, 261
Beyer, Tom, 299
Bialy, Harvey, 46
Bickerton, Ashley, 140, 141, 152, 157, **158**, 159, 176–77, 335
Biederman, James, 45, 137, 157
Bielski, Janek, 236
Billian, Cathy, 88, 157
Billops, Camille, 65, 110, 158, 240
Bilquist School, 237
Binion, McArthur, 28
Binkley, Sam, 251
Binkley, Tomthy, 47, 157, 276
Birch, Willie, 261
Birnbaum, Dara, *64*, **87–88**, 157, 162
Birrell, James, 104
Bishop, Jim, 298
Bjorkman, Nina, 311
Black Cat Collective, 235, 243
Black, Iosta, 96
Black Phoenix, 107
Blackmon, Prophet William J., 242
Bladen, Ronald, 28
Blagg, Max, 222
Blair, Dike, 92, 157
Blanca, Paul, 171
Blanchard, Nancy, 93
Blanchon, Robert, 277, 292
Blane, Marc, 68, **68**, 157
Blankets, 254, 332
Blau, Douglas, 175, **182**, 184
Bleier, Rick, 169, 176, 184, 214, 220
Blinderman, Barry, 173
Bliss, 290
Block, Corliss, 169, 176
Blondeel, Claude, 173
Blood, 290
Bloodworth, Sandra, 184
Bloom, Barbara, *66*, **74**, *74–75*, 92, 155, 277, 296, 335
Blum, Sydney, 261

Blumenthal, Lyn, 153, 171, 185
Blush, B., 290
Bobby G, 136, *136*, 157, 162
Bocanegra, Suzanne, 248
Bochner, Mel, 23, 29, 46
Body Language, 238, 332
Body Politic, 240
Boes, Richard, 134
Bogawa, Roddy, 236
Bogosian, Eric, 66–67, 80, 91, 99, **101**, *101*, *116*, 118, 119, 145, 162
Boice, Bruce, 68
Bolande, Jennifer, 145, **146**, 157
Boltanski, Christian, 93
Bonet, Juan Manuel, 187, 329
Bonita, Pena, 187
Bookchin, Natalie, 244
Boone, Mary, 64, 109
Boord, Dan, 234
Border Art Workshop – Taller de Arte Fronterizo, 216–17, *216–17*, 223, 331
Bordo, Robert, 248
Bordowitz, Gregg, 176, 177, **215**, 216, 235, 330
Bordwin, Andrew, 298, *298*, 308, **309**
Borelli, Caterina, 182
Borofsky, Johnathan, 25, 28, **28**, *28, 56*, 57, 71, 107, 137, 157, 162, 171, 222
Bos, Saskia, 178, 180, 223, 330
Bosman, Richard, 335
Boston Film and Video Foundation, 237
Bouckhaert, Harm, 140
Bougatsos, Liz, 298, 314
Bourdon, David, 68
Bourgeois, Louise, 23, 45, 337, *337*
Bourges, Alain, 180
Bowens, Kabuya, 220, 236, 254, 284
Bower, Gary, 74, 137, 157
Bowers, Andrea, 296
Bowman, Arlene, 188
Bowyer, Sylvia, 253
Boxes, 241
Boyd, Don, 140, 157
Boyd, Robert, 251
Boyden, Martha Hall, 84
Boyle, Kevin, 81
Brack, Charles, 235
Braderman, Joan, 236
Bradley, Warren K., 255
Brafman, Marcy, 173
Braithwaite, Christopher, 284
Brand, Axel, 158
Brand, Bill, 88, 125
Brandl, Eva, 166
Brandt, Susie, 229, 254, 333
Brantley, Darryl, 253
Brathwaite, Fred, 49
Brattin, John, 280, 297
Bratton, Chris, 177, 235, 237, 277
Brault, Sebastien, 312
Brauntuch, Troy, 61, 78, 81, 84, 86, 91, **92**, 137, 146, 157, 162
Bray, Anne, 180
Brazelton, Tom, 158
Breitz, Candice, 300
Brekke, John, 254
Breuer, Marco, 299
Brew, Kathy, 247
Brewer, Nema, 237
Brewster, Michael, 86, 162
Brice, Freddie, 242
Brickhouse, Farrell, 92, 137, 157
Bridgers, Janice, 276
Bridgwood, Barry, 158

Bright, Deborah, 246
Brinkmann, Vinzenz, 236
Britton, Susan, 125
Broadfoot, Keith, 234, 331
Brockman, Susan, 29
Brody, Nancy Brooks, 158
Bronk, Keiko, 158
Bronstein, David, 235
Brooke, Kaucyila, 236
Brooks, Dorrie, 237
Brose, Larry, 188
Brother Tongue Collective, 253
Broughel, Barbara, 139, 157, 167, 215
Brown, Dan, 312
Brown, Elizabeth, 140
Brown, Gavin, 265
Brown, James Andrew, 237
Brown, James, 75, 173
Brown, Kay, 73
Brown, Kevin, 284
Brown, Marie-Annick, 251
Brown, Trisha, 78
Brubach, Holly, 278, 334
Bruce, Chris, 241, 332
Bryant, Linda, 110
Bubley, Esther, 240
Bucalo, Domenica, 298
Buchan, David, 125
Buchanan, Nancy, 221
Buchanon, Nancy, 93
Buchmuller, Eva, 288, **288**, 290, 292, 334
Buckler, Diane, 149, 157
Buczak, Brian, 292
Buell, Dexter, 311
Buffalo Artists Against Repression and Censorship, 243
Buffum, Sarah, 285
Buhler, Ken, 249, **251**, 252, 260, 313, 333
Bull, Catherine, 289
Burchill, Janet, 234
Burckhardt, Rudy, 23, 34
Burden, Chris, 93, 173
Burden, Rhea, 214
Bureau of Inverse Technology, 290, 292
Burg, China, 96
Burgy, Donald, 93
Burke, Elizabeth, 260
Burke, Michael, 261
Burkett, Lois, 311, 312
Burkhart, Kathe, 240, 242, *242*
Burnley, Gary, 107, 137, 156, 157–59, 162, 166
Burns, Tim, 88, 95, 107, 125, **134**, 168, 276
Burnside, Madeleine, 92
Burson, Nancy, 72, 126, 157
Bursztyn, Dina, 252
Burton, Jim, 45, 93
Burton, Scott, 28, 33, *36*, 39–40, 52–53, 57, 69, *69, 70, 70*, 71, 73, 81, 107, 137, 156, 157, 162, 222, 296
Burton, Sigrid, 72
Burwell, Charles, 276
Busch, Charles, 253
Buschke, Frances, 158
Buschmen, The, 253
Bush, George, 172, 206
Bush, Kimberly, 214, 220, 244
Bussman, Bruno, 125
Busto, Ana, 177, 330
Butler, Connie, 196, 203, 205, 214, 220, 234–36, 238–40, 242, 244, **245–46**, 248–51, 253, 254, 286, 287, 331–33, 338
Butler, Pam, 255
Butler, Rex, 234, 331

Buying In and Selling Out: Dealing with the Forms of Broadcast Television, 182
Byron, Michael, *120*, **143–44**, 152, 157, 162, 190, *190*, 222
Byssodomein, 279

C

Cable Excess, 291
Cabrera, David, 139, **152**, 153, 157
Cadmus, Paul, 260
Cage, John, 23, 45, 171, 173
Cahill, Thomas, 155, 169, 176, 184, 214, 220
Caire, Patricia, 123, 157
Cajuste, Raymond, 174
Callahan, Janet, 167
Callard, Andrea, 88, 157, 254
Callas, Peter, 247
Calvo Serraller, Francisco, 167, 329
Cameron, Dan, 175, 329
Camille, Michael, 252, 333
Campano, Miguel Angel, 167
Campbell, Natasha, 237
Campbell, Paul, 125
Campion, Jane, 240
Campus, Peter, 33, 276
Canal, Nina, 96
Canaux, Didier, 248
Candace Street Free Arts Program, 237
Candan, Can, 235
Canogar, Daniel, 240, 332
Cantor, Ellen, 290
Cappelletto, Marina, 184
Carcharodon carcharias, 277
Cardillo, Rimer, 261
Cardoso, Jose, 174
Caris, Valerie, 292
Carlomusto, Jean, 216, 235
Carlos, Jose, 157
Carlos, Laurie, 240, 276
Carlson, Cynthia, 34, **34**, 69, 137, 157, 162
Caron, Elizabeth, 250
Carpenter, Bert, 166, 329
Carpenter, James, 166, 167
Carstens, Nicole, 287
Carter, Daniel, 299
Carter, Steven, 291
Carty, Larry, 236
Carvalho, Josely, 158
Carver Center, 237
Carvin, Robert, 144, 157
Casebere, James, 104, *104*, 106, 148, 149, 157, 162, 177
Casey, Tim, 236, 254
Cassidy, Naval, 291
Castelli, Leo, 47
Cathcart, Linda L., 80, 81, 90, 96, 110, 145, **147**, 162, 184, 226, 328, 329
Cavanagh, 157
Cazabon, Lynn, 310
Celant, Germano, 159
Celebrity Ribbon Cavalcade, 229, 253
Celli, Peter, 280
Ceppi, Mau, 298
Cha, Theresa Kyung Hak, 145
Chamoun, Jean, 222
Chan, Terry, 236
Chance, James, 71, 82, 96
Chann, Barry, 254
Charlesworth, Bruce, 140, 157
Charlesworth, Sarah, 285
Chase, Louisa, 45, 157, 162
Chatham, Rhys, 82, 93, *93*, 96, 131, 157

Chavoya, C. Ondine, 278
Cheang, Shu Lee, 218, 236
Chenzira, Ayoka, 185
Cherepak, Corinne, 298
Chernick, Meryl, 131, 157
Chesley, Tom, 221
Chester, Jeffrey, 182
Chevins, Chris, 158
Chiang, Jean, 254
Chiarini, Doriana, 159, 329
Child, Abigail, 241
Chimeric Architectures, 315
Chin, Andrew, 254
Chin, Mel, 252, 254
China Mary Series, The, 256, 333
Chittenden Community TV, 243
Cho, Seoungho, 276, *276*
Choi, Christine, 214
Choi, Sung Ho, 254
Choice Histories, 251, 333
Cholo, 216
Chong, Ping, 229, 252, 276, 333
Christel, Martin, 310
Christenson, Don, 96
Christgau, Robert, 82
Christie, Robert, 278
Christo, 23, 45, 127
Christopher, Phyllis, 185
Chrono, 253
Chu, Ken, 254
Chu, Kristy, 255
Chua, Lawrence, 254
C-Hundred Film Corp., 245
Chung, Y. David, 254
Chunn, Nancy, 140, *140*, 144, 157
Cicerone, Josh, 298
Cifuentes, Guillermo, 312
Ciment, Jill, 82
Ciniglio, Vincent, 92
Circle Fine Arts Galleries, 173
Clark, Ed, 234, 332
Clarke, Cheryl, 184
Clarke, Chris, 252
Clarke, Jim, 126
Clarke, Kevin, 126, *126*
Clarke, Robert, 255, 336
Clary, Braden, 254
Clayton, Jay, 49
Cleater, John, 309, 310
Cleator, Molly, 178, 180
Close, Chuck, 22–24, 30, **31–32**, 34, 105, 260
Close, Leslie, 30
Clough, Charles, 53, 55, 80–82, **82**, 84, 94, 96, 137, 154, 157, 162, 171, 173
Clyde, Rayshan, 284
Coates, Nancy, 244, 254
Coates, Peter, 163
Cobb, Christina, 298
Cobb, J. B., *22*, 28, *28*, 157
Cochran, Dorothy, 169
Coggeshall, Calvert, 183, 330
Cohen, Elaine Lustig, 173
Cohen, Jem, 245
Cohen, Martin, 107, 157
Cohen, Maxi, 171
Coito, Deborah, 240
Cokes, Tony, 182, 243, 251, 333
CoLab (Collaborative Projects), 40, 47, 75, 92, 172, 219
Colburn, Jon, 126, 157
Cole, Kenneth, 236
Cole, Willie, 9, 220, 239, 267, **287**, 288, 292, 337, *337*
Colebrook, Binda, **277**
Coleman, Craig, 158
Coleman, James, 193, *193*, 223, 237, 330
Colicchio, Rich, 158
Colin, Paul, 28, 84, 157

Collective Clubhouse Project, 299
Colliding: Myth, Fantasy, Nightmare, 149, 192, 330
Collins, James, 88, 157
Collins, Michale, 158
Collins, Tricia, 163, 329
Collyer, Robin, 125
Colo, Papo, 173
Colomina, Beatriz, 175, 182, 329
Colvin, Bruce, 72
Coming Attractions, 236, 242
Common Object Has Special Powers, A, 263, 297
Communists, The, 96
Composer's Collective, 33
Compton, Candace, 171
Conceptual Art from the Bay Area, 278, *278*
Condo, George, 158
Conduit, Cecelia, 192
Connelly, Arch, 127, 157, 162
Connerton, Kim, 298
Connor, Tim, 240
Connors, Maureen, 74
Conrad, Tony, 84, 181, 188, 190
Constant, 311
Constantino, Valerie, 169, 176
Contained Attitudes, 178, 180, *180*, 330
Contortions, The, 57, 71, 82, 87, 96, 131
Coogan, Jay G. 131, 157
Cook, Cathy, 247
Cooney, Dan, 297, 310, 311
Cooney, Robert Smith, 49, 95, 172
Cooper Contemporary School, 237
Cooper, Dennis, 167, 169
Cooper, Elizabeth, 302
Cooper, Ellen, 10, 136, 157
Cooper, Paula, 32, 47
Copeland, Noel, 244
Coplans, John, 23, 34, 276
Copley, Claire, 166, 329
Coran, Ruth, 45
Corber, Mitch, 87, 88, 93, 95
Corner, Phil, 45
Cornwell, Regina, 168
Correa, Catherine, 158
Corritore, Regina, 251
Cortés, Esperanza, 220
Cortez, Diego, *47*, *53*, 73, 84, 87, 93, 95, *288*
Cossio, Miguel Angel, 253
Costan, Chris, 158
Costanzo, Jim, 251
Cottingham, Cicely, 237
Cottis, Jane, 236
Cotton, Paul, 82, 87
Couacaud, Sally, 234, 331
Couture, Lise Anne, 183
Couzin, Sharon, 170
Cowan, Bob, 29
Cowie, Norman, 178, 222, 236
Cowles, Virginia, 9, 12, 241, *314*, **315**
Cox, Renée, 260, *261*
Coyne, Petah, 228, 250, *250*
Cozzi, Louise Fischer, 244
Cramer, Douglas S., 173
Crane, Gregory A., 158
Crane, Sumner, 96
Creative Learning Community School, 237
Creative Time, Inc., 248
CREATIVE/WILL, 284
Cremers, Roger, 311
Crenson, Ethan, 290, 297, 298, 311
Creston, Bill, 290
Crilly, Anne, 217

Crimp, Douglas, 60, 61, 68, 73, 81, 82, **89–90**, 124, 135, 216, 328
Critics Voices Volume IV, The, 175, 182
Critics' Responsibility to the Artist, 68
Crockett, Bryan, 138, 266, **284**, 315
Cross, John, 84
Crum, David, 28, 157
Crutchfield, Robin (Lee), 86, 96, 157
Cruz Azaceta, Luis, 260
Cuba: Facts, Fiction, and Film, 256
Cullen, Catherine, 290
Cullman, Brian, 175, 182, 184
Cultural Politics Between the First and Third Worlds, 215
Cummings, Michael, 255
Cunningham, Mark, 96
Curio Shop, The, 254, *254*
Curtis, John Cates, 84
Customized Terror, 138, 266, 284, *284–85*, 334
Cutforth, Roger, 88, 157
Cutschall, Colleen, 158
Cypis, Dorit, 148, 157, 221
Cypriano, Tania, 249

D

D'Agostino, Peter, 99
D'Amato, Senator, 198
D'Arcangelo, Christopher, **97–100**
D'Arrigo, Elisa, 126, 157
Daboll, Susan, 248
Dado, Celeste, 199, 202, 205, 244, 246, 248, 249, 333
Daily Life, 96
Daitch, Susan, 184, 290, 293
Dalby, Marcia, 144, *144*, 157, 162
Damian, Ahmed, 222
Daniels, Mark, 219
Daniels-Endesha, Giza, 119, 215, *215*, 223
Dannemeyer, William, 196
Darden, Douglas, 175
Daris, Julie, *195*
Dark Rooms, 116, 144, 222–23, 245; (1–2/83), 148, *148*; (1–2/85), 166, *166–67*, 329; (2–3/87), 180, 330; (3–4/89), 217, 331
Dashow, Carrie, 311
Dassin, Jules, 276
Daube, Michael, 261
Davey, Michael, 104, 157
Davey, Moyra, 236
David, Anita, 169
David, Jiří, 219
David, Julie, 203
Davidek, Greg, 238
Davidovich, Jaime, 173
Davidson, Nancy, 238
Davis, Betsy, 253
Davis, Collis, 174
Davis, Debby, 149, 157
Davis, John T., 125
Davis, Julie, 204, 205
Davis, Lisa Corinne, 236, 244
Davis, Mary V., 253
Davis, Scott, 84, 157
Day Without Art, 204, 210, 226, 227, 239, 270
Day, Pip, 265, 267, 291, 298, 300, 301, **310–12**, 313, *327*, 334
Daze, 276
de Beer, Sue, 312
De Biaso, Tom, 95
de Camp, Kyle, 254
De Cesare, Donna, 277
de Cointet, Guy, 93, 124, 125
de Costere, Stefaan, 173
de Hirsch, Storm, 29
De Hoyas, Joe, 292, 298
De Jong, Constance, 93, 153, **153**, 182, 184, 193
de la Barrera, Gerardo, 278
de la Casiniere, Joelle, 238

De La Paz, Neraldo, 175
De Landa, Manuel, 95, 125, 134, 168
de Montaut, Philippe, 95, *134–35*, 136
de Mundo, Link, 314
De Niro, Robert, 136
de Sana, Jimmy, 95, 158
De Vuono, Catherine, 254
de Wit, Dirk, 289
deAk, Edit, 23, 24, 27, 34, *35*, *37*, **37–41**, 46, *47*, 68, 70–74, 85, 86, 114, 168, *288*
DeAk, Norma Jean, 92, 93
Dean, Marge, 124, 192
Dean, Mark, 158
Dear Joe, Dare Dreams (Tribute to Joe Beam), 251
Dearborn High School, 237
Debbaut, Jan, 158
DeBiaso, Tom
Decade of New Art: Artists Space, A, 70, 129, 147, 162
DeCapite, Mike, 280
Decker, Greg, 254
Deconstruction, Quotation and Subversion: Video from Yugoslavia, 219
Dee, Michael Patrick, 311
DeForest, Kevin, 260
Dekeukeliere, Charles, 181, 186
DeLeo, Maryann, 182
DeLeon, Ann Flash, 88, 96
DeLucia, Nicholas, 169
Demi, 93
Denari, Neil M., 193
Dennis, Donna, 276
Dent, Darius, 68
Dercon, Chris, 173, 178, 180, 330
Deren, Maya, 186
Derry Film and Video, 217, 277
Dertnig, Carola, 298, *299*, 310, 311
Design/Writing/Research, 15, *15*, 287, 334
Designers Republic, 138, 266, 284
Desmond, Katherine, 296
deSoto, Lewis, 256, 333
DeSwann, Sylvia, 261
DeVito, Cara, 171, 240
DeWitt, Louie R., 84
Dewys, Margaret, 96, 157
Diamond, Jessica, 163, 276
Dibble, Douglas, 276
Dick, Kirby, 140
Dick, Vivienne, 106, 125, 172, 290
Dickie, Robin, 178
Dickson, Jane, 136, **136**, 153, 157, 172, 221
diCorcia, Philip-Lorca, *206*, 221
Diebboll, John, 252, 336
Dienes, Sari, 45
Dieu Donné Papermill Lecture series, 252–55
Digital Mapping, 266, *308*, 309, *309*, 310, 311
Diller, Elizabeth, 175, 181, **182**, 183, 192, 278, 315, 330, 337
Dimensional Typography, 15, 287, 334
Dinnematin, Gilles, 222
Dion, Mark, **176–77**, *177*
Direct Art Productions, 167
Disarming Genres, 236, 332
Diurnal Experiments and Nocturnal Investigations, 234, *234*, 332
Divine Comedies, 253, 333
Dixon, Terence, 293
DNA, 96
Dobens, Larry, 254
Dobson, Jane, 29
Document and Dream, 218, 331
Doering, Christoph, 158
Dohna, Anne, 176, 184, 214, 220, 236, 244, 254
Doktori, Kochi, 126, 157
Dolinko, Jamie, 290

Dolmatch, Blanche, 302
Dominguez, Isabel, 278
Dominquez, Maria, 254
Donaldson, Rory, 312
Donegan, Cheryl, 298
Donkersloot, Peter, 93, 126
Doran, Anne, 163
Doron, 290
Dorzillier, D. D., 312
Doty, Fernando, 127
Dougherty, Cecilia, 241
Doughton, Steve, 290
Downer, Carol, 251
Downey, Juan, 45
Downing, Glenn, 284
Downsborough, Peter, 93, 126
Doyle, Judith, 153
Dr. Earl, 93
Drake, Peter, 144, 157
Draper, Lou, 240
Drasler, Greg, 238
Dress, Lou Ann, 237
DressCode, 264, *277*, 278, 334
Dries, Danny, 253
Driver, Sarah, 134
Drobnick, Jim, 261
Droll, Donald, 119, 155, 156, 158, 159, 166, 298
Drucker, Charles, 182
Drummond, Sally Hazelet, 158, 329
Drury, Sarah, 177, 178, 330
Dryer, Moira, 176
Dubler, Linda, 170
Dučev, Hristo Pop, 219
Dudar, P., 86
Duff, Dana, 167
Dugdale, Elizabeth, 126
Dumb Type, 248
Duncan, Carol, 48
Duncan, John, 93
Dunham, Carroll, 101, **130**, 131, 135, 157, 162, 270
Dunkerley, Susan, 254
Dunn, Fontaine, 74, 84, 157, 182
Dupuy, Jean, 46, 88, 140, 157
Durant, Mary Alice, 260, 334
Dureau, George, 171
Durham, Jimmie, 187, *187*, 189, 223, 330
Dvorkin, Michael, 311
Dwyer, Nancy, 60, 80, **80**, 84, 85, 94, 127, 131, 157, 162, 260, 335
Dynamic Systems, Inc., 8
Dynel, Johnnie, 96

E

Earley, Brendan, 311
Easter, Mary, 193
Easterson, Sam, 297, 311
Ebersol, Dick, 171
Ecker, David, 21
Edelheit, Martha, 22, *22*, 28, 29, 47, 157
Edelson, Mary Beth, 260
Eder, Susan, 72, 84
Educational Video Center, 237
Edwards, Mel, 23, 45, 46
Egan, Tracy, 173
Ehrenreich, Barbara, 240, 332
Ehrich, David, 253
Eiferman, Lee, 153
Eight Upstate, 34
Eins, Stefan, *53*, 95
Eisenberg, Ed, 251
Eisenman, Peter, 267, 285, 286, 334
Eisenstark, Doug, 152
Eisenstein, Sergei M., 186
Ekks, Redd, 145
Elaine, James, 260
Elam, Jo Anne, 170
Elie-Rivera, Clarence, 221
Elizabeth, 277
Ellis, Darrel, 221
Ellison, Lori, 302
Ellsworth, Barry, 242
Ellzee, Ram, 290
Elovich, Richard, 204, 222
Emergency: New Films by 13 New York Filmmakers, 134

Emshwiller, Susan, 153
Enders, Anthony, 12
Enders, Elizabeth, 12, **247**, 252, 260, 337
(Energeia), 239, *239*, 332
Eng, Angie, 291, 314, 334
Eng, Lily, 86
Engler, B. J., 253
Engler, Brigitte, 291
Engler, Elise, 244, 254
Eno, Brian, 57, 82, 131, 173
Enslin, Theodore, 46
Enteen, Bob, 284
Erawa-Era Was, 235, 332
Ericson, Kate, 162, 163
Eros, Bradley, 290
Ess, Barbara, 96, 157, 260
Essenhigh, Inka, 293
Estenger, Max, 276
Estridge, Christopher, 255
Etkin, Suzan, 173
Evans, Andrea, *122*, 140, 157
Evans, Anona, 220
evansandwong, 264, 267, 277, *277*, 278, 286, 337
Eveleigh, Romany, 156, 157
Events (11–12/76), 78, *81*, 81, 82; (2/77) 84; (3–4/77) 86; (5/77) 88; (4/82) 139; (5/82) 140; (3/84) 158
Evening of New Music, An, 299
Eves, Bruce, 255, 256
Ewing, Lauren, 72, 76, 157
Exhibit A, 15, 287, 334
Exploring Media Program, 237
Export TV, 235
Export, Valie, 185, *185*
Extended Definitions: Video Experiments in Perception, 221, 331

F

Fab 5 Freddy, 29
Faber, Mindy, 238
Fabo, Andy, 235
Fabulous Sex, 260
Facades, Landscapes, Interiors, 116, *122*, 140, 160, 222
Facility for the Channeling and Containment of Undesirable Elements, A, 229, 252, 333
Fagin, Steve, 234, 332
Fahoum, Ziad, 222
Fairy Tale: Politic, Desire, and Everyday Life, The 176–78, *176–77*, 330
Falcione, Dominic, 253
Falk, Gary, 131, 157
Fallon, Camilla, 244
Famous for 30 Seconds: Artists in the Media, 171, 173
Fantasy, L.A., 173
Farber, Robert, 226, 227, 247, 252, 292, 333
Fares, William, 96, 162
Farina, Ralston, 45, 88, 107, 157
Farkhondeh, Simone, 236
Farmer, Frank, 255
Farrell, Fred, 49
Farris, John, 284
Fasanello, Denise, 228, 261, **264–72**, 277, 284, 285, **286**, 314, 334
Fathan, Ridzwa, 309, *309*, 310
Fay, Ming, *236*, 237, 276
Feckner, John, 126
Feigen, Richard, 31
Feingold, Ken, 95, 104, 157
Feinstein, Rachel, 280
Fels, Antje, 158
Fenley, Molissa, 173, 284
Fenner, Andrew, 260
Ferguson, Bruce, 219, 331
Ferguson, Edy, 310
Ferguson, Kathleen, 49
Fernandez, José Gabriel, 246
Ferrara, Abel, 143
Ferrara, Jackie, 72
Ferrer, Rafael, 23, 46
Ferris, Robert, 253
Fiddle, Lorraine, 169, 176, 184
Field, Bradley, 96

Field, Dorothy, 253
Fiengo, Robert, 184
Fier, Bruce, 93, 124
Filan, Michael, 155
Film (4/79) 106; (11/79) 107; (2/80) 125; (4/83) 152; (5/83) 153; (10/85) 170
Film in the Cities, 237
Films-In-Progress: Coming Soon, 219
Fin, Amanda, 276
Fine, Albert M., 45, *45*
Fine, Sari, 45
Finkelpearl, Tom, 214, 330
Finkelstein, Avram, 216
Finley, Jeanne C., 247, 260, 334
Fischer, John, 33
Fischer, R. M., 92, 100, *100*, 137, 157, 162, 173, 335
Fisher, Ellen, 253
Fisher, Gareth, 104, 157
Fisher, Jean, 177, **189–90**, 187, 193, 223, 330
Fisher, Morgan, 95
Fitch, Claudia, 156, 157
FitzGerald, Jared, 247, 333
Fitzgerald, Taryn, 289–91
Fitzgibbon, Colleen, 88, 95
Five Artists, 163
Five Spanish Artists, 105, 167, 329
Flack, Audrey, 46
Flamm, Carol, 49
Flanery, Gail, 254
Flavin, Dan, 33, 100
Fleischer Brothers, 186
Fleischer, Bob, 186
Flick, Robbert, 253
Flint, Gavin, 246, 250
Floating Values: A Survey of Gendered Investigations, 185, *185*, 188
Floating Point Unit, 314
Floyd, Nancy, 253
Flux Information Sciences, 312
Focke, Anne, 169, 329
Foley, Fiona, 234
Foley, J., 167
Fonseca, Harry, 187
For Beauty's Sake, 277
For My Brother, 252
Forbes, David, 216
Forced Sentiment, 163, 329
Ford, Hermine, 74, 137, 156, 157, 162, **170**, 183, 218, 276
Ford, Stephen, 255
Foreign Relations, 174, 175, 187
Formica, Jennifer, 314
Forms of Experience: Speaking Through Mass Culture, 237
Forti, Simone, 68, 173
Fortunato, Mimi, 155
Fortuyn, Irene, **155**, *155*, 158, 329
Forum on Artforum, A, 34, 40
Foster, Guy-Mark, 251
Foster, Hal, 215
Four Artists (Murray), 170, 220, 329
Four Artists, (Lawson), 104, *104*, 328
Four Humors, The, 276
four person untitled exhibition (Reiring), 98–100, *99*, 100, 328
Four Walls, 228, 248, 249, 333
Fouratt, Jim, 222
4(to)5, 303, *303*, 334
Fox, Howard, 138
Fox, Terry, 93, 278
Frailey, Stephen, **148**, 149, 157, 162
Frame, Allen, 221, 248
Frampton, Jerald, 171
Franceshi, Edgar, 260
Francis, Jeff, 293, 334
Franco, Jean, 235, 332
Francoeur, Norm, 311
Frank, Elizabeth, 218, 331
Frank, Mary, 23, 48
Frank, Peter, 140, 328
Frank, Robert, 290, 293

Frankenthaler, Helen, 72
Frasconi, Pablo, 245
Fraser, Andrea, 176, 177, **178**, 249
Fraser, Philip, 95
Fray, Leslie, 260
Frazier, Jacqueline, 178
Fred, 131
Freed, Hermine, 171, 185
Freedman, Deborah S., 46, 157
Freeman, Roger, 169
Fremont, Angela, 254, 261
French, Kari, 298
French, Stephanie, 6, 333
Freund, Peter, 310
Fried, Howard, 152, 278
Friedberg, Richard, 25
Friedman, Barbara, 156, 157
Friedman, Fern, 93
Friedman, Ken, 140, 328
Friis-Hansen, Dana, 235, 332
Fritz, Gary, 68
Frohnmayer, John E., 172, 173, *195*, 198, 199, 202–207, 247
From Here to Eternity: Fact and Fiction in Recent Architectural Projects, 175, 329
X/Y Feminin-Masculin, Le Sexe de L'Art, 289
Fuerst, Shirley, 47
Fujiyoshi, Aki, 280, 290, 291
Fulmer, Scott, 308
Fung, Richard, 185, 240
Futura 2000, 141, 158

G

Gabriel, Janice, 184, 214
Gajić, Goran, 219
Gale, Peggy, 125, 328
Gallagher, Ellen, 143, **256**, 260, 315, 337
Gallagher, Steven, 167
Gallo, Doreen, 126, 156, 157
Gambling, William T., 34
Garcia Sevilla, Ferrán 167
Garcia, Alvaro, 255
Garcia, Ana Maria, 251
Gardère, Paul, 237
Gardiner, Anne, 308, **310**, *310*, 311, 312, 334
Gardner Post Emergency Broadcast Network, 298
Gardner, Andrea, 214
Garett, Dana, 158
Garratt, Robert, 158
Garris, Laurie, 332
Garwood, Deborah, 241
Gassinger, Ilse, 238
Gasteazoro, Eva, 252
Gaulke, Cheri, 93
Gautier, Fabienne, 298
Gazella, Ernie, 48
Ge Kiere, Madeleine, 45
Geffner, Greg, 297
Gehry, Frank, 252
Geisman, Jarg M., 236
Geist, Sidney, 24, 25, 30
Geleynse, Wyn, 175
Geller, Wendy, 261
Geluso, Paul, 299
General Growth, 242
Generic Memorial (for Wm. Schwedler, 1942–1982), 253
George, Bob, 124
George, Carl, 229, 256, 239
Georges, Daniel O., 287
Gerber, Ava, 241, *241*, 260
Gerber, Matthÿs, 234
Gerlovin, Rimma, 140
Gerlovin, Valery, 140, 157
Gero, Robert, 239, *239*, 332
Gesualdi, David, 184
Get it in Writing, 167, 169
Gfeller, Reinhard, 126
Ghez, Susanne, 175
Gholson, Craig, 95
Gianakos, Steve, 110, 335
Giard, Robert, 251
Gibb, Russ, 237
Gibbons, Arthur, 34
Gibbons, Joe, 167, 249
Gibson, Ann, 9, 12

Gibson, Jeff, 234
Gibson, Linda, 251
Gibson, Ross, 331
Giegerich, Jill, 154, 157
Gilbert, Sharon, 158
Gilbert, Sid, 167
Giles, Jonathan, 221
Gilhooley, Jack, 30
Gili, Anna, 296, *296*, 334
Gilje, Kathleen, 131, 157
Gill, Leslie, **193**
Gillespie, Peter, 245
Gimenez, Carmen, 329
Ginzel, Andrew, **46**, 276
Giordano, Joan, 220
Giorno, John, 222, *231*, 260, 337
Girouard, Tina, 33, 47
Giroux, Joan, 246
Gitai, Amos, 222
Giuntini, Gilles Jean, 140, **140**
Givigliano, Roni, 289, 290
Glantzman, Judith, 158
Glass, Philip, 21, 32, 33, 47, 90, 96, 173
Glassman, Audrey, 169
Glassman, Stephen, 190
Glenn Branca, 96
Glimcher, Arne, 235
GODZILLA, 254, *254*, 333
Golan, Ron, 236
Goldberg, Brian, 260, 276
Goldberg, Jeff, 95
Goldberg, Joan, 34, 157
Goldberg, Neil, *289*, **290**, 290, 291, 311
Goldberg, RoseLee, **111**, 168, 173
Goldberg, Sidney Leon, II, 96
Golden, Deven, 175
Golden, Kenneth Sean, *276*
Golden, Nancy, 310
Golderman, Mark, 126
Goldin, Eunice, 29, 157
Goldin, Nan, 49, 94, 131, 136, 153, 157, **172**, 183, 196, 202, 203, 207, 214, 221, 222, 242, 246, 260, 315, 331, 337
Goldman, Shifra, 331
Goldsmith, Silvianna, 29
Goldson, Annie, 177, 181, 185, 187, 217, 236, 277, 330, 331
Goldstein, Barbara, 236, 332
Goldstein, Eric, 253
Goldstein, Jack, 55, 71–73, 80, 81, 90, *90*, 91–94, 98, 124, 136, 137, 146, 157, 162, 168, 173, 267
Goldstein, Marge, 41
Goldwater, Marge, 169, 329
Goldson, Annie [duplicate]
Golub, Leon, 48, 72, 73
Gomez, Marga, 253
Gomez, Marsha, 187
Gomez, Odris, 284
Gomez-Peña, Guillermo, **216**, *216–17*
Gonchar, Nancy, 246
Gonzalez, Arthur, 158
Gonzalez, Daniel, 237
Gonzalez, Maria Elena, 276
González, Reynaldo, 235, 332
Gonzalez, Rita, 298
González-Torres, Félix, 141, 177, 184, 185, **186**
Goo, Gwen-Lin, 220, 236, 244
Goodden, Caroline, 96
Goodman, Donna, 175
Goodman, Ken, 123, 157
Goodman, Steven, 238
Goodyear, Jessica, 290
Gordon, Bette, 134, 172, 276
Gordon, John, 104
Gordon, Juliette, 47
Gordon, Kim, 57, 180
Gordon, Lee, 238
Gordon, Peter, 49, 96
Gordon, Richard, 289, 290, 301, 308, 311, 312
Gorewitz, Shalom, 173
Gosfield, Annie, 299
Goss, Gary, 159, 329
Goss, James, 127, 153, 157

Goss, John, 247
Gottesfeld, Linda, 236, 244, 254
Gould, Claudia, 10–12, 15, 64, 105, 110, 131, 138, 148, 153, 182, 218, 220, 241, 260, **264–72**, *266, 268*, 277–80, 284, 286–91, 297, 298, 301, 302, 310, 313–15, 334
Goulet, Cie, 157
Goycoolea, Adrian, 299
Grace, Trudie, **20–26**, 27, 28, 37, 38, 40, 52, 53, 58, 82, 85, 106, 156, 195
Grafstrom, Karin, 125
Graham, Dan, 33, 35, 69, *69*, 85, 87, 157, 168
Grajales, Elizabeth, 214, 220, 236
Gramet, Ilona, 93
Gramming, Walter, 158
Grand Galop, 148, *148*, 149, 328
Grass, Peter, 49, 84, 86, 88, 131, 157
Graves, Michael, 95, *233*, 252
Graves, Nancy, 22, 23, 28, 32, 34, 47, 57, 168
Gray, Bradley Rust, 311
Gray, Spalding, 173
Gray, Tony, 244, 254
Greczynski, Bolek, 214
Green, Charlene, 34
Green, George D., 34, 157
Green, Renée, 237, *237*, 238, **239–40**, 287, 332
Green, Vanalyne, 192, 240
Greenberg, Clement, 69
Greenberg, Wendy, 74
Greenblat, Rodney Alan, 158
Greene, Jimmy James, 254
Greenfield, Louise, 173
Greenly, Colin, 84, 157
Gregory, Scott, 297
Grennan, Simon, 244
Greyson, John, 236
Greytak, Sharon, 139, **141**, 153, 157, 218, 331
Griffin, George, 88
Grimonprez, Johan, 289
Grooms, Red, 23, 46
Groot, Paul, 158, 329
Grosser, Benita-Immanuel, *262*, 291, *291*
Grossman, Nancy, 46, 261
Group Material, 141, 142
Grove, Kathleen, 158
Gruenberg, Hannah, 155
Grundberg, Andy, 166, 171, 329
Grünewald, Axel, 277
Grynsztejn, Madeleine, 243, 333
Gržinić, Marina, 219
Guagnini, Nicolás, 310
Gualtieri, Roberto, 68
Guardiola, Juan, 280
Guatti, Albano, 106, 157
Guberman, Rebecca, 292, 298
Guerrier, Philippe, 130
Guerrilla Girls, 110
Guest, Tim, 156, 328
Guilleminot, Marie-Ange, 289
Guillot, Robert, 156, 157
Gummer, Don, 28, 35, *44–45*, 137, 157, 162
Gund, Agnes, 235
Gunderson, Greta, 276
Gunning, Lucy, 289
Gurrin, John, 182
Gustafson, Julie, 171
Gutierrez, Benjamin, 237
Gutierrez, Marina, 158
Gutierrez-Solana, Carlos, 218, 220, **226–32**, *227*, 235, 244, 245, 247, 249–56, 260, 270, 286, 312, 313, 315, 333, 334
Gutman, Walter, 29, 45
Gutzeit, Fred, 92, 157
Guy, Jolie, 290
Guyot, Fabrice, 311
Guyot, Fred, 156
Gwendolyn, 238, 239

Gyalwa Karmapa, 46
Gynecologists, 96

H

Haacke, Hans, 46, 68, 118
Haberstroh, Matthew, 255
Hacker, Marc, 193
Haendel, Karl Frederick, 311
Haerer, Carol, 234, 332
Hafif, Marcia, 88
Hagedorn, Jessica, 182, 187, 240, 254
Hahn, Alexander, 221
Hahn, Christine, 96
Hahn, Kimiko, 254
Haimsohn, Jana, 93
Halasz, Andras, 288, 290, 334
Halbreich, Kathy, 169, 329
Hall of Fame, 312
Hall, Penny, 278
Hall, Robert, 182
Halle, Howard, 215
Halleck, Dee Dee, 235, 332
Halley, Peter, **159**, 163, 291, 334
Hallwalls, 80, *80*
Halsey Brown, Laurie, 290
Ham, Soomin, 311
Hambleton, Mary, 261
Hambleton, Richard, 158, 173
Hamill, Janet, 48
Hamill, Juan, 33
Hamilton, Ann, 126, 190, **191**, *191*
Hamilton, Pat, 152
Hamilton, Ray, 242
Hammel, Stephen, 253
Hammersley, Frederick, 183, 330
Hammett, Doug, 261
Hammond, Robert, 159
Hammond, Valerie, 176, 214, 236, 244, 254
Hammons, David, 66, 110
Han, Dongho, 215
Handzel, Jane, 126, 157
Hanh, Thi Pham, 240
Hanhardt, John, 148, 166, 290, 329
Hankwitz, Molly, 245, 333
Hanlon, Terry, 93
Hannah, Duncan, 95
Hansell, Freya, 123, 157
Hansen, Al, 47
Happel, Marc, 226, 247, *247*, 253
Har Kim, Michelle, 290
Harbutt, Charles, 166, 329
Harding, Bob, 30, 47, 49
Hardinger, Ruth, 68, 126, 157
Haring, Keith, 173
Harmonics Choir, 87, 93
Harris, Grant, 308
Harris, Jody, 96
Harris, Lyle Ashton, 260
Harris, Suzy, 23, 30, 33, 45, 47
Harris, Thomas, 255
Harrison, Margaret, 106, 107, 141
Harrison, Newton and Helen, 93
Hart, Kevin, 290, 311
Hart, Kitty Carlisle, 62, 135
Hartel, Jim, 243
Hartnett, Elaine, 45, 74
Harvestworks, 265
Harvey, Bessie, 242
Harvey, Michael, 80, 88, 92, 93, 157
Harvey, William, 171
Haslanger, Martha, 95, 157
Hasselbrink, Ed, 49
Hastanan, Skowmon, 254
Hatch, James, 65, 240
Hatch-Billops Collection, 65
Hatoum, Mona, 222, 337
Hauft, Amy, 163
Haury, Peter, 290
Hausman, Beth, 169, 176, 236
Hausman, Jerome, 21
Hawkins, Cynthia, 184, 260
Hawkins, Pamela, 49

Hawkins, Yolanda, 141
Hawkinson, Laurie, 175
Haxton, David, 95, 162, 168
Hayes, Garry, 253
Hayes, Tom, 243
Haynes, Todd, 192
Hays, K. Michael, 193, 330
Hazelwood, Carl E., 237, 260, 332
Hazlitt, Don, 126, 157
Healy, Julia, 220, 236, 244, 254
Heap of Birds, Edgar, 189
Hearn, Pat, 240
Hearne, Betsy, 177
Hearst, Patricia, 108, *108*
Heart of Glass, 251
Hedstrom, Cynthia, 30
Heft, Carol, 220
Heidel, Deborah, 215
Heiferman, Marvin, 172, 175
Heilbut, Anthony, 214, 330
Heilmann, Mary, 72
Heinemann, Susan, 48, 157
Heiss, Alanna, 23, 27
Heist, Eric, 246
Heizer, Michael, 28
Hejduk, John, 193, 330
Held, Al, 23, 32, 34
Hell, Richard, 222
Heller, Didi, 177
Heller, Neddi, 220
Hellman, Kit, 170
Helman, Phoebe, 48
Helms, Jesse, 172, 196, 198, 199, 204, 220
Henders, Doug, 276
Henderson, Mike, 235, 332
Henderson, Victor, 154, 157
Hendricks, Geoff, 45, 267, 292, 293, 298, 334
Henrich, Biff, *148–49*, **149**, 157, 162, 192
Henry, Janet, 110, 255, 261
Henry, Max, 167
Herman, Laura, 311
Hernández, Camilio, 235, 256, 332
Herrera, Carmen, 229, 260, 334
Hershman, Lynn, 221, 278
HerStories in Color, 251, 333
Hertel, Barbara, 254
Hertz, Betti Sue, 251, 276
Herzberg, Julia, 278
Herzog, Elana, 236, 244, 254
Hess, Elizabeth, 202
Hessler, Douglas, 107
Hestand, Mary, 240
Heterogeneity and Alienation, 183, 330
Heurta, Benito, 222
Heyn, John, 218
Heyward, Julia, 47, 84, 87, *91*, **91**, 92, 93
Hicks, Emily, 216
Higgins, Dick, 45
High, Kathryn, **170**, 171, 192, *192*
Highstein, Jene, 20, 25, 33, 96
Higuchi, Akihiro, 248
Hilderley, Jeriann, 34
Hildreth, Joe, 34
Hill, Chris, 185, **188**, 243
Hill, Gary, 221, 247
Hill, Richard, 240
Hill, Robin, 169
Hillen, Andrea, 158
Hill-Montgomery, Candace, 107, 157
Hills, Patricia, 73
Hilton, Joseph, 175
Hirschhorn, Michelle, 253
Hirshorn, Harriet, 188
Hirst, Michael, 173
History Lessons, 238, 332
Hiuni, Dahn, 298
Hoberman, Perry, **148**, *148*, 157, 177, 290, 291
Hock, Louis, 183
Hodgekin, Carter, 255
Hodges, Jim, 215, *215*
Hoffman, Barbara, 202
Hoffmeister, Knut, 158

Hoke, Lisa, 171
Holden, Barry, **70,** 252
Holder, Robin, 214, 220, 236
Holechek, John, 237
Holl, James, 127, *127*, 157
Hollander, Anita, 284
Holstein, Pieter, 104, 157
Holup, Wapo, 126
Holzer, Jenny, 13, *136–37*, **137**, 157, 262, 173, 222, 252, 336, *336*
Home on De Range, 254
Hong, Hyunhwa, 215
Hong, Yun-ah, 251
Honor Their Dignity, 226, 247, *247*
Hoot, W. E. Scott, 293
Hope High School, 237
Hopkins, Budd, 48
Horn, Andrew, 219
Horowitz, Beth, 88
Horowitz, Jonathan, 218
Horowitz, Leonard, 29
Horrigan, Bill, 234, 332
Horvatić, Hrvoje, 219
Hot Coffee, 270, 275, 296, *296*, 297, 334
House of Field, 253
Houser, Page, 241
Hovagimian, Gerry, 96
Hoven, Bryant, 253
Howe, Nelson, 45
Howland, Rebecca, 136, 154, 157, 158, 162, 276
Hoyt, Dale, 241
Huang, Arlan, 254
Hubard, Olga, 284
Hubaut, Joël, 130, 157
Hubbard, Kim, 154, 157
Hubbell, Ken, 34, 68
Hudlin, Reginald, 182
Hudson, (Hudson/Buzz Tone Outlet),138, **138**, 157
Huebler, Douglas, 85, 93, 138
Huerta, Benito, 331
Huff, Robert, 190
Huff, Tom, 187
Huffman, Kathy Rae, 219, 331
Hughes, Ian, 302
Hughes, Robert, 182
Hugill, Tannis, 82, 157
Huillet, Daniele, 152
Hujar, Peter, 202, *206*, 207, 210, 221
Hultman, Irene, 250, *250*
Hundreds of Drawings, 127, *156*, 157
Hunt, Miranda, 254
Hunter, Alexis, 107
Hunter, Christian X., 280
Hunter, Paul, 153, 157
Hutchinson Park Elementary, 237
Hutchinson, Peter, 33
Hutchinson, Stephen, 312
Hykes, David, 87, 93
Hyndman, Dave and Marilyn, 217

Ingraham, Susan, 308
Innerst, Mark, 156, 157
Insley, Will, 329
International Projects, 117, 155, *155*, (11–12/1983),156; (1–2/1984 & 2–3/1984), 158; (4–5/1984),159, 328, 329, 223
INTERROGATION!, 256
Iorizzo, Peter, 253
Irazabal, Prudencio, 248
Irby, Ken, 46
Ireland, David, 278, 336, *336*, 337
Irvine, Louva, 47
Is There a Renaissance Woman?, 47
Ischar, Doug, 240
Isermann, Jim, *136–37*, 137, 138, 157
Islam, Runa, 311
Israel, Bob, 30
It Should Have Been the Happiest Moment of My Life, 255, 333
Itami, Michi, 254

Jaar, Alfredo, **162**, *162*, 163
Jackson, Derek, 253
Jackson, Ronald, 155
Jackson, Scott, 253
Jackson, Suzanne, 184
Jacobs, Diane, 92
Jacobs, Ken, 181, 186
Jacobsen, Carol, 246
Jacobson, Lia, 244
Jacoby, Roger, 181, 186
Jaffe, Shirley, 170, 218, 261, 331
James, David, 170
Jameson, Fredric, 177, 330
Jamieson, Malcolm, 312
Jang, Younhee, 214
Jannetti, Tony, 276
Janowich, Ron, 156, 157
Japan: Outside/Inside/In Between, 247–50, 333
Jaramillo, Virginia,158
Jarden, Richards, 99, 157
Jarmusch, Jim, 134, 290, 293, 298
Jarmusch, Tom, 290, 298
Jaroslavsky, Mariana, 290
Jashinsky, Judy, 261
Jasper, Maura, 297
Jean, Guy, 254
Jefferson High School, 237
Jemison, G. Peter, 187
Jenik, Adrienne, 332
Jenkins, Amy, 290, 298
Jenkins, Kiely, 158
Jenkins, Tom, 93
Jenrette, Pamela, 52–53, **69**
Jesionka, Henry, 190
Jessop, Colin, 243
Jesurun, John, 106, 139, 157
JFK Library Corps, 237
Jhingan, Shikha, 251
Jin, Che, 215
Jo, Seung-Jae, 289
John and Alessandro, 290
Johns, Jasper, 87
Johnson, Gail, 188
Johnson, Glenys, 106, 136, 157
Johnson, Janice, 280
Johnson, Larry, 158
Johnson, Liza, 298
Johnson, Poppy, 78, *78*, 93, 157
Johnson, Ray, 107
Johnson, Scott, 93, 95
Johnson, Sue, 279
Johnson, Susan, 157
Johnson, Suzanne, 153
Johnson, Tim, 234
Johnson, Tom, 45
Johnston, Jill, 45
Joint Ventures, 235, 237, 332
Jolley, Patrick, 312
Jonas, Joan, 72, 91, 95, **96**, 178, 185
Jonelle, 237
Jones, Art, 243

Jones, Ben, 287
Jones, Chris, 30
Jones, Henry, 95
Jones, Kellie, 65, 184, **185**, 234, 330, 332
Jones, Leroy, 73
Jones, M. Henry, 290
Jones, Ronald, 9, 12, 60, **138**, *138*, 157, 244, **264–72,** 284, 334
Jones, William, 247
Jones-Griffith, Philip, 277
Jones-Sylvester, Caryl, 184
Jottar, Berta, 216, 280
Joyce, Joe, 253
Jubela, Joan, 237
Jubelin, Narelle, 234
Judd, Donald, 22, 30
Jugnet, Anne Marie, *270*, *286*, 287, 334
Jung, Boksoo, 214
Jung, Sungjin, 215
Jung, William, 254
Just, Marcel, 74, 78, 84

K
K, Katy, 253
K.O.S., 141, *142*, 157, 335
Kahane, Lisa, 141, 157
Kahn, Eric A., 236
Kahn, Kim Lee
Kahn, Robin, 260
Kaiser, Diane, 49
Kalil, Michael, 175
Kalin, Tom, 242
Kalpakjian, Craig, 248, 260
Kamin, Franz, 45, 48
Kamrowski, Gerome, 175
Kano, Betty, 254
Kaplan, Corey, 170
Kaplan, Howard, 240
Kaplan, Kenneth, 175
Kaplowitz, Jane, 156
Kaprow, Allan, 93
Kara, Vinzula, 253
Kardestuncer, Sermin, 158
Karhof, Yasmyn, 310
Karp, Andrew, 170
Karrer, Lisa, 299
Kashi, Ed, 277
Kasher, Steven, 169
Kashi, Ed, 277
Kass, Deborah, 115
Kasuli, William, 244, 254
Katchadourian, Nina, 300, *300*, 301
Katz, Alex, 72
Katz, Cherly, 48
Katz, Joel, 238, 332
Katz, Leandro, 88, 93, 95
Katzman, Maria, 244, 254
Kaufman, Betsy, 277
Kaufman, Jane, 28
Kawachi, Taka, 220
Kay, Karyn, 134
Kazama, Sei, 248
Kazovszkij, El, 219
Kazuko, 158, 254
Keading, Hilja, 190
Keane, Patrick, 309, 310
Kearns, Jerry, 173
Keeley, Shelagh, 176
Kelder, Diane, 34
Keller, Andrea Miller, 145
Kelley, Jeff, 216, 331
Kelley, Kevin, 290
Kelley, Mike, 116, 126, *164*, 167, 169, 178, **180**, 219, 261, 265, 336, *336*
Kelly, Andrew, 92
Kelly, John, 253
Kelly, Mary, 106, 107, 177, 276, 336
Kempster, Jim, 250
Kendall, Nancy, 29
Kendrick, Mel, *18–19*, 25, 28, **28–29**, 137, 162
Kennedy, Andrew, 302, *302*
Kennedy, Brigid, 131, 157
Kennedy, Laura, 107
Kern, Richard, 167, 260, 280
Kernan, Margot Starr, 218
Kerns, Robert, 49

Kerr & Malley, 253
Kertess, Klaus, 31
Kesoglides, Anatasio, 68
Kessler, Jon, 126, **152**, *152*, 153, 157, 162, 335
Kessler, Ladd, 106, 131, **131**, 157
Ketchum Communications, 192
Khiang, Hei Han, 314
Khleifi, Georges, 222, 331
Kidd, Julia, 177
Kiesel, Thomas, 158
Kikel, Ridy, 222
Kilchesty, Buddy, 170
Kim, Byron, 254
Kim, Dongwon, 214
Kim, Joyce, 251
Kim, Misun, 215
Kim, So Yong, 308, 310, 311
Kim, Yeon Jae, 289
Kim, Yongtai, 214
Kim, Youngjong, 215
Kimler, Wesley, 175
Kimmel, Karen, *299*, 300, **301**, 311, 334
Kimmel, Michael, 332
Kimmerling, George, 312
Kimoto, Komiko, 290
King Middle School, 237
King, Kathleen, 106
King, Tony, 126
King, William, 74
Kinney, Robert and Donald, 241
Kipke, Željko, 219
Kipnis, Laura, 218
Kipper, Harry, *168*
Kipping, Brian, 86
Kiraly, Anna, 290
Kirby, Lynn, 218
Kirby, Seth, 298
Kirsch, Andrea, 188
Kirshner, Judith Russi, 218, 331
Kitchell, Nancy, 33
Klahr, Lewis, 167
Klauber, Richard, 68, **70**, 157
Kleier, Roger, 299
Klein, Barbara, 237
Klein, Calvin, 171
Klein, Michael, 124
Klein, Sheila, 236
Kleinhans, Chick, 170
Klemm, Harold, 310
Klemperer, Wendy, 298
Klick, Laurel, 93
Klien, Tom, 251
Kline, Katy, 252, 333
Kliros, Hilary, 163, 177, 251, 330
Klonarides, Carole Ann, *171*, 173
Klove, Lars, 215
Kluge, Alexander, 234
Kluver, Olga, 46
Knapp, Lucretia, 298
Knauer, Lisa Maya, 251
Knecht, John, 180, 234, 332
Knoebel, David, 126, 157
Knowles, Alison, 45, 124
Knowles, Christopher, 93
Knowlton, Win, 144, 157
Knudsvig, David, 2621
Kobland, Ken, 106, 157, 168
Kocman, J. H., 140
Kocur, Zoya, 240, 332
Koenig, Janet, 251
Koff, David, 152
Kohler, Matthias, 312
Koivisto, Steven, 163
Kojima, Junji, 248
Koken, Tom, 127,157
Kolatan, Susan, 315
Kolbowski, Silvia, **123–24,** 125, *125*, 157, 176, 177
Kolhofer, Christof, 49, 131
Kolker, Andrew, 247
Konyk, Craig, 314
Koons, Jeff, 61, *121*, 139, **139**, 154, 157, 162, 222, 267, 315
Koós, Anna, 288, 290, 292, 334
Korenc, Jurij, 219
Koretsky, Elaine, 254

Korman, Ann, 284, 289, 290
Korsak, Sandra, 261
Kostelanetz, Lucy, 20, 21
Kosuth, Joseph, 9, 141, *288*, 290, 336
Kotz, Liz, 241, 332
Kouguell, Susan, 152
Koury, Elizabeth, 158
Kovačić, Mare, 219
Kovanda, Jiři, 219
Kovel, Joel, 181, 330
Kozloff, Joyce, 68
Kozloff, Max, 34
Kramer, Margia, 49, 84, 123, 157
Krapes, Shelley, 176, 184, 214, 236
Kraus, Chris, 290
Krauss, Rosalind, 34, 61, 68, 89
Krayenbuhl, Sabine, 242
Kriegman, Mitchell, 106
Kriesberg, Irving, 29
Krishnan, Indu, 251
Kroesen, Jill, 92, 93, 157, 168
Kroll, David, 175
Krueger, David, 260
Krueger, Ted, 175
Kruger, Barbara, 28, **28**, *28*, 33, 34, 35, 48, 78, 93, 109, 153, 157, 162, 176, 220
Krughoff, Fred, 30
Kruk, Mariusz, 219, 221
Krulik, Jeffrey, 218
Ku, Alexander, 254
Kubota, Shigeko, 250
Kuchard, Geroge, 280
Kufert, Iris, 214, 220
Kuffler, Suzanne, 84, 87
Kugler, Ann, 297
Kulik, David, 130
Kummer, Raimund, *266*, 279, 334
Kunda, Brenda, 314
Kuni, R., 125
Kuo, Nina, 254, 276
Kuoni, Carin, 251
Kurahara, Ted, 234, 332
Kuri, Gabriel, 302, *302*
Kurka, Piotr, 219, 221
Kurland, Justine, 314
Kursaal for a Evacuee, 330
Kurze, Heather, 236
Kwan, Jerry, 276
Kwangju Visual Art Research Institute, 214
Kwon, Sowon, 244, 254, 261
Kybartas, Stashu, 218, 246, *247*
Kyser, Amanda, 156, 157

L
L'Hotsky, Tina, 95, 125
La Mantia, Paul, 175
Labadie, Kevin, 153, 157
LaBarbara, Joan, 49
Labat, Tony, 175, 190, *190*, 308
Lable, Eliot, 49, 84, 157
Lack, Stephen, 158
Lacy, Suzanne, 93, 192
Ladda, Justen, **159**, *159*
Laderman, Seth, 123, 157
Ladrón de Guevara, Miriam, 278
Lafky, Ernie, 253
Lake, Mayumi, 312
LaMarr, Jean, 187, 190
Lamas, Menchu, 157
Lamb, Gina, 237, 238
Lamelas, David, 72
Land, Owen, 185
Landers, Sean, 126
Landry, Richard, 33, 47, 87, 96
Lane, Lois, 28, 107, 137
Langdon, Chris, 73
Language of Paradise, The 245, 333
Lanigan-Schmidt, Thomas, 45, *60*, 107, 137, 157, 162, 253, 276
Lankton, Greer, *207*, 221
Laor, Leora, 158

LaPorta, Tina, 290
Lapping, Julie, 155, 169, 176, 184
Lapthisophon, Stephen, 138,157
LaRico, Benje, 182
LaRiviere, Mark, 220, 222, 236, 244, 254
Larmon, Kevin, 163
Larrabee, Eric, 21
Larsen, Alfred, 126
Larsen, Ernest, 235, **237**, 247, 248, 332
Larsen, Susan C., 154, 175, 328, 329
Larson, Kay, 169, 329
Larson, Laura, 242
Las Americas: The Return of Martin Steel, 280, 334
Lassnig, Maria, 29, 45
Lastreto, Alberto, 261
Latham, Barbara, 171, 192
Latinovich, Gina, 243
Lattanzi, Barbara, 163, 238, 243, 247, 333
Latuchie, Karen, 240
Latzky, Eric, 256
Lauf, Cornelia, 290
Law, Alan, 276
Lawler, Louise, 89, 98, 99, **100–101**, *100*, 137, 138, 157, 177, 267, 336
Lawrence High School, 237
Lawrence, Robert, 298
Lawson, Thomas, 61, 78, 88, 92, 98, 104, 137, 138, 157, 162, 176, 178, 244, 253, 267, **296**, 328, 334
Le, Dinh, 244
Learned, Jamie, 155
Leavitt, William, *62*, 106, **107**,157
LeBoff, Gail, 9
Lechner, Inge, 310
Ledoux, Jacques, 181
Ledwith, Irene, 251
Lee, Bing, 254
Lee, Charles D., 236
Lee, Choon-Jin, 298
Lee, Colin, 254
Lee, Jeagu, 215
Lee, Jeanne, 49
Lee, Jonggu, 214
Lee, Kuozhong, 260
Lee, Lanie, 254
Lee, Lanie, 261
Lee, Lindy, 234
Lee, Michael, 255
Lee, Myungja, 215
Lee, Pamela, 254
Lee, Sangbin, 214
Lee, Susan, 255
Lee, Thomas, 68
Lees, John, 96, 162
Leggat, Graham, 291
Legros, Marie, 280, 285
Lehane, Gregory, 23, 30
Lehmann, Elke, 334
Lehrer, Phyllis B., 311
Leicht, Don, 126
Leigh, Carol, 243
Leites, Susan, 72, 84, 157
Lemaître, Maurice, 186
Lemieux, Annette, **156**, 158, *158*, 336
Lenkowsky, Marilyn, 30, 84, 157
Lenny, Candace, 107
Lenski, Willy, 40, 87, 88, 107, 157
Leo, Vince, 240
Leonard, Zoe, **214**, 215
Leone, Hillary, 239
Leong, Evelyn B., **194–210**
Lerner, Jesse, 280
Lesage, Julia, 170
Leshé, Greg, 311
Lessa, Maria Jose, 290
Lethbridge, Julia, 169
Letitia, Joe, 260
Letterman, David, 173
Letters, 46

LeVeque, Les, 234, *234*, 247, 290, 297, 332
Levine, Ed, 125
Levine, Les, 93, 157
Levine, Michael, 261, 267, 296, 335
Levine, Sherrie, 61, 73, 84, 91, 98, 100, 107, 137, 139, 146, 157, 159, 162, 335
Levy, Barbara, 104, 157
Levy, Don, 186
Lew, Jeffrey, 27, 226
Lew, Rachel, 30
Lew, Walter, 254
Lewczuk, Margrit, 170
Lewis, Jason Clay, 311
Lewis, Jesse Jane, 284
Lewis, Mark, 298
Lewis, Susan, 84
Lewis, Wendy, 287
LeWitt, Sol, 22, 28, 33, 57, 86, 141
Leys, Rejin, 284
Liberty, Marsha, 34, 157
Libeskind, Daniel, 182,183
Lichtenstein, David, 249
Lichtenstein, Roy, 119, 335
Liddell, Siobhan, 221, 261
Light, Flash, 251
Ligon, Cathy, 123
Ligorano, Nora, 182
Likely Story, A, 116, 138, *138, 139*,222
Li-Lan, 260
Lim, Ocksang, 214
Lin, Janet, 254
Lin, Lana, 280
Lindberg, David, 300
Lindgren, Gary, 312
Lindhardt, Hank, 245
Lindsay, Arto, 82, 96, 265, *288*
Lindstrom, Kathleen A., 236
Lines of Loss, 266, *271*, 302, *302*,334
Linn, Judy, 184
Lino, Maria, 260
Linwood, Elliott, 292, 293
Lipfert, Theo, 310
Lipp, Jeremy, 95
Lippard, Lucy, 24, 28, 41, 52, 62, 73, 76, 86, **106**, 109, 110, 189, 214, 215, 330
Lipski, Donald, 99, 157
Liss, Andrea, 253, 333
Liss, Barbara, 157
Liss, Carla, 140
Lister, Ardele, 171, 178
Littke, Ron, 289
Living Testament of the Blood Fairies, A, 292, *292*, 293, *293*, 298, 334
Llewellyn, Sue, 250
Loaisiga, Miriam, 181
Lobell, Katherine, 119, 247, 315
Loch, Joan, 171
Lockpez, Inverna, 72, 157, 199
Lockwood, Anna, 45
Loevy, Ram, 183
Logis, Niki, 260
Logue, Joan, 173
Lohn, Jeffrey, 96
Loncar, Bob, 250
London Project, The, 192, 193, *193*, 330
London Women's Film Group, 178
London, Barbara, 298, 311
Long Prairie High School, 237
Long, Charles, 180
Longendyke, Paula, 84, 88
Longo, Robert, 53, 55, 57, 61, 71, 78, 80, *80, 81*, **81–82**, 84, 85, 89, 91, 94, 98, 101, 109,131, 137, 139, 149, 157, 162, 163, 168, 244, 267, 296, 297, 329, 335, *335*
Lonnerton, Kim, 311
LOOP 2, 236, 332
López Cuenca, Rogelio, 276
Lopez, Abelardo, 278
Lord, Chip, 183, 236
Lorenz, Patrice, 236, 254

Los Angeles – New York Exchange, 154, 328, *329*
Lotringer, Sylvère, 222
Lou, Richard A., 216
Loughlin, Robert, 158
Lounge Lizards, 265
Lounsbury, Ruth, 250
Lovejoy, Kristin, 152
Lovell, Mike, 29
Lovell, Whitfield, 215
Lowe, Jenny, 130
Lowe, Pelle, 280
Lowe, Steven, 47
Lubelski, Samara, 312
Lucas, Gary, 290
Lucas, Kristin, *263*, 265, 289, 290, **291**, 292, 297, 298
Lucero, William, 184
Lucier, Mary, 45
Luddy, Sarah, 278
Luers, Wendy, 205
Lukasik, Robert, 276, *276–77*
Lum, Ken, 145, **145**, 157
Luña, James, 261
Lunch, Lydia, 82, 96, 290
Lundy, Nell, 243
Lupton, Ellen, 277, 287
Lurie, John, 107
Lutes, Jim, 175
Lutes, Linda, 45
Luttrell, Joseph, 253
Lyczko, Judith, 218
Lynch, Kara, 251
Lynch-John, Rachel, 250
Lynn, Greg, 95, 267, **285**, 286, *286*, 297, 300, 334
Lyons, Lisa, 140
Lyons, Marcia, 244

M

MacArthur, Johanna, 298
MacArthur, Johnna, 312
MacBride, Oistin, 277
MacCaig, Art, 277
MacDonald, Colleen, 188
MacDonald, Nick, 152
MacDonald, William, 315
Machado, Agosto, 276
Machaty, Gustav, 276
Machet, Cari, 312
Machida, Margo, 238, 254, 260
MacKenzie, Kathleen, 289
Maclaine, Christopher, 186
MacLow, Jackson, 45
MacQueen, Kathleen, 240, 332
Madison High School, 237
Magid, Eleanor, 74
Magnuson, Ann, 290
Mahlmeister, Suzanne, 126
Maiwald, Christa, 88
Majore, Frank, 130, 157
Makos, Christopher, 95
Makuuchi, Munio T., 254
Maldonado, Linda, 248
Malle, Louis, 276
Mallory-Jones, Phillip, 193
Malloy, Michael, 92
Malpede, John, 127
Maltz, Russell, 126, 157
Mandansky, Cynthia, 277
Mandela, Nelson & Winnie, 143–44
Mangold, Robert, 337
Manhoff, Ira, 243
Mann, Lisa, 184
Manrique, Jaime, 256
Mantell, Eva, 248, 284
Manzo, Helene, 155, 169, 176, 184, 214
Mapplethorpe, Robert, 109, 171, 196, 198, 220
Mar, Stefani, 184, 260
Marangoni, Federica, 99, *99*
Marano, Lizbeth, 170
Marclay, Christian, 290
Marcopoulos, Ari, 290
Marcos, the Mountains and Mao (Video, Reading, and Film on the Philippines), 182
Marcus, Paul, 158
Marden, Brice, 23, 46
Margarucci, Anthony, 261

Margileth, Lynn, 220, 236, 244, 254
Margolis, Aimee, 290, 298
Marioni, Joseph, **35**, 46
Marioni, Tom, 278
Mariscal, Mighel, 216
Marisol, 261
Marker, Chris, 186, 188
Markgraf, Horst, 158
Markovitz, Sherry, 169
Marks, Jack, 30
Marlhens, Audrey, 312
Marras, Amerigo, 86
Marrero, Ernest, 152
Marrow, Lonnie, 68
MARS, 96, 131
Marshall, Albert, 193
Marshall, Anthony Kenneth, 255
Marti, Gloria, 312
Martin, Agnes, 89
Martin, Jean-Marie, 293
Martin, Katy, 88, 95
Martin, La Tanya, 284
Martin, Miss Robbie, 253
Martin, Tom, 100, 105
Martinez, Daniel J., 253
Martinez, Dominick, 284
Martinez, Hugo, 68
Martinez, José, 243
Martinez, Rodolfo, 68
Martinis, Dalibor, 219
Marton, Janos, 214, 330
Marton, Pier, 185
Martone, Jeanette, 248
Marxer, Donna, 47
Masayesva, Victor, 188
Mascatello, Tony, 144, 157
Maschmann, Anette, 158
Masheck, Joseph, 34, 156, 157, 328
Mashrawi, Rashid, 222
Mason, Bob, 96
Masri, Mai, 222
Mastraccio, John, 126
Matakos, Asterios, 242
Mateo, Julio, 255
Materić, Mladen, 219
Mathew, Jan, 240
Mathis, Thelma, 298
Matta-Clark, Gordon, 27, 33, 47, 96, 226
Mattaschka, Mara, 238
Mattelart, Michèle, 181, 330
Matulic, Yelena, 220
Matyas, Diane, 244
Maul, Tim, **152**, 153, 157
Maurer, Evan M., 175, 329
Maurer, Susan M., 175, 329
Maya, Frank, 253
Mayer, Aline, 95
Mazzella, Marcello, 298, 330, 301
McAlpin, Loring, 260
McBride, Rita, 241, *241*, **242–43**
McCain, Gillian, 280
McCain, Sheila, 253
McCalebb, Howard, 276
McCall, Anthony, 29, **29**, 45, 78, 88, 125
McCarthy, Doreen, 261
McCarthy, Paul, 93
McCary, Lynn, 251
McCauley, Robbie, 240
McClard, Michael, 47, 71, 78, 84, 87, 95,157
McClelland, Bruce, 46
McClure, Bruce, 299
McCollum, Allan, 92, 125, **127**, 137, *156*, 157
McCormick, Carlo, 40, 312
McCullin, Don, 277
McCullough, Barbara, 170, 193
McCullough, Mark, 237
McDonald, Anne, 248
McDonald, Jillian, 311
McElhenney, Sidney, 131, 157
McFarland, Art, 173

McGee, Micki, 124, 170, 184, 188, 192, 214, 236, 238–40, 244–47, **248–49**, 250, 330–33
McGrath, Jerry, 125
McGuirl, David, 237
McKay, Joe, 299
McKay, Ralph, 290. 202
McKendrie, Jo, 250
McLaughlin, Mundy, 141, 157
McMahon, Paul, 55, 63, 68, 70–74, 76, 78, **85–87**, 88, 90, 91–94, 96, 109, 114, 124, 140, *140*, 157, 168, 173, 175, 182, 296
McMenamin, Brendan, 217
McNeur, Lorna, 130
McPhillips, Ramsey, 172, 214, 221
McShine, Kyanston, 52, 55
McWeeney, David, 253
Me and My Mink, 216
Media Against Censorship, 243
Media Coalition for Reproductive Rights, 247
Meehan, Deborah, 219
Meet the Artists, 292, 293
Mei, Dean-E, 254
Mekas, Jonas, 40
Melamed, Brad, *122*, 140, 141, 157
Melamid, Monica, 235
Méliès, George, 186
Mellinger, Jeanine, 192
Meltzer, Larry, 125
Meltzer, Sara, 9
Memory Jam: A Retrospective of Films and Performances at Artists Space, 1973–85, *165*, 168, *168*
Mendelsohn, John, 84, 157
Mendelson, Michael, 9
Mendez, Jorge, 125
Mendini, Alessandro, 267, 296, 334
Mendizabal, Alex, 299
Mendoza, Jeffrey, 131, 157
Mennick, Andy, 253
Menyhàrt, Jenô, 290
Mercado, Eduardo "Wingy," 284
Merchant, Michael, 248
Meredith, Ann, 289
Merenstein, Lawrence E., 155, 169
Mertes, Cara, 221, 240, 331
Mesic, Jelena, 331
Mesina, Editha, 276
Mesmer, Sharon, 280
Messager, Annette, **136**, *136*, 337, *337*
Metaphysical Visions: Middle Europe, 194, 219, 221, 223, 331
Metcalfe, Rohesia Hamilton, 218, 311
Metz, Mike, 131, 157
Meuser, 178
Meyer, Ellen, 155
Meyer, Ruth, 138
Miasata, Rose, 308
Michalak, Megan, 312
Michalakakos, Maro, 314
Michals, Robin, 177
Michelson, Alan, 187, **189**
Michelson, Annette, 34
Michelson-Bagley, Henrietta., 157
Middle College High School, 237
Middleton, Alain, 96
Mieli, Paola, 249
Migliorino, Laura, 260
Mignone, Gerard, 253
Miguens, Martica, 45, 147
Mikhail-Ashrawi, Hanan, 222, 331
Milazzo, Richard, 163, 329
Millán, Lucero, 181
Millar, Norman, 236
Miller, Brenda, 72
Miller, Branda,171, 173, 183, 237, 238
Miller, George, 93

Miller, J. Abbott, **15**, *15*, 277, 287, **287**
Miller, John, 144, *144*, 157, 167, **169**
Miller, Larry, 93, 140, 175
Miller, Laura, 240, 251
Miller, Matt, 255
Miller, Nachume, 154
Miller, Richard, 84
Miller, Stephen, 139, 157
Millner, Sherry, 171, 235, 240, 246, 247, 261
Milner, Richard, 45
Min Joong Art, 186, 214, *214*, 215, 223, 330, 331
Min, Byoung, 34, 157
Min, Jungki, 214
Min, Yong Soon, 215
Miracle House, 276
Miralda, Antonio, 84
Miranda, Sonia, 95
Miss Guy, 253
Miss Lulu, 253
Miss, Mary, 30, 47, 72, 119, 157, 163, **168**, *294*, *295*, 296
Mistress Formica, 253
Mitchell, Eric, 92, *92*, 95, 107
Mitchell, John, 81
Mitchell, Peter, 192
Mobile Forces, 297
Model City, 217, 331
Moderns in Mind, 175, 329
Moffatt, Tracey, 251
Mogol, Susan, 93, 171
Moisdon, Stéphanie, 289
Molenaar, Renny, 143, 260
Molinaro, Ursule, 153
Molnar, Gail, 236, 254
Money Commission Project, 278, 334
Monk, Meredith, 93, 173
Monsod, Emerald Trinket, 252
Montano, Linda, 93, 192, 278
Montaug, Haoui, 134, 157
Monteza, Oriela, 237
Montgomery, Candace, Hill, 141
Montgomery, Jennifer, 236
Monti, John, 241
Mooibroek, Eveline, 297
Moore, Alan, 95
Moore, Frank, 9, 144, 157, 158, 226, 247, *247*, 260, 267, 292, 293 **298**, 334
Moore, George, 215
Moore, Patrick, 252, 333
Moore, Rebecca, 190
Moore, Sabra, 158, 251
Moores, James, 314
Morehead, Gerry, *73*, **73**, 84, 157
Morelli, François, 240
Morgan, Robert, *72*, **72**, 73, 84, 86, 88, 157
Morgan, Susan, 297
Mori, Ikue, 290
Morin, Robert, 218
Moritsugu, Jon, 218
Morosan, Ronald, 131, 157
Morris, Meaghan, 234, 331
Morris, Robert, 68
Morrisroe, Mark, 171, 172, 207, 221
Morrow, Charlie, 45
Morse, Holly, 238
Morton, Leo, 253
Morton, Ree, 22, *22*, 27, 28, 34, 57, 107, 137, 157, 162
Moses, Andy, 176, 181, 186, 330
Moss, Donald, 249
Motherwell, Robert, 68, 70, 206
Motta, Camila, 242
Mountain, A Bed, and a Chair, 333
Mouris, Frank, 29
Mr. Dead & Mrs Free: A History of Squat Theatre, 265, *270*, 273, 275, 288–90, *290*, 291–93, 334
MTV, 173
Muehl, Otto, 181, 186

Mueller, Cookie, 136, 172, 182, 196, 207, 221, 222, 331
Mulero, Lillian, 238
Mullen, Joan, 176, 184
Mullen, Maureen, 220, 236, 244, 254
Muller, Dave, 296
Mullican, Lee, 175, **175**, *175*
Mullican, Matt, **55–67**, **71**, *71*, 72, 73, 78, 81, 84–87, 94, 137, 157, 162, 163, 175, 176, 261, 296, 335
Mullins, Lynn, 289, 298, 312
Munoz, Celia Alvarez, 240
Munoz, Susaña, 278
Munroe, Don, 173
Muntadas, Antonio, 148, *148*, 157, 183, 276, 292
Murphett, Richard, 125
Murphy, Charlotte, 199, 205
Murray, Alison, 289
Murray, Elizabeth, 30, 72, 170, **220**, 252, 260, 329
Murray, Ian, 93
Murray, Judith, 126, 157
Murray, Julie, 190, 290
Murray, Rachel, 253
Murrill, Gwynn, 34, 157
Murrin, Tom, 229, 260, 334
Muschamp, Herbert, 221, 331
Myers, Kathryn, 255
Myles, Eileen, 222

N

Nadin, Peter, 157, 158
Nagata, Osamu, 248
Nagy, Peter, 158
Nahas, Dominique, 280, 334
Namuth, Hans, 335
Nance, Marilyn, 261
Naphtali, Dafina, 299
Nares, James, 87, 88, 95, 107, 134, 157, 221
Nash, Andrew, 131, 157
Nash, Charlie, 96
Nathan, Gail, 84
Nathenson, Howard, 84
Navarro, Ray, 216
Neaman, Laurie, 171
Neaman, Linda, 153
Nearly the Solstice party, 312, *316*
Nechvatal, Joseph, 141, 157, 265
Necochea, Miguel, 181
Neff, Eileen, 248
Neill, Joe, 34, 157
Neiman, Leroy, 173
Nelson, David, 292
Nelson, Dona, 170
Nemec, Vernita, 184
Nengudi, Senga, 260
Nenner, Paulette, 141, 157
Nereaux, Joyce, 96
Neri, Louise, 290
Nerwen, Diane, 247, 290
Neshat, Shirin, 277, **280–81**, *280*
Neu, Jim, 219
Neuhaus, Itty, 248
Neumann, Andrew, 221
Neurotic Art Show II, The, 249
Nevaquaya, Joe, 187
New Art Auction and Exhibition, 84, *84*
New Capital, The, 40
New Galleries of the Lower East Side, 115, 158, 328
New Image Painting, 62, 82
New World Order, Part 1, 251, 333
New World Order, Part II, 253, 333
New World Order, Part III, 229, 254, *254*
New Year, New Work, 247
Newman, Betsy, 237
Newman, Donald, 63, 76, 84, 86, 87, 94, 104–106, 108, **109**, *109*
Newman, Nurit, 289, 290, 311
Newton, David, 214
Niblock, Mark, 253

Nichols, Garry, 261
Nickard, Gary, 228, 252, 260, 276–78, 286, 334
Nicol, Heather, 214, 220, 236, 244
Nicolau, Luis, 217
Nicosia, Nic, 145, *145*, 147, 157, 162
Nielsen, Margaret, 260, 333
Niest, Sharon, 222
Nieuwenhuis, Jesse, 284
Nigger Drawings, The, 31, 41, 62–66, 76, 104–106, 108–110, *109*, 114, *118*, 135, 142, 143,185
Night of 1,000 Drawings (1993), 260; (1994), 279; (1995), 287; (1996), 293; (1997), 302; (1998), 314
Nikolić, Milan Peca, 219
Nix, Bern, 290
Nixon, Richard, 88
No New York, 71, 82, 131
No Wave Music Shows, 49
No. 7, 28
Noah, Barbara, 145
Noble, Kevin, 130, 157, 162
Nochlin, Linda, 46
Nodjoumi, Nickzad, 247, 333
Nolfi, Dyland, 235
Nonas, Richard, 20, 21, 25, 28, 33, 93, 157
Nordstrom, Kristina, 47
Norris, Paige, 236
North of Ireland, 217, 331
Northwest Film and Video Center, 237
Norwood, Nancy, 237
Noschese, Christine, 245
Noval, Trena, 276
Nurudin, Azian, 238, 241

O

O'Brien, Glenn, 184
O'Brien, Mark, 251
O'Brien, Robert, 155, *155*, 158, 329
O'Connell, Patrick, **94**
O'Connor, Cardinal, 172, 196, 198
O'Grady, Lorraine, 260
O'Mara, Beverly, 244
Obejas, Achy, 222
Obering, Mary, 28, 157
Obermeyer, David, 170
Oblowitz, Michael, 88, 95, 125
Obrosey, Aric, *122*, 140, 157, 277
Ochs, Jacki, 88, 95
Of a Space, Solitary/ Of a Sound, Mute, 219, 331
Office Killer, *269*, 272, 302, *304*, *305*
Ogilvy & Mather, 192
Oh, Jungock, 215
Oh, Yoon, 214
Ohtsu, Hatsune, 248
Oja, Marjatta, 310, 311
Oji, Helen, 158, 248, 254, 260
Oken, Marian, 45
Oko, Annette, 34
Okuhara, Tetsu, 248
Okuyan, Selime, 254
Old Orchard Beach High School, 237
Oldenburg, Claes, 69
Oldham, Todd, 277
Oleszko, Pat, *227*, *233*, 252
Olitski, Jules, 69
Oliver, Andrew, Jr., 199, 202, 207
Oliver, Deborah, 130
Oliver, Valis, 214
Omabegho, Billy, 45
Onslow-Ford, Gordon, 175, 329
Ontani, Luigi, 171
Oo, Sanda Zan, 254
Open Dialogue, 276
Open Video Call, 265, 267, 277, 286, 291; (4/96), 289; (5/95), 284; (6/96), 290; (6–7/97), 298; (9/97), 301; (2/98), 308; (4–6/98), 311

Ophuls, Max, 276
Oppenheim, Dennis, 33, 39, 87, 88, 93, 157
Orozco Ochoa, Victor, 216
Orozco, Gabriel, 267, 302, 334
Orr-Cahall, Christina, 203
Ortega, Damian, 302
Ortega, Julian "Chiquilin," 216
Ortiz-Torres, Ruben, 280
Osa Hidalgo, T., 261
Osgood, Charles, 173
Other Countries: Black Gay Men Writing, 228, 251, 255
Other Schools: Student Producers in the Community, 237
Other Versions (Perversions), 190, *190*, 330
Otterness, Tom, 67, 94, 96, **96**, 107, 157, 162, 260, 310, *335*, 335, 336
Ottersen, Michael, 158
Otterson, Joel, 163
Our Bodice, Our Selves, *243*, 333
Our Film Yard Collective, 214
Overlie, Mary, 30
Overstreet, Edgar and Joe, 189
Owen, John, 153
Owen, Michael, 173
Owens, Craig, 153, 178
Owens, Laura, 296
Owens, Michael, 171

P

Packer, Eve, 49
Padua, Jose, 280
Pagnucco, Jayne, 251
Paha, Michael, **174**, *174–75*, 175
Pajaczkowska, Clair, 125
Palaia, Franc, 237
Pale Soft Plane, A, 314
Palestine, Charlemagne, 86, *86*, 87, 93, 173
Paley, Laura, 253
Pally, Marc, 154, 328
Palmer, Laurie, 218, 331
Palumbo, George, 156
Panas, Lydia, 171
Paper as Ceremony, 252–55
Paper Tiger TV, 171, 182, 236, 237, 247
Paquin, Ralph, 235, 332
Parachini, Allan, 203–205
Paraculture, 234, *331*
parAIDS, 254
Paraiso, Nicky, 276
Parcero, Tatiana, 284
Pardovani, Eddie, 298
Paris, Bob, 298, 308
Park, Buldong, 214
Parker, Bill, 173
Parker, Jonathan, 253
Parker, Laura 253
Parker, Mike, 292
Parkins, Zeena, 290
Parkinson, Carol, 265, 299
Parkinson, Chrysa, 250
Parmar, Pratibha, 251
Parnes, Laura, 284
Parnes, Uzi, 218
Parra, Catalina, 158
Parrino, Steven, 158, 163
Parsons, Ivy, 261
Partenheimer, Jürgen, 146, 157
Participation Projects Foundation, 45
Passentino, Rosemary, 278
Pastor, Perico, 221
Patton, Andy, 156, 157
Paul, Janice, 155
Pavam, Carlos, 181, 330
Pavlicovic, Jim, 73
Payne, Lan, 88
Paz, Marga, 167, 329
Pazos, Carlos, 93
Pearlstein, Alix, 280, 298
Pearlstein, Philip, 22, 30

Peciura, Auste, 100, 105, 137, 157
Peckham, Linda, 219
Peer, Linda, 158
Pelka, Ken, 130, 157, 162
Pell, Claiborne, 204
Pelletier, Margo, 221
Penland, Michael, 245
People's Art School, 214
Perez, Antonia, 220, 244, 254
Perfidia, 253
Performance series, 30, 49, *76–77*, 78, 79, 92, *92*, 106
Perimeters of Protest, 46
Perkins, Gary, 156, 157
Perlman, Cara, 107, 136, 157, 172
Permutations, 266, 300, 301, 311, 334
Perreault, John, 31
Perrone, Jeff, 175, 182
PersonA series, 23, 31, *32*, 33, 35, *35*, *36*, *42*, *43*
Perspective: The State of Existing in Space Before the Eye, 221
Pervin, Gilda, 247, 333
Peterson, Vicki, 47
Pezo, Zoran, 219
Pfaff, Judy, 25, 28, 30, *30*, 31, 34, *349*2, 100, 126, 136, 137, 156, 157, 162, 173, 220, 261
Pfeiffer, Paul, 254
Pham, An Ngoc, 254
Phelan, Ellen, *72*, 157, 162, 173, 220
Philbin, Annie, 131, 267
Phillip, Kelvin Zachary, 242
Phillips, Alice, 60
Phillips, Gifford and Ann, 85
Phillips, Jerry, 255, 333
Phillips, Liz, 33
Phillips, Michael, 276
Phillips, Patricia C., 184, **184**, 330
Phillips, Paulette, 193
Phipps, Cyrille, 237
Photo Collective for Social Movement, 214
Picard, Lil, 46, 84
Pictures, 60–62, 81, *81*, 89–91, *90–91*, 92, 101, 105, 124, 136, 146, 159, 240, 270, 297, 328
Pierce, Sarah, 311
Piersol, Brian, 92
Piersol, Virginia, 45, 88, 92, 157
Pierucci, Massimo, 126
Pillette, Patricia, 193
Pincus-Witten, Robert, 34
Pindell, Howardena, 31, 62, 63, 76, 105, 106, **110**, 142
Pineyro, Yvette, 242
Piper, Adrian, **31**, 33, *39*, 40, 63, 85, 98, 99, 100, 110, 131, *132–33*, 162, 328
Pitrone, Anne, 141
Pittman, Lari, **154**
Place, Pat, 96, 107, 130, 157, 290
Plate, Catya, 296
Pleasants, Craig, 215
Pletsch, Gary, 254
Poe, Amos, 95
Pogrebin, Letty Cottin, 240
Pohl, Timotheus R., 9
Points de vue, 289
Polak, Jenny, 261
Political Advertment (1952–1996), 292
Pollack, Barbara, 290
Pollack, Stephen, 145, 157
Pomeroy, Jim, 99, 124, 162
Pool Show, 126, *126*
Poons, Larry, 52, 69
Poool, The, 312
Pop Art, 23, 34
Pope, Carl Robert, Jr., 261
Pope, William L., 284
Porcel de Peralta, Alicia, 284
Porter, Jenelle, 313–15
Porter, Liliana, 158, 261

Portillo, Llordes, 278
Portnoy, Michael, 311
Post-Boys & Girls: Nine Painters, 232, 238, 239, 332
Potelle, Scott, 237
Pou, Alyson, 254, 276
Powell, Gregg, 88
Power, Kevin, 167, 329
Poyo, Txuspo, 311
Pozzi, Lucio, 126, 157
Present Tense, 301, *301*, 334
Pressly, Nancy, 202
Price, Liza, 312
Price, Luther, 280
Primer (for Raymond Williams), 141, *141*, 143
Prince, Richard, 57, 98, **124**, 125, *125*, 127, 137, 139, 157, 158, 162, 171, 173, 267, 296, 337
Princethal, Nancy, 10
Priore, Christopher, 244
Private/Public, 248
Project (11/93–1/94), 260; (6–7/94), 277; (10/94–1/95), 278, 279; (1–4/95), 280; (5–7/95), 284; (9–10/95), 286; (11/95–1/96), 287; (1–3/96), 15, 287, 334; (9–10/96), 291; (11/96–1/97), 293; (1–3/97), 296; (11/97–1/98), 301; (1–3/98), 303, *303*
Project series, 214, 244; (11/88–1/89), 216; (1–2/89), 217; (11/89–1/90), 222; (11/90–1/91), 239; (1–3/91), 240; (3–4/89), 218; (3–4/90), 234; (3–5/91), 241; (4–5/89), 219; (4–5/90), 235; (5–6/90), 236; (5–6/91), 243, *243*; (9–11/90), 238; (9–11/91), 245;
Project Space, 278, 310; (6–7/97), 298; (11/98–1/99), 314; (1999), 315
Project Space 2 (1999), 312, 313, 315
Prol, Rick, 158
Protovin, Richard, 45
Prouveur, Jean-Marc, 171
Prown, Lise, 177, 251, 330
Przybylak, Jagoda, 236
Psychotic Eve, 253
Pugh, Megan, 251
Pujol, Ernesto, 276
Pustay, Maureen, 131
Putman, Andrée, 267, 287, 334
Putt-Modernism, 229, *230, 233*, 249, 251, 252, *252*, 260, 313, 333, 336

Q

Quasha, George, 45, 46
Quasha, Susan, 45
Queer Kind of House, A, *276*
Quinilin, Kathy, 214

R

Ra'ad, Walid, 276
Raciti, Cherie, 192
Radio Show, The, 228, 249, 250, *333*
Radloff, Tom, 93, 157, 176
Raff, Orit, 291
Rage and Desire, 255
Rainer, Yvonne, 90, 91, 152, 157, 261
Ramey, Cathy, 236, 244, 254
Ramirez, Jaime, 68
Ramirez-Jones, Paul, 238, 244
Ramos, Tony, 236
Ramotar, Leela, 251
Ranalli, George, 301, *301*, 334
Rankaitis, Susan, 253
Rankin, Aimee, 177
Rankin, Scott, 221

Rapaport, Pola, 218
Rappaport, Mark, 29, 260
Rashid, Hani, 181, 182, **183**, *183*, 267, 309, 310, 330, 334
Ratcliff, Carter, 40, 48
Rath, Edwin, 149, 157
Rather, Dan, 173
Rauchberg, Ron, 234
Rawlings, Stacy, 236
Rawlins, Patrick, 251
Rawlison, Jennifer, 289
Ray, Richard (Whitman), 187
Ray-Chaudhuri, Debi, 254
Read, Howard, 124
Reagan, Ronald, 110, 114
Rebo, Mark, 293
Recchion, Tom, 93
Recent Art from Chicago, *174–75*, 175, 329
Reckinger, Candace, 171, 183
Reconstruction Project, 158
Reconstructions, 241, 332
Recycling L. A., 236, 332
Reddy, Shawn, 301
Redgreene, Karen, 280
Reed, Jason, 244, 251
Reeder, Jennifer, 312
Reese, Marshall, 182, 292
Reeves, Jennifer, 261
Reframing the Family, 240, *240*, 245, 248–49, 332, *332*
Reich, Murray, 70, 218, 331
Reich, Steve, 32
Reid, Don, 255
Reiniger, Lotte, 178
Reiring, Janelle, 59, 85, 89, **98**, 99, 100, 124, 138, 142, 328
Reiser, Jesse, 193, *193*
Remapping Boundaries: Video Art and Popular Culture, 241, 332
Remapping Tales of Desire, 253, 333
Remembrances for Tomorrow, 104, 107, 127
RENEW, 245
Reno, 253
Renvall, Seppo, 298
REPOHistory, 251
Representing School, 237
ReproVision, 251
Resemblance, 80, 86
Resnick, Marcia, 88, 95
Retrovizija, 219
Return of the Repressed, The, 228, 249, 250, *333*
Reunanen, Tina, 311
Reverend Jen, 311, 312
Reynaud, Bérénice, 183, 330
Reynolds, Hunter, 184
Reynolds, Marilyn, 169, 176, 184, 214
Reynolds, Reynald, 290, 312
Reynolds, Robert, 276
Rhein, Eric, 220
Rhoads, Thomas, 260, 333
Rhone, Jody, 312
Ribé, Gloria, 234, 251
Ribot, Marc, 290
Ricard, Rene, 222
Riccardo, Lyn, 220
Rice, Tennese Dixon, 278
Richard, Mark, 240
Richards, James, 169
Richards, Michael, 251
Rickaby, Tony, 107, 157
Rickard, Jolene, 187
Ridanovic, Igor, 219
Rifka, Judy, 46, 84, 88, 95, 137, 157, 261
Rigg, Jean, 45
Riggs, Marlon, 239, 255
Riley, Debra, Bosio, 310
Rinden, Thor, 84, 157, 169
Rinder, Lawrence, 245, 333
Ringgold, Faith, 84
Ripling, Earl, 92, 123
Rise & Shine Productions, 237
Rist, Pipilotti, 289
Rittimann, Jim, 241, 332
Rivas, Francisco, 167, 329
Rivera, Dhara, 155

Rivera, Eddie, 284
Rivera, Pedro, 174
Robbett, Bart, 96, 106, 157
Robbins, Andrea, 276
Roberti, Fabio, 167
Roberts, Liisa, 261, 310
Robins, Joyce, 49, 157
Robinson, Abby, 126, 157
Robinson, Colin, 251
Robinson, Jonathan, 247
Robinson, Steve, 301
Robinson, Walter, *37*, *37–41*, *47*, 84, 88, 98, 136, 137, 157, 162, 219
Rocha, Mauricio, 302
Rocha, Manuel, 302
Roche, Jim, 124
Rocheieall, Ron, 284
Rockburne, Dorothea, 22, 28, 29, 260
Rodan, Don, 88
Rodrigues Gil, Diana, 26
Rodrigues, César, 181
Rodrigues, Richè, 261
Rodriguez, Eduardo, 68
Roeschlein, Timothy, 236, 244, 254
Rogers, Roy, 157
Rollins, Tim, 127, **141–43**, *142*, 157, 162, 335
Romberg, Osvaldo, 280
Room 207, 74, 86–88, 95, 96, 104
Rope Show, The, 228, 248, 250, *333*
Rorimer, Anne, 169, 193, 329, 330
Rose, Barbara, 23, 34
Rose, Mary Ann, 169, 176, 184, 254
Rosen, A. G., 12
Rosen, Barry, 124, 328
Rosenbaum, Daniel, 176, 184, 236, 244, 254
Rosenbaum, Joan, **20–26**
Rosenberg, Maddy, 254
Rosenblum, Robert, 23, 34
Rosenfeld, Marina, *275*, 296, 308
Rosenfeld, Susan, 153, 170
Rosenthal, Barbara, 290
Rosenthal, Mark, 152
Rosis, John, 255
Rosler, Martha, 124, 171, 185, 192, 240, 276
Rosmarin, Cari, 184
Ross, Michael, 289
Rossellini, Roberto, 178
Rosser, Jesse, 171
Roth, Jacques, 169
Rothenberg, Erika, 131, 157
Rothenberg, Stephanie, 308
Rothenberg, Susan, 72, 96, 220
Rothschild, Gail, 239
Rothstein, Barbarie, 34
Rothzeid, Mitchell, 153
Rouse, Michael, 183
Rousseau, Ann Marie, 49
Rowden, Stephanie, 261
Rowe, Sandra, 253
Rowher, Chen, 237
Roxbury Boys and Girls Club, 237
Rubenstein, Meridel, 136, 157
Rubenstein, Meyer Raphael, 218, 331
Rubin, Jon, 166, 167, 245
Rubio, Jeff, 192
Rubnitz, Tom, 131, 157
Ruda, Edwin, 28
Rudman, Lisa, 243
Rudolf, Adam, 180
Ruiz, Beth, 216
Rumm, Ellen, 157, 162
Rupp, Christy, 84, 96, 135, 154, 157, 162
Russell, Greg, 169
Russell, Susan, 78, *78*, 88
Ruva, Doug, 253
Rychlak, Bonnie, 176
Ryman, Robert, 23, 45

S

Saalfield, Catherine, 261
Saar, Alison, 252
Saatchi, Charles, 109, 126
Sabalis, Aldona, 84, 157
Sacks, Glen, 276
Safety Belt, 291, 334
Safford, Kimberly, 152
Saganic, Livio, 92, 157
Saghbazarian, Anita, 155, 169, 176
Said, Edward, 175, 187, 215
Saijo, Yumi, 247, 250
Saito, Dawn, 254
Sakai, Eiko, 45, 298
Sakamoto, Hiromi, 252
Sakamoto, Kerri, 254, 256, 333
Sale, Mike, 290, 291
Salerno, Nina, 153
Salgado, Angela, 248
Salgado, Eduardo, 68
Saliske, Maggie, 140, 157
Salle, David, 55, 56, 60–61, 74, *74–75*, 78, 81, 84–96, **90–91**, 109, 137, 156, 158, 162, 220, 241, 296
Salloum, Jayce, 218, 222, 276
Salmen, Tania, 252
Saltz, Jerry, 297
Salvest, John, 237
Salzer, Nancy, 245
Samaras, Lucas, 23, 28, 34
Samatowicz, D., 47
Sammons, Susan Hong, 244
Samoa, 254
San Clementi, Charles, 163
Sanborn, Keith, 140, 158, **181**, 186, 218, 330
Sánchez, Cecilio, 278
Sanchez, Juan, 177, 261
Sanchez, Rafael, 237
Sanchez, Robert, 216, **217**
Sandborn, Jim, 138, 157
Sanders, Joel, 333
Sandler, Irving, 9, 12, 21, 23, **20–26**, 28, 34, 38, 48, 52, 53, 55, 64, 65, 68, 81, 106, 107, 126, 135, 156, 158, 183, 195, 218, 235, 277, 279, *282–83*, 302, 329, 334
Sandlin, David, 260
Sandrow, Hope, 158
Sang Kyeidong Community, 214
Sangaris, Michael, 158
Sans, Jérôme, 287, 334
Santamarina, Guillermo, 302, *302*
Santana, Nelibel, 284
Santes, Carlos, 173
Santiago, Filemón, 278
Santos, René, 130, 157
Santos, Susana, 187
Sapp, John, 255
Saret, Alan, 88, 100
Saslow, James, 238, 332
Satellite Choices: Young Curators Explore, 284, 334
Satellite exhibit (1–2/94), 261; (12/94–1/95), 279
Sato, Norie, 291
Saturday Night Live, 173
Sauer, Michel, 148, 157
Sauer, Ruth, 236
Saunders, Joel, 254
Savinar, Tad, 140, 157
Savor, 300, 301, 311
Sawin, Martica, 175, 329
Sayre, Sue, 49
Scanga, Italo, 73
Scape, 314, 334
Scarpati, Vittorio, 172, 221
Schafer, David, 241
Schapiro, Teddy, 220
Scharf, Kenny, 173
Scher, Julia, *216–17*, 217
Scherer, Sean, 220
Schicker, Eva, 236
Schiff, Steven, 171, 177, 330
Schimert, Kathleen, 276
Schipper, Merle, 183, 330
Schiro, Gary, 253

Schjeldahl, Peter, 25, 40, **68**
Schlattman, Craig, 170
Schlesinger, John, 276
Schloss, Arleen, 290
Schmidt, Bruno, 158
Schmittroth, Teresa, 248
Schneemann, Carolee, 29, *29*, 45, 88, *88*, 157, 180, 186
Schneider, Cynthia, 192
Schneider, Gary, 86
Schneider, Karin, 310
Schneider, Rosalind, 29
Schnorr, Michael, 216, 331
Scholz, Christopher, 175
Schönwiese, Fridolin, 290
Schonwit, Irene, 251
Schor, Mira, 92, 157
Schreiner, Rachel, 290
Schuldt, 139, 157
Schulman, Sarah, 222
Schuyff, Peter, 158
Schwabacher, Christopher, 9
Schwartz, Barbara, 46, 107, 137, 157
Schwartz, Charles, 46
Schwartzman, Allan, 9, 12, 152, 157
Schweder, Robin, 251
Schwerner, Armand, 45
Sclavonas, Jim, 96
Scofidio, Ricardo, 175, 182, 183, 278, 337
SCOPE 1, 310
SCOPE 2, 311, *312*
SCOPE 3 (7/98), 312
Scott, Deirdre A., 193
Scott, George, III, 96
Scott, John, 125
Scott, Marlene, 33
Scott, Matthew, 311
Scully, Julia, 166, 329
Séchas, Alain, 178
Seckinger, Regine Anna, 252
Segal, George, 20, 23, 24, 34
Seid, Dui, 237, 254
Sekula, Allan, 240
Selbo, Vivian, 243
Selections, 127, *130*, 131, 186, 195, 245, 286, 298; (3–4/81), 131, 328; (9–10/82), 144, *144*, 328; (10/83), 156, 328; (11–12/84), 159, *162, 163*, 163, 329; (9–10/85), 169, 329; (9–10/86), 176, 330; (10/87), 184, 185, 186, *186*, 330; (11/88–1/89), 215, *215*, 330; (9–11/89), 220, 331
Selections: Aljira & Artists Space (9–11/90), 237, 332;
Selections (9–10/94), 277, *280*
Self, Jim, 253
Sellers, Terence C., 95
Seltzer, Joanne, 92, 157
Semenec, Elyce, 308
Seminara, Gian, 278
Semmes, Beverly, 235, *235*, **236**, 332
Sennett, Arthur, 34
Serlen, Bruce, 23, 30
Serra, Richard, 22, 28, 32, 33, 35, 90, 96, 125, 168, 170
Serrano, Andres, 196, 198, 220, 337
Serrano, Efrain, 284
Sester, Marie, 309
Seubert, Emelia, 187, 188
Seubert, Emelia, 330
Seven-person untitled exhibition, 136
Seven Toronto Artists, 125, 328
Severine, Terence, 95
Severson, Ann, 186
Shafir, Lisa, 289, 311
Shah, Ela, 284
Shane, Jo, 221
Shang Shang, 298
Shapiro, Joel, 30, 72
Shapiro, Sherry Kromer, 238
Sharits, Paul, 84, 167
Sharp, Elliott, 290, 292
Sharp, Willoughby, 87

Sharpe, Deborah, 170
Sharpe, Leslie, 246
Shaw, Jim, 193
Shaw, Kendall, 247, 333
Shea, Geoffrey, 193
Shea, Larry, 290
Shearer, Hartley, 217, 222
Shearer, Linda, 24, 52, 56, 65–67, 72–74, 80, 105, **114–120**, 127, 130, 131, 136–39, 143, 144, 147, 154–56, 158, 159, 166–70, 173, 187, 195, 218, 222, 234, 247, 270, 312, 328, 329
Shebairo, Richard, 9, **280**
Shelley, Ward, *233*, 252
Shelton, Christopher, 28
Shelton, Lynn, 290
Shelton, Peter, 146, 157
Shen, Hilda, 244, 254
Shepard, Mark, 312
Sheppard, Ileen, 220
Sherk, Bonnie, 278
Sherk, Scott, 254, 333
Sherman, Cindy, 9, 30, **52–67**, 71, 78, 80, *80*, 81, **84–85**, 89, 90, 94, 98, 99, *99*, 100, 101, 108, 109, 111, 119, 124, 127, 130, 131, 136, 137, 147, 149, 157, 162, 173, 220, *241*, 244, 252, 260, 267, *269*, 271, 272, 385, 293, 296, 297, 302, *304*, *305*, 334, 335, *335*, 336
Sherman, Genie, 49
Sherman, Robert, 253
Sherman, Stuart, 93, 98, *98*, 124, 127, 157, 168, 183
Sherman, Susan, 46
Sherry, Jane, 107, 260
Sherwood, Katherine, 220
Shicoff, Rochelle, 155, 244
Shim, Kwang Hyun, 214, 330
Shimano, Yoshitaka, 248
Shinn, Barbara, 248
Shlensky, Lincoln, 219
Sholette, Greg, 251
Shoyer, Lisa, 253
Shuhan, Olga, 252
Shulman, David, 74
Sicilia, José-Maria, 167
Sighting the Gallery, 254, 333
Sigler, Jeremy, 314
Signs of Fiction, 218, 331
Sillman, Amy, 228, 248, 333
Silva, Ernest, 46
Silver, Shelly, 182, 238
Silverman, Dara, 248
Silverman, Sandy, 188
Silvestrini, Anthony, 163
Silvia, Pet, 298, 308, 311
Simenuk, Chris, 280
Simmons, Gary, 9, 82, 267, 286, 291, 292, 297, 308, 310, 334
Simmons, Laurie, 98, **101**, *101*, 104, 127, 135, 137, 157, 162, 171, 173, 267, 270, 285, 335
Simmons, Sally, 173
Simon, Adam, 176, 228, 248, 333
Simon, Gabriella, 290
Simon, Jason, 192, 245, 249, 261, 280
Simonds, Charles, 23, 34, 45, 107, 137, 162
Simons, David, 299
Simpson, Gordon, 284
Simpson, Lorna, 336, *336*
Sims, Lowery, 110
Sims, Patterson, 169, 176, 184, 214
Sims, Robert, 255
Singer, Debra, 300, 311, 334
Singer, Leslie, 238, 241
Sinn Fein Information, 277
Sins, Katheryn, 155
Siporin, Michael, 47
Sisco, Elizabeth, 216
Sistema Sandinista de Television, 181
Sit Down and Watch It, 280, *280*
Six Moons Over Oaxaca, 278, 279, 334

Six Sculptors, 171, 329
Sixth Anniversary Exhibition, 56, 60, 107
Skinner, Doug, 255, 256, 280
Skiptares, Theodora, 72
Skoglund, Sandy, 252, 261
Skolimowski, Jerzy, 221
Skou, Lise, 310, 312
Sky's the Limit: Live Performances by Artists with Disabilities, 284
Slater, Jeremy, 289
Slaughter, Todd, 277
Slaughter, Tom, 12
Slides and Music, 131
Sloan, Jennifer, 276
Sloan, Rebecca, 314
Sloane, Patricia, 29
Slonem, Hunt, 173
Slotkin, Terise, 92, 157
Slye, Joe, *195*, 204
Small, Deborah, *243*, 333
Smid, Aina, 219
Smith, Alexis, 93
Smith, Barbara, 93
Smith, Bob, 156, 157
Smith, Duncan, 95
Smith, F. O. 49
Smith, Gavin, 291, 298, 308, 311
Smith, Jack, 33, 40, *42*, 45, 49, 71, 86, 131, 181, 186
Smith, Jaune Quick-To-See, 158
Smith, Julian Maynard, 106
Smith, Kiki, 9, 96, 107, 134, 136, 153, 157, 172, *197*, **219**, 221, 256, 260, *266*, 317, 336, *336*, 337
Smith, Lindzee, 95, 107, 134
Smith, Mark, 255
Smith, Michael, **78**, *79*, 93, 99, 124, 157, 162, 168, *168*, 173, 256, 280
Smith, Mimi, 34, 124, 157
Smith, Patti, 63, 64, 100, 105
Smith, Paul, 187, 330
Smith, Philip, 89, 91, 157, 162
Smith, Robert, 107, 131
Smith, Roberta, 109, 154, 182, 328, 330, **222**
Smith, Seton, 136
Smith, Shelly, 276
Smith, Stephanie, 289
Smith, Valerie, 10, 13–14, **52–67, 114–120**, 127, 138–40, 143, 145, 148, 152, 153, 159, 163, 166, 167, 169–71, 174–76, 180–83, 190, 193, 194, 196, 214, 215, 217, 217–19, 221, **222–23**, 245, 264, 265, 329–31
Smith-Miller, Henry, 175
Snapp, Marcey, 169, 176
Snider, Jenny, 84, 125, 137, 157, 170
Snyder, Huck, 158
Snyder, Joan, 45, 252
Snyder, Kit-Yin, 254
Social Spaces, 190, *190*, 191, *191*, 330
Soe, Valerie, 251
Soechting, Joerg, 290
Sogo, Stom, 298, 299
Sojourner: Black Gay Voices in the Age of AIDS, 255
Sokol, Lee, 170
Sokolowski, Thomas, 330
Sola, Joe, 298, 311
Solomon, Alisa, 288, 334
Solomon, Holly, 126, 152
Solomon, Tom, 152
Somatogenics, 285, 334
Some Questions Concerning Technology, 234, *234*, 332
Somebodies: Fairies, Queens, Emperors, and their New Clothes, 278
Somerville, Michele Madigan, 280
Sondheim, Alan, 33, 39, 74, 84, 169, 185, 188, 329
Sonenberg, Jack, 276
Song, Chang, 214

Song, Susan, 253
Sonic Youth, 178, 180, 265, 315
Sonnier, Keith, 47, 93, 124
Sons & Daughters, 253
Sontag, Susan, 214
Sonzogni, Debi, 277, 279
Soo, Choi Byung, 214
Sorkin, Michael, 217, 301, 334
Sosa, George, 237
Sosa, Irene, 242
Sound Selection: Audio Works by Artists, 124, 328
Sousa, Jean, 170
Southern, Hugh, 198
Southwest Alternate Media Project, 237
Spak, Roza, 158
Spear, Jeremy, 254
Spector, Buzz, 239, 332
Speight, Alonzo, 237, 238
Spelling, Aaron, 173
Spence, Andy, 163
Sperandio, Christopher, 244
Spero, Nancy, 46, 100, **105**, 157, 158, 336
Spiegel, Olga, 29
Spiller, Barbara, 244, 254
Spiro, Ellen, 239
Spitters, 312, *316*
Spitz, Ellen Handler, 249
Split/Vision, 171, 329
Spohn, Jessica, 139, 157
Sporn, Pam, 237, 238
Spotted Eagle, Chris, 188
Spretnjak, Stephen, 182
Springer, David, 141
Springfield, Susan, 95
Squat Theatre, 265, *270*, *273*, *275*, 288–90, *290*, 291–93, 334
Squavo, Chris, 298
Stahl, Jolie, 158
Stahl, Mark, 153
Staller, Eric, 173
Stamets, Bill, 170
Stamm, Ted, 45, 126, 157, 162
Stanbridge, Jeremy, 292
Stancil, William L., 312
Standing, Alastair, 193
Stankovski, Aleksandar, 219
Stanley, M. Louise, 192
Starn, Mike and Doug, 260
Stathacos, Chrysanne, 240, **242**, *242*
Station to Station, *271*, 291, 297, 308, 310, 334
Staudt, Birgit, 290
Stavrou, Alexandra, 49
Stecchini, Brendan, 48
Steele, Ana, 199
Steele, Lisa, 185, 235
Steele-Perkins, Chris, 277
Stein, Carole Clark, 68, 157
Stein, Charles, 45
Stein, Donna, 188
Stein, Gertrude, 23, 45
Stein, Jane, 221
Stein, Janet, 125, 153, 260
Stein, Louis, 107, 157
Steinbach, Haim, 107, **111**, *111*, 157, 176, 267
Steiner, Charles, 243
Steinhardt, Susan Margules, 9
Steininger, Anna, 238
Steinman, Barbara, 219
Steir, Pat, 96
Stephenson, Mindy, 134
Sterbak, Jana, 217
Sterck and Rozo, 285
Stern, Monike Funke, 158
Sterne, Hedda, 183, 330
Stevens, May, 46, 48, 72, 73, 141, 261
Stevenson, Diane, 45
Stevenson, Gordon, 96, 125
Stevenson, John, 169, 176, 184
Stewart, Carrie, 311
Stidworthy, Imogen, 289
Stikker, Carolien, 244
STILL SITTING?, 256
Stinson, Don, 221, 331
Stockholder, Jessica, 126, 169

Stoddard, Ann, 235, 332
Stone, Diana, 289
Stone's Throw: Television from Cuba, Island in Goliath's Sea, 235, 332
Storey, Lou, 276
Storr, Robert, 251, 315
Stracke, Caspar, 290
Strategies of Art Criticism, 48
Strategy Hinted At, A, *262*, 291, 292
Straub, Jean-Marie, 152
Strider, Tom, 260
Strom, Mary Ellen, 240
Strosser, Margie, 167
Stroud, Leisa, 95
Studio's Independent Theatre, 180
Subway to the Outside, 315
Sukop, Sylvia, 251
Suleiman, Elia, 187, 222, 331
Sulit, Abhe, 158
Sulkes, Robin, 169, 176, 184
Sullivan, Coleen, 170
Sullivan, Ellen, 260
Sullivan, Patricia, 244, 254, 276
Sullivan, Rich, 308
Sultan, Donald, 84, 94, 100, 105, **105**, 137, 157, 162, 167, 260, 328, 329
Sumler, Radiah, 176, 184
Sumner, Holly, 260
Sumner, Stephan, 34
Sun, Carol, 184, 229, 254, 256, 333
Sundiata, Sekou, 184
Sung, Wankyung, 214, 223, 330
Super 8 Film Exposition, 88, *88*, 89
Super-8 Solar System, 167
Suprenant, Anne, 163
Sur Rodney (Sur), 267, 292, 334, 293, 298
Sussler, Betsy, 88, 95, 125, 134
Sussman, Elizabeth, 172
Sutherland, Frederick, 158
Sutter, James S., 157
Sutton, Debbi, 284
Sutton, Eva, 260
Suzuki, Miho, 290, 331
Svoboda, Terese, 234
Swanson, Charles, 34
Swithenbank, Gail, 140
Switzer-Kohler, Skyler, 220, 236
Symbolic Gestures, 276, *276*
Syrop, Mitchell, 153, 154, 157
Szymanski, Fred, 153

T
Taft Middle School Media Project, 237
Tahimik, Kidlat, 182
Taho, Ritsuko, 171
Taillepierre, Julio Dicent, 255
Tajiri, Rea, 153, 236, 250
Takagi, J. T., 214
Takagi, Kiki, 236
Takagi, Orinne J. T., 193
Talan, Dianne, 84
Talking Cure, 249
Talking Photograph, 308
Tallichet, Jude, 314
Tampering with the Reel, 298, 311, 334
Tan, Fiona, 311
Tañedo, Rochit, 182
Tanger, Susanna, 84, 157
Tannenbaum, Judith, 248, 333
Tapia, Juan, 68
Tarn, Nathaniel, 46
Tartaglia, Jerry, 181
Tashjian, Tabboo! Stephen, 221
Taubin, Amy, 78, 134
Taylor, Fred, 152
Taylor, Steed, 261, 276
Taylor, Tawana, 284
Taylor, Valery, 72, 157
Teaching TV, 237, 238
Teen Aid High School, 237

Teenage Jesus and the Jerks, 96, 131
Telling Tales, 193
Tellus, 265
Temkin, Merle, 252
Templeton, Fiona, 222
Ten Artists/Artists Space, 107, 152, 328, 329
Terminal, 96
Terrible Beauty, 277, 334
Terris, Albert, 48
Testing the Limits Collective, 236
Teufelsbergproduktion, 158
Texier, Catherine, 290, 293
Theoretical Girls, 96
Theys, Koen, 180
Thirty Five Artists Return to Artists Space: A Benefit Exhibition, 30, 127, 137, 328
Thomas Jefferson High School, 237
Thomas, Austin, 284
Thomas, Richard, 277
Thompson, Anthony, 104, 137, 157
Thompson, Carol, 252
Thompson, Peter, 234
Thompson, Thom, 48
Thomsen, Russell N., 236
Thomson, Colin, 156, 157
Thornley, Patricia, 169, 217
Thornton, Leslie, 152, 183, 219, 234
Thornycroft, Ann, 96, 157
Thrall, Bart, 93, 157
Three Artists Select Three Artists, 156, 158, *158*
Through Our Eyes, 237
Through the Tulips & the Red Red Rose, 334, 310, *310*
Thurber, Shellburne, 221
Tiers, Wharton, 96, 314
Tietelbaum, Richard, 173
Tillett, Seth, *53*, 88
Tillman, Lynne, 153, **153**, 184, 222
Timoney, Tess, 251, 333
Timpanelli, Giola, 154, 157
Tisa, Ken, 221
Tiscornia, Ana, 261
Tisdale, Daniel, 193, 284
Titolo, Ted, 87, 157
Tkacheff, Peter, 84
To Dario, 250
Toa Film Collective, 214
Tobias, Julius, 45, 126
Tolle, Brian, 138, 266, 284, *284–85*
Tolman, Mary Ann, 188
Toman, Mary Anne, 242
Tomaselli, Fred, 234, *234*, 251, 332
Tomczak, Kim, 125
Tomic, Biljana, 219, 331
Tondrick, Lynn, 298
Tone Death, 96
Tonkonow, Leslie, 9, 144, 157
Too Black, Too Strong!, 193
Top Stories, 153
Torffield, Marvin, 25, 30, 157
Torlen, Michael, 156
Torr, Diane, 284
Torreano, John, 30, **30**, *30*, 31, 40, 107, 137, 157, 162, 173, *230*, 252, 260, 335
Torres, Francesc, 46, 157
Torres, Rigoberto, 276
Torruella-Leval, Susana, 28
Toshida, Mitsuo, 254
Tot, Endre, 140
Toufic, Jalal, 298
Tourist Attractions, 182, 184
Townsend, John, 276
Traditions/Five Painters, 96, 328
Training of a Fragile Memory, 260, 334
Trajkovski, Zlatko, 219
Trasobares, Cesar, 216, 330
Trasov, Vincent, 81, *81*
Trattner, Marsha, 254
Travers, Phillip, 242

Treitz, Gretchen, 155, 169, 176
Tremley, Nicolas, 289
Tribe, Jim, 33
Tribe, Kerry, 312
TriBeCa Open House, 248
Triggs, Lula, 237
Trinh, T. Minh-ha, 174
Tripp, Brian, 261
Tripp, Kristin, 311
Troyano, Ela, 218
Tsao, Richard, 276
Tschinkel, Paul, 48, 157
Tschumi, Bernard, **95**, *95*, 130, 157, 192, 264, 315, 328
Tsien, Billy, 278
Tsuda, Rumiko, 254
Tucker, Marcia, 68, 80
Tuesday Night at the Movies, 261, 276
Tuft, Sarah, 192
Tupahache, Asiba, 188
Turkel, Alice, 169, 176
Turnbaugh, Douglas, 47
Turpin, Franck and Oliver, 310
Turtletaub, Jeffrey, 173
Turyn, Ann, 147, 153
Tuttle, Richard, 29, 45, 171
TV Gallery, 219
TV Program "A-Studio," 311
TV Sandino, 181, 187, 330
Twitchell, Lane, 314
Tynan, Dana, 277
Tyndall, Andrew, 125
Type A, 310, 311

U

U.S. Projects, 117, (10–11/1981),136; (1–2/1982 & 2–3/1982), 138; (4–5/1982),140; (11–12/1982),145, *145*;(12/1982–1/1983), 146, *146*; (2–3/1983),152; (5–6/1985),169, 329
Um, Hyuk, 214, 223, 330
Umland, James, 93
Unacceptable Appetites, 192, *192*, 330
Unband, 312
Underexposed: A Selected History of Neglected Films, 186, 330
Underground, 236, 238, 244; (11/90–1/91), 239; (1–3/91), 240; (3–5/91), 241; (5–6/91), 243; (9/91–1/92), 246
Underhill, Linn, 240
Unemoto, Nanako, 193, *193*
United Graffiti Artists, 40–41, *41*, 68
Univesity Film Alliance, 214
Unnaturally Yours, 287, *287*, 288, 292, 334
Unruh, Jennifer, 311
Uprising: Videotapes on the Palestinian Resistance, 187, 222, 331
Urban Space, 245, 333
Urbanski, Adrienne, 285
Ute Indian Tribe Audio-Visual, 188

V

Vachon, Gail, 153
Vaisman, Meyer, 158
Valenta, Barbara, 176, 184, 214, 220, 236, 244, 254
Valente, Antonio, 248
Valenti, Nadine, 47
Van Assche, Christine, 289
van Berkel, Ben, 95, 297, **300**, 334
van Cook, Marguerite, 276
van der Heijden, Liselot, 311
Van Doxell, Nathalie, 311
Van Genderson, Monique, 253
van Heeswijk, Jeanne, 315
Van Lamsweerde, Inez, 285, *285*
Van Oost, Jan, 178
van Riper, Peter, 68, 84, 88, 140, 157

van Rolleghen, Constance, 248
VanderHeyden, Marsha, 34
Vanderhofstadt, Alain, 158, 328
Varela, Myriam, 298
Vargas, Roberto, 174, 187
Vasulka, Steina and Woody, 247
Vazquea-Pacheco, Robert, 255
Vejvoda, Ivan, 331
Velarde, Kukuli, 260, 276
Velazquez, Carlos, 254
Velez, Edin, 173, 247
Venet, Berner, 93
Verabioff, Mark, 190, 289
Veras, Jorge, 292
Vereano, David, 184, 214
Vermeiren, Didier, 158, 328
Verrochi, Barbara, 236, 244, 254
Vevers, Tony, 74
Vezjak, Peter, 219
Vicente, Mercedes, 289
Vicuna, Cecilia, 260
Vidas Perdidas/Lost Lives, 216, 216–17, 331
Video Witnesses: Festival of New Journalism, 243, 333
VIDKIDCO, 237
Viemeister, Tucker, 277
Vinci, John, 193, 330
Viola, Bill, 247
Vipotnik, Miha, 219
Virilio, Paul, 173
Visual Brains, 248
Vitiello, Stephen, 280, 298, 311
Vizenor, Gerald, 188
VJ Lo$$Vega$, 299
Vladimer, Meryl, 45, 157
Vodicka, Ruth, 47
Vogel, Conrad, 131, 157
Vogwill, Sarah, 251
Voice Group, 49
Voight, Kay, 237
Vokovic, Dragica, 219
von Bruch, Klaus, 173
von der Lippe, Gail, 84, 157
von Osten, Coop, 276
von Rydingsvard, Ursula, 276
Vorhest, William, 126
Vundla, Mfundi, 174

W

Wachtel, Julie, *130*, **131**,157, 171, 267
Wacs, Darin, 251
Wada, Yoshimasa, 140
Wade, Ken, 107, 157
Wadsworth, David, 235
Wagner, Merrill, 260
Wagner, Sokhi, 139
Wagner, Warren, 236
Wagoner, Gerry, 176, 184, 214
Wailing Wall, 255
Waite, Peter, 145, 157
Walczak, Marek, 193
Waldman, Diane, 114
Walker, Cid Collins, 82, 157
Walker, Kara, 65, 185
Walker, Nancy Meli, 291
Walker, Philip, 248
Walkingstick, Kay, 187
Wallace, Patty, 167
Wallach, Alan, 73
Wallis, Brian, 182
Wallner, Martha, 181
Walsh, Alida, 23, 29, 45, 47, 157
Walsh, Connie, 298
Walsh, Jack, 218
Walworth, Dan, 139, 152, 157, 169, 170, 174, 178, 180–82, **187**, 188–90, 193, 214, 215, 217–19, 222, 223, 308, 330, 331
Walz, Kevin, 84
Wanggaard, Amy, **226–32**, 277
Wang-Lee, Elizabeth, 236
Ward, Jay, 178
Warhol, Andy, 73, 86, 171, 173

Warneke, Ken, 175
Warp and Woof, 244, *244*, 333
Warren, Art, 203–5
Warren, Lee, 190
Warrick, Jane,184
Wasow, Oliver, 158
Waters, Jack, 229, 256
Watkins, Ragland, 82, 90, 101, 108, 124, 125, 127, 130, 131, **135**, 270, 328
Watson, Carl, 280
Watson, Simon, 115
Watts, Rolanda, 157
Way, Jeff, 20, 48, 84, 157
We the People, 187, *187*, 223, 330
Wearing, Gillian, 289
Webb, William Edward, 236
Webber, Albert, 237
Webber, Cleve, 244
Webber, Neel, 236, 244, 254
Weems, Carrie Mae, 240, 276, 336
Weep Not for Me But for Your Children, 253
Wegman, William, 39, 56, 72–74, 88, 90, 93, 114, 124, 157, 173, 336
Weiffenbach, Jean-Edith, 136
Weil, Brian, 130
Weiner, Cathy, 97
Weiner, Chris, 237
Weiner, Lawrence, 72, 85, 93, 124, 157
Weinhardt, Seth, 171
Weinstock, Jane, 125
Weir, John, 240
Weis, Cathy, 284
Weise, Rick, 188
Weiss, Gary, 173
Weiss, Harvey, 255
Weiss, Rocio, 216
Weissglass, Jeannie, 261
Weissman, Benjamin, 167, 169
Welch, Roger, *32*, 88, 162
Welling, James, 85, 107, 127, 296
Wells, Mac, 229, 260, 334
Wen Yi Hou, 254
Wenders, Wim, 136
Wentz, Gerry, 106
Wergius, Pia, 312
West, David, 312
West, Mark, 175
Wester, Bradley, 256
Western Agenda, 241, 332
Westfall, Stephen, 251
Westmoreland, LaMonte, 193
Westwater, Angela, 29, 34
Weyergraf, Clara, 125, 168
Whalen, Benji, 310
What Are the Issues in Art Today?, 23, 34
What Does She Want?, 171
What's a Mother to Do?, 261
Whirlwind, 313, *318–19*, 334
Whisler, Stephen, 153, 157
White, Charles, 285
White, Dondi, 158
White, Iverson, 170
White, James, 71, 82, 96
White, Peter, 169
White, Steve, 244, 254
White, William, 74, 157, 241
Whitehouse, Dennis, 169
Whitfield, Kevin, 73
Whitman, Sylvia, 45
Whitney, Deborah, 255
Whitney, Peter, 287
Wiitasalo, Shirley, 125
Wiley, Dan, 251
Wiley, Tad, 169, 261
Wilhite, Bob, 93
Willams, Bert, 256
Willams, Steve, 255
Williams, Chris, 169
Williams, Grace, 276
Williams, Lee, 284
Williams, Megan, **154**, *154*, 157
Williams, Pat, 204, 234
Williams, Reese, 124, 125, 141, 142, 154, 157, 158

Williams, Sue, 242, 337
Williams, Todd, 278
Wilson, Ann, 123
Wilson, Fred, 65, 119, **186**, *186*, 184, 252, 287
Wilson, Marcia, 245
Wilson, Martha, 65, 73, **76**, *76–77*, 78
Wilson, Millie, 238
Wilson, Peter, 130, 157
Wilson, Stewart, 146, 157, 169, 176, 184, 335
Winer, Helene, 24, 26, 31, 41, **52–67**, 68, 70–76, *73*, 78, 80–82, 85–87, 89, 90, 92, 94, 95, 98, 101, 105, 107–11, 114, 116, 118, 124, 127, 130, 131, 135, 136, 138, 142, 146, 147, 158, 159, 168, 222, 264, 267, 296, 328
Winn, Martin, 177, 190, 330
Winograde, Edie, 314
Winsor, Jackie, 22, 28, 72
Winter Flush, 218, 331
Winter, David, 176
Winter, Julie, 45
Winter, Stephen, 253
Winters, Robin, 47, 57, 71, **75**, 78, *79*, 84, 87, 95, *165*, 168
Witlarge, Leopanar, 299
Witnesses: Against Our Vanishing, 136, 153, 172, 173, 186, 196–216, 218–22, 234–36, 246–48, 270, 312, 315, 331
Wodiczko, Krzysztof, 96
Wodkowski, Mike, 314
Wojnarowicz, David, 94, 120, 136, 158, 172, 196, 198, 203–4, 207, 210, *211*, 214, 219, 221, 222, 234, 236, 246, 331
Wolf, Tom, 136, 157
Wolfe, Michael, 167
Wolff, Beverly, 9, 196, 198, 202, 203, 205, **234–35**
Wolff, Robert, 45
Wolkenstein, R. S., 158
Wong, Martin, 254, 276, 292
Wong, Tony, 260
Wong, Victor, **278**
Woodard, Catherine, 9, 260
Woodberry, Billy, 240
Woolery, Reginald, 193
Woon, Sheralyn, 311
Wooster, Ann, 92
Working, 245, 246, 333
World Television Makes: Critical Work on the Media, The, 237
Wright, Allen, 251
Wright, Charles, 228, 244, 249
Wu, De-Chuen, 289
Wu, Yung-Te, 289
Wurtz, B., 171
Wyatt, Susan, 10–12, 24, 38, 65, 68, 71, 74, 85, 90, 94, 100, 118, 127, 135, 169, 171–73, 176, 178, 182, 183, 187, 193, **194–210**, 218, 220, 222, 234, 235, 237, 243, 244, 246, 248, 249, 251, 264, 270, 286, 312, 313, 315, 329–33
Wye, Pamela, 215
Wynn, Don, 34

X

Y

Yablonsky, Linda, 136, 221, 222, 280, 331
Yacila, Oscar, 169, 176, 184, 214
Yamaguchi, Yuriko, 171
Yamamoto, Lynne, 254
Yankowitz, Nina, 252
Yarber, Robert, 158
Yarrington, Jo, 220
Yasecko, Nancy, 170
Yasuda, Robert, 126, 157
Yates, Marie, 107
Yates, Sidney R., 204
Yau, John, 234, 332
Ybarra-Frausto, Tomás, 278
Yelavich, Susan, 131, 157
Yeomans, Erika, 298, 312
Yli-Annala, Kari, 311
Yo, Yana, 158
Yonemoto, Bruce and Norman, 178, 185
Yood, James, 175, 329
Yoshida, Minoru, 45
Young and Rubicam, 192
Young Fluxus, 140, 328
Young, Frank, 126, 157
Young, Graham, 180, *180*
Young, Kent, 296
Young, Mimi, 254
Young, Purvis, 216, 331
Youngerman, Jack, 33
Yourgrau, Barry, 139, 157, 290
Youth International Party, 188
Youth Vision, 237
Yu, Cheng Chien, 250
Yu, Garson, 254
Yuen, Charles, 163, 254, 260
Yung, Susan L., 254
Yunque, Peggy, *126*, 131, 157, 162

Z

Zafar, Omar, 314
Zahn, Michael, 291, **292**
Zalopany, Michelle, 163
Zaloudek, Duane, 166, 329
Zamudio-Taylor, Victor, 278
Zando, Julie, 185, 218, 238, 332
Zane, Arnie, 173
Zapkus, Kes, 20
Zeig, Susan, 174
Zeitlin, Marilyn A., 222, 331
Zeller, Chris, 49, 157
Zemel, Carol, 238, 332
Zephyr, 158
Zero, Mark, 289
Zhang, Hongtu, 237, 254
Ziegler, Mel, **162–63**, *163*
Zimmer, William, 137, 328
Zimmerman, Philip, 169
Zipes, Jack, 177, 330
Zittel, Andrea, 244, *244–45*, 251, 260, 337
Ziv, Ilan, 175
Zoltners, Mara, 310
Zorn, John, 93, 157
Zox, Holly, 158
Zucker, Barbara, 261, 277
Zucker, Joe, 30, 31
Zulueta, Ricardo, 248, 276
Zwack, Michael, 57, 71, 80, **82**, 92, 94, 96, 101, 106, *106*, 131, 157, 162
Zwerver, Ton, 178
Zwickler, Phil, 235
Zwillinger, Rhonda, 158

Colophon

Design and Production by Design/Writing/Research:
J. Abbott Miller, Paul Carlos, Scott Devendorf, John Corrigan.

This book has been set in FF Balance designed by
Evert Bloemsma of the Netherlands in 1993.

The paper is 120 gm² Nippon Paper International.

Film separations, printing and binding through
Palace Press International, China.

THERE IS A TERRIBLE PHASE WHEN ABUSED ANIMALS OR CHILDREN ACT POLITELY AND TRY TO DO EVERYTHING RIGHT. BY THIS STAGE, THOUGH, THEY ARE SO OBVIOUSLY WEAK AND UNAPPEALING THAT THEY GET LITTLE RESPONSE. IF THEY DON'T DIE THEY BECOME SAVAGE.

IT TAKES A WHILE BEFORE YOU CAN STEP OVER INERT BODIES AND GO AHEAD WITH WHAT YOU WERE TRYING TO DO.

IT'S A SAFE GAME TO PLAY WITH YOUR NOSE, SHUTTING OFF THE AIR AND LETTING IT FLOW AGAIN. THEN YOU CAN ESCALATE AND SEE HOW LONG YOU LAST UNTIL YOU PASS OUT, YOUR HAND RELAXES AND YOU BREATHE NORMALLY AGAIN.

IT'S EASY FOR YOU TO FEEL BETRAYED WHEN YOU'RE JUST WAVING YOUR ARMS AROUND AND THEY COME CRASHING DOWN ON A SHARP OBJECT.

JUST ONE ROTTEN SPOT IN YOUR HEAD CAN MAKE EVERY MOVEMENT PAINFUL. YOU CAN'T ROLL YOUR EYES, BEND DOWN OR JUMP AND LAND WITH IMPUNITY. EVEN THINKING HURTS.

WITH BLEEDING INSIDE THE HEAD THERE IS A METALLIC TASTE AT THE BACK OF THE THROAT.

ANY NUMBER OF ADOLESCENT GIRLS LIE FACE DOWN ON THE BED AND WORK ON ENERGY, HOUSING, LABOR, JUSTICE, EDUCATION, TRANSPORTATION, AGRICULTURE AND BALANCE OF TRADE.

THERE IS A PERIOD WHEN IT IS CLEAR THAT YOU HAVE GONE WRONG BUT YOU CONTINUE.

SOMETIMES THERE IS A LUXURIOUS AMOUNT OF TIME BEFORE ANYTHING BAD HAPPENS.

MORE THAN ONCE I'VE AWAKENED WITH TEARS RUNNING DOWN MY CHEEKS. I HAVE HAD TO THINK WHETHER I WAS CRYING OR WHETHER IT WAS INVOLUNTARY, LIKE DROOLING.

THERE IS PLEASURE IN STAYING HOME TO ADJUST EACH PHYSICAL DETAIL SO THAT WHEREVER THE EYE FALLS, THERE IS HARMONY. THEN YOU GO OUTSIDE AND DO THE SAME.

SOME DAYS YOU WAKE AND IMMEDIATELY START TO WORRY. NOTHING IN PARTICULAR IS WRONG, IT'S JUST THE SUSPICION THAT FORCES ARE ALIGNING QUIETLY AND THERE WILL BE TROUBLE.

SOMEONE WANTS TO CUT A HOLE IN YOU AND FUCK YOU THROUGH IT, BUDDY.

IF THINGS WERE A LITTLE DIFFERENT YOU WOULD DIGEST YOURSELF THROUGH A CUT IN YOUR MOUTH. IT'S A RELIEF TO KNOW THERE ARE PROVISIONS AGAINST THIS.

THE FOND OLD COUPLE WAS DISAPPEARING TOGETHER THROUGH SUCCESSIVE AMPUTATIONS.

SOMETHING HAPPENS TO THE VOICES OF PEOPLE WHO LIVE OUTSIDE. THE SOUNDS ARE UNNATURALLY LOW AND HOARSE AS IF THE COLD AND DAMPNESS HAVE ENTERED THE THROAT.

THERE ARE PLACES THAT ARE SCARRED AND THE SKIN IS PULLED AROUND, LIKE THE NAVEL OR THE HEAD OF THE PENIS, THAT LEAVE YOU THINKING THE BODY IS FRAGILE.

IN A PARADISAIC CLIMATE EVERYTHING IS CLEAR AND SIMPLE WHEN YOU ARE PERFORMING BASIC ACTS NECESSARY FOR SURVIVAL.

TWO CREATURES CAN WANT TO MOVE AND REST IN CLOSE PROXIMITY EVEN IF THEY ARE AFRAID OF EACH OTHER.